Y0-GFK-623

TO THE STUDENTS:

The fact that this volume is being used as a text or reference in FaithWay Baptist College does not mean that the College endorses its contents from the standpoint of morals, philosophy, theology, or scientific hypotheses. In order to standardize the work and validate the credits of the College, it is sometimes necessary to use books whose contents the College cannot wholly endorse because no entirely satisfactory publication is available.

FAITHWAY BAPTIST COLLEGE
MEMPHIS, MICHIGAN

Faithway Baptist College
Library

# FOSTER AND HEADLEY'S EDUCATION IN THE KINDERGARTEN

**FOURTH EDITION**

REVISED BY **NEITH E. HEADLEY** 1898-
Nursery School-Kindergarten-Primary Department
College of Education
University of Minnesota
Minneapolis, Minnesota

C131
1965-66

**D. VAN NOSTRAND COMPANY**
New York Cincinnati Toronto London Melbourne

Faithway Baptist College
Library

**D. VAN NOSTRAND COMPANY** Regional Offices:
**New York Cincinnati Millbrae**

**D. VAN NOSTRAND COMPANY** International Offices:
**London Toronto Melbourne**

**Copyright © 1966 by LITTON EDUCATIONAL PUBLISHING, INC.**
ISBN: 0-442-21642-4

All rights reserved. Certain portions of this work copyright © 1959, 1948, 1936 by **Litton Educational Publishing, Inc.** No part of this work covered by the copyrights hereon may be reproduced or used in any form or by any means — graphic, electronic, or mechanical, including photocopying, recording, taping, or information storage and retrieval systems — without written permission of the publisher.

Manufactured in the United States of America

**Published by D. VAN NOSTRAND COMPANY**
450 West 33rd Street, New York, N.Y. 10001

15 14 13 12 11 10 9

66-1073

LB1169
.H4
1966

# PREFACE

"Over the expressway and through the tollgates to grandmother's condominium we go." . . . Yes, both the experience and the vocabulary of today's young children differ greatly from the experience and the vocabulary of children of bygone days. But, by and large, the children themselves are not very different. To be sure, tables in this book indicate that today's five-year-olds tend to be a bit taller and a bit heavier than their ancestors were at five years of age, and television has extended the young child's here-and-now to encompass even outer space. Nevertheless, basically today's five-year-olds have the same social, emotional, intellectual, and physical urges and capabilities that young children have had through the years.

Because the urges and capabilities of children are basically the same as they have been for years and because there is undoubtedly a wider range of capabilities within one group of kindergarten children than the range that exists between generations of five-year-olds, this fourth edition of *Education in the Kindergarten* continues to stress the importance of pacing education to meet the needs of individuals.

The explosion of knowledge and the awareness of the extended here-and-now have convinced some subject-matter specialists, as well as some do-it-yourself educators and others of the lay public, to suggest—and in some instances almost to demand—that children become subject-matter oriented at an earlier age. There is proof that children can indeed be taught reading and various other skills at a very early age. But the question remains: does *can* mean *should?*

This fourth edition of *Education in the Kindergarten* takes a definite stand in regard to having information for information's sake and skill for skill's sake crowded down into the school experience of children who have had but sixty months—plus or minus—to acquaint themselves with the many challenging experiences of everyday living. An equally definite stand has been taken in regard to the importance of bringing into focus the unending number of opportunities for learning and development which can be found in everyday kindergarten living.

The many new curriculum guides that include the "K" through Three, or

Six, or Eight, or Twelve span attest to the fact that the kindergarten is currently thought of as an integral part of the educational program. We are grateful for the extended awareness of this concept, and yet we are somewhat apprehensive lest the impression be given that the kindergarten should be block- or subject-matter oriented.

In this as in earlier editions of *Education in the Kindergarten* attention is directed to the fact that the very noncompartmentalized nature of the good kindergarten program affords opportunities to utilize experiences that clarify understandings and build foundations for further learning. Throughout this edition emphasis is placed on the importance of (1) helping children clarify their present understandings and (2) challenging children to use their present knowledge to solve problems and thus acquire new knowledge which in turn will go toward developing a broader base of understanding. It takes a "heap of living" to make symbols, facts, and general information meaningful!

Bringing out a new edition of a book is like rearranging a room to make space for new furniture. Room arrangement usually involves moving *all* the furniture, discarding some items, refurbishing or redoing others, and then regrouping so that old and new pieces make a harmonious whole. If the arrangement was well done in the first place and if the rearrangement maintains the same artistic quality, the addition of the new enhances all.

It is our hope that the analogy is apparent to the reader of this fourth edition of *Education in the Kindergarten*. The text has been taken apart chapter by chapter and paragraph by paragraph; a new section has been added on the pros and cons of the name kindergarten; a section designed to help teachers challenge children to think has been written for the language arts chapter; the chapter on science and social studies has been recast to show more clearly the many educational implications to be found in simple, everyday experience; all the bibliographical material has, as far as possible, been brought up to date; and the index has been redesigned to make it more functional. New illustrations have been added, but many, with intent of purpose, have been reprinted from earlier editions. The re-runs have been used as proof that, though children's experience and vocabulary may have greatly changed, children themselves are not so very different from children of bygone years.

It would be impossible to mention by name all the people who have contributed, in one way and another, to this edition of *Education in the Kindergarten*. Kindergarten children themselves, kindergarten teachers, students, my student assistant, teachers in whose kindergartens students have been privileged to observe, workshop participants, and colleagues have all made contributions. I am deeply grateful, too, for the courtesy extended by the libraries of such colleges as Macalaster, St. Olaf, and Carleton—and, of course, the library personnel of the education and reference rooms at the University of Minnesota.

N. E. H.

# CONTENTS

# ILLUSTRATIONS

# TABLES

# 1

# THE FIVE-YEAR-OLD

Five candles on a birthday cake! What will the next year bring? Almost certainly a period of interesting development, a year in which babyhood is left behind and a year in which the child will throw himself into his widening experience arena with a zest for doing and feeling and learning that might well arouse the envy of the grown-up. For many American children, age five also means school. A small percentage of our five-year-olds will be entering first grade, Montessori ungraded groups, and pre-primary units; a far larger percentage will be entering kindergartens—if kindergartens are provided in their district.[1]

What kind of kindergarten is best? Obviously, one that is best adapted to the needs of its children. The socioeconomic group served by the school, the ability range and the age range within the enrolled group—these and other factors must be taken into consideration in determining what kind of kindergarten is best in a particular situation. Since the factor most common to all American kindergartens is the chronological five-year-oldness of the enrolled children it seems wise to review what is known of the development, abilities, and needs of the five-year-old child before considering what might be the best kinds of experience for the kindergarten to provide.[2]

Even before we review the facts which we have long accepted as guides to the child's maturity, let us heed an admonition! Educators need to become more informed about neuro-maturation. The development of the child's nervous system is closely related to his ability to perceive ideas and perform tasks. Pediatricians use the term "developmental quotient" rather than "intelligence quotient." "The DQ considers all phases of the child's growth pattern such as motor development, adaptive behavior, social-

[1] See Chapter 2.
[2] See Chapter 3.

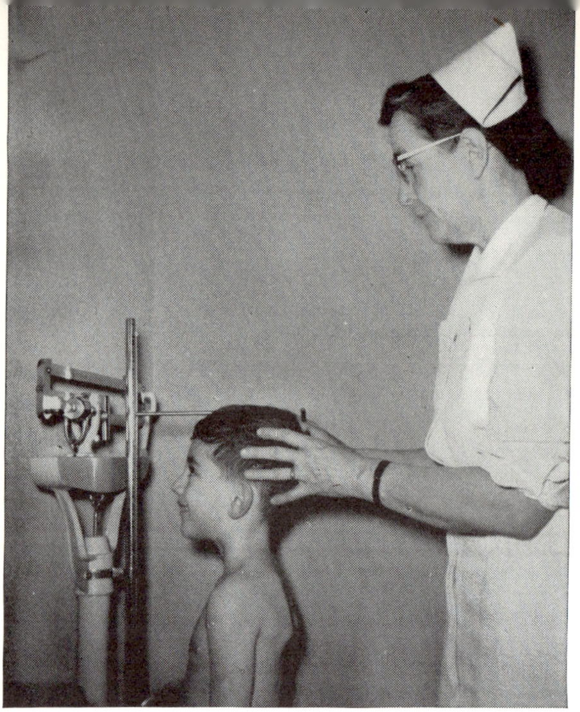

*"I'm big."*
*"You're 45 inches tall and you weigh 43 pounds."*

personal relationships and facility in the use of language."[3] Now, keeping this "DQ" in mind, let us consider some of the various phases of the five-year-old's development.

## Physical Development

The five-year-old is at the end of a period of very rapid growth, known in the language of physical development as "early childhood."[4]

The following table indicates that the kindergarten child is apt to be somewhere between thirty-five and forty-nine inches tall and to weigh between twenty-nine and fifty-five pounds. It also gives us an estimate of the average weight for children of different heights at ages four, five, and six.

In this table, age is taken to the nearest birthday, height to the nearest inch, and weight to the nearest pound. Children from birth to five years are not considered to be seriously undernourished unless they are from 7 to 10 percent below these figures.

[3] From a paper presented by Helen Heffernan at the Conference of the Association for Childhood Education International, Portland, Oregon, 1964. Miss Heffernan is citing Dr. Shelby Dietrick, a physician for the Los Angeles schools and formerly Director of Pediatrics at the California Hospital in Los Angeles.

[4] In the field of education this term usually refers to the period of time from nursery school and kindergarten through the primary school.

**Table 1** Height-Weight-Age Table for 4-, 5-, and 6-Year-Old Children[5]

| HEIGHT IN INCHES | WEIGHT IN POUNDS: BOYS | | | GIRLS | | |
|---|---|---|---|---|---|---|
| | Age 4 | Age 5 | Age 6 | Age 4 | Age 5 | Age 6 |
| 35 | 29 | | | 29 | | |
| 36 | 31 | | | 30 | 31 | |
| 37 | 32 | 32 | | 31 | 32 | |
| 38 | 33 | 34 | | 33 | 33 | |
| 39 | 35 | 35 | | 34 | 34 | 34 |
| 40 | 36 | 36 | 36 | 36 | 36 | 36 |
| 41 | 38 | 38 | 38 | 37 | 37 | 37 |
| 42 | 39 | 39 | 39 | 39 | 39 | 39 |
| 43 | 41 | 41 | 41 | 40 | 41 | 41 |
| 44 | | 43 | 43 | | 42 | 42 |
| 45 | | 45 | 45 | | | 45 |
| 46 | | | 48 | | | 47 |
| 47 | | | 50 | | | 50 |
| 48 | | | 52 | | | 52 |
| 49 | | | 55 | | | |

Prepared by Robert M. Woodbury

In using this or any other height-weight table, we should remember that the more recent studies in child development tend to measure the child's deviation from the average in relation to physical types and familial patterns rather than in relation to height, weight, and age. However, from this table we do get certain interesting facts. There is, for example, very little difference between the ratio of weight to height for boys and girls at this age. Generally speaking, we can use forty-five inches and forty-five pounds as guide figures when thinking about five-year-olds and their body build. For the shorter child the number of pounds is usually less than the height in inches, and for the taller child it is generally greater.

Before fixing too firmly in mind the range of expectancy in height and weight and expected ratio of height to weight presented in the above chart, let's look briefly at some figures quoted in a study of mean weight for height presented in a 1957 pediatrics journal, and consider also some facts presented in other recent studies.

The figures in Table 2 are taken from a set presented by G. M. Naimark.[6] Although the relationships between heights and weights are essentially the

[5] Table and notation from Marion L. Faegre and John E. Anderson, *Child Care and Training*, 7th ed., rev., Minneapolis, University of Minnesota Press, 1947, pp. 22–23.

[6] "The Growth Spectrum: A Simplified Chart for Assessment of Growth," *Journal of Pediatrics*, May, 1957, 50:586–590, chart p. 587.

**Table 2** Mean Weight for Height

| Age Yrs. | RETARDED OR SLOW GROWING GROUP Height Inches | RETARDED OR SLOW GROWING GROUP Weight Pounds | AVERAGE GROWING GROUP Height Inches | AVERAGE GROWING GROUP Weight Pounds | ACCELERATED GROWING GROUP Height Inches | ACCELERATED GROWING GROUP Weight Pounds |
|---|---|---|---|---|---|---|
| GIRLS | | | | | | |
| 4 | 39.4 | 33.7 | 40.6 | 37.5 | 41.3 | 42.1 |
| 5 | 41.7 | 37.9 | 43.1 | 41.2 | 44.1 | 48.1 |
| 6 | 44.5 | 43.0 | 45.9 | 46.7 | 46.9 | 53.2 |
| BOYS | | | | | | |
| 4 | 39.6 | 35.7 | 40.8 | 39.0 | 41.5 | 41.4 |
| 5 | 42.3 | 40.3 | 43.7 | 42.8 | 44.5 | 45.9 |
| 6 | 44.9 | 44.1 | 45.8 | 47.6 | 47.2 | 51.8 |

same as those in Table 1, they give us a slightly different slant on weight-height expectancies. There seems to be a tendency for today's children to be slightly heavier for height than those of a decade ago. Too, the overall height-weight pattern of average growing children today approaches that of the accelerated group a quarter of a century ago. No wonder we often hear adults say, "My, but these children seem large for their age!"

An interesting fact in relation to increase in physical size is found in the following. The expected average increase in weight between the child's fifth and sixth birthdays is about 5 pounds and 2 ounces and in height, 2.5 inches. These figures are easy to remember because the digits reverse themselves—weight 5.2, and height 2.5.

Now, if you are not bogged down by figures, suppose we turn our attention to some that are even more revealing. The figures in Table 3 are taken from a survey made by W. Edgar Martin. They represent action or postural measurements made in the spring of the year on 207 children enrolled in kindergartens. For two reasons the averages may be a bit high. First, since the measurements were made between March and the first weeks in June, most of these children were six at the time; and second, the measurements were made with the children wearing clothing and shoes. But by and large, these are the children whom any kindergarten teacher might have in her group in the spring of the school year. If you can't bear to look at any more figures at this point, just skip this set for the present and come back to it sometime when you are wondering how high to hang a picture, what height the new workbench should be, how deep or how high the new set of shelves should be, how many inches should be added or removed from your present table legs, where you

**Table 3** Postural Measurements of Kindergarten Children[7]

| | | MEAN | S.D. | RANGE |
|---|---|---|---|---|
| Weight in Pounds | Boys | 47.3 | 6.72 | 27.1-67.4 |
| | Girls | 46.1 | 6.80 | 25.7-66.5 |
| Height in Inches | Boys | 45.7 | 1.78 | 40.4-51.1 |
| | Girls | 45.5 | 1.80 | 40.1-50.9 |
| Eye Height from Floor | Boys | 41.1 | 1.78 | 35.8-46.4 |
| | Girls | 40.8 | 1.80 | 35.4-46.2 |
| Shoulder Height | Boys | 35.7 | 1.70 | 30.6-40.8 |
| | Girls | 35.3 | 1.64 | 30.6-40.4 |
| Elbow Height | Boys | 27.5 | 1.52 | 22.9-32.0 |
| | Girls | 27.3 | 1.31 | 23.3-31.2 |
| Maximum Reach | Boys | 55.4 | 2.61 | 47.5-63.2 |
| | Girls | 55.1 | 2.47 | 47.7-62.5 |
| Maximum Seat Height | Boys | 11.5 | 0.57 | 9.8-13.2 |
| | Girls | 11.6 | 0.61 | 9.8-13.5 |
| Lumbar Height Above Seat | Boys | 8.3 | .64 | 6.4-10.2 |
| | Girls | 8.4 | .69 | 6.4-10.5 |
| Table Height from Seat | Boys | 7.1 | 0.45 | 5.8- 8.5 |
| | Girls | 7.2 | 0.58 | 5.5- 8.9 |
| Table Height from Floor | Boys | 18.7 | .76 | 16.4-21.0 |
| | Girls | 18.2 | .60 | 16.4-20.0 |
| Standing Working Position | Boys | 26.1 | 1.58 | 31.4-30.8 |
| | Girls | 26.3 | 2.34 | 19.3-33.3 |
| Maximum Forward Reach | Boys | 18.8 | 1.60 | 14.0-23.6 |
| | Girls | 18.0 | 1.53 | 13.4-22.6 |

[7] W. Edgar Martin, *Children's Body Measurements for Planning and Equipping Schools,* Washington, D.C., United States Department of Health, Education, and Welfare, Office of Education, 1955.

should put the back support on the chair you are making, or at what level the easel should be adjusted.

At age five the body has attained about 38 percent of its mature development, though different parts of the body are developing at different rates.[8] The brain has developed so rapidly that by five or six it is almost as large as it will ever be. By age five the lymphoid organs have attained about 80 percent of their growth, the nervous system about 88 percent, and the genital organs about 8 percent. All the baby teeth have appeared, and possibly one or two have already fallen out. (What a red-letter day it is when that first tooth drops out!) While he is in his sixth year, the child may be expected to acquire the first four of his permanent teeth.

Apparently eye maturation, like much other human development, is greatly dependent on the individual growth pattern. We do know that for young children low vision is likely to be the rule rather than the exception during the preschool years and even up to nine years of age. Park and Burri have brought to our attention the following facts relating to vision in the early years of childhood. Using 20-20 as perfect vision, they report that approximately 50 percent of preschool children have less than perfect vision, while from 65 to 80 percent may be expected to achieve a 20-20 rating in the early elementary and junior-high-school period. The study also points out two other findings which may help in making an estimate of the five-year-old's visual maturity. Between the prereading period and the eighth grade, good fusion increases from 54 to 80 percent; and in approximately the same period of time, good stereopsis increases from 18 to 75 or 80 percent.[9]

It has been said that more American children of primary-school age wear glasses than do children of similar age groups in those countries where formal reading is not introduced until children are seven. Of course we do not know whether this is because our children get an earlier opthomological diagnosis or because we tend to place children, ready or not, into an earlier reading program. Nevertheless, the second possibility should not be overlooked in any consideration of eye maturation.

## Motor Development

More striking than mere growth of individual parts of the body at this age is the gain in control which the child has acquired over his muscles. In the first five years of life, the individual changes from a newborn infant

[8] Richard E. Scammon, "The Growth of the Body in Childhood," *Measurement of Man*, Minneapolis, University of Minnesota Press, 1930, p. 193.

[9] George E. Park and Clara Burri, "Eye Maturation and Reading Difficulties," *Journal of Educational Psychology*, December, 1943, 34:535–546.

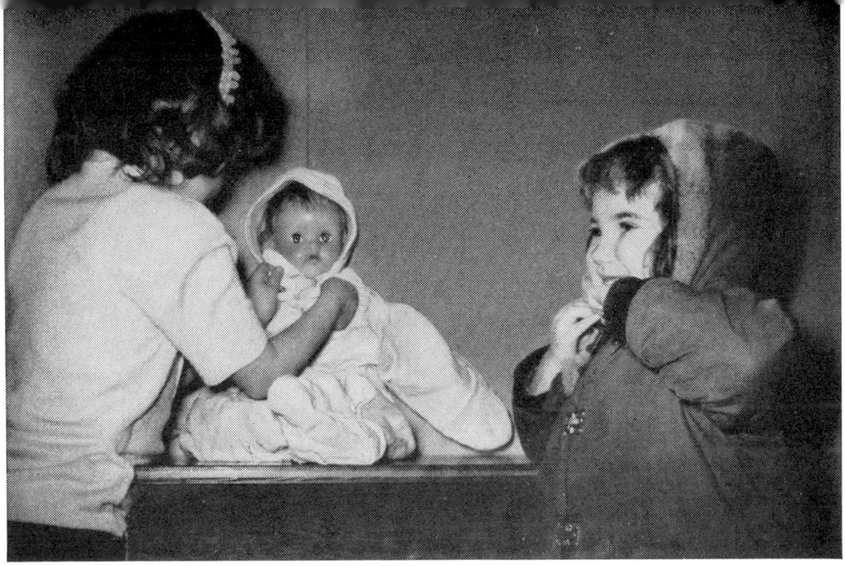

University of Minnesota

*"Tying is fun. I can do it without looking. See!"*

whose random movements are completely uncoordinated to an alert child who, in gross muscular control, is very much the master of his motor self. The five-year-old walks with an easy swinging gait; he runs freely—and, it might be noted, about as often as he walks; he hops with reasonable ease, though usually better on one foot than on the other; he jumps down from one level to another and across space but does not find it easy to jump up and over hurdles. Most five-year-olds can gallop, but skipping is something many are "working" on. Between 72 and 91 percent can be expected to acquire an easy skip by the time they are six.

Outfitted with the right kind of clothing, he can be expected to dress himself. He is learning to tie bows and may be observed minutes on end struggling to master the art. Once he has achieved the skill of bow-tieing, his joy seems complete, and he often goes about tieing and untieing everything in sight, from shoelaces to mother's apron strings. Occasionally he still needs some help with rubbers and boots, but with a little adult encouragement at the outset, he can soon learn to manipulate fastenings, such as buttons, large snaps, and buckles. He finds it very difficult to start an open-end zipper but, once it is started, delights in "zipping." He handles pencils and crayons, usually with a thumb and forefinger grasp, and is able to copy a square and a triangle, or perhaps even a diamond.

About 90 percent of all five-year-olds have become right-handed. The others are either still experimenting or are by nature distinctly left-handed.

One of the interesting facts about the motor development of the kindergarten child is that this physical development is not a reliable indicator of his mental ability. Generally speaking, motor development depends on chronological age or maturation, and only in part on practice and mental ability. It is interesting to note that a very able child may appear to be only average or less than average in his motor development and that forced drill and practice, though it may actually be harmful to the individual, may make almost any child appear to be more mentally able than he really is.

## Intellectual Development

Though the physical growth curve indicates a slowing down of physical development at the five-year level, there is no real evidence that the same is true of intellectual development. Although the curve for the normal child usually continues in a gradual ascent, it is not until the five-year level that we begin to get a significant correlation between scores on mental tests given at this age with scores on tests given at a higher age level. Scores on mental tests given at two years of age have a low correlation—only .46—with scores on tests given at seven years of age.[10] And with the seven-year score we find the intervening ages correlated in this fashion: three years, .56; four years, .66; five years, .75; and six years, .81.

Keeping in mind the tremendous difference in individual patterns of development, we should not take even the five-year-old scores too seriously. The child being measured by the tests may be either a slow- or a fast-developing individual and, quite apart from a slow or fast start in development, there are other factors to be kept in mind in evaluating the intelligence of an individual. Earlier emphasis on the constancy of the IQ has diminished as a result of longitudinal testing programs. Testing of individuals over a long period of time has revealed that, while there is some persistence in the individual's performance ratings, there are indications that mental growth does not proceed at a uniform rate, nor does it always proceed in a predictable fashion. We have long realized that a single test is not a valid measure of a child's mental ability and, although a series of tests helps us determine where the child is in his present stage of mental development, we must never think of even a battery of tests as being a definite prognostic instrument.[11]

## Language

The child's speech has shown a somewhat amazing increase, from an average of 3 words at one year to 272, 896, and 1,540 words for the suc-

[10] G. G. Thompson, "The Meaning and Measurement of Intellectual Development," *Child Psychology*, Boston, Houghton Mifflin Company, 1952, pp. 586–590.

[11] Jean Walker MacFarlane, "From Infancy to Adulthood," *Childhood Education*, March, 1963, 39:336–342.

cessive years. At five he may be expected to have an average vocabulary of 2,072 words.[12] He will probably have at his command a greater selection of nouns than any other parts of speech; but he also frequently uses verbs, adjectives, conjunctions, and pronouns. Adverbs, however, are not so common. In the development of language, chronological age, again, seems to be more important than mental age. Children from families high in the socioeconomic scale ordinarily show a high degree of language development.[13] Recent studies have indicated (1) that television has been a contributing factor in raising the language developmental level in lower socioeconomic groups; (2) that kindergarten-aged children use a wider variety of words and talk more than they did twenty-five years ago; and (3) that the more advanced children tend to use more verbs, more direct sentences, and fewer dangling phrases than less advanced children. We know that twins frequently show a retarded language development and that, for better or worse, children of kindergarten age will have acquired most of the language patterns commonly heard on television or used by the adults with whom they are most closely associated.

The five-year-old is still experimenting with language, trying out new words, inventing forms by combining words or adding endings which he has used on other words. Not infrequently the kindergarten teacher has to translate what comes to her ears in order to get the idea the child is attempting to convey. For example, when she hears a child report that his father "hired the fence" she gleans from context that the child's father made the fence higher, and when she hears that a child's big brother "mored the lawn" she rightfully concludes that the big brother cut the grass with a lawnmower. Verbal play is still interesting. The kindergarten

[12] Florence L. Goodenough, *Developmental Psychology*, 2nd ed., New York, D. Appleton-Century Company, 1945, p. 280.

[13] The socioeconomic status of a family corresponds roughly to the father's occupation. A classification of occupations is given by Florence L. Goodenough and John E. Anderson in *Experimental Child Study*, New York, The Century Company, 1931, p. 237. The following is a much abbreviated form of this classification: Group I (about 3 percent of the total) architects, civil, electrical, and mechanical engineers, clergymen, teachers, dentists, physicians, lawyers; Group II (about 5 percent of the total) managers, superintendents, railroad officials, bankers, stockbrokers, wholesale dealers, importers, accountants, draftsmen, state and federal officials, and inspectors; Group III (about 14 percent of the total) retail dealers, bookkeepers, cashiers, stenographers, real-estate and insurance agents, telegraph operators, carpenters, electricians, jewelers, machinists, plumbers, ticket agents, steam railroad conductors, veterinary surgeons, city and county officials; Group IV (about 19 percent of the total) farmers, florists, poultry and stock raisers; Group V (about 27 percent of the total) salesmen, policemen, soldiers, bakers, blacksmiths, painters, cobblers, tailors, street-railway conductors, firemen, motormen, chauffeurs, barbers, waiters; Group VI (about 13 percent of the total) messengers, bundle and office boys, miners, teamsters, switchmen, watchmen, janitors, servants; Group VII (about 19 percent of the total) laborers in coal and lumber yards, street and railroad laborers, longshoremen, farm laborers, gardeners, lumbermen.

child mumbles and gurgles, experimenting with new sounds and inventing combinations just for the fun of feeling and hearing them.

His conversation with his peers begins to have some of the element of discussion, but much of his hour-by-hour verbalization is little more than a series of soliloquies. He talks about what he is doing, and if his audience fails to hear or to reply, he is not too concerned. He asks an ever-increasing number of questions.[14] Most (some 86 percent) are asked of adults, and almost 90 percent refer to the immediate situation rather than to the past or future. His questions are no longer primarily concerned with the names of things. More and more they reflect his concern about causal relations and social relationships. Boys appear to be more concerned with causes and girls with social relationships.

Along with the improvement in expression goes, of course, an increase in comprehension, and we find that the five-year-old is much more able than the four-year-old to understand verbal explanations. We cannot rely on his understanding words accurately, however, and must constantly aid him by presenting the real article.

English is a complex and confusing language. As adults, we sometimes overlook two facts in relation to the learning of new words and grasping word meanings. We forget what it is like to have only an auditory awareness of a new word; and we forget that one word frequently has more than a single meaning. The kindergarten teacher at times has to be something of a mental telepathist to figure out what the child is trying to say; yet all the time the child may merely be repeating a word as he has heard or understood it. For example, Barbara once reported quite confidentially to her teacher, "I brought my revival lipstick today. My mother bought it for me Sunday." The "revival" lipstick turned out to be *Lip-ivo,* a camphorated "lipstick" often used for chapped lips. As we have noted, a child is not always aware of all the meanings of a word and may interpret in the light of what he knows. A group of children and their teacher were discussing the planting of bulbs. They seemed to be proceeding satisfactorily until one little girl reported that they had a bulb at home that she could bring for the school garden but she didn't know whether it would grow or not. And then, by way of explanation, she added, "It won't light any more."

## Information

Through firsthand experiences, books (especially science picture books), stories, newspapers, comic books, TV, radio, recordings, filmstrips, films

[14] E. A. Davis, "The Form and Function of Children's Questions," *Child Development,* March, 1932, 3:57–74.

and sometimes movies, the five-year-old has been exposed to a wide variety of information. Fortunately or otherwise, the readiness factor has acted as a stop valve to control the amount actually taken in. In the process of sorting out and putting together the information absorbed, the child is likely to arrive at some rather surprising conclusions. Having been given an explanation of the way in which the taxidermist has prepared the birds for the museum case, for instance, he may ask in all seriousness if a statue used to be alive. Back in the nineteen thirties, a test devised to ascertain kindergarten children's general information revealed that, among other things, a kindergarten child might be expected to know the name of a paper published in his city, the number of hands on a clock, legs on a horse, and horns on a cow, but not the number of wings on a butterfly, pennies in a dime, or eggs in a half dozen. He might be expected to know who cuts hair, who pulls teeth, who removes tonsils, and who brings letters to the house, but not who makes the laws of the country. He would probably know what ice, snow, and skis are made of, but not what lightning and paper are made of. He might be expected to know how a drum is played, but not how a cornet is played, to know that apples grow on trees, but not—unless he lived in the South—where we get cotton. And, no doubt, he would know what Jack and Jill did, but not what kind of coach Cinderella rode in. One child, when asked what Cinderella lost at the ball, said "I'm not sure but I think it was six to nothing."

*The Snow Plow—Neither Snow Nor Sleet Can Dull Their Curiosity.*

This same test, when given to five-year-olds in the middle nineteen fifties, produced both some expected and some rather surprising results.[15] The children usually did not know the name of a local newspaper, but they knew the names of TV stations, TV news reporters, and TV programs. When they were asked the name of the nearest large city, the one most frequently named was New York. And one child, when asked what part of a plant is underground replied, "the shelter." In general the test revealed that though children may seem "brighter" today it is not so much a case of their being "brighter" as it is of their having been exposed to a greater and a different body of information than that to which children of an earlier day were exposed. Some information common to children in the early and even the middle nineteen hundreds is almost completely outside the realm of today's children. Today's five-year-olds speak easily of astronauts orbiting the earth but they know very little about a streetcar and even less about a horse and buggy as modes of transportation. They enjoy orange juice and potatoes but many have little idea of their source—as far as they are concerned orange juice comes in cans or bottles and potatoes come in small cardboard packages.

The child's lack of experience makes him unable to see relationships or to generalize as readily or as accurately as an adult does. Many of his erroneous conclusions are due, not to his failure to think, but to insufficient information. Consider, for instance, some of the deductions early man made about the world or some of the deductions we are currently making about life on the moon and you will find that these are not unlike some of the conclusions of an uninformed child. When an adult is faced with unfamiliar material, he makes the same kind of mistakes the child makes—and is no more concerned by his errors than the child is!

Many five-year-olds can count by rote to 19 without help, and with help at the deciles can go on and on toward 100 or more.[16] They love to bandy about such words as *thousands, millions, billions,* and *trillions,* and even "finity," but, of course, have little idea of their meaning. Counting objects is a different thing from rote counting or the mere verbalization of numbers. A five-year-old's performance is average if he can point to and count accurately as many as thirteen objects.

The five-year-old can recognize his own first name usually without much difficulty when it is set down in uppercase letters, and with some study he can learn to recognize his name when both upper- and lowercase letters are used. He often attempts to print his name and finds it much easier

[15] Mildred Templin, "General Information of Kindergarten Children: A Comparison with the Probst Study after Twenty-Six Years," *Child Development*, March, 1958, 29:87–96.

[16] See the Gesell books in "Selected References" at the end of this chapter.

*The Thinker*

to use capital letters. These efforts at printing are sometimes amusing; he frequently scatters large, irregularly shaped letters at random over his paper. Even when he has them in sequence, it is not unusual for the sequence to lead from right to left. Frequently this early interest which a young child shows in naming and writing letters is taken by parents as an indication of the child's being ready to be "taught reading"—though no one would dream of saying that a child's first interest in learning to move about in an upright position indicates that he should be "taught dancing"!

When the kindergarten-aged child defines an object, he usually does so in terms of its use—a chair is to sit in, an airplane is to fly in; and when he tells about a picture he still often simply enumerates objects, though he is beginning to go further and give an *overall* description of what he sees in the picture. When he draws or paints he frequently puts into his picture much more than others can see in the finished product. Purely as an experiment, a teacher once attempted to interpret a child's picture (see illustration above) as the story of "The Sun and the Wind." When she had finished, the child said, "That's not it at all. You see this is the thinker and he's sitting under this tree and over here is the 'servatory and that thing on the top is a telescope. At night you can see the sky and also the thinker." The five-year-old is often very adept at telling fairly long stories, but again individual differences dictate the flow of words. Some children can tell all they have to say in a sentence or a sentence fragment; others spin their tales as long as time permits.

## Learning

The five-year-old is learning rapidly. He wants to find out about things, he is eager for information. One kindergarten child expressed the feeling of his age group very well when, unabashedly and with great enthusiasm, he said, "I just *love* to learn new things." Fostering intellectual curiosity[17] is one of the major responsibilities of the kindergarten teacher.

The kindergarten child investigates, examines, and questions. He frequently appears to be an animated question box with inquiries ranging from such comparatively simple questions as "Where does wood come from?" to such complex ones as "Where does the electricity go when you turn off the light?" He is consumed with curiosity as to the weight, strength, taste, and smell of all sorts of materials. He wants to know how things work and turns handles and punches switches to find out. He yearns to test his strength and exhibit his prowess. There is little, in fact, that he is not willing to attempt. Scissors, paints, saws, brooms, gadgets, and gymnasium apparatus all challenge him. He is very fond of books and stories. He knows that they are sources of information and frequently produces a book in proof of a point. His immediate environment offers him unending challenges. The alert five-year-old is seldom idle.

Generally speaking, the greater the mental ability of the child, the more rapidly he will learn. If a problem is made interesting and pleasant, the average kindergarten child will learn rapidly; if he dislikes the work, his progress will be slow. But learning, it must be remembered, never proceeds at a uniform rate. Some individuals show considerable irregularity, gaining at times rapidly and at other times gaining apparently not at all. Sometimes such periods of no visible improvement are ultimately advantageous. It takes an artist teacher to know when and under what conditions information should be featured. Some teachers offer a vapid information program while others seem almost to force-feed information.

Of the daily skills, the kindergarten child may be expected to know how to take off his wraps and hang them where they belong, to go to the toilet by himself, to wash and dry his hands reasonably well, and to get his rug for rest period, folding it according to the rules of the school. Simple habits of this type can be acquired easily if the teacher will only remember that the child needs motivation, that he needs much opportunity for practice, and that he needs to know reasons for his behavior and to feel that the goal is within reach. In the words of an early White House Conference: "Youth wishes to see results. We all do. Youth wishes

[17] Kenneth Wann, Miriam Dorn, Elizabeth Ann Liddle, *Fostering Intellectual Development in Young Children*, New York, Bureau of Publications, Teachers College, Columbia University, 1962.

to carry responsibility. The two things must be joined together under conditions that will secure more and ever better consideration of the broader consequences."[18] Experiments in the psychological laboratory have shown that people learn more quickly if they are rewarded for their correct responses and mildly penalized for incorrect responses. It has been found also that both punishment and reward are more effective if they are natural (or apparently natural) results of the activity.

## Imagination

Imitative and representative play (impersonation) make up a large part of the play of five-year-olds. They pretend they are other people, animals, fire engines, airplanes, locomotives, and even trees, flowers, rocks, wind, and waves. During the third or fourth year, there are sometimes evidences of a fantastic imagination that may disturb the conscientious and truthful adult, but as long as the child recognizes the difference between fact and fancy, there is little danger. We do not want the individual to live completely in a land of dreams; yet from a combination of vivid imagination and high intelligence come many of our creative artists and scientists. The creative instinct is common to all children, but only through much opportunity to experiment with materials and ideas can the child realize his potential creative ability. Creativity, Torrance reminds us, can be primed.[19]

The kindergarten child's imagination is strong enough to let him see the possible effects of bad behavior; thus, when he is asked to explain some past irregularity in conduct, he occasionally tries to misrepresent or to shift the emphasis, hiding some facts, stressing more desirable angles, all in an attempt to produce the conclusion that will be most pleasant for him.

His imagination lets him realize that someday he will be "grown up," and he talks and plans about what he is going to do when that happy time arrives. He apparently is concerned (at least as far as we can trust the evidence of dreams) with fire, animals, death, people, and his play. When we ask him what he would like if he were granted one wish, most often he asks for some material object, and much less frequently for amusements, a new baby in the family, money, or supernatural power. An investigation of children's wishes has shown that as children grow older, they gradually

[18] White House Conference, *The School Health Program*, New York, The Century Company, 1932, p. 28.
[19] E. Paul Torrance, "Priming Creativity in the Primary Grades," *Elementary School Journal*, October, 1961, 62:34–41.

come to realize that a general desire—for example, to have all the wishes they wanted—if granted, will automatically bring with it many specific desires. The investigation also indicates that children's wishes are directed toward actual objects rather than the acquisition of strength and power.[20]

## Interests

Many five-year-olds are interested in hoarding and collecting, as is evident from an inspection of their pockets and lockers. It is not unusual at this age for such acquisitiveness to lead to mild flings of pilfering. Girls seem more interested in collecting fancy pins, small boxes, paper cuttings, and paper dolls. Boys prefer such things as small notebooks, cards, marbles, comic books, stones, and bottle tops. Conclusions concerning kindergarten children's favorite play materials vary greatly. Farwell found that for boys blocks were the most popular indoor play materials, with paints and modeling clay coming next. For girls, paints and clay headed the list. Girls seem to be more interested in other people and in furniture, and boys in such things as tricycles, wagons, and trucks.[21] Van Alstyne found that children in a five-year-old group were equally interested in active and quiet play.[22] More recent observations (study by Margolin and Leton)[23] indicate that, when childen have a wide variety of play materials to choose from, blocks do not retain their earlier high interest rating.

With each type of play material the nature of the activity changes as the child matures. For example, the young child carries his blocks about, places them one on or beside the other, pushes the pile over, and starts all over again. By the time the child is five, he usually starts building an enclosure or high structures, and his building shows an awareness and appreciation of form and design.

## Emotional Development

Emotionally also the five-year-old child is on the road to maturity. From the comparatively simple and clear-cut emotional responses of his early

[20] A. T. Jersild, F. V. Markey, and C. L. Jersild, *Children's Fears, Dreams, Wishes, Daydreams, Likes, Dislikes, Pleasant and Unpleasant Memories,* Child Development Monograph No. 12, New York, Bureau of Publications, Teachers College, Columbia University, 1933.

[21] L. Farwell, *Reactions of Kindergarten, First, and Second Grade Children to Constructive Play Materials, Genetic Psychology Monographs,* 1930, 8:431–562.

[22] Dorothy Van Alstyne, *Play Behavior and Choice of Play Materials of Pre-School Children,* Chicago, University of Chicago Press, 1932, p. 51.

[23] E. B. Margolin and D. A. Leton, "Interest of Kindergarten Children in Block Play," *Journal of Educational Research,* 1961, 55:13–18.

years, he has now developed finer shades and gradations of feeling, more subtle responses to a greater variety of stimuli, and his responses are more varied. He responds, also, in a more controlled manner. Although he is still likely to burst into furious or joyous activity, he will occasionally restrain himself. Sometimes he will recover from an outburst promptly; at other times he may harbor an emotion and sustain a mood for a fairly long time. He resorts to tears as an expression of emotions much less frequently than he did at earlier ages, though there is of course a wide range of individual difference.

Tears seem to be a woman's right even at this age, for the girl who cries is not nearly so likely to lose face as is the boy. The boy who cries is quickly dubbed "crybaby" or "sissy." It has been suggested that our cultural nonacceptance of tears from men and boys may be responsible for emotional buildups which contribute to the shorter life-span of the male portion of our society. Apparently crying can be a wholesome emotional expression—tears can be therapeutic. The child who never cries and the child who cries over every little thing both may be in need of help.

Probably the most commonly observed emotion in young children is anger, the causes of which vary with the age of the child. Generally speaking, the younger the child, the more likely he is to become angry at any interference with his physical activities. Perhaps he is struck by another child, perhaps someone withholds a toy he desires, or perhaps he cannot steer his "walker" around a chair. If he is very young, his response to such situations will probably be a display of temper, but a few years later he may fight back or calmly endeavor to overcome the difficulty. As he grows older, his anger is more likely to be aroused by interference with his possessions, plans, and purposes, and by such things as being ridiculed or called names. In general, boys are more quarrelsome than girls. Of the common activities of the nursery school and kindergarten, sand play produces more quarrels than any other single cause, probably because the sand is not easily divided into equal shares.

Few fears appear in the ordinary school environment. The fears of most young children are very definitely influenced by the attitudes of the people about them; thus there is often a close similarity between the fears of a child and those of his mother. Since the teacher has usually been taught to conceal whatever foolish fears she may have, the children see little to imitate at school, and few fears appear there. In five-year-olds at home, the most common fears are of animals; supernatural events, such as mystery and death; "bad" people, such as robbers; darkness; being alone; strange sights; and deformities. Less frequent are fears of dreams and apparitions, gestures, noises, frightening tales, bodily injury, or physical danger.

Jealousy, which is usually the accompaniment of strong affection, is most often evoked in the five-year-old by attention or privileges accorded younger or older siblings. The five-year-old working and playing with a peer group under the guidance of a friendly but impartial teacher is less likely to have occasion for feeling jealous than the same child in the more highly emotionally affectionate climate of the home.

One of the emotions which may appear at this age is rivalry. By the age of five, many children will be spurred on to greater effort and higher accomplishment if they are working beside another child. At the younger ages, this proximity has no influence, except possibly to serve as a distraction and sometimes actually to lower the output of each child.

Laughter has been greatly overrated as an attribute of childhood. Laughter is often near the surface but, if one watches a group of kindergarten-aged children for a period of time, it becomes quite apparent that they are surprisingly serious about their play. Boys laugh aloud more than girls, but girls smile more than boys. Most young children are ready to smile back at anyone who smiles at them; they seem to interpret an adult smile as in indication of friendly feeling and of a satisfactory state of affairs. Children of five are amused by such things as noises; grotesque faces and figures; dramatic situations, such as someone falling down; funny dancing; bumping into each other; and things falling upside down or turning inside out. The appreciation of jokes and of varied types of humor comes only with experience and training. A five-year-old often tries to tell jokes he has heard from older children—particularly the moron jokes—and frequently he has missed the point entirely, but he laughs uproariously at the conclusion. Other children will often laugh with him, but a more sophisticated child may simply frown and say, "I don't get it!" Gradually the child will come to recognize absurd physical phenomena, surprising relationships, word plays, and incongruities. At first he laughs only at what he himself actually experiences; later he is able to laugh at pictures and at stories without any demonstration or pictorial representation. Absurdities which seem delightfully amusing to grown-ups often get little response from five-year-olds. For example, until the humor of the situation is pointed out to them, five-year-olds are likely to see nothing funny about the frog who jumped out of the pond and found himself in the rain and then said, "I'll get wet and I may catch cold," and thereupon jumped into the pond again. Although generally speaking the children who are mentally most alert are those first to see the funny side of things, such recognition depends not only on mental development but on training as well.

## Social Development

The five-year-old is definitely more social than he was the year before. Records show that the percentage of solitary children decreases steadily from year to year from 8 percent at age 3 and 5 percent at age 4 to 2 percent at age 5.[24] Not only is the older child less solitary but he is also gradually coming to enjoy larger groups of companions. About a third of the groups of five-year-olds are composed of two members only; groups of more than five members are rare. In these groups the children are usually of the same sex. The groups hold together for brief periods, with only about a third staying together more than twenty minutes. Friendships become stronger and quarreling with playmates less frequent as the child grows older. Boys' friendships seem to be somewhat stronger than those of girls. Girls tend to "mother" boys, and boys tend to accept the mothering.

Some solitary children find their social satisfaction in imaginary companions. These phantom companions usually appear, if at all, between the ages of four and ten.

Gradually the child comes to appreciate the value of certain types of social behavior. He tries out various ways of approaching other children. Some prove to be successful all or most of the time, some are successful with only a few playmates, and some fail under all conditions. Sooner or later the child learns how to modify his behavior so as to avoid trespassing on the rights and feelings of others, while at the same time accomplishing the aims which he has in mind.

There is considerable discussion today about "training for leadership." Certain individuals apparently attain the ability to lead others from their own experience without specific training. In any group of children we are likely to discover a leader. At age five, we find some who lead because of their domineering attitude; they are perhaps stronger than the others and threaten their playmates into acceptance of their leadership. Others lead because they have at their command benefits and privileges which their companions lack: they are able to "treat" the others to candy or to movies, or have a home which offers marvelous opportunities in the way of toys and a playroom. These leaders are successful only temporarily; their followers drop away whenever something more interesting appears. The most successful leader is the one who is resourceful, who thinks up more fascinating things to do than the other children, who can always vary play to include a newcomer and make everyone happy.

Such a leader was Michael. Michael, decked out in a purple cape and a golden crown, had just proclaimed himself as king when Peter, a much larger boy, rushed in and said, "You're not the king. I was the king yesterday and I'm going to be the king today." Unflustered, Michael said, "I know! We'll have two kings. I'll be the first king and you can be the second king.". . . "No," said Peter, "I'll be the first king and you can be the

[24] E. H. Green, "Group Play and Quarreling Among Pre-school Children," *Child Development*, December, 1933, 4:302–307.

Faithway Baptist College
Library

*Chronologically—Five All!*

R. K. Headley, University of Minnesota

second king.". . . "OK," said Michael. "You be the first king and we'll pretend that you are old and sick and have to stay in bed. OK?" "OK," said Peter. With Peter, bedecked in a red cape and a golden crown, confined to his bed, Michael's throne seemed unshaken. Thus the true leader incorporated the intruder into his play with no serious modifications of his own plans. Although the leader generally is somewhat more intelligent than his playmates, if the difference in mental ability is too great, he may fail to reach a common ground of interest with the others.

## Individual Differences

Throughout this chapter we have been discussing general tendencies and traits which we may expect any five-year-old to show, but we must remember that each one of these five-year-olds is a distinct personality. Each one not only has a heredity that is all his own, but he has had five years of experience that will have been very different from the five years of each of his classmates.

We need only compare siblings of our acquaintance to realize that even children in the same family differ not only in physical and mental equipment but also in the atmosphere in which they live. The attitude of the rest of the family toward a child may be influenced by some trait unrelated to the child's own behavior, such as his curly hair or his crossed eyes. The many individual differences in ability and in experience mean, of course, that every child in school must be considered as an individual and not simply as a sample typical of all children.

## SUMMARY

The kindergarten child is at an age where physically he exhibits no startlingly new development in his growth pattern. But he is daily adding to his stature and perfecting already acquired skills. He shows distinct advances in language, in interests, in the amount of his information, and in the breadth and control of his emotional responses. Although many broad trends of development can be found, each child is an individual, different from all other individuals.

## QUESTIONS AND PROBLEMS

1. A five-year-old girl weighs thirty-six pounds and her height is average for that weight. What is it?
2. Observe a four-year-old child. How does he compare with the average five-year-old in motor and language development?
3. Observe a six-year-old child. How does he compare with the average five-year-old in social development?
4. If you were to purchase a gift for a five-year-old boy, what would it be? Why? For a five-year-old girl? Why?
5. Observe two five-year-old children. How are they alike and different in their emotional responses? How are they alike and different in their interests?
6. Recall two sisters whom you know. In what ways are they most alike? What are the most striking differences between them?
7. Try to recall an experience you may have had, as an adult or as a child, when you either confused the meaning of words or actually "heard" the wrong word.

## SELECTED REFERENCES

Department of Elementary School Principals, *Those First School Years,* Washington, D.C., National Education Association, 1960.
Hymes, James L., Jr., "Starting with a Child," pp. 10–15.

Lindberg, Lucile, and Mary W. Moffet, "The Program and the Child," pp. 50–125.

Gesell, Arnold, and Others, *The Child From Five to Ten*, New York, Harper and Brothers, 1946.

Gesell, Arnold, and Others, *The First Five Years of Life*, New York, Harper and Brothers, 1940.

Hammond, Sarah Lou, Ruth J. Dales, Dora Sikes Skipper, and Ralph L. Witherspoon, *Good Schools for Young Children*, New York, The Macmillan Company, 1963.

Hurlock, Elizabeth B., *Child Development*, 3rd ed., New York, Prentice-Hall, 1956.

Ilg, Francis, and Louise B. Ames, *The Gesell Institute's Child Behavior*, Dell Publishing Company, 1960 (paperback).

Imhoff, Myrtle, *Early Elementary Education*, New York, Appleton-Century-Crofts, 1957.

Jenkins, Gladys, and Others, *These Are Your Children*, revised, Chicago, Scott, Foresman & Company, 1953.

Jersild, Arthur T., *Child Psychology*, 4th ed., New York, Prentice-Hall, 1960.

Lambert, Hazel, *Early Childhood Education*, New York, Harcourt, Brace & Company, 1960.

Langford, Louise, *Guidance of the Young Child*, New York, John Wiley and Sons, 1960.

Martin, W. Edgar, *Functional Body Measurement of School Age Children*, Washington, D.C., United States Department of Health, Education, and Welfare, Office of Education, 1955.

Merry, Frieda Kiefer, and R. V. Merry, *First Two Decades of Life*, New York, Harper and Brothers, 1958.

Murphy, Lois Barclay, and Collaborators, *The Widening World of Childhood: Paths Toward Mastery*, New York, Child Study Association, Inc., 1963.

National Education Association, Washington, D.C.—Bulletins:
*Foundation Learnings*, 1958.
*Freedom to Move*, 1962.

Olson, Willard C., *Child Development*, 2nd ed., New York, D. C. Heath & Company, 1959.

State of Minnesota, A *Guide for Teaching in the Kindergarten*, State of Minnesota Department of Education, Curriculum Bulletin No. 25, St. Paul, 1963. See particularly "Some Things We Know About Kindergarten Children and Their Implications for Teaching," pp. 13–66.

Stone, Joseph, and Joseph Church, *Childhood and Adolescence: a Psychology of the Growing Personality*, New York, Random House, 1959.

White House Conference on *Children and Youth in a Changing World*, Washington, D.C., White House Conference on Children and Youth, Inc., 1960.

Wills, Clarice D., and William H. Stegeman, *Living in the Kindergarten*, 2nd ed., Chicago, Follett Publishing Company, 1956.

# 2

# FACTS ABOUT THE KINDERGARTEN

The word *kindergarten* means many things to many people the world around, and for that reason it can be used only generically. If you were to speak with twenty people from twenty different countries, each of whom was familiar with the early-childhood education program in his own country, you would probably get nearly twenty different points of view concerning kindergarten education. And this is as it should be; schools for young children, as well as for older children, should be adapted to the cultural needs of the society in which the schools exist. Even within any one culture, the schools should always be subject to change in the light of the demands of a changing world.

## Age Range

No matter what the cultural demands of a society may be, however, it is safe to say that, because of the surprisingly patterned sequence of development common to all children, certain practices and procedures can be evaluated in relation to the age range within a kindergarten. Although in our country the kindergarten child is about five years of age, we must not assume that kindergarten children in other countries are the same age. The following is a sampling of age ranges within school or welfare groups corresponding to kindergartens: two and one-half to seven years; four to seven years; three to six years; four to six years; four to five years; and five to six years. One factor that all kindergartens seem to have in common is the presence of five-year-olds in their midst.

We must always remember that whenever we evaluate the practices and procedures of kindergartens outside the United States, and sometimes even within the United States, we should first ascertain the age range of the children enrolled in the group. A few communities in the United States have both four- and five-year-old kindergarten groups in their public schools, and in some of the Southern states it is not uncommon to have three- and four-year-olds enrolled in private or church schools called kindergartens.

## Admission Age Practices

Legal provisions set up by the states for kindergarten entrance age seem to bear little relation to actual practice. We find, for example, that in three states the authorized kindergarten entrance age is as low as three years; in fifteen states it is four years; in thirteen states five years, and in eight states simply under six years. In the report from which these figures were taken, nine states appear to have no legal provisions governing kindergarten entrance age, and data for Hawaii and Alaska were not included.[1]

Excluding the relatively few communities which support four-year-old public kindergartens, the public-school practice for kindergarten admission in the United States may be roughly stated as follows: approximately 70 percent of the schools having kindergartens require their entrants to be between four years and eight months and four years and nine months of age at the beginning of the school year, this usually being thought of as September 1. The remaining 30 percent of the schools having kindergartens require the entering children to be from four years and nine and one-half months to five years of age at the opening of the school year. In other words, in 70 percent of our kindergartens a child may enter in September if he will be five on or before the following January 1; and in 30 percent of our schools the entering child must be five on or before September 1 or November 15. Although these percentages give us little indication that there is a growing tendency to require more chronological maturity at the date of kindergarten entrance, other figures seem to point in that direction.

## Early Admission Policies

Relatively few school systems make any provision for admitting children to kindergarten before the date set by the state law or local board regulations. When such provision is made, it is on the basis of the child's

[1] A. K. Steiner, "A Report of School Laws, Early Elementary Education," *School Life*, April, 1957, 39:1–8.

all-round maturity and his ability to profit more then than later by the challenge of the kindergarten experience. Specialists from the ranks of psychologists, psychometricians, and physicians, and the parents, principals, and teachers are usually expected to pool their findings and observations before the administrative authorities admit the underage child to the kindergarten group. In situations where provision is made for early kindergarten entrance, there seems to be less parent pressure to seek early admission for their children. There appears to be a growing awareness of the fact that, while some few children can profit by early school entrance, others can profit by delayed school entrance. Today it is not too unusual to have parents seek advice on delaying kindergarten entrance for the child who appears immature, even though chronologically he might slip under the admission wire.

## Kindergarten Enrollment

Friedrich Froebel (1782–1852), the founder of the kindergarten in Germany, predicted that of all the countries into which the kindergarten movement might spread, its growth would be most vigorous in the United States of America—and he was right! From 1873, when the first United States public kindergartens were established in St. Louis, until 1930, when there was a leveling off in the growth pattern of the kindergarten movement, the number of children enrolled in public and private kindergartens increased from 1,252 to approximately 778,000. From 1930 to the early 1940's, though there was curtailment of the kindergarten program in some cities, there was expansion in others. Critics of a more lugubrious nature looked only at the retrenchment and shook their heads ominously as they ventured their opinions about the future of kindergartens in America. More farsighted individuals, however, saw in this era not a slowing down of growth in the kindergarten movement but rather a gathering of strength for vigorous development in the years to come. Let the figures tell their own story:

**Table 4** Kindergarten Enrollments in the United States[2]

**1888–1940**

| | 1888 | 1900 | 1930 | 1934 | 1940 |
|---|---|---|---|---|---|
| Public Schools | 15,145 | 131,657 | 723,443 | 601,775 | 594,647 |
| Private Schools | 16,082 | 93,737 | 54,456 | 37,506 | 50,621 |
| Total | 31,227 | 225,394 | 777,899 | 639,281 | 645,268 |

[2] *Early Childhood Education,* Forty-sixth Yearbook, Part II, Chicago National Society for the Study of Education, 1957, Chapter IV, p. 46.

The 1940 figures might seem to indicate waning strength in the kindergarten movement; but the figures which follow are proof of the vigorous growth of the movement. Note that in Table 5 the figures are for public-school kindergarten enrollment only.

**Table 5** Public-School Kindergarten Enrollment in the United States[3]

**1944–1954**

| | | | |
|---|---|---|---|
| 1944 | 734,000* | 1949 | 1,051,200 |
| 1945 | 733,000 | 1950 | 941,150 |
| 1946 | 873,850 | 1951 | 1,272,150 |
| 1947 | 984,700 | 1952 | 1,399,050 |
| 1948 | 1,016,200 | 1953–54 | 1,479,000 |

*All figures have been rounded to approximate 50 or 100.

It is evident from these figures that there has generally been a constant increase in kindergarten enrollment since 1944. Adding to these public-school figures the number of children in private and parochial school kindergartens in the United States gives a total of some 1,654,000 children attending kindergarten in 1953–1954.

In the fourteen years from 1940 to 1954, the number of children in kindergartens increased almost 150 percent. In the same period, first-grade enrollment increased 21 percent, second-grade 26 percent, and fifth-grade 16 percent.[4] From these percentages we can conclude not only that more children are coming to kindergarten but also that new kindergarten units are being organized.

From 1954 to the present, figures have continued to show a steady increase in the number of children enrolled in public-school kindergartens in the United States:

| | |
|---|---|
| 1954 | 1,479,000 |
| 1958 | 1,771,753 |
| 1962 | 2,098,913 |
| 1964 | 2,131,473 |

[3] Biennial Survey of Education in the United States, "Statistics of State School Systems, 1953–1954," Organization, Staff, Pupils and Finances, Washington, D. C., United States Department of Health, Education, and Welfare, Office of Education, 1954, p. 54.

[4] "Statistics of State School Systems, 1953–1954," p. 9.

The following table is of interest in that it indicates public-school kindergarten enrollment by both regions and states:

**Table 6** Kindergarten Enrollment Figures—Fall, 1963[5]

Enrollment figures for full-time kindergarten public schools in the United States—50 states, District of Columbia, and outlying parts of the United States:

| | Total Kindergarten |
|---|---|
| | 2,098,913 |
| NORTH ATLANTIC | 685,761 |
| Connecticut | 48,405 |
| Delaware | 1,168 |
| Maine | 16,781 |
| Maryland | 28,020 |
| Massachusetts | 52,231 |
| New Hampshire | 4,353 |
| New Jersey | 112,129 |
| New York | 274,808 |
| Pennsylvania | 125,000 |
| Rhode Island | 9,015 |
| Vermont | 1,975 |
| District of Columbia | 11,363 |
| GREAT LAKES AND PLAINS | 886,505 |
| Illinois | 155,306 |
| Indiana | 57,796 |
| Iowa | 53,599 |
| Kansas | 37,328 |
| Michigan | 186,475 |
| Minnesota | 56,558 |
| Missouri | 52,250 |
| Nebraska | 28,043 |
| North Dakota | 2,472 |
| Ohio | 168,529 |
| South Dakota | 7,172 |
| Wisconsin | 80,977 |
| SOUTHEAST | 31,603 |
| Alabama | ...... |
| Arkansas | ...... |
| Florida | 5,082 |
| Georgia | 10,792 |
| Kentucky | 1,173 |
| Louisiana | 6,783 |
| Mississippi | ...... |
| North Carolina | ...... |
| South Carolina | ...... |
| Tennessee | 937 |
| Virginia | 6,836 |
| West Virginia | ...... |
| WEST AND SOUTHWEST | 527,604 |
| Alaska | 2,823 |
| Arizona | 7,082 |
| California | 342,600 |
| Colorado | 34,997 |
| Hawaii | 13,031 |
| Idaho | ...... |
| Montana | 3,433 |
| Nevada | 7,692 |
| New Mexico | ...... |
| Oklahoma | 17,265 |
| Oregon | 9,517 |
| Texas | 29,000 |
| Utah | 13,459 |
| Washington | 41,482 |
| Wyoming | 5,223 |
| OUTLYING PARTS | |
| American Samoa | ...... |
| Canal Zone | 1,038 |
| Guam | ...... |
| Puerto Rico | 1,593 |
| Virgin Islands | 448 |

[5] *School Life*, Jan.–Feb., 1964, 46:22.

As the figures indicate, children have the opportunity to attend public-school kindergartens in all but eight of our fifty states. However, if we compare the number of children enrolled in kindergartens and the number of children enrolled in first grade, we find that states vary greatly in the proportion of their kindergarten-aged population for which they provide kindergartens. Some of the Southern states provide public-school kindergartens for as little as 1 to 6 percent of their kindergarten-aged populations. Other states provide public-school education for anywhere from 10 percent to all of their kindergarten-aged children. Oddly enough, in at least four states kindergarten enrollment exceeds first-grade enrollment. There are two possible reasons: (1) the number of five-year-old children in the United States in 1963 exceeded the number of six-year-old children by some 14,000, and (2) because of crowded conditions, many parochial schools have closed their kindergartens, and children who will be attending parochial first grades are now attending public-school kindergartens.

According to figures published by the United States Department of Commerce, approximately 43.5 percent of the total five-year-old population were enrolled in kindergarten in 1953; 14.5 percent were enrolled in other school-grade units, and 41.6 percent were not in school. Today between 54 and 65 percent of all five-year-olds are enrolled in kindergarten. Nevertheless some 1,500,000 of our five-year-olds are even now being deprived of kindergarten experience; many more urban than rural children have the opportunity to attend kindergarten; and some kindergarten units have far too many children enrolled for the good of the children.

## Group Size

In some instances the number of children enrolled in a single kindergarten unit far exceeds the ideal of from twenty to twenty-five children, but every effort is being made to keep the size of the group near that number. Class size in American kindergartens varied in the late 1940's from twenty to forty-five children in a single half-day session. The median class size was twenty-nine, and the most frequent size was thirty to thirty-five. In many cities additional kindergarten units have been added to accommodate the increase in enrollment, and in only a relatively few communities—usually those suburban communities that have sprung up almost overnight—is the kindergarten enrollment sometimes quite beyond the bounds of reason. New Jersey is credited with being the first state to enact a law providing that state aid be withheld where honest effort is not made to approach a twenty-four maximum kindergarten enrollment.

## The Importance of Kindergartens

It was in the Depression, the war, and the early postwar years that the attention of the American public was focused more sharply than ever before on the needs of young children. Research results in the area of child development were presented to the public through exhibits, films, radio programs, and popular articles. In both England and the United States, federal programs were set up to provide for the welfare of young children. In the United States we had first the WPA programs, which established schools for nursery-school-age children, and later the federally supported Extended School Service program for nursery-school and older children. The Extended School Services, or Lanham Act Schools, established chiefly for the care of children whose mothers were employed in war-production plants, indicated that a changing pattern in our society called for a re-evaluation of the type of schools which we were providing for young children. It was in these years that the public in general and parents in particular gained new insights into the needs of young children, and more adults became actively aware of the importance of early childhood education.

## Laws Relating to the Kindergarten

Today in practically every state we have laws which authorize the use of public, local, and/or state funds for financing kindergartens. In at least twenty-seven states, state funds are available for financing kindergartens. In at least forty states, laws regarding the establishment of kindergartens are permissive in nature, and where legislation of this sort exists, kindergartens may be established in communities by vote, by action of the local school authorities, or in response to a petition of the public. In six states the laws relating to the establishment of kindergartens are mandatory—that is, kindergartens must be established under certain conditions. Arkansas, Georgia, and North Dakota stand alone in having no funds allocated for the support of public kindergartens, and only Arkansas and Georgia have no laws at all relating to the establishment of kindergartens in their states.[6]

## Kindergarten Backing

National organizations, including such groups as The American Association of School Administrators, The American Association of University

[6] A. K. Steiner, "A Report of School Laws, Early Elementary Education," *School Life*, April, 1957, 39:1–8.

Women, The Association for Supervision and Curriculum Development, The Department of Elementary Principals and the Elementary-Kindergarten-Nursery School Division of the National Education Association, The Association for Childhood Education International, The Southern Association for Children Under Six, The Council of Chief State School Officers, The National Kindergarten Association, National Congress of Parents and Teachers, and The National Council of State Consultants in Elementary Education, as well as many state and local groups, have gone on record in support of kindergartens.

Of 670 recommendations which came out of the thinking of the 7,000 delegates at the 1960 White House Conference on Children and Youth "235 either explicitly or implicitly pointed at elementary school education." In recommendations 153, 154, and 209 the following proposals were made:

> that the scope of free public education be extended downward and upward to include kindergarten through community college.
>
> that kindergarten be made an integral part of the tax supported public school system in all communities; and that state departments of education be authorized to extend public education to include nursery schools.
>
> that it be mandatory for state departments of education to establish standards for certification for nursery school and kindergarten teachers.

Other recommendations, although not specifically mentioning the kindergarten, proposed that programs for young children should be flexible enough to meet children's early social, physical, intellectual, and psychological needs and that early efforts should be made to identify the needs and talents of individuals. The United States Office of Education, in its official journal, *School Life*, reports that "The 1960 White House Conference repeatedly asked schools to provide early childhood education" and recommended that every elementary school have a kindergarten by the end of the 1960's.

Thus it seems quite obvious that the kindergarten has truly "come of age" and no longer is it necessary for the kindergarten to defend its position in the elementary school. To be sure, when lack of funds seems to impede an ongoing educational program in a community, almost always the threat is made that the community's kindergarten program must be dropped. But usually the impending catastrophe never materializes. In most instances parents, principals, and teachers rally forces and the threat is soon dropped.

## The Role of Research

In the latter part of the nineteenth century and early part of the twentieth, the kindergarten, though housed and included in the public school, existed as a unit almost completely apart from the rest of the school. Patty Smith Hill, S. C. Parker, Alice Temple, John Dewey, and others did much to bring about the unification of the kindergarten and the primary program. But it was not until the research of the twenties that we had any information establishing the importance of kindergarten education in relation to later school adjustment and progress. The research of this period brought out the following facts:

1. Children with kindergarten training tend to make relatively more rapid progress in the first five grades than those who have not attended kindergarten.
2. The proportion of first-grade "repeaters" in cities without kindergarten programs is much greater than in cities with kindergartens.
3. In grades one through three, kindergarten-trained children show a marked advantage in both rate of reading and comprehension.
4. In grade one kindergarten-trained children surpass others in the rate and quality of their handwriting.
5. In grades one through three, children who have had kindergarten experience tend to establish better person-to-person and person-to-group relations than do those who have not.
6. Kindergarten-trained children tend to receive higher teacher ratings on such traits as industry, initiative, and oral language than those without kindergarten training.[7]

In the thirties and early forties, much of the research in early childhood education concerned itself with formulating tests and establishing norms of development. Sometimes, however, research workers went into the kindergartens and, through their studies, brought helpful and illuminating facts to the attention of the public. Among other things, they found that

1. In their efforts to raise standards, teachers spend more time with boys than with girls.
2. Five-year-olds respond better to suggestions and requests than to commands, and the length of time required for a response to a suggestion is shorter than the time involved in responding to a command.
3. The spontaneous conversation of children during a work period is chiefly about people and materials in the immediate environment.

[7] Elizabeth Fuller, "Kindergarten Education," *Encyclopedia of Educational Research,* Walter Monroe, ed., New York, The Macmillan Company, 1960, pp. 385–398.

4. Though five-year-old boys tend to talk more than five-year-old girls during a work period, the topics of conversation show no marked sex differentiation.
5. The upper notes in many of the older songs written for children are uncomfortably high for the voices of the five-year-olds.
6. Kindergarten children in afternoon groups tend to rest more quietly than those in morning groups.
7. Children rest more quietly in small than in large groups.
8. The amount of participation in a group of five-year-olds is in inverse proportion to the size of the group.

In the 1950's, with the further resurgence of vigor and growth in the kindergarten movement, research bearing on kindergarten education was concerned chiefly with accounting, maturity in relation to school achievement, the physical aspects of the school plant, the developmental sequence in learning, factors influencing human relations, exceptionality—with special attention to the gifted child—and methodology. The research of the 1950's brought out the following facts:

1. Class enrollment in the late 1940's varied from twenty to forty-five children and the median class was twenty-nine. The most common class size was from thirty to thirty-five. The next most common was twenty-nine.
2. Kindergarten teachers felt that a class enrollment of twenty-five children, with an average attendance of from twenty to twenty-four, would be practical and desirable.
3. There was some trend toward the raising of kindergarten entrance age. Whereas children had been admitted to kindergarten in September if their birthdays came before January or even in April, the trend was to require fall entrants to be five in September, October, or November.
4. In one study, it was found that 16 percent of the children who entered kindergarten before they were four years and nine months of age had difficulty in making the school adjustment. On the other hand, only 4 percent of the older children had difficulty in making the adjustment.
5. In another study, the achievement scores of two groups of sixth graders (each with IQ's ranging from 90 to 110) showed that the group entering the first grade between six years and five months and six years and eight months of age had higher scores than the group entering first grade between five years and eight months and five years and eleven months of age. Eleven from the two groups had been retained at one time or another; of the eleven, ten were from the younger group and

eight were boys. This seems to indicate that a delayed start in reading is important to all, but more important to boys.

6. Kindergarten teachers tended to feel that there was wisdom in raising the age for kindergarten entrance, but they trusted that the change in entrance policy would not deprive four-year-olds of school opportunities.
7. Bodily measurements based on working or action positions have helped teachers make better provisions for children's work and play needs.
8. A consensus of kindergarten teachers indicated that a minimum floor space of from fifty to sixty square feet per child would be more reasonable than the usually designated minimum of thirty-five square feet per child.
9. Predictable developmental skills and concepts involved in speech, writing, reading, and arithmetic have become useful guides for the teacher working with young children.
10. Boys generally choose to play masculine roles as early as four, five, and six years of age; girls do not show a definite preference for feminine roles until six, seven, and even eight.
11. Children are aware of racial differences as early as three years but have no feeling of discrimination until considerably later.
12. Blind children can profit by early group experiences, and deaf children can gain much by being included in groups of children with normal hearing.
13. New stress laid on individual growth patterns has led teachers to be less quick to type children from either their own observations or test scores.
14. Kindergarten teachers felt that the first days of kindergarten should be limited in two ways. (a) The number of children attending kindergarten on the first day should be limited to a third or half of the total entering group. (b) The first week's session should be limited to a half or three-fourths of the scheduled time allotment.
15. The nursery school, kindergarten, and primary groups were more and more frequently being thought of as a single educational unit, and many kindergarten teachers felt that it might be desirable to have this unit housed in its own building.

Today research in the kindergarten appears to be concerned chiefly with creativity, neuro-maturation, methodology related to the introduction and presentation of subject matter skills, teacher certification, culturally disadvantaged children, maturity factors related to school entrance, extension of kindergarten education, and the enrichment of the content of the kindergarten program. Research of the 1960's tells us that

1. The IQ is not a valid prediction of achievement. Creativity, neuromaturation, and other factors enter into the child's ability to achieve.
2. Creativity can be "primed."
3. Through such programs as the Initial Teaching Alphabet, The Omar Moore Reading Experiment, The Denver Reading Program and others, it has been proved that three-, four-, and five-year-olds *can* be taught to read.
4. There is no *evidence* that the early introduction of formal subject matter (reading, writing, and arithmetic) *has any real* value for young children.
5. There is a tendency for workbooks and worksheets to be used in kindergartens, in spite of the fact that there is no evidence that they increase reading readiness.
6. Workbooks and worksheets tend to take time away from other kindergarten activities which would, in the long run, be more profitable to children's all-round development.
7. Culturally disadvantaged children can profit from *compensatory* programs,[8] and these programs are in operation.
8. There is a strong trend toward requiring a four-year degree for kindergarten teachers. Along with this is a trend toward requiring those teachers who have taught only in the grades, junior high school, or high school to take child development courses and do practice teaching in the kindergarten before being certified as kindergarten teachers.
9. The number of musical recordings on the market is increasing by leaps and bounds and there is a tendency, good or bad, for kindergarten teachers to substitute recordings for their own piano playing.
10. State guides for kindergarten teaching are increasing in number. Thirty-three states now have such guides.
11. Reading, mathematics, and science programs are being designed for K–3, K–6, and K–12.
12. There is a strong evidence that the kindergarten program needs to be more challenging; but there is no evidence to support the desirability of pushing formal subject matter down into the kindergarten.

## SUMMARY

There are between 3,500,000 and 3,750,000 kindergarten-aged children in the United States, and of these approximately 65 percent have the

[8] Some 30,000 federally supported "Head Start" programs were in operation in the summer of 1965. These programs were designed to provide compensatory experiences for culturally disadvantaged children who would be entering kindergartens and first grades in the fall.

opportunity to attend kindergarten. About 10 percent of those attending kindergartens are enrolled in private schools. States vary greatly in their provisions for kindergarten attendance and in their financial support of kindergartens. Many national and other organizations, as well as the members of the 1960 White House Conference on Children and Youth, foresee a day when the kindergarten will be a part of every public elementary school.

Research has played an important role in supplying us with facts which have (1) helped the public understand that the kindergarten should be an integral part of the American system of education; (2) helped alert the public to the developmental needs of young children; (3) helped teachers evaluate their own procedures; and (4) helped administrators and policy-directing groups plan for the welfare of five-year-olds. Research has also contributed to making Froebel's prediction concerning the vigorous growth of the kindergarten in America come true. We know that today's children are growing up in a world smaller and yet vastly more complex than the world of yesterday, and it seems logical to conclude that kindergarten programs need to be enriched and extended. But there is no evidence that formal subject matter should be pushed down into the kindergartens.

The kindergarten needs the further support of research as it strives to meet the needs of today's television and space-minded five-year-olds. May new facts always be forthcoming!

## QUESTIONS AND PROBLEMS

1. What are some of the factors behind the rapid growth of public-school kindergartens in the period from 1955 to 1965?
2. What reasons are there for teaching reading in the kindergarten? What reasons for *not* teaching reading at that level?
3. In a situation where workbooks are being used in a kindergarten, try to identify children who appear to find the assignment too easy; those who seem comfortably challenged by the assignment; and those who appear baffled, confused, or oblivious of the problem presented by the assignment. What was the evidence that led to your conclusions?
4. List factors you feel should be considered in recommending the under-aged child for kindergarten admission.
5. What elements in kindergarten programs seem to have more appeal to girls than to boys? How could you redesign the program so that the boys would seem to be more fairly challenged?
6. What further areas about the kindergarten or about kindergarten children would you like to have research explore?

## SELECTED REFERENCES[9]

Albera, R. G., "Validity of Early School Entrance into Kindergarten," *Journal of Educational Research*, September, 1962, 79:29–46.

Bain, Winifred E., "With Life So Long Why Shorten Childhood," *Childhood Education*, September, 1961, 38:15–18.

Blakely, W. Paul, and Erma Shadle, "A Study of Two Readiness for Reading Programs in the Kindergarten," *Elementary English*, November, 1961, 38:502–505.

Butler, Annie L., "Hurry! Hurry! Hurry! Why?" *Childhood Education*, September, 1962, 39:10–13.

Council of Chief State School Officers, *Responsibilities of State Departments of Education for Nursery School and Kindergarten*, Washington, D.C., National Association of Education, 1961, p. 21.

Davis, David, *Patterns of Primary Education*, New York, Harper and Row, 1963.

Davis, H. M., "Don't Push Your School Beginners," *Parents Magazine*, October, 1956, 27:140–141.

*Encyclopedia of Educational Research*, Monroe, Walter S., ed., Sections on child development and kindergarten education, New York, American Educational Research Association, The Macmillan Company, 1941, 1951, 1960.

Durkin, Dolores, and William D. Sheldon, "Should the Very Young Be Taught to Read?" *NEA Journal*, November, 1963, 52:20–24.

Fancher, Betsy, "Speaking Out: Let's Stop Cheating Our Children Out of Their Childhood," *Saturday Evening Post*, September, 1962, 29; 235:10.

Fuller, Elizabeth M., *Values in Early Childhood Education*, Bulletin, Washington, D.C., National Education Association, Department of Elementary Kindergarten, Nursery Education, 1960.

Fuller, Elizabeth M., *About the Kindergarten: What Research Says to the Teacher*, Bulletin No. 22, Washington, D.C., National Education Association, Department of Classroom Teachers, 1961.

Gabbard, Hazel, "Status and Trends in Early Childhood Education," *Those First School Years*, Washington, D.C., National Education Association, 1960.

Headley, Neith E., "Kindergarten Comes of Age," *NEA Journal*, March, 1954, 43: 153–154, Condensed: *Education Digest*, May, 1954, 19:49–51.

Heffernan, Helen, "Pressures to Start Formal Instruction Early," *Childhood Education*, October, 1960, 37:57–60.

[9] See further references in the Appendix, "Research and Articles Helpful to Kindergarten Teachers."

National Education Association, Department of Elementary School Principals, *Those First School Years,* Washington, D.C., National Education Association, 1960.

National Education Association, *Admission Policies for Kindergarten and First Grade,* Circular No. 3, Washington, D.C., National Education Association, 1958.

Pines, Maya, "How Three Year Olds Teach Themselves to Read—And Love It," *Harper's Magazine,* May, 1963, 226:58–64.

Torrance, E. Paul, *Education and the Creative Potential,* Minneapolis, University of Minnesota Press, 1963.

Wann, Kenneth, Miriam S. Dorn, and Elizabeth Ann Liddle, *Fostering Intellectual Development in Young Children,* New York, Bureau of Publications, Teachers College, Columbia University, 1962.

White House Conference on Children and Youth, *Children in a Changing World,* Washington, D.C., White House Conference on Children and Youth, Inc., 1960.

# 3

# THE AMERICAN KINDERGARTEN POINT OF VIEW

## New Schools From Old

Today's American kindergarten is a direct descendant of the German kindergarten of Friedrich Froebel (1782–1852), but in the course of the near-hundred years of its existence in America—the first public-school kindergartens were established in St. Louis, Missouri, in 1873—the kindergarten has undergone many changes. It was only natural that a school planned for the youth of an old country steeped in tradition should fail to fulfill completely the requirements of a pioneering and intensely practical land. The wonder is that so many of the original materials and methods clung to the transplanted school for so long. Gradually, however, the procedures of the kindergarten were altered and when, in the early part of the twentieth century, the theories and practices of Madame Maria Montessori (1870–1952) became known, these were absorbed with little difficulty into the kindergartens already in existence.

At present there are few if any kindergartens in the country which can be labeled strictly "Froebelian." With the upsurge of interest in the Montessori movement in America in the late nineteen fifties and early sixties there are some *American* Montessori and *pure* Montessori schools for young children being established.[1] There are no Montessori groups in our public schools.

[1] Nancy Rambusch, *Learning How to Learn: An American Approach to Montessori*, Baltimore, Helicon Press, 1962.

## What's in a Name?

It is interesting to note that the German name Kindergarten or "children's garden" has continued to be the name common to the school year that immediately precedes the first grade. Some contend that this fact—that the pre-first-grade unit bears the name "kindergarten"—is a distinct disadvantage as far as the kindergarten itself is concerned. Others enthusiastically support the name. Edna St. Vincent Millay, in one of her poems, mulls over the question of "what's in a name" and comes to the conclusion that a name locks one into quite as much as it locks one out of. So it is with the name "kindergarten." Suppose we take time out to consider the pros and cons of retaining or rejecting the name.

### The Case for Discarding the Name "Kindergarten"

(1) The name seems to make the kindergarten something quite different from the other grades in the elementary school.

(2) "Kindergarten" is a German word. Why do we use a German word to describe a unit in the educational system of an English-speaking nation?

(3) The term "kindergarten" has come to have a negative connotation.—"That's just kindergarten stuff."—Why put kindergarten teachers and children as well, on the defensive?

(4) Some tend to think of kindergarten as little more than a glorified play school, a place where children go before they start school. The name reinforces the thinking that school begins with the first grade.

### The Case for Retaining the Name "Kindergarten"

(1) The word "kindergarten," children's garden, tends to place emphasis on children rather than on subject matter.

(2) The name does set the kindergarten group apart from the rest of the school, but this has a good result: *pressures* for achievement are not so great and the teacher can feel freer to give thought to the well-being of the "whole child."

(3) The word "kindergarten" brings to mind the image of a pleasant place.

(4) The garden concept leads to many striking analogies between growing children and growing plants:

(a) Each flower has its own time and season for maturing.

(b) Some flowers, like sunflowers, reach great height; others, like pansies, are low growers.

(c) Different plants need different plant foods.
(d) Most plants thrive best in a rich environment.
(e) Plants need time for rest.
(f) Plants thrive best when they have a good balance of sun *and* rain.
(g) Plants need space for growing.
(h) Plants need light, sunshine, and fresh air.
(i) Variety adds interest and charm to a garden.
(j) The good gardener makes an overall plan for his garden.
(k) The good gardener knows that physical effort is involved in carrying out his plans.
(l) Weeds and unpleasant outcroppings have to be coped with in every garden.
(m) Growth must come from within the plant—it is not something to be added to the plant.
(n) Some things in a garden grow well together. Others destroy or choke off growth.
(o) Forced growth usually results in a weaker plant.
(p) Flowers last longer in their own environment than when picked and singled out for show purposes.
(q) Individual plants sometimes need special treatment.
(r) The gardener needs the right tools to cultivate his plants.
(s) In certain stages of their development, some plants need props and supports.
(t) Some plants need carefully designed frames on which to grow.
(u) The garden is more effective if it is designed to fit harmoniously into its surroundings.
(v) When blight strikes, the good gardener seeks the advice of a specialist.
(w) Research has done much to help the gardener have a better garden.
(x) The gardener himself can contribute to research.
(y) Written records are helpful in knowing what to expect in the garden and in planning for the garden.
(z) The best gardener's plans and hopes for a good garden can be thwarted by seeds, the soil, or the climate.

THE NAME PROBLEM RESOLVED. As the case stands, it seems that the name "kindergarten" truly does let the kindergarten into quite as much as it locks it out of. Current practice in educational bulletins and guides sets a precedent which appears to be a very neat resolution of the name problem. The practice, in referring to any span of education in which the kindergarten is included, is to use the letter "K" to represent the kindergarten: "K through Three," "K through Twelve," and so on. When this practice is followed, kindergarten appears as an integral part of the educational program and yet the "K" brings the kindergarten into focus as being somewhat different from grade-school education and so removes from it the *pressures* of formal academic work which can easily take over in the grade school.

## Features Retained and Modified

Many of the activities of the Froebelian School, such as singing, playing, talking, painting, gardening, modeling, weaving, looking at pictures, and listening to stories, have been incorporated into our American kindergartens. These have been modified in accordance with research findings or to conform more closely to American habits. For instance, we have enlarged the play materials of the Froebelian school in an attempt to guard the child's eyesight, and we demand less fine muscle coordination in the manipulation of materials. We have reduced our demands for accuracy in handwork in the light of greater knowledge of motor development, and we have lengthened the time spent on certain activities as a result of our accumulated experience in dealing with children.

From the Montessori program we have taken over both procedures and materials dealing with the social and self-help aspects of the school. We have adopted Montessori's notions of children's responsibility for the housekeeping of the room. We have heartily agreed with her insistence on the importance of self-help and the exercises of practical life, though we have substituted the child's own clothing for practice in place of the formal lacing and buttoning frames used in her schools. We have accepted her belief that, to a large extent, the teacher should keep herself in the background and be an inspiration, a guide, and an "ever-present help in time of trouble," rather than a person concerned primarily with cramming information into the minds of her children.

## American Thinking Reflected in the Kindergarten Program

In addition to its inheritance from Froebel and Montessori, the American kindergarten has been greatly influenced by the thinking, teaching, writing, and research done in our own country. G. Stanley Hall helped educators appreciate the significance of play in education. From the opposing philosophies of kindergarten education represented by Susan

Blow and Patty Smith Hill came the beginning of our present scientific outlook on kindergarten education. As a result of the teachings of John Dewey, educators have come to recognize that the present as well as the future is of vital importance to the young child's development. Education is not only preparation for what is to come; it is the enrichment and interpretation of the present. William Heard Kilpatrick, through both his teaching and his writing, did much to bring new dignity to the profession of kindergarten teaching. He helped educators and the public in general appreciate the fact that young children deserve and need teachers who can find educational implications in everyday experiences, and who can challenge children to make good use of the knowledge and understanding they already have. From the 1920's on, research in child development and education has contributed richly to our awareness of the needs and capabilities of the kindergarten-aged child.[2] We are aware that past, present, and future must all be taken into consideration in developing a good educational program for children.

At the mid-century point, considerable emphasis was placed on the importance of meeting the needs of children who deviated from the average in their development. Now new emphasis is placed on the needs of those in our society who may be thought of as culturally disadvantaged. In some commuities special opportunity groups are being set up for four-year-olds and five-year-olds, and older children as well. These educational programs, sometimes referred to as compensatory programs, are set up in an effort to give children experiences which will broaden and strengthen their base of appreciation and understanding. In the regular kindergarten, although the teacher tailors her program to the developmental needs of most of her group, she must be mindful at all times of ways in which she can enrich, simplify, or otherwise alter her program to meet the needs of the unusual children in her group.

## Types of Kindergartens

There are and should be different types of kindergartens. Many factors enter into determining these types: (1) the demands and expectations of society, (2) the philosophy of the teacher and/or the school, (3) the socioeconomic group served by the school, (4) the age range of the enrolled group, (5) the ability range of the group, (6) the number of children enrolled and the ratio of boys to girls, (7) the length of the session—both the yearly and the daily session, (8) the physical plant, (9) the geographical location, and (10) the education and strengths of the teacher.

[2] See Chapter 2.

## The Teacher

The teacher in the early kindergarten, like the school in which she was taught, was a Victorian institution. She had been taught by beautiful quotations and precepts and was first and foremost a "lady" concerned with "beautiful thoughts" and "sentiments," and she often rejected as unladylike and unrefined all else. Through her training, the kindergarten teacher of the early days grew to be more and more a charming and gracious lady who stressed beauty, art, and grace—and when things were not beautiful or graceful, she avoided them. Such a teacher served her day well, but she would hardly fit into the modern school, of course. She has given way to the teacher who, while recognizing the values of beauty and art in life, does not believe that outward signs necessarily indicate inward security and well-being. The new teacher is a searcher for truth, an investigator into ultimate and often hidden causes. She is concerned not with polishing the veneer of perfect behavior required of "little ladies" and "little gentlemen" but with the fundamental underlying concepts and attitudes of very human girls and boys.

## Aims of the Modern Kindergarten

The American kindergarten today attempts to give the child of five an education which is appropriate to his stage of development, which will be immediately satisfying to him, and which will help him build good foundations for the years ahead. In such an education, the child will develop all his powers—physical, emotional, mental, and social. Obviously, we do not seek to give him all the information he may need either now or in the future, but we do hope to help him develop the power to meet new situations by showing him how to use the information he posseses and how to gain other information he may need. We try through practice to help him develop skill in thinking. We are interested in discovering the traits and abilities of each child and in helping each child make the most of his potentialities.

More specifically, it is the aim of the kindergarten to provide each child with:

1. An opportunity to be in a social situation where his all-around readiness can be appraised before he must face the challenges of the first grade.
2. An opportunity to have a wide variety of experiences particularly adapted to his developmental needs.
3. An opportunity to mesh old and new learnings and, in so doing, to build for himself a broad base of understanding.

4. An opportunity to be in many situations that will help him perceive relationships through problem solving.
5. An opportunity to be in social situations where he can feel needed.
6. An opportunity to be in situations where he can become increasingly aware of the relationship between freedom and responsibility.
7. An opportunity to have many experiences that will help him "grow into reading."

## Physical Development

From the point of view of health and general physical development, the early years are of great importance. Some kindergarten children have a background of careful medical attention, excellent diet, adequate sleep and rest, and many opportunities for desirable activity and exercise. In contrast, some come from overcrowded and congested areas, where contagious diseases and unhygienic conditions abound. Still others come from homes where there is only the most meager awareness of standards of health and sanitation, and where little thought is given to the physical needs of the growing child.

The kindergarten must try to meet the needs of all these children. The school must not interfere with the helpful regimen of the fortunate children, but it must work to better the conditions of the less fortunate. No plan for a kindergarten can be satisfactory if it disregards the fact that a healthy body is prerequisite for good development of any kind.

## Mental Development

It should be unnecessary to say that the kindergarten is interested in promoting the mental development of the child. But often visitors to the kindergarten do not understand that absence of set lessons does not mean absence of learning. The kindergarten child is learning constantly. He is acquiring a great mass of information, broadening his range of interests, learning techniques of problem-solving, developing his language powers, and improving many other skills. In short, he is building good foundations for a wide variety of subject matter skills.[3] Later chapters will suggest specific ways in which the kindergarten encourages learning of various kinds.[4]

[3] See Chapter 23.
[4] See particularly Chapter 6.

## Emotional Development

In discussing the characteristics of the five-year-old, we mentioned the gradual maturing of emotional responses. The kindergarten can encourage this process by helping the child understand the kind and degree of emotional response appropriate in various situations. It can help him learn how to behave in the face of anger-provoking or dangerous situations. There is opportunity to help him learn how to behave in the hazards of traffic, how to respond effectively when another child interferes with his work, or how to act when a bee lights on his hand.

The kindergarten which works only for the physical and mental development of its children is not discharging all its duties or using all its opportunities. It has the further task of attempting to help the child control or redirect those emotional responses that are likely to lead to unhappiness for himself or others, and to help him express other responses which may prove beneficial. Chapter 5 contains a discussion of some of the ways such expression may be fostered.

## Social Development

Children from the age of three frequently exhibit a strong desire for the company of others. By the time they are ready for kindergarten, they should have at least a beginning appreciation of their personal responsibility both to themselves and to the group.

The kindergarten stresses the child's responsibility for himself. If he cannot care for himself, he is a drag on the group. He learns to understand that increased responsibility means increased freedom. For example, as he learns to take care of his toilet needs, to tie his shoes, to put on his own wraps, he becomes less dependent on others and therefore has greater freedom. In the kindergarten many children are away, for the first time, from the supervision of relatives, baby-sitters, or adult family friends. For the first time they find they must really "stand on their own." Sometimes it takes a kindergarten child a long time to realize that he has the same rights, neither fewer nor more than the others in his group. But, in general, kindergarten children soon indicate their awareness of the responsibility entailed in group living. They learn to respect the property rights of others, and their less tangible right of speaking without being interrupted and working without being annoyed. They learn also to contribute to the work of the group and to do their full share whether in the way of working or talking.

The kindergarten helps the child assume responsibility not only for mate-

*Advice Offered!—*
*Advice Not Needed!*

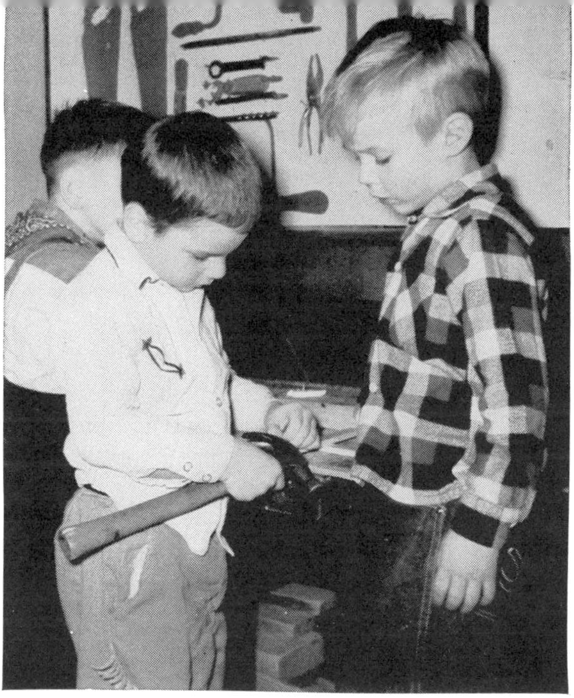

rials belonging to himself but also for those belonging to other children and to the school. It provides opportunities for children to share materials when necessary, to take turns or to divide, to give and to accept help when it is needed, and to refrain from giving help when another child prefers to work things out for himself. In the give-and-take of everyday kindergarten play, the child has an opportunity to try out social techniques, to learn what kind of behavior is pleasing to other individuals in the group, and what is pleasing to only a few or to none. He has a chance to test various methods for holding the attention of the group when he is talking or showing something, for persuading others to follow his lead, and for being a good follower when some other child leads.

Under the example and suggestion of the wise teacher, the kindergarten child learns the fundamentals of courtesy. He learns, for example, to listen when others are talking; he learns to limit his activities when they infringe upon the rights of others; he learns to understand and to appreciate the efforts and the accomplishments of others; and he learns to give and accept constructive criticism.

Although in some schools the outward forms of politeness are stressed, and in all schools, such simple forms of speech as "Please" and "Thank you" are encouraged, there is always an attempt to make the child feel that these words are not bribes or rewards but simply common forms of speech, equivalent to smiles, which are used to express gratitude or appreciation. An attitude, a look, or a glance can often be more expressive of sincere appreciation than the spoken word. The point is well illustrated by the small boy who, when reminded by his mother that he hadn't said "Thank you," said in all sincerity, "I *know;* but he could tell by the way I looked that I felt that way."

## Some Guiding Principles

Today's kindergarten teacher plans her program and guides her children in accordance with certain fundamental principles. Some of these are conclusions from psychological experiments, some the fruit of much experience, and some mere statements of faith. They may be summarized as follows:

1. There are many habits, skills, and attitudes essential to the successful adjustment of the individual which can profitably be developed in a pre-formal instruction school program.
2. Every child needs experiences that will foster his physical, social, emotional, and *intellectual* development.
3. Every child should be given the information he craves and is able to assimilate.
4. Every child has many interests.
5. Every child needs to work and play with others.
6. Every child needs to learn to think for himself.
7. Generally speaking, at this age level every child learns more readily through doing than through words.
8. Generally speaking, every child, if deprived of actual experience, learns more readily through models and pictures than through words.
9. Every child learns more readily if he has incentives for greater effort.
10. Every child learns more effectively if he can review his experiences through such means as dramatic play, discussion, drawing, painting, and modeling.
11. Every child craves success or at least appreciation of his efforts.
12. Every child is sensitive to the attitudes of others toward himself.
13. Every child responds more readily to appreciation and constructive criticism than to being ignored or severely criticized.
14. Every child differs from every other child in inherited abilities and past experience.
15. Every child has his own growth pattern.

## Acquainting Parents with the Aims of the Kindergarten

In many cities and towns there has been an effort on the part of school officials to acquaint the public with the aims of the kindergarten. In some cities, either at the time of the spring or summer "roundup" or very early in the school year, the building principal, the school nurse, and the kindergarten teacher meet with the parents of new kindergarten entrants to outline the plans for the school year and to answer any questions the parents may have. Frequently much is done through newspaper publicity to acquaint the public with what it means to the child to become a member of an entering kindergarten class. Within the last fifteen or twenty years, many schools have prepared kindergarten handbooks, which they give to the parents of all kindergarten entrants.[5] These handbooks, which are usually very attractive, supply the parents with information about school procedures and outline the general kindergarten program, its aims and goals. The handbooks vary greatly in details, but they all stress the importance of home-school cooperation in the child's development. In many instances, the handbooks may be purchased for a nominal sum from the department of education of the city in which the book is published.

## Acquainting the Public with Kindergarten Education

Never before in the history of education have newspapers and popular periodicals carried so many items and articles on early childhood education. By and large, it is a good thing to have early childhood education brought to and kept before the eyes of the public; but we have just passed through an era in which particularly the "do-it-yourself" enthusiasts have outdone themselves in featuring in newspapers and periodicals the "Hurry! Hurry! Hurry!" program in early childhood education. We have also had many —but need more—articles on the "Does *Can* Mean *Should?*" angle of the question, and we need more articles on the ways in which young children are being challenged to make profitable use of the information which is theirs because of the widening horizons of their "here-and-now" experience. We also need more articles to show how kindergarten teachers can and are building good foundations for further learning without resorting to the pressures being exerted to push formal subject matter down into the kindergarten. (See Chapter 23.)

## Kindergarten Teaching Evaluated

A concerted effort is needed to acquaint the public with what is meant by *good* education for young children. The following two paragraphs quoted from the State of Minnesota *Guide for Teaching in the Kindergarten* will be useful in evaluating the kindergarten teaching program. (A word of caution! In each of the cited examples in the first paragraph—the

[5] See listing in Appendix.

fourth example excepted—there are undoubtedly elements of good kindergarten education; but any program predominantly in the character of any one of the pictures presented in the first paragraph is definitely not to be classified as a *good* kindergarten.)

> Unfortunately the lay public and educators who do not understand the needs of young children are frequently unable to recognize truly effective kindergarten teaching. Some are unduly impressed by "well controlled" children, a "well organized day" and a room in which confusion is at an absolute minimum. They are unaware of the fact that in such a situation the teacher may be manipulating children like puppets rather than providing them with worth-while educational opportunities. Others, apprehensively concerned with the current explosion of knowledge, may feel that more information at an earlier age is a logical way of preparing children to cope with the modern world. They are delighted to see a kindergarten in which subject matter and skills are presented as isolated formal lessons—complete with phonic, number and speech drills, workbooks and worksheets, for example. Still others are prone to measure the quality of kindergarten experiences by the "clever things" the children make, the "cute things" they do and their "smiling faces." A good kindergarten for these observers means a "pretty room," a "pleasant teacher" and "happy children." Still a fourth misconception of good kindergarten teaching grows out of the belief that unlimited freedom, laissez-faire behavior and complete permissiveness are measures of a wholesome kindergarten atmosphere.
>
> Present-day knowledge of growth and development have led us to "realize that our educational goals are attained best when we make it possible for a child to learn things which he is physically, mentally, emotionally and socially able to learn. We realize that learning is dependent upon maturation and the kinds of experiences that are provided. Teaching is knowing what the child is like and exerting skill in selecting and guiding activities that contribute to the child's total development."[6] It takes a well-educated person, specifically prepared in the area of childhood education to teach kindergarten effectively.[7]

And, we might add, today it takes an individual with considerable perspective to reconcile what is known about the developmental needs of children with the pressures our complex society is placing on our educational institutions.

[6] *Those First School Years,* Yearbook of the National Elementary Principal, Vol. XL, No. 1, September, 1960, p. 50.

[7] *A Guide for Teaching in the Kindergarten,* State of Minnesota Department of Education, Curriculum Bulletin No. 25, 1963, p. 5.

## SUMMARY

The modern American kindergarten retains the name of its German founder, Friedrich Froebel, though many of its practices and procedures reflect the thinking and teaching of Madam Maria Montessori and outstanding American educators. Research in child development and education has also done much to shape the American kindergarten program. Starting with a set of guiding principles, the kindergarten teacher endeavors to offer every child, "regardless of race, belief, economic status, residence or physical condition"[8] (sounds amazingly current, doesn't it?), an opportunity for the fullest development of his individual powers. The kindergarten lays stress on the child's all-around development, not overlooking, as some tend to feel, his intellectual development. The kindergarten has always helped parents realize that the school and the parents need to work closely together for the good of the child. Handbooks advise parents of the aims of the kindergarten. The kindergarten teacher today is faced with the challenge of helping the public appreciate that the educational pressures of our complex society are at times in conflict with what is known about the developmental needs of young children.

## QUESTIONS AND PROBLEMS

1. Visit a kindergarten and list those activities most like and those most unlike the things a child does at home.
2. Devote an hour of your class time to a discussion of the Froebel and the Montessori materials. If possible, have the materials for exhibit purposes. What adaptations of these materials can you find in a modern kindergarten? What activities in the kindergarten can be classified as "exercises of practical life?"
3. Cite a specific case in which you observed a teacher helping a child clarify and solve his own problem.
4. Give examples of activities in the kindergarten that fulfill each of the guiding principles listed on page 48.
5. Why should the kindergarten be concerned with physical, social, and emotional development?
6. Cite an instance in which it was apparent that one child in a kindergarten group had much greater information on a particular subject than his peers. Is this necessarily an indication of greater intelligence?
7. How would you convey to your public the concept of good kindergarten education?

[8] "Platform of the National Education Association," *Journal of the National Education Association*, 1934, 23:169.

## SELECTED REFERENCES


Association for Childhood Education International, Washington, D.C.:

*Basic Human Values*, Bulletin No. 8-A, 1962.

*Don't Push Me*, Bulletin No. I-A, 1960.

*How Good Is Our Kindergarten?* Bulletin No. 65, 1959.

*Implication of Basic Human Values*, Bulletin No. 10-A, 1964.

*What Are Kindergartens For?* Membership Bulletin No. A, 1961.

Berson, Minnie Perrin, *Kindergarten—Your Child's Big Step*, New York, E. P. Dutton & Company, 1959.

Bruner, Jerome, *The Process of Education*, Cambridge, Massachusetts, Harvard University Press, 1960.

Hammond, Sarah Lou, Ruth J. Dales, Dora S. Skipper, and Ralph L. Witherspoon, *Good Schools for Young Children*, New York, The Macmillan Co., 1963.

Heffernan, Helen, "Significance of Kindergarten Education," *Childhood Education*, March, 1960, 36: 313–319.

Heffernan, Helen, "Pressures to Start Formal Instruction Early," *Childhood Education*, October, 1960, 37:57–60.

Lambert, Hazel, *Teaching the Kindergarten Child*, New York, Harcourt, Brace and Company, 1958.

Langdon, Grace, and Irving W. Stout, *Helping Parents Understand Their Child's School; A Handbook for Teachers*, New York, Prentice-Hall, 1957.

Moore, Eleanor Haegle, *Fives at School*, New York, G. P. Putnam's Sons, 1959.

National Education Association, Washington, D.C.—Bulletins:

*Foundation Learnings in the Kindergarten*, 1958.

*Let's Look at Kindergartens*, 1959.

*Why Kindergarten?* 1959.

National Education Association Department of Elementary School Principals, *Those First School Years*, National Education Association, Washington, D.C., 1960.

Rudolph, Marguerita, and Dorothy H. Cohen, *Kindergarten—A Year of Learning*, New York, Appleton-Century-Crofts, 1964.

Wann, Kenneth, Miriam Dorn, and Elizabeth Ann Liddle, *Fostering Intellectual Development in Young Children*, New York, Bureau of Publications, Columbia Teachers College, 1962.

Wills, Clarice D., and William H. Stegeman, *Living in the Kindergarten*, rev., Chicago, Follett Publishing Company, 1956.

# 4

# THE KINDERGARTEN TEACHER

In the life of any small child, people are more important than things. The "poor little rich girl" has come to symbolize the individual child who has everything in the way of material blessings but no human being to turn to for comfort and wise, understanding guidance. A parallel to the poor little rich girl's situation would exist if a group of kindergarten children—no matter how beautifully and perfectly their room might be equipped—lacked the leadership of a teacher who had warmth, insight, and understanding. Fortunately, most people who choose to teach in the kindergarten do possess these qualities! But what other qualities, abilities, and strengths should the kindergarten teacher have?

## Personal Characteristics of the Kindergarten Teacher

Since the teacher is almost sure to be admired and copied by the children, some people conclude that she should be a paragon. One list of "desirable attitudes and traits" in a teacher gives the following: "alert, altruistic, approachable, charitable, clean, co-operative, courageous, democratic, dependable, dignified, fair, faithful, generous, happy, honest, idealistic, impartial, just, kind, loyal, magnanimous, modest, neat, noble, open-minded, optimistic, patient, patriotic, poised, positive, progressive, pure (morally), reverent, sensitive to humor, serene, strong (physically), sympathetic, tactful, tolerant, true, and truthful." We cannot help wondering whether the person who seriously compiles such a list can have the desired "sensitivity to humor." Another impressive list says that the kindergarten teacher should possess "good health, youth, patience, voice control, sense of humor, love of children, tact, training, and experience." Still another assumes that a teacher must be a leader and lists the four qualities essential to leadership as "(1) the courage of the pioneer . . . of the adventurer; (2) the kind of courage that will take a chance, will try a new thing, will experiment; (3) the ability to keep things from becoming static; (4) the ability to influence the actions of others."

Abandoning any attempt to enumerate the desirable characteristics of a kindergarten teacher, we may say that in selecting a teacher for young children we want the very finest person we can get, a person who would still be a fine person if for one reason or another she gave up her teaching. In other words, a teacher should be thought of as a human being primarily and as a teacher only secondarily—a human being who is greatly interested in teaching. We cannot take space here to discuss the qualities that make up a fine person, but we can suggest some of the additional characteristics she would need as a teacher of young children.

Most teachers of young children in America are women, though some nursery schools have found that young men doing graduate work in psychology make excellent assistants in work with children. A few men, though not many, have ventured into the kindergarten teaching field. When we note how much the visits of such men as the principal, the doctor, the psychologist, a father, and the building caretaker mean to the children, we wish that more young men would choose to work with young children.

In spite of the fact that some of our very best kindergarten teachers are among those who have been in the teaching field for many years, the business of kindergarten teaching, generally speaking, is better suited to those who are chronologically young. An older teacher, however, who is *young* in spirit is much preferred to a young teacher *old* in spirit. We have all seen some people in their twenties or early thirties who were much older, more static, and more labored in their bearing than other people in their fifties or sixties. These latter, in contrast, were alert, tuned to the present, agile in both thought and action, and filled with a zest for the challenge of the day. The teacher of young children needs to be alert physically as well as mentally. She needs to be quick to change as her group changes, or as studies in the field of research and the experiences of others suggest change.

A good kindergarten teacher cannot have a one-track mind. Although, artfully, she appears to be giving her undivided attention to a single child or to a single problem she must be at the same time mindful of and attuned to the total group situation. This seems to be one of the most difficult arts for a beginning teacher to acquire.

An observer sitting on the sidelines is often amazed to note how many details the alert kindergarten teacher is aware of. Perhaps she is helping John at the workbench as he tries to figure out a way to fasten a propeller on his plane. She may appear to be completely absorbed in John's problem, but at the same time asks Betty if she would take time to replenish the supply of manila paper in the far cupboard. She smiles her approval of Jim's new stunt on the jungle gym, then catches Blair's questioning glance and raises her eyebrows as Blair, in the playhouse corner, threatens to break the dishes. She notices that the light is inadequate in the library corner, and asks Clark if he will be kind enough to snap on the switch. She suggests that Lois put the ribbon she has just found into the lost-and-found bag instead of in her own locker. She praises Tom for the way he handled the situation when Mike took blocks from his airport enclosure without asking. She nods her hearty approval as Peter turns from posting a picture he has just finished. She reads and signs a note that has been sent from the principal's office. With a quick glance at the clock, she sets out the tray and napkins just as two fourth-grade boys come through the door with milk. She does all this, and yet apparently she has been giving her whole attention to John and his propeller problems!

## What Children Like

Kindergarten children do not have a sufficiently clear-cut appreciation of values to give us an exact idea of what they like in a particular teacher; but it is obvious from their remarks that they like their teacher to be attractive. Fortunately, this does not mean that the teacher must have a Grecian profile, nor must she have perfection in grace and movement. The little Russian picture storybook, *My Mother Is the Most Beautiful Woman in the World,* which depicts a plain—very plain—woman, affords solace for many of us.

At kindergarten age, both boys and girls are very much interested in what the teacher wears. They like color, either in the material itself or in the trimming; they love jewelry with an almost savage ardor, and they like the texture of materials. But above all, they like variety. What kindergarten teacher has not been confronted with, "You wore that dress yesterday" or "Why do you always wear that dress?" The "same old dress," assuming it is well-styled, may seem unobjectionable to the teacher, but not to the children. Far better, from their point of view, to wear a still older dress than always the same one.

Oddly enough, the teacher's "different" shoes seem to have a special appeal to children. On second thought, maybe it isn't so odd! In the first place, since kindergarten children often sit "at the teacher's feet," they probably get tired of seeing the same old shoes. And in the second place, since they themselves have only one or at the most two pairs of shoes that fit their growing feet, it probably seems amazing that the teacher can wear so many different shoes. High heels, in spite of the fact that they are a hazard to the teacher and a source of danger to children, have their own special appeal to young children. High heels are a symbol of being grown up, and what child doesn't look forward to being grown up? When a little girl "plays lady," one of the first things she seeks out is a pair of high-heeled shoes. Can you imagine "playing lady" in a pair of sneakers?

Sometimes a change of shoes, a change of jewelry, or just a bright scarf or handkerchief added to a teacher's costume will give the effect of a fairly varied wardrobe. In spite of the fact that children are fond of color, on a day when their usually gaily attired teacher may have occasion to appear in something like an all black outfit, the children are likely to be carried away with admiration. On that day the teacher is royalty in their midst!

But far more important than her physical features or her clothes is the teacher's facial expression. A ready smile will win the confidence of practically every small child, and a merry laugh will straighten out many a near-tragedy. An interchange of glances or smiles will often bring about a sense of security and happiness that is suddenly greater than it was a moment before. A teacher may get something of a shock when a child brings in a picture cut from a magazine and says, "This looks like you." The person may look centuries older than the teacher feels, but if the picture shows a countenance lit up by a smile, then that teacher may consider herself deeply complimented.

## Teacher-Child Rapport

Many behavior difficulties have their root in a child's belief that the teacher dislikes him. Such a belief, however lacking in foundation, is a potential source of difficulty. The belief carried home to parents has a potential for *gross* misunderstanding. While no teacher can be human and still remain equally fond of all the children in her classes year after year, all must respect the individuality and the potentialities of each child and strive to help each one become his best self. The teacher can be the friend of each individual but must limit the display of enthusiasm for any one in particular. Showing favoritism will often cause difficulties for both the teacher and the "teacher's pet"; and no good kindergarten teacher would dare say, even to herself, "I can't stand that child!"

Not only must the teacher guard against being unfair in her treatment of individual children, but she must at all times be absolutely fair in her dealings with the whole group. Unfairness on the part of the adult will encourage insecurity, dishonesty, and even open hostility on the part of the children.

When it comes to things and situations, the expression of preference, the expression of likes and dislikes, is quite another matter. The teacher will be much more appreciated if the children know that she has definite likes and dislikes—with, of course, emphasis on the likes—for special things and situations.

Kinships can be established through the expression of these feelings. A teacher who shows her enthusiasm for ice-cream cones will at once have strengthened the bond between herself and all the children in the group who are also fond of ice-cream cones. If a child expresses a dislike for cabbage, and the teacher says that she can understand it because she herself had to learn to like it, there is a similar effect. Of course, there are some things which it is one's personal privilege to prefer over others. In most instances the teacher will not care for certain radio or television programs or comic strips which the children may like very much, but she can do little good by condemning them completely. It is always wise for her to keep in touch with children's current enthusiasms so that she can discuss them, laugh with the children and, in some instances, lead them to an appreciation of higher types of entertainment.

## The Teacher's Voice

No discussion of the characteristics of a good teacher would be complete without some mention of her voice. We Americans are rightly criticized for our harsh, high-pitched voices. Every new teacher can profit from a first-hand observation of the techniques used by our better public lecturers. The best speakers are not those who speak the loudest. On the contrary, those who hold their audiences spellbound and who move them and carry them on from one point to another are those who enunciate clearly, so that every word is audible, who have a pleasingly modulated voice, who seem to speak without effort or strain, and whose voice is pitched considerably lower than the average woman's voice in ordinary conversation. Such a voice neither tires nor irritates its hearers; instead, it invites listening.

A further word about the teacher's voice. Certainly we do not want the teacher to speak in hushed and whispered tones but on the other hand it is well to remember that a raised voice is frequently a sign of feared defeat. A teacher's voice can do much to give children a sense of security in and respect for her as their leader.

## Patience

It is often suggested and usually implied, that a kindergarten teacher must have unbounded patience. True! She must not be impatient with children's awkward but well-meaning endeavors; she must not be impatient when children err in the process of learning. She must be able to adjust to the rhythm of young children's living; but her patience need not and should not be the patience of a Pollyanna. If occasion warrants, she should not hesitate to express dissatisfaction. Even five-year-olds can and do appreciate "righteous indignation."

## A Child's-Eye-View of a Good Kindergarten Teacher

A third-grader, spotting her kindergarten teacher in a grocery store said, "Mother, I liked her. She was a good teacher." And when, on the way home, her mother asked her if she knew why she liked the kindergarten teacher and why she thought she was a good teacher, she came forth with these rather sage remarks—remarks which teachers and parents alike might well ponder. "Well, for one thing, she had lots of good ideas; but even though she had lots of good ideas of her own, she always liked our ideas too. For another thing, she always gave us time to do things. Then too, I remember she used to tell us good stories, and she never seemed to be in a hurry. For another thing, I remember she was always fair; she always let us tell how we thought it happened. Then too, she always seemed to know what was going to happen next. And another reason I liked her was because she seemed to like us—she liked *all* of us. . . . And I guess another reason I liked her was because I liked her clothes. I just loved the feeling of her coat. It wasn't very long but o-o-h it was soft."

## Training of the Kindergarten Teacher

There was a time when any "lady" was accepted as a teacher of young children, but times have changed. Originally, the change was in the direction of giving the lady a four- or five-weeks' course in Froebelian methods. Today a good general education is stressed as a prerequisite for special training in teaching methods.

Fifteen states require their kindergarten teachers to have bachelors degrees, twenty-eight states require some other designated certification for teaching in the kindergarten, and at least seven states do not appear to have any certification requirements.[1]

The individual states designate the training and general course requirements for certification, but an overview of the requirements may be had

[1] Elizabeth H. Woellner and M. Aurilla Wood, *Requirements for Certification—Elementary Schools–Secondary Schools–Junior Colleges*, 29th ed., Chicago, Chicago, Press, 1964–65.

by reviewing the standards for early childhood education which were developed by the Teacher Education Committee of the Association for Childhood Education International:

Standards for Teacher Education in Early Childhood[2]

Qualified teachers for nursery school and kindergarten as well as those in primary grades, both public and private, should become recognized as professional people in their field. To do this it is necessary to meet requirements for certification by State Departments of Education.

*Requirements*

The qualified teacher should be a graduate of an accredited four-year college with a major in Early Childhood Education. The major may be completed at the under-graduate level or by additional courses at the post-graduate level.

I. Study in the area of the physical and biological sciences, mathematics and philosophy, language and literature, the social and behavioral sciences and the fine arts.

II. Professional preparation in the specialized field of Early Childhood Education

  A. To develop basic understandings of:

    1. Human growth, development and learning, mental and physical health.
    2. School, parent, home and community relationships and interactions.
    3. Curriculum content, methods, materials, experiences and resources.
    4. Current problems, history and philosophy of education.
    5. Administration and organization of school; relationship to upper elementary school.

  B. Through:

    1. Supervised experience with children including observation, participation and student teaching, with opportunities to coordinate theory with practice.
    2. Classroom discussion, lectures and readings.
    3. Guidance of student teachers toward keener awareness of themselves and their environment; of young children and their families.

In addition to the above requirements, special certification is essential for administrative positions in public and independent elementary schools, including nursery schools and kindergartens. Preparation for these positions

[2] ACEI Teacher Education Committee, "Standards for Teachers in Early Childhood Education," *Childhood Education*, 1958, October, 35:65–66.

includes successful teaching experience; study of the organization, administration of programs for young children; and professional development of staff.

*Professional Advancement*

Periodic refresher courses or workshops are required so that teachers can keep themselves abreast of current trends and research and their application to the understanding of children and curriculum development. Teachers should maintain their certification status with their State Education Department.

Sometimes students feel that the requirements in the area of physical and biological sciences, mathematics, philosophy, language, literature, the social and behavioral sciences, and the fine arts are unnecessary for a person not planning to teach these subjects. Those who have had kindergarten teaching experience, however, realize that, no matter what the breadth of their knowledge and experience may be, they never seem to have enough information to answer the many questions that arise in the kindergarten situation. When a child brings an unusual stone to school, an odd bird's nest, a discarded snake's skin, or a foreign book, when a child misquotes facts on a satellite launching, or when a child reports that his grandmother is going to Bazutaland, there is opportunity for educational discussion if only the teacher knows enough herself to make the discussion profitable. In addition to having a broad academic training, the teacher who has traveled, who has become acquainted with all sorts of people, and who is widely read has the potential of being a much better teacher than the one whose horizon is limited to the four walls of the schoolroom or to her immediate community.

## Observation

Before the young teacher actually begins to work with groups of children, it is essential that she have the opportunity to observe experienced teachers at work. While at this stage she will not appreciate fully the skill of the teacher, yet through repeated observations and questions she should come to recognize the outstanding points in the teacher's plans and techniques. It is quite possible, also, that occasional observation of poor teaching can make the student aware of pitfalls to be avoided.

## Student Teaching

Study and observation will give the student the theory of kindergarten teaching, but before she is ready to teach a group of her own, she needs an opportunity to serve as an apprentice under an experienced teacher. When we watch a skilled artist at work, we are impressed by the ease with which he creates; when we try it ourselves, the tools suddenly become clumsy, and our fingers all thumbs. So it is in teaching. Under the skilled teacher, the children behave and respond as they should; under the novice, they turn suddenly into problem children, bent upon embarrassing the teacher. The nursery schools report that three-year-old children will "try out" the new assistant and will think of all sorts of negative behavior the moment the regular teacher is out of sight. Probably contributing to this trying-out process of the new teacher is the fact that the children sense the young teacher's feeling of inexperience and inadequacy.

Children are sometimes uncanny beyond belief in their analysis of a situation. In one instance, a student teacher who, from the adult point of view, exhibited marked poise, found herself in charge of the rest period. She assumed a relaxed but expectant manner and all seemed to be going well until two children began chatting. She made a gesture which was meant to signify that it would be well for one child to turn over. The child turned over and the teacher half-breathed a sigh of relief. The second child looked at the teacher, then moved closer to the first and said, "Don't pay no attention to her; she's just a young thing."

If she can succeed in having the children believe that she is the master of the situation and knows it, the young teacher will probably be successful. Usually, however, it is only through experience that the teacher gains confidence in her own ability and learns the methods with which she is most successful. Some educators have predicted a day when beginning teachers will have a year or two of apprenticeship, comparable to the young doctor's internship, in which they will have opportunities to gain a mastery of essential techniques while still under the observation and guidance of experienced teachers. At any rate, during this time or as early as possible in her teaching experience, a teacher needs to develop a personal philosophy of education. Once having established a personal philosophy, educational approaches and procedures can be evaluated in the light of that philosophy. Practices and procedures will and should change to meet the demands of an ongoing culture, but a sound basic philosophy will help the teacher withstand pressures when the demands of society and the needs of children seem to be in conflict.

## The Teacher in the Community

Four principles summarize the teacher's role in society: (1) In a democracy the public-school teacher has the same rights as any other citizen.

(2) There should be a vital relationship between what she teaches and what takes place in the world outside the classroom. (3) The teacher must know her children, not only as members of her school group, but as members of families and members of a community as well. (4) Because the teacher has had certain cultural opportunities and because she has chosen teaching as a profession, she has certain responsibilities and obligations to the profession and to society. There should be no compartmentalization of classroom life and life outside the classroom. Whether inside or outside the school, the teacher should conduct herself as one worthy of her citizenship in a democracy.

There are, of course, certain responsibilities. Like the doctor, the teacher will learn much of the intimate home life of her pupils. She will be told many things about the family and the child confidentially, and she must make sure that she keeps inviolate all such trust. If there is any question as to whether or not anything should be told about a child or a family, the safest procedure is not to tell it. Another safe rule is to use no names. A story will be just as amusing if it is told about "one of the boys in my room," and the policy will save possible embarrassment for both teacher and family and perhaps untold misery for the child.

Accepted as an integral part of a community, the teacher should try to live as a real member of that community. Some cities require that their teachers reside in the city itself and not in some nearby community. In these days of easy transportation, such a rule at first sounds somewhat ridiculous, and yet there can be no doubt that the teacher's concern for and pride in those civic affairs which have to do with the parents and children of the school are greater if she is a resident of the community in which she teaches. When a young teacher goes to a new community, she frequently tends to compare the place unfavorably with other communities. No one type of conversation can do more to turn the townspeople and a teaching staff against a new teacher. It is tactless and often really destructive to the teacher's professional reputation.

The teacher is ordinarily expected to participate in the activities of the community. Such participation is helpful because it brings about social relationships with the parents and in addition provides an opportunity for a personal social life. In some localities, however, the teacher will have to beware of a too-close social alliance with any one group. The one definite alignment that is accepted without question by most communities is church affiliation. If there is a church of her faith in the community, the teacher is perfectly free to affiliate with that church. If, on the other hand, there is no such church, or if she has no church affiliation, then, in today's society most communities respect the teacher's right to "worship as she sees fit."

## A Teacher's Code of Ethics

A code of ethics developed by the National Education Association long ago still seems applicable today. The part which applies to relations with pupils and with the community is as follows:

1. The schoolroom is not the proper theater for religious, political, or personal propaganda. The teacher should exercise his full rights as a citizen but he should avoid controversies which may tend to decrease his value as a teacher.
2. The teacher should not permit his educational work to be used for partisan politics, personal gain, or selfish propaganda of any kind.
3. In instructional, administrative, and other relations with pupils, the teacher should be impartial, just, and professional. The teacher should consider the different interests, aptitudes, abilities, and social environments of pupils.
4. The professional relations of the teacher with his pupils demand the same scrupulous guarding of confidential and official information as is observed by other long-established professions.
5. The teacher should seek to establish friendly and intelligent cooperation between the home and the school.
6. The teacher should not tutor pupils of his classes for pay.[3]

## In-Service Education

Too often teachers become so absorbed in the details of the day-by-day program that they lose sight of more distant goals. Many school systems attempt to correct this condition by requiring their teachers to attend conferences, take university courses, attend workshops, travel, or otherwise broaden their outlook. Just meeting certain academic requirements, however, does not assure that the individual has in any way come to have new interests and new understandings, been imbued with the scientific spirit, come to have new respect for personalities, or become more world-minded. The desire to improve, the will to become a vital and proficient teacher, can come only from within. School systems may set up requirements, but only the individual teacher can decide whether or not she will benefit from in-service education. In-service education programs need to be carefully reviewed. Sometimes the credit rating and/or the lure of increased pay which comes with taking additional course work leads teachers to overextend themselves. Too many meetings, too many study groups, too many

[3] *Ethics in the Teaching Profession*, Research Bulletin of the National Education Association, IX, No. 1, January, 1931.

late afternoon or evening classes, and too many summer school courses can exhaust rather than re-create and build teaching strength.

## SUMMARY

The teacher is the most important element in the make-up of the kindergarten. To be a superior teacher, an individual must be a superior person who has a broad general education as a basis for her specific training. She must possess certain qualities and characteristics that enable her to work with and be liked by young children.

The student should have many opportunities to observe and work with good teachers before she tries to work with a group of children of her own. The teacher and the classroom should not be isolated factors set aside from society. The teacher is first of all a citizen and then a teacher. Today's superior teacher approaches her problems with scientific curiosity, has sincere respect for personalities, sees her teaching efforts in relation to the total span of human development, and is concerned with the progress of humanity in its broadest sense.

## QUESTIONS AND PROBLEMS

1. Write a description of the grade-school teacher you liked best and a description of the one you liked least. Compare your two descriptions to determine the good teaching characteristics of each.
2. Based on at least five hours of kindergarten observation, indicate situations which challenged the teacher to draw on her background of academic learning—science, history, sociology and so on.
3. What would be the considerations relating to a public-school teacher's filing for an elected civic office?
4. Granted that in-service education is a forward step in raising teacher standards, can you cite an example of a situation where you felt that a teacher overextended herself in trying to better her academic rating? Discuss.
5. Suppose a group of mothers of the children in your kindergarten asked you, for remuneration, to run a series of birthday parties in the various homes. From a professional point of view would you feel justified in doing so? Explain your answer.
6. Children love to wear pins and buttons. Suppose it is several weeks before the time of the Presidential election and you have dozens of campaign buttons on hand. Would you feel justified in giving them out to the children in your kindergarten? Give reasons for your answer.

## SELECTED REFERENCES

American Association of School Administrators, *Who's a Good Teacher?*, Washington, D.C., National Education Association, 1961.

Berson, Minnie Perrin, *Kindergarten—Your Child's Big Step*, New York, E. P. Dutton and Company, 1959.

Biber, Barbara, and Claudia Lewis, "What Children Expect from Their Teachers," *Child Development*, March, 1954, 25:45–50.

Heffernan, Helen, and Vivian Todd, *The Kindergarten Teacher*, Boston, D. C. Heath and Company, 1959.

Imhoff, Myrtle, *Early Elementary Education*, New York, Appleton-Century-Crofts, 1959.

Jersild, Arthur T., *When Teachers Face Themselves*, New York, Bureau of Publications, Teachers College, Columbia University, 1956.

Langdon, Grace, and Irving W. Stout, *Teaching in the Primary Grades*, New York, Macmillan Company, 1964.

Leonard, Edith, Dorothy Van Deman, and Lillian Miles, *Foundations of Learning in Childhood Education*, Columbus, Ohio, Charles E. Merrill Books, Inc., 1963.

Moore, Sallie Beth, and Phyllis Richards, *Teaching in the Nursery School*, New York, Harper and Brothers, 1959.

Murphy, Gardner, *Freeing Intelligence Through Teaching*, New York, Harper and Brothers, 1961.

"Research in Comparative Education of Training and Further Training of Pre-Primary Teaching Staff," Bureau of Educational Bulletins, 1961, 4th quarter, 35:195–202.

Ryans, David G., "Prediction of Teacher Effectiveness," *Encyclopedia of Educational Research*, New York, Macmillan Company, 1960.

# 5

# SOCIAL CLIMATE OF THE KINDERGARTEN

Social climate, though most difficult to describe, is something one senses almost the moment he steps into a room in which human beings are functioning. It is conceivable that a kindergarten could be rated almost perfect on all other factors and still fall far short of being an ideal kindergarten if the social climate were not good. The kindergarten group might be composed of an ideal number of normal children; the room might contain the best equipment laid out in the most desirable fashion; and the teacher might have taken all the courses necessary to teach in kindergarten. But without a good social climate, this kindergarten would not even approach the ideal of wholesome kindergarten living.

## Ideas Flow Freely in the Desirable Social Climate

If the social climate of the room is wholesome, one will be able to sense at once that ideas are flowing freely, that the media through which the ideas flow and the outward forms the ideas take are as varied as the personalities, interests, and capabilities of the individuals in the group. Obviously in such a case there is not simply an outpouring of ideas from a single source—the teacher—but a flow of ideas to which both teacher and children contribute. A teacher who "has all the answers" is not receptive to ideas and, no matter how hard she strives otherwise, cannot create a desirable social climate.

## Ideas Accompany Problems

Ideas flow freely under the stimulus of problems. Problem solving, whether academic or social, always involves thinking and reasoning. We are inclined to overlook the importance of problem solving in child development. There is so much about the child's day that seems trivial to busy grown-ups that we have a tendency either not to give the child time to solve his own problems or to solve them for him, not realizing that the situation might give him profitable experience. In many cases the child really does have enough background experience to solve the problem himself, if the adult will but clarify it a bit. Failure to recognize a child's ability results in waste of valuable educational opportunities.

We may illustrate this point with Patrick, who is sitting at a kindergarten table on which there are several glasses of paint. One glass is very near the edge. Patrick, in a somewhat dreamy mood, is painting the third leg of the chair he has made. He paints the same leg over and over again. The teacher sees the problem of the paint glass being dangerously near the edge of the table, and she notes that Patrick is only seemingly occupied in purposeful activity. Obviously Patrick is not aware of either problem. In order to get the glass moved to a safe position and to get Patrick back to purposeful activity, the teacher might say, "Patrick, move your paint glass back away from the edge of the table and start painting the other leg of your chair." Or she might say, "Patrick, your glass is so near the edge of the table. It might get knocked off. Move your paint, then you can start painting the other leg of your chair. You have been painting the same one over and over again." Or she might say, "Patrick, your glass is so near the edge of the table I think it might get knocked off." Patrick will doubtlessly move the glass. The teacher might then shift attention to the chair and say, "Just one more leg to finish. We'll have to be cleaning up soon. Do you think you will be able to get the painting job done today?"

In the first two instances the problem for the child would become one of simply carrying out the commands of the adult. In the second instance, reasons are added but only after the commands have been given. The reasons do not clarify the problem for the child's own solution. In the third case the child has his attention directed to the problem itself, and since the problem is twofold, the teacher tries to clarify one part at a time. Once the problems are clarified the child's task becomes that of thinking out his solutions and acting on them. The results in any one of the three cases would be the same: the paint glass would be moved to a safe position and Patrick would return to purposeful activity. But the actual solving of the problem by the child himself would result in two special benefits: Patrick would have experience in using his present knowledge in an effective fashion, and he would have the satisfaction of solving his own problems.

## Problem-Solving Opportunities

Kindergarten teachers often fail to utilize the many opportunities for problem solving which are available. It is possible even today to go into kindergarten rooms where every detail of the day's program is directed by the teacher herself. If the observer is not aware of the values inherent in having the children meet and solve problems, it is possible that he will be impressed by the efficiency of the kindergarten teacher and the smoothness with which the program seems to progress. The problem-solving kindergarten, however, works on the theory that there is not always going to be a "superior" individual about to direct the child's every act. It is advantageous to give the child opportunities to use his present knowledge to try to solve those problems for which his present knowledge is adequate. He will then get into the habit of relying on himself and attempting to meet new situations in the light of his present knowledge. The child will make many mistakes in this process also, but if we can guide him so that his conclusions are sound, the efforts of both the teacher and the child will be worthwhile. As adults we may be pleased with beautifully finished art work and highly organized social conduct, but we should remember Piaget's contention that "mistakes" are an essential part of the reasoning process.[1]

In our complex civilization, the child could not possibly have sufficient knowledge to solve many of the problems with which he is faced. We must try, however, not to overlook the opportunities which many common experiences offer for problem-solving at the child's level. The solution of a problem, no matter how simple it may be, is accompanied by a feeling of satisfaction. Since effort accompanied by satisfaction is one of the primary laws of learning, it is not difficult to comprehend why the free flow of ideas which accompanies problem-solving is conducive to the establishment of a desirable social climate.

## Environment and Maturity Level of the Group

The degree to which the environment is adapted to the maturity level of the group is a second element in social climate. In the environment there should be a variety of challenges to meet the range of developmental levels represented. No matter how rich it may be, we absorb from our environment only that for which we are ready. A group of advanced mathematicians, for example, might be challenged by being set down in an empty room in which there was nothing but involved equations written on the walls, but it is scarcely conceivable that such an environment would be a

[1] J. Piaget, *Judgment and Reasoning in the Child*, New York, Harcourt, Brace & Company, 1928.

challenge to most of us. And so it is with kindergarten children: the environment must offer something that will challenge all members of the group.

## Sources and Organization of Knowledge

If the child's present knowledge is not adequate for the solution of his problems, then new sources of information must be tapped. Sometimes the teacher serves as the guide who directs the child to new knowledge, and sometimes she is the source of the new knowledge itself. Whether guide or source, she tries to plan so that the new information can be interwoven with old learnings. Formerly it was not uncommon to observe the teacher giving out information wholesale. The brighter children seized upon it and built for themselves great towers of learning. The less able had to let it fall about, making nothing but clutter and confusion for their minds. In our newer schools, the teacher tries to help the child fit his information and learning together, not so that he can form great towers of learning, but so that he can build for himself strata of learning. The broader and thicker the base, the better will be the foundation for later learning. In the tower concept, we note that the child builds many isolated groups of facts, all of which may be quite impressive at first glance. On further scrutiny, however, the new learning usually appears to be unrelated. If we can think of education on a strata rather than a tower basis, it is possible that that alone will do much to help establish a desirable social climate in the kindergarten.

## Running Account of a Kindergarten Visit

The following paragraphs are a brief account of a morning in a kindergarten. As you read them, try to pick out those elements which suggest that (1) ideas seem to be flowing freely, (2) the children are faced with problem-solving situations, (3) the environment, both social and physical, is challenging, (4) the teacher is helping the children build new learnings into strata rather than towers, and (5) the teacher, though aware of the needs and strivings of the individuals in the group, does not sacrifice the good of the group for the benefit of the individual.

### A HALF-DAY IN KINDERGARTEN

School XXX — Date of observation *April 26th*
Duration of session: *8:30 to 11:30*

Approximate date on which this group was enrolled in kindergarten: *September 16*
Approximate age range: 5 *yrs.* 6 *mo. to* 6 *yrs.* 1 *mo.*
No. of children enrolled: *12 girls, 13 boys*
No. of children present: *10 girls, 13 boys*
No. of teachers: *1*
Socioeconomic background of the group: children coming from homes of professional men, *10;* business executives, *6;* tradesmen, *5;* skilled laborers, *4;* day laborers, *0.*
Health inspection: The children are checked by the nurse before coming into the kindergarten room.

8:30 The kindergarten teacher is mixing paint and putting fresh paper on the easel. Jimmy opens the door and says, "Good morning, Miss B. Can I paint?" "Good morning, Jimmy. Things are all ready. You know where the paint smocks are kept, don't you?" Jimmy smiles, puts his sweater and cap in his locker, and comes back to the easel pulling on a smock.

Four more children appear in the doorway, wave to Miss B., and go to play in the outside sandbox. Miss B. props open the outside door to supervise both inside and outside activities. Peter comes in with his older sister, who says, "Peter didn't get to sleep last night until eleven o'clock. We had company." Miss B. says, "Thanks for telling me. Peter, if you feel tired or cross today, we'll know that you need some extra rest, won't we?" Peter takes off his things and joins Jimmy at the easel. He watches Jimmy outline a blue house with windows and doors and struggle to paint a gabled roof. Beside the house Jimmy paints what might be a robin. The robin is the size of the house.

Betsy, Joan, and Perry have come in and are playing in the doll corner. Perry is "sent to the store" for some milk for the baby. Jeffrey and four cohorts have arrived and are building an airplane with blocks and planks. They are working just outside the kindergarten door in the patio. Barbara and Jean are sitting at a small table, coloring. Barbara is making a picture of a bluebird, and Jean is trying to copy her idea.

Gretchen and Peggy go directly from the locker to the cupboard for puzzles. "Oh, look!" says Gretchen, "Mine is a new one. It looks like a hard one." Miss B. says, "It is a hard one. I put it on the shelf just this morning. I wondered if there would be anyone in this group who could work it." "Bet I could," says John, swaggering over and practically snatching it out of Gretchen's hands. "After Gretchen finishes, why don't you take a turn?" suggests Miss B. John releases his hold on the puzzle and goes over to the jungle gym, hangs upside down, swings back and forth, then climbs to the top and pretends he has a telephone. "Bombardier to pilot. Bombardier to pilot." Archer joins him. They talk together a minute, then rush to get their helmets. Miss B. walks to the jungle gym. Glancing up at the ceiling, she says, "You won't forget about how close you are to that upstairs floor, will you? They're trying to study in that room, you know." "OK," says Archer, and drops his voice to a lower level.

9:00 Miss B. stands outside the door offering a suggestion here and a word of approbation there. Jeffrey and Billy each have ideas about the wingspan of their plane. Jeffrey tries to explain his idea to Billy, but Billy picks up the board and runs off with it. Jeffrey and Danny force Billy to give up the board, but not without a struggle. Billy takes a good right swing at Jeffrey. "Miss B.," says Danny, looking at Jeffrey, as he holds the board in one hand and rubs his chin with the other, "Don't you think Billy had better go inside?" "Maybe so," says Miss B., "at least until he gets control of himself and can make it pleasant for others." She nods in the direction of Billy, and Billy plods heavily toward the door, Miss B. following. Billy hangs up his jacket and stands by his locker, looking sulky. Miss B. says, "Better get washed up and maybe you'll feel more like yourself. It wasn't a very pleasant experience you had, was it?"

9:20 Billy washes, then stands in the washroom door. "What are your plans?" asks Miss B. "Haven't any," says Billy. "In that case," says Miss B., "perhaps you had better get your rug so you can stretch out and relax. You'll be able to plan better when you feel relaxed." Billy spreads his rug by the library corner and stretches out. He stays there about five minutes, then folds up his rug and goes to get paper and crayons from the cupboard.

Janice has been wandering about the room ever since she put her sweater in her locker. Miss B. has been observing her, but has said nothing. Finally she says, "Janice, if you're not busy, would you see about sorting these crayons? The blues and the purples and the blacks seem to be mixed up." Janice picks up the pan of black crayons and Miss B. places the purple and the blue box on the table. Janice looks at a purple and then at a blue. It seems to be difficult to tell one from the other. "Maybe if you had a testing paper it would be easier to tell those blues and purples apart," says Miss B. Janice goes to the cupboard and brings back a piece of scrap paper. Barbara passes the table and says, "What are you doing?" Janice does not answer. Barbara turns to Miss B. and says, "May I do it, too?" Miss B. says, "You'll have to talk that over with Janice; she has the job now." Janice calls out, "Get another piece of paper so you can tell which is blue and which is purple." Barbara brings a piece from the cupboard and the two girls visit together as they sort. Miss B. says, "How lucky! You're just finishing your sorting, and it's time to get things put away. The children will certainly appreciate having those colors in the right boxes. Thank you!"

The cleanup word passes along. One by one, materials are put away, toilet needs are taken care of, and hands are washed. Miss B. has signaled to the children outside that it is time to come in. As she signals, she notes that the boys seem to hesitate. Miss B. picks up one end of a long board and says, "Tom, if you'll help me with this, and if Jeffrey and Danny will be responsible for the other blocks, we'll have everything taken care of." She hands the children in the sandbox a basket for their toys and promises to give them a broom so that they can sweep around the sandbox. Dorothy volunteers to be the sweeper. Miss B. starts to go in, saying, "I'll see you inside soon. Some children are practically ready for the meeting right now." Miss B. hands Dorothy the broom, washes her own hands, and joins those children who are standing by the piano. She plays a gay tune, and they sing as she plays.

9:30 All toys and materials are back in place, and all the children except two are seated on the floor by the piano in front of the teacher's low chair. Dorothy is still sweeping outside, and Jean is struggling to get some crayon marks off the table. While they wait for the two children, they enjoy a "true-false" game. Miss B. says, "Beans grow under the ground." Since the statement is not true, the children give one clap. Next, "Peas grow on vines." Since the statement is true, the children raise their hands. "Oh, oh," says Miss B., "Jeffrey, you forgot to wash your hands. Don't forget your chin. That was a dirty hit you got this morning. But you certainly handled the situation well! Congratulations!" "By the way, Billy, after you rested and relaxed, you really got hold of yourself, didn't you? That ship picture you are working on is a beauty. When it's finished I hope we can hang it up so everyone can enjoy it." Billy raised his downcast eyes and says, "It'll be finished tomorrow. I'm going to work on it the first thing I get here in the morning."

The children take turns telling what they have learned about the arrival of spring and discuss preparations for their garden.

9:50 As they leave the discussion group, each child goes off with a purpose. Jim and Bill go to the workbench to make markers for the garden rows. Ten children go to get plasticine to make models of the things needed to prepare the ground for gardening. Three others choose to draw pictures of how they would like to have the garden look. Barbara asks if she may paint her idea of the garden. Jean also wishes to paint, but Miss B. suggests that in her locker Jean has a doily with spring flowers on it which she hasn't finished. Jeffrey volunteers to print signs which "you can read so you'll know what you planted." He gets his paper and crayons, then asks Miss B. how "peas" would look. She prints it, and he copies it. Then he takes it to the boys at the workbench and consults them as to how they can best fasten his paper onto their sticks. They decide to tack it on. Three children have produced unfinished work from their lockers.

10:30 As the children finish their work, they clean up, go to the toilet, wash, and go to the library corner. About half of the children are still at work. The teacher plays a slow, quiet signal on the piano, and everybody stands at attention. The teacher asks those who have not finished to put their work in their lockers and to join the others in the library.

10:50 All are in the library. Individual books have been put back into the bookcase with "the bindings pointing out," and the group is seated on the floor in front of Miss B., who is holding up a copy of *The Little Gardeners*. They look at the pictures together, and then Jean says, "Read it." First they observe that in two places it says *The Little Gardeners*. Miss B. runs her finger under both captions. "Now if everybody is comfortable, I suppose I can begin." There is much settling back and some fussing about not being able to see. Miss B. waits quietly; everyone is settled. Now she begins to read, holding the book so that all can see the pictures. After the story, the children stretch up tall and go over to the piano.

11:10 The children ask for a skipping tune. Miss B. plays with clear accent, but light tone. As the music stops, they stand where they are and listen to the next music, which they have never heard before. They look puzzled and then begin to swing into many different responses. Some show much feeling for the music, and others seem merely to feel they should be doing *something*. Those who do not not have the feeling for the music begin to act silly, crowding together and bumping into one another. Miss B. stops the music and says, "Will you all sit down just where you are?" Then Miss B. says, "Archer, John, Betsy, Nancy, and Jean, would you show us the dances which you made up to that music? I think the rest of the group would enjoy seeing them." The five children dance freely, seemingly oblivious of anything but the music. All the children try again, many of them reflecting the patterns of the five. Betsy asks for "The Brownies." She is asked to choose five children for the dance. After much counting and recounting, the dance proceeds. The observing audience chuckles with delight.

11:30 The children are all seated by the piano. As request numbers they have sung "Tirra, Lirra, Lirra," "Now at Last Winter's Past," "He Dug His Garden," "Swinging," "Roller Skates," and "It's Raining." Then Miss B. plays some music she had played for them yesterday. The children recognize it and ask her what the song is about. She tells them it is about a Maypole. They chat about a Maypole, many confusing the word with "maple." Miss B. clarifies the meaning and then sings the song for them. They listen and join in. Some have difficulty with the whole song, and so Miss B. sings a single phrase and then they sing it with her. Now she sings a single phrase and they sing it back to her. Now they put the whole together. Barbara says, "Maybe we could have a Maypole dance in our kindergarten." With that thought for future planning, the children go in small groups to get their wraps.

First Miss B. asks all those who wore coats to get their wraps, then all those who wore jackets, then all those who wore sweaters. As they slip into their wraps, they say casual good-bys and disappear through the playground door. Kindergarten's over—until afternoon, when a new group will arrive!

## The Artist-Teacher

The teacher who is able to create a social climate which approaches the ideal may well be called the "artist-teacher." To the untrained observer, the artist-teacher often appears to be but an interested onlooker. In one sense she is just that, but in another sense she is much more. With the help of her observations, she is able to guide the children so that they can grow in their ability to gain meaning and understanding from their experiences. She knows just when and under what circumstances she should share with the child bits of her greater fund of information. She always shows empathy for children and is keenly aware of those values which are of significance to the individual child. Somehow, through her own artistry, the good kindergarten teacher is able to grasp the total group situation without losing sight of the many individual problems and strivings within the group.

## Evaluating the Social Climate

It is difficult for the individual teacher to evaluate the social climate within her own group. If on any one day she feels that she has succeeded in being a true friend to the children, if she has been able to create a balance between freedom and responsibility, if she has been a wise leader, a thought-provoking guide, an honest contributor, a just critic, a fair judge, a wise counselor, a cooperative aid, an enthusiastic participant, a source of sound information, and an understanding and efficient executive, then she may know that on that day the social climate of her room has approached the ideal. There are relatively few such days in the lives of the best kindergarten teachers, but the satisfaction they bring makes the ideal worth the struggle.

### SUMMARY

The social climate of the kindergarten is something one senses immediately on entering the room. In a good social climate, the children have a feeling of responsibility, and it will be evident that this feeling has been developed and not superimposed. The children and the teacher seem to be co-workers, and between them is a comfortable give-and-take. Ideas flow freely and the children use their present knowledge and understanding to solve their own problems and those of the group. The teacher is adept at keeping the welfare of the entire group in mind even when she appears to be giving undivided attention to immediate problems. Although it is apparent that the teacher is not the dominating force in the room, it is equally apparent that she has set up goals and is helping both the individuals in the group and the group as a whole to progress in the direction of those goals. The children will be jubilant and gay or serious and intent in their bearing as the situation demands. The artist-teacher creates within her room that social climate which approaches the ideal.

## QUESTIONS AND PROBLEMS

1. Why is it impossible for the teacher who is not receptive to ideas to create a desirable social climate in her room?
2. Visit a kindergarten. (a) Note the instances in which the teacher makes use of available problem-solving situations. (b) Note those problem-solving opportunities which seem to be overlooked or ignored.
3. Cite an instance either from your kindergarten observation or from your own early school experience in which you feel that "towers of learning" were erected.
4. In the running account of a kindergarten morning included in this chapter, (a) did you note any instance in which the teacher tried to give the timid, withdrawn child an opportunity to be the leader? Who was the child? (b) How did the teacher handle the situation when it appeared that the boys who were building the airplane outside were about to question her authority? (c) What did the teacher do to lower the voices of the boys on the jungle gym?
5. Were there any "missing links" in this account—that is, were any parts of the usual routine kindergarten daily program omitted? Explain.

## SELECTED REFERENCES

Ashton-Warner, Sylvia, *Teacher*, New York, Simon and Schuster, 1963.

Dollins, Joseph G., Henry Andeline, and Edmund Mech, "With Words of Praise," *Elementary School Journal*, March, 1961, 61:314–316.

Headley, Neith, *Foundation Learnings in the Kindergarten*, Bulletin, Washington, D.C., National Education Association, 1958.

Heinz, Mamie, *Growing and Learning in the Kindergarten*, Richmond, Virginia, John Knox Press, 1959.

Lane, Howard, and Mary Beauchamp, *Human Relations in Teaching: The Dynamics of Helping Children Grow,* New York, Bureau of Publications, Teachers College, Columbia University, 1955.

Leonard, Edith, Dorothy Van Deman, and Lillian Miles, *Foundations of Learning in Childhood Education,* Columbus, Ohio, Charles E. Merrill Books, Inc., 1963.

Lindberg, Lucile, and Mary Moffit, "The Program and the Child," *Those First School Years,* Washington, D.C., National Education Association, 1960.

McConkie, Owen W., and Marie M. Hughes, "Quality of Classroom Living in Relation to Size of Kindergarten Group," *Childhood Education,* May, 1956, 32:428–432.

Nesbitt, Marion, *A Public School for Tomorrow,* New York, Harper and Brothers, 1953.

Rasey, Marie E., and J. W. Menge, *What We Learn from Children,* New York, Harper and Brothers, 1956.

Wann, Kenneth, Miriam Dorn, and Elizabeth Ann Liddle, *Fostering Intellectual Development in Young Children,* New York, Bureau of Publications, Teachers College, Columbia University, 1962.

Zirber, Laura, *Spurs to Creativity,* New York, G. P. Putnam and Sons, 1959.

# 6

# PROVISIONS FOR PHYSICAL WELFARE

The kindergarten was the first division of the school system to stress the importance of the physical health of its children. The kindergarten still tends to show greater concern for the health and general welfare of its enrollees than many other school units—and with good reason.

In the first place, an early discovery of physical weakness or deficiencies is important so that remedial steps may be taken or planned for before the child enters into more competitive phases of school and society. In the second place, it is important to alert parents early to what may be done to improve the physical well-being of their children. Never again, in all probability, will parents be so solicitous about the child's health. Later on, school grades, gracious manners, personal appearance, and a general concern for "keeping up with the Joneses" may assume overwhelming importance to parents who have become used to a jerky gait, a seemingly slight speech defect, a tendency to ask for the repetition of words, an unusual way of looking at reading material, or perhaps just a lack of normal vim and vigor. Although the teacher, the school nurse, and the school doctor are responsible for pointing out any apparent physical problems the child may have, the actual treatment of the problem, of course, is the responsibility of the family's medical consultant. Teachers and school authorities have the responsibility of making every possible provision for the child's well-being by maintaining a safe, hygienic, and wholesome school environment for all enrolled children.

## Safe Buildings

While there is little or nothing the individual kindergarten teacher can do about the overall physical plant, yet it is essential that she know what is really adequate and where improvement should and could be made.

The most important consideration in the construction of any school building is safety. Since, for most parts of the country, the greatest danger lies in the possibility of fire, it is absolutely essential that every precaution be taken against this hazard. If it is possible, buildings should be of fireproof construction. Halls and stairways should always be kept open and free. Even in a supposedly fireproof building there should be enough fire escapes and fire extinguishers, and halls should be equipped with fire alarm bells. In large units, fire drills should be held frequently enough to acquaint both teachers and children with the routines to be followed at the sound of the fire alarm bell. The heating plant should be shut off from the rest of the building by fire doors, and the heating units within the rooms should be recessed or otherwise shielded, so that the children cannot come into direct contact with the units. Doors should swing outward and should not be so heavy that they cannot be operated easily by the youngest children. Heavy doors that swing easily should be equipped with a control which will keep the door from crashing shut and catching fingers or children themselves between door and frame.

Stairs should be wide enough to preclude crowding, and landings should be arranged at distances sufficient to discourage jumping. Every stairway should be provided with handrails on both sides and, perhaps most important of all, every stairway should be well lighted. If the steps are covered with composition treads or if they have metal bands at the edges, great care should be taken that these are kept in excellent condition. Many a serious fall has resulted from a foot caught in a loose metal edging or worn floor covering.

Within the room the teacher can do much to provide for safety by setting up area units—an area for woodworking, an area for block building, an area for large-muscle equipment, an area for rhythms, and so on. The location and design of shelves and counter space used for the storage of materials is also an important factor in providing for a maximum of safety. Shelves should be neither too high nor too deep—and cupboard doors that swing out into a lane of traffic can be hazardous as can some types of sliding doors.

## Contact with the Out-of-Doors

Most kindergarten rooms are located on the main floor of the school building near an exit and entrance to the out-of-doors. It is desirable that at least one exit from the kindergarten room lead directly onto a fenced or hedged play yard, so that the activities of the kindergarten day can be carried on either in or out of doors. Recess, the term often used by grade-school children for out-of-door playtime, is seldom used in connection with the kindergarten program, for kindergarten activities can be carried on both in and out of doors.

## Hygienic Kindergarten Rooms

Children of kindergarten age need plenty of space. They will and should spend much of their time moving about; and much of their activity is accompanied by verbalization or other sound effects. If they are expected to work and play in an area crowded with other children, and if they have no opportunity for retreat to the relative privacy which they have known at home, their adjustment to school ways may be difficult.

From fifty to sixty square feet of floor space is needed per child. In estimating available floor space, it is not unusual to overlook the fact that cabinets, counters, library shelves, tables and chairs, a piano, and other pieces of furniture and equipment will occupy much floor space. The estimated floor area should exclude locker and washroom space. All this means that in a kindergarten room to be used by twenty-four children there should be between 1,200 and 1,500 square feet of floor space exclusive of washroom and locker areas. A room slightly longer than it is wide is somewhat less formal looking than a square room, and it seems easier to divide such an elongated room into interesting units.

Heavy battleship or inlaid linoleum slightly mottled but not highly figured still heads the list as the most desirable floor covering in kindergarten rooms. Rubber, cork, and asphalt tile might at first seem to be more desirable, but it is found that with the constant moving of chairs and tables, the tiles are likely to loosen and crack. From the standpoint of comfort, it is unfortunate that building codes stipulate that the floor covering in school buildings be laid on cement. In many instances teachers find that shoes with resilient composition soles are the only answer for comfort. They also find that breakage is great on flooring laid directly on cement. Kindergarten teachers look forward to the day when a resilient pad between the cement and the floor covering will be installed in every kindergarten room. The kindergarten floor should be kept clean, swept between morning and afternoon sessions, and cleaned thoroughly at least once a week. Kindergarten children spend much time working, playing, and sitting on the floor. No child should be required or allowed to sit on a dirty floor. A clean floor is a must; but the shiny, highly waxed floor, though it may be the pride and joy of the maintenance staff, can lessen the comfort and safety of kindergarten living.

## Lighting

Climatic conditions must be considered in planning for good lighting. But generally speaking, a southern or eastern exposure is better than a western exposure, while a northern exposure has nothing in its favor. The window areas should be approximately one-fifth of the floor area, and the windows should be low enough that the children can see outside as they go about their work and play. There is such a thing, though, as having too much window space in a kindergarten room. This is especially true when it comes to darkening the room for rest time. Again, climatic conditions will be a factor in determining the best type of window. In warm climates it may be highly desirable to have windows of shatterproof glass extending to the floors, so that they may be rolled or folded back to provide an open side to the room. In cold climates, it is impractical to have ceiling-to-floor windows, especially the kind that roll or fold back, for the cold air all too easily finds its way into the room and across the floor. Wherever possible, there should be windows on two sides of the room. Pull shades, venetian blinds, and fireproof draw curtains each have points in their favor. Window coverings should be such that they can make the room dark enough for the projection of pictures.

Adequate light for dark, cloudy days can best be provided by fluorescent lights, arranged so that they afford a mellow, diffused, nonglare radiance. A bulletin of the United States Department of Health, Education, and Welfare states that a kindergarten room seems adequately lighted when forty-foot-candle intensity is maintained throughout the room.[1] An electrician testing the light intensity of various classrooms and offices on one campus indicated that halls and corridors are adequately lighted if the light there registers five- to fifteen-foot-candle intensity; light in an office is adequate if a fifty-foot-candle intensity is maintained in the desk area. Bright sunlight gives a 10,000-foot-candle intensity. No wonder we find it difficult to read in the bright sunlight, and no wonder we need shades, draperies, or blinds to screen out the *bright* sunlight from our classrooms.

## Walls

Walls should be finished with a nonglaze paint which can be cleaned easily. The best color for the walls will depend largely on the room exposure. Soft greens or any of a variety of delicate pastels may well be used in

[1] *Designing Elementary Classrooms*, Special Publication No. 1, Washington, D.C., United States Department of Health, Education, and Welfare, 1953.

rooms which get much sunshine, but in rooms with a northern exposure, it will be wise to use only the strongest of light-reflecting colors. Yellow in its various tints will best compensate for lack of sunshine in the room. In general, it is best to leave the walls plain and to provide pictures and hangings that can be changed frequently. The woodwork of the room is easy to clean and pleasing to look at when painted with a glossy—but not too glossy—enamel in soft neutral tones. A tiled dado is easy to keep clean, but chips readily; some people feel it is too austere for a kindergarten. Where groups of young children work and play, sound absorbent ceilings are almost a must; they help no end in lessening tension and confusion.

## Lockers

Open, wooden, individual locker space should be provided in the main room or in space immediately adjoining the main room. It is desirable that lockers be so arranged that their contents are not visible from the main room. Each locker should be large enough to hold treasures brought from home, unfinished work, an apron or smock and, of course, the child's outside wraps, including rubbers or boots. Obviously, it would be practical to have the locker space located near the entrance door. In some climates it is desirable to have the locker area designed so that a flow of hot air can be circulated to dry rain- and snow-soaked wraps.

## Plumbing Facilities

Every kindergarten room needs toilet and washroom facilities of its own. Two lavatories and two toilet seats will be adequate for twenty-four children. The location of the toilet and washroom area, like other parts of the kindergarten unit, should be such that it can be easily supervised by the teacher. The five-year-old usually seeks a degree of privacy when taking care of toilet needs, but some can become quite fearful when they find that heavy solid doors are going to shut them off from contact with the others. It is desirable to have either latticed or free-swinging booth doors in the toilet area. Separate toilet facilities for girls and for boys are acceptable but certainly not necessary.

A low counter sink which can be used by both the children and the teacher is an ideal area for mixing paint, washing brushes, scrubbing clay boards, and doing other things such as squeezing out sponges. If it has a good stopper, it is also good for all kinds of water play, including testing and sailing boats made at the workbench.

A drinking fountain in the room encourages children to stop for a drink whenever they feel the urge, and it does away with the time-consuming and boring business of waiting in line for the single drink of the morning or afternoon. Children should be encouraged to take care of toilet needs and take drinks during those periods of the day when these activities will interfere least with group activities.

## Area Dividers

A workroom or playroom adjoining the main kindergarten room, if designed so that the activities of the two rooms can be observed easily by a single adult, has its advantages. This room can be used in any number of ways. In some schools it serves as a woodworking room, in others as a paint shop, and in still others as the room for the apparatus for big-muscle activity. To whatever use it is put—and it can be used in a host of ways not mentioned here—such a room tends to help lessen group tensions by distributing children and more or less segregating certain types of activity. The placement of an upright piano and movable storage units as well as the use of temporary screens can aid in making a room more functional. Accordion-like folding screens which run on an overhead track may be installed, providing the added advantage of making the total kindergarten area available as a unit.

## Ventilation

To a certain extent, the kindergarten teacher can control the ventilation of her room. She can try to keep the temperature between 67° and 70° Fahrenheit and the air fresh, guarding against direct drafts in the colder months while encouraging the circulation of air on all days. If the children must be in the room with their wraps on while waiting to be picked up, the teacher should adjust the room temperature to protect them from becoming overheated. The teacher can prevent the accumulation of dust in the air by keeping the room as clean as possible and by helping the children learn to avoid or control activities likely to raise dust, such as clapping the blackboard erasers together, waving rugs or outdoor wraps, tracking in mud, and sweeping too vigorously or waving a dust-filled broom.

If there is a humidifying system in the building, the teacher should acquaint herself with its control and find out whether she has any responsibility for its functioning. If there is no humidifying system, there are ways in which the teacher and the children can provide for better humidity. An open aquarium, a large pan or small tank kept filled for water play, or just a container of water placed somewhere in the room will help. If the teacher finds the room damp and humid, she should mention the matter to the proper person. Each school system seems to have its own pattern for channeling requests concerning the physical plant, and it is well for a new teacher to acquaint herself with the procedure early in the school year.

## Protection from Hazards

Although the teacher can seldom make radical changes, she should report to the principal of the building any conditions that may endanger the health or safety of children. Hazards such as unscreened windows which open onto ball fields, unguarded hot radiators, unsanitary drinking fountains, and exposed or worn electric wires should be reported. If these dangers cannot be removed, the teacher must teach the children to protect themselves and others against them. Children of five are mature enough to appreciate the dangers of certain elements in their environment, and yet many come to kindergarten surprisingly unprepared to use judgment in caring for themselves.

## Safety Measures

In kindergarten, children can acquire the habit of handling scissors and tools in such a way that maximum safety is assured both for themselves and for others in the group. It is wise to establish with the children a uniform way of handling certain tools, such as saws and scissors. For example, the children should be taught to carry a saw pointing down and held close to the body and to carry scissors by grasping the closed blades in their fists and carrying the scissors with the points toward the floor. If the members of the group know what to expect of others as well as what to do themselves in handling the tools, hazards can be minimized. They can learn to beware of and to report such things as sharp splinters, broken glass, torn bits of wire, and rough edges of tin cans. And they can come to recognize the dangers involved in such activities as playing at the head of stairs, approaching too near a child who is swinging, interfering with others when they are doing gymnastic stunts, or daring less able children to perform feats of which they are not capable.

Every year we read in the papers accounts of young children who have become temporarily lost on their journey to and from school. If the child can tell his name and address, the police or other adults can easily direct him or take him to his home. At the time of the spring or summer registration, it is wise to remind parents that five-year-olds should know their own full name, their father's name, and their own address. Early in the year, the kindergarten teacher should make sure that each child knows and can state this information clearly.

A name and address tag designed to be worn by the kindergarten child during the first days of school can be not only a help to teacher and/or the school bus driver but it can be a status symbol for the child as well. If the tag matches in color the symbol displayed in the bus which the child is to ride, much confusion can be avoided in the business of bus-loading during the early days of kindergarten attendance.

After the first few days or the first week, most children who are able to walk to school will be able to do so by themselves. If traffic is heavy near the school, police patrols, the teacher, or a police officer may be needed to see the children across certain streets. Children need to be encouraged to go directly to and from school, and they need to learn that they should always check in at their homes before going to play with other children.

Children who have to walk where there is no sidewalk need to know that in walking in the road they are expected to keep to the left so that *they* will be facing approaching traffic. All children must understand that streets are for traffic and not for play. Children should be taught to look both ways when crossing a street and then to proceed with care, avoiding lagging, running, or darting into the street. The kindergarten teacher can help children see the necessity for traffic requirements by taking the class on excursions, and by stimulating discussions and dramatic play in which traffic regulations are featured.

Five-year-olds are unusually interested in fire and matches. They should be given opportunities to learn of the care which must be used in approaching them.

Electricity has come to be such a common source of light, heat, and power in most homes that its proper use should be something kindergarten children are aware of. The inquiring six-year-old who was caught just as he was about to plunge the electric heater into the bathtub to see whether it would make the water boil should have learned its proper use before he reached this age.

## Physical Examinations

In many schools, parents are required to bring or send to the school a record of their child's physical examination made by the family doctor or the child's pediatrician. Usually these come in at the time of either the spring or the summer registration: it is hoped that any remedial attention needed can be given before school opens in the fall. This record, along with other information about each child[2] will inform the teacher about the kind of group she can expect and it should forewarn her of individual children who will need special observation or special treatment throughout the year.

If it is difficult to obtain the record of a physical examination made before the child enters school, one should be obtained soon after. In those schools where a physical examination is given by the school physician, the parents are usually invited to be present. In some instances the school nurse gets from parents a medical history while the doctor gives the physical examination.

During the year it is desirable to have two or three measurements of children's height and weight. If a child of kindergarten age loses weight or fails to gain over a period of several months, a complete physical examination is in order.

## School Attendance

For many years the public schools have stressed the importance of regular attendance. Although it is quite true that the child will benefit more from his school if he is present every day, there is another side to regular attendance which has frequently been overlooked. If a child attends school when he does not feel well, or is actually ill, he will hardly profit as much from this one day's schooling as he would from remaining at home indoors or in bed. He may "learn" more on this one day by remaining in school, but the loss of physical vigor caused by going to school when he should be resting and receiving special care may mean a number of days of lessened ability to learn, and at the end of the week he may actually know less than if he had rested on the day he was not up to par.

Because the school is trying to offer the greatest good to the greatest number of pupils, we must consider the effect of absences not only on the child but on the rest of the class as well. Suppose, for example, that Johnny appears at school one day with a fresh cold. He sneezes his way through the day and is perhaps able to absorb only a little less of the schoolwork than he would ordinarily. Being in school has not greatly injured him. But within a day or two, he breaks out in a rash and is in bed with a severe case of measles. That is unfortunate for Johnny, though his mother may rejoice that, since she didn't keep him out of school for his "cold," he is missing no more school than is absolutely necessary. But how about the

[2] See Chapter 22.

rest of the class? Ten days after Johnny's appearance with his "cold," ten or a dozen of his playmates may be out of school with measles too. Thus we must balance the gain of Johnny's attendance at school on one or two days when he didn't feel well not only against the schoolwork he would have lost if he had stayed home on those days but also against all the time his classmates lost as a result of their contacts with him. When everything is considered, Johnny's attendance at school proves highly expensive.

The records of the United States Public Health Service show many school absences due to colds. The number steadily decreases as the children grow older, but for the younger ages, it is high. If every child with a new cold were kept home for a period of two or three days, we might prevent the spread of colds.

## Contagious Diseases

The alert teacher can do much to prevent the spread of contagious diseases, especially in schools where the nurse sees a child only when he returns to school after an absence or when the teacher refers him to her for examination. The teacher should keep herself informed of the prevalence of diseases in the community. Although most such information comes through the daily papers, usually there is no report on chicken pox and measles. The teacher can acquaint herself with the illnesses prevalent in the school often by overhearing the children's conversations, which may include such items as "My brother is sick with speckles all over him," "The people upstairs have a sign saying you can't come in." During an epidemic the teacher will naturally be alert for signs of the disease, but at all times she must be quick to recognize certain conditions which suggest contagion and provide sufficient reason for sending the child to the nurse for examination.

In keeping alert for signs of contagious disease, we must remember that many illnesses start as a common cold, with watery eyes, running nose, sneezing, and inflamed throat. Other symptoms of illness which every teacher should be quick to recognize and report are the flushed face and hot dry skin of the feverish child; the spotted face, neck, or chest, and perhaps the itching of the child with a rash; the vomiting or abdominal distress of the child with a digestive disturbance; and such general symptoms as discharge from eyes, ears, or nose, and indications of pain, particularly in the head, ears, or stomach. To the experienced teacher, changes in a child's behavior will often indicate oncoming illness. Any type of behavior that is unusual deserves close observation. Lassitude in the ordinarily alert child, irritability in the ordinarily placid child, sensitiveness in the ordinarly well-poised child, and depression in the ordinarily happy child call for further investigation or at least for careful watching during the next few days.

While the kindergarten teacher should not consider herself qualified to diagnose an illness, there are times when the school nurse and doctor are not available and when a mother wants an immediate answer to her question of how long her child must remain out of school with chicken pox, or how soon he is likely to become ill after an exposure to measles. The following section briefly presents facts which a kindergarten teacher should have at the tip of her tongue, or at least at the tip of her fingers.

### CHICKEN POX

*Incubation period:* fourteen to twenty-one days.
*Onset:* usually slight fever, eruption in twenty-four hours.
*Isolation period:* ten days or until disappearance of scabs.

### DIPHTHERIA

*Incubation period:* two to five days, occasionally longer.
*Onset:* sore throat, fatigue, chilliness, aches and pains, fever; child seems sicker than his temperature indicates.
*Isolation period:* until three consecutive negative cultures have been obtained.

### GERMAN MEASLES

*Incubation period:* fourteen to twenty-one days, usually about sixteen.
*Onset:* rash, swelling glands, symptoms of any acute infection.
*Isolation period:* four to seven days or from first appearance of the symptoms until two days following the appearance of the rash.

### INFLUENZA

*Incubation period:* one to three days.
*Onset:* fever, headache, fatigue, cough.
*Isolation period:* while fever lasts and until active symptoms subside, or approximately seven days from onset.

### MEASLES[3]

*Incubation period:* about ten days, the rash usually appearing on the fourteenth days after exposure.

[3] Highly effective vaccines make it quite probable that a kindergarten teacher will never observe the onset of real measles, polio, or whooping cough.

*Onset:* fever, cough, watery eyes, running nose, rash appearing on third or fourth day.

*Isolation period:* from first appearance of symptoms until four or five days following the appearance of the rash.

### MUMPS

*Incubation period:* twelve to twenty-six days, usually eighteen days.

*Onset:* swelling of gland below and in front of ear, sometimes limited to swelling under jaw, usually one side at first.

*Isolation period:* seven to ten days or until swelling has subsided.

### POLIO[3]

*Incubation period:* about seven to fourteen days.

*Onset:* headache, fever, sore throat, stiff neck, nausea, vomiting, and loss of appetite.

*Isolation period:* one week following the appearance of symptoms or for the duration of the fever if this lasts more than one week.

### SCARLET FEVER

*Incubation period:* one to nine days, usually three or four, rarely longer than seven.

*Onset:* vomiting, fever, sore throat, rash in twenty-four hours.

*Isolation period:* seven to ten days, occasionally longer.

### WHOOPING COUGH

*Incubation period:* seven to sixteen days.

*Onset:* cold, cough followed in two or three weeks by a characteristic cough, usually occurring paroxysmally at frequent intervals and often accompanied by vomiting.

*Isolation period:* three weeks after appearance of paroxysmal cough or whoop.

## Skin Infections

Impetigo, scabies or itch, ringworm, and eczema are all common in the early school years. All except eczema are contagious and should be referred to a physician for treatment. Some children may have hives occasionally. Hives are not contagious and disappear, usually, without treatment. If the mother or the school nurse reports that the child has hives, the teacher need not worry beyond making sure that the child is under the care of a physician to ensure against a mistaken diagnosis.

[3] Highly effective vaccines make it quite probable that a kindergarten teacher will never observe the onset of real measles, polio, or whooping cough.

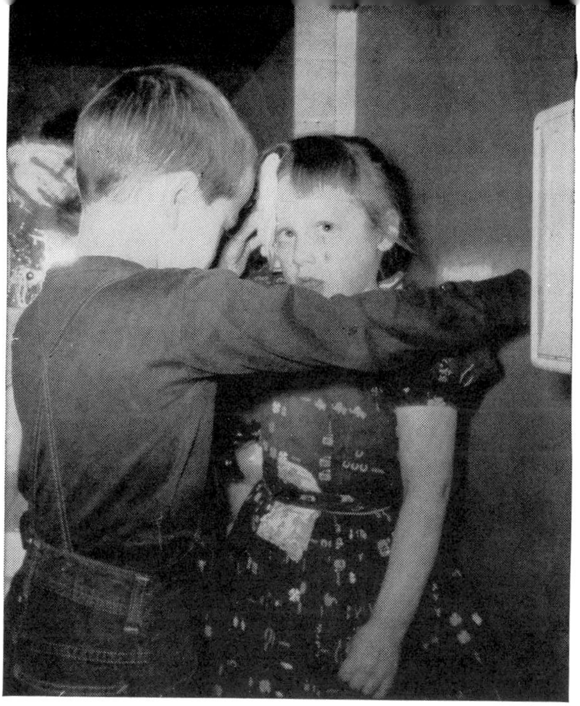

*First—First Aid*

## Other Infections and Diseases

The teacher must be alert to any changes of behavior, particularly behavior indicating unusual fatigue, which might be related to rheumatic fever, hepatitis, and various other virus infections.

## Minor Mishaps and More Serious Injuries and Illnesses

If there is a full-time nurse on duty in the building, all minor injuries, such as scratches, cuts, bruises, and scraped knees, should be cared for in the health unit. If the nurse is not on full-time duty, it is practical for each kindergarten to have its own supply of first-aid materials and for each kindergarten teacher to be prepared to treat those injuries which are classified as minor. The first-aid equipment for the room should be stored in an airtight cabinet. The stock might be expected to include band-aids of various sizes, sterile bandages of various widths, adhesive tape, a few sterile gauze packs, Zephiran, alcohol, boiled water, butesinpicrate ointment for burns, a lotion such as caladryl for mosquito bites, swabs in a sterile airtight jar, and sterile needles, tweezers, scissors, and a thermometer.

In most cases the kindergarten teacher's major responsibility for the sick or seriously injured child is that of establishing contact with the home. For this reason if for no other, the teacher should have available the parents' home and business phone numbers, as well as the name and phone number of the family doctor. The teacher makes the contact with the doctor only if she has the parents' written permission to do so, and then only if she is unable to get in touch with the parents and the child needs immediate medical attention. There should be provision for caring for the child until the parents can call for him. The kindergarten should have at least one cot on which the sick child can be isolated and some blankets.

## Health Habits

Besides doing her best to protect the child, the teacher can help him learn to protect himself by establishing desirable health habits. Every child needs a considerable intake of water each day. If the school does not provide a good drinking fountain, the children should learn how to get a clean drink of water, either through the use of paper cups or by learning the best way to use the inferior, bubble-type fountain still found in many schools. The teacher is quite within her rights to ask the mother to supply her child with a handkerchief or cleansing tissue. The school should be supplied with paper handkerchiefs for emergencies. All the children should learn to cover their mouths when they sneeze or cough and to wash their hands with soap before eating and after using the toilet. If a child is making his first acquaintance with paper towels, he will probably need a little instruction and practice in the best way to dry his hands. Habits for the preservation of health may be built up directly through practical application and discussions, and they may be emphasized through dramatic play.

One of the most important health habits a child can acquire is to keep hands, clothing, pencils, and everything else except food out of the mouth. Most diseases are spread easily by the route of hand to mouth. Toys which are held in the mouth, like horns and mouth organs, have no place in the kindergarten.

The carry-over of health habits from school to home is not great unless parents and teachers cooperate. Too often at this age the child seems to feel that he has one set of standards for home and another for school. Discussion of the importance of an early bedtime, a darkened, well-ventilated sleeping room, milk and vegetables in the diet, and the effects of outdoor play may influence the home behavior of the child, but the effect will probably not be great unless the standards of the home and school are somewhat comparable.

## Healthful Activity in the Kindergarten

The kindergarten child is at an age when he demands and needs considerable activity. Spending the entire kindergarten session sitting rela-

*"My sister teached me to do this."*

tively quiet in a chair is very hard work for a five-year-old. As healthy active adults we can appreciate this more fully if we contrast the fatigue involved in walking a mile or standing absolutely motionless for fifteen minutes. For part of the kindergarten session it is essential that opportunity be provided for big-muscle activity. If the kindergarten room is equipped with a jungle gym or a climbing rope, a ladder up the wall, a slide or merely a platform with steps at either end—and if the children are free to relieve cramped muscles by an occasional lively scramble over such a piece of apparatus—many behavior difficulties will be forestalled.

The younger the child, the shorter the time he can be expected to maintain attention and interest. Experiments have shown that if activity is varied the attention can be held longer than when a monotonous repetition of one act is called for. Generally speaking, fifteen to twenty minutes is the maximum for a kindergarten activity. Self-initiated tasks, however, evoke greater persistence than do assigned or required tasks. Watch a kindergarten child trying out his newly acquired bow-tying technique—an older boy trying to perfect his batting! If a work period has been launched so that each child feels challenged by the task ahead, if he can use his own creative and problem-solving ability, and if he is free to move about as he works at one phase and then another phase of his problem, the period may extend from forty-five minutes or an hour and more without loss of interest and attention.

When planning the program of the day, the teacher must remember that active periods and quiet periods must alternate so that the children will get the full benefit of each. If one active period follows another, the second is not a rest from the first. The fatigued child often becomes irritable and unhappy; he is also more susceptible to disease. The prevention of fatigue is an important consideration in planning the kindergarten program.

## Provision for Snacks and Rest[4]

Offering fruit juice, milk, or other snacks in the daily kindergarten session provides not only an opportunity for the renewal of energy but opportunity for children to pause, relax, and enjoy the give-and-take of conversation. Although the nutriment may not seem essential in all groups, we are reminded that the limited stomach capacity and rapid metabolism of young children call for a quick energy pickup during the kindergarten session. Snacks can include such items as carrot sticks, raisins, celery, bite-sized sandwiches, crackers, cookies, and cocoa, as well as the customary fruit juice or milk. It may be wise to look into the possibility of having such snacks prepared in the school cafeteria or by mother helpers. Public health regulations would have to be looked into, however, before the institution of such a policy. At present, for example, because of the danger of hepatitis, in many schools no unpackaged or unbottled food is permitted in some kindergartens.

In addition to the cot provided for the child who might become ill at school, there should be prone resting facilities available for the entire group. A routine rest period may or may not be part of the daily schedule. Many factors, such as length of the daily session, size of the group, weather conditions, types of activities engaged in and tension within the group, will enter into the scheduling of a rest period. We must remember, however, that group living, even at best, is likely to be strenuous for young children, and there are times when there is nothing quite so comfortable or quite so refreshing as to stretch out—or curl up—and block from one's attention the awareness of people and things in the immediate environment.[5]

### SUMMARY

Much can be done to provide for the protection and physical welfare of the kindergartner. The school building should be fireproof and as free

[4] Mary Elizabeth Keister, "Relation of Mid-Morning Feeding to the Behavior of Nursery School Children," *Journal of American Dietetics Association*, 1950, 26:25–59. State of Minnesota *Guide Teaching in the Kindergarten*, Curriculum Bulletin, No. 25, St. Paul, State Department of Education, 1963.

[5] See Chapter 17 for a further discussion of rest and relaxation.

from other hazards as possible. The kindergarten room should be arranged so as to provide sufficient space, good light, and fresh air of the proper temperature and condition. There should be an exit leading directly from the kindergarten room to the play yard. When dangers cannot be avoided, the children can be taught how to behave in their presence. Children need physical examinations before entering kindergarten or early in the school year, and they need constant observation for symptoms of contagious diseases and fresh colds. The teacher should be prepared to care for minor injuries of a superficial nature, and she should know what to do in case of illness and serious accidents. Much can be done also to help children acquire desirable health habits. However, merely talking about health habits will do little good. The school environment must be such that the habits can be put into practice, and teacher and parents must cooperate if the habits are to be carried over into daily living. The kindergarten program should provide for alternating periods of activity and quiet; the five-year-old needs and demands activity, yet he also needs—though he seldom demands—rest and quiet.

## QUESTIONS AND PROBLEMS

1. List the things you have seen five-year-old children do which you consider dangerous to the child himself or to others.
2. Which of those activities you have listed might appear in a kindergarten? What do you think the teacher should do in each case?
3. Give all the reasons you can for the greater number of absences due to colds at the younger ages.
4. After the age of seven, the percentages of school absence due to infectious disease drop sharply. What factors may cause this?
5. Consult old newspapers for each month of the past year and note the number of new cases of each contagious disease reported. What differences appear from month to month?
6. Why is prone resting preferable to having children rest sitting at tables with their heads on their arms?
7. Fire drills are often frightening to kindergarten children. What preventive measures could the teacher take to avoid undue alarm on the part of the children?

## SELECTED REFERENCES

Allen, W. Paul, and George E. Raab, "The School Plant," *Those First School Years,* Washington, D.C., National Education Association, 1960.

American Association of School Administrators, *Planning American School Buildings* (Report of AASA School Building Commission), Washington, D.C., National Education Association, 1960.

California State Department of Education, Bureau of Elementary State Curriculum Commission, *Teacher's Guide to Education in Early Childhood,* Sacramento, California, State Department of Education, 1956 (see particularly pp. 443–460).

Gallagher, J. Roswell, *Your Child's Health—A Handbook for Parents and Teachers,* Better Living Booklet, Chicago, Science Research Associates, 1952.

Grout, Ruth E., *Health Teaching in Schools,* 4th ed., Philadelphia, W. B. Saunders Company, 1963.

Hochman, Vivienne, "Kindergarten-Primary Rooms Reflect Interests," *Space Arrangement, Beauty in Schools,* Washington, D.C., Association for Childhood Educational International, 1958.

Lambert, Hazel, *Early Childhood Education,* Boston, Allyn and Bacon, 1960 (see particularly pp. 16, 17).

Martin, W. Edgar, *Children's Bodily Measurements for Planning and Equipping Schools; A Handbook for School Officials and Architects,* Special Publication No. 4, Washington, D.C., United States Department of Health, Education, and Welfare, Office of Education, 1955.

# 7

# EQUIPMENT AND SUPPLIES FOR THE KINDERGARTEN

In an earlier chapter we stressed the fact that children work and think with things more easily and naturally than with abstractions. It is important, therefore, for the kindergarten to be well equipped with materials suitable to the age and development of the children. Anyone, of course, would prefer a superior teacher in a poorly equipped room to an inferior teacher in an elaborately equipped room. The ideal, naturally, is a combination of the two. Our aim in this chapter is to consider some of the many acceptable and desirable materials that one will find in a well-equipped kindergarten, and to make some estimate of the costs involved in providing them.

Many studies have been made to ascertain children's body measurements. One study most helpful to the classroom teacher is summarized in the bulletin entitled *Children's Body Measurements for Planning and Equipping Schools.*[1] In this study, made on a sampling of the total school-age population, measurements were taken as children assumed a variety of positions, such as standing, sitting, reaching, bending, and writing. Because of the findings in this study, the heights and proportions of furniture and other kindergarten equipment given in this and the third edition of *Education in the Kindergarten* vary substantially from those quoted in the first and second editions. This is a nice example of how research is helping us meet the needs of children.

## Furniture

Kindergarten children should not be expected to sit at fixed desks, nor should they be expected to sit in a single position or place very long. The

[1] See p. 5 for complete reference.

kindergarten room should be provided with movable chairs and tables of proper height and proportions. Because of a considerable range in the heights of kindergarten children, the seats of some chairs should be an inch or more higher than others. For most groups of kindergarten children, the chairs should have seat heights ranging from 10 to 13 inches, but most of the chairs should be 11 or 12 inches high.

The chairs should permit the child to sit in a relaxed position with his feet on the floor. A full saddle seat and a lumbar support approximately 8 inches above the seat seems to be best for the postural needs of kindergarten children. The chair base should be broad and sturdy, and yet the total chair weight should not exceed 8 to 10 pounds. The chairs need to be of such weight and design that they can be carried easily and safely by the children. When space is at a premium it is a great advantage to have both chairs and tables that can be stacked.

The distance between the seat height of the chair and the surface area of a kindergarten table should be approximately 7½ inches. Table surfaces that are covered with linoleum, formica, or other plastic coatings are more resistant to wear and scrubbing than are stained, shellacked, or painted wood surfaces. Worktables that are approximately 30 inches square afford practical working space and opportunity for children to work in small informal groups. Square tables have the additional advantage of being able to be combined into a variety of larger units. The tables, though square, should have slightly rounded corners as protection against children's bumping into or being pushed against sharp corners. Although round, hexagonal, or trapezoidal tables may appeal to the eye, they do not provide as much working area as square tables.

Round, hexagonal, or trapezoidal tables can be used, however, in the library area of the kindergarten room, where surface working area is not a major factor. And it is desirable that the furniture in the library should make that area seem quite different from the main working areas of the kindergarten room. The library might well be equipped with several comfortable, child-sized armchairs and perhaps something as cozy and homelike as a comfortable couch or divan made from an old set of springs and a crib mattress. It is almost unbelievable to see how much the kindergarten library area gets slighted—oddly enough, often by the very teachers who devote an amazing amount of time to workbooks for reading readiness!

## Provisions for Big-Muscle Activities

The kindergarten child is an active individual, and he needs to have a great deal of work and play involving use of the big muscles. Such work and play is best when it can take place out of doors in the sunshine; but during certain months, in many of our states, bitter cold, snow, or rain make it necessary for children to be indoors long hours on end. Since the average home, particularly the city apartment, does not lend itself, in either space or equipment, to the jumping, climbing, pushing, lifting, stretching, crawling needs of the five-year-old, it is fortunate that the kindergarten tries to provide space and equipment for big-muscle activity. Often it is the only place where the child has an opportunity during the winter months for large-muscle activity unrestrained by the limitations of relatively small quarters or bulky winter clothing. We might express a word of appreciation at this point for the efforts of researchers who have made it possible for manufacturers to make less heavy and less bulky winter wearing apparel for children. Now if someone would come up with a foolproof zipper and warm winter boots that would stretch to fit new shoes, he would win the undying thanks of nursery school and kindergarten teachers —and mothers!

## Space and Equipment for Indoor Activity

In some schools the kindergarten children are taken either to the school gymnasium or to a room known as the "activity room" for a period of games and activity. It is fine to have access to such space, but scheduled

H. Armstrong Roberts

*"I feel much better now!"*

periods of activity are not the whole answer to the needs of the active five-year-olds.

Whether or not the kindergarten children have access to a special room for active play, the kindergarten room itself should have at least one piece of apparatus which not only provides for but encourages active play. Five-year-olds, as yet unaccustomed to some of the necessary restrictions of group living, need a chance to exercise their muscles at odd times during the session. A scramble over the jungle gym, a zip down the slide, a climb up a rope ladder, or a few rolls or somersaults on a tumbling mat will often relieve the strain of confining activity or the tension of seemingly unending social demands.

For such indoor play, the piece of equipment best for a particular room will depend on the amount of space available. A jungle gym, for example, while an excellent piece of equipment for a large room, takes up far too much space for crowded quarters. But for the small room one might use a small section of a jungle gym fastened securely to the floor and wall. And, of course, even in a relatively small room there is always space for a climbing pole or climbing rope, and possibly for a balancing board and a ladder combined with floor blocks.

## Space and Equipment for Outdoor Activity

In warm, pleasant weather, many five-year-olds—when not eating or watching TV—spend much of their out-of-school day playing outdoors; even so, the kindergarten should make some effort to supplement or further encourage such play.

It is generally accepted that the area allotted for the outdoor activities of kindergarten groups should be a minimum of 100 square feet per child. This sounds like a tremendous amount of space, but if the kindergarten enrollment approximates the ideal twenty-four, the overall area would not be much more than 40 x 60 feet. Whatever size the allotted area, it should be enclosed by a fence, wall, or hedge, and it is desirable to have some portion of the enclosed area set aside for planting a garden.

A most satisfactory arrangement for outdoor play is found in the kindergarten which has its own private entrance opening directly onto a patio or playground planned especially for the use of kindergarten and first- and second-grade children. In schools where the children must share the playground with older children, the teacher should schedule the kindergarten children's use of facilities for times when the older children are not outside.

Ideally the kindergarten should be so located that at least a portion of the playground affords a natural extension of kindergarten living. When it is, certain vehicles can be especially reserved for use in this area, and yet the kindergarten children can mingle with the other primary-school children and use the equipment and space provided for the entire primary unit.

Equipment for the kindergarten playground should include some or all of the following items: a climbing tower; turning bars—set at different heights; a horizontal ladder; a slide; swings with rope, canvas, or air-cushioned seats; a teeter-totter; and perhaps a horizontal tree trunk with extending branches. Hollow blocks, planks, sawhorses, balls, jumping ropes, shovels, rakes, hoes, and wheeled toys will all encourage large-muscle activity.

Wheeled toys, particularly velocipedes, tractors, airplanes, and trucks, rank high in popularity, but there is some evidence that these delightful vehicles tend to make solitary children more solitary and thus have a somewhat antisocial influence if not used as part of group or dramatic play. Thus, it is wise to select those vehicles which lend themselves to cooperative play, such as tricycles with back stands, trailer-hitch units, tractors which pull loads, and commercial delivery trucks. It has been found that wheeled vehicles designed for one age group neither fit older children nor withstand the use "tendered" them by the older children—hence the reservation of certain vehicles for kindergarten children only. It probably goes without saying that outside storage should be provided for wheeled vehicles, blocks, sand toys, and other equipment.

## Adult Supervision

Kindergarten children need the supervision of a teacher when playing outdoors at school. If the playground has apparatus, the teacher will be needed to establish and maintain standards for its safe use; if the playground has the most meager equipment, the teacher can encourage games and dramatic play. Whether there is much or little equipment, playground time should be thought of as an essential part of the kindergarten program. It is always something of a shock to hear an adult observing kindergarten children on the playground say, "When is kindergarten going to begin?"

## Equipment for Kindergarten Housekeeping

Just as outdoor activity is a part of kindergarten living, so is housekeeping. The adult who reported that the kindergarten children wasted twenty minutes "just cleaning up the room" did not grasp the significance of such activity at all. If housekeeping is to be an integral part of kindergarten living, provision must be made for its being carried on in a satisfying and reasonably efficient fashion.

Every kindergarten should have several wastebaskets. A broom, preferably a pushbroom, large enough to be effective but of a size easily handled by children themselves, will encourage neatness and order. A regulation 16-inch-wide floor brush with its handle cut to 40 inches will make a good implement for children's use. A dustpan, either long- or short-handled, is essential. The long-handled dustpan theoretically keeps the child from inhaling the dust, but its manipulation is somewhat involved, and the sweeper usually ends by either balancing his dustpan against a wall or table and getting down to push the dirt into the container or enlisting another child to get down to push the dirt into the container. Much clattering and banging can be avoided if a least the edge of the dustpan is rubber-tipped. An entirely rubber or soft-plastic dustpan is a joy in any kindergarten. Cleaning rags, dust cloths, sponges, scrubbing brushes, and turpentine and soap are indispensable in the kindergarten. (Turpentine, incidentally, will remove crayon marks from hard-finished floors, walls, and tables.) Just give the kindergartner some soap and a sponge, and the scrubbing—which not infrequently turns into finger painting—produces marvelously clean surfaces. Picking the scraps from the floor is often facilitated—and made more enjoyable, too—by the carpet sweeper borrowed from the playhouse.

## Equipment for Rest

Although some rest and relaxation are provided by alternation of quiet and vigorous activity, there are times when children can profit by stretching out on a flat surface. Obviously, for this kind of rest period, there must be something to lie on, something other than the very hard and often not very warm or clean floor. Some schools have lightweight cots, weighing no more than four pounds each, which can either be set up quickly or permanently set up in a separate room. Most schools have only something that can be laid directly on the floor. The variety in resting mats available seems almost endless. There is, however, a 20 x 30 inch mat specifically designed for kindergarten resting, a filled plastic mat stitched crosswise in several sections. It is easy to clean and easy to fold into sections, but even so there is still the problem of finding storage space, for the folded mat is somewhat bulky. Perhaps the most satisfactory resting mat for the short, ten- to twenty-minute rest period is still the small rug (24 in. x 48 in., or even 20 in. x 36 in.), which can be folded up after the rest period and returned to the child's own locker. Such rugs may be laundered easily and they wear very well. The chief problem in using the rugs is to teach the children to fold them so that they know which side goes away from the floor. A piece of masking tape on which the child's name has been written either with a felt-point or a ballpoint pen will not only denote ownership but also indicate the side to be kept away from the floor and the head of the rug.

Other kinds of resting mats include small linoleum rugs or pieces of compo board (usually piled in the corner of the room between rest periods), pieces of brown paper folded over and pasted down on the edges, several layers of newspapers bound together with colored yarn and, of course, pieces of just plain newspaper. In addition to the resting mats supplied by the school, there can be a variety of equipment brought from home: small cotton blankets, terry cloth towels, old baby blankets, squares of flannel, and so on. With these, as with some of the others, storage is often a problem.

## Materials for Manipulation

Many children who enter kindergarten have had a surprisingly meager collection of good play materials at home: a doll or two, perhaps some cardboard puzzles, and some flimsy mechanical toys. These children are fascinated with sturdy, well-designed manipulative toys and need a few weeks of just getting used to them before they are ready for more constructive activities. It is well to have on hand beads (plastic or wooden, ½ in.), bead strings, pegs and pegboards (10 in. x 10 in.), nests of rings, figures and boxes, small blocks of various shapes and colors, and puzzles varying from the simple (9 to 16 pieces) to the more complex (17 to 27 pieces). Paper or aluminum foilplates and baskets used as containers or frames will add to the pleasure and satisfaction in the use of beads, pegs, and puzzle pieces. A few manipulative toys of each kind will be more useful and interesting than a large supply of any one kind.

Although children who have attended nursery school will have had the opportunity to experiment with many of these materials, one must remember that many of them can be used in other than a purely manipulative fashion. There is frequently a revival of interest in such things as beads and pegs toward the end of the kindergarten year, when the children use them for creating designs sometimes composed of amazingly intricate numerical units.

## Materials for Construction

Much of the work of the kindergarten year centers around construction of one type or another. The greater the variety of constructive materials available, including waste materials, the more opportunities the children will have to (a) gain experience and skill in handling materials, (b) try out and develop their creative urges, (c) discover and test the possibilities and limitations of each kind of material, and (d) come up against concrete problem-solving situations requiring them to make plans and test ideas and conclusions.

BLOCKS Blocks have long, and deservedly, held an important place in the kindergarten—small blocks for manipulation and designs and larger blocks for more ambitious undertakings. There are good sets of blocks on the market ranging from five to two hundred dollars. Often perfectly satisfactory sets may be made by local carpenters or by industrial-education groups. Beware of trying to make a set yourself unless you have power tools; the slightest variation in the angle of cutting can make a block totally useless in block building. The chief requirement of any set is that the measurements of the larger blocks be exact multiples of those of the smallest block.

Since it makes little difference what measurement is taken as the unit block, this decision can often best be left to the carpenter or designer, who will know to what measurements the available lumber can be cut most economically. If, for example, two-by-four lumber is to be used, it will probably be best to use units of 3½ in. x 1¾ in., cut into various lengths that will all be multiples of 3½ in.—3½ in., 7 in., 14 in. and so on, with some sticks cut 1¾ in. x 1¾ in. in various lengths. A set of small blocks for three or four children would include about 110 blocks; a set for ten children, about 215 blocks; a set for fifteen children, about 450 blocks. A full set for thirty children might include a thousand blocks. A study done at the University of Minnesota[2] indicates that, regardless of how many blocks an individual five-year-old is given, the most he will use is approximately 130.

Life-size constructions will need large, sturdy blocks which can be held together to prevent the structure from tumbling over on its builders. Some sets of blocks have metal rods to be run through holes in the blocks, some have nuts and bolts, and still others interlock. Along with any set of blocks, it is wise to have large sheets of pegboard or other lightweight composition material, to be used as roofs and partitions.

BLOCK STORAGE Blocks require storage space near where they are used. Ordinary cupboards and shelves will do, but shelves, chests, and platforms

[2] Eleanor Robinson, "The Form and Imaginative Content of Children's Block Building," (Ph.D. Thesis), Minneapolis, University of Minnesota, 1958.

on wheels are more satisfactory. Movable block storage serves a double function: it makes the blocks available for any building area, and it separates one building area from another. A low, movable, block-storage case, if pushed into a low three-sided enclosure, can both seal the blocks from dust and dirt and be placed wherever extra table or counter space is needed.

PAPER Many kinds of paper are needed in the kindergarten. For all-around, everyday use, such as painting or cutting, newsprint—unprinted newspaper, or expression paper, as it is sometimes called—heads the list. This paper is most easily handled in 18 in. x 24 in. sheets, which come in 100-sheet packages. Even though the 24 in. x 36 in. paper or the 500-sheet packages seem more economical, their bulk and dimensions make them impractical for kindergarten use. When large areas of paper are needed, they can better be secured by pasting sheets of paper together or by using paper from a roll. Manila paper for drawing is often most economically purchased in large-size sheets, 12 in. x 18 in., which can be cut if smaller sizes are needed. Construction and poster paper, 12 in. x 18 in., and some 18 in. x 24 in., is more economically supplied in packages of one color rather than in packages of assorted colors. Certain colors are almost sure to be used in quantity at particular seasons of the year—for example, orange and black at Halloween, red and green at Christmas time, and the pastels in the springtime.

Poster paper is usually less expensive than construction paper and often will serve the kindergarten child's purpose just as well or better. For the odds and ends of pieces of colored paper, it is well to have a small open cabinet 10 in. x 14 in. and 15 in. high equipped with a pull-out shelf for each color.

Brown wrapping paper fills many a need throughout the kindergarten year, and a holder for a roll of 30 in. wide paper is a good investment. Another good investment for art work, particularly finger painting, is a roll of white paper 24 in. wide glazed on one side and rough on the other. Tissue paper and crepe paper will be wanted in small quantities, as will tag board, aluminum foil, Saran Wrap, and cellophane.

For use with the paper, children need scissors (4 in. to 5 in. in length), a few with rounded blunt points but others with semipointed or even pointed blades, and perhaps a pair of plastic scissors; paste, preferably semiliquid and unpalatable; a few pencils, rather larger than ordinary and with soft leads; crayons (4 in. x 7/16 in.), preferably hexagonal or at least flat on one side; an easel (adjustable in size); aprons (terry cloth); watercolor poster paint (liquid and powder); finger paint (cream and powder), and starch and vegetable coloring for making finger paint; and large paintbrushes.

All these materials are not, of course, limited to use with paper. They should be available for a variety of expressive activities along with many of the following additional materials: chalkboard and chalk (white for the most part, but some colored), house and enamel paint, varnish brushes, shellac, denatured alcohol, and turpentine or other commercial solvents for shellac and paint.

Wood Soft wood, white pine preferably, in various shapes and sizes will simplify the problems of the amateur carpenters in the kindergarten. The tools needed will vary with the skill of the particular groups of children, but certainly hammers, cross-cut saws, a screwdriver, pliers, nails, and sandpaper will be essential. Coping saws, bits and braces, files, screws, bolts, and burrs are not so essential. A plane might be needed, though if semifinished wood is available, the necessary smoothing can usually best be done with a wood file or sandpaper. Tools should be kept in an enclosed area. A wall cabinet large enough so that the tool needed may be removed without disturbing the other tools will provide most satisfactory storage. If their outlines are painted on the storage background, tools are more likely to be replaced properly.

The main requirement of the workbench is that it be sturdy and of such a size (24 in. x 42 in. is a functional size) that it will fit into an area out of the way of traffic. The bench should have at least one strong gripping vise. The bench can serve a dual purpose if it has a cover.

Sand Early in the year some of the less mature or more timid children seem to find great security in attaching themselves to the sand table and viewing the new kindergarten situation from this retreat. Here they can occupy themselves and feel a part of the whole group without having to meet the many new challenges created by group living. If the kindergarten group as a whole has had little experience with indoor sand play, they may at first enjoy just playing at the sand table with rolling pins, scoops, cookie cutters, and pans of one sort or another. But usually kindergarten children soon exhaust the manipulative possibilities of sand; then small, hard rubber trucks, boats, planes, trains, trees, and houses, as well as measuring units of various sizes, stimulate engineering and dramatic play.

A watering can and syringe are helpful in keeping the sand moistened and, if kept in good condition, they can also be used for the terrarium and garden activities. There should be some provision to store the sand toys after they have been thoroughly rinsed. Kept in bins or in a box or even a basket on a shelf beneath the sand table, they are handy without creating a gritty mess in the room. The sand table is not complete without a brush and dustpan to sweep up accidental—and, one might add, expected—

spillings. If a cover is provided for the sand table, then, like the block storage and the workbench, it too can serve a dual purpose. The sand table is usually approximately 26 inches high, and usually the metal or plastic lined wooden box is at least 7 inches deep. There is some evidence that a higher and deeper sand table might be desirable. The top of the higher sand table comes between the elbow and armpit height of the children, and the box, being some 12 to 16 inches deep, allows the children to dig and build without having to be too cautious about spills.

MODELING MATERIALS Clay and plasticine are excellent materials for modeling. Pieces of oilcloth or plywood board (12 in. x 18 in.) will protect the table, and aprons can be brought from home or provided by the school to protect clothing. It is well to stretch a washable rug under the chairs of the clay modelers in order to collect the clay bits that naturally scatter on the floor around them. When children are finished with their modeling, they can fold up the rug and shake it in the wastebasket, thus preventing the clay from being tracked across the floor.

Plasticine has the advantage of remaining in a pliable state, and clay that of hardening into a form which can be preserved. Clay needs to be kept in an airtight container in which moisture can be retained. Plasticine, on the other hand, is best kept in a metal or plastic container, and, since it becomes hard to manipulate when cold, it is wise to keep the container near a source of mild heat—in the sunshine or on or near a warm heating unit. For work with clay or plasticine, tools are not essential. Children sometimes request knives, sticks, or nails, but almost invariably the tools detract from rather than stimulate the child's creativeness. In addition to clay and plasticine there are many other materials that can be used for modeling.[3]

NEEDLES AND THREAD Because of the fine muscular and eye-hand coordination involved in sewing, the use of needle and thread is not to be encouraged at the kindergarten level. However, for stringing bread and popcorn or sewing an occasional seam, it is well to have some needles and thread at hand. The needles, usually to be threaded by the teacher, should have long eyes but not very sharp points. A tapestry needle #20 meets most kindergarten needs. If a sharp-pointed needle is needed, a Crewel #5 to #9 is desirable. The thread to be used should be of a loosely twisted variety, such as silkalene or yarn, so that the point of the needle, after the thread has been put through the eye, can be run back through the short end of the thread, thus preventing the needle from coming unthreaded. Cloth should be available for those times when a seam needs to be stitched

[3] See Chapter 11.

or for construction work and dramatic play. Most five-year-olds will find it difficult to cut cloth. Glazed chintz and other treated materials are among those easiest for children to use.

## Materials for Dramatic Play and Special Days

Kindergarten dramatization is at its best when informal and spontaneous. The teacher does set the stage, however, by providing materials. Generally speaking, simple materials which may be used to construct "properties" and which demand considerable imagination in their use are as satisfactory as highly specialized materials, perhaps more so. A square of cloth, for example, may become a scarf, a cape for Superman, a bride's veil, an apron, a flag, a tablecloth, a window curtain, a blanket for the doll, a bedspread, or any of a number of other things, whereas once the cloth has been fashioned into a complete costume, it usually has only one use. A single clown, fairy, or other costume is certainly fun to have in the kindergarten, but it would be unwise to invest kindergarten funds in a number of complete costumes. On the other hand, a trunk full of grown-up hand-me-downs is always intriguing. In the costume trunk or on the costume rack, one might expect to find old ties, belts, vests, safety razors (without blades, of course), gloves, purses, scarves, beads, ribbons, veils, flowers, glass-less glasses, skirts, sweaters, smocks, shoes, and hats as well. Such things as guns, pistols, and swords would no doubt stimulate a kind of dramatic play, but that kind of play, so far as the kindergarten is concerned, needs no stimulation! The teacher must exercise real discretion in her selection of costume effects and dramatic play materials.

Hand puppets, either very simple commercial ones or those made by the children themselves, should be included in any list of dramatic play material, but marionettes, except as operated by skilled adults, really have no place in the kindergarten.

As a center for dramatic play, the playhouse corner ranks high. Some permanent furniture for house play is desirable, but too much is—well, just too much. A table, two or three chairs, a cupboard, a stove, a doll carriage, and a bed may well suffice as far as original furniture goes. Two or three unbreakable dolls of a composition or cloth type, not less than 12 inches in size and outfitted with clothes that can be taken off and put on easily, are definitely a "must" in the playhouse corner. Young homemakers will also need utensils for cooking, play food, and dishes for feeding "the family." Equipment for washing, ironing, sweeping, and dusting will stimulate much dramatic play, as will toy animals, telephones, a milkman's carrying case, suitcases, lunch boxes, briefcases, shopping bags, and shopping carts.

The playhouse area needs to be separated from the rest of the room, but not by any permanent partition. A furniture arrangement that provides an apparent exit and entrance or low movable screens will often serve adequately.

Many times toys and materials which the children bring from home and even the clothes they wear inspire wholly delightful activity. A ballerina skirt, a pair of binoculars, a bag full of buffalo bones, a life-size toy dog, a nurse's kit, a cowboy hat or an astronaut's suit—what an impetus each of these, in its own way, can give to the dramatic play of the day!

## Equipment and Supplies for Special Occasions

Special calendar days and other days, such as cooking days, entertaining days, and picnic days, make their own special demands. Holiday decorations, Easter egg dyes, paper plates and cups, plastic or paper spoons, food for visiting pets, Saran Wrap for the experimental terrarium, greens for the aquarium, batteries for the playhouse doorbell, a just-published book to be used in connection with a special interest—these and many more things must be included in the teacher's buying. It would be utterly impossible for any teacher to foresee all the materials which might be needed for the many worthwhile, and sometimes quite unexpected, experiences of the kindergarten year.

## Petty-Cash Fund

A petty-cash fund for teachers is a wise budgetary provision. A kindergarten survey which included among other things teachers' estimated yearly output of personal funds for school materials revealed that some teachers spent more than $50 and that the average expenditure was about $15. Since this survey was made in the early nineteen fifties, it is probable that the average expenditure of personal funds will now approximate $25 or $30.

## Science Materials

Much of our science material is all about us and is ours for the taking. It is well for each kindergarten to have a special science counter, cupboard, or table—which should not be relegated to the corner as it often is. Among the many things that may appear in this area from time to time are shells, stones, seeds, leaves, treebark, caterpillars, cocoons, insects, bird's and hornet's nests, a magnifying glass, magnets, scales, pulleys, wire, electric bells, and batteries. There is really no end to the number of things that may show up in a kindergarten science collection!

Usually we cannot plan on what "livestock" we may expect to have in the kindergarten during the year. A small cage for such visitors as white mice, baby squirrels or hamsters; an aquarium for goldfish, guppies, or even turtles; and a large cage for rabbits, small dogs, cats and kittens, ducks, geese, and chickens will encourage the children and interested friends to share their pets with the kindergarten. A deep metal tray, like a sandbox tray, will often be sufficient for some of the smaller or less daring visiting creatures. Strong rope should be available for tethering such visitors as ponies, calves, or goats. If the school does not have a variety of enclosures or tethers, the arrival of a visiting pet may be something less than an enjoyable experience!

Gardening belongs in the realm of science experiences, too, and provision should be made for experimenting with various kinds of growing. Observable germination, chemical gardening, the forcing of growth by artificial light, and many other experiences can be a part of indoor gardening. But gardening at its best for the kindergarten is carried on outside, in fresh air and sunshine. A few good garden tools, not just play tools, are essential for garden work.

Some kindergarten rooms have recessed cupboards or shelves for the exhibition of precious or delicate objects. A cupboard, perhaps two feet wide by three feet high, lighted by electricity from the inside or above and equipped with sliding glass doors that lock against too-curious hands, may be used to exhibit such things as stuffed birds and animals; foreign costumes and books; original pictures from books which are popular with the children; and valuable or delicate products which might tie in with the current interests of the group. If a case of this sort is to serve a real purpose, the contents must be changed with changing group interests. It is better to have no case at all than one the contents of which are never changed.

## Material Specifically Designed for Reading and Number Readiness

Included in these supplies would be all kinds of lotto and domino games, form board and card games involving identifying likenesses and differences, three-dimensional letter and numeral forms, sequi and completion cards, number frames, numeral and number matching games, word and picture match games, and various flannel board materials. Even some of the workbook pages may be included in these materials if they, like puzzles, are available to those individuals who want to work with them. In the last several years the market has been flooded with so-called educational materials—the "teach your baby to read" and "teach your baby to count" sort of things. Many of these are gimmicks and nothing more. All too often, instead of teaching, they get in the way of learning and take valuable time from or preclude more worthwhile developmental experiences. Leland Jacobs speaks of these gimmicks and educational trappings as "paraphernalia that get in the way of learning."

## Music

Because the piano is so often and so comfortably the center for music activity, we think of it as an absolutely essential piece of kindergarten equipment. Either a low upright or a spinet piano is a desirable musical instrument for the kindergarten room. Fortunate indeed are kindergarten children who have opportunity to experiment with making piano music, and most fortunate are the children who have the opportunity to spend their kindergarten year with a teacher who plays the piano well. But the teacher who is not a skilled pianist no longer needs to feel that she must deprive children of musical experiences. Good portable record players are available, and there are now on the market thousands of records—many of them specially designed for children's listening and doing—which can be used with kindergarten children.[4] Every kindergarten needs a good supply of recordings, and the teacher who does not play the piano will want to be particularly selective in her choice of records.

When we find even five- and six-year-olds coming to kindergarten with their transistor radios, we sometimes wonder if we ought not list radios as an essential part of our classroom equipment; but then when we find how little there is for them to listen to and how little they actually do listen, we can conclude that a radio is not a must in kindergarten equipment. It is possible that a TV set will become a desirable piece of kindergarten equipment, but to date there seems little to warrant the expenditure of money. Most schools have a set which can be borrowed for kindergarten use if and when the occasion for in-school viewing does arise.

A tape recorder, like a TV set, may profitably be available to but not necessarily owned by the kindergarten. A tape recorder can be used to record summaries of experiences, as a "caught" experience which can be shared with children who missed the original experience; and it can also be used to help children hear and improve their way of speaking.

Rhythm band instruments made available to children can do much to help them enjoy and appreciate rhythm and musical sound effects.

[4] See Chapters 14 and 15.

## Books

The kindergarten teacher needs to keep aware of good new books for children even though her book order may have to go through the school library. Kindergarten children derive greater pleasure from the books if the area of the room designated as the library is somewhat set apart from the rest of the room by special shelves, tables, chairs, and so on. Since most kindergarten children do not actually read, it is desirable to have the books arranged on the shelves so that the children can seek out a particular book without having to handle all the books and thus upset the whole arrangement. In order to make this possible, shelves can be designed so that some books can be placed in small partitioned sections and others can be spread out, covers showing, on the shelves. A case designed in the style of a magazine rack, with space for three or four tiers of books, will serve the same purpose, but somehow it does not seem quite so casual or inviting as does the bookcase arrangement. No more than twenty or thirty books need to be out at any one time. As interests change, new books will be added and others taken away.

## Pictures

Pictures for the kindergarten fall into three general classes: (1) framed pictures, murals, wall hangings, and plaques; (2) mounted pictures of current interest, to be posted on bulletin boards or studied at tables; and (3) pictures made by the children themselves.

Pictures of the first group can add to the general attractiveness of the room, supply a note of color, and be interesting to young children. It is more pleasing to the eye if there are only a few of these pictures on the wall at one time. A picture that always hangs in one place is soon ignored. If, therefore, we want children to observe and enjoy pictures, they must be changed every few weeks. If the school provides only one framed picture for the kindergarten, it is better to take it down sometimes, returning it later or perhaps hanging it in a different place. Sometimes one frame can be used for different pictures at different times. Pictures for the kindergarten should be hung reasonably near eye level. (Mean eye level for kindergarten children when standing is approximately forty-one inches; sitting, approximately thirty-one inches.)

Smaller mounted pictures are almost indispensable. The kindergarten teacher will be quick to see in magazine covers, calendars, advertisements, posters, and the like many pictures of interest and value to the children. If, when such pictures are cut out, the teacher files them according to some simple system, she will be able to locate quickly pictures relating to Thanksgiving, farms, birds, home life, and so on. These pictures may be posted on bulletin boards or placed in the bookcase or on the library table. When a good book reaches a stage where repairs are no longer possible, some of the illustrations may be salvaged by cutting them out and mounting them on any stiff paper, such as heavy tagboard or cardboard. A word of caution! If this is done, care must be taken to avoid suggesting that cutting pictures from books is accepted procedure. It is warranted only when the book is no longer in a condition to give satisfaction as a book. Children delight in coming upon pictures like those already familiar to them in books. Book characters to be used as stick puppets can also be made from old book illustrations.

## Films

Filmstrips, 2 x 2 inch slides, and movie films all have their place in the kindergarten program. In many instances filmstrips and slides—as well as opaque-projected illustrations from books—are more satisfying than movie films in that discussion can accompany the showing of the pictures. Movie films can often profitably be shown more than once, either immediately following the first showing or at a later date. This is not surprising: it is not unusual for us as adults to find that we get much more from the second showing of a film than we got from the first showing.

The modern stereoscope offers opportunities for individual viewing of three-dimensional slides and reels, and there is now available a Junior Projector which makes it possible for Viewmaster films to be enjoyed by groups. Since movie films are usually rented or borrowed from the local visual education center, we need not concern ourselves with them in our discussion of kindergarten equipment.[5]

## Cost of Equipment, Materials, and Supplies

The following section presents approximate prices, as of 1966, for equipment, materials, and supplies which one would find in a well-equipped kindergarten. Since prices vary greatly from one part of the country to another and from one year to another, the quoted prices are merely indicative of what the expense might be in setting up and continuing a kindergarten unit. As one compares these 1966 figures with those in earlier edi-

[5] See Chapter 21 for a listing of films and slides for young children.

tions of this book, one is impressed anew with the fact that the dollar "isn't what it used to be." It cost, for example, approximately $480 in 1958 to purchase materials which could have been purchased in 1940 for $225. In 1966 the cost is approximately one-third higher than it was in 1958—and so the spiral goes. Things cost more, but we must remember that wages and salaries are higher, too!

## KINDERGARTEN ROOM AND ROOM FURNISHINGS

Acoustical ceiling, $.60 per sq. ft., tile; $3 per sq. yd., plaster.
Block storage case, $30 to $70.
Bookcases (9 to 12 cu. ft.), $3 to $5 per cu. ft.
Bulletin boards (20 to 30 sq. ft., cork), $.40 to $.80 per sq. ft.
(4 to 6 sq. ft., steel-baked enamel with magnets), $5 to $6 per unit.
Chairs (adult size, 17 in. seat height, at least two), $7.50 to $12 each.
(wicker or modern, 12 in. seat height, four for the library unit), $5 to $10 each.
(wooden or plastic with metal tubing, 11–12 in. and 13 in. seat height), $6 to $10 each.
Chalkboard (12 to 18 sq. ft., green), $1 to $1.50 per sq. ft.
Clock (electric, wall), $8 to $20.
Cupboards (storage space, 125 to 200 cu. ft.), $.75 to $1 per sq. ft.
Desk (adult size or table and file case), $60 to $100.
Draperies or blinds, $10 to $15 per window.
Drinking fountain (slant stream, 27 in. basin height), $50 to $100 plus installation.
Fire extinguisher (1 qt. size), $12 to $18.
Linoleum floor covering (heavy duty), $4 to $5 per sq. yd. plus installation per sq. yd., $1.
Lockers (individual for wraps and other personal property, approx. 12 in. x 14 in. and 54 in. high), $16 to $20 per unit.
Mirror (approx. 15 in. x 45 in.), $12 to $15.
Paper-towel container (white, metal), $3.50 to $5.
Pictures and wall hangings, $2 to $15 each.
Sand table (with cover, 3 ft. x 6 ft., metal box 7 in. deep, overall height 26 in.), $25 to $50.
Screen (36 in. x 48 in., pegboard, removable feet), $12 to $14 each.
(30 in. x 54 in., 3 or 4 panels), $16 to $25 per total unit.
Soap dispenser (liquid soap), $3 to $9.
Storage space for wood (2 ft. x 3 ft. x 4 ft.), $18 to $20.
Tables (work, 30 in. x 30 in., plastic top, 18 in. to 21 in. high), $20 to $30 each.
(library, 36 in. in diameter, plastic top, 20 in. high), $30 to $40 each.
Toilet facilities (lavatory, two, 28 in. high), approx. $50 each plus installation.
(toilet, two, 12 in. high), approx. $50 each plus installation.
Tool storage unit (24 in. x 36 in. and 8 in. deep, wood), $9.50 to $14.
Workbench (24 in. x 42 in. and 26 in. high, two vises), $35 to $50.

## EQUIPMENT AND SUPPLIES FOR HOUSEKEEPING

Broom (lightweight, adult size, 40 in. overall measurement), $1.30 to $3.
Brush (counter style), $2 to $2.50.
(long-handled, push broom style), $3 to $5.
(5 in. scrub brushes), $.25 to $.30 each.
Cleanser, $.27 per can.
Dust cloths, $.25 to $.40.
Dustpan (rubber or rubber tipped), $1 to $2.30.
Mop (small, lightweight, sponge), $2.25 to $3.45.
Sponges (1 in. x 3 in. x 4 in. or in animal or toy shapes), $.16 to $.33.
Vases or bowls (with flower holders), $.35 to $2.
Whisk broom (small size), $.47.

## EQUIPMENT FOR REST

Resting mats (20 in. x 48 in., durable plastic cover), $1.95 to $3.95 each.
Rugs (washable, 27 in. x 48 in.), $1.25 to $3.

## EQUIPMENT AND SUPPLIES FOR FIRST AID AND HEALTH

First-aid cabinet (stocked in accordance with individual school regulations), $5.25 to $15.
Paper handkerchiefs (hospital size), $.08 to $.12 per box.
Paper towels (junior size, 150 towels in pkg.), $.30 to $.45 per pkg.
Soap (liquid), $1.85 to $2.30 per gallon.
Toilet paper (rolls), $.12 to $.15 per roll.

## EQUIPMENT FOR BIG-MUSCLE ACTIVITIES

Ball (rubber 4 in., 6 in., 8 in., 10 in.), $.75 to $3.95.
Climbing rope (8 ft.), $4.75.
Climbing tower (jungle gym or other), $80 to $200.
Hollow blocks (12 in. x 12 in. x 6 in., 12 in. x 24 in. x 6 in., and other unit sizes), $2 to $4 per block.
Ladder (rope rungs with a snap hitch), $9.50 to $10.
(wooden, 6 ft.), $7 to $8.
Planks (60 in. x 5 in.) (finished) $3 to $5.
Skipping ropes (solid wooden handles), $.75 to $1.50.
Slide (wooden trough, 8 ft. stand), $75.
Swing (rope, canvas, or air-cushion seat, preferably hung from tree, 10 ft. suspension), $6 to $15.
(two-swing outfit, metal standard, 10 ft. high), $60 to $100.
Teeter-totter (9 ft. plank, 18 in. sawhorse), $13 to $16.
Velocipede (20 in. pedal wheel, 10 in. rear wheels, chaindrive), $26.50.
Velocipede trailer (two wheels), $9.50.
Wagon (rubber tires, wooden box, 16 in. x 34 in. x 3½ in. deep), $16.50.
Wheelbarrow (rubber-tired wheel, wooden box), $11 to $17.

## MATERIALS FOR MANIPULATION AND PROBLEM-SOLVING: READINESS MATERIALS

Beads (plastic, ½ in. cubes, etc.), $6 to $8.50 per 1,000, assorted forms.
(wooden, ½ in. cubes, etc.), $6.50 to $10 per 1,000, assorted forms.
Bead-counting frames, $2.50 to $12.
Bead laces, $.40 to $.50 per dozen.
Counting rods, $2.50 to $6.
Dominoes and other game blocks, $.90 to $12 per set.
Flannel board and visual-aid units, $12.50 to $18.
Lotto games (bird, flowers, store, zoo, etc.), $.90 to $2.
Mechanical form boards and simple bolt and lock sets, $2 to $3.
Nest of rings or boxes, $.90 to $2.50 per set.
Pegboards (10 in. x 10 in., wooden), $.75 to $1.25.
Pegs (⅛ in. in diameter, 2 in. long, hard wood), $.90 to $3.50 per thousand.
Puzzles (9 to 16 pieces, wooden, 9 in. x 12 in.), $1 to $1.75.
(one or two advanced puzzles, 17 to 27 pieces), $1 to $3.

## EQUIPMENT AND MATERIALS FOR CONSTRUCTION AND ART WORK

Alcohol (denatured), $.78 per qt.
Ball bearing clips (2½ in. x 2⅜ in.), $.27.
Blocks (unit floor blocks), $20 to $170.
(interlocking or large hollow blocks), $28.50 to $199.
Chalk (white), $1.25 per gross.
Chalk (colored), $.45 to $.55 per dozen.
Clay (semimoist, 120 lbs.), $.12 to $.15 per lb.
(powder, 100 lbs.), $.12 per lb.
Clay container (polyethylene pails with tight-fitting covers), $1.50 to $2.95.
Cloth (material like glazed chintz or paper cambric), $.63 to $.75 per yd.
Conductor's punch, $1.15 to $4.95.
Cotter pins (assorted sizes), $.50 to $.60 per box.
Crayons (hexagonal, 4 in. long, 7/16 in. in diameter), $4 to $6 per gross.
Easel (double, adjustable height, aluminum), $20 to $25.
(double, adjustable height, wooden), $14 to $20.
Eraser (art gum), $.05 to $.09.
(felt for chalkboard), $.35 to $.50.
Felt or flannel board (18 in. x 24 in.), $4 to $4.50.
Felt packages (12 pieces of felt 9 in. x 12 in., assorted colors), $2.
Flour (5 lb. sack), $.07 to $.09 per lb.
Glue (an all-purpose adhesive), $.24 to $.49.
Masking tape (½ in. wide x 60 yds.), $.75 to $1.18 per roll.
Mending tape (Scotch, permanent mending tape, transparent, ¾ in. wide x 60 yds.), $.59 per roll.
Modeling boards (3 ply, 12 in. x 18 in.), $.40 to $.75 each.
Mounting board (22 in. x 28 in.), $.35 to $.45 per sheet.

Mystik Tape (cloth with plastic finish, ¾ in. to 1½ in. x 108 in.), \$.29 to \$.59 per roll.
Needles (tapestry, #20), \$.10 per pkg. of six.
Paint (enamel), \$.20 and up per ¼ pt.
(flat, household), \$.40 and up per ½ pt.
Paint (finger, cream), \$2 per qt.
(finger, powder), \$1 per 8 oz. can.
(starch for making finger paint), \$.15 to \$.20 a box.
Paint (watercolor, thick liquid), \$1.80 to \$2 per qt.
(watercolor, powder), \$.71 to \$1.04 per lb.
Paint jars (with covers, plastic), \$.15 to \$.20.
Paintbrushes (flat, ¾ in. to 1½ in. spread), \$.35 to \$.80.
(round, for easel, 1¼ in. hair length, 9 in. handle), \$.20 to \$.85.
Paper (brown wrapping, 45 lb. roll, 30 in. wide), \$7.20 to \$7.50.
(wrapping paper holder for 30 in. roll), \$4.50.
Paper (colored construction, 9 in. x 12 in.), \$.36 to \$.50 per pkg. of 50.
(colored construction, 12 in. x 18 in.), \$1 to \$1.14 per pkg. of 50.
(colored poster, 9 in. x 12 in.), \$.27 to \$.42 per pkg. of 100.
(colored poster, 12 in. x 18 in.), \$.66 to \$.84 per pkg. of 100.
Paper (crepe, 20 in. x 7½ ft.), \$.19 to \$.25 per fold.
(tissue, 20 in. x 30 in.), \$.10 to \$.25 per fold of 24 sheets.
Paper (frieze roll, one side glazed, other rough, 24 in. x 180 ft.), \$3 per roll.
Paper (manila, for drawing, 12 in. x 18 in.), \$2.50 to \$3.56 per ream.
Paper (unprinted news or newsprint, sometimes called expression paper, 18 in. x 24 in.), \$3.20 per ream.
Paper bags (approx. 8 in. x 14 in.), \$5 to \$6 per thousand.
Paper clips, \$.10 per box.
Paper cutter (12 in. blade), \$10 to \$15.
Paste (semiliquid), \$4 per gal.
Paste jars (10 oz., plastic), \$.15 to \$.20 each.
Paste sticks, \$.75 per pkg. of 500.
Pencils (soft thick lead without eraser), \$.05 each.
Pins (safety, medium size), \$.15 per box.
Pins (straight, common), \$.25 per roll of 300.
Plasticine (single color), \$.40 to \$.75 per lb.
Roving (heavy rug filler), \$.85 per hank.
Rubber binders (assorted sizes), \$.35 per 1 oz. box.
Ruler (1 in. and ½ in. markings), \$.10 to \$.25.
Sand (white for inside box, brown for outside box), \$.01½ to \$.02 per lb.
Sand toys (spoons, measures, molds, etc.), \$.10 to \$1.
Sandpaper (10 sheets, assorted, sizes 000 to 3), \$.45 per pkg.
Scissors (semipointed, forged steel, some blunt points, one or two plastic), \$.16 to \$.50.
Scotch Tape (½ in. x 36 yds.), \$.51 to \$.68 per roll.
Scotch Tape dispenser (for 22 or 36 yd. rolls), \$1.50 to \$2.75.
Shears (adult size), \$1 to \$3.

Shellac (white, clear), $1.40 per qt.
Silkalene (assorted colors), $.12 per ball.
Stapler and staples, $1 to $4.
Starch (box), $.21, 12 oz. box.
String (carpet warp, colored), $.69 per ½ lb. spool.
Tagboard (medium weight, 24 in. x 36 in.), $.08 to $.12 per sheet.
Thread (black and white #60), $.10 per spool.
Thumbtacks (solid head, 7/16 in. length), $.20 per box of 100.
Tools for woodwork:
- Bits (½ in., ¼ in., ¾ in., and 1 in.), $1.25 to $1.95.
- Brace (adult size, 1½ lbs.), $4.95 to $5.70.
- Clamps (metal, 3 in., 4 in., and 5 in. opening), $.30 to $1.60.
- Coping saw (wooden handle), $.68 to $1.
- Coping saw blades (assorted sizes), $.35 per pkg. of 12.
- Hammers (13 oz. and 16 oz., flat head, claw), $1.85 to $3.50.
- Hand drill and drill sets, $1.95 to $3.95.
- Nails (3d, 6d, 7d), $.14 to $.22 per lb.
- Pliers and wirecutter, $.60 to $1.35.
- Saws (cross cut, 16 in. and 20 in., 8 teeth to the inch), $1.50 to $3.59.
- Screwdriver (8 in. and 12 in.), $.75 to $1.35.
- Screws (assorted sizes, flat-headed steel), $.35 to $.50 per box.
- Sloyd knife, $.85 to $1.10.
- Square (8 in. blade), $1.50 to $2.

Turpentine (plain), $.78 per qt.
Wood (mill ends, any soft wood), up to $4 per 6 cu. ft. load.
(pine, rough measure, 3 ft. lengths), $.18 to $.20 per bd. ft.
Yarn (red, green, and yellow), $.35 per 4 oz. skein.

## EQUIPMENT FOR DRAMATIC PLAY AND SPECIAL DAYS

Block play:
- Figures (individual and set, animals and people, rubber or wooden), $.40 to $10.50.
- Vehicles and machines (individual and set, trucks, trains, planes, boats, hoists, etc.), $.75 to $15.

Dolls and doll play:
- Doll carriage or stroller (24 in. to 27 in. handle), $9.95 to $29.95.
- Doll clothes, $.75 to $1.50 per garment.
- Dolls (unbreakable, 10 in. to 40 in.), $2 to $9.95.

Dress-up properties:
- Trunk for storing clothes (30 in. x 14 in., 15 in. high), $8.75.
- Old clothes kit, $.00.
- Rack and hangers for hanging dress-up clothes (40 in. uprights and 36 in. connecting pole), $5 to $7.50.

Playhouse cleaning equipment (broom height 36 in. to 38 in., other articles in proportion):

Broom, \$.75 to \$1.50.
Carpet sweeper (one that really picks up dirt), \$3.95.
Clothes bars (30 in. to 36 in. high), \$2.50 to \$3.
Dust mop, \$.75.
Dustpan and small counter brush, \$1 to \$2.
Iron (wooden or metal), \$.95 to \$1.25.
Laundry set (tub and board), \$2.50 to \$3.
Push broom, \$.75 to \$1.25.
Sponge mop, \$1 to \$1.25.
Sponges, \$.16 to \$.33.

Playhouse furniture and equipment:
Bed (wooden, approximately 28 in. x 14 in. and 10 in. high), \$8 to \$10.
Cupboard (wooden, approx. 12 in. x 20 in. and 40 in high), \$15 to \$20.
Cutlery (aluminum, 4 in. to 5 in. long), \$1 to \$1.25.
Dishes (tea set, unbreakable), \$2 to \$5.
(cooking set, aluminum), \$4.95 to \$5.50.
Milk carrier and bottles (wooden), \$1 to \$2.50.
Refrigerator (wooden, approx. 12 in. x 20 in. and 36 in. high), \$25 to \$27.
Rocking chair (10 in. to 12 in. seat height), \$8 to \$12.
Sink (wooden with plastic pan, approx. 12 in. x 24 in. and 24 in. high), \$20 to \$25.
Stove (wooden, approx. 12 in. x 20 in. and 24 in. high), \$18 to \$22.
Table and two chairs (18 in. to 20 in. high, chairs fitted to slide under), \$22 to \$28.
Telephone with operating dial (wood or metal), \$.90 to \$2.

Puppets and puppet play:
Puppet stage or screen (approx. 36 in. wide, 54 in. high, with side wings), \$17.95 to \$33.50.
Puppets (hand, rubber, or cloth), \$1 to \$4.95.

Special-day materials:
Birthday ring or cake (wooden or plastic), \$2 to \$4.
Christmas tree (fireproofed), \$1.25 to \$2.50.
Flags (2 ft. x 3 ft.), \$2.85 to \$6.40.
(12 in. x 18 in.), \$9 per dozen.
Paper cups (5 to 6 oz. size), \$.55 to \$.85 per hundred.
Paper napkins (white, plain), \$.60 per pkg. of 250.
Paper plates (5 in. and 6 in. diameter), \$.25 to \$.30 per pkg. of 24.
Pumpkins (3 to 5 lbs. or perhaps one considerably larger), \$.10 to \$.35.
Straws, \$.48 per pkg. of 500.

## EQUIPMENT AND MATERIALS FOR SCIENCE

Animal cage (36 in. x 36 in. x 36 in.), \$20 to \$35.
(all metal, 12 in. x 28 in. and 14 in. high, with exercise wheel), \$5 to \$8.
Aquarium (10 in. x 18 in. and 14 in. high), \$8 to \$10.
Bird cage (hanging), \$2.50 to \$8.79 and up.

Cocoons (butterfly, moth), $.00 to $.25 to $.30 each.
Electrical invention kit (batteries, bells, switches, wires, etc.), $5 to $11.95.
Food (fish, turtle, bird, etc.), $.15 to $.25 per box.
    (hamster, rabbits, mice, etc.), $1 to $5.
Garden tools (junior-size but sturdy, sometimes called "ladies' tools"), $6.50 per set.
Globe (9 in. or larger), $5 to $17.50.
Hot plate and oven, $10 to $15.
Kaleidoscope kit, $.50 to $2.
Level (6 in. to 9 in., wooden), $.75 to $1.
Magnet (horseshoe and block), $1 to $3.50.
Magnifying glass (3 in. to 4 in. in diameter), $1.50 to $3.
Measuring unit (cup, pint, quart, etc.), $.25 to $.35.
Plants, $.25 to $3.50.
Plastic bags (assortment of sizes from 3 in. x 5 in. to 12 in. x 15 in.), $.75 to $1.25.
Prism, $1 to $1.75.
Scales (table model), $6.
Steel bulletin board (18 in. x 24 in., plus 20 magnet discs), $6 to $8.
Syringe (large bulb, for watering plants), $.35 to $.75.
Terrarium (10 in. x 18 in. and 12 in. high), $7 to $10.
Thermometer (outside and inside, large figures, red indicator), $.75 to $5.
Watering cans (long spout), $1 to $1.50.
Pets:
    Baby chicks, ducks, geese, $.30 to $.50.
    Canary, $3 to $5.
    Goldfish, $.10 to $.75.
    Hen (for setting), $1.50 and up.
    Parakeet, $2 to $4.
    Hamster and rabbit, to be borrowed from laboratories.
    Snails, $.10 to $.25.
    Turtles (small, Japanese), $.15 to $.30.
        (garden and shore variety), $.00.
    White mice and white rats, to be borrowed from laboratories.

## EQUIPMENT FOR MUSIC AND LISTENING

Books (musical games, rhythms, and songs), $.50 to $4.75.
Intruments:
    Auto-harp (5 or 12 chord), $18.75 to $29.95.
    Barrel drum, $3.50 to $8.95.
    Bells, $.35 to $.75 each.
    Chinese tom-tom, $6.50 to $7.50.
    Cymbals, $1.05 to $3 each.
    Hand snare, $2.25 to $3.50.

Jingle clogs, $.50 to $.60 each.
Maracas, $1.25 to $1.50 per pair.
Phonograph needles (long-life needle, 1,000 to 10,000 plays per needle), $.50 to $1.50 each.
(Sapphire-tipped, lifetime), $4 to $5.
Piano (midget size, upright or spinet), $400 to $800.
Phonograph, $30 to $60.
Records (music appreciation, musical games, rhythms, songs, and stories), $1.25 to $7.50 each.
Rhythm sticks, $.20 to $.45 per pair.
Tambourine, $2.40 to $3.95.
Tape recorder, $129.95 to $220.
Tape reels, $.42 to $6.65.
Tone block, $.50 to $1.35.
Triangle, $1.
Xylophone (wooden), $3 to $17.

## EQUIPMENT FOR VISUAL EDUCATION[6]

Books (story and picture), $.25 to $3.50 each.
(reference materials for children and teachers), $.25 to $5.
Filmstrips, $2 to $6.
Junior Projector, $9.95.
Pictures (carefully mounted current pictures), $.00 to $.50.
(framed without glass), $2.50 to $18.
Plaques (tile and wood), $.50 to $5.
Projector for filmstrips and slides, $59.95 to $149.50.
Screen for classroom (36 in. x 48 in.), $21.95.
Slides (2 in. x 2 in.), $.55 to $1.35 each.
Stereoscope, $1.75.
Stereoscope reels (full color, 7 views), 3 for $1.25.
Wall hangings (washable prints or embroideries), $2.50 to $6.

## EMERGENCY, SEASONAL, AND "BEST BUY" SUPPLIES—$15 TO $25

(a) Greens for the fishbowl, replacements of snails and goldfish, flower bulbs, plants, gourds, starch, flour, vegetable coloring, Easter egg dye, etc.
(b) Illustrative and craft materials often needed in the development of a particular angle of an interest or in the development of an unforeseen interest.
(c) Those articles which may be found by the creative teacher in her travels.

[6] Filmstrips and slides may be rented from audio-visual companies or are usually available from your state visual-education department. A projector and tape recorder are usually thought of as the property of the entire school rather than as kindergarten equipment.

## A MASTER SHEET

A roughly blocked-out master sheet providing for setting up and equipping a kindergarten for thirty children might look something like this:

| | | |
|---|---|---|
| I. | Kindergarten Room and Room Furnishings | $3,500.00 |
| II. | Equipment and Supplies for Housekeeping | 30.00 |
| III. | Equipment for Rest | 60.00 |
| IV. | Equipment and Supplies for First Aid and Health | 70.00 |
| V. | Equipment for Big-Muscle Activities | 575.00 |
| VI. | Materials for Manipulation | 75.00 |
| VII. | Equipment and Materials for Construction and Art Work | 640.00 |
| VIII. | Equipment and Materials for Dramatic Play and Special Days | 300.00 |
| IX. | Equipment and Materials for Science | 125.00 |
| X. | Equipment and Books for Music | 765.00 |
| XI. | Equipment and Books for Visual Education | 220.00 |
| XII. | Emergency Materials | 25.00 |
| | TOTAL | $6,385.00 |

## Selection of Equipment and Expendable Supplies

A new teacher often has little to say about the kind or amount of permanent equipment supplied for her room. Sometimes she finds it meager beyond imagination, sometimes she finds the room overequipped for the available space and the number of children enrolled, and sometimes she walks into that dream room which seems almost ideally equipped from every point of view. Many school systems are making an effort to standardize kindergarten equipment, but since the equipment must fit both the area of the particular room and the needs of the particular group of children, as well as the individual teacher's way of working with children, standardization does not seem to be the complete answer to the equipment problem.

Occasionally the teacher is fortunate enough to come into a situation where she is consulted about equipment. She should be prepared to exercise studied judgment in the expenditure of money for the selection of both materials and supplies. The teacher who continues in the same building and room can easily become oblivious to the shortcomings of her room equipment and sometimes needs to be reminded of her responsibility for keeping up her equipment and adding to or replacing outmoded pieces. In selecting equipment and materials for the kindergarten, the teacher should realize that it is neither necessary nor desirable to have enough of each kind of material to supply every member of the group. It is extremely desirable, on the other hand, to have a variety of material, even though the number of pieces in many instances is limited.

The teacher is usually expected to determine the kind and amount of expendable materials needed for the ensuing year. At present few kindergarten teachers seem to know even approximately how much or how little the budget allows. It is true that supplies come to the kindergarten sometimes by way of the art, science, library, or other departments, but even so, it would result in a feeling of greater security for the teacher and possibly in a better investment of funds if she could know, within a certain range, how much money she could expect to spend for expendable supplies. The present amount per pupil available for expendable supplies seems to range from $1.50 to $15 per pupil.

The following section lists expendable materials and new or "going forward" materials and equipment that will cost currently between $280 and $300.

## A YEAR'S ALLOTMENT FOR EXPENDABLE AND "GOING FORWARD" SUPPLIES FOR A KINDERGARTEN OF TWENTY-FIVE CHILDREN

Books:
- 2 Music Books, songs or rhythms
- 10 Picture Storybooks

Clay:
- 100 lbs. of powdered clay

Cloth:
- 3 yds. of cloth, assorted colors and designs

Crayons:
- 18 doz. crayons

Emergency Supplies:
- Articles to be selected as needed by the teacher

Equipment:
- A replacement or new piece of equipment for indoor or outdoor use

First Aid and Health Supplies:
- 36 boxes of paper handkerchiefs, hospital size
- 1 refill for first-aid cabinet
- 3 cases of paper towels (junior size, 25 pkgs. to case)
- 2 gals. liquid soap
- 3 doz. rolls of toilet paper

Housekeeping Supplies:
- 4 cans cleansing powder
- 1 doz. dust and cleaning cloths
- 6 sponges

Miscellaneous:

- 2 erasers (art gum)
- 1 box each of fish and turtle food
- 5 lbs. of flour
- 1 pkg. of greens for aquarium
- 1 roll of masking tape
- 1 roll of Mystik Tape
- 9 lbs. of nails
- 1 pkg. of needles
- 3 or 4 colorful plants
- 1 box of refills for stapling machine
- 1 box of rubber binders
- 1 box of safety pins
- 1 roll Scotch Tape
- 2 boxes of starch
- 1 roll of straight pins

Paint:

- 1 qt. of enamel, white with an assortment of oil paints in tubes
- 3 pts. of flat house paint, 1 pt. each of green, red, and yellow
- 12 qts. of poster paint, 3 qts. red; 2 each of yellow, green, and blue; 1 each of brown, black, and white
- 1 qt. of alcohol
- 1 qt. of white shellac or a fixative
- 2 qts. of turpentine
- 8 cans finger paint powder

Paintbrushes:

- 6 easel brushes
- 2 varnish brushes

Paper:

- 20 pkgs. colored construction paper, 9 in. x 12 in., 3 each red, orange, blue, green, and black; 2 each yellow and white; 1 brown
- 4 pkgs. colored construction paper, 12 in. x 18 in., assorted colors
- 4 reams of buff, manila drawing paper, 12 in. x 18 in.
- 1 roll frieze paper, 24 in. x 180 ft.
- 15 pkgs. of 100 sheets expression or unprinted newspaper, 18 in. x 24 in.
- 10 pieces of tagboard, 24 in. x 36 in.
- 4 pieces of colored mounting board, 22 in. x 28 in.
- 8 pkgs. of tissue paper, pastels, and red, green, and white
- 1 roll of wrapping paper, 30 in. wide

Paste:

- 1 gal. semiliquid paste
- 1 4 oz. bottle of liquid adhesive

Pencils:

½ doz., thick, soft lead

Phonograph Needles:

1 needle designed for 1,000 or more plays

Phonograph Records:

1 record for quiet listening
1 record for rhythmic activities
3 records for song story or story content

Plasticine:

5 lbs. of plasticine

Playhouse Equipment:

Doll, doll clothes, dishes, etc.

Puzzles, Manipulative Materials, and Games:

1 new puzzle
1 new floor or table plaything
2 new readiness packets

Sand:

200 to 300 lbs. for indoor sandbox
800 to 1,000 lbs. for outdoor sandbox

Science Materials:

Aquarium plants
3 cocoons
2 fish
1 box fish food-turtle food
2 house plants

Special and Holiday Supplies:

2 pkgs. of paper cups
2 pkgs. paper napkins, white
5 doz. paper plates
3 doz. paper or plastic spoons
1 carton of straws, 500

String and Yarn:

3 balls of yarn, 1 each of red, yellow, green
1 spool of colored carpet warp
3 hanks of roving, 1 each of red, yellow, and green
2 balls of silkalene

Wood:

Approx. 6 cu. ft. of mill ends (soft wood)
30 pieces of soft wood in 3 ft. lengths, ¾ in. thick and in widths from 2 in. to 8 in.
8 discs ¾ in. thick and 5 in. to 6 in. in diameter

## A SAMPLE REQUISITION

A section taken from a requisition submitted to the principal might look like this:

REQUISITION FORM

Expendable Supplies
Kindergarten

Articles selected from the 19. . . . . .
Brown Book and Stationery Catalog

Day. . . . . . . .Month. . . . . . . .Year. . . . . . . .

By. . . . . . . . . . . . . . . . . . . . . . . . . .

| Quantity Ordered | Article and Description | No. of Item in Catalog | Cat. Page | Unit Price | Total Price |
|---|---|---|---|---|---|
| 4 reams | Drawing Paper<br>Buff Manila, 12 in. x 18 in. | No. 1408 | 90 | $2.00 | $8.00 |
| 3 reams | Expression Paper, 18 in. x 24 in.<br>500 sheets per pkg. | No. 368 | 92 | $3.20 | $9.60 |
| 1½ gross | Crayons, Kindograph,<br>4 in. x 7/16 in.<br>4 doz. red<br>3 doz. each, green, blue, black<br>15 sticks each, orange, yellow, brown, purple | No. 934 | 54 | $5.00 | $7.50 |
| 5 lbs. | Plasticine<br>Harbutt's, dark green | . . . . . . . | 61 | $0.60 | $3.00 |

## A SUPPLY COMPANY ORDER[7]

An order to be sent directly to the supply company might be set up in the following fashion:

Name of Company________________
Street________________
City, State, Zip Code________________
________________
Ship to________________
Street or R.F.D.________________
City, State, Zip Code________________
________________
Shipping Point________________

Date________________19______
Ship by________________
Freight, Express, Mail
Enclosed find________________
Check, Money Order, Draft
or
Charge to________________
Individual, Firm or School District
No.________________

For FREIGHT OR EXPRESS DELIVERY

| Quantity Ordered | Article and Description | No. of Item in Catalogue | Cat. Page | Unit Price | Total Price | Shipping Cost |
|---|---|---|---|---|---|---|
| | | | | Total Price $ | 000.00 | $0.00 |
| | | | | Shipping Cost $ | 0.00 | |
| | | | | Complete Charge | $0,000.00 | |

[7] A letter written on a separate sheet should always accompany the order blank.

## SUMMARY

Although anyone would prefer a superior teacher in a poorly equipped room to an inferior teacher in an elaborately equipped room, the selection of equipment and supplies deserves most careful consideration. Chairs, tables, workbenches, climbing apparatus, and other equipment for big-muscle activity must be selected to meet the needs of active children—five-year-olds *are* active. Research has given us many good guides for selecting such equipment. Equipment and supplies for housekeeping are needed by both teachers and children. Materials for science, dramatic play, construction, and manipulation afford children opportunities to experiment with and clarify ideas (and learn about their world). Books, musical equipment, pictures, and films all play a part in the educational program of five-year-olds. Every teacher needs to know not only what, how much, and how to order but also the approximate costs of desirable equipment and supplies.

## QUESTIONS AND PROBLEMS

1. Using the school supply catalogs from your own community, make out an order to be submitted to your principal for a year's supply of expendable materials to be used by a group of 25 kindergarten children.
2. In the Appendix on page 546 and following, you will find floor plans of different kindergarten rooms. Study each carefully and select one room in which you feel you would like to work with children.
   a. List those features which seem to make this a particularly desirable room.
   b. Indicate the changes you would like to make in the room.
3. On graph paper, 10 in. x 12 in. or larger, draw a floor plan for a kindergarten room which would approach your ideal, indicating the materials and supplies you would hope to find in the various storage units about the room.
4. Observe a kindergarten room of your own choosing; then answer the following questions:
   a. Is adequate storage space provided for materials in active use? For materials on reserve?
   b. Does the room provide needed space and privacy for a variety of activities?
   c. Are the chairs and tables of proper height for five-year-olds?
   d. What provision is made for big-muscle activity? For manipulative activity? For creative use of materials?
   e. Does the room seem well integrated?

## SELECTED REFERENCES


Association for Childhood Education International, *Equipment and Supplies*, Bulletin No. 39, Washington, D.C., ACEI, 1965 (revised biennially).

"Equipment and Materials for the Kindergarten and Primary Grades," *Kindergarten Education in California: A Report of a Study*, Bulletin, Sacramento, State Department of Education, April, 1960.

*Instructional Supplies and Equipment for the Five and Six-Year-Old of the Good Elementary School*, Monograph No. 3, San Francisco, California Elementary School Admin. Association, 1956.

*Instructional Supplies and Equipment for the Four- and Five-Year-Olds of the Good Elementary School*, Monograph No. 2, San Francisco, California Elementary School Admin. Association, 1956.

Kawin, Ethel, *The Wise Choice of Toys*, Chicago, University of Chicago Press, 1938.

Manufacturers Equipment and Material Catalogs:[8]

*Community Play Things*, Community Playthings, Rifton, New York.

*Equipment and Supplies for Early Childhood*, Child Craft Equipment Company, 155 E. 23rd Street, New York 10010.

*For Effective Creative Teaching Materials by Judy*, The Judy Company, 310 North Second Street, Minneapolis, Minnesota, 55401.

*Mor-Play Block Play Program*, R. H. Stone Products, P.O. Box 414, Detroit, Michigan 48232.

*Play Art*, Play Art Educational Equipment Company, 437–439 Arch Street, Philadelphia, Pennsylvania 19106.

*A Prepared Environment—Parent Guide to Play and Learning in the Home*, Creative Playthings, Inc., Princeton, New Jersey 08504.

*Sifo Educational Toys*, Sifo Company, 353 Rosabel Street, St. Paul, Minnesota 55501.

Minneman, Rudolph, "Equipment Materials and Supplies," *Those First School Years*, Washington, D.C., National Education Association, 1960.

Pitts, Clara L., "Materials for Young Children," *Those First School Years*, Washington, D.C., National Education Association, 1960.


[8] See also other manufacturers' catalogs and catalogs put out by your local distributors, catalogs such as *3 to 7 Playways*, St. Paul Book and Stationery, Corner of Sixth and Cedar Streets, St. Paul, Minnesota 55501.

# 8

# CREATIVE SELF-EXPRESSION

In an earlier chapter we noted that the kindergarten offers opportunities for two kinds of emotional development: the gradual controlling of certain undesirable responses, and the furthering of certain desirable ones. It is necessary, of course, to help the child grow in his ability to control expressions of undesirable emotions. At the same time, by giving the child sufficient practice in expressing himself acceptably, we reduce his desire to act in an unacceptable manner. One of the primary rules for breaking any bad habit is to replace the habit with a good one.

Perhaps if we were not concerned with the happiness of the individual or with the improvement of our civilization, we could be content with mere destruction of undesirable traits. Under such conditions, we could spend our days cramming children full of rules. If, however, we want children to grow to be alert, thinking, creative, contributing, progressing adults, we need to give them opportunity to experiment, freedom to question custom, an understanding of what is done by others, and a chance to develop the imagination to see new possibilities and new relationships in materials.

## Affecting the Environment

One of the fundamental urges of the human individual is to affect his environment, to do something to the things or the people around him. His acts may be destructive or constructive. The child who smashes a vase into a thousand pieces on the floor may get as much satisfaction from his activity as the glassblower who made the vase. The baby takes enormous delight in knocking down the pile of blocks which some adult has built so carefully for him, and he obviously takes greater joy in the destruction than in either the activity of the adult or the finished construction. It is our own actions, not someone else's, that satisfy us most.

## Learning Through Experimentation

Trying out our strength or our skill on materials brings us not only joy in the activity but also a much clearer understanding of the properties of the materials themselves. Adults gain much information through words; children profit more from experience. Experimentation with materials is a way of thinking and may make a distinct contribution to the individual's mental development. But while using materials in accordance with the explicit suggestions of others may improve a child's skill, it will add little to his ability to meet other new situations.

Throughout the day, the kindergarten teacher should be ready to further the self-expression and creative work of her children. When activities of this kind do not interfere with the rights and happiness of others, and particularly when they show an advance in the thinking or in the performance of the child, the teacher should give the child an opportunity to carry out his own ideas. One kindergarten group, for example, had made a wooden horse and wanted a horseman to ride on his back. The teacher was somewhat surprised when the children chose wood for the horseman too. The finished doll-horse-man had a disc head with features outlined in thumbtacks, hair made from yarn, and a rectangular body with legs and arms jointed by screw eyes. Such a construction gave wide scope to experimentation and cooperative planning. If the teacher had insisted on some other more conventional medium, a splendid opportunity for invention and ingenuity would have been lost.

The urge for self-expression may appear at any hour in the kindergarten day, though there are certain times when it is more likely to appear and when it can most easily be encouraged and, of course, times when originality and unpredicted variations are undesirable. As one teacher of older children said, "When my children show originality in spelling, I discourage it; when they show originality in composition, I greet it with joy."

Continued experimentation with materials (or with words, social contacts, and so on) leads not only to improvement in our own techniques but to a truer appreciation of the work of others. Experience and increased ability make the individual far more appreciative of other people's skillful work. The amateur musician appreciates the skilled musician far more than does a wholly inexperienced individual. We often marvel at things completely outside our own experience, but our highest admiration is given to accomplishments in fields we understand.

## What Is Creative?

The term "creative self-expression" is ordinarily used to mean the giving forth of something that is tinged with personal attitudes, convictions, or desires. When we ask a child if he likes dogs, an answer "Yes" tells us little of the child as distinguished from other children. If, however, he answers, "I would if they sang songs instead of barking," we can be fairly sure that the child has expressed his true self in his answer. He has added something of his own; he has created. Whenever a statement or a product is not merely a report or copy of something seen or heard but, rather, a report or representation colored by the personality and enriched by the ideas of the maker, we have true creativity.

We cannot create out of nothing. Even in imagination, we create by recombining earlier experiences and memories and imaginings. Suppose the adult tries to invent a brand-new sort of human being who is supposed to inhabit another planet. He can do so only by combining parts of living things he has seen in life or in pictures. The result may have six feet, one arm, the head of a horse with the horn of a unicorn and the voice of a crow, but there will be nothing absolutely new. And so in any other sort of creation: we merely put together bits of our previous experience. The creations of the child are drawn from his experience and are often crude and extremely simple. They are frequently like creations made by other people at other times, but as long as they are original with the child, they are as truly created as if they were occurring for the first time.

A delightful example of the way in which creative expression is an outgrowth of experience is the account of the kindergarten child whose father played cello in the city symphony. Because of illness the child had been absent from school for several weeks, and when he returned he had not only a wonderful coat of tan from sunlamp treatments but also an amazing shock of uncut hair, about which he was very self-conscious.

As he settled himself with paper and crayons, he smiled and said aloud to himself, "I know! I'll make a cello." With a flourish of his orange crayon, he made a somewhat oval figure and to this appended the peg which supports the cello. But when the picture was finished it was obvious that his thoughts had not stayed long with the cello. The cello peg had been fashioned into a neck, the somewhat oval figure now bore facial features almost completely covered with brown, and from the top of the "head" there was a heavy and bristly outcropping of orange. He asked the teacher to write down the story of his picture and this is it:

"Once there was a man. His hair grew longer and longer. Then he grew sunburnt. Then they took him to the barber. He snipped the hair off. And he used the scissors. Then he used the brush, then he used the powder.

Then he went home. Then his hair felt so-o-o prickly. Then it was time for bed."

## The Importance of Creativity

Getzel, Jackson, Guilford, Torrance, and others have brought to our attention the fact that creativity is an important factor in determining the way in which native intelligence is used. The individual with the high IQ is not always the one whose academic achievement is of top-ranking quality, nor is he the one who can be counted on to make the greatest contribution in the fields of art, literature, or science. Given two individuals with equal intellectual ability, the more creative one can be counted on to do more with his ability. Recent studies help us appreciate the importance of helping children make creative approaches in problem solving. Torrance reminds us that creative thinking can be primed in the early grades.[1] Bruner points up the values of hypothesizing in the face of problems rather than simply waiting and then accepting a single solution to the problem.[2]

## The Arts in the Kindergarten

Creative expression is the characteristic which most distinguishes the artist from the skilled routine worker. In the following paragraphs we shall consider the various arts as they appear in rudimentary form in the kindergarten. Few children will ever go beyond a very elementary type of artistic development, but all children, for the sake of their own satisfaction and their own emotional and intellectual development, need opportunities for experimentation and practice in self-expression. It is largely through experimentation and practice that the child clarifies his concepts and finds new patterns of interrelatedness among his ideas. Thus we should not measure the value of creative expression by the perfection of the product, for it is not what the child does to the material or the medium of self-expression that counts, but rather what using the material or the medium does for the child.

## The Writer and the Speaker

Words—spoken or written—are the most common medium of creative self-expression. The kindergarten child is not yet ready to write down words

[1] E. Paul Torrance, "Priming Creative Thinking in the Primary Grades," *Elementary School Journal*, October, 1961, 62:34–41.

[2] Jerome Bruner, *The Process of Education*, Cambridge, Mass., Harvard University Press, 1960.

for himself, but he is able to dictate letters and stories to be written by adults and teachers.[3] Teachers and other adults can also jot down some of the many and refreshing expressions children use.[4] In oral expression the kindergarten child is fairly proficient. He has mastered a working vocabulary and many grammatical forms. He has little difficulty expressing his desires and meanings. To be sure, he lacks some necessary words, but when the right word or phrase is lacking, he frequently coins his own words. One five-year-old, trying to explain to a student teacher how she had gone wrong in trying to get the group up from rest, said, "You made a mistake; Miss B. calls us one-by-one and you called us all-by-all."

The kindergarten child learns new words easily and those for which he has use and meaning quickly become part of his everyday vocabulary. All most kindergarten children need to increase and refine their vocabularies is (a) the opportunity to hear well-spoken English, (b) something to talk about, and (c) practice in speaking.

Sometimes five-year-olds seem almost too creative in their use of words, and the fascination of the tall tales they find themselves spinning leads them to confuse fact and fancy. Then it is well to help the child distinguish between the factual report and the fanciful tale. Each can be creative in its own way, but the kind of creativity acceptable in one situation is not acceptable in the other. When the child obviously begins to ramble out of bounds in his factual report, the teacher may question (in a light mood) the factualness of specific details or ask him to save that kind of material until some time when they will be having "make-up" stories. She may then ask him to continue further with his present interesting statements of facts. But the technique doesn't always work! When Alan, reporting on a week-end experience, said that he went into the woods with his father and he (Alan) shot a bear, the teacher lightly said, "Oh, I don't believe you really shot a bear, Alan," Alan promptly replied, "Well, I nicked him anyway."

## The Actor

When words fail us, we all fall back on gestures to express our meanings. We shrug our shoulders, we gasp with surprise, we laugh, and we cry. Such simple gestures are the elements of dramatization. The small child does all these things; moreover, he delights in walking like a lame man, crowing like a rooster, tooting and rumbling like a train, and blasting off like a rocket. These are ways of expressing himself in the character of different persons, animals, and machines. The rooster is even cockier and more strenuously vocal if we have known how it feels to crow. And the rushing of the train

[3] See Chapters 10 and 18.
[4] See Chapter 18.

down the track and of the rocket into space afford even a greater thrill if we have ourselves rushed and sounded off like them. In the kindergarten, dramatization often starts in some such simple form as representing the feature most striking to the child. A rooster, for example, may strut around the barnyard while crowing, but the child will usually remember only the crowing. As the child develops, he will reproduce larger units, using more details and introducing elements that may go far back in his experience.

Dramatization not only fulfills the child's desire for self-expression but also is a means of clarifying his experiences and understanding. If a little girl plays house, for example, her understanding of the tasks of the housekeeper becomes clearer in trying to reproduce them. If at some point she realizes that she does not know just how her mother holds the broom or just what dishes are used in the oven, she will be motivated to observe more carefully when she goes home. Similarly, dramatization of a story may clear up vague notions or lead to an appeal to the teacher for explanations.

## The Musician

Few people classify themselves as musicians or claim any of the traits of musicians; yet which one of us does not straighten his shoulders and step in time as he walks down the street when a band plays? Rhythm appears in many of our everyday activities, and many people find that tasks which are uninteresting and boring become much less disagreeable when accompanied by music. More than that, quick music will speed up the rate at which we move, while slow music will retard our movements.

Small children delight in music. They enjoy experimentation with musical sounds. The young child often sings or hums songs he has heard or tunes he makes up or happens on. His fingers strike varying successions of notes on the piano, he taps with rhythm sticks, beats the drums, shakes the rattles, rings the bells, and otherwise experiments to produce satisfying —and sometimes not so satisfying—sound effects. All these are youthful ways of creative self-expression in the realm of music. Some of the many specific opportunities which the kindergarten offers for music experiences will be discussed later.[5]

## The Dancer

The dancer combines an interest in bodily movement with an interest in music. Most people cannot listen to music without at least some small

[5] See Chapters 14 and 15.

*"A dab here, and a dab there, and there it is."*

University of Minnesota

bodily movements, and some people interpret and enjoy music best when they move their entire body in keeping with it. We find even the baby waving his arms rhythmically; later, when he is fairly stable on his feet, he hops and jumps, at first clumsily, but gradually with more and more facility and grace. Dancing is probably one of the most natural ways for young children to express themselves. They enjoy dancing so long as there is not too much exact movement involved; they love to march, run, gallop, hop, and skip. Although many opportunities for such expression occur during the kindergarten day, in the rhythm period special encouragement is given to bodily response to music. Free bodily response, rather than patterned steps, is the ideal.

## The Sketcher and the Painter

The person who works with pencils, paints, and crayons expresses himself through reproducing his observations and feelings in the form of pictures. These range from the detailed photographic type, which attempts to depict everything seen, to the expressionistic, which tries to portray an emotion or a feeling rather than give a representation of objects.

The pictures of most five-year-olds may be said to be schematic or symbolic. The child's chief concern is setting down an idea, and he is never limited by what he actually sees. For example, he may include in the picture of a house both the exterior and the interior. It does not seem to him the least bit unusual to see both the people and the furniture through the opaque walls. He knows there are people and things in the house, and so he puts them there!

Making pictures, like other forms of self-expression, furnishes joy and satisfaction to the child. Pictures are also an excellent check on memory—particularly on the number and kinds of details that have made an impression on him. Children often tell more about an experience or an idea through graphic art than through words.

## The Modeler

Many objects are more easily reproduced in three-dimensional material than in pictures. Elephants and chairs, for example, are more easily recognized in a crude bit of clay work than in an equally crude paper-and-pencil reproduction. The child likes to work with clay, likes to manipulate the material and watch it change as he exerts pressure here and there. He presses his fingers into the damp clay and leaves their impression. He is delighted to find that the impression is a picture of his own fingers in the clay. Gradually he becomes more expert in his manipulation of the clay and comes to feel the joy of making snakes, eggs, nests, baskets, dishes, animals, people, and many other things.

## The Architect and Builder

The child who builds with blocks or hammer and nails, the carpenter, the builder, and the architect have in common the desire to give expression to an idea through building materials. Large building blocks, those based on the six-to-twelve-inch unit block, afford opportunities for children to make structures in which they can actually play. Large interlocking blocks encourage the construction of mechanical things such as pumps and hoists and vehicles or more permanent housing structures. Small blocks, those based on the two-to-four-inch unit block, lend themselves to the construction of designs, repetitive units, and all sorts of small structures, from furniture, houses, trains, and airplanes to turreted castles, fabulous skyscrapers, and even whole communities.

The dramatic use of building blocks increases until six or seven, at which time children seem to substitute paint, clay, and woodworking. There is some indication, however, that the interest in block building would still be running high at eight and nine years if the adult attitude toward the activity did not seem to suggest that it is for babies.[6]

Children of four, five, and six delight in creating with wood, hammer, and nails. Two crossed pieces of wood secured by a nail will suggest an airplane to the four- or five-year-old, and the five- and six-year-olds get no end of satisfaction from their more elaborate experimentation with wood and tools. To make something as impressive as a picture frame, a TV stool, or even a "TV set" itself is both a creative and a satisfying experience.

## SUMMARY

While it is possible that in any kindergarten group there may be a child who one day will become a great artist, a great inventor, a great scientist, or a creative thinker of great renown, there is small chance of our recognizing him as such when he is a child of kindergarten age. Although some individuals will simply plod through life most of them will show, some way, somehow, that within them there is a real spark of creativity. Creativity can be primed in the early grades.

If the kindergarten fails to give children the satisfaction of enjoying their work, of realizing that their own ideas, memories, and plans have real value; if it teaches children to follow directions blindly, to do only what they are told to do and no more, to keep their thoughts, questions, ideas, and wishes wholly to themselves, it will be encouraging the development of dull routine workers. The kindergarten should aim, rather, to help children develop into alert, interested, thoughtful workers—workers who, through their cooperative and creative efforts, can add something to both the wisdom and the happiness of the world. Creativity, though often thought of in connection with the arts, is something that can be encouraged in all areas of living and learning.

## QUESTIONS AND PROBLEMS

1. Select an art medium that is relatively unfamiliar to you—clay, papier-mâché, pipestone, or something as simple as a piece of string—and try to express a single idea in it. How does this experience extend your appreciation of children's creative attempts?
2. Place a segment of a circle on a piece of paper and ask five or more kindergarten children—or for that matter, five or more adults—(a) to

[6] Eleanor Robinson, "The Form and Imaginative Content of Children's Block Building" (Ph.D. Thesis), Minneapolis, University of Minnesota, 1958.

tell you what they think it looks like, and (b) to add lines to the segment form to make it look like something else. Record the number and the variety of ideas expressed.

3. Observe two or more children in the playhouse area. What roles are they playing and how do they enact their roles?
4. Listen to a group of five-year-olds in a work or free time activities period. Record all statements which indicate that they are extending their thoughts beyond the factual "here and now."
5. Try to catch and record at least three creative musical expressions —either vocal or instrumental—made by children.
6. Cite a situation in which the observed teacher encouraged creativity. How was it done? Cite another in which creativity was discouraged. In your opinion, was the discouragement of creativity wise or unwise? Why?

## SELECTED REFERENCES

Association for Childhood Education, *Creative Dramatics,* Bulletin 2-A, Washington, D.C., Association for Childhood Education, 1961.

Barkan, Manuel, *Through Art to Creativity,* Boston, Allyn and Bacon, Inc., 1960.

Barron, Frank, "Creative Vision and Expression," *New Insights in the Curriculum,* 1963 Yearbook, Association for Supervision and Curriculum Development, Washington, D.C., National Education Association, 1963.

Conrad, George, *The Process of Art Education in the Elementary School,* Englewood Cliffs, N.J., Prentice-Hall, 1964.

Fraiberg, Selma H., *The Magic Years,* New York, Charles Scribner's Sons, 1959.

Franseth, Jane, "Freeing Capacity to be Creative," *New Insights in the Curriculum,* 1963 Yearbook, Association for Supervision and Curriculum Development, Washington, D.C., National Education Association, 1963.

Getzel, J. W., and P. W. Jackson, *Creativity and Intelligence,* New York, John Wiley and Sons, 1962.

Landeck, Beatrice, *Children and Music,* New York, William Sloane Associates, 1952.

Lindstrom, Miriam, *Children's Art,* Berkeley, California, University of California Press, 1959.

Lowenfeld, Viktor, *The Meaning of Creative Expression for the Child,* New York, Bank Street Publications, 1957.

Lowenfeld, Viktor, *Your Child and His Art; A Guide for Parents*, New York, Macmillan Company, 1954.

Marksberry, Mary Lee, *Foundations of Creativity*, New York, Harper and Row, 1963.

National Education Association, *The Step Beyond: Creativity*, Bulletin, Washington, D.C., National Education Association, 1964.

Sheehy, Emma, *Children Discover Music and Dance*, New York, Henry Holt and Company, 1959.

Torrance, E. Paul, *Education and the Creative Potential*, Minneapolis, University of Minnesota Press, 1963.

Torrance, E. Paul, "Priming Creative Thinking in the Primary Grades," *Elementary School Journal*, October, 1961, 62:34–41.

Wilt, Miriam E., *Creativity in the Elementary School*, Appleton-Century-Crofts, 1959.

# 9

# STARTING THE KINDERGARTEN YEAR

Most kindergarten teachers are faced with the responsibility—and the privilege—of introducing the young child to school life. If the introduction is a wholesome one, the child will develop an attitude toward school that can carry him through those occasional difficult situations which everyone is bound to meet in his climb up the educational ladder.

Most children look forward eagerly to starting school. They come to kindergarten enormously pleased with their own advanced age, and they are usually prepared to like everything they will be doing. A few, it is true, may be upset at the prospect of an absent mother, and some will at first be overstimulated by the group experience and will tend to rush from this to that, showing little concentration and responsibility. Under the guidance of a wise and capable teacher, this heterogeneous collection of children should develop during the year into a fairly homogeneous, responsible group. As individuals these children should not only grow in their ability to conduct themselves according to the standards of the group but also should learn to work together without losing their individuality. While it is always possible later on for a teacher to help children who have had an unfortunate start, it is much easier to work with students who have had an auspicious introduction to school.

## Morning or Afternoon Enrollment?

Many factors enter into the placement of children in morning or afternoon groups. Not the least important of them are transportation, and the schedules of working mothers.

In communities where children are brought to school by bus, it seems practical to have a single delivery or a single pickup of all kindergarten children. In other words, kindergarten children can ride the buses with the older children in the morning and then all kindergarten children can be taken home at noon; or all kindergarten children can be picked up at noon and then ride the buses with the older children in the afternoon. When this is the practice, it can sometimes be worked out so that the kindergarten bus children will attend the morning session during the first half of the year and the afternoon session during the last half. Their sessions can alternate with the non-bus children's. This seems a practical and, as far as the children are concerned, profitable way of letting them spend at least half of the year with the teacher when she is fresh to meet the challenges of the day. When this scheduling is followed communities sometimes have station wagons available for transportation so that the children and a single bus driver will not have to cover the whole territory. If there are too many children for a single kindergarten session, the morning and afternoon enrollment is sometimes divided on a North-South, East-West, or some other basis.

As far as possible, kindergarten enrollment—that is, morning or afternoon—is made to fit the mother's work schedule. Surprisingly enough, however, if this cannot be done the working mother often finds that she can make a change in her work schedule or can arrange to have her child taken care of in the home. It is strongly recommended that kindergarten children not be enrolled in other groups during that part of the day when they are not in kindergarten.

When transportation and work schedules do not have to be considered, it is best to enroll children on the basis of chronological age or other maturity factors. When this practice is followed, the younger children can be enrolled in the morning group and the older children in the afternoon group for the first half of the year. At mid-year each group can be "promoted" to the other session. This policy gives each group a chance to be with the teacher a half-year in the morning session and permits the younger children to continue home afternoon rests during the first half of the year. The plan has at least one other strong point in its favor. In those cases where a child may be extending his kindergarten experience beyond a single year, he will have the opportunity to live his second year of kindergarten in a group which is, for five-year-olds, reasonably mature.

## First-Day Program

What shall the program be for the first day of kindergarten? That is a question asked not only by teachers-to-be but by teachers of long experience as well. The personnel of the entering group greatly affects the answer to this question. Obviously one cannot plan a detailed program that will be equally appropriate for all entering groups. The safest plan for the first day—and for other days, for that matter—is to have merely a skeleton program.

## Knowing the Children

The kindergarten teacher should know in advance something about the individuals who will make up her group. There are several ways in which the information can be acquired, some of which are discussed in Chapter 22 under "Records from the Home for Use in the School." In general it is wise to assume that the formalities of registration have all been taken care of before opening day. If any of the paper work of registration must be taken care of on the first day, this should be done in the office of the principal and not in the kindergarten room. The kindergarten teacher ought to be free from all clerical work, so that she can devote her whole attention to the children. And if you think that isn't enough to keep her busy, just step into a kindergarten room some opening morning!

The teacher may have read and reread information about her entering group, but until she actually meets the children, the information is only statistical material. In order that every child's chances for a good school start may be reasonably assured, the teacher needs to know them as individuals from the first day on. This she cannot do if the entering children appear in the kindergarten en masse.

## Staggered Entrance

A staggered entrance program is probably the most important way to assure a good school beginning. The following is but one of the many ways in which the entrance can be staggered: on each of the first three days of school, only a third of the group can be scheduled to appear. If this plan is followed, every child in the group can have equal school hour opportunities, and the teacher can have a chance not only to see the children as individuals but also to help each child orient himself to the ways of kindergarten living.

## Length of Sessions

If the kindergarten day is longer than two and one-half hours, it is well to limit at least the first week's session to approximately three-fourths of the

*"Kathy's mother is just leaving."*

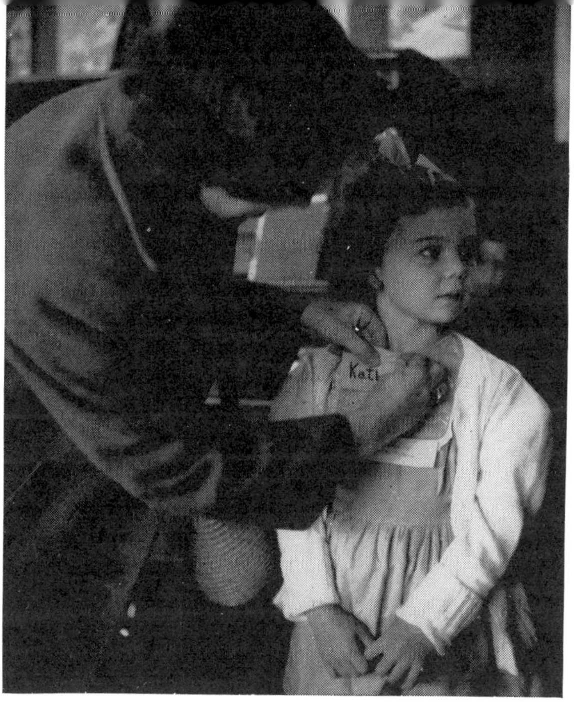

Paul L. Mathews

usual time. And if the kindergarten day is more than four hours, it is well to limit perhaps the first two weeks to approximately one-half the usual time.

## Parents' Leave-Taking

Usually the five-year-old makes an easier and more wholesome adjustment to kindergarten if the mother or other adult bringing the child to school does not linger after the exchange of casual and informative pleasantries with both the teacher and the child. Of course the child needs to have the assurance that he will be picked up or welcomed home at the conclusion of the kindergarten session, but once he has been "checked in," it is easier for him to align himself with his school family if he does not feel torn between home and school, as represented by the presence of both mother and teacher. If the mother remains with the child, he is more than likely to display some kind of confused behavior. He may actually refuse to leave his mother's side; he may leave her momentarily but still look to her for approval of his every move; or he may enter into activities in such a manner that his behavior will tempt her to interfere, in which event he is confronted with direction and control from both mother and teacher.

Occasionally we find a child who is actually embarrassed by his mother's lingering, oversolicitous, protective, and interfering presence. Seeming to size up such a situation, one kindergarten boy approached his mother and somewhat perfunctorily said, "Mother, I think you had better go home now. I think the baby might need you. I'll be seeing you when school is out." Of course, at the other extreme is the child who is so inexperienced, so insecure in his own social adjustment, or just so timid that it would be little short of emotional cruelty to thrust him into a group without giving him the assurance of parental presence. In general, however, if the child has had opportunities to function as an increasingly mature individual, it is safe to say that the first day in kindergarten will be more successful for both the child and the teacher if the adult representing the home does not stay with the child.

## First-Day Orientation

If a staggered entrance program is functioning, the teacher will have time to greet each child in a warm, friendly fashion. In these first minutes both the teacher and the child can learn a great deal about each other. Suppose the teacher, after pointing out the need for name and locker tags, asks the child to select from an assortment of primary colors a piece of paper on which he would like to have his name printed. The child, consciously or otherwise, will undoubtedly appreciate the teacher's approach in consulting him concerning his choice of materials to be used.

The child's response will tell the teacher a great deal about his social, emotional, and intellectual maturity. He may refuse, for example, to make any response; the mother standing by may choose the color for the child; he may point to a color and not name it; he may point and name a color incorrectly; or he may point to and correctly name the color of paper on which he wishes his name to be printed. As the teacher prints the name in manuscript on the pieces of paper, she may note that the child pays little or no attention to the process; she may find that he volunteers to spell or even write his name; or she may find that he actually disclaims the name because it is not written as he knows it, in capital letters. The teacher may pin a name tag on the child and give him the matching tag for the hook or locker which will be his. When offered the tag and some form of adhesive, the child may refuse to accept the materials; his mother, standing by, may take them for him; he may take the materials but hesitate long before selecting a hook or locker; he may post his name upside-down—and the chances are about fifty-fifty that he will; he may be uncertain as to how to post the name; or he may post his tag in a most meticulous and business-like fashion, and be ready for the next bit of business at hand. The teacher who has thoughtfully observed the children's reactions to the various chal-

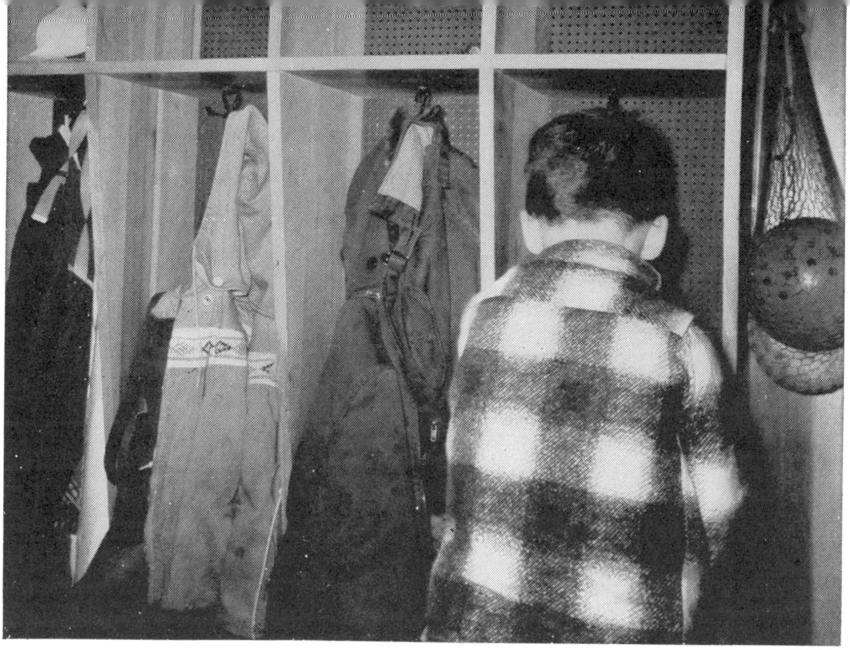

*A Property-Owner in His Own Right*

lenges of this first orientation period will already know much about the characteristics and abilities of the individuals she has just met.

The teacher, of course, does not expect the entering kindergarten child to be able to read his name; however if he can do so, this fact might well be recognized. The respect and importance given the child's name and the personal posting of the name tag will do much to help him feel that he has a special place in the kindergarten group. So far as recognizing his locker or hook is concerned, he will do this not so much by the printed name as by the color of his name tag and his own, probably unique, way of posting his tag. After he has made himself a part of the kindergarten by taking a hanger or cubicle, he should be ready and anxious to acquaint himself with the rest of what henceforth he is to know as *his* kindergarten.

### The Kindergarten Room—Activity Areas

The kindergarten should be arranged so that there will be various challenging centers of interest. On one table the child may find a variety of manipulative toys, including such things as beads and strings, pegs and pegboards, and a few simple inset puzzles. Other similar materials may be found on open shelves nearby. The more complicated puzzles, while not on open shelves the first day, should be available for the child who seems ready to meet their challenge. On another table the child may find paper and crayons in bright-colored containers. Over in the corner he may see dolls and near at hand a suitcase or two containing any variety of things. Close by the dolls there may be building blocks which will perhaps suggest chairs and beds for the dolls, or garages, hangars, and lighthouses for the toy trucks, planes, and boats. On low shelves or on the library table there may be a few both familiar and new picture storybooks, such as Tengren's *Mother Goose,* Beatrix Potter's *Peter Rabbit,* Romney Gay's *Corally Crothers,* Majorie Flack's *Angus and the Cat,* Lois Lenski's *Little Auto,* and a train and an airplane book, perhaps those by George Zaffo called *The Big Book of Real Trains* and *The Big Book of Real Airplanes,* together with Franklyn Branley's *Mickey's Magnet,* Ethel Wright's *Saturday Walk,* Margaret Winkoop's *Mac Goes to School,* and Jo Ann Stover's *If Everybody Did.*[1] Attractive books will invite the child's attention, and the welcoming and comfortable chairs in the library area will suggest settling down to enjoy the books.

In one corner or on one side of the room there may be apparatus for big-muscle activities, such as a jungle gym, a teeter-totter, a slide, a climbing rope, or just a walking board. The sand table, with its moist sand and variety of simple sand toys, will lure even the most timid child, except, perhaps, the rare very timid child who sees nothing in all the kindergarten to move him from the spot in which he seems to be rooted.

## The Timid Child

Often the timid child may be a very practical-minded child, and for just such children as this the teacher will reserve specific tasks. The goldfish or turtles must be fed, or certain tables must be dusted, or the flowers need watering. If the child feels he is doing something worthwhile, he often loses his timidity. And once uprooted from his spot, he can more easily and graciously bring himself to explore the rest of the room. He is like a grown-up who enjoys himself in a group of strangers more when feeling himself a necessary part of the group. Most timid children become more shy if the teacher makes obvious efforts to make them feel at home, while they lose some of their shyness if accepted naturally and given something to take their minds off themselves and their own behavior.

## A Signal—Its Importance

At some time during the first hour of play, the teacher may sound a few notes on the piano. The children will naturally turn toward the piano, and

[1] See Chapters 13 and 19.

she can explain what the signal means. There are many signals the teacher may use, but one that has repetition and some length is preferable because, while it calls for the immediate attention of every child, it does not require a tense military response. A very satisfactory musical signal is

The thought accompanying is, "Stand up, stand straight, stand tall, stand still, if you please." It can be explained to the children that this response is desired from them so that everyone in the room can get the message the teacher has to give them. At first the signal is little more than a game. The teacher plays the signal again while all are assembled and of course much praise goes to those who stand up when they hear it. Perhaps the teacher asks them to close their eyes to see whether they know what to do even if they don't see the signal being played. Again more praise for those who stand and little if any comment about those who do not stand. By the end of the second or third week, the signal should be automatic for everyone. The response to the signal is established not because the teacher wants to impress her authority on the group, but as a safety device. If the teacher knows that no matter what the emergency, she can count on having the attention of each child simply by playing the signal, much more real freedom can be enjoyed during the kindergarten days.

On the first morning the teacher should make it a point to move with apparent casualness from child to child and from group to group, entering into the children's activities. She may sit down to string beads with some of the children, she may make passing comments on sand or doll play, she may put a few blocks together to make a "bed" on which the dolls could rest, or she may sit down with the children at the library table to enjoy the books with them. Upon request she may read from some of the books. It is always better for her to be occupied than to seem to be standing about as though on guard duty.

If the materials at the child's disposal on this first day require little or no restriction on their use, the suggestions the teacher makes to the children can be positive in their nature, and she will find little if any occasion for using commands. If the necessity for using a command does arise, she must be sure that it is obeyed.

Toward the end of three-quarters of an hour of such exploratory play, some of the children may be shown individually how to return their playthings to the cupboards. The signal may be sounded and all the children invited to sit down by the piano. If the teacher has a list of the children enrolled, a game may be made of calling the names and seeing which child responds to each name. If each child stands as his name is called, this not only gives him bodily exercise, but it lets the others identify him. If the teacher calls her own name and responds in the same way, the children enjoy the camaraderie and learn the teacher's name as well. Sometimes a child fails to answer to the name given in the records. Much trouble will be saved if the teacher knows in advance not only the child's real name but the name by which he is usually called. Many a Richard has failed to answer in kindergarten because he thought his name was Dick or Junior.

After this game of calling the roll, the group may enjoy repeating with the teacher some of the familiar nursery rhymes and learning to perform a finger play or two. If possible, at least one of the finger plays ought to be a new one—one which older brothers and sisters and mothers and fathers have never heard before. It can be deflating to come home, bursting with "new learning," only to be greeted by, "Oh, yes, I remember we learned that when I was in kindergarten." On the other hand, in some instances it may give status to the kindergarten child to find that he has joined the ranks of those "who know." Just to play it safe, it is wise to introduce one old and tried finger play and one that will be sure to be new to older siblings and parents. The teacher may have to make up the new finger play, and it may not be of top literary quality, but the novelty of the material will perhaps compensate for its lack of quality. Can't you just imagine how impressed older siblings and parents might have been if in the fall of 1962 Johnny had come home with:

> This is the astronaut (Fist clenched, thumb upright)
> And this is his rocket (Palms together, fingers pointed upward)
> Wh-ish-sh-sh goes the take off (Hands pushing upward into space)
> And now he's in orbit
> . . .
> Round and round (Fingers of the left hand point toward fingers of the right hand.)
> Round and round (Hands and arms revolve about each other.)
> and
> Round and round
> The world he goes.
> . . .
> Time for landing! (Hands drop loosely into lap.)

## Getting Acquainted With Toilet Facilities

If there are toilet facilities in the kindergarten unit, probably many of the children will discover or be directed to them within the first hour. If the toilet facilities are in another part of the building, the group's attention must be formally directed to their location, and possibly to their use.

The first trip outside the kindergarten room is a great adventure. Some children may be loath to leave the security of the room, in which case the teacher must make sure that the timid child senses extra security by being near her. When girls go to one toilet room and the boys to another, the building janitor or one of the older grade-school boys can be of great help. After two or three days, or at most a week or so, the toilet procedures should become a routine matter. This is true also of drinking fountain procedures.

## Music

On returning from this last adventure—getting acquainted with toilet facilities—the children may be attracted by a bit of running music played on the piano. A signal such as

will bring the group to the piano, where they may listen to heavily accented music in four-four time. Perhaps many children who did not respond to the running music will respond to this with various hand movements, such as clapping, tapping the floor, and beating an imaginary drum. Original responses may be commented on, thus from the first day encouraging the child to use his initiative. Sometimes it is wise to leave singing out of the program until a later day. If, however, the teacher herself has a pleasant singing voice, the children will enjoy listening while she sings and many may even join in.

## Snack and Rest Time

The lunch period, if there is to be one in the kindergarten, is often not initiated on the first day. The rest period—if introduced at all on the first day—may well be a very short one, perhaps not more than five minutes. If there are some children who object to stretching out on the rugs in the darkened room, it is well to let them observe the others, with the suggestion that the reluctant ones can learn how to do it by watching.

## Story Time

When the rugs are folded and either put onto shelves or hung on racks, the children may group themselves about the teacher for a story. Depending on the teacher's ability to tell stories and on the supply of attractively illustrated books available, the story is either read or told. The story, if told well, gives the teacher a more direct contact with her listeners; however, a story which is read from a book, with gay and attractive pictures shown at the same time, has the advantage of appealing to the eye as well as the ear.

## Time for a Game

After this, a simple game, such as "Mother Kitty and Baby Kitty," may be played before it is "going-home-time." Most kindergarten children will enjoy this simple game; but if the group is too sophisticated to be talking about "kitty this and kitty that," the game can be played substituting such animals as monkeys, koala bears, tigers—and even prehistoric animals. It is amazing to note the fascination the dinosaur family holds for some kindergarten children! Sometime it would be interesting to experiment with running the game through with "mother tyrannosaurus and baby tyrannosaurus" as the main characters. It is quite probable that kindergarten children might accept it without question; but can't you just imagine the reaction of parents and older siblings when, at home, Danny suggests that he would like to have the family play the Tyrannosaurus game:

> Mother tyrannosaurus and baby tyrannosaurus were fast asleep.
> Baby tyrannosaurus woke up and lumbered off to hide.
> When mother tyrannosaurus woke up and found baby tyrannosaurus gone
> She thumped her tail, THUMP-THUMP-THUMP!
> And baby tyrannosaurus thumped his tail. THUMP! THUMP! THUMP!
> Then mother tyrannosaurus lumbered off to find baby tyrannosaurus.

## Out-of-door Play

Out-of-door play is not recommended for the first day unless the kindergarten has a private playground. It is asking too much of the children to acquaint themselves with both indoor routine and outdoor regulations all in one day.

It is always well in planning for the initial days to make sure that the children have something desirable to look forward to. The anticipated activity may be out-of-door play; it may be the use of certain materials, such as hammers and saws and paints; or it may be something as simple as the use of a particular section of the room, such as the workshop or the balcony.

## Dismissal

If parents call for the children, it is usually better for them to wait outside the door. The children should be praised and encouraged for putting on their own wraps, but they should also be helped if necessary, so that they can learn the technique without too great a struggle.

If the traffic is heavy in the vicinity of the school, members of the school police patrol or city traffic officers will be needed to see that the children get across the first busy intersections. It must be remembered that two or three five-year-olds can be counted on to exercise more caution in traffic than can a larger number of five-year-olds. After the first few days of school attendance, most five-year-olds living within walking distance of the school can be expected to go and come without being escorted by an adult or older child. Both teachers and parents must emphasize the importance of the child's going and coming directly to and from school and complying with traffic regulations. Out of a group of fifty children, there may be two or three whose mothers feel that, for one reason or another, they must be "delivered and called for."

If kindergarten children ride school buses, loading and delivery will be facilitated by having children wear a colored name tag which matches the color symbol displayed near or on his bus door. The name tag should bear both the full name and the address of the child. In some cases loading is further facilitated by having police patrol members display the bus color symbol on a long stick high above the crowd of children. Most teachers group children for dismissal according to the routes they walk or the buses they ride.

## The Successful First Day

The success of the first day in kindergarten cannot be measured by the smoothness with which the day proceeds. The smoothness depends largely on the character of the entering group. The combination of personalities making up the group can make it enthusiastic or unresponsive, alert or dull, cooperative or defiant, timid or forward, self-reliant or dependent. The details of the program must be adapted to the specific group.

No matter how smoothly or how haltingly the day may have progressed, the individuals making up the group should have formed the following opinions of school from their first day in kindergarten: first, school is a pleasant place; second, in school there are many interesting and worthwhile things to do and learn; third, being a member of a group necessitates conforming to certain rules; fourth, the teacher is a friendly and poised individual, whose sympathy, judgment, and sense of justice may be relied upon; and fifth, each child is an important part of the school.

## The Nursery-School Graduate in Kindergarten

If many of the children entering kindergarten have had nursery-school experience, the program suggested above would be inadequate. Most nursery-school children have already experimented with many kinds of manipulative play materials and apparatus for physical activity.[2] They have all had the experience of belonging to a social group outside the family unit. Most nursery-school children have learned to care for their own toilet needs, and many, if not all, have had daily opportunity for practice in self-help. Songs, rhythms, and stories have been included in their programs. The teacher is already recognized by these children as a friendly person of considerable wisdom.

Often in a kindergarten made up of nursery-school graduates and children without nursery-school experience, the nursery-school graduates dominate the situation to the extent of almost overriding those children who have had little or no experience in a social group. To forestall such a happening in one case, the children who were to enter kindergarten directly from home were enrolled three days before the other group so that those without nursery-school experience might get something of a group feeling to match that of the nursery-school group. After this preliminary three-day period, the two groups met and were then blended into a new whole.

Some people feel that because the child has had nursery-school experience, he is prone to be bored by his kindergarten experience. Such a condition may result from one of two causes: either the nursery school which the child has attended has been conducted too much like a kindergarten, or the kindergarten which the child enters fails to offer enough in the way of materials, experiences, subject matter, and problem-solving situations to stimulate the child. The same difficulty arose when the kindergarten was first appended to the grade school. Through the cooperation of first-grade and kindergarten teachers, a unified kindergarten and first-grade program was worked out. When the nursery-school and kindergarten teachers coop-

[2] Many nursery schools admit children between two and one-half and five.

erate in the same fashion, a unified and equally smooth nursery-school and kindergarten program can evolve.

The teacher must see that the nursery-school child has some first kindergarten experiences which will make him feel that he is now in a school for "big" children. He will come back to and enjoy through the year many of the materials which he encountered in nursery school, but on the first day of kindergarten we need to be sure that he meets some truly new experiences and some truly new materials. Meeting new experiences will come in the way of adapting to new routines and exploring the new environment. It would be a pity if the child coming into kindergarten found just the same sets of blocks he had used in nursery school and no more. How disappointing it would be to find the same old puzzles and no others, and what if the library table held only the same old books which he had looked at over and over again in the nursery school! It is a thrill to see something of the old and familiar but also disappointing to meet with nothing new. The kindergarten teacher must plan so that the child will not be disappointed by the available materials and the standards of conduct.

For those children who have come through the nursery school, the purely manipulative table toys would hold little charm, and they might be replaced by such things as untried nine-to-twelve-piece puzzles, fairly complex form boards, plasticine, and an abundance of large drawing sheets and new crayons. The sand table, if there is one, might contain some small transportation toys, some animal and human figures, a few good digging and pushing tools, some gaily colored measuring cups and spoons, and perhaps even a sturdily constructed scale unit. The doll corner, without much of the necessary housekeeping equipment, would be a challenge to block builders, especially if a set of interlocking blocks were stored nearby. The library table might be supplied with new and familiar books in a two-to-one proportion. In the rhythm period, conformity to particular standards might well be emphasized on the first day. By stressing the ability to stop exactly when the music stopped, a new element might be introduced. Old songs would be enjoyed and one new song might be introduced or the music for one new song presented and the words promised for the following day. Playing a circle game such as "Postman"[3] with a large rubber ball helps children get the idea that in the kindergarten there are times when the fun of the group depends on everyone's self-control and cooperation.

The nursery-school child who enters the kindergarten gets almost as great a thrill out of his promotion as the child who enters the kindergarten directly from home. In one sense, the nursery-school child's pleasure and joy are greater: he can share his anticipation with his group. Because of the motor coordination, good health habits, interest in music and stories, inde-

[3] See page 317.

pendence, and social balance he has acquired through his nursery-school experience, his actual entrance into the kindergarten is likely to be an experience of unalloyed joy, with no intense emotional disturbances. The nursery-school graduate, usually with little delay, can throw his energy and intelligence into creating with the teacher a purposeful program centered around a variety of interests.

Perhaps a word of warning ought to be interjected at this point. We think of those children who have attended nursery school for two or three years as having had a great deal of experience in group living. For that reason we often assume that their kindergarten adjustment will be a very happy and simple matter. Usually it is, if a group of children who have been in nursery school moves on as a group into the kindergarten. But if a child leaves his group and makes his entrance alone into kindergarten, he may be as "homesick" for his old group as some children are for home. This is understandable: probably each of us can attest to the fact that there exists no more lonely feeling than being alone in a crowd of people all of whom seem to know one another very well.

## The Kindergarten Time Schedule

A sampling of kindergarten time schedules in various parts of the United States indicates that there has been little effort to standardize them. This may be thought by some to be undesirable, by others most desirable: perhaps the lack of conformity shows allowance for individual differences. Kindergarten sessions vary greatly in duration. Some begin as early as eight-thirty and run until three-thirty. Some begin at eight-thirty and run until noon. Most kindergartens operate on a two- or three-hour schedule, one session beginning at nine and a second session, with a different group of children, beginning about one-thirty. One of the most deplorable situations so far as scheduling is concerned is that in which a single kindergarten teacher has to run three separate sessions in one day, one group arriving at eight-fifteen and remaining until ten-fifteen, a second arriving at ten-thirty and leaving at twelve-thirty, and a third arriving at one-thirty and being dismissed at three-thirty.

In the early days of kindergartens, the teacher spent only the mornings with the children, her afternoons being devoted to making contacts with the parents. There are a few schools in which this practice is continued or is being initiated. In one fairly large school system, two teachers are provided for the two groups; each teacher has her own group but assists the other when her group is not in attendance. In the same system the kindergartens are in session part time during the first two weeks of school, while the teachers spend the rest of the time calling on the families, getting background information, and seeing the child in his own environment.

The length of the kindergarten day depends on many factors, such as size and preparation of the staff, number of children enrolled, available space both indoors and out, adequacy of equipment and supplies, and provisions for luncheon and rest.

Sample Time Schedules These examples of kindergarten time schedules will show the variations in present-day kindergarten scheduling:

### TYPE I—TWO-HOUR SESSION

8:30– 8:40—Inspection, roll call, good-morning greeting
8:40– 9:30—Work period, construction, and evaluation of work accomplished
9:30– 9:45—Lavatory
9:45– 9:55—Singing
9:55–10:05—Rhythms
10:05–10:15—Story
10:15–10:45—Games

### TYPE II—TWO-AND-ONE-HALF-HOUR SESSION

9:00– 9:15—Conversation and greetings
9:15– 9:55—Group work
9:55–10:00—Housekeeping
10:00–10:10—Recess and toilet
10:10–10:35—Games
10:35–10:50—Milk
10:50–10:55—Rest
10:55–11:30—Varied activities, music, dramatics, stories, rhythms

### TYPE III—THREE-HOUR SESSION

8:45– 9:15—Arrival, inspection, and free play
9:15–10:10—Conference and rhythmic activities
10:10–10:35—Snack period
10:35–10:45—Rest period
10:45–11:15—Music and language
11:15–11:45—Varied activities, games, outdoor play, excursions

### TYPE IV—THREE-AND-ONE-HALF-HOUR SESSION

8:30– 9:00—Individual greetings, health inspection, room interests
9:00– 9:45—Social living (part or all of the group assembled)
9:45–10:00—Cleanup and preparation for snack
10:00–10:30—Social snack followed by rest

10:30–11:00—Active rhythms followed by music appreciation and singing
11:00–11:30—Various guided activities
11:30–11:55—Language arts—books, stories, dramatic play, creative expression, sharing, and listening
11:55–12:00—Dismissal

## TYPE V—AN ALL-DAY SESSION*

8:20– 8:45—Arrival and nurse's inspection
8:30– 9:45—Free play and work time
9:45–10:00—Housekeeping and toileting
10:00–10:20—Group meeting—sharing interests and observations, discussing plans and evaluating activities
10:20–10:30—Fruit juice
10:30–10:50—Singing and rhythmic activities
10:50–11:10—Varied activities—outdoor play, games, special work period
11:10–11:20—Preparation for luncheon
11:20–11:45—Library and story time
11:45–12:15—Luncheon
12:15– 1:15—Outdoor play[4]
1:15– 1:30—Preparation for rest
1:30– 2:30—Rest period (on cots)
2:30– 3:00—Dressing, making beds, snack time
3:00– 3:15—Varied activities—music, games, story
3:15– 3:30—Departure

* This program is tentative and may vary greatly according to the group composition, the season, the weather, group interests, and individual needs.

The kindergarten devotes approximately 36 percent of its day to physical education, including play on apparatus, outdoor play, games, rhythms, rest, and lunch; 33 percent to general arts, including housekeeping activities, fine and industrial arts, and dramatic art; 16 percent to general assemblies, including plans for work, evaluation of work, behavior, hygiene, and nature; 9 percent to literature and language, including stories told and read, poems read and repeated, conversation, and original stories; and 6 percent to music, including singing, music appreciation, and rhythms.[5]

Some of the schedules given above seem much more idealized than others. We must remember that innumerable factors in any kindergarten may affect the daily schedule. The program details, as well as the time

[4] As suggested earlier, each schedule is dependent on many factors. Logically, rest on beds would follow immediately after luncheon, but in this particular kindergarten all activities, including eating and resting, are carried on in a single room, and it seems best to have the children outside while the dishes are being cared for and the room is being set in order for the rest hour.

[5] *Encyclopedia of Educational Research*, Monroe, Walter S., ed., Section on Child Development-Kindergarten Education, New York, American Educational Research Association, Macmillan Company, 1960.

scheduling, will be influenced by such things as the background of the children, the personality of the teacher, the place of the kindergarten in the organization of the school, and the location of the school itself. Thus any kindergarten schedule set down on paper is merely suggestive of what may be happening in the kindergarten at any hour or any minute. Needs and interests will determine what actually is happening.

In planning her program, the wise teacher will first of all find out what experiences most of the group have had in common. If she finds that the group has had a great many opportunities to participate in either family or other group musical activities, she may well feature music at the beginning of the year. If many in the group have had camp, field trip, travel or summer outdoor experiences, she may well feature an activity built around the out-of-door world.

Sometimes a negative factor should be influential—for example, the fact that a particular group had had very little in the way of play materials at home. The free-play period would then be the part of the program most emphasized. The range of IQs, the emotional stability, the physical poise, and the initial social behavior, as well as the past experience of the group, must all be taken into consideration in making out a time schedule.

It is often fallaciously assumed that teachers who have been graduated from institutions of good standing or who have proved themselves to be skilled in the art of teaching are equally proficient in every phase of their teaching. Almost every teacher, however, recognizes that she can make some parts of the daily program more worthwhile and stimulating than others. It is well for the teacher to capitalize on her particular abilities. If she is able to get the most wholehearted and purposeful response from her group in the work period, she is justified in giving more time to it than the teacher who is seldom able to get the children up to their best in that period. In capitalizing on her own abilities, the teacher must guard, however, against the danger of slighting that part of the program which she herself may not enjoy. The children have a right to a well-rounded program, and the teacher must not ignore the importance of any particular phase of the program simply because she herself feels more adequate in other situations.

Building rules and regulations and the class and recess schedules of the other grades necessarily affect the kindergarten time program. Obviously, it would be unwise to schedule a kindergarten rest period while the upper-grade children were having recess period outside the kindergarten windows. Generally speaking, it is also unwise to have the kindergarten children on the playground when the older children are out for their recess. The sharing of an activity room or a gymnasium or the toilets with the rest of the school means, of course, that the kindergarten must adhere to a very rigid schedule. The modern kindergarten, equipped with its own lavatories, drinking fountains, and toilets, and having ample play space, is obviously not particularly affected by the schedules of other classes.

The location of the kindergarten, whether we consider it from the point of view of the building, the neighborhood, or the city, will have an effect on the time schedule. If the kindergarten room has an exit directly into a private play yard, the children will probably spend more time in outdoor activities than those children in rooms where the door leads into the main hall of a great city school. If there are many places of interest near the school—parks, stores, firehouses, and the like—the time allotted for excursions will be greater than in a school situated in a purely residential community. In particularly congested districts, the kindergarten hour of dismissal may depend on the class schedules of the school police boys or the time when the official traffic officer is on duty. Obviously it is quite impossible to devise a single time program that would be satisfactory for all localities. The activities recommended for a sunny winter's day in California would differ markedly from those advised for that same cold and blustery winter's day in Minnesota.

## SUMMARY

The child's attitute toward school may be highly colored by his early kindergarten days. The kindergarten teacher needs to be free from all kinds of registration details so that she can welcome and put children at ease. A staggered registration helps the teacher provide good experiences for entering groups. Considering the many combinations of factors in any one kindergarten situation, it seems that too great standardization of the kindergarten time program is undesirable. A program based on a percentage of time allotment and adapted to local community conditions can be expected to meet the needs of kindergarten children more fully than any standardized one. Of the many factors which affect the drafting of a time schedule, the following are probably the most significant: the background and past experiences of the children, the training and personality of the teacher, the physical plant (both indoor and outdoor space, materials, and equipment), and the location of the school. A kindergarten time schedule set down on paper is merely suggestive of what may be expected to be happening at any particular time of the day. In a good kindergarten the needs and the interests of the group will determine what actually does happen.

## QUESTIONS AND PROBLEMS

1. Plan a kindergarten program for the month of January in Florida; one for the month of January in northern Michigan. In each case, make the session two and a half hours long.

2. On the first day of school Dorothy is brought to the kindergarten by her fourth-grade brother and bursts into tears when the brother leaves. What should the teacher do?
3. In a small school on the opening day, the teacher finds that she will have in her kindergarten ten children who have already had half a year of school and fifteen children who are entering for the first time. What situations are likely to arise? How can these be met or forestalled?
4. In a private school in Michigan, the parents ask to have the kindergarten children stay all day, from 9 A.M. to 3 P.M. Assume that the school can provide the necessary space, equipment, and assistance. Plan a program for this six-hour day in the winter and in the late spring.
5. For the purpose of presenting thinking on both sides of the case, debate the question of the staggered entrance of children into kindergarten versus the en masse entrance.

## SELECTED REFERENCES

Association for Childhood Education International, "The Kindergarten Program," *Portfolio for Kindergarten Teachers*, No. 2, Washington, D.C., Association for Childhood Education International, 1951.

California State Department of Education, *A Teachers Guide to Education in Early Childhood*, Sacramento, California, California State Department of Education, 1956.

Colorado State Department of Education, *A Guide to Teaching in the Kindergarten*, Office of Instructional Service, Denver, 1956.

Hammond, Sarah Lou, Ruth J. Dales, Doris Sikes Skipper, and Ralph L. Witherspoon, *Good Schools for Young Children*, New York, Macmillan Company, 1963.

Lambert, Hazel, *Teaching the Kindergarten Child*, New York, Harcourt, Brace, & Company, 1958.

Leavitt, Jerome E., ed., *Nursery-Kindergarten Education*, New York, McGraw-Hill Book Company, 1958.

Logan, Lillian M., *Teaching the Young Child: Methods of Pre-School and Primary Education*, Boston, Houghton Mifflin, 1960.

Minnesota State Department of Education, *A Guide to Teaching in the Kindergarten*, Curriculum Bulletin No. 25, State Department of Education, St. Paul, 1963.[6]

[6] Most states have issued kindergarten guides of one sort or another. The ones listed are those bearing reasonably recent publication dates. Local curriculum guides, such as those issued by Baltimore, Cincinnati, Cleveland, Long Beach, Los Angeles, Minneapolis, New York, Philadelphia, St. Paul, Tulsa, and other communities, also offer helpful leads for starting and progressing through the kindergarten year.

# 10

# PROGRESSING THROUGH THE YEAR

Through a parent interview or home visit, it is possible for a teacher to gain an understanding of the background and interests of the children to be enrolled in her kindergarten group. After observing and working with the group for a few days, she should be able to determine roughly the abilities represented. Then, with the group's background, interests, and abilities in mind she can analyze and evaluate the tentative plans she has set up for the year's work. Certain types of activity will come into any kindergarten program. Stories, music, and rest will be very much the same from one year to another. There will be differences in techniques, of course, determined by the particular group of children, and there will be differences in the actual stories and music used. But these will be minor differences. The major difference between the program for one kindergarten year and that for another will lie in the centers or areas of interest around which the program is built.

## Areas of Interest

The old schools organized their programs around the teacher's intention to teach, while later schools organized their programs around the child's desire to learn. The old schools believed in knowledge for knowledge's sake; later schools, in activity for activity's sake. Schools today take a middle course, recognizing the importance and necessity of having the child's intention to learn and the teacher's intention to teach incorporated into one program. The area of interest—area of experience, center of interest, activity, unit of work, or whatever other name one chooses to use—has become the vehicle for bringing activity into the classroom and carrying knowledge out.

The outstanding advantage of the area-of-interest approach to learning is the many challenges it offers for real thinking. Problems are always in the foreground inviting solution. The teacher has the responsibility of helping children clarify problems and of supplying information, experience, and materials that will aid in the solution of problems. It is the teacher's business to teach the child *how* to think, not *what* to think.

If the teacher cannot see this last point, if she is going to make all the plans for the children and direct all the activity, then the area-of-interest plan has no more value in kindergarten than did the daily program which was carefully broken up into ten- and fifteen-minute periods of occupation, entertainment, and busywork. Attitudes which grow out of real, not superficial, understanding are among the most significant concomitants of learning.

## Selecting Interests

In formulating a plan for the kindergarten year, one must keep in mind the fact that there are many activities, centers of interests, or units of work which may serve as vehicles for bringing activity into the classroom and carrying knowledge out. The following is only a random listing of some of the many areas of interest that may be explored: homes, schools; trains; buses; trailers; airplanes; rockets and satellites; sources of light, sound, heat, and power; birds; animals; fish; trees; gardening; food and clothing; fire and police protection; circus; orchestra; band; postal services; books; libraries. There is practically no end to areas of interest that can be explored in the kindergarten. And fortunately, in most instances, kindergarten teachers feel free to cut across the great bodies of knowledge. It is only later on, of course, that children will be ready to go more deeply into some areas of interest that have been explored in the kindergarten.

In many kindergartens today the curriculum is developed around from six to ten major areas of interest, while ample opportunity is provided for the development of a diversity of minor interests. Major interests, if properly handled, will not exclude other interests. However, they will tend to channel the main efforts and thoughts of the group over a period of time. It is frequently found that what appeared in the beginning to be a minor interest develops later into a major interest. In one case, for example, the teacher had not planned to give any considerable amount of time to building and construction, but when a steam shovel and a crew of men moved in not fifty yards from the kindergarten door, obviously that was the time to guide the thinking of the group along the lines of building and construction. Such an opportunity for daily observation might never again be so available. An interest like this may continue from a few days to several weeks, depending in part on how pertinent the particular interest is to the group and in part on the values the group may be deriving from the activity.

### Criteria for Evaluating Interests and Accompanying Activities

If the unit of work is to be worthwhile, it must measure up to certain standards. (1) It must be an activity which grows out of the children's experience, preferably real experience but sometimes vicarious experience gained through books or stories. (2) It must be sufficiently complex to demand a variety of responses, so that many children can make contributions according to their abilities. (3) It must be an activity that will broaden the outlook and social understanding of the group. (4) It must lead into other related units of work. (5) It must be one that will further the children's physical health and well-being. (6) It must afford the children some degree of satisfaction.

It is not likely that two kindergartens will explore the same areas of interest, and it is also quite possible and most desirable that the interests in any one kindergarten will vary from year to year. Fixed and unchanging programs are objective evidence that the teacher or the school system is giving little heed to the educative possibilities of the variety of profitable experiences available in the immediate environment. The following very brief statements, some of which were made during kindergarten children's play activities and some of which are obviously imaginative, serve to prove that education even in the kindergarten must keep pace with the times.

### Children's Conversation Reflects the Times

In reading the following, try to put each in its own era. Chronologically they have been jumbled but they can be put in such an order that the past, present, and future will be represented: "Look, look, I've made a horseless carriage.". . ."Bombardier to pilot—O.K. Roger!". . ."You be Marie, you be Yvonne, you be Cecile, you be Annette, and what's the other one's name?" . . ."Bang! Bang! Bang! Look out, the Huns are coming.". . ."Hey! Get that message—it's from Telestar.". . ."I'll fill the lamps while you go out and bring in a pail of water.". . ."Is that an airplane? N-o-o. It's a *rocket* and I'm going to the moon.". . ."Oh, no, Father, you won't need any points for Pablum, just money.". . ."I'm the Spirit of St. Louis!". . ."My mother is going to fly us to Mexico tomorrow.". . ."Kling! Klank! Quick, blow harder. The iron is getting cold!". . ."Watch out, kids, I got an atom bomb.". . .

"I'll get in and you crank the car." . . ."Come on: let's play this is an escalator." . . ."Last night on our TV I saw a football game." . . ."My daddy and me went around the world last week."

## Teacher Planning

Although it is the privilege and responsibility of the school or the teacher to set the stage for exploring an area of interest and to make tentative outlines of the desirable outcomes of any interest, often unforeseen elements enter into the program to such an extent that the adult's prediction of the development and the value of the activity proves to be entirely false. Sometimes, as suggested earlier, what seems to be but a minor interest develops, through the enthusiasm of the group or through external circumstances, into one of the main projects for the year. In one kindergarten the children were sidetracked from pursuing the planned interest by the occurrence of a series of fires in the neighborhood. Out of this experience grew a very stimulating unit of work on the fireman, which, with many ramifications, grew into an interest in different community helpers and the interdependence of the members of the community.

## Dangers To Be Avoided

There are two particular dangers which any teacher must guard against in launching a program centered around any specific area of interest. The first is the danger of seeing in her own mind a unit carried through to adult perfection, while those she is working with are but children. The second is the danger of expecting each succeeding group to reach similar levels in developing an interest. The teacher tends to measure the value of the undertaking in the light of gross output rather than in the light of individual achievement and growth. Occasionally the teacher, having adult perfection and gross output in mind, cannot resist thinking for the children or supplementing their manual efforts so that her own aspiration can be realized. Some of the work on display in kindergarten rooms would do credit to high-school art and woodworking departments!

## The First Major Interest

The year's work should be based on a succession of wisely guided activities and interests. In the main, these will grow out of the common experience of the group and, therefore, will be very simple.

The home, as it is reconstructed and reinterpreted in the kindergarten playhouse corner, is often the first interest around which activity is launched. In many kindergartens this interest develops immediately out of the arrangement of the kindergarten itself. Dolls and a limited amount of furniture and other equipment are supplied by the teacher. As the necessity arises for tables, cupboards, beds, and chairs, the teacher will see to it that the materials are available for the construction of these pieces of furniture. Large blocks often satisfy the first needs. Later the children will want to make "real" furniture and perhaps a "real" house out of something more permanent. At this time wood, clay, cloth, paper, crayons, and paint will be needed for making such things as tables, dishes, rugs, curtains, pictures, wallpaper, books, bookends, and flower boxes.

## Later Interests

The subject of homes may well lead to an interest in the children's new school or in the many kinds of homes which may be observed in the community. The birds, the bees, the ants, the spiders, the caterpillars, the squirrels, the chipmunks, the rabbits, and any other living creatures in the immediate environment will offer interesting subject matter for consideration. While the life of the animal and insect world may be made vivid for the children by bringing the creatures into the kindergarten for short periods of time, in general, it is better to observe animal life in its own environment. It is ideal when the children can have an opportunity to make such true friends with wild creatures that they will feel free to come to the children or even to come into the kindergarten room. In one kindergarten, a pigeon that the children had enticed into the room by offering corn and grain used to come to the kindergarten daily at story time and sit on the balcony railing while the children were listening to their story.

This interest in living creatures may lead to an interest in the preparation which all living things make for the changing seasons. An excursion into the neighborhood offers a wealth of concrete evidence of the actual changes taking place in nature during autumn. A collection of seeds gathered by the group, or contributions made by individuals will prove fascinating and educational. A discussion of the various seeds, for example, and their modes of traveling and maintaining life through the winter months brings to the child an appreciation of some of the many details of nature's preparation for the coming seasons.

The life and work of the farmer as he gathers his harvest and stores food and seeds for the winter may well be considered at this time. A study of the farm, particularly if an excursion can be made to a farm, may profitably be developed into a major interest for some groups.

## Halloween

Halloween fun may interrupt the work on the farm interest, but surely the joy of preparing for the Halloween parade or party, to say nothing of the importance of the experience of sharing in the planning and execution, would warrant its inclusion. The discussion of the planting of the pumpkin seeds, the rambling of the vines, the harvest of the pumpkins, and the travels of the pumpkins as they find their way from producer to consumer is fascinating and thrilling. Halloween also offers a wonderful opportunity for the five-year-olds to begin to get an appreciation of weights, sizes, and values. It is a big step in the five-year-old's development to be able to appreciate values—to appreciate, for example, that the biggest is not always the best. In one kindergarten the group spent some time discussing the relative merits of large and small pumpkins. When the medium-sized pumpkin seemed to have many points in its favor, scales and tape measure were brought to determine what might be a pumpkin of the right size for a five-year-old's jack-o'-lantern. After much weighing and measuring, an ideal size was arrived at and, from that time on, each child who brought his pumpkin to school took pride in weighing and measuring it to show that he had made a good choice.

## Thanksgiving

Whether or not to observe Thanksgiving as a historical holiday is a frequently debated question among kindergarten teachers. Even though the complete significance of the first Thanksgiving is beyond the understanding of the five-year-old child, the story of the Pilgrims and their first Thanksgiving is one that always appeals. When analyzed, it is found to have all the elements of a good story. A small boy's comment assures one that the story belongs in the kindergarten program. "That," he said, "was a good story. I bee-d so still, I didn't want to miss a word."

A work unit on either farm or home will dovetail very nicely with Thanksgiving plans. In the first place, the experience the children have had in constructing and stocking their classroom playhouse or experimenting with plants has not been too unlike that of the Pilgrims, who struggled to set up their homes and thought of the fruits of the harvest. In the second place, the further consideration of foods as products of nature helps show what the Pilgrims were relying upon. In the third place, collecting food and sharing it with people whose larders are not so amply filled is quite comparable to the Thanksgiving Day on which the Pilgrims shared their somewhat meager "bounties" of nature with their Indian neighbors.

## Christmas

Current pressure is on the side of de-emphasizing the public school's recognition of Christmas. There is probably virtue in this in that, in many cases, the public schools have taken over functions and rights which should be the prerogative of the church or the home. But to attempt to drop all recognition of Christmas in the school life of young children would seem to be a pity—and, furthermore, it would seem quite futile as well. The impact of the mystery and wonderful pageantry of Christmas is so great in the lives of young children that it would be next to impossible to ignore it.

Some people contend that, as an area of interest in the kindergarten, celebrating Christmas is a violation of religious freedom. If handled properly, it need not be that at all. It need not be thought of as an attempt to impose doctrines on children any more than the pursuit of any other area of interest might be thought of as an attempt to impose the ways and values of others upon young children. When we "study" the contributions and ways and life of the farmer, for example, we are not trying to suggest that all people should be farmers. When we "study" about air and space travel, we do so with no intent to belittle earthbound modes of travel. And so it is, or can be, with Christmas as we "study" about and live Christmas in the kindergarten. As a broadening cultural experience and as an experience which affords many opportunities for creative expression in the field of art, music, and drama, it has much to offer. In developing an area of interest built around the Christmas theme, the spirit of Christmas *can* be retained without in any way imposing religious doctrines on young children.

CHRISTMAS RULED OUT In these changing times, however, it behooves every kindergarten teacher to acquaint herself with the policy which the local school authorities have adopted regarding the recognition of Christmas in the public school of the community. If its recognition has been ruled out, then it is the obligation of the teacher to abide by the ruling.

In those communities where it is understood or stipulated that the Christmas theme shall not be developed in the public school, kindergarten teachers sometimes feel at a loss to know which area of interest may profitably be substituted. Since in most communities children are going to be surrounded by people who are actively engaged in the business of getting ready for Christmas, it would seem wise to develop an interest that would tie in with this. The following might be given consideration: books, toys, foods, trees, buying and selling, postal services, and transportation.

*"It's beautiful. And look! I can make it twirl!"*

Graphic Laboratory, University of Minnesota

CHRISTMAS RETAINED The kindergarten teacher may have to struggle to keep Christmas interests down while Thanksgiving is being considered. Christmas, as a holiday, is not so simply handled as Thanksgiving Day. If the approach to Christmas is not carefully planned, the teacher finds herself involved in a succession of trying situations. Whether Christmas is approached from the religious or the purely secular side, one is faced with quandaries. Probably no other country in the world has a wider variety of ways of celebrating this particular day or season. Since, however, Christmas is based on the story of the birth of the Christ Child, it seems only fitting to start the Christmas unit of work with the story of the first Chrismas. The story need not be told with any implication of religious dogmatism, but it *is* an account of the first Christmas, and all of the many customs and traditions associated with the Christmas season have grown out of this story.[1]

The idea of Santa Claus leads the teacher into a maze of situations which must be handled most carefully. If parents have instilled the idea that Santa Claus is real, it is hardly fair for the kindergarten teacher to contradict their story, though there are not many teachers who are willing to

[1] The teacher must always keep in mind the fact that there are children who do not have Christmas in their homes. Almost every religion, however, has some day or days in the year which are set aside, as is Christmas, for the thought of others. The Jewish Festival of Lights, or Hanukkah, or the customs of Turkish children of Moslem faith in celebrating their Candy Day and Spare-a-Sheep Day mark significant holidays.

further this concept of mythical personality. Still, stripped of its mystery and folklore, Christmas would lose half its charm. How, then, is the kindergarten teacher to proceed in order to retain the charm of Christmas without encouraging the belief that Santa Claus is a real person? It may be done by saying that in different parts of the world children have different ways of receiving their gifts. The German children play that the *Weihnachtsmann* brings gifts to their tree; the French children play that *Bonhomme Noël* goes about distributing the gifts; and the Swedish children go to sleep on Christmas Eve dreaming of all the lovely things which the *Yuletummte* will bring. After a consideration of these various traditions, the question may then be put: "Who do we pretend brings gifts to us at Christmas?" The answer will, of course, be "Santa Claus." After it has once been stated by teacher and group alike that "we pretend" that Santa Claus brings our Christmas gifts, then one may dramatize and play Santa Claus as much as one likes without believing something which must one day be unlearned.

GIFTS The kindergarten Christmas is usually the first Christmas in which the child personally gives gifts. The first discussion of gifts for mothers and fathers will probably result in such suggestions as balls, wagons, dolls, and the like. It is always interesting to see a group of five-year-olds as they reach a dawning consciousness that suitable gifts must be those that will be enjoyed not by the doner but by the recipient. Often the children suggest articles which would be far beyond their powers to make or obtain, such as a TV set, a necktie, or shoes. When, after looking about at home and asking a few searching questions, the children next discuss gifts, some novel but practical and interesting suggestions develop. One such list was as follows:

### FOR FATHER

A can for nails (coffee can painted and decorated)

An ashtray (clay dish painted)

A spindle (clay or wooden base with long nail run through it and standing upright)

A book to write things in (small book of blank pages with painted cover design)

A footstool (wooden stool with cloth upholstering)

A pencil holder (block of clay, painted and decorated, in which holes have been made to stand pencils)

A tool to wash windows (a wooden T with a crosspiece covered with tire tubing).

FOR MOTHER

A tray (made of wood and painted)
A candleholder and candles (clay or wood holders, painted; hand-dipped candles made of melted paraffin colored with paint powder)
A pocketbook (oilcloth coin purse stitched with yarn)
Doilies (paper set, designed and colored)
A little table (end table of wood)
A dish for paper clips, pins, and other odds and ends (clay dish painted)
Something to set plants on (wooden square 4 in. x 4 in., wooden beads, fastened on with nails, used for legs)
A box for buttons (individual ice-cream containers decorated with wallpaper, button knob for cover).

Preparation for Christmas Preparation for the kindergarten Christmas must be started in time to prevent a rush just when both teacher and children ought to be free to enjoy the festivities. It is usually not too early to begin the actual work on Christmas gifts immediately after Thanksgiving. If a program or a party is to be given, it is wise to have it as the outgrowth of the work and play of the preceding weeks. A stilted program, with verses and dances practiced and drilled for the occasion, does not have nearly the charm or wholesomeness of the program growing directly out of the many recent song, game, and rhythm experiences common to the group. Since many parents visit the kindergarten at no other time, the Christmas party should give them an idea of the kindergarten as it ordinarily is. They will enjoy watching and helping the children in stringing the popcorn, bread, and cranberries for the birds' Christmas tree; tying the peanuts to the squirrels' Christmas tree; and making the doilies and napkins or frosting the cookies and setting the tables for their own Christmas party. While the last and perhaps surprise touches are being added by an assistant, the parents and children alike may enjoy listening to a story told by the teacher, or short stories or rhymes by the children. After the party proper (something as simple as fruit juice or milk and a cookie), the children may gather by the piano or festive Christmas tree for a period of songs, rhythms, games, or a bit of dramatization. If each child is supplied with a large paper bag in which he can carry home his gifts and party favors safely, the day has reasonable assurance of coming to a happy close.

## The Winter Term

After the holiday season, the group comes together with renewed but undirected interests. As one youngster put it on coming back to the kindergarten after the holidays, "Well, we have studied about homes, we have studied about farms, we have studied about Thanksgiving, we have worked hard for Christmas—now I wonder what we had better do."

The program at this time of year will depend somewhat on the climate, and on current city or neighborhood happenings. If there is a great deal of snow on the ground, an area of interest may be centered around the care and feeding of the birds; or if the snow is not too dry, the building of a snowhouse may well lead to a consideration of the many ways in which people adapt their environment to their needs.

## Winter Circus

If the city has a winter circus, the interest of the kindergarten group is often centered around its coming and around dramatization of the performances and the study of the circus animals. It is interesting to note, however, that when five-year-olds go to a circus they are invariably impressed not so much by the animals and the feats of skill exhibited by the acrobats as by the clowns. Children are often surprised to learn that clowns are ordinary men who have chosen clowning as a vocation. Youngsters are further surprised and impressed to know that much practice and experience is necessary before some of the clowns, particularly those who do acrobatic stunts, can enter the circus. This interest in a specific vocation sometimes leads to a consideration of choices of occupation and the need which exists in our society for a tremendous variety of workers. Sometimes the arrival and departure of the circus leads to an interest in modes of travel and transportation. Or it may lead to an interest in wild animals and creatures of the zoo.

## Valentine's Day

Valentine's Day, like Halloween, will probably interrupt a major unit of work; but, like Halloween, it has its justification in the joy derived by the children. The kindergarten often has a box into which the children put the valentines they make for one another. The school does not usually encourage bringing valentines from home, but in many cases the pattern set by older brothers or sisters is reflected in the kindergarten. It is a good idea to supply each child with a large envelope and ask him as he looks at his valentines to slip them into his envelope. If the teacher then volunteers to staple the envelope so that the valentines won't fall out on the way home, hurtful comparisons of numbers of valentines received can almost completely be eliminated. This will avoid that dreadful moment when the gay little butterfly of the group lifts her nose and says to her neighbor, "Is that all you got? Just look at all I have!" Sometimes, in an effort to avoid such a situation, lists on which all of the children's names appear are sent home and children are encouraged to bring valentines to all class members. This may take care of one problem, but it brings up another—the quantities of valentines to be distributed. In some cases each child has his own personally decorated bag hanging on a large wire or taped to a ledge. On each bag the teacher has printed in large manuscript letters the child's name. Children have fun trying to match the names on their valentine envelopes with the names on the bags. Some children can read the names without difficulty but most will need the help of the teacher in delivering their valentines to the proper bag. Confusion can be avoided by having each child sit on his own rug as he opens his valentines.

## National Holidays

The birthdays of Abraham Lincoln and George Washington are holidays whose significance it is difficult for the kindergarten child to understand. A kindergarten teacher, in attempting to explain the reason for the forthcoming holiday, went into some detail about the life and death of our first President, and concluded by saying "and tomorrow is the birthday of George Washington." A somewhat cynical child in the group said, "Hmph, I don't see how he could have a birthday if he isn't even living." Before the teacher could explain, a mite of a girl retorted, "Of course he could have a birthday—don't you suppose someone else could eat his ice cream for him?"

The displaying of the flag, which for young children is a large part in the celebration of these two holidays, is a concrete experience around which the kindergarten teacher may build. Beyond the aim to give our children an honest respect for the flag of their country, we have here an excellent opportunity to present the idea that there are many flags in the world and that the children of various lands have special days and occasions on which they display their particular flags. If the children have had access to many books, they will enjoy associating the flags of the various countries with the characters in the books. "Ameliar Anne" and "Christopher Robin" would put up an English flag on their holidays, "Pelle" and "Olle" would hang out a Swedish flag, "Madeline" and "Pierre" a French flag, and "Pitia" and "Pancho" a Mexican flag. Many kindergarten children are interested in flags and they enjoy making for themselves or for the decoration of the kindergarten a variety of flags painted or crayoned on either cloth or paper.

The long weeks between February and the coming of spring offer time for the exploration of interests centered around the community. The community, extended as it is in our modern world, will stimulate interests ranging from the immediate neighborhood to outer space. Children are interested in "studying" about stores and storekeepers, fire stations and firemen, traffic and policemen, libraries and librarians, construction and construction workers, and many other phases of neighborhood community living. But they are also interested in things beyond their immediate neighborhood. Young children today have much information about, and are fascinated by, satellites, rockets, astronauts and outer space in general. It is not uncommon to find kindergarten children and their teacher pursuing together an interest on space and space travel.

At this point a word of caution might profitably be interjected! All too often teachers and parents get carried away with a kindergarten interest on space. They are unduly impressed by the fact that young children are talking about such things as rockets orbiting the earth, astronauts being sent into space, and messages being received by way of Telestar. They forget that in years gone by other adults were equally impressed by hearing children speak of telephones, automobiles, airplanes, radios, and television sets. These distant or "modern as tomorrow" interests tend to be greatly overrated. Many of the kindergarten interests which are developed around things in the immediate environment actually afford equally, if not more valuable, learning experiences for young children.

## Easter

The long pull from February to late March or early April is climaxed by the arrival of Easter. The Easter season, like Christmas, has its maze of religious beliefs and folk legends. The idea of the Easter Bunny, like Santa Claus, brings to the kindergarten teacher the delicate problem of manipulating her program so that the children may retain all the fun and joy of play centered around the Easter Bunny without believing in his physical existence. The old German story of "Mr. Easter Rabbit"[2] helps the children understand the secret of the Easter rabbit, yet does not rob them of the joy of joining heartily into the business of playing Easter Bunny.

From the spiritual viewpoint, Easter may be considered simply as a time of new life and new hope. The whole world of nature is beginning to stir itself once again, and those tiny seeds which the children observed with

[2] See reference, p. 243.

such amazement and wonder in the fall are now about to burst into life. The moth may be felt stirring in its cocoon; the polliwogs may be seen "sprouting" legs; and even the baby chicks may be heard and seen as they peck their way through the shell. Everywhere, if attention is but called to it, one sees evidence of new life.

## The Spring Term

Following Easter, spring comes quickly.[3] The birds have begun to return, trees are green again, flowers are blooming, the farmer is sowing his seeds, and gardening time has arrived. Plans are made for the kindergarten garden. Seeds and tools are brought from home. The ground is turned and raked; fertilizer is worked into the soil. At length the planting is done, and signs are made and posted to designate the fruit, flower, or vegetable which may be expected to appear in each row.

Sometimes the garden seems to be a long time starting, but during those weeks of waiting, there is much of interest in the environment which calls for attention. Perhaps new construction work that was held up by the ice and snow of the winter is under way; the neighborhood florist may have some particularly interesting developments in his greenhouses; a planned trip to the country may provide opportunities for the children to observe

[3] This applies, of course, only to the Northern states. The local climate will naturally determine the time for considering seasonal changes.

*"Pansies must be picked every day."*

the newly seeded fields and to see the colts, calves, baby pigs, and lambs with their mothers. A trip could be planned so that the children would be at the farm on a day when the sheep were being sheared. In that case, a whole new area of interests would be opened. In any event, once spring comes, the outside world will be begging the children to come out to see what surprises it has to offer. Spring birds, spring blossoms, and spring life of all kinds will be beckoning for attention.

Sometimes in the spring of the year it is pleasant to do as the children did "when my big brother and sister were in kindergarten," or as the English people did long ago. It is pleasant to set up and make preparations for a very simple Maypole dance. Simple as it all may be, it gives the children a feeling of unity and helps them understand the importance of having each one do his part. The undertaking is much more worthwhile if the children can make their own streamers for the pole. One satisfactory method seems to be that of making streamers, chain fashion, from strips of colored paper. To some the making of paper chains seems little more than an "occupation" carried over from the old Froebelian kindergartens of the nineteenth century. To make paper chains *per se* would be exactly that. But to have the group make an effort to solve the problem of appropriate materials and procedure and to have each child working on his own paper chain of a chosen color—how very different this is from giving each child strips of paper and telling him to sit down and paste paper rings together!

With summer in the offing, vacation plans will be in the minds of most of the group. The prospect of a holiday at the lake or the beach may lead to an interest in boats. Travel may well center the interests of the group around the study of trains, buses, airplanes, or other modes of transportation.

Late in May or early in June, a final challenge will be getting the room ready for the children who will be entering the kindergarten in the fall. Books will need to be mended, blocks scrubbed and packed away, lockers cleaned, pictures removed, and the playhouse dismantled. And last of all, as a fitting ending to a busy school year, plans may be laid for a farewell picnic. The garden will no doubt supply such foods as lettuce, carrots, and radishes for sandwiches; the bees may have supplied honey in a sufficient quantity for tarts, and butter for the bread or ice cream for dessert can be made in the kindergarten.

As the kindergarten year comes to a close, it will be the teacher's hope that through playing, planning, observing, exploring, testing, and learning each individual in the group will have realized many of his ever-increasing motor and intellectual potentialities, and that he will have been able to establish within himself an emotional control which will make his conduct socially desirable. In addition it is to be hoped that each child, through daily living, "study," and experimentation in the kindergarten, will have been helped in building for himself some sort of beginning appreciation of the way in which life as a whole fits together.

The following story was dictated in the month of March by a five-year-old kindergarten child who had just finished painting a picture. The picture itself was in no way unusual—just a yellow house with a scattering of red and yellow flowers about it—but the story which accompanied it serves to alert us to the fact that kindergarten experiences and pursued interests can help children begin to sense relationships as they work and play. Here is the story: "Once upon a time there was a garden that had flowers in it. Roses grew in the garden and dandelions. One day some honeybees came. They were going to make honey. After they made it, they stored it in their tree. Then one day it rained. The next day it was winter. The flowers died. Don't worry. The flowers will come in the spring. Inside the golden house which stood by the garden the children were sleeping. And the next day they made a snowman. Then they put up a Swedish flag by the snowman . . . their grandfather had come from Sweden. The next day they went to the United Nations Building and they saw all the flags and they even saw their own flag. Best of all, they saw the United Nations flag. Then they went home and they went to sleep. 'The End.' "

## Developing an Interest

It has been said by some that it is better not to set down on paper an outline for any given interest to be developed with young children. The reason obviously is that an outline, once set down, tends to make the teacher cling too closely to it. The teacher who clings too closely to an outline is likely to be oblivious of the many unpredictable but often valuable concomitants inherent in pursuing an interest. She is also inclined to lose sight of that very important factor which we might call "the factor of human variableness." But the fact that the teacher does not set down her outline in "lesson plan" fashion does not mean that she will not have thought an interest through before developing it with the children.

For the purpose of helping the teacher think her problem through, the following outline in the form of a summary has been made. It has been purposely drawn up as though the interest had already been developed, so that the teacher will be encouraged to think of her plans as involving both the interest and the children. Too often, teacher planning concerns itself more with interests and ideas than with children!

## OUTLINE FOR THE SUMMARY OF A DEVELOPED INTEREST

*General Area of Interest*
- Specific area

*Factors Considered in Relation to the Pursuit of the Interest*
- Group composition
  - How many children in the group?
  - What is the ratio of girls to boys?
  - How long has the group been together?
  - What is the chronological age range?
  - What is the apparent level and range of ability?
  - What is the socioeconomic background of the group?

*Initiation and Duration of the Interest*
- From what did the interest arise?
- How was it stimulated?
- What was the duration of the interest?
  - Date initiated?
  - Apparent peak of interest?
  - Date terminated?

*Exploring the Interest*
- Sources of shared information
  - Verbally presented information given by either the children or the teacher
    - Specific sources: previous experience, firsthand observations made as a result of present interest, parents or other adults, experts or authorities, newspaper pictures or articles, magazine pictures or articles, books, movies, radio and TV programs, or other sources
  - Materials brought in by either the children or the teacher
  - Models, samples, pictures, books, raw materials
  - Excursions taken by the group
  - Films and slides seen by the group
  - Science experiments observed or participated in by the group
  - Radio and TV programs, records, and the like, enjoyed by the group
- How did the interest find expression in the various phases of the daily activities?
  - Stories, rhythms, music appreciation, games, dramatizations, poetry, songs, creative songs, free play, conversations
- How did the interest find expression through the use of materials?
  - Wood, clay, paper, crayons, paint, blocks

*Culmination of the Interest*
- When, if ever, were summaries or checkups made on learnings? How?
- Was there any culminating activity? If so, of what nature?
- How did the interest terminate or blend into a new interest?

*Evaluation of the Interest*
- How many children made contributions?
- How closely have the new learnings been related to the children's living?

What were the significant and desirable results in attitudes and understandings? Were there any undesirable outcomes?
What challenges were offered for building foundations for further learning in the areas of reading? mathematics? science?
Did the results justify the expenditure of the teacher's time? children's time? output of teacher energy? output of children's energy? teacher interest and enthusiasm? child interest and enthusiasm?
Would another group of kindergarten children be likely to pursue the same interest another year?
What suggestions do you have for making the pursuit of the interest more profitable?

At the conclusion of a unit, it is desirable for the teacher to fill in, in outline, the developed interest in some detail. This will show how circumstances and the human elements in the kindergarten have affected the total experience.

The following is a fictitious account of an interest developed by a student teacher. As you read it, note how many of her learnings she has put to use. She is assuming that she *is* the teacher:

## A HALLOWEEN INTEREST

Our school—the Bay Park School at Knight and Bay Park Place—is one of the newest schools in Baysville. The kindergarten room is spacious, pleasant, and conveniently located on the ground floor. My morning group was enrolled in September, and was the first group to use the new room.

There are twenty-six children in the morning session—twelve girls and fourteen boys. They range in age from four years and ten months to five years and eight months. Ratings on the Goodenough Draw a Man Test indicate that the IQ range in the group is from approximately 95 to 137. About half the children are from families whose fathers are professional people or business executives; the other half are from families whose fathers are tradesmen, laborers, and university students; one child in the group lives in an orphanage. Miss K, the student teacher, and I have this group each school-day morning from 8:30 to 11:30.

The children had already become highly interested in the many signs of fall which were everywhere in evidence. The park outside the school offered many opportunities for gathering leaves and, believe me, we had an unusually large collection. A sampling of the most perfect leaves of each kind was kept under a large piece of heavy glass laid over a dark-green desk blotter. The other leaves formed room bouquets or, dipped in wax, served as bulletin board decorations. Introducing the Halloween interest seemed very natural; it was just another part of the fall idea.

After a few years of teaching, one becomes very much aware of the neighborhood surroundings and seeks out all possibilities for developing interests in simple, meaningful ways. I had happened, a week before this, to see a bin of pumpkins (all sizes) near one of the cow barns on the farm campus. I stopped to ask Mr. Petersen, who works in the barns, all about the pumpkins, and to my surprise he told me they were experimental. He said the pumpkins were not being used for any further experimental purposes and were just waiting to be fed to the cows. I asked about the possibility of getting some for our kindergarten, and he seemed to think it would be quite possible that we might have some. This experience of mine really sparked our week and a half of Halloween fun in the kindergarten.

On October 19 at our group meeting, after our usual discussion of interesting observations and objects brought in by children, including more leaves, I told the children of my visit with Mr. Petersen on the farm campus. We talked about the "experimental" pumpkins, how pumpkins grew from seeds, and about what happened to pumpkins after they had ripened. Peggy said that she and her brother had a jack-o'-lantern last year. Their mother had helped them carve the face and put the candle inside. This brought many Halloween memories to the group and they were "buzzing" with excitement. Kristin wondered if we were going to have a jack-o'-lantern. It was decided, of course, that we definitely should have a jack-o'-lantern, perhaps more than one. When we talked about where and how to get a pumpkin, Joan wondered about some farm-campus pumpkins. I said that it was quite possible that Mr. Petersen could give us some pumpkins and perhaps it would be a good idea to ask him—but how could we ask him? Telephone? Yes; however, it was difficult to reach him in the barn. Walk up to the campus? Yes; though it was quite a distance and we couldn't be sure to find him in the barn. Finally Caroline hit on the idea of writing a letter. The children couldn't write, but I could print one for them. We were anxious for a quick reply, and so we decided, since I lived only a block from the campus, that I could deliver it at noon on my way home. This was how the letter read:

> Dear Mr. Petersen:
>
> We are looking for some pumpkins. We would like to make some jack-o'-lanterns for our room. Would you have some extra pumpkins for us?
>
> The morning kindergarten<br>Bay Park School

To this Mr. Petersen replied:

> Dear morning kindergarten,
> I will expect to see you about 10:00 o'clock Friday outside the big white cow barn. We have a bin of pumpkins there, and you will be able to choose some for your room.
>
> Sincerely,
> Mr. Petersen

The next morning I read Mr. Petersen's letter and everyone was eager to go to the big white cow barn for the pumpkins.

Some time previously, I had checked with our principal about school policy on excursions. Excursions were encouraged; however, it was necessary to have a signed permission slip from a parent of each child before I could take them from the school premises.

We discussed why their mothers should know when they went away from school and how important it was for them to tell me that their mothers wanted them to go. It was decided that, since it had been so much fun to write a letter to Mr. Petersen, maybe we could write a letter to the mothers. This was the result:

> Dear Mother,
> Mr. Petersen is giving us some pumpkins for our kindergarten jack-o'-lanterns. We would like to go to the farm campus at 9:30, October 22, to get the pumpkins. Please sign your name and my name if I may go. I must have your signature before Mrs. Keller and Miss Koen can take me.
>
> ..................................
>
> ..................................

While Miss Koen was duplicating the letter, we discussed the coming excursion and some of the things we should consider: staying in a group; stopping at all street corners before crossing a street; and being especially careful at Bay Street. We considered the courtesy which we should extend to motorists and bus drivers.

When it was time to go home that day, Miss Koen and I pinned the letters on the children. The following morning all but two signed letters came back. All the mothers had pinned the slips on the children. I checked with the mothers of the children whose slips we did not receive, and all the slips were in by Friday morning.

It was necessary to anticipate the size of the pumpkin we should have and the way we could get the pumpkin back to school. I took a pumpkin to school with me to stimulate interest in size, shape, and weight that would be suitable for a jack-o'-lantern for a five-year-old.

Someone wondered about how much the pumpkin I brought weighed, and so Miss Koen got our scales and the tape measure. She set the pumpkin on the scales and the indicator sped around to 12½! We counted around the scale with the indicator—1, 2, 3, and so on—almost everyone counted accurately. Then we measured the pumpkins. We counted on the tape measure—1, 2, 3, up to 33. Only a few children could count to 33. This was a pretty big pumpkin. Siggy said he thought he would like to be able to carry his pumpkin. We all agreed he had a good idea. I asked him if he wanted to try to lift the pumpkin off the scale and he jumped up immediately. He had a little trouble with it and of course everyone was eager to rush up to help him. To avoid a stampede and to study the situation better, I suggested that we all stand up and pretend to lift a 12½ pound pumpkin from the floor. Some fairly tossed their pumpkins into the air and others struggled with the weight. In the end we concluded that a pumpkin which weighed as much as 12½ pounds would be much too heavy to carry. We finally decided on a three- or five-pound "carrying pumpkin," but all agreed that a larger one would be fun to have in the room as a decoration. Then came the problem of getting the pumpkins back from the farm campus. After some discussion we finally decided to take the kindergarten wagon.

Friday we reviewed how we were going to walk to the farm campus. Two back captains and two front captains were selected to guide the group safely. Mr. Petersen was very patient with the children; he answered many questions and carefully set out pumpkins on the ground before the children as they saw ones that might be about the right size. After much lifting, feeling, and eliminating, three pumpkins were finally selected and placed in the wagon.

I told Mr. Petersen I was very grateful and wanted to thank him for his time and for the fine pumpkins. Some of the children picked this up and also thanked Mr. Petersen, and bumpity bump bump—we were off.

On our return to kindergarten, the children were all set to carve the pumpkins immediately; but Miss Koen reminded them that it was Friday and that if the pumpkins were carved and left in the warm building over the weekend they would probably be all soft and spoiled before Halloween day. Peter suggested putting them in the icebox, but Miss Koen thought that the pumpkin smell might get into and spoil other foods. Jim suggested putting them outside in the yard, but other children thought they might get carried away. In the end the pumpkins were set near the outside door, and the carving was delayed until the next week. The children discussed how they would like their pumpkins to look, and I shared with them the poem called "Smiling," by Dixie Willson, which is found in *The Golden Flute.*

On Monday several of the children brought in colored pictures from the Sunday newspaper about jack-o'-lanterns, and one child brought a beautiful harvest picture which she had found in a magazine. One boy brought in a mask which he had bought while shopping on Saturday with his mother.

Miss Koen and I had put several new books on the library shelves. The new books included the following: *Now It's Fall,* Lois Lenski; *The Man Who Lost His Head,* Robert McCloskey; *Autumn Harvest,* Alvin Tresselt; *The Proud Pumpkin,* Nora S. Unwin; *Georgie,* Robert Bright.

We had also arranged new fall and Halloween pictures on the bulletin board. The pictures were some Miss Koen had selected and mounted in one of her university courses. During the week many orange and black, and yellow and green creations took form as the children used their clay, crayons, and paint. John made a reasonably convincing black cat, but most of the other children's creative expressions tended to be in the nature of "modern abstracts." Some children, however, who till this time had seemed to have little feeling for form gained confidence and direction in creating the big shape of the pumpkin, and from these shapes there emerged jack-o'-lanterns with real character.

While about twelve of the children worked with a variety of art media, a group of thirteen children gathered with me to carve the first jack-o'-lantern. Our plan was to surprise the others. First we spread several layers of newspapers on the floor; then, with a plastic bowl to put the seeds in and a large plastic wash basin to put the refuse in, we were ready. But were we? We needed some long-handled spoons and a strong but short sharp knife, preferably a sloyd knife. The sloyd knife we found in a special case high on a shelf, and the spoons came from the paint cupboard. Now we really were ready. As I cut the top the children quoted "I found an orange pumpkin in the barn. I cut a big slice off the top," then, "I scooped out the whole inside, because nobody told me to stop." The spoons and the pumpkin were passed around the circle, and each child had a turn "scooping." Ricky took charge of the seeds. Then, with the inside cleared, we set about planning the surprise—the character of our jack-o'-lantern. John got a pencil from the cupboard, and we drew the jack-o'-lantern's face on a smooth but rounded side of the pumpkin. Of course, the actual cutting had to be done by an adult but the planning was all a group experience. Then came the test! The flashlight was put inside, and Mr. Jack-o'-lantern glowered in a proper fiery fashion. This first group rolled up its newspapers and turned to using other creative materials as the second group of children spread out their papers and made plans for their surprise jack-o'-lantern. Later Miss Koen told the children the story of "The Jack-o'-Lantern" as found in *Told Under the Blue Umbrella.*

The first-grade children whose room adjoined ours brought in a note inviting us to a parade and party. We sent a note of acceptance, and the next days were busy. The children suggested bringing costumes from home, but since this was just our school Halloween and not our home Halloween, we decided to make everything we would wear or carry in the parade. Some made heads from stuffed paper bags which, with the teacher's help, they fastened on long sticks onto which they had nailed a shoulder crossbar. When an old doll blanket or pillow case was slipped over the shoulders, the effect was delightfully grotesque. Others made pointed hats in Halloween colors, and still others made eyeglasses, long paper curls, bracelets, shoe buckles, or just huge orange and black paper buttons for their clothes.

Music was an important part of our Halloween fun. Children like scary fun songs, and it is fun to sing in a minor key for a change. Miss K. and I selected "Halloween Is Coming" from the *Kindergarten Book* and "Jack-o'-lantern" from the *Sing and Play Book.* The first grade used "Halloween Night" from the *Music Hour, Kindergarten and First Grade* for the parade music.

The day after the Halloween party, we gave our soft droopy pumpkin to Mr. Jones, the building engineer. We don't know what he did with it, but we kept the seeds and added them to our collection of seeds that we had been making all fall. We may experiment with planting some this winter. If we don't, we will surely put some in our garden next spring. John says the seeds are good to eat, and so we may roast some, or perhaps we will use some to feed to the birds and squirrels this winter.

Miss K. and I were especially pleased with the opportunities which the interest provided for letter-writing and problem-solving. There was also opportunity for the children to weigh, measure, and count, and to consider the wise and safe use of such things as lighted candles and sharp knives. The social situation afforded by the first-grade entertainment was a most valuable experience, as was the contact made with Mr. Petersen on the farm campus. From a science point of view, the children—and I—learned a great deal about horticulture.

All in all, I felt that the unit was a satisfying experience for both the children and the teachers.

## Preparing the Child for the First Grade

No plan for a kindergarten year can be complete unless it recognizes the necessity of giving the children good preparation for the school work they will undertake in the next year and in the years to come. Gertrude Hildreth, in making a few generalizations on readiness for learning, says "A broad preparatory program is more successful than narrow techniques in developing readiness for learning. The activity program . . . with emphasis on functional learning and meaningful experiences, is the best preparation for later progress in learning skills. The activity program affords children natural opportunity for language development, manipulating materials, sensing meanings and relationships, developing work habits, and attaining social maturity."[4]

There is some statistical evidence to show that children who have had a year of kindergarten experience may be expected to do better work in first grade than those children who enter first grade straight from home.[5] The advantage for the kindergarten graduate lies not in any provable increase in intellectual status but in the fact that the child has had an opportunity to become accustomed to working with a group, to conforming to school rules, to accepting criticisms and suggestions, to expressing himself, and to solving problems. Certain kindergarten experiences are planned with the thought of facilitating the child's work in the more formal school subjects which he will meet during the next year or two.

## Reading

Anyone can read with greater ease and more speed if the subject matter and vocabulary of the text are reasonably familiar. The kindergarten affords many experiences, both group and individual, which will broaden the child's interests and add to his fund of information and vocabulary, thus building up for him a reading background. By having his attention called to careful enunciation and pronunciation in the kindergarten, the child learns to hear the exact sounds of the words he will later learn to read.

The kindergarten child learns to recognize the importance and the function of the printed word not only by having stories read to him but also through his experience in dictating letters, identifying labels, recognizing common street signs, and attempting to print his own name. Through the library and story hour, he comes to have an interest in books and a regard for their care and handling. By turning the pages and following the picture stories in a book, he learns the mechanics of turning pages, and he learns in which part of the book a story begins. The pictorial indexes found in some of our story and song books help the child understand the significance

[4] Quoted by permission from *Readiness for Learning,* p. 6. See reference at end of chapter.

[5] See Appendix, "Research Reports and Articles Helpful to the Kindergarten Teacher."

*"Your shell is like this one."*

of the index; and attempting to find the story or song by referring to the index gives him practice in interpreting printed symbols. By watching the teacher as she reads and by having the fact specifically called to his attention, he learns that the eye movement for reading carries through from left to right. This eye movement he practices in his own "play reading." Occasionally the kindergarten teacher will run her finger or place a marker under the title of a familiar story, or she will pause to show the children a printed refrain rather than reading it to them. Although actual reading has little or no place in the kindergarten, the kindergarten teacher tries always to be alert to the many opportunities in the program which can help pave the way for the actual experience of learning to read later on. Reading readiness, not reading ability, is the concern of the kindergarten teacher.[6]

## Arithmetic

Through many concrete and meaningful experiences, the kindergarten child is building a background for his later work in arithmetic. He often has occasion to count objects. If he is setting the table or pouring the orange juice, he must count the number of chairs or the number of glasses that will be needed. In stringing beads or making paper chains, the children

[6] See Appendix, "Research Reports and Articles Helpful to the Kindergarten Teacher."

invariably measure and count as they progress. Sometimes they stand about in a circle and a child is asked to count the children in the circle. A second and a third child counting the same group help verify the answer. Certain games necessitate "counting out" the children. The kindergarten child comes to know and use with perfect understanding arithmetical terms and ideas, such as add, take away, more, less, equal, longer, shorter, half, whole, and so on. Written numbers are recognized by the kindergarten child as meaningful symbols because he has followed the thermometer up and down, or he has checked the calendar, perhaps while waiting for the arrival of baby chicks. He has sought special page numbers through the index or by finding the number which has been marked with a slip of paper or some other marker. Simple addition and subtraction problems often come within the experience of the kindergarten child. He may find, for instance, that if he and his friend are to have an equal number of blocks he must "take away" two blocks from his pile and "add" two blocks to his friend's pile.

## Science

In the kindergarten which is set up for wholesome living for five-year-olds, the opportunities for science experiences are legion—plants are in the room to be observed and cared for; outdoor space is provided for gardening; experiments are set up for the observation of germination; goldfish, hamsters, white mice, parakeets, and canaries are in the kindergarten permanently or temporarily; scales, thermometers, and measuring units, both those made in the kindergarten and commercially produced ones, are available for experimentation and for providing answers to real problems; magnifying glasses, magnets, air pumps, batteries, and other such materials are available for experimentation and practical purposes as well. In addition, one must remember that just in the ordinary business of daily living a kindergarten teacher stands ready to answer or to help the child find the answers to such questions as "What kind of insect is this?" "Is this a seed or a stone?" "Why do leaves fall?" "How do bees make honey?" "Why do some birds go south in winter?" "What do the birds that stay here in the winter eat?" "Where do turtles go in winter?" "Why did the milk in our milk bottle push the top off the bottle?" "Why can't we eat this white snow?" "How much does this pumpkin weigh?" "How can they grow oranges if the oranges don't have any seeds in them?" "What makes it get dark at night?" "Why do satellites stay up in the sky?" "How does God keep the sun hot?" And on and on the questions go! Each question answered, or better yet, each question made answerable by experimentation or observation, provides the child with experience and understanding in science.

## Writing

Any of the many activities in the kindergarten, such as drawing, painting, modeling, cutting, and pasting, which involves the coordination of eye and hand movement tend to make learning to write more simple. The child who is helped to hold his crayon correctly or who is taught to use the side of the chalk when marking on the chalkboard is learning some of the fundamentals of writing. Many children learn to print their own names while they are in kindergarten, and some even venture to make captions for their pictures or to print signs for the kindergarten store, airport, garden, and the like. One never knows where an interest in printing may lead among kindergarten children. In one group the collecting of autographs flourished for days. In some instances the names were indicated by a scribble only. Some names were composed of a series of scattered letters, others were set down sequentially in capital letters, a few names were set down in manuscript writing, and in one case a name was laboriously set down in script. At the kindergarten level we are not too concerned, of course, with the form the child's autograph may take. We can expect, though, that because capitals are easier to make than lowercase letters and because he probably sees more capitals than lowercase letters in billboard, magazine, and TV advertising, he will naturally use capital letters in setting down his name. We can show him how his name will look in manuscript and the way he will learn to write his name in the first grade if we use manuscript writing to identify his locker, his possessions, or his work projects. As the year progresses, it is to be expected that a child will identify his own products by appending to them his own signature. Capitals or capitals *and* lowercase letters—let's accept the child's choice as his signature in the kindergarten. Whenever the teacher writes, as she frequently does, on the chalkboard or the easel, she will always use capital or lowercase letters as the situation demands, and further she will frequently direct the children's attention to the direction she must follow in correctly forming her letters.

## Music

Most kindergartens have daily music periods, as well as incidental music throughout the day. These music experiences not only afford the child immediate joy and satisfaction but also provide opportunities for developing music skills and appreciation. The kindergarten child has frequent opportunities to listen carefully and to respond freely to the rhythm and mood of music. He has practice in matching tones, in singing phrases, and in picking out tunes on instruments. By the end of the year he has acquired a repertoire of songs and rhythmic patterns. Furthermore, he has begun to appreciate and enjoy good folk music and simple classical and good modern music. In short, the kindergarten has helped the child build a good foundation for his further study and enjoyment of music.

## SUMMARY

Seasonal happenings, current events, and the background experiences and needs of the group determine to a large extent the areas of interest which will be pursued during the kindergarten year. The area of interest may be thought of as the vehicle which brings activity into and carries knowledge out of the classrom. Major interests simply channel the group thinking; they do not in any way exclude other interests and experiences. As the child progresses through the year, he comes to have some appreciation of the way in which life as a whole fits together, and he builds for himself foundations for future learning. No plan for the kindergarten year is complete unless it recognizes the necessity of building good foundation learnings. Foundations for reading, arithmetic, science, writing, and music are all structured in a good kindergarten.

## QUESTIONS AND PROBLEMS

1. Outline one of the following subjects as though you had developed it as an area of interest in your kindergarten: the farm, the home, the grocery store, the circus, the seashore, airplanes or trains.
2. Would you plan to develop the same interests with your group each year? Why or why not?
3. What leads for activity interests do you find in the following statements made by kindergarten children:
   a. "Next summer my daddy and my mother and I, we are all going to England on a big boat."
   b. "We went out to the lake yesterday and my mother was digging and down under the old wet leaves she found some little blue flowers just starting to grow. They were all kind of fuzzy looking."
   c. "There is a hole in our big tree and I saw a bird fly into it; but I didn't see him come out."
4. Make a list of those things in your community around which areas of interest might be developed. Which, if any, of these interests would be geographically limited to your community?
5. Assume that you are developing with your children an interest dealing with airplanes. How might this interest differ if it were to be developed early in the school year or late in the school year?
6. Reread "A Halloween Interest" and classify under such headings as reading, science, arithmetic, and so on, the many experiences involved in the development of the interest.

## SELECTED REFERENCES

Association for Childhood Education International, Washington, D.C.:
*How Good Is Our Kindergarten*, Bulletin No. 65, 1959.
*Portfolio for Kindergarten Teachers*, Bulletin No. 2, 1951.
*Reading in the Kindergarten?* Bulletin 6-A, 1962.

Berson, Minnie Perrin, *Kindergarten—Your Child's Big Step*, New York, E. P. Dutton & Company, 1959.

Ellis, Mary Jackson, *The Kindergarten Log*, Minneapolis, T. S. Denison & Company, Vol. I, 1955, Vol. II, 1960.

Hammond, Sarah Lou, Ruth J. Dales, Doris Sikes Skipper, and Ralph L. Witherspoon, *Good Schools for Young Children*, New York, Macmillan Company, 1963.

Hildreth, Gertrude, and Others, *Readiness for Learning*, Bulletin, Washington, D.C., Association for Childhood Education International, 1941.

Imhoff, Myrtle, *Early Elementary Education*, New York, Appleton-Century-Crofts, 1959.

Leonard, Edith, Dorothy VanDeman, and Lillian Miles, *Foundations of Learning in Childhood Education*, Columbus, Ohio, Charles E. Merrill Books, Inc., 1963.

Logan, Lillian, *Teaching the Young Child: Methods of Pre-School and Primary Education*, Boston, Houghton Mifflin Company, 1960.

National Education Association, Washington, D.C.:
*Foundation Learnings in the Kindergarten*, Bulletin, 1958.
*Your Child and Reading*, Bulletin, 1963.

Sheehy, Emma D., *The Fives and Sixes Go to School*, New York, Henry Holt and Company, 1959.

State and Local Guides for Kindergarten Teaching.[7]

Wills, Clarice D., and William H. Stegeman, *Living in the Kindergarten*, rev., Chicago, Follett Publishing Company, 1956.

[7] See text and footnote, p. 157.

# 11

# THE WORK PERIOD

The work period in the modern kindergarten

- Offers frequent opportunities for the child to meet concrete problem-solving situations.
- Helps the child acquire the ability to plan and carry out individual or group projects.
- Encourages the child to complete a task once begun.
- Acquaints the child with the various materials available for self-expression.
- Offers an opportunity for the child to learn to work harmoniously with others, sharing ideas and materials.
- Offers the child opportunities to engage in activities that will develop motor skills.
- Helps the child establish habits of orderliness in both room upkeep and care of materials.
- Affords the child the joy and satisfaction which experimentation and achievement bring.

## Types of Kindergarten Work Periods

There are three types of work periods found in the kindergarten today. While this chapter is concerned chiefly with only one of these types, we shall mention briefly the techniques of the other two.

The first, the directed-lesson type, really belongs to another kindergarten age, but it is still used today and, under some conditions and on some occasions, has value. The directed lesson is planned in detail by the teacher. When the children sit down at their tables they are expected to wait for the materials with which they are to work and the instructions for handling them. The group proceeds to carry out, step by step, the directions given by the teacher. Much help usually has to be given the less able children. This type of work period, when used, is allotted from fifteen to thirty minutes in the program of the day; it is frequently accompanied by tears!

The second type of work period, the semidirected or semicreative, is—as its name suggests—neither one thing nor the other. In this period the children may be seen scattered about the room using a variety of materials and making many different things. Each child seems to be doing creative work. The child usually feels that he is doing his own thinking and his own work; but when the situation is examined, it is found that the teacher is merely couching her directions in such a fashion as to convince not only the child but herself that the planning and executing are being done by the child. This type of work period can consume from thirty to forty minutes of the kindergarten session.

The third type of work period, the problem-solving or truly creative, is one in which the children are challenged with real problems. It may be that a fence is needed to keep the dogs from running into the garden. How and by whom shall it be made? The playhouse may need new dishes. What material is there in the kindergarten that can be used for dishes, what dishes are most needed, and how can they be made attractive? Or it may be that some pictures are needed, both for room decoration and as a record of a trip the group made to the house under construction down the block. What materials shall be used and what are some of the most interesting things to tell about the trip? Perhaps Jimmy was not present on the day the group went on the trip. How about making a special record of the trip to show him? Individual problems, as well as group problems, can be met in a work period of this type. Perhaps some child has been thinking a great deal about boats or has enjoyed a book about boats from the library. The wood is in the wood box; how can he make a boat he can float in the tank of water? Or perhaps some child's mother has a birthday. The child has thought about making her a tray, or maybe a pad for jotting down notes in the kitchen, but then he sees other children designing doilies for the luncheon tables, and he decides he will make his mother a set of doilies for her birthday. Now he is really faced with a problem! What shape shall they be? What paper shall he use? What colors would his mother like?

Whatever the problem, and whether it is group or individual in its nature, the process by which a solution is reached involves combining and testing ideas. It is through this that a broad base is built for future learning. In the problem-solving type of work period, the children are usually to be found scattered about the room using a variety of materials. The teacher is not conspicuously in evidence, but she is there, with each child's problem pretty clearly in mind. A laboratory atmosphere pervades the room, and the teacher stands by, ready to suggest, guide, praise, criticize, judge, and admire both effort and achievement. She is ready to give help when help is really needed, but she makes it a point to do neither the child's thinking nor his work for him. A work period of this kind may be anywhere from thirty to sixty minutes in length, and it often extends beyond its allotted time.

The materials used and the articles made in the three types of work periods may be identical, but the teaching techniques used during the periods differ tremendously. The following sections give examples of the way in which the making of a cardboard house might be handled from the three points of view.

## A Directed Experience

In the directed-lesson type of period, the children are usually working as a group sitting about the table. In this case the children have before them their half-finished cardboard houses. The wallpaper has been pasted on two walls; one wall has as yet no wallpaper. The teacher has marked the wallpaper so that if the child cuts on the line marked, the paper will exactly fit the wall. Each child has a pair of scissors, and when the paper is passed out, the children are instructed to cut very carefully "on the line." When the child has cut his paper he is requested to wait until all are through, when further instructions will be giver. The children are directed to turn their paper over so that the design of flowers is underneath, and then they are directed to put paste all around the edge. When the paste has been applied, the teacher helps each child in turn to put the paper smoothly and neatly into place. The teacher writes the name on each child's house, and the houses are collected and put in a row in the cupboard. At the end of the day they are taken home to admiring parents.

## A Semidirected Experience

In the semidirected and semicreative work period, the children are usually working on individual projects. One child is working on a cardboard house, which is finished except for the wallpaper on one side and the chimney. The child comes up to the teacher with his house. "Have you pasted the wallpaper on this side?" asks the teacher, pointing to the side on which there is no wallpaper. "No," answers the child. "Well," says the teacher, "then you will have to do that next, won't you?" "Yes," answers the child. Thereupon the teacher picks up a piece of wallpaper and measures it on the wall of the house, cuts it to fit the side of the wall, and hands it to the child, saying, "Put your paste just along the edge, here and here and here." Soon the child, walking about the room, is showing everyone the house that *he* has made. When he takes it home, mother and father marvel at the *child's* ability.

## A Problem-Solving Experience

The children are scattered about the room working on a variety of individual and group problems. One child is making a cardboard house like the one his big sister's friend made. It is made from a large hatbox which he has brought from home and, except for the wallpaper on one side and the chimney, it appears to be complete.

The child stands by his worktable, and as the teacher passes he looks up to see if she notices his work. She smiles her appreciation and says, "Your work is progressing nicely, isn't it? I notice that you already have the wallpaper on two walls of your house." The child smiles back and says, "And now I need some paper for the other wall." Whereupon the teacher says, "I think there is some paper in that box which will match yours." The child goes to the box and comes back beaming in a few seconds, saying, "Here's a piece just like mine, only it's too big." "So it is," says the teacher. "What are you going to do about that?" The child looks up and says in a very knowing tone, "I'm going to cut it off." With that he gets a pair of scissors, puts the paper on the outside of his house, holds it with one hand, and cuts it with the other. The imperfections in the result, the inaccuracy in size, and the occasional jagged cut in the side disturb neither teacher nor pupil. Filled with the desire to carry out his purpose, the child gets his paste, applies it to the inside wall of the house, and spreads his paper. Then he brings his box house over to the teacher again. While the teacher looks at it he remarks, "The paper won't go on very smooth," and the teacher suggests that the next time it might be wise to put the paste on the paper, that perhaps it would stay in place if paste were put only on the edges; and she adds that then it would not take so much paste. The child says, "That's a good idea." He takes his finished house over to show it at the meeting which will be held later. He then starts to clean his work area.

The child may have spent his entire work period or even several work periods on his house. His finished product is crude, and unless the parents are educated to understand the importance of problem-solving, they may not appreciate it fully. Perhaps the teacher can find an excellent reason for leaving the house at the kindergarten. Then someday when Mother is visiting kindergarten, she will see her child's product and hear about its evolution. Mother will note that the product is comparable to the achievements of other five-year-old children. What is more, if she is an intelligent observer, she will note that every child in the group is doing not only his own work but also his own thinking.

## Initiating the Work Period

In helping the children outline their plans for the work period, the teacher must be sure that a variety of rich ideas has been presented to the group. These ideas grow out of experience and are usually shared and discussed in the period directly preceding the word period. The teacher must guide the planning so that not all the children will want to use limited material or space simultaneously.

For example, a discussion period centered around the needs of the kindergarten playhouse, if not wisely directed, can lead to three-fourths of the group's wanting to start work on chairs and tables for the house. Obviously twenty or more children cannot be working at the workbench and sharing the tools at the same time. Three to five would be a much better number. The teacher need not dictate what each child is to do; but through her suggestions she can guide the choice of activities into different channels. In handling large groups of children, it is sometimes wise for the teacher to write down, as they develop in the discussion period, the possible activities which may be engaged in. Then under each heading she can list the names or the number of the children who plan to engage in each activity. If this list is put on the blackboard, the children can see for themselves just how their plans are working out. The kindergarten child cannot really read the printed words, but from the teacher's explanation and the grouping of the symbols he can see how many people plan to engage in a particular activity. Incidentally, this is one of the many experiences that help lay a foundation for reading.

If, after the plans for the work period have been discussed and most of the children have decided on their undertaking for the day, there are still children who do not know what they would like to do, the teacher may take further time to help them formulate their plans. Some of these children may not be up to the level of the others in development, and may be interested in little beyond the manipulation of beads, pegs, sand, and blocks.[1] As the teacher observes such children go about their work, she must be alert to behavior that may indicate causes of their apparent immaturity. She must guard against letting these children get into the habit of waiting until the others have started working before they pretend to think or plan. Or, more serious than this, they must not be allowed to get into

[1] See pp. 454–456.

the habit of expecting the teacher to do all their thinking for them. It is hoped that as the year progresses there will be fewer and fewer occasions for separate discussions with these children.

When the discussion meeting is concluded, each child ought to have clearly in mind the particular problem he is going to attack. The child's plans may change tremendously as he works but, no matter how much his plans will be altered in the work period, he ought to leave the discussion period with some definite undertaking in mind.

In order to avoid congestion at the beginning of the work period, the teacher will have to devise some method for dismissing the children a few at a time from the discussion group. Sometimes she suggests that all the children who are going to use a particular material leave the group at the same time. Often the division into small groups is made on the basis of those who have work to finish and those who are starting new work. At times the teacher may find it well to choose first those children who have in mind exactly what they plan to do. Occasionally the group may be asked to observe how a particular child goes about his work, noting how very businesslike his manner is. The approach to the work period can lend tone to the whole hour.

## Arrangements for the Work Period

The room itself has much to do with the type of work done in the work period. Too often the teacher dresses the room up to such an extent that the children do not feel free to be creative. In general, the kindergarten room should resemble a laboratory more than a parlor, conservatory, or museum.

The equipment of the room ought to be such that the child can use it without feeling unduly inhibited. For example, it would be folly to have a carefully painted workbench in the room. Since a workbench is meant to be used for hard, rough work, it should be made of solid, unstained wood that will stand many blows and an occasional misdirected nail. If possible, the regular tables should be finished so that the children can wash them when they need to remove crayon marks, clay, or paste. Battleship linoleum similar to that used in floors makes an adequate table top; but Formica, a covering frequently found on restaurant or kitchen counters, is most satisfactory. There should be enough wastebaskets, brooms, dustpans, cleaning cloths, and brushes to suggest to the children their responsibility for the care of the room. The children should always feel that the room belongs to them and that they are therefore responsible for its appearance and care.

There ought to be in the kindergarten room an abundance of material to which the children have access. Much of it should be in low, spacious cupboards. Materials which are used every day, such as paper, crayons, scissors, paste, and wood, should be within easy reach, while such things as cloth, enamel paints, tissue paper, tagboard, and the like may be kept on shelves that are less accessible. In stocking the cupboards, the teacher must consider the allocation of materials and put together those materials which will be used together. In order to avoid congestion when the materials are being taken out or replaced, she must try to scatter types of supplies in different sections of the room. It would be unwise, for example, to have the supplies of paint, crayons, clay, and wood all in one area of the room.

## The Function of the Teacher in the Work Period

It is probably more difficult for the observer to discern exactly what the teacher is doing in the work period than in any other period in the kindergarten day. Though she keeps herself as much as possible in the background, she is alert to the whole environment, and she tries to have a friendly, earnest, scientific curiosity about all she observes.

At all times she attempts to give the impression of being interestedly occupied. One teacher who failed to give this impression was accosted by a small girl who said: "Say, Miss D——, don't you ever do any work?" Then, finding the teacher at a loss for an answer, the child added, "Oh, I suppose you do your work at home, don't you, Miss D——?" Often the teacher settles down with the children to do work with them. She makes their interests her interests and attempts to use the materials in much the same way as they are used by the children.

She must always be ready to admire or justly criticize the efforts and work of the children. Thus she will help the individual child keep up to his own best accomplishment, and make sure that through the year the child is advancing not only in the number of materials with which he is experimenting but also in the number of ideas he is venturing to express through the materials. The teacher must also encourage the child to see one piece of work finished before he starts on another. This does not, of course, preclude the possibility of immediate interests' taking precedence over remote interests.

If work such as pouring paint or lifting a large board into place for the roof of a house is really too difficult for the child, the teacher must be willing to help. Most inexperienced teachers err on the side of offering help when it is not really needed or desired. But if a child is using tools in a dangerous manner, the teacher must redirect his use of the tools. If a particular grouping of individuals seems to result in undesirable social behavior, the teacher must take steps to reorganize the group. She must be alert to the opportunities which arise for establishing good health habits and habits of courtesy. Through her own example, she can do much to raise the standard of politeness and encourage the use of quiet, well-modulated voices.

Throughout the period, the teacher must strive to help the children maintain a workshop or laboratory spirit. She must stimulate the sharing of both materials and ideas. The children should be encouraged to learn when and how to get help when help is needed, and they should be encouraged to know when and how to give help when help is needed.

If for one reason or another the teacher feels that the work period is not proceeding profitably for most of the group, it is her responsibility to call the group together and, through further discussion, arrive at a better approach.

## Cleaning Up After the Work Period

If properly conducted, the cleaning-up period can be one of the most enjoyable, and it certainly is one of the most valuable, periods in the kindergarten day. Each child ought first of all to be responsible for the condition and order of his own materials and work space. If, after he has finished his own cleaning, he is willing to help another child, the work will progress rapidly and happily. The children may be expected to wash their own paintbrushes, wipe or scrub their easels, put away their own crayons in the proper box, replace their carpentry tools, brush off the workbench, put back into the cases blocks which are not part of structures to be left standing, close the sandbox, sweep up the sand, put small paste jars in the cupboard, wash paste sticks, remove paste and crayon marks from the table, pick up or sweep up the scraps from the floor, and arrange the furniture for the next activities. If the program can be so planned that a library period will follow the cleaning period, then no organized group activity will be interrupted by those who are somewhat slow. Plenty of brooms, dustpans, wastepaper baskets, cleaning cloths, and scrub brushes will help make this an interesting activity period. Responsibility shared by every child in the group and backed by as little teacher dominance as possible will enliven what might otherwise be mere drudgery.

## Adapting the Activities to the Progress of the Group

There are so many activities carried on in a good work period, and the activities vary so greatly from day to day and from one part of the year to another, that it is difficult to give any clear ideas of the program of the activities of the work period for either a day or a year. Certain general trends, however, may suggest the developmental program through the year.

In the beginning of the year the teacher will be stressing the social side of the work period. Many of the activities, therefore, are really socializing activities, not, technically, work activities at all. However, while dollhouse play, play on the gymnasium apparatus, looking at books, manipulative play of all sorts (including play with beads and pegs, and purely manipulative block and sand play) might all legitimately belong in the work period in the beginning of the year, to continue the same activities in the work period throughout the year would be to build up an erroneous idea of work. First-grade teachers sometimes say that when kindergarten children enter first grade they lack a sense of responsibility about an undertaking. One can readily understand how this criticism might be made of those kindergarten teachers who never, through the opportunities offered in the work period, help the children acquire good work habits.

As the year progresses, kindergarten children may be expected to profit by purposing for themselves, with the aid of the teacher, quite definite undertakings. They should be able to profit also by seeing their work through to completion. This does not mean that the kindergarten child is expected to "keep his nose to the grindstone" and work to exhaustion. Not at all! For the kindergarten child, the work period is one of the happiest and most delightful periods in the day; it is a time of achievement.

Before the kindergarten year is ended, the children may be expected not only to organize their own efforts toward a given purpose but also, with the aid of the teacher, to organize their efforts into cooperative undertakings centered about a variety of interests. The plan of the kindergarten year as outlined in Chapter 10 can be a guide to the interests around which the activities of the work period may be organized.

There are unlimited possibilities for the activities of the work period. These activities will be determined primarily by the interest of the week or of the month. They will be determined in part, of course, by the abilities and previous experiences of the group, and in part, necessarily, by the limitations of the kindergarten equipment.

If the interest is centered about the home, for example, the teacher need only begin a discussion of those things in a real home which could be made for the playhouse, and she will be flooded with suggestions for making play furniture, curtains, dishes, rugs, pictures, books, kitchen equipment, and so on. Some of the articles suggested require considerably more skill to make than others. Suppose some child suggests making a "piano." If the group has just entered school, it will be well to make a countersuggestion of making some simpler article first, with the hope of advancing to the play piano later on.

No comprehensive list could be drawn up of all the constructions which could be made by the children in connection with any one interest. Suffice it to say that the alert teacher will be quick to recognize which of the children's ideas are feasible, which can be developed with little adult help, which will require the cooperation of several children, and, above all, which will seem important and worthwhile from the point of view of the child. Unless the child feels that his work is worth his time and effort, the main incentive of the work period is lost. The child who does not sense any purposefulness in his work may well feel as the kindergarten child did in the cartoon—sitting at a table with six or seven others, he threw up his hands and cried, "Color, cut out, and paste! Color, cut out, and paste! Where does it get me, anyway?"

## Equipment and Materials—Their Care and Use

On the following pages you will find a few suggestions concerning (a) work period materials and equipment and (b) the teacher's and the children's responsibility for these materials and equipment. No attempt has been made to set down the many things which might be made from the materials; for specific suggestions concerning the many, many ideas that might be developed through the use of available materials, see the starred references at the end of this chapter.

APRONS The kindergarten usually has a few aprons on hand for emergencies, but it is wise to encourage the children to bring from home something in the nature of a "coverall." Father's old shirt—with sleeves cut short and the collar removed—when worn with buttons down the back makes a surprisingly satisfactory substitute for a smock. Aprons designed like those worn by the neighborhood butcher are adjustable. If these aprons have long wrap-around ties, the children can easily tie them in a loose knot in front. Those aprons made of plastic, oilcloth, or similar materials have the advantage of thoroughly protecting the garments under the apron, but since they are nonabsorbent, the paint often runs down the apron onto clothes or shoes below. A heavy gingham, or perhaps better yet, a thoroughly absorbent terry cloth, is probably as satisfactory a material as any for the kindergarten work apron.

BLACKBOARDS AND CHALK When is a blackboard not a black board? When it is a green board! Many green boards are better than black boards for chalk work, and certainly they are much more attractive. In most kindergarten rooms adapted from former classrooms, far too much wall space is given over to chalkboards. A chalkboard three feet high and six feet long is probably large enough for the ordinary kindergarten room. If there is surplus chalkboard space, it may be covered with burlap, compo, or cork board and used as bulletin board space. Sometimes the covering is fitted over a removable frame so that the space can be used alternately as a chalkboard or a bulletin board.

Chalkboard painting is fun. Pictures which vanish like magic can be made by painting on the chalkboard with clear water. Either a brush or a sponge can be used. Although most of the chalkboard drawing is done with white chalk, there ought to be a limited amount of colored chalk on hand for very special work. Colored chalk may also be used to good advantage on either wet or dry paper.

If too many erasers are supplied, the children tend to become more interested in the erasing activity than in the drawing itself. Two or three erasers should be sufficient for the ordinary kindergarten. Erasers should be cleaned frequently, and erased chalkboards should be washed daily. Nothing makes a room look more untidy than great expanses of chalkboard covered with chalk dust. Children from other grades often enjoy coming into the kindergarten after school to wash the boards and to help the kindergarten teacher with other simple housekeeping duties.

BLOCKS Whenever possible, the teacher should suggest that block-building take place in an area of the room where there is likely to be little congestion. If the blocks are stored in movable chests or shelves, these can frequently serve as boundary enclosures for building activities. Large block structures which can remain intact and grow—or at least be used—from day to day afford some of the best opportunities for both problem-solving and dramatic play.

While the large building blocks may serve many purposes in the kindergarten, we must not overlook the fact that the small blocks also have a place. These blocks not only lend themselves to certain kinds of building but also frequently have special appeal for the shy, unaggressive child, who seems to get great satisfaction from working with construction materials he can manipulate by himself.

CLOTH Although one tends to associate cloth with sewing, there are other things which can be done with it that are far better adapted to the kindergarten child's stage of motor development. It can be used, for example, for upholstering furniture, for making tops for automobiles, for making sails for sailboats, and for making puppet-stage curtains. It also makes a good background for certain crayon and paint work, and, of course, squares of bright colored material are always a welcome addition to the dress-up box or trunk.[2]

[2] For further suggestions concerning the use of cloth, cutting, and sewing, see Chapter 7.

"The nose on the rocket is tipping—I'll fix it."

University of Minnesota

Cooking Equipment and Supplies The kindergarten needs to be equipped with some kind of cooking unit—an electric plate will do. A few utensils, such as spoons, knives, a measuring cup, a mixing bowl, and a cooking pan, along with a baking pan or cookie sheet, should also be available. Children enjoy participating in cooking experiences, and part of the fun lies in the planning. Hands, aprons, and kitchen area should be clean, of course, before the actual preparation of food gets under way.

In most communities children can be counted on to bring from home the ingredients to be used in cooking. Cooking experiences must be planned several days in advance in order to assure the arrival of the ingredients, and it is usually wise to have several volunteers for specific ingredients just in case the child forgets or is unable to bring in his contribution. Sometimes it helps children remember that they have volunteered to bring such ingredients as apples, sugar, cream, or vegetables if they draw and cut out pictures of the item or items they hope to be able to bring. The picture of the article which the teacher pins on the child's coat may in no way resemble the real article, but at least it will challenge mother to ask about the symbol, and it will remind the child to speak about his plans. In some communities or at times where there is a high incidence of a disease such as hepatitis, cooking is not permitted in the kindergarten. In situations where cooking is permitted but where extra precautions must be taken, supplies are not brought from home, and the children do not take an active part in the mixing process. Instead the teacher does the actual mixing, but she makes a point of using a transparent bowl, so that all can see just what is happening. The baking process is much more interesting, too, if it can be observed. A device as simple as an electric skillet with a pyrex top will provide this opportunity.

CRAYONS In most kindergartens the children do not have individual boxes of crayons but use crayons from the general supply. The cupboard in which crayons are kept should be in such a position that it gets the best of light. In order to help the children identify crayon colors easily, crayons of different colors may be kept in small open metal boxes painted to match the crayons they hold. On the cupboard door or on a shelf nearby there should be a piece of paper on which the children can test the color of the crayons: frequently blue, purple, and black crayons are indistinguishable even when the boxes are marked.

If the child is working on a picture or design that necessitates his crayoning to the edge of his paper, he is almost sure to make marks on the table. He may be reminded to put newspaper or other paper under his work to save himself the job of scrubbing off the marks with soap and water. Crayon marks on wood, linoleum, or other hard surfaces can be removed with turpentine but, since the smell is not pleasant, it is probably wise to expect the child to remove his accidental table or floor marks with soap and water and a little muscle work.

Kindergarten children are usually in a symbolic or schematic stage of drawing. They do not draw what they see before them, but rather what they know about the thing before them. It is better to let them express and clarify their ideas through their drawing than to provide patterns to copy.

EASELS AND PAINT CONTAINERS An easel is certainly not essential for kindergarten painting, but it does afford the child a painting experience he usually has not had at home. In some schoolrooms the easel and the chalkboard area can be used interchangeably. The whole area, including chalkboard trough, can be pulled out to form one long easel at which from three to five children can paint at one time. In other rooms the easel is provided by tying a board, approximately twenty inches by twenty-six inches, to the back legs of a chair which has been inverted on an ordinary table. The commercial double easel which comes in adjustable heights has some things to be said in its favor.

Containers for paint jars, cups, or glasses are sometimes attached directly below the easel board, but unless they are well below the painting area, the brushes which stand in the paint tend to be in the way of the painter. Often the paint stands on a table near the easel, or on the floor if the child is painting on a floor board or "floor easel." If jars, cups, glasses, or even empty cream or cut-down milk cartons are secured by being sunk in a wooden frame or heavy corrugated paper box, there is little danger of the paints being tipped and spilled. It is desirable to place under any painting area a piece of linoleum or compo board from which inevitable paint drippings can be wiped easily. A cloth should always be at hand for emergency "paint runs," as well as for the paint drips.

## Modeling Materials

Clay, plasticine, modeling dough, sawdust and paste, papier-mâché, homemade salt-and-flour dough, asbestos powder and paste, and wallpaper cleaner all afford the child the opportunity to make a three-dimensional impression of one sort or another.

Clay Clay is best kept in earthen or plastic containers which can be tightly covered. With three containers, each approximately three gallons in capacity, the clay can always be kept in usable condition. In the first jar the teacher can put dry bulk clay or old, discarded, unpainted clay articles, and the clay can then be covered with water. After the clay has soaked for a day or more, part of it can be drained by lifting portions with a trowel or spoon and permitting surplus water to run back into the container. This drained clay, as it is ready, can be placed in the second container. Next some of the clay from the second container can be removed and put into a mound on a tray or board. The total mass of clay on the tray or board should be covered with paper towels or a heavy cloth to prevent a crust from forming as the clay dries. When the clay is dry enough to work into balls (it may take five or six hours or longer, depending on the humidity in the room), they can be dropped onto a slightly raised wooden platform in the third container. If there is approximately an inch of water under the platform the balls—which, by the way, are about the size of an orange—will remain properly moist for use. They will, that is, if the cover is kept on the container! If the cover is kept on and if it is tight fitting, the balls of clay should remain moist almost indefinitely. Once the cycle of clay containers is started, clay will always be on hand when needed. If powdered instead of dry clay is used, the supply in container number three can be made ready for use almost immediately upon demand. With powdered clay, a three-to-one proportion of clay to water will form a mixture which can be made into a pliable ball. If the objects made are to be baked, or even if the unbaked articles are to be expected to hold together well, then the clay must be both wedged and aged. The already-prepared clay is somewhat more expensive than the dry bulk or the powdered clay, but it is certainly easier to handle and if the airtight plastic bags in which it is shipped are not punctured, it is ready for use at any time. The larger five pound lots in which it is packaged can be easily cut by placing a strong string or pliable wire under the mass of clay, bringing the two ends of the string or wire up, crossing them and pulling them downward with a firm steady draw.

Oilcloth, heavy paper, old magazines, or individual clay boards made of plywood may be used on the table when clay work is being done. The clay board has several advantages over the oilcloth or paper. First, the clay board will serve as a tray on which to carry the clay; second, it provides a firm surface on which to work; and third, it can be scrubbed and put away as each child finishes his work. A washable rug placed under the modeler's chair saves a tremendous amount of clay trackage about the room. When the child has finished his modeling, he can fold the corners of the rug to the middle and carry the clay crumbs to the wastebasket. Kindergarten children need few if any tools to manipulate their clay; a pencil or a nail and perhaps a jar cover will usually answer most of their needs. When elaborate tools are supplied, children tend to become so engrossed in the manipulation of the tools that they frequently lose sight of their plans.

Kindergarten children are usually more successful with clay if they work from the ball or mass rather than using a coil technique. If an article is to be worked on over a period of two or more days (which is not likely), it is well to wrap it in a damp cloth and store it in an airtight container, such as a plastic bag twisted at the end and secured with a piece of wire twist. Clay articles must dry thoroughly before being painted. The five-year-old child does not profit greatly by having a model before him. He may look at, study, and talk about an object before he begins modeling, but when he actually does begin, it is well to remove the model, for if he tries to follow it, he often becomes so absorbed in particular details that he loses sight of or becomes discouraged about the whole which he is trying to achieve.

Plasticine Plasticine is not intended as a substitute for clay. It is simply another medium through which the child can express himself. Plasticine is like clay in that it can be pinched and molded into any desired shape. It is unlike clay in that it never hardens. Some teachers contend that plasticine is neither sanitary nor pliable enough for young children to use; others maintain that it carries its own disinfectant. If kept in a covered tin box like a breadbox and placed on or near the radiator, the plasticine will always be ready for use. Old plasticine which has become dry and lifeless can be reconditioned by working a bit of Vaseline into it.

Play Dough Play dough is a modeling material which is excellent for those who are in the manipulative or symbolic stage of modeling. It is pliable, colorful, nontoxic, and reasonably long-lasting. The play dough on the market retains its pliability over a long period of time. Homemade play dough is not so long-lasting as the commercial product, but it can afford the young child equally satisfying experiences. The dough can be made by combining one part of flour, a half part of salt, a fourth to a half part of water, and adding to this several teaspoons of alum and some vegetable coloring. If this homemade dough is kept in a plastic bag and placed in a cool place, it will be usable over a period of days and even weeks.

Other Materials Asbestos powder mixed with semiliquid paste, or even with powdered paste and water, will also produce a doughlike modeling material. Articles made from this composition will dry to a fairly hard consistency, but they tend to disintegrate or crumble easily. Pliable wallpaper cleaner also makes a good doughlike modeling material, and we must not overlook plain gingerbread or other cookie doughs as modeling materials. Gingerbread men, houses, hearts, and flowers made from cookie dough have the added advantage of being bakable and edible—a feature most distinctly in their favor!

If the articles are designed for eating, the same concern for sanitary conditions must be exercised, of course, as in an actual cooking experience. Children should be provided with clean smocks or aprons, hands should be thoroughly washed, and the table on which the modeling is being done should be thoroughly scrubbed. It is well for each modeler to have under his work a piece of heavy wax paper.

Sawdust and Paste The fine sawdust which comes from hardwood or, for that matter, any sawdust which has been put through a reasonably fine sieve makes a good base for a modeling material which will dry, if given days and weeks, to a hard, woodlike consistency. A pliable mix made from two cups of sawdust and one cup of semiliquid paste can be used to make mass, hard-drying forms, such as balls and eggs, or relief surfaces on solid backgrounds. Sawdust and paste can also serve as a good substitute for the more expensive commercial wood-fillers.

Papier-Mâché Strips and Papier-Mâché Pulp Papier-mâché strips which have been made from newspaper cut into approximately one-half inch strips and run through flour and water or some other liquid-paste mixture may be used for construction work. They may be applied in diagonal designs over basic forms such as bowls to make masks; to grapefruits or oranges to make rattles; or to wooden or wire frames to make animals. If this kind of work is undertaken in the kindergarten, it is usually in the nature of a group project. Each interested child contributes a bit of his time and effort to applying the six or more coverings essential for a finished product. If the finished product is to be removed from its form, the original base must be well covered with Vaseline or petroleum jelly. Papier-mâché pulp to be used for solid or relief-modeling is made by pouring boiling water over torn scraps or strips of newspaper and allowing the mixture to stand overnight. After the whole is mashed into a pulp and the excess water squeezed out, wallpaper paste or plain flour-and-water paste is mixed with the pulp. Salt is often added to keep the mixture from spoiling.

## Paint

Poster Paint The first requisite of water colors to be used by young children is that they be opaque in quality. Poster paint having an opaque quality comes in either powder or liquid form. If powdered paint is used, the teacher usually has it ready-mixed for the children's use. About two tablespoons of the paint powder is needed to make one glass of paint. In mixing the powder and water, it is well to add the water slowly. Red paint is by far the most difficult to mix, and it has three other distinguishing characteristics. It is the most popular color, it is usually the most expensive powder, and its stain is the most difficult to remove from garments. The paint purchased in liquid form seems much more expensive than that in powder form, but it can be diluted to such an extent that it really is no more expensive in the end. Liquid paint is easier to prepare for use. Not too much of any poster paint should be mixed at one time, for if it is allowed to stand over a period of several weeks, the odor can become very disagreeable. Paint which has been mixed should be kept in tightly covered jars. Plastic syrup pitchers also make good containers for mixed poster paints.

When filling the containers into which the children will dip their brushes, one should always remember that the young child is sure to dip his brush to the very bottom of the container. Therefore, if the brush handle is to remain reasonably free from paint, the amount of paint in the container should never be more than will cover the brush hairs. If

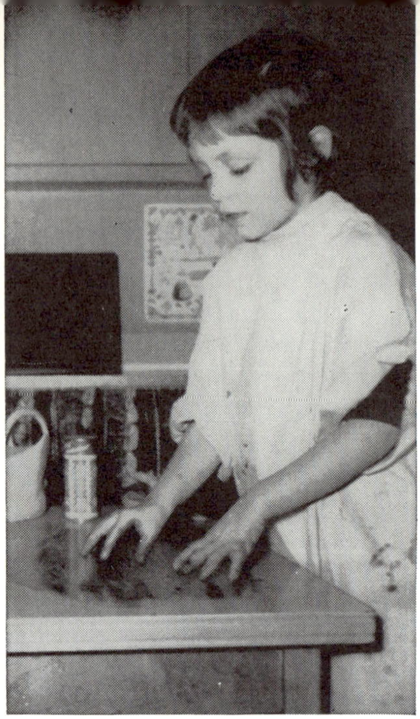

*"After I mix the powder and water, I make my picture."*

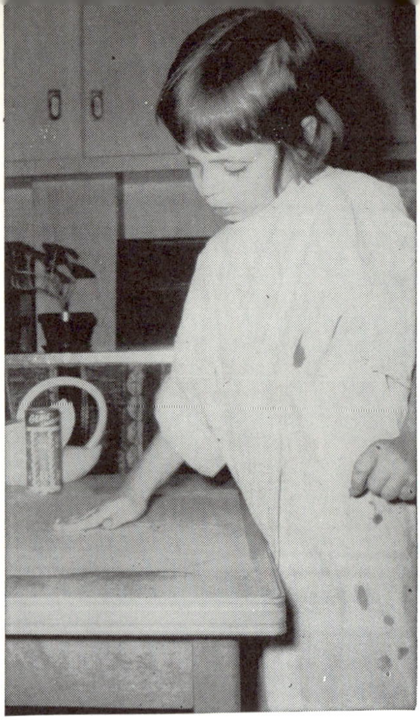

*"Now I'm making a print of my picture."*

the handles of the paint brushes are painted to match the color of paint in which they are to be used, the child will be encouraged to dip his brush always into the same color of paint. Paint which, by accident or by intent, has become muddied by other colors need not be thrown away. If all such mixtures are put into a single container, a functional brown paint will usually evolve. Children should be encouraged to wash their brushes when they have finished painting. Brushes may get their first washing by being sloshed up and down in a container such as a fish bowl. Children love to watch the resulting color effects. After they have been thus soaked, it is well to encourage the children to rinse the brushes in the sink outlet. This procedure gives the child the opportunity to observe the fascinating color combinations and at the same time prevents the sink and the surrounding area from becoming splashed with paint and water. Washed brushes should be pinched to a point or edge and placed brush-end-up in a holder. According to some artists, they should be laid flat on a tray to dry. Under no circumstances should they be allowed to stand brush-down in a container.

When opaque water paint is used on articles made from clay or wood, a coat of white shellac should be added to give the finish a gloss and to prevent the paint from rubbing off on hands and clothing. Pictures which have been painted with opaque water paints may be preserved by being sprayed with a commercial fixative or a very thin liquid paste.

*"And here's my picture. Do you see the doorbell?"*

Finger Paint Finger paint may be purchased in a semiliquid state, ready for use, in one-fourth-pint, one-half-pint, pint, and quart jars. The quart jars are most economical. It may also be purchased in powder form. Both the semiliquid and the powdered finger paint are somewhat expensive for everyday use but, fortunately, homemade substitutes are relatively inexpensive and easy to prepare. A substitute for the semiliquid paint may be made in a variety of ways. One simple formula calls for mixing together a cup of starch and a bit of cold water and then pouring over this, while stirring, two cups of boiling water. The starch should appear clear or silvery. If it does not appear so, the mixture will have to be cooked. Vegetable dyes, powdered paint, or regular commercial cloth dyes can be added for color. This semiliquid homemade finger paint does not keep very long; therefore, only small quantities should be mixed at any one time. Powdered alum, sodium-benzoate, oil of cloves, and other ingredients will tend to prolong the usability of the homemade finger paints. As a substitute for the powdered finger paint, one may use paste powder. This is a good way to use up some of those paste powders which do not function well as adhesives.

As the name suggests, fingers—and, we might add, hands and arms—instead of brushes are used to apply the paint and give expression to feelings and ideas. The paper, either commercial finger-painting paper or glazed—but not plastic—shelf paper, is dipped in a pan of water and spread onto a flat, nonabsorbent surface. Then the semiliquid or powdered paint is applied to the paper. In order to provide unhampered and rhythmic expression, paper that is at least twelve by eighteen inches in size should be used. The child, carefully covered with an apron or smock, rubs the paint all over the surface of the paper with the palms of his hands and then with his fingers, hands, or arms makes all sorts of impressions on the paper. Finger painting can also be done directly on marble, enamel, Formica, or other hard-finished surfaces. If pictures made on these surfaces are to be saved, a print can be obtained by smoothing a sheet of newsprint over the picture before the paint gets dry. A variety of colors may be used for finger painting, but for the kindergarten child it seems to be more satisfactory if at least his early attempts are limited to a single color.

Enamel and Flat Housepaint Sometimes an article seems to demand a finish a bit less crude than that given by poster paint and shellac. For example, at Christmas time clay candleholders and bowls are more truly festive if they are covered with clear bright enamels. Sometimes pieces of furniture made by the children are worthy of real house paint. Articles such as fences, chicken coops, or signs, which are to be put out-of-doors, need to be painted with flat paint rather than with poster paint and shellac. A varnish brush with a one- to one-and-one-half-inch spread is suitable for applying the flat paint, and a regular brush used for shellac may be used also for the enamel if it is thoroughly cleaned afterwards. Brushes used in shellac should be cleaned in alcohol; those used in enamel and flat paint should be cleaned in turpentine. Whenever children use enamel or flat paint, they should spread papers under their work and, in order to protect their clothing, should wear aprons, smocks, or perhaps real coveralls. A small container of turpentine and a cloth should be available for cleaning up drops and smudges of paint.

## Paper

Construction and Poster Paper Construction paper is heavier than poster paper and for that reason should serve better for three-dimensional effects. But since it is heavy it is hard to fold and sometimes tends to crack along the line of the fold. Poster paper, however, lends itself to folding so well that baskets and other three-dimensional articles are often fashioned from it. Children usually find that construction paper is easier to cut and absorbs less paste than poster paper; for that reason it is often chosen for making posters.

Construction and poster paper in 9 in. x 12 in. sheets ought to be available in small amounts for the children's use. A reserve supply should be kept out of the children's reach. A box of odds and ends of colored paper may be kept on a low shelf with the easily available new, unused paper. The children should be encouraged to pick the size of paper best suited to their needs, and they should learn to trim off and return to the box any usable bits of paper. If the used paper can be kept in a box which provides separate storage for various colors, the paper will be less likely to be wasted. Large pieces of construction and poster paper 18 in. x 24 in. in an assortment of colors should be available for picture mounting.

MANILA PAPER Manila paper, available in buff, gray, and white, is especially satisfactory for crayon work. White paper, though often more fine in quality, has the disadvantage of showing finger marks; almost before the child has an opportunity to start his work, he finds that his paper is soiled. Manila paper for drawing may be purchased in 12 in. x 18 in. sheets. If smaller paper is needed, these pieces can be folded and cut. Manila paper 18 in. x 24 in. would be most satisfactory for painting, but it is so much more expensive than the newsprint that it seems reasonable to use the newsprint for young children's experimentation.

UNPRINTED NEWSPAPER Newsprint—unprinted news or expression paper, as it is sometimes called—is suitable for most kindergarten poster painting. It comes in both pastel colors and in white. The white sheets in an 18 in. x 24 in. size seem to answer the day-by-day desire for experimentation; but it is always fun to be able to bring out the colored sheets for special occasions (white per ream $3.10; colored per ream $4.90). The newsprint is usually secured to the easel by large spring clips; to secure the newsprint on a floor board, Plasti-tak, thumbtacks, or masking tape can be used. Sometimes children enjoy making murals, particularly train pictures, by pasting sheet after sheet of newsprint together. The process usually involves painting a unit and then pasting a fresh piece of paper to the first unit, painting on that piece, and so on.

No end of trouble and confusion can be avoided by having specific storage spaces set aside for the various sizes and kinds of sheets of paper used in the kindergarten.[3]

WRAPPING PAPER A large roll of wrapping paper, in a neutral tone and from eighteen to thirty inches in width, affords children abundant opportunity to experiment freely and expansively. Wrapping paper also serves as an excellent background for large posterlike pictures, which can be built up by using colored construction paper, paste, and scissors. The wrapping

[3] This is true, of course, for storage of all such materials.

paper is easier to use if it can be installed on a roller in a conveniently located cupboard.

In addition to the papers discussed in this section, the kindergarten should have available for limited use various other kinds of paper, including tissue and crepe paper, foil, cellophane and Saran Wrap, wallpaper, and contact paper. Glazed shelf paper or commercial finger-painting paper should also be available.

## Pencils

Sometimes kindergarten children find that their large crayons are not satisfactory for setting down such things as their names or "writing a book." To meet the request of the child who asks for a pencil, the kindergarten should have on hand a few marking pencils, such as those large, soft-lead pencils often found in the first and second grades. These pencils, together with those needed by the teacher, may be kept in holders made from clay. Pencils should be placed in the holders with the points up.

## Sand

The sand in the sandbox should come no more than halfway to the top of the box. It should always be kept moist; whenever possible it should be aired in the sun. The sandbox with a cover is more satisfactory in the kindergarten room than the one without a cover. When the cover has been put on, the temptation to loiter at the box or to dangle the fingers through the sand while passing is removed, and the covered sand table gives extra table space in the room.

If most of the group of kindergarten children have come through nursery school, where they have had experience in sand play, it is questionable whether an indoor sandbox is an essential part of the kindergarten room.

## Scissors

The kindergarten needs to be supplied with both blunt and semipointed scissors, and it is well to have on hand a single pair of plastic scissors, to be used by the individual who cannot resist cutting clothes and hair. Sometimes scissors are kept in covered cardboard or wooden boxes, into which holes which exactly fit the points of the scissors have been drilled. A clay holder for scissors can be fashioned by the children themselves. Other devices for scissors storage are boards on which the scissors can be hung or carrying frames designed for transport as well as storing. When the children carry scissors from the storage cupboard or frame to their tables, they should be admonished to keep the points together and pointed down, to lessen the danger of accidents.

If a child finds it difficult to cut with scissors, it is well to encourage him to open the scissors wide and attempt to cut close to the screw which joins the two blades. Then there is much less danger of the paper or cloth slipping between the blades. If the child can learn to pull the material to be cut toward himself and at the same time to push the scissors away from himself, his cutting efforts will meet with greater success.

## Waste Materials

The kindergarten teacher must reserve ample space for the storage of such waste materials as aluminum foil plates, cardboard boxes, cork and bottle tops, cartons, sticks, magazine and calendar pictures, orange and apple crates, reels and spools, and scraps of cloth, wood, string, and yarn, pieces of hose, rope, and wire, plastic bags and containers, wheels and other parts of discarded toys . . . and on and on the list might go! The children ought to be familiar with the available materials and encouraged both to use the materials and to make contributions to the supply. These materials themselves are often the inspiration for creative work. The articles in the collection of waste materials, like those in the costume box, encourage much imaginative play and fill many a need in carrying a project to completion.

## Wood

Pine and poplar are probably the most satisfactory kinds of wood for use in the kindergarten. Wood cut into three-foot or shorter lengths is easier to store and handle than longer lengths. Odds and ends of soft wood from milling companies will stretch the supply, and the variety of shapes in a mill-end load of lumber may give many suggestions to kindergarten carpenters. The wood should be kept either on shelves or in a large chest. If the shelves or the chest can be divided into sections to fit the various lengths and shapes of wood on hand, the search for the right piece of wood can be less tedious. Tools should be stored in a space that can be enclosed.

All work with carpentry tools should be done at a workbench, and the number of children working around a workbench at one time should be limited to three or, at most, five.

## Evaluating Work and Raising Standards

Mere repetition of activities connected with materials will give the child some information as to the properties of the material in question, and may to some extent improve his skill in handling the material; but it is likely to result in more and more careless work. If he is to show steady improvement, the child needs not only to receive constructive criticism but also to be given the desire to do better or different work. Psychological experiments have shown that improvement in performance appears when the subject really wants to improve and when he has some knowledge of what his past performance has been.[4] This is quite evident in the kindergarten. Constant working, without ever trying to do better or without ever realizing that past performances showed shortcomings, avails little. The kindergarten child works best when his efforts are appreciated and when his mistakes as well as his successes are noted. No child respects a teacher who can be hoodwinked into believing that poor work is good work.

### Individual Evaluation

As the teacher moves about the group during the work period, she makes remarks which tend to raise the standard of the work being done. Some seems to be absolutely essential if the child is to better his work. To comment favorably on the features which the child has included in his drawing of a man and then to suggest that the man will need arms if he is going to be able to carry anything will bring much greater improvement than to say merely that the drawing of the man is poor and really doesn't look much like a man.

### Group Evaluation

In most kindergartens there is a time set aside for the group to gather for the purpose of evaluating children's work and raising the standards of effort and achievement. This group meeting may either precede or follow the work period, or meetings may be held both before and after the work

[4] Theta H. Wolf, *The Effect of Praise and Competition on the Persisting Behavior of Kindergarten Children*, University of Minnesota Institute of Child Welfare, Monograph Series, No. 15, Minneapolis, University of Minnesota Press, 1938. See also Joseph Dollins, Henry Angeline, and Edmund Mech, "With Words of Praise," *The Elementary School Journal*, May, 1960, 60:446–450.

period. The discussion which follows the work period considers the work which the children have just finished; the discussion which precedes the work period considers the work of the previous day or days and gives impetus for the work of the period to follow. Experience seems to indicate that the evaluation period which precedes the work period does more to raise the standards of effort and achievement than the evaluation period which follows.

To this group meeting the children may bring the articles on which they have been working; or, if the work is of such a nature that it cannot be brought to the meeting, the children may report on their achievement and, perhaps, invite the group to see their work. In the discussion, directed by the teacher, some of the following points are considered: the general plan of the work, the suitability of the medium used, the care the child has exercised, the industry behind the work exhibited, the relation of the product to the child's ability, ways in which the product might be improved, and specific plans for continuation.

The children should be encouraged to give their criticisms at all times in a helpful, constructive manner. Those children whose work is being criticized ought to feel free to justify their procedures, but they should also profit by the criticism of their work.

Children who have problems with which they would like help are asked to present their difficulties to the group. Children and teacher together offer possible solutions of the problems. If the teacher feels that a particular child needs help and does not himself recognize the fact, she will ask that child to bring his work before the group.

At times the teacher will ask the child who does not need help, but who has ideas incorporated in his work which might be helpful to others, to present his work to the group for their enjoyment, appreciation, and inspiration. Though the teacher may feel that the example of originality and good workmanship exhibited ought to be a real inspiration to the others, she must remember that the criticism and praise which she gives to this very superior piece of work is probably beyond the understanding of the less able child. The teacher must guard against letting herself fall into the habit of asking only the able children to show their results. If she does this too frequently, she is giving the time of the whole group to the very few able children; and the less able children, who, perhaps, need more encouragement and help than those who have already met with success, are neglected. In almost every effort, the alert teacher can find something worthwhile on which to comment.

It would not be wise to bring the work of every child before the group every day; this would result in little more than boredom. But certainly the teacher ought to be mindful of the fact that every child needs at some time to have his effort and his achievement evaluated. In some large kindergartens, the teacher follows the practice of discussing with the group only one type of work each day. On one day, for example, only those children who have worked with paper bring their work to the group. Another day it may be only those who have worked with wood, and so on. All the children in the kindergarten are expected to be at the meeting, whether they used that particular material or not. Both individual and group criticism are needed if the children are to be expected to raise the standard of their work.

## SUMMARY

There is great variation in the types of work periods found in the modern kindergarten. By and large, the problem-solving type seems to have the most points in its favor. The room and the equipment have much to do with the type of work done in the period. The teacher tries to keep herself in the background as much as possible; yet she has each child's problem clearly in mind and is alert to the whole environment. As the year progresses, certain occupations once accepted as work activities become play activities. The child needs to feel that his work efforts are really purposeful. As he is confronted with and solves his problems through a variety of media, he assembles and tests his ideas, thus building for himself a broad horizontal base for future learning.

## QUESTIONS AND PROBLEMS

1. Consider the three situations described on pages 189–191. Show to what extent each fulfills the purposes of the work period outlined at the beginning of the chapter.
2. If you were the teacher in charge and Sally said, "I can't draw a man; you draw one for me," what would be your response? Why?
3. In some kindergartens there is a clean-up committee designated for each day. What arguments can you make for or against this practice?
4. Suppose your kindergarten group has visited a fire station. List at least six ways in which the experience may find expression in the work period.
5. At the end of a discussion of work to be undertaken, one child has set his heart on attempting something the teacher knows is completely beyond his capability. What attitude should she take?
6. The text suggests that a daily group evaluation period should be part of every kindergarten program. What dangers can you see in such a procedure?

## SELECTED REFERENCES


Association for Childhood Education, Washington, D.C.

*The Color Book Craze*, 1964.

*Children Can Make It—Experiences in the World of Materials*, 1955.*

*Creating With Materials for Work and Play*, Portfolio No. 5, 1957.*

California State Department of Education, Bureau of Elementary Education, *Teacher's Guide to Education in Early Childhood*, Sacramento, State Department of Education, 1956 (see especially pp. 407–424).

Conrad, George, *The Process of Art Education in the Elementary School*, Englewood Cliffs, N.J., Prentice-Hall, 1964.

Harris, Dale, *Children's Drawings as Measures of Intellectual Maturity*, New York, Harcourt, Brace and World, Inc., 1963.

Lambert, Hazel, *Teaching the Kindergarten Child*, New York, Harcourt, Brace and Company, 1958.

Lants, Beatrice, *Easel Age*, Monterey, California, California Test Bureau, 1955.

Margolin, E. B., and D. A. Leton, "Interest of Kindergarten Children in Block Play," *Journal of Educational Research*, September, 1961, 55: 13–18.

National Education Association, *Block Building in the Kindergarten*, Washington, D.C., National Education Association, 1960.

National Education Association, "The Kindergarten Program," *Those First School Years*, Washington, D.C., National Education Association, 1960.

Shaw, Ruth, *Finger Painting*, Boston, Little, Brown and Company, 1939.

Turner, G. Alan, *Creative Crafts for Everyone*, New York, The Viking Press, 1961.*

# 12

# FREE-TIME ACTIVITIES PERIOD

The kindergarten free-time activities period provides opportunity for the child to

- Choose his own activity.
- Experiment freely with materials and apparatus.
- Engage wholeheartedly in dramatic and imaginative play.
- Solve his own social problems.
- Converse freely with other children.
- Lead the group without depending on teacher direction.
- Cooperate with the group without depending on teacher direction.
- Experience the joy which spontaneous play brings.

## Free-Time versus Free-Play

The old and still commonly used term "free-play period" has led to much misunderstanding about the activities engaged in during the period. Because of its name and the relatively unstructured nature of the period, some people have inferred that an atmosphere of "do as you please" and license is characteristic of the period. Others have felt that the name is a misnomer, since children are not completely free to do as they like in the period. A lay observer commented, "I felt it was anything but a free-play period. There were many regulations controlling behavior."

True! In the kindergarten in which the observation was made, these regulations were in effect: (1) children who forcibly rocked the jungle gym were not allowed to stay on the apparatus; (2) children were welcome to play the piano, but only if it was not being used by another child; (3) crayons, scissors, paper, and paste could be used, but when a child had

*"Sometimes I like to get away from it all and lose myself in a good book."*

finished with his activity, he was supposed to clear his table for the use of others; (4) puzzles and books were available, but each child was expected to share materials and to replace his materials or turn them over for others before beginning some other activity; (5) after using books, children were expected to return them to shelves, so that they might be kept in good condition and made more easily available to others.

This observer needed to develop a keener awareness of the fact that freedom is limited by concern for the good and welfare of all. You and I live in a free country, yet there are many things we are not "free" to do. For example, we are free to drive on our highways only if we conform to the regulations set up for the good of all. We cannot proceed through a stop sign at will; we cannot drive down the left-hand side of the road; we cannot park on the highway; and we cannot drive when we are not in a condition to control our car. In the free-play, or as we are now more correctly calling it, the free-time activities period, there are certain regulations and agreements made for the common good. Beyond these there are no fixed rules and formal procedure, and generally there is no climax toward which the play is directed. Insofar as the activities do not interfere with the good of the group, they will be guided by the interests and the fancies of the individuals of the group. The available equipment, not the teacher's prepared plan, will provide the inspiration for the activities of the period. One small boy, in response to a teacher's attempt to outline a plan of activity for playtime, said, "But Miss F., we don't want to play something; we just want to play." And that, if the period is to be truly a free time, is exactly the spirit in which the children may be expected to enter into its activities.

## Time

Free-time appears most often at the beginning of the daily kindergarten session. When scheduled at this hour, it gives both children and the teacher opportunities to exchange news, renew friendships, observe and pursue special interests before coming together into any kind of an organized group.

Sometimes free-time is placed in the middle of the day's program for the purpose of offering rest and relaxation from more organized activities. If it is scheduled for the middle of the session, the teacher must make sure that the children do not confuse its activities with the activities of the work period. It is easy for the children to confuse the drifting informality of the one with the informal purposefulness of the other.

Free-time scheduled for the beginning of the session is likely to be longer than that scheduled for the middle of the session. Either period, however, may run from ten to thirty or more minutes.

## Arrangements for Free-Time Activity[1]

In some schools the children go from their own room into a special-activity or gymnasium room for their free-time activities. In other schools the kindergarten room itself or a combination of the kindergarten room and the play yard is used for the activities of the period. Of course, if the kindergarten room is too small to allow the children to move about freely, it is wiser to go to another room for play. But there is so much in the kindergarten room itself which can be used to advantage in the free-time activities period that it is profitable, if practical, to remain there for the period. If the kindergarten has an exit leading into its own play yard or a section of the main school playground, then both the playground and the kindergarten room can be used for free-time activities.

[1] See the running account of free-time activities on pp. 70–77.

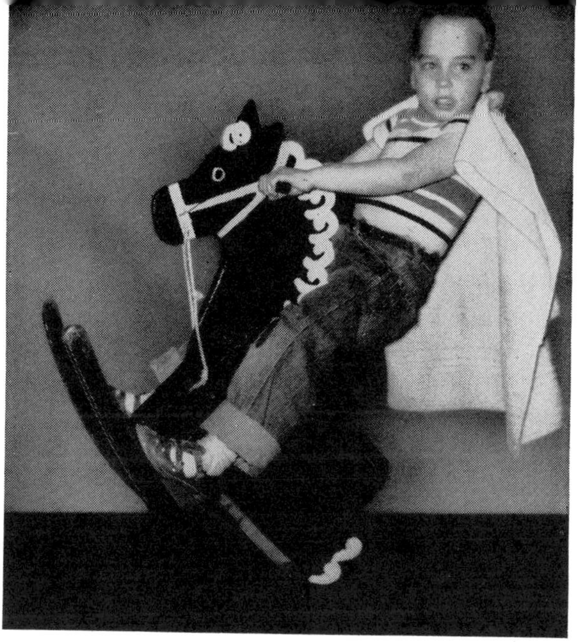

*"Sometimes I'm Superman."*

## Special-Activity Room

The special-activity room is usually the school gymnasium or a vacant classroom which has much clear floor space. In this room there may be one or two pieces of playground apparatus, such as a slide, a teeter-totter, a rocking board, a climbing rope, a swing, or a jungle gym. Tricycles, wagons, jumping ropes, balls, and ring-toss games may also be available. Sometimes a play corner or a playhouse is set up on one side of this room. The special-activity room is more often used in the middle of the morning than at the beginning of the daily session.

## The Kindergarten as Its Own Activity Room

If the space is economically apportioned, a place can be found in most kindergarten rooms for at least one piece of playground or gymnasium apparatus. The jungle gym offers more play possibilities for more children than any other piece of play equipment. As many as eight or ten children can be on it at one time, and if a slide is made by hooking a removable plank to one of the rungs, even more children can be accommodated. Not only is the jungle gym used as a piece of physical-activity apparatus, but it also figures largely in the dramatic play of the children. Sometimes it is a cage, sometimes an airplane, sometimes a house or tower, sometimes, as its name suggests, a jungle.

The doll corner of the kindergarten offers numerous possibilities for dramatic play. In addition to being used for housekeeping play, it is a center for dramatizing the work of many of the community helpers. The milkman, the fireman, the policeman, the postman, the doctor, the TV repairman, the plumber, the electrician, the deliveryman, the door-to-door agents, all come in for their share of dramatization. During the work period, the children may have been making such things as trains, airplanes, boats, barns, jails, post-office buildings, supermarkets, and general stores. If so, they will welcome the opportunity the free-activities period gives for further play centered about these constructions.

Many of the materials, particularly those of the manipulative type used in the work period, may be experimented with and enjoyed during the free-time period. There are many ways in which one may experiment with blocks during this period. Towers, designs, and all kinds of fanciful structures may be built. A good deal of fascinating representative play often centers around this block play. Play in the sandbox using the various measures, molds, and toys offers excellent opportunity for wholesome cooperative interplay. Even the pegs and beads and other manipulative materials which may have long since been ruled out of the activities of the work period may be enjoyed in the free-time period. Some children enjoy spending their free time looking at books, while others are eager to experiment with some of the art media. The piano, xylophone, sets of chimes, or percussion instruments have appeal for others.

For some children the so-called educational or readiness materials, such as lotto and domino games, sets of flannel board materials, three-dimensional numeral and letter materials, numeral and number matching cards, word- and picture-matching cards, phonics games, and even work sheet materials will have a strong appeal. In the free-time period the teacher should be free to circulate so that she can answer questions and give help, praise, and commendation.

Some children find pleasure and satisfaction in organizing their own small groups for such games as ring toss, bowling, ball-in-the-basket, and other games of skill.

Except in the free-time period there is often little opportunity for children to enjoy watching the activities of the fish, turtles, polliwogs, chipmunks, birds, and other live pets which may be in the kindergarten. Some children will spend much time with these pets.

Unless there is a scheduled free-time activity, it is possible for children to spend their days in a beautifully set-up kindergarten room and yet have little opportunity to take advantage of its offerings. In that time when the children come into the room, hang up their wraps and sit down to wait for the group to assemble, many educational opportunities are wasted. Why have a kindergarten room beautifully set up if little or no free time is to be made available for the use of the various facilities? The kindergarten that provides for free time on Fridays only is usually the kindergarten in which the program is so highly structured that hundreds of worthwhile learning opportunities are completely ignored.

## The Play Yard[2]

The first requisite for a play yard is plenty of safe space in which to play. If the play yard is near the street, it should be shut off by a fence or thick hedge. The second requisite is a good surface on which to play. Grass is the ideal covering for a play yard, of course, but even for kindergarten children it does not hold up very well. Perhaps the best substitute is tanbark. This is certainly not nearly so attractive, but it is clean, provides a reasonably soft surface on which to tumble, and also provides for good drainage.

Some cement surface, preferably in a circular construction, should be provided for wheeled vehicles. A real or artificial hill or slope adds greatly to the possibilities of a yard, as does a "climbable" tree. An outdoor sandbox, a climbing apparatus, swings, tricycles, wagons, and maybe a scooter, a few pieces of rope, an airplane inner tube, several balls, some large hollow building blocks, a few boxes and boards—and the playground makes a pleasant complement to the kindergarten room. Outside storage space should be provided for the outdoor equipment.

## Activity

Play of all kinds will be inspired by such an arrangement. Even though the play yard or playground is not adjacent to the kindergarten room, the teacher ought to make an effort to offer some opportunity for daily out-of-door play when the weather permits. The teacher in the Northern states should consider snow one of the priceless play materials. Southern guests, visiting a kindergarten in Minnesota on a snowy winter day, marvel at nature's contribution to the playgrounds of the North.

## The Function of the Teacher in the Play Period

The teacher will have to encourage children in certain activities and discourage them from others. She must be ready to encourage all kinds of wholesome, wholehearted play, and to discourage play that interferes with

[2] See Chapter 7.

Public Schools, Oakland, California

*Dramatic Play—Simple, But Obviously Satisfying*

the freedom and rights of others. Yet she must be careful not to set herself up as a tribunal to which all arguments and disputes are brought. When individuals come to report the misbehavior of others, the teacher should refer the one reporting to the offender, making it clear to the child that the offender and not the teacher is the one to talk with in such cases.

## The Teacher Observes

Sometimes, when invited by the children, the teacher may join in the children's play. As an observer she can learn much about the interests and the background of the children. Such remarks as the following, overheard in the free-time period, can have a significant bearing on the teacher's later dealings with the children:

One small girl to another as they played in the doll corner: "I don't know why my mother never wants me at home. She likes me, but she never wants me at home."

A boy to his companion as they played in the kindergarten store: "Mr. Grownowski is mean. He wouldn't let my mother get cigarets on her 'lotment order."

A boy talking to himself as he built cliffs in the sand: "When I was in London I had tea at the zoo with my nurse. Here is where we sat."

The two following bits of representative play observed in the playhouse give amazing insight into the two kinds of experience to which the individuals must have been exposed:

> Jane picked up the toy phone, dialed "O" and said, "Give me the Jim Porter's house, and make it snappy too.". . . After a second she continued, "Hello, I want to talk to Betty! That's what I said . . ." and so the conversation continued. A few minutes later Barbara picked up the same phone. She lifted the receiver, waited for a brief moment and then very carefully dialed DR 5631. After a brief interval she said, "Oh, hello, this is Barbara speaking. Is Emily at home? . . . Yes I would: but don't disturb her if she is resting. . . . No, please don't. I'll call back later around three o'clock perhaps. . . . Thank you! Goodby."

## The Teacher Acts

The teacher must be ever present in both mind and body during the free-activity time. She must encourage children to engage in a variety of activities. The child, for example, who always plays the piano during the period ought to be encouraged to do other things, not only for his own sake, but for the sake of others who want a turn at the piano. The child who always plays alone ought to be encouraged or invited to join the play of others.

If the teacher observes that a very aggressive child has come to be the solon of his party, she should find a way to invest another member of the group with power to offset his control. Perhaps the young dictator brought a ball from home, and he is specifying just how and when and what everyone is to do in *his* game. The teacher may casually toss out a second ball so that two games can be organized, thus "relieving" the aggressive child of some of his dictatorial power.

Sometimes children seem to run out of ideas for wholesome fun and activities degenerate into tomfoolery. Then the teacher must be ready to offer suggestions that will stimulate further interest in wholesome activity. Sometimes all that is needed is a favorable comment on the interesting activity of another child or another group. At other times the teacher will need to direct activities into very practical channels. For example, she may ask the apparent leader of the group to help in preparing the paints, watering the flowers, or feeding the goldfish.

Occasionally a child becomes overstimulated in the free-time activity period and loses all sense of self-control. In such a case the teacher is justified in asking the child to leave the group to get control of himself. Often it will suffice if he simply sits down to watch the others, or it may be necessary for him to be quite apart from the other children. The way the teacher handles the situation will make all the difference in the world in the child's and the children's reactions to the situation. She may command the child to leave the group and sit in a chair, or she may say, in a calculated but offhand manner, "Pretty excited, aren't you, Peter? Better sit down and watch the others for a while until you can get control of yourself." In the second instance, the teacher seems to be part of the total situation, she does not swoop in from the outside, and her judgment seems to be based on a somewhat careful appraisal of the total situation. The child may be expected to accept the second approach more readily than the first, and the group will not think of the teacher as a creature who might descend on them at any moment.

## Free-time and Desk Work

The teacher who thinks of the free-time activity period as a time in which she can be free to do desk or other work removed from the general activity arena is not being fair to the children. The teacher, though careful not to intrude or interfere any more than necessary, must always have the total situation in mind, and when the period is ended the children and the teacher, working together, should see that materials and equipment are put back in their proper place.

### SUMMARY

The free-time activities period gives the child the opportunity he needs to exchange ideas, to cooperate in a child-directed group, to play with things he has made, to investigate and explore the possibilities of many old materials, to become acquainted with new materials, to play on the apparatus, to observe live animals, and to engage in special pursuits peculiar to his liking. The period provides opportunities for dramatic play and the accompanying review of what has been learned. The period will also help the child distinguish between the somewhat drifting informality of such a period and the informal purposefulness of the work period. It is not intended to provide time for the teacher to do desk work or other work which removes her from the general activity arena.

### QUESTIONS AND PROBLEMS

1. List the relative advantages and disadvantages in having the free-time activity period at the beginning of the kindergarten session.

2. Describe the activities in the playhouse area when it is being used (a) in the free-time period and (b) in the work period.
3. During a thirty-minute period of out-of-door free-time play, observe particularly one boy and one girl. How many activities did each engage in? How long did each stay with a single activity?
4. From your observations of both in- and out-of-door free-time activities, would you say that any particular activities appealed more to girls than to boys? What is your evidence?
5. During an observation of an indoor free-time activity period, what evidence did you find of the teacher's awareness or lack of awareness of the total situation?
6. How was the free-time activity period terminated? What part did the teacher take in helping put away materials and equipment? What part did the children take?

## SELECTED REFERENCES

Fleming, Robert S., *Curriculum for Today's Boys and Girls,* Columbus, Ohio, Charles E. Merrill Books, Inc., 1963.

Hartley, Ruth, and Robert M. Goldenson, *A Complete Book of Children's Play,* New York, Thomas Y. Crowell Company, 1957.

Inhoff, Myrtle, *Early Elementary Education,* New York, Appleton-Century-Crofts, 1959.

Jenkins, Gladys, and Others, *These Are Your Children,* rev., Chicago, Scott Foresman & Company, 1953.

Kepler, Hazel, *The Child and His Play: A Planning Guide for Parents and Teachers,* New York, Funk & Wagnalls Company, 1952.

Ledermann, Alfred, and Alfred Trachsel, *Creative Playground and Recreation Centers* (translated from the German by Ernst Priefert), New York, Frederich A. Praeger, Inc., 1957.

Moustakas, Clark E., *Children in Play Therapy: a Key to Understanding Normal and Disturbed Emotioins,* New York, McGraw-Hill Book Company, 1953.

National Education Association, *Freedom to Move,* Bulletin, Washington, D.C., National Education Association, 1962.

# 13

# LIBRARY AND STORY TIME

Through library and story experiences, the kindergarten program gives the child

- An opportunity to share pleasure of the highest type.
- Frequent opportunities for role-playing in the group as leader, director, listener, observer, contributor.
- An opportunity to learn to appreciate good literature.
- A respect for books and a technique for handling books.
- An opportunity to build a strong foundation for first-grade reading.
- A fund of general information.
- An opportunity for guided flights into the world of fancy.
- An awareness of the joy of living with books.

## The Kindergarten Library

With the publication in the last thirty or forty years of hundreds of books written especially for the child who has not yet learned to read, or who is just beginning to read, the library has become an essential part of the kindergarten. Some kindergartens are more fortunate than others in the number of books their libraries can boast; but no kindergarten library, particularly with the appearance on the market of many excellent picture storybooks selling for $1.25 and less, need be without a variety of good books.[1] There are also some very good books on the market for as little

[1] Association for Childhood Education International, *Children's Books for $1.25 or Less*, Bulletin No. 36, Washington, D.C., Association for Childhood Education International, 1961.

as twenty-five and thirty cents, but because these books are usually not durable enough for group use, it is wise to spend school money for the better-bound books.

Many good books, even some of the better inexpensive ones, can be secured with especially durable library bindings. Some of the Little Golden Books, for example, which sell in their original bindings for thirty-five and fifty cents can be had in library bindings for seventy-five cents. If the text and the illustration are of top quality, then it is well worth spending the extra money to secure the library-bound copies. The Cadmus and the Huntting library-bound books also hold up particularly well under kindergarten use.[2]

We are grateful for the inexpensive good books that are on the market but, from an educational point of view, it does not seem wise to put these books on our kindergarten library shelves. In the first place, it would be a poor investment of school funds, and in the second place, we could hardly expect to help children develop an attitude of respect for books if the books we provided simply fell apart in their hands. Children will bring to kindergarten many of the inexpensive and poorly constructed books and many times these can be enjoyed for their content. If or when they fall apart or get damaged, attention can be drawn to the difference in the well-designed construction of the better books and the poorly designed construction of the less expensive books.

[2] Cadmus Books, E. M. Hale and Company, 1201 S. Hastings Way, Eau Claire, Wisconsin. The H. R. Huntting Company, Inc., 300 Burnett Road, Chicopee Falls, Massachusetts.

*The Library Atmosphere Invites Lounging and "Reading."*

University of Minnesota

## The Library Setting

The library area ought to have something about it, aside from its books, to distinguish it from other parts of the room. An easel-like bookrack with attached benches set down between a block building area and the lavatory will make the area look different, but that is about all that can be said in its favor. The library area, in addition to being different from any other area, needs to be a unit apart from traffic and noisy activity, and it needs to have a pleasant, casual atmosphere that will invite lingering and lounging. If possible, the furniture in the library unit should be quite different from that in the rest of the kindergarten room. And if the same type of chairs and tables must be used, the arrangement ot the furniture should be casual and the chairs should perhaps have colorful back and seat pads.[3]

## Book Storage and Display Features

There must be a place, of course, to store the books. A rack similar to the kind used in public libraries for magazines has the advantage of permitting the book covers with their pictures to be visible at all times, a very real advantage since the kindergarten child must identify his book by the cover. However, the low bookcase with open shelves seems somewhat less formal and therefore more inviting. The shelves of a kindergarten bookcase should never be "filled" with books, for two reasons. Having too many books encourages the child to go from one book to another without stopping to enjoy any one in particular; and locating the desired book in a filled bookcase is a complicated problem when one cannot read and can see only the spine of the book. Keeping only eight or ten books on a shelf which could hold as many as twenty-five or fifty books enables the child to find a book with ease. Some of the books will be standing and others lying flat on the shelf, but it should be possible to take any book from the shelf without upsetting the whole order. Variation in shelf heights will help children keep books of similar size together, and a few upright partial partitions in the shelves will be a further aid to organization.

At first the number of books in the entire bookcase will probably not exceed fifteen or twenty. As the year progresses and the interests of the group develop, more and more books will be added. Some books that are seasonal in their interest will be on the shelves for a few days or a few weeks at most; others, as they are added, will remain on the shelves for the rest of the school year. Ordinarily, however, the number on the shelves at any one time should not exceed about thirty-five.

[3] See pp. 96 and 112 for a further discussion of library furnishings.

An area of the bookcase—or better yet, a second bookcase—may be set aside as a "home-school library case." Here into the designated space would go any books children bring from home to share with the group and later take home again. This "home-school" unit will serve to keep the home and school copies of the better books from being interchanged; it will remind the children of the standards for care of books; and it will illustrate the necessity of standards for the selection of books. Each book in the kindergarten library bookcase, it is hoped, will be chosen with the age interests of kindergarten children, the content, and the format of the book in mind, whereas many of the books brought in by the child will not be so carefully selected.

## Types of Books for the Kindergarten Library

Though the kindergarten child usually cannot read, he demands that there be printed material in his books. The younger child is often satisfied with a picture book, but not so the kindergarten child. There are, of course, exceptions. Moreover, in one or two unusual picture books, the pictures follow the action of the story so closely and have such storytelling value that the child is intrigued by telling the story himself as he turns the pages.

For the child a picture is more interesting if it is gaily colored, full of action, and free from distracting details.[4] Photographic illustrations, probably because they have so much detail in them, seem to be more interesting to adults than to children. Silhouette pictures are often confusing to young children; monotone and line pictures are satisfying but not intriguing. The young child is highly critical of inconsistencies in pictures. If, in a continuous story, a character is wearing blue socks on one page and red socks on another, the kindergarten child will be quick to note the inconsistency.

Even though the average kindergarten child does not read, he is beginning to take an interest in the appearance of printed words. For that reason, some thought should be given to the size of print used in the picture storybooks. In general the print should not be smaller than 14-point and not larger than 18-point or 20-point. (The type used for this line is 10-point.) You might look at the word "type" in most standard dictionaries to visualize desirable type sizes for picture storybooks for young children. If manuscript or script is used in picture storybooks, it must be clear in outline and letters, with words and lines well spaced. The page background should be a dull, grayed white, and on or opposite every page on which

[4] C. L. Freeman and R. S. Freeman, *The Child and His Picture Book*, Chicago, Northwestern University Press, 1933.

there is text, there should be an illustration. For the youngest kindergarten children, a two-to-one proportion between text and picture seems to be entirely satisfactory.

The size of the book which is most enjoyed by young children is still a much debated question. It is quite probable, however, that in our habit of supplying large play equipment in general, we have more or less forced upon the child a book that is really awkward for him to handle. The book which measures 8½ in. x 7½ in. and opens on the shorter side is handled with ease by kindergarten children. While both smaller and larger books are enjoyed for variety's sake, it would be well if most of the books were about the size mentioned above.

The subject matter of the books found in the kindergarten library will vary greatly according to the background of the children in the particular school district. It may be suggested, however, that books bearing on the following interests should appear on the shelves sometime during the year:

Mother Goose and folk tales
Realistic experiences of animals, children, and grown-ups
Imaginary adventures of animals, children, and machines
Information about nature—plants, animals, birds, fish, and human beings
Information about mechanical things—trains, boats, hoists, shovels, trucks, buses, airplanes, rockets, and satellites
Information about the community and community helpers—markets, bakeries, shops, general stores, libraries, and museums; policemen, firemen, mailmen, bus drivers, construction workers, and repairmen
Information about the world and the universe—earth, air, water, sun, moon, stars and outer space, rain, snow, hail, electricity, and other sources of heat and energy.

## Choosing Books for the Kindergarten Library

There was a time when we looked to Germany, Sweden, and other European countries for the best of a somewhat meager selection of picture books and picture storybooks for young children. But not any more! It is estimated that between one thousand and two thousand children's books are published here each year. Some are excellent, some good, some fair, and some downright poor. It would be possible for a child to attend a kindergarten a whole year, have a different book or story every day, and yet not have had the opportunity to become acquainted with those books which would be deemed "too good for a kindergarten child to miss." The books marked with an asterisk in the book list at the end of this chapter are those which appear on a list of "Kindergarten Books Too Good to

Miss" which came from a random sampling of kindergarten teachers throughout the United States. From a carefully selected list of 257 books, some fifty teachers were asked to name those which they would select as "too good to be missed"—those they would not want to be without. Interestingly enough, the two books which headed the list were written long years apart! Clement Moore's *'Twas the Night Before Christmas* and Robert McCloskey's *Make Way for Ducklings*. Beatrix Potter's *Peter Rabbit* and Virginia Burton's *Mike Mulligan and His Steam Shovel* followed closely.[5]

## Guides for the Selection of Books

Among the many publications designed to be of help in the selection of books for children, the following, published regularly, are especially helpful:

*Adventuring with Books* Elementary Reading List Committee of the National Council of Teachers of English, 704 South Sixth St., Champaign, Illinois 61820 (published biennially)
*Bibliography of Books for Children*, Association for Childhood Education International, 3615 Wisconsin Avenue N.W., Washington, D.C. 20016 (published biennially)
*Books of the Year*, Children's Book Committee of the Child Study Association of America, 9 East 89th Street, New York, New York 10038 (published annually)
Bulletin of the Center for Children's Books, University of Chicago Press, 5835 Kimbark Avenue, Chicago, Illinois 60637 (11 issues yearly)
*The Horn Book Magazine*, The Horn Book, Inc., 585 Boylston Street, Boston, Massachusetts, 92116 (published six times a year).

Local libraries and the Sunday book sections of various newspapers and periodicals such as *Childhood Education*, *Elementary English*, and *Parents Magazine* also carry listings and reviews of new books. Twice a year, in the fall and in the spring, the Sunday book section of such papers as The New York *Times* and the Chicago *Tribune* are given over to children's books. May Hill Arbuthnot's, *Books Too Good to Miss*, put out irregularly —most recent issue 1963—by the Western Reserve University Press of Cleveland is also helpful.

For books that have been tried and tested in the kindergarten see the book list at the end of this chapter and similar book lists in other books dealing with early childhood education.

[5] State of Minnesota Department of Education, A *Guide for Teaching in the Kindergarten*, Curriculum Bulletin No. 25, St. Paul, 1963, pp. 129, 130.

## Library Activities

Frequently there is no definite time set aside in the kindergarten for the use of the library, but the children are free to look at the books during the free-time activities period or whenever else they have a bit of leisure. In some kindergartens, however, there is a ten-to-fifteen-minute period definitely scheduled as a library period. Sometimes a child will sit by himself to enjoy his book; at other times he will get pleasure out of sharing his experience with a friend or a small group of friends. The children usually pass running comments on the pictures as the pages are turned. If a particular book is a favorite with the group, it often happens that the children will gather around the child who holds the book, and the child holding the book will, by popular acclaim, become the storyteller.

At all times the children should be encouraged to exercise care in handling books. It is not too much to expect kindergarten children to exercise judgment as to when their hands are or are not clean enough to handle books. It is not unusual to see a kindergarten child sit down at the library table and then get up immediately in order to wash his hands before using a book. If a child finds that the pages of a book have been torn or if, by chance, a particular child has the misfortune to tear a page, he should be encouraged to report the fact and to set the book aside so that it may be repaired before further damage is done. That all may enjoy the library equally the children in the library or in the vicinity of the library may be expected to show respect for the rights of others. Loud conversation, hoarding books, and unnecessary moving about should all be discouraged. When a child has finished looking at a book, he may be expected to put it back on the shelf or in the rack so that the picture cover can be seen. Library time can quite naturally blend into story time.

## The Story Hour

The first story hour may well grow out of a library experience. In compliance with a request to "read this," the teacher may sit down beside the child to tell or read the story in the book the child offers her. When others in the group note that a story is being read aloud, they will gather about to listen. As the group grows, it will be increasingly difficult for all the children to both see the pictures and hear the story. A suggestion about sitting down may then be in order. Chairs can be used, but the simplest procedure is to have the children seat themselves on the floor. In some kindergartens a rug is provided for the group to sit on at such times. When the teacher is sure that everyone is comfortably seated and not in the way of any other viewer or listener, she may continue or, better yet, start the story again from the beginning.

## Reading versus Telling Stories

Before the appearance of the many attractively illustrated children's books, the teacher found it more desirable to tell than to read most of her stories. It is still wise for every teacher to have many stories at her command for telling, but if a book with attractive illustrations is at hand, it is pointless not to let the children enjoy the pictures as well as the story. Few kindergartens can claim to have complete libraries; a teacher, therefore, who can tell stories can give her group stories they might be deprived of if they were to rely solely on the books at hand.

There are some stories that are much better told than read under any conditions. Many of the old folk tales and some very simple realistic stories lose a great deal of their charm if they are read. The story that is told has the advantage of creating a more informal and friendly atmosphere and affording the teacher the opportunity of making direct contact with her group. This direct contact and the freedom achieved through it help the teacher sense the mood of her group so that she can better adapt her manner of telling to that mood. Both facial expressions and gestures may be used more freely if the story is told rather than read. Children get a great deal of enjoyment out of watching as well as listening to the storyteller. This last point is clearly illustrated when the teacher operates some form of projector and tells the story at the same time. Although the pictures are interesting and quite in keeping with the text, the children will frequently turn to watch the teacher as she speaks.

The story that is read has the advantage of always presenting to the children an example of well-chosen English and of building up in the child's mind a connection between stories and books, books and reading. This association does much to create an interest in reading. The mere act of watching the teacher read helps the child build reading habits. The child learns, among other things, that the line is read from left to right, that the page is read from top to bottom, and that pages are turned singly or run through quickly. Frequently the child's attention is called to particular words on the printed page or to the general make-up of the book—index, page numbers, chapters, and so on.

Thus both the story that is told and the story that is read have their own special function; neither should be used to the exclusion of the other. The proportion of stories told to stories read will depend chiefly on the size of the kindergarten library and the kindergarten teacher's skill in storytelling.

## Techniques of Preparing the Story

Whether the story is read or told, the teacher ought to be so familiar with the sequence of events that the whole story will move smoothly. In preparing a story to read or tell, she ought first to read it over just for her own enjoyment; then she should try to recall the events in the story so that in presenting it she can have in mind the event or incident to which the account is leading. If the story is to be told without the text, she should know the outline of her story and a few of the words of the text, along with any rhyming jingles; but beyond that it is probably better for her to rely on her own ingenuity. Nothing is more disappointing than to have a perfectly good story cut short or broken into simply because the teller cannot recall the next sentence or the next word. It is well to practice either reading or telling the story to an imaginary audience, or better yet to a single child of the age to which the story is adapted.

## Techniques of Presenting the Story

While it seems more friendly and informal to tell stories to small groups of kindergarten children, one study on the relation of the size of the group to the amount of the story retained by individuals has indicated that the size of a group has little to do with children's ability to enjoy and retain the facts of the story.[6] Neither the number of children in the group nor the child's position in the group seems to have any real effect on the amount of the story that is grasped. The teacher, however, should be careful to see that the child who is hard of hearing or who has poor eyesight is well up in the front of the group. Five-year-olds may be expected to exert some effort to respect the listening enjoyment and pleasure of the group.[7]

When everyone is comfortably settled and in an expectant mood—the teacher included—the telling or reading of the story may proceed. The storyteller who begins her story with the hope that interest in the story will quiet the group has no assurance whatsoever that the story hour will be a pleasant one. Ideally, of course, the story and the manner of telling will be so delightful that interest alone will hold the group together. But the ideal cannot always be achieved. The storyteller must recognize that no single story is equally appealing to all listeners and, if she were to rely

[6] Helen C. Dawe, "The Influence of Size of Group upon Performance," *Child Development*, June, 1934, 5:295.

[7] See Owen W. McConkie and Marie M. Hughes, "Quality of Classroom Living Related to Size of Kindergarten Group," *Childhood Education*, May, 1956, 32:428–432.

on interest alone to hold the group together, she might find the group's enjoyment of the story hour entirely out of her control.

A deliberate telling, with pauses judiciously inserted, is far better than a rapid one. There is a tendency for inexperienced teachers to hurry through one story after another, almost as if they were afraid to stop talking lest the group disintegrate. An experienced storyteller has been known to spend two hours—that is, the story hours on two consecutive days—in telling a story which an inexperienced storyteller might tell in eight or ten minutes. A few gestures consistent with the thoughts being presented will add much to the vividness of the story being told, but the teacher must always remember that she is telling and not dramatizing the story. It is desirable to have the voice pitched just low enough so that the children will have to pay close attention in order to hear. The teacher who shouts her story at the group not only wears herself out but, by forcing her story on the children, tends to antagonize them. At all times the teacher must guard against the use of any unpleasant mannerisms or a "storytelling" voice. Any teacher who wants to evaluate her own mannerisms or voice can do so by listening to the children as they retell or "read" the stories for themselves. Children are remarkably good imitators!

Interruptions are bound to come in one way or another, particularly early in the year. A whole story hour may be ruined if the teacher does not know how, tactfully, to meet outbursts of relevant and sometimes irrelevant remarks. The teacher must learn to handle these interruptions firmly but in such a way that the children will not feel rebuffed. The children can be led to know that their contributions will be most welcome when timely. Sometimes an understanding glance or nod in the direction of the child who is about to burst forth will take care of the situation. At other times a long pause on the part of the storyteller and an eager request from the group to have the story continued will forestall further interruptions.

It is not the audience alone that does the interrupting. At times the storyteller herself falls into the habit of interrupting her own story. It adds nothing to the story to have the teller stop to throw out questions or to have her digress in the way of explaining new words. The questions may better be omitted and the new words, if the context does not make their meaning clear, may well have a synonym or two or an explanatory phrase used in conjunction with them. The story can then proceed without interruption. If the teacher does find it necessary to interrupt her story for one reason or another, she ought to apologize to the group for the interruption, making it clear that she herself not only regrets but disapproves of the interruption.

The picture storybook which has an illustration on every or nearly every page offers a problem. Some feel that the pictures should be shown before or after each page is read, and others feel that the story should be read or told completely before the pictures are shown. Though either of these techniques is usable, it seems more natural for the children to be able to enjoy both text and illustrations at the same time. With a little practice and sufficient familiarity with the story, the teacher can manage this. It is sometimes interesting, while waiting for the group to assemble, to run through the pictures before beginning to read the story. If the teacher holds the book somewhat to the side and in front of herself, the children will be able to see the illustrations as the pages are turned, and by glancing occasionally at the text, she can proceed with the account. If the book is tipped backward, the children will have a tendency to stretch or rise up to see the picture; if the book is tipped forward, the children will find it to their advantage to remain seated while the story is read.

## Children's Storytelling

Too often the teacher feels that the responsibility or privilege of telling the story is hers alone. Kindergarten children not only enjoy but profit by retelling and creating stories. At times the teacher may make it a special point to impress on the group that a story from the children will be appreciated by both the children and herself. It is probably not quite fair either to the teller or to the audience to ask a child, unless he is one of the rare artists at storytelling, to tell a story with which the group is already familiar. Often, as suggested in Chapter 18, the children may share with the group stories they have heard outside the kindergarten. Original stories may be encouraged and stimulated by asking the children to make up or tell dreams. The dream story allows for unbounded flights of imagination. There should be a distinction between the story that really happened or might happen and the imaginary tale. Wooden or felt figures of characters from several familiar stories—*Three Billy Goats Gruff, The Three Bears, Little Black Sambo*—may be set out to encourage the children to make up new stories in which the familiar characters appear. Picture books with either poor or foreign texts offer an inducement for original story contributions. Even the child who lacks imagination seems to feel that making a text for a book is a worthy cause.

## Dramatization of Stories

Kindergarten children enjoy dramatizing or, as they say, "playing the story." Watch and listen to them on the playground! Find a set of steps with an opening undernearth or a slide with someone crouched beneath it and you are almost sure to hear someone call out, "Who's that going across my bridge?" Over in the sandbox you may hear one child calling to another, "Here, wait a minute. Here comes Mary Ann. I'll play I'm Mike Mulligan and we'll dig that hole for you. Watch out! She's taking hold." Sometimes a story such as *Three Billy Goats Gruff* will be played with the entire sequence being carried through; but most often you will hear only snatches of the story being dramatized. When children dramatize stories in the kindergarten, the teacher should realize that a story will seldom be played in its entirety unless she as a teacher pretty much dictates each step in the procedure. And if she does that, the fun and spontaneity of the play usually are lost. Frequently nursery rhymes or brief narrative poems, such as the rhymed account of the snowman who stood outside the door and then was blown inside the house only to become a puddle on the floor, will give greater impetus to creative dramatization than will stories of greater length and more detail.

Stories should be dramatized in the kindergarten chiefly for the enjoyment which role-playing affords. A dramatization worked up solely for an audience often defeats its own purpose. Because of values to be derived from role-playing, it is desirable for the children to feel and play the parts informally and then, if they want to, to present "the play" to an audience simply in the belief that the audience too will enjoy what has been enjoyed by the players. Even when "the play" has been worked out in considerable detail, its presentation is usually enjoyed more by the actors than by the audience.

Stage properties need not be elaborate; the children's imagination can do much to supply missing effects. A box of odds and ends, including among other things a basket, a square of cloth to be used interchangeably as a shawl, scarf, apron, tablecloth, or doll blanket, and a few fancy bits of ribbon, a man's cap, a pair of "ears," and maybe a "tail" or two will do much to stimulate dramatic play. Other costumes or stage properties may be evolved by the children themselves. Elaborate costumes designed by the teacher and made by the mothers or the teacher are not necessary for kindergarten dramatization.

Simple hand or stick puppets—either commercially made or made by the children themselves—paper dolls on sticks, potato-head puppets, small squash, stuffed paper-bag puppets, and many others are sure to encourage the children in role-playing. The children will enjoy building their own puppet stage of large floor blocks, or they can even have fun manipulating the puppets as they crouch behind screens or movable storage cases. The use of puppets will often encourage even the most timid child to speak up in order to have his character heard. Although the children sometimes dramatize familiar stories with their puppets, more often than not they make up their stories as they go along.

The following rhymes, stories, and poems suggest the type of written story material which lends itself well to dramatization:[8]

| | |
|---|---|
| Nursery Rhymes | 8, 51, 204, and 215—"Jack and Jill," "Jack Be Nimble," "Little Miss Muffet," "Hickory Dickory Dock," and "Little Jack Horner" |
| Stories | "Three Billy Goats Gruff" (1), (3), (21), and (29); "Little Duckling Tries His Voice" (4), (8), (12); "Three Bears" (1), (16), (21), (23), and (29); "The Story of Dobbin" (2); "The Boy and the Goats" (3); *The Funny Thing* 87; "The Poppy Seed Cakes" 43; and *One Little Indian Boy* 29 |
| Poetry | "Baby Seed Song" 206; "Lines and Squares" 149 (27); "Little Turtle" 10, 112, 206, (21), and (27); "Once There Was a Snowman" 112; "Whisky Frisky" 91, 112, and (21) |

## Poetry

To set aside a period in the day for poetry and during this period simply to read and check the poems which each child has memorized is to approach the whole field of poetry in the wrong fashion. It is putting poetry and the learning of poems on a drill level. Poetry ought to mean much more than memorizing words or even ideas.

Poetry can scarcely be said to belong to any specific period in the day. Though it is often a narrative, it does not truly belong in the story period. To be thoroughly appreciated and enjoyed by the group, poetry must be presented when it seems to summarize or epitomize a group experience. If, for example, after raking and cleaning the yard in the fall, the children can have a chance to settle back to watch the bonfire made of the dried leaves and debris, then, and not at some later hour, is the time to introduce such a poem as "Autumn Fires."[9] If the children have walked to school on streets wet from an all-night rain, then, early in the session and not "next Friday," is the time to introduce "Rain in the Night."[10] Poetry is often introduced during a conversation or discussion period because at that time the group as a whole is thinking purposefully along one particular line.

Children like the "feel" of poetry, and they will frequently join in as the teacher reads or recites a poem. If a poem is really appreciated and enjoyed by the children, they make short work of memorizing it. Poems which have

[8] The numbers in parentheses refer to references on pp. 246–247. Other numbers refer to references on pp. 247–258.

[9] See reference, p. 243.

[10] See reference, p. 244.

already been introduced or which have been memorized may be reviewed profitably at the beginning or end of the story hour; but if poetry is substituted for the story itself, the children will express their disappointment openly.

Part of the beauty of poetry lies in the pattern presented as a whole, and for this reason it is well to encourage the children to listen to a poem as though they were listening to music. If there are interruptions in the reading or reciting, it is well to start again from the beginning, so that the children can get the feeling of the whole pattern.

Children's own poetical expressions are often a delight and worthy of being recorded—Jackie: "The rain drops are like a thousand and thousand of prisms." Billy: "The snow is like God's hand stretched out over all the world." Betty: "I can hardly wait. Just two sleeps until Christmas!" However, unless these poetical expressions are woven into a pattern by some poetry-minded adult, they are seldom more than refreshing and unique sentences or phrases.

Rhyming jingles, such as "I see the man, the man has a pan," which the older kindergarten child enjoys creating, may serve as a prephonic work. The rhymes to be found in many books will do much to stimulate kindergarten children's interest in rhyming sounds. And, of course, children take great delight in playing games that involve hearing or supplying rhyming words. A word of caution however! The appreciation of poetry is something that extends far, far, beyond the satisfaction derived from rhyming words.

## Finger Plays

Finger plays are not to be confused with poetry. Finger plays are usually nothing more than rhyming jingles accompanied by finger dramatization intended to amuse and hold the attention of the children for short periods of time. They have their place in the kindergarten, sometimes as games and sometimes as one of the many devices which help keep the group running smoothly. In the early part of the school year, they are sometimes substituted for poems, but they in no sense take the place of poetry. Few lay any claim to real literary value. A few finger plays which may be used as games or devices are listed below:

> Here's a ball. (Small circle made with thumb and index finger of one hand)
> And here's a ball. (Larger circle made by using both thumbs and index fingers)
> And a great big ball I see. (Huge circle made by using both arms)
> Shall we count them? Are you ready?
> One! Two! Three! (Each of three circles made as counted)

Two little houses all closed up tight! (Fists closed, thumbs closed in)
Open up the windows and let in the light. (Fingers and thumbs stretched)
Ten little finger people tall and straight, (Palms to the front, fingers erect)
Ready for kindergarten at half past eight. (Fingers erect, hands and arms move jerkily forward.)

Two tall telegraph poles, (Index fingers erect)
Across them a wire is strung, (Points of middle fingers touching)
Two little birds hopped on, (Thumbs touching "wire" made by middle fingers)
And swung and swung and swung. (Finger position held, arms swung)

These are my great sunglasses. (Circles made around the eyes with thumb and index finger of each hand)
This is my great sun hat. (Hands placed over head, forming pointed hat)
This is the way I fold my hands, (Hands clasped in the air)
And rest them, just—like—that! (Hands relaxed and resting on lap)

Here is the steam shovel, (Right forearm raised, hand hanging)
And here is the ground, (Two arms extended to inclose ground area)
See how the boom swings round and round, (With right forearm raised and hand hanging, let the arm pivot from the elbow.)
Dipping—(Let forearm with hand hanging descend to the area designated as the ground.)
Biting—(Thumb and fingers open and close)
Lifting—(Raise forearm slowly and let it pivot from the elbow)
Throwing—(Thumb and fingers open to deposit load)
Dipping—Biting—Lifting—Throwing—(Repeat above actions)
See how the hole in the ground is growing! (Peer into the hole made by two hands inclosing the hole area)

Five little black birds sitting in a line, (Left arm raised from elbow, fingers outstretched)
The first one said, "My the weather's fine." (Right hand touching thumb of upraised left hand)
The second one said, "But I feel a chill." (Pointer finger touched)
The third one said, "It's coming round the hill." (Third finger touched)
The fourth one said, "We had better not delay." (Fourth finger touched)
The fifth one said, "Let's strike right out today." (Little finger touched)
In the sky a "V" they drew, (Wrists crossed, hands up forming a "V")
As away to the sunny south they flew. (Wrists still crossed, move hands in a flying motion.)

## Selection of Stories, Picture Storybooks, and Poems

Just as surely as there is a field of literature for high-school students, so there is a field of literature for kindergarten children. In making a selection of the literature, the teacher must try to include the best of the old, tried, and tested materials and a wise sampling of more recent publications. The lists which follow suggest the stories, picture storybooks, and poems which might be incorporated into the program of the kindergarten year.

## Stories, Picture Storybooks, Finger Plays, Poetry and Story Recordings[11]

### STORIES AND PICTURE STORYBOOKS

#### ABC BOOKS, AND MOTHER GOOSE RHYMES

*ABC Books* 86, 146, 225
*Mother Goose* 8, 51, 84, 204, 214, 223

#### FOLK STORIES

"Boy and the Goat, The" (3)
"Cat and the Parrot, The" (9)
"Elves and the Shoemaker, The" (1) (3) (21) **59**
"Gingerbead Boy, The" (1) (9) (19) **20**
*Gone Is Gone* 88 (7)
"Gudbrand-on-the-Hillside" (30)
"Henny Penny" (1) (21)
"Journey Cakes Ho" 182
"Little Old Woman and Her Pig" (1) (3) (9) (21) (27) (29) **34**
"Little Pine Tree Who Wanted New Leaves" (6) (9)
"Little Red Hen" (29)
"Little Sojo" (4)
"Little Wee Woman" (29)
"Pancake, The" (1) (3) (21)
"Race Between the Hare and the Hedgehog" (3)
"Scrapefoot" (3)
"Story of the Three Bears, The" (1) (16) (21) (23) (29)
"Story of the Three Little Pigs, The" (1) (3) (21) (23) (29)
"Street Musicians" (3) (21) (23)
"Three Billy Goats Gruff" (1) (3) (21) (29) **63**
"Three Wishes" (16) (29)
"Travels of a Fox" (1) (3)
"When the Husband Kept House" (1) (23) **68**

#### EXPERIENCES OF CHILDREN, CHILDREN AND ANIMALS, AND ANIMALS

*All Falling Down* 233
*All My Shoes Come in Twos* 106
*Angus and the Cat* 73a
*Angus and the Ducks* 73b, (1)

[11] Numerals in ordinary type refer to books in picture storybook listing on pp. 247–258. Numerals in parentheses refer to books in story collections listing on pp. 246–247. Numerals in boldface type refer to recordings in story recordings listing on pp. 244–246.
See pp. 432–434 for listing of film and filmstrip stories.

## IMAGINARY ADVENTURES OF TOYS, ANIMALS, AND CHILDREN

"All About Copy Kitten" (1)
*And to Think That I Saw It on Mulberry Street* 188 (16) (23)
*Ask Mr. Bear* 74 (1) (4) (16)
*Blowaway Hat* 3 (66)
*Brownie's—Hush!* 4
*Brownie's—It's Christmas* 5
*Curious George Wins a Medal* 173
"Elephant's Child, The" (1) (16)
*Five Chinese Brothers* 24
*Five Hundred Hats for Bartholomew Cubbins* 190, **16**
*Funny Thing, The* 87
*Golden Egg Book, The* 34
*Happy Lion, The* 69
*Hercules* 98
*Horton Hatches the Egg* 191, **22**
*If I Ran the Zoo* 192
*In the Forest* 65, **24**
*Katy No-Pocket* 159 (11)
*Little Bear's Visit* 150
*Little Black Sambo* 13 (8) (19) (27) **30**
*Little Carousel* 30
"Little Duckling Tries His Voice" (4) (8) (12)
*Little Island* 145, **36**
*Little Toot* 99 (17) **39**
*Little Rabbit That Wished for Red Wings* 12 (19) **40**
*Little White Teddy Bear* 194
*Mellops Go Flying* 219
"Merry-Go-Round and the Griggses, The" (4) (16)
*Millions of Cats* 89, **48**
*Mr. Rabbit and the Lovely Present* 239
*Mr. T. W. Anthony Woo* 67
"Muddy Mouse" (14)
*New House in the Forest* 151
"Olle's Ski Trip" (20)
*Picnic Woods* 175
"Pooh Bear Goes Visiting" (1) (16) (23)
*Pussy Willow* 37
*Runaway Bunny, The* 39
"Space Ship to the Moon" (16)
*Story of Babar* 52 (23)
*Story of Ferdinand* 130 (16)
*Tale of Peter Rabbit* 169, **56, 57**
*Timothy Turtle* 50
"Two Little Shoes" (4)
*When the Root Children Wake Up* 72

## INFORMATION ABOUT NATURE[12]

*All Ready for Summer* 1
*All Ready for Winter* 2
*All Things Bright and Beautiful* 166
*Animals Everywhere* 49
*Autumn Harvest* 207
*Big Rain* 84
*Big Snow, The* (10)
*Bobby Follows a Butterfly* 201
*Carrot Seed, The* 127
*Country Noisy Book* 33, **50**
*Day We Saw the Sun Come Up, The* 97
*Fruit Is Ripe for Timothy* 177
*Gilberto and the Wind* 64
*Green Thumb Story, The* 70
*Little Gardeners, The* 62
*Hi! Mr. Robin* 208
*Hole in the Tree* 95
*Johnny Maple Leaf* 209

[12] For additional books on nature and mechanical things, see pp. 415–420, "Science Books for Children (and Teachers!)."

## INFORMATION ABOUT MECHANICAL THINGS[13]



## INFORMATION ABOUT THE COMMUNITY[13]



## HOLIDAY AND SPECIAL DAY STORIES

BIRTHDAYS



CHRISTMAS



[13] For additional books on nature and mechanical things, see pp. 415–420, "Science Books for Children (and Teachers!)."

## FINGER PLAYS[14]



## POETRY



[14] See also pp. 237, 238.
[15] Dolores Knipple (compiler), *Poems for the Very Young Child*, Racine, Wisconsin, Whitman Publishing Company, 1932. This book is out of print, but it seems to be the only source of the "Icicle" poem, just the right thing for a January thaw experience.

## STORY RECORDINGS[16]

1. Andy and the Lion WWS
2. Babar Stories DECCA
3. Big Snow, The WWS
4. Biggest Bear, The WWS
5. Blueberries for Sal WWS
6. Busy Man and the Night-time Noises BOW
7. But Muffin Can Hear YPR
8. Caps for Sale WWS
9. Carrot Seed, The CRG
10. Casper the Friendly Ghost GOL
11. Christmas Kitten BOW
12. Circus Baby WWS
13. Curious George Rides a Bike WWS
14. Emperor's New Clothes, The YPR, GOL
15. Finders Keepers WWS
16. Five Hundred Hats VIC
17. Follow the Sunset FOL
18. Frog Went A-Courtin' WWS
19. Georgie BOW, WWS
20. Gingerbread Boy, The DECCA
21. Hercules BOW, GOL, WWS
22. Horton Hatches the Egg MGM

[16] See listing of record companies, p. 246.

23. How the Singing Water Got to the Tub YPR
24. In the Forest WWS
25. In Which a House Is Built at Pooh Corner for Eyore VIC
26. Jenny's Birthday WWS
27. Johnny Crow's Garden WWS
28. Laughing Jack-O'-Lantern, The MER
29. Lentil WWS
30. Little Black Sambo VIC
31. Little Cowboy YPR
32. Little Engine That Could, The VIC, BOW
33. Little Hawk Indian Boy, The YPR
34. Little Hero, The (Lentil) YPR
35. Little Indian Drum YPR
36. Little Island WWS
37. Little Red Hen, The DECCA
38. Little Red Lighthouse WWS
39. Little Toot CAP, COL, WWS
40. Little White Rabbit That Wished for Red Wings BOW
41. Littlest Angel, The DECCA
42. Long-Name-No-Can-Say VIC
43. Madeline and Other Bemelmans Stories CAED
44. Madeline's Rescue WWS
45. Magic Clock, The YPR
46. Make Way for Duckling WWS
47. Mike Mulligan and His Steam Shovel BOW, WWS
48. Millions of Cats WWS
49. Muffin in the City YPR
50. Muffin in the Country YPR
51. Old Woman and Her Pig MER
52. Paddy's Christmas BOW
53. Pancho WWS
54. Peter and the Wolf (simplified) MER
55. "Peter Please! It's Pancakes!" CRG
56. Peter Rabbit BOW, DECCA
57. Peter Rabbit and Other Tales DECCA
58. Rolito DECCA
59. Shoemaker and the Elves, The DECCA
60. Stone Soup BOW, WWS
61. Story About Ping, The WWS
62. Story of Ferdinand CAP
63. Three Billy Goats Gruff DECCA, VIC
64. Tree Is Nice, A WWS
65. "'Twas the Night Before Christmas" DECCA
66. Two Little Trains YPR
67. Walk in the Forest YPR
68. When the Husband Kept House VIC

69. White Easter Rabbit, The MER
70. White Snow, Bright Snow WWS
71. Winnie the Pooh COL
72. Winnie the Pooh and the Heffalump VIC

| RECORD COMPANIES | CODE LETTERS | ADDRESSES |
|---|---|---|
| Bowmar Records | BOW | 12 Cleveland St., Valhalla, New York |
| Caedmon Records | CAED | 461 Eighth Ave., New York 10001 |
| Capitol Records | CAP | 1290 Ave. of Americas, New York 10019 |
| Children's Record Guild | CRG | 27 Thompson St., New York 10013 |
| Columbia Records | COL | 799 Seventh Ave., New York 10019 |
| Decca Records | DECCA | 445 Park Ave., New York 10002 |
| Folkway Records | FOL | 165 W. 46th St., New York 10036 |
| Golden Records | GOL | 630 Fifth Ave., New York 10020 |
| Mercury Records | MER | 228 N. LaSalle St., Chicago 60601 |
| MGM Records | MGM | 1540 Broadway, New York 10036 |
| RCA Victor Records | VIC | 155 E. 24th St., New York 10010 |
| Weston Woods Records | WWS | Weston, Connecticut 06880 |
| Young People's Records | YPR | 27 Thompson St., New York 10013 |

## STORY COLLECTIONS

1. ARBUTHNOT, MAY HILL, *Arbuthnot Anthology of Children's Literature,* Chicago, Scott, Foresman, 1953.
2. Association for Childhood Education International, *Told Under the Blue Umbrella,* New York, Macmillan, 1933.
3. Association for Childhood Education International, *Told Under the Green Umbrella,* New York, Macmillan, 1930.
4. Association for Childhood Education International, *Told Under the Magic Umbrella,* New York, Macmillan, 1939.
5. BACMEISTER, RHODA, *Stories to Begin On,* New York, E. P. Dutton, 1943.
6. BAILEY, CAROLYN S., *For the Children's Hour, Book II,* Springfield, Mass., Milton Bradley, 1921.
7. BJOLAND, ESTHER (compiler), *The Story Hour,* Chicago, Standard Education Society, 1956.
8. *Book Trails,* Vol. I., Chicago, H. Lawrence, 1928.
9. BRYANT, SARA CONE, *Best Stories to Tell Children,* Boston, Houghton Mifflin, 1912.
10. Child Study Association, *Holiday Story Book,* New York, Thomas Y. Crowell, 1952.
11. Child Study Association, *Read Me Another Story,* New York, Thomas Y. Crowell, 1949.
12. Child Study Association, *Read Me More Stories,* New York, Thomas Y. Crowell, 1951.

13. Child Study Association, *Read-to-Me-Again*, New York, Thomas Y. Crowell, 1961.
14. Child Study Association, *Read-to-Me-Story Book*, New York, Thomas Y. Crowell, 1947.
15. CONOVER, CHARLOTTE, *A Holiday Story Sampler*, Chicago, Albert Whitman, 1941.
16. GRUENBERG, SIDONIE (ed.), *Favorite Stories Old and New*, rev., New York, Doubleday, 1955.
17. GRUENBERG, SIDONIE, *Let's Hear a Story*, New York, Doubleday, 1961.
18. HARPER, WILHELMINA, *Easter Chimes*, New York, E. P. Dutton, 1942.
19. HARPER, WILHELMINA, *The Gunniwaolf and Other Merry Tales*, New York, David McKay, 1936.
20. HARPER, WILHELMINA, *Merry Christmas*, New York, E. P. Dutton, 1935.
21. JOHNSON, EDNA; SCOTT, CARRIE; and SICKLES, EVELYN, *Anthology of Children's Literature*, rev., see "Preschool to About Six," Boston, Houghton Mifflin, 1948.
22. KRAMER, NORA, *Nora Kramer's Story Book for Fives and Sixes*, New York, Julian Messner, 1956.
23. MARTIGNONI, MARGARET, *Illustrated Treasury of Children's Literature*, New York, Grosset & Dunlap, 1955.
24. MITCHELL, LUCY SPRAGUE, *Another Here and Now Story Book*, New York, E. P. Dutton, 1937.
25. MITCHELL, LUCY SPRAGUE, *Believe and Make Believe*, New York, E. P. Dutton, 1956.
26. MITCHELL, LUCY SPRAGUE, *Here and Now Story Book, rev.*, New York, E. P. Dutton, 1948.
27. O'CONNOR, BETTY (compiler), *Better Homes and Gardens Story Book*, Vol. I, Des Moines, Iowa, Meredith Press, 1950.
28. O'CONNOR, BETTY (compiler), *Better Homes and Gardens Story Book*, Vol. II, Des Moines, Iowa, Meredith Press, 1952.
29. ROJANKOVSKY, FEODOR, *Tall Book of Nursery Tales*, New York, Harper, 1944.
30. THORNE-THOMSEN, GUDREN, *East o' the Wind and West o' the Moon*, Evanston, Illinois, Row, Peterson, 1946.

## PICTURE STORY, FINGER PLAY, AND POETRY BOOKS[17]

†Adelson, Leone

1. †*All Ready for Summer*, New York, David McKay, 1956.
2. †*All Ready for Winter*, New York, David McKay, 1952.
3. †*Blow-Away Hat*, New York, David McKay, 1946.

[17] Daggers indicate entries with social studies implications. Starred titles indicate books deemed to be the rightful heritage of every kindergarten child. (See pp. 228, 229 of this chapter.)

| | | |
|---|---|---|
| Adshead, Gladys | 4. | *Brownies—Hush!*, New York, Henry Z. Walck, 1938. |
| | 5. | *Brownies—It's Christmas!*, New York, Henry Z. Walck, 1955. |
| Aldis, Dorothy | 6. | *All—Together*, A Child's Treasury of Verse, New York, G. P. Putnam, 1952. |
| | 7. | *Everything and Anything*, New York, Minton Balch, 1934. |
| *Anderson, Ann | 8. | **The Old Mother Goose*, New York, Thomas Nelson, 1925. |
| †Anderson, C. W. | 9. | †*Billy and Blaze*, New York, Macmillan, 1959. |
| Anglund, Joan Walsh | 10. | A *Pocketful of Proverbs*, New York, Harcourt, Brace & World, 1964. |
| Association for Childhood Education | 11. | *Sung Under the Silver Umbrella*, New York, Macmillan, 1962. |
| *Bailey, Carolyn | 12. | **The Little Rabbit That Wished for Red Wings*, New York, Platt and Munk, 1945. |
| *Bannerman, Helen | 13. | **Little Black Sambo*, New York, Frederick A. Stokes, 1923. |
| †Bannon, Laura | 14. | †*The Best House in the World*, Boston, Houghton Mifflin, 1952. |
| | 15. | †*Manuela's Birthday*, Chicago, Albert Whitman, 1945. |
| | 16. | †*Patty Paints a Picture*, Chicago, Albert Whitman, 1946. |
| †*Bate, Norman | 17. | †**Who Built the Bridge?* New York, Scribner's, 1954. |
| | 18. | †*Who Built the Highway?* New York, Scribner's, 1953. |
| *Bemelmans, Ludwig | 19. | **Madeline*, New York, Viking Press, 1939. |
| | 20. | *Madeline and the Bad Hat*, New York, Viking Press, 1957. |
| | 21. | *Madeline's Rescue*, New York, Viking Press, 1957. |
| †*Beskow, Elsa | 22. | †**Pelle's New Suit*, New York, Harper, 1929. |
| Bianco, Pamela | 23. | *The Valentine Party*, Philadelphia, J. B. Lippincott, 1955. |
| Bishop, Claire | 24. | *Five Chinese Brothers*, New York, Coward-McCann, 1938. |
| | 25. | *Twenty-two Bears*, New York, Viking Press, 1964. |
| *Bragg, Mabel, retold by Watty Paper | 26. | **The Little Engine That Could*, New York, Platt and Munk, 1930. |

| | | |
|---|---|---|
| Bright, Robert | 27. | *Georgie,* New York, Doubleday, 1944. |
| †Brock, Emma | 28. | *The Greedy Goat,* New York, Alfred A. Knopf, 1931. |
| | 29. | †*One Little Indian Boy,* New York, Alfred A. Knopf, 1932. |
| *Brown, Marcia | 30. | *Little Carousel,* New York, Scribner's, 1946. |
| | 31. | *Stone Soup,* New York, Scribner's, 1947. |
| | 32. | **Three Billy Goats Gruff,* New York, Harcourt, Brace, 1957. |
| †*Brown, Margaret Wise | 33. | **The Country Noisy Book,* New York, Harper, 1940. |
| | 34. | **The Golden Egg Book,* New York, Simon and Schuster, 1947. |
| | 35. | *Little Brass Band,* New York, Harper, 1950. |
| | 36. | *Little Chicken,* New York, Harper, 1943. |
| | 37. | *Pussywillow,* New York, Simon and Schuster, 1952. |
| | 38. | †*The Runaway Bunny,* New York, Harper, 1942. |
| †Bryan, Dorothy, and Bryan, Marguerite | 39. | †*Just Tammie,* New York, Dodd, Mead, 1951. |
| †*Burton, Virginia L. | 40. | †**Katy and the Big Snow,* Boston, Houghton Mifflin, 1943. |
| | 41. | †**The Little House,* Boston, Houghton Mifflin, 1942. |
| | 42. | †**Mike Mulligan and His Steam Shovel,* Boston, Houghton Mifflin, 1939. |
| Clark, Margery | 43. | *Poppy Seed Cakes,* New York, Doubleday, 1921. |
| Colver, Anne | 44. | *Nobody's Birthday,* New York, Alfred A. Knopf, 1961. |
| Crockett, Johnson | 45. | *Harold and the Purple Crayon,* New York, Harper, 1955. |
| | 46. | *Will Spring Be Early—Will Spring Be Late?* New York, Thomas Y. Crowell, 1959. |
| †Dalgliesh, Alice | 47. | *Bears on Hemlock Mountain,* New York, Scribner's 1952. |
| | 48. | †*Thanksgiving Story,* New York, Scribner's, 1954. |
| †D'Aulaire, Ingri, and Edgar D'Aulaire | 49. | †*Animals Everywhere,* New York, Doubleday, 1940, 1954. |
| *Davis, Alice Vaught | 50. | **Timothy Turtle,* New York, Harcourt, Brace, 1940. |

| | | |
|---|---|---|
| *de Angeli, Marguerite | 51. | **Book of Nursery and Mother Goose Rhymes*, New York, Doubleday, 1954. |
| de Brunhoff, Jean | 52. | *The Story of Babar, The Little Elephant*, New York, H. S. Smith and R. Haas, 1933. |
| DeJong, Meindert | 53. | *The Singing Hill*, New York, Harper, Row, 1962. |
| *Delafield, Celia | 54. | **Mrs. Mallard's Ducklings*, New York, Lothrop, Lee and Shepard, 1946. |
| †Dudley, Nancy | 55. | †*Linda Goes to the Hospital*, New York, Coward-McCann, 1953. |
| Duvoisin, Roger | 56. | *Easter Treat*, New York, Alfred A. Knopf, 1954. |
| | 57. | *The Happy Hunter*, New York, Lothrop, Lee and Shepard, 1961. |
| | 58. | *Petunia*, New York, Alfred A. Knopf, 1950. |
| Earle, Olive L. | 59. | *The Swans of Willow Pond*, New York, William Morrow, 1955. |
| †Earle, Vana | 60. | †*The Busy Man*, New York, Lothrop, Lee and Shepard, 1951. |
| | 61. | †*The Busy Man and the Night-time Noises*, New York, Lothrop, Lee and Shepard, 1954. |
| †Encking, Louise | 62. | †*The Little Gardeners*, Chicago, Albert Whitman, 1933. |
| Estes, Eleanor | 63. | *A Little Oven*, New York, Harcourt, Brace, 1955. |
| Ets, Marie Hall | 64. | *Gilberto and the Wind*, New York, Viking Press, 1963. |
| | 65. | *In the Forest*, New York, Viking Press, 1944. |
| | 66. | *Mr. Penny's Circus*, New York, Viking Press, 1961. |
| | 67. | *Mr. T. W. Anthony Woo*, New York, Viking Press, 1951. |
| Ets, Marie Hall, and Aurora Labastida | 68. | *Nine Days to Christmas*, New York, Viking Press, 1959. |
| Fatio, Louise | 69. | *The Happy Lion*, New York, Whittlesey House, 1954. |
| Fiedler, Jean | 70. | *The Green Thumb Story*, New York, Holiday House, 1952. |
| Field, Rachel | 71. | *Prayer for a Child*, New York, Macmillan, 1941. |
| Fish, Helen D. | 72. | *When the Root Children Wake Up (Etwas von den Wurzelkindern)*, New York, Frederick A. Stokes, 1930, 1941. |

| | |
|---|---|
| †*Flack, Marjorie | 73a. *_Angus and the Cat_, New York, Doubleday, 1931. |
| | 73b. *_Angus and the Ducks_, New York, Doubleday, 1930. |
| | 74. _Ask Mr. Bear_, New York, Macmillan, 1958. |
| | 75. †_Boats on the River_, New York, Viking Press, 1946. |
| | 76. _Happy Birthday Letter_, Boston, Houghton Mifflin, 1947. |
| | 77. †*_The Restless Robin_, Boston, Houghton Mifflin, 1937. |
| | 78. †*_The Story About Ping_, New York, Viking Press, 1933. |
| | 79. *_Tim Tadpole and the Great Bullfrog_, New York, Doubleday, 1932. |
| | 80. †*_Wait for William_, Boston, Houghton Mifflin, 1935. |
| Flothe, Louise Lee | 81. _Cowboy on the Ranch_, New York, Scribner's, 1959. |
| Foster, Doris | 82. _A Pocketful of Seasons_, New York, Lothrop, Lee and Shepard, 1961. |
| †*Françoise | 83. †_Big Rain_, New York, Scribner's, 1961. |
| | 84. *_The Gay Mother Goose_, New York, Scribner's, 1938. |
| | 85. _Spring Time for Jean-Marie_, New York, Scribner's, 1955. |
| †*Gag, Wanda | 86. *_ABC Bunny_, New York, Coward-McCann, 1933. |
| | 87. _The Funny Thing_, New York, Coward-McCann, 1929. |
| | 88. †_Gone Is Gone_, New York, Coward-McCann, 1935. |
| | 89. *_Millions of Cats_, New York, Coward-McCann, 1928. |
| Galdone, Paul F. | 90. _The Hare and the Tortoise_, New York, McGraw-Hill, 1962. |
| Gay, Romney | 91. _Picture Book of Poems_, New York, Grosset & Dunlap, 1940. |
| Gay, Zhenya | 92. _The Nicest Time of Year_, New York, Viking Press, 1960. |
| | 93. _Wonderful Things_, New York, Viking Press, 1954. |
| Geismer, Barbara, and Antoinette Suter | 94. _Very Young Verses_, Boston, Houghton Mifflin, 1945. |
| George, Jean | 95. _Hole in the Tree_, New York, E. P. Dutton, 1957. |

| | | |
|---|---|---|
| †Gilbert, Helen E. | 96. | †*Mr. Plum and the Little Green Tree,* Nashville, Abingdon Press, 1946. |
| Goudery, Alice E. | 97. | *The Day We Saw the Sun Come Up,* New York, Scribner's, 1961. |
| †*Gramatky, Hardy | 98. | *Hercules,* New York, G. P. Putnam, 1940. |
| | 99. | †**Little Toot,* New York, G. P. Putnam, 1939. |
| Grayson, Marion F. | 100. | *Let's Do Finger Play,* Washington, D.C., Robert B. Luce, 1962. |
| †*Hader, Berta, and Elmer Hader | 101. | †**The Big Snow,* New York, Macmillan, 1948. |
| | 102. | †*Little Stone House,* New York, Macmillan, 1944. |
| | 103. | †*Lost in the Zoo,* New York, Macmillan, 1951. |
| | 104. | *Mighty Hunter,* New York, Macmillan, 1943. |
| *Heyward, Dubose, and Majorie Flack | 105. | **Country Bunny and the Little Gold Shoes,* Boston, Houghton Mifflin, 1939. |
| Hoberman, Mary Ann, and Norman Hoberman | 106. | *All My Shoes Come in Twos,* Boston, Little, Brown, 1957. |
| Hogan, Inez | 107. | *Bear Twins,* New York, E. P. Dutton, 1953. |
| | 108. | *Koala Bear Twins,* New York, E. P. Dutton, 1955. |
| †Horwich, Frances, and Reinald Werenrath, Jr. | 109. | *A Big Coal Truck,* New York, Rand McNally, 1953. |
| | 110. | †*A Day Downtown with Daddy,* New York, Rand McNally, 1953. |
| | 111. | *Suitcase with a Surprise,* New York, Rand McNally, 1953. |
| Hubbard, Alice, and Adeline Babbit (compilers) | 112. | *The Golden Flute,* New York, Rand McNally, 1932. |
| Institute of Child Development | 113. | *Finger Plays,* rev., pamphlet, Minneapolis, University of Minnesota, 1956. |
| †Ipcar, Dahlov | 114. | *Black and White,* New York, Alfred A. Knopf, 1963. |
| | 115. | †*One Horse Farm,* New York, Doubleday, 1950. |
| Jacobs, Frances | 116. | *Finger Plays and Action Rhymes,* New York, Lothrop, Lee and Shepard, 1954. |
| Jacobs, Leland | 117. | *Goodnight, Mr. Beetle,* New York, Holt, Rinehart and Winston, 1963. |
| Johnson, Johanna | 118. | *Sugar Plum,* New York, Alfred A. Knopf, 1955. |

| | |
|---|---|
| Kahl, Virginia | 119. *The Habits of Rabbits*, New York, Scribner's, 1957. |
| †Kay, Helen | 120. †*One Mitten Lewis*, New York, Lothrop, Lee and Shepard, 1955. |
| | 121. *Snow Birthday*, New York, Farrar and Rinehart, 1955. |
| Keats, Ezra Jack | 122. *Snowy Day*, New York, Viking Press, 1962. |
| | 123. *Whistle for Willie*, New York, Viking Press, 1964. |
| †Krauss, Ruth | 124. *The Backward Day*, New York, Harper, 1950. |
| | 125. †*Big World and the Little House*, New York, Harper, 1956. |
| | 126. *A Bouquet of Littles*, New York, Harper, 1963. |
| | 127. *Carrot Seed*, New York, Harper, 1949. |
| | 128. †*The Growing Story*, New York, Harper, 1947. |
| La Fontaine | 129. *North Wind and the Sun* (Brian Wildsmith, ill.), New York, Franklin Watts, 1964. |
| Leaf, Monroe | 130. *The Story of Ferdinand*, New York, Viking Press, 1936. |
| †Lenski, Lois | 131. †*Cowboy Small*, New York, Henry Z. Walck, 1949. |
| | 132. †*A Dog Came to School*, New York, Henry Z. Walck, 1955. |
| | 133. †*Little Airplane*, New York, Henry Z. Walck, 1948. |
| | 134. †*Little Auto*, New York, Henry Z. Walck, 1937. |
| | 135. †*The Little Sail Boat*, New York, Henry Z. Walck, 1937. |
| | 136. *On a Summer Day*, New York, Henry Z. Walck, 1953. |
| | 137. †*When I Grow Up*, New York, Henry Z. Walck, 1960. |
| †*Lindman, Maj | 138. †*Flicka, Ricka, Dicka, and Their New Friend*, Chicago, Albert Whitman, 1942. |
| | 139. †*Snipp, Snapp, Snurr, and the Big Surprise*, Chicago, Albert Whitman, 1937. |
| | 140. †**Snipp, Snapp, Snurr and the Red Shoes*, Chicago, Albert Whitman, 1932. |
| †*McCloskey, Robert | 141. †**Blueberries for Sal*, New York, Viking Press, 1948. |
| | 142. †**Make Way for Ducklings*, New York, Viking Press, 1941. |

| | |
|---|---|
| | 143. †*One Morning in Maine*, New York, Viking Press, 1952. |
| | 144. †*Time of Wonder*, New York, Viking Press, 1958. |
| †McDonald, Golden | 145. †*Little Island*, New York, Doubleday, 1946. |
| †McGinley, Phyllis | 146. †*All Around the Town*, Philadelphia, J. B. Lippincott, 1948. |
| Memling, Carl | 147. *I Can Count*, New York, Golden Press, 1963. |
| Milne, A. A. | 148. *Now We Are Six*, New York, E. P. Dutton, 1927. |
| | 149. *When We Were Very Young*, New York, E. P. Dutton, 1924. |
| Minarik, Elsie Homelund | 150. *Little Bear's Visit*, Harper, New York, 1961. |
| †Mitchell, Lucy Sprague | 151. †*New House in the Forest*, New York, Simon and Schuster, 1946. |
| †Moeschlin, Elsa | 152. †*Little Boy with the Big Apples*, New York, Coward-McCann, 1932 OP. |
| †Monsell, Helen A. | 153. †*Paddy's Christmas*, New York, Alfred A. Knopf, 1942. |
| *Moore, Clement | 154. **Night Before Christmas*, New York, Houghton Mifflin, 1958. |
| Munari, Bruno | 155. *Birthday Present*, New York, Harper, 1959. |
| | 156. *Bruno Munari's Zoo*, Cleveland, World Publishing, 1963. |
| †*Newberry, Clare | 157. †**April's Kitten*, New York, Harper, 1940. |
| | 158. **Mittens*, New York, Harper, 1936. |
| *Payne, Emmy | 159. **Katy-No-Pocket*, Boston, Houghton Mifflin, 1944. |
| Petersham, Maud, and Miska Petersham | 160. *The Box with the Red Wheels*, New York, Macmillan, 1949. |
| | 161. *The Christ Child*, New York, Doubleday, 1931. |
| | 162. *Circus Baby*, New York, Macmillan, 1950. |
| | 163. *The Rooster Crows*, New York, Macmillan, 1946. |
| †Petrides, Heidrun | 164. †*Hans and Peter*, New York, Harcourt, Brace, 1962. |
| Pierce, June | 165. *Finger Plays and Action Rhymes*, New York, Wonder Books, 1955. |
| †Politi, Leo | 166. *All Things Bright and Beautiful*, New York, Scribner's, 1962. |

| | | |
|---|---|---|
| | 167. | †*Little Leo*, New York, Scribner's, 1951. |
| | 168. | †*Song of the Swallows*, New York, Scribner's, 1949. |
| *Potter, Beatrix | 169. | **The Tale of Peter Rabbit*, Philadelphia, Henry Altemus, 1903. |
| Poulson, Emily | 170. | *Finger Plays for Nursery and Kindergarten*, New York, Lothrop Lee, 1893, 1921. |
| Reed, Philip (ed.) | 171. | *Mother Goose and Nursery Rhymes*, New York, Atheneum, 1963. |
| *Rey, H. A. | 172. | **Curious George*, Boston, Houghton Mifflin, 1941. |
| | 173. | **Curious George Gets a Medal*, Boston, Houghton Mifflin, 1957. |
| †Rice, Inez | 174. | †*March Wind*, New York, Lothrop, Lee and Shepard, 1957. |
| Robertson, Lillian | 175. | *Picnic Woods*, New York, Harcourt, Brace, 1949. |
| Rossetti, Christina | 176. | *What Is Pink?* New York, Holt, Rinehart and Winston, 1963. |
| Rothschild, Alice | 177. | *Fruit Is Ripe for Timothy*, New York, William R. Scott, 1963. |
| †Sage, Juniper | 178. | †*The Man in the Man-Hole*, New York, William R. Scott, 1946. |
| †Sasek, Miroslav | 179. | †*This is London*, New York, Macmillan, 1959. |
| | 180. | †*This is New York*, New York, Macmillan, 1960. |
| †Sauer, Julia | 181. | †*Mike's House*, New York, Viking Press, 1954. |
| Sawyer, Ruth | 182. | *Journey Cake, Ho!*, New York, Viking Press, 1953. |
| Schlein, Miriam | 183. | *Deer in the Snow*, New York, Abelard-Schuman, 1956 |
| | 184. | *Elephant Herd*, New York, William R. Scott, 1959. |
| †Schneider, Nina | 185. | †*While Susie Sleeps*, New York, William R. Scott, 1948. |
| †Selsam, Millicent | 186. | †*You and the World Around You*, New York, Doubleday, 1963. |
| Sendak, Maurice | 187. | *Very Far Away*, New York, Harper & Brothers, 1957. |
| *Seuss, Dr. (Pseud.-Geisel, Theodore) | 188. | **And to Think that I Saw It on Mulberry Street*, New York, Vanguard Press, 1937. |
| | 189. | **Cat and the Hat*, New York, Random House, 1957. |

| | |
|---|---|
| | 190. *Five Hundred Hats of Bartholomew Cubbins*, New York, Vanguard Press, 1938. |
| | 191. *Horton Hatches the Egg*, New York, Random House, 1940. |
| | 192. *If I Ran the Zoo*, New York, Random House, 1950. |
| †Shapp, Martha, and Charles Shapp | 193. †*Let's Find Out About Cowboys*, New York, Franklin Watts, 1963. |
| Sherrill, Dorothy | 194. *The Story of a Little White Teddy Bear*, New York, Holt, Rinehart and Winston, 1931, 1961. |
| †Slobodkin, Florence, and Louis Slobodkin | 195. †*Too Many Mittens*, New York, Vanguard Press, 1958. |
| †Slobodkin, Louis | 196. †*Circus*, New York, Macmillan, 1962. |
| | 197. †*Trick or Treat*, New York, Macmillan, 1959. |
| | 198. *The Late Cuckoo*, New York, Vanguard Press, 1962. |
| Slobodkina, Esphyr | 199. *Caps for Sale*, New York, William R. Scott, 1947. |
| | 200. *The Clock*, New York, Abelard-Schuman, 1956. |
| Steiner, Charlotte | 201. *Bobby Follows the Butterfly*, New York, Macmillan, 1959. |
| Stevenson, Robert Louis | 202. *Child's Garden of Verses* (Tasha Tudor, illustrator), New York, Henry Z. Walck, 1947. |
| Stover, JoAnn | 203. *If Everybody Did*, New York, David McKay, 1960. |
| *Tenggren, Gustav | 204. **Tenggren's Mother Goose*, Boston, Little, Brown, 1940. |
| Tensen, Ruth M. | 205. *Come to See the Clowns*, Chicago, Reilly and Lee, 1963. |
| Thompson, Blanche | 206. *Silver Pennies*, New York, Macmillan, 1927. |
| †*Tresselt, Alvin | 207. †**Autumn Harvest*, New York, Lothrop, Lee and Shepard, 1951. |
| | 208. †**Hi! Mr. Robin!* New York, Lothrop, Lee and Shepard, 1951. |
| | 209. *Johnny Maple Leaf*, New York, Lothrop, Lee and Shepard, 1948. |
| | 210. *The Rabbit Story*, New York, Lothrop, Lee and Shepard, 1957. |
| | 211. †**Rain Drop Splash*, New York, Lothrop, Lee and Shepard, 1946. |

| | |
|---|---|
| | 212. †*Wake Up City*, New York, Lothrop, Lee and Shepard, 1957. |
| | 213. †*White Snow Bright Snow*, New York, Lothrop, Lee and Shepard, 1947. |
| †Tudor, Tasha | 214. †*Around the Year*, New York, Henry Z. Walck, 1957. |
| | 215. *Mother Goose*, New York, Henry Z. Walck, 1957. |
| | 216. †*Pumpkin Moonshine*, New York, Henry Z. Walck, 1938, 1962. |
| †Udry | 217. *Let's Be Enemies*, New York, Harper, 1961. |
| | 218. †*A Tree Is Nice*, New York, Harper, 1957. |
| Ungerer, Tomi | 219. *The Mellops Go Flying*, New York, Harper, 1957. |
| Unwin, Nora | 220. *The Proud Pumpkin*, New York, E. P. Dutton, 1953. |
| †Ward, Lynn | 221. †*The Biggest Bear*, Boston, Houghton Mifflin, 1952. |
| †Weisgard, Leonard | 222. †*Treasures to See*, New York, Harcourt, Brace, 1957. |
| Wells, Carolyn | 223. *Mother Goose*, Garden City, Garden City Books, 1946. |
| Werner, Jane | 224. *Golden Book of Poetry*, New York, Golden Press, 1947. |
| Wildsmith, Brian | 225. *Wildsmith's ABC*, New York, Franklin Watts, 1963. |
| †Will and Nicolas | 226. *Even Steven*, New York, Harcourt, Brace, 1952. |
| | 227. †*Finders Keepers*, New York, Harcourt, Brace, 1951. |
| †Wright, Ethel | 228. †*Saturday Walk*, New York, William R. Scott, 1951, 1954. |
| †Wynkoop, Margaret | 229. †*Mac Goes to School*, New York, Doubleday, 1941, 1961. |
| †Yashima, Nitsu, and Taro Yashima | 230. *Momo's Kitten*, New York, Viking Press, 1961. |
| | 231. †*Umbrella, The*, New York, Viking Press, 1958. |
| †Yashima, Taro | 232. †*Crow Boy*, New York, Viking Press, 1955. |
| †Zion, Gene | 233. *All Falling Down*, New York, Harper, 1951. |
| | 234. †*Jeffie's Party*, New York, Harper, 1957. |
| | 235. *The Meanest Squirrel I Ever Met*, New York, Harper, 1962. |

| | | |
|---|---|---|
| | 236. | *No Roses for Harry*, New York, Harper, 1958. |
| †Zolotow, Charlotte | 237. | *Mr. Rabbit and the Lovely Present*, New York, Harper, 1962. |
| | 238. | *Over and Over*, New York, Harper, 1957. |
| | 239. | †*Park Book*, New York, Harper, 1944. |
| | 240. | †*Storm Book*, New York, Harper, 1952. |
| | 241. | †*A Tiger Called Thomas*, New York, Lothrop, Lee and Shepard, 1963. |

## SUMMARY

The library area is an essential part of any kindergarten room, and there should be something about the area which makes it a very special place. Although most kindergarten children do not read, they can build up certain prereading skills by watching the teacher read and by handling and using books themselves. The teacher, through reading and storytelling, can share with the group pleasure of the highest type. In selecting books for the kindergarten library, she should try to include the best of both the old and new in the way of picture storybooks. Not too many books should be on the shelves at the same time. A section called the home-school library may be reserved for those books which children bring from home. Children enjoy both listening to and telling stories. They frequently enjoy dramatizing bits of stories and poems. Nursery rhymes and finger plays may be thought of as forerunners to poetry appreciation.

## QUESTIONS AND PROBLEMS

1. Why should the library of a kindergarten have a setting quite different from that of the rest of the room?
2. If there is a school library room or a branch of the public library in the building, how may this be used? Is it desirable for the kindergarten to go there for their period with books?
3. Ask a five-year-old to name his favorite story or stories. Where in the classification given on pages 239–243 do these appear?
4. How can you incorporate books which the children bring from home into the kindergarten program and yet make sure that those books which are "too good to miss" are not slighted?
5. Try first reading and then telling a story to a group of three or four young children. Which is easier? Why? Which is more satisfying? Why?
6. What would you think of the advisability of having a daily ten-minute period set aside for poetry?

## SELECTED REFERENCES


Arbuthnot, May Hill, *Children and Books,* Chicago, Scott, Foresman & Company, 1947, 1957, 1964.

Arbuthnot, May Hill, *Children's Books Too Good to Miss,* Cleveland, Western Reserve University Press, 1948, 1953, 1963.

Association for Childhood Education International, *Bibliography of Books for Children,* Washington, D.C., Association for Childhood International, 1937 . . . first printing, biennial revisions from 1948 on.

Dalgliesh, Alice, *First Experiences with Literature,* New York, Charles Scribner's Sons, 1932.

Duff, Annis, *Bequest of Wings,* New York, The Viking Press, 1945.

Durant, Ruth Sawyer, *The Way of the Story Teller,* New York, The Viking Press, 1942. 1964 (paper)

Herrick, Virgil, and Leland Jacobs, *Children and the Language Arts,* Englewood Cliffs, N.J., Prentice-Hall, 1955.

Huck, Charlotte S., and Doris A. Young, *Children's Literature in the Elementary School,* New York, Holt, Rinehart and Winston, 1961.

Shedlock, Marie, *The Art of the Story Teller,* 3rd ed., New York, Dover Publications, 1951.

Tooze, Ruth, *Story Telling,* Englewood Cliffs, N.J., Prentice-Hall, 1959.

# 14

# SINGING THROUGH THE DAY

In group-singing time and throughout the day, the kindergarten program affords the child opportunities to

- Hear and enjoy a variety of good vocal music.
- Experience the pleasure of ensemble singing.
- Express his feelings, moods, and thoughts in song.
- Enjoy and learn how to control his singing voice.
- Build up a repertoire of songs.

There are comparatively few people who have the ability to sing on a professional level, but practically everyone, unless he suffers from some organic difficulty, can learn to sing satisfactorily and to enjoy singing. From infancy on, most children display an interest in and a love for music, and singing time can encourage and stimulate them to sing with others for the pleasure and satisfaction the experience affords. Although it is true that, with tremendous pressure, the kindergarten child can be taught to use his voice with a considerable degree of skill, such procedure usually so reduces the child's pleasure that often much time must be spent re-educating him to enjoy music. It seems wholly unwise, therefore, to destroy, through formal prolonged practice and drill, the child's native enjoyment of music.

The revival of interest in folk music, an interest probably as old as man himself, has led us to sense anew the joy of participation in singing. No longer do we think of singing solely as an end product, a performance, but rather as an expression through which an individual or a group of people can give voice to thoughts, feelings, and emotions. As with painting and drawing, we recognize that study, technique, talent, and hard work are involved in the production of a masterpiece, but we are also aware that young children, and adults as well, can get and sometimes give great satisfaction through their own untutored creative expression.

The teacher must still have in mind a measure of the child's musical accomplishment, and she can help him try to raise his own standard of achievement and enjoyment.[1] Through simple, enjoyable tone and phrase drill, through her own appreciation of the creative musical expressions of the children, and through offering delightful examples of vocal music, the teacher is constantly raising musical standards. At one and the same time, she makes an effort to enrich the child's musical experience and preserve the spontaneous and satisfying joy of singing.

## Group Singing in the Daily Schedule

There seems to be no uniform time in the daily schedule for group singing. In some kindergartens, it is used as an "opening exercise," in others it is scheduled for the middle of the session, and in others it is the last or almost the last period in the day. There is probably no one "best" time for group singing, though for various reasons it seems wise to have it scheduled for the middle of the session. If it comes at the beginning, it is like eating the frosting off the cake first, and if it comes at the end, the children are likely to be too tired to give it their best attention and enthusiasm. There are two precautions which ought to be taken, however, in scheduling a time for group singing. The period ought not follow one of violent activity, when the children will be out of breath; and it ought not precede or follow a long period requiring sustained attention, for the children, obviously, will be in need of bodily activity. A period of group singing is usually not more than ten or fifteen minutes, but as the year progresses, there will be days when the group will enjoy singing together for a much longer time.

Though a certain period of the kindergarten day is set aside for group singing, if a good social climate exists the children will sing together at other times during the day as well. Children frequently sing together as they work and play, and if there is within the group a child or several children who have experienced the thrill and fun of picking out familiar tunes on the piano, other children will naturally gravitate to the piano to add their voices to the fun. Children also enjoy the "sing-along" experience that many recordings inspire.

## Arrangement for Group Singing

In some schools the children are expected to bring their chairs to the piano for singing time. Their vocal technique is probably better if they

[1] Unfortunately, this must be a measure based only on her own judgment. No scientific music tests are available for children under eight. Herbert Wing's *Standardized Test of Musical Intelligence*, Sheffield, England, Sheffield City Training College, 1948, is for age 10 and possibly as young as age 8.

sit in chairs, but for enjoyment the informality of having the children group themselves on the floor is more desirable—and sometimes it is fun just to stand around the piano and sing.

If it can be achieved casually, it is good to have those children who have the greatest difficulty in matching tones sit near the teacher or the piano. In some school systems, as the year progresses, the teacher is expected to assign each child to one of three rows. The skillful in matching tones are assigned to a back row, and the others, in accordance with their musical performance, are assigned to rows closer to the piano. If this must be done, some of the original informality may be retained by arranging the rows in a semicircle. According to Seashore and others, five-year-olds are at a stage of development wherein the more informal type of musical experience is most profitable.[2]

The piano, if used in the singing period, should be in front of the children and so placed that the teacher can sit at it and see the group at the same time. The piano should be tuned at least once a year, and if atmospheric conditions within the room vary greatly from one part of the year to another, it should be tuned more frequently. Other stringed instruments, such as an autoharp, banjo, guitar, or violin, are often used to provide musical accompaniment in the singing period.

## Presenting A New Song

When a new song is presented, the children should hear the whole melody before beginning to learn either the melody or the words. Sometimes the new song is played through on the piano or hummed by the teacher the day before it is to be taught to the children. In this case, the teacher may just play the song through as a surprise listening experience, or she may say that she is playing or humming a tune which she enjoys and which she hopes they will enjoy learning. If the children enjoy the melody, they will usually ask the teacher to play it again, so that the group hears the whole song twice before trying to sing it.

## Using the Teacher's Voice as a Pattern for Teaching the Song

If the teacher is fortunate enough to have a voice that is musically enjoyable, it is well for her to sing the whole song through to the children without accompaniment. After this, she may invite the children to sing with her

[2] See reference at the end of this chapter.

as much of it as they can remember. Some children will feel lost and probably say or imply by their expressions that they don't know the song. The teacher may then say, "Suppose I sing just a phrase of the song and then after I have finished, you sing that phrase right back to me—you be my echo." The children will need to listen carefully to the teacher's pattern. Sometimes the teacher can ask for a repeat of the echo, suggesting that it was not quite like the music she sent out. The children will probably be delighted with the echo idea and shortly the song will be theirs—another treasure to be added to their repertoire.

## Using an Instrument as a Pattern for Teaching the Song

An instrument is a poor substitute for a pleasant singing voice, but it is to be preferred to an unpleasant or a distinctly untrue singing voice. When an instrument is used, the teacher should play the song through first from beginning to end. She may at first play it through with the accompaniment, but before the children begin to learn it, she will certainly play it through using only the melody. As she plays the melody alone, she will suggest that they listen now for just the singing part of the song. Next she may tell the children the story of the song, giving them the exact words of the book but telling them in such a way that it will sound like a continuous story. Then she may ask the children to listen carefully as she plays the melody through once more to see whether they can hear any music that seems to tell a certain part of the story. If a child does find a measure or a phrase that matches the story, the children may join in singing that bit. Phrase by phrase, the teacher may present the words and the music. While the teacher plays the music, she may ask the children to "think" the words—not *sing* them, but just *think* them—and then, when the music is repeated, they may sing the words. Sometimes the children and the teacher can take turns singing the phrases back to each other. Almost before all the different parts of the story have been sung, a child or a group of children will usually say, "Now let's put it together." And lo—when the phrases are put together, the song fairly "sings itself." A word of caution! This may not be so the first day, but on succeeding days the entire song will be recalled quite easily.

When we realize how quickly children pick up songs from hearing them on the radio and TV, we can see that sheer repetition of a hearing experience is one of the best ways for children to learn new songs. Taking a cue from this, we would perhaps do well to give groups more opportunities to hear songs sung over and over again in their entirety. Many listening repetitions and less drill might be a good policy.

## Tone and Phrase Drill

There is a place for some kinds of drill in the singing program. It is important that children get the feel of matching tones and phrases. This is often achieved by playing certain simple drill games. For example, the children may play the echo game. In this game the teacher calls a name or phrase and then designates someone to be the echo—to return it exactly as she called it. Sometimes the children play they are vendors selling fruit, flowers, vegetables, or papers, and they take turns calling their wares. Each child who has a turn tries to think of a new and different thing to call, but he calls his wares in a musical pattern designated by a piano pattern played by the teacher, such as

Generally, the musical interval should not be greater than fifths, and it is usually easier for children to match tones in a descending than in an ascending scale.

Children also enjoy singing simple phrases and challenging the teacher or another child to match them on the piano. Of course, some children and some teachers have real difficulty with this challenge, but it is great fun, and the attempts afford a good listening experience for the group. Another interesting drill experience is humming a phrase from a song and asking the children to identify the song. After the game has been played with the teacher supplying the phrase to be identified, she may ask a child to sing a song to himself and then to hum a phrase aloud. Play with ascending and descending musical patterns also offers opportunities for interesting tone drill. For this experience children may stand by the piano as the teacher slowly plays a broken or a running series of notes. As the children listen, they lower or raise themselves when the music falls or rises. These and many other such experiences come under the general heading of tone or phrase drill—quite different from formal, regimented practice and drill procedures.

## Encouraging the Use of Light Pleasant Tones and a Smooth Flow of Song

The pattern offered by the instrument or the teacher's own voice can do much to induce the children to use light, pleasant tones. If the child finds it difficult to achieve light, clear tones, it may help him to accompany his vocal effort with bodily movement, such as pretending to toss a ball or balloon into the air as he sounds a high note. At least two or three times a week, some help should be given those children who cannot seem to sense the pitch. This may be given either in the music period or during the free-time activities period.

Sometimes the children can get the idea of singing smoothly if they diagram with their hands the way the song sounds and the way it might be sung. For example, if the song is rough and choppy, the design will look like this:

If the song is smooth and flowing, the design will be like this:

To help the child sing so that his music will float out on the air rather than drop to the floor as he sings, the children may dramatize a song such as "Apples Ripe." One child will sell his fruit on one side of the street (the room) and another child will be on the other side. If the person on

the opposite side of the street can hear what the vendor is selling, he will call back his wish to buy. If the person selling can understand that he wants to buy the goods he is selling, he will sell them to him and the play will begin again, with the children exchanging roles.

A song should be taught at the tempo at which it is to be sung. Inexperienced teachers are inclined to teach the song very slowly and then attempt to speed it up after it has been learned slowly. This necessitates two learnings instead of one.

## Singing in the Group and Singing Alone

The greater part of any singing period is usually devoted to group singing. The children may sing as an ensemble, or different groups may take turns singing to other groups. Sometimes at the conclusion of a song the teacher may comment that she heard some especially lovely tones coming from a particular section of the group and name two or three children who might have been responsible for them. Upon invitation these children may come to the front of the group to share their singing with the others. These children in turn may be asked to listen to the others as they sing and then to select voices they especially enjoyed listening to. Shortly a second and a third group will be chosen to stand with the singers. When approximately half the group is standing, the teacher may say, "Now suppose you all stand and let's have one big chorus." Or she may say, "Suppose the children who are now standing move over here. . . . And now let's have the people who are sitting stand over here. . . . Now we have two singing groups—two choirs, let's call them." The two choirs may take turns singing to each other. In this way every child is part of the singing group, and yet an opportunity is provided for the less skilled to hear the singing of those who are perhaps more skilled musically. Occasionally a child may be found who seems almost oblivious of the fact that all the others are singing "by mouth." He may be singing inside and he may be the child who sings at home every song he has heard at kindergarten. Of course, we would like to have him experience the fun of singing with a group but that, with a little help from the teacher, may come later.

At this age children frequently enjoy and even request the privilege of singing alone. This affords the teacher a nice opportunity to ascertain the musical proficiency of individuals. The artist-teacher will be quick to feature particular skills and be alert to finding ways to help those less musically skilled children find their "singing voices." There will be an endless number

University of Minnesota

*"Play it again."*

of ways which she will use in helping these children hear and appreciate differences and likenesses in sound. On the playground, for example, as a child taps on a metal fence with his sand shovel, she may say, "My, but that fence makes a high sound, doesn't it? Let's see if we can discover anything around here that makes a low sound." And together they may find that the metal wagon box or the manhole cover or something else on the playground makes a low sound. Or, when a child uses a pleasing inflection as he calls to a friend, the teacher may comment on his lovely *singing* tones, and she may even repeat his call, showing him how really musical it sounded to her.

An experience that will add great pleasure to group singing is having an artist come into the group with an instrument—preferably a stringed instrument, but a flute is lovely, too—to play songs which the children already know and perhaps to teach them a new song. If the artist is a person who really understands children and enjoys singing, the children will appreciate having him sing both with them and for them. The artist who comes to the group with an autoharp always receives a warm welcome, probably because the children themselves can produce beautiful tones on the instrument, and because the music of the autoharp so complements the singing voices that its music becomes a part of the singing experience, rather than something added to it.

## Original Songs

Thoughts, feelings, and moods often get translated into music. And since it is true that kindergarten children delight in playing with vocal sounds, it is only natural that many of their experiences should find expression in song. Sometimes the children develop simple chants to accompany their rhythmic motions, sometimes they use songs for the simple recounting of the steps in an activity in which they are engaged, sometimes they use song in their dramatic play, and often they sing purely as an expression of feeling and mood. Perhaps the best way to gain an appreciation of the five-year-old's song-making is to listen as children go about their work or play. Try to think of yourself as an observer as you read the following accounts of children at work and play in the kindergarten. Consider the many ways in which these particular children have expressed themselves creatively through song. You will note that in most instances these "songs" are but phrases or sentences; however, they are often phrases and sentences repeated almost ad infinitum. Five-year-olds do not usually create whole songs; they may paraphrase song verses or make up new verses to songs already familiar to them, but generally their own song-making is confined to musical expressions.

Let's start by observing Barbara. She is standing by the sink washing her paintbrushes by sloshing them up and down in an aquarium-like container. As she washes, she develops a rhythmic dipping motion and a lovely soft chant. With her curls bobbing and her whole body attuned to her dipping rhythm, she makes a lovely picture. But the chant, is it *too* something beautiful? Far from it—this is her chant, "Now I'm making poi-son . . . Now I'm making poi-son. . . ." And on and on the chant continues until the brushes are more than washed.

George is sitting at the piano striking clearly but lightly these notes over and over again in one unbroken pattern. Without breaking his rhythm he begins to sing, "I love you. Yes I do. I love you. Yes I do. I love you. Yes I do."

Jeff, sitting on the floor with a wooden xylophone and a rhythm stick, says, "Listen, it's a fire engine." Then as he strikes high C three times and lets his stick glide down the bars, he sings, "Ding Ding Ding. Wh-o-o-o-sh, Ding Ding Ding wh-o-o-o-sh."

Benjie, standing alone and half hidden by the piano, is beating out a rhythm on a tom-tom and singing to himself, "This is how the big tall Indian beats upon his drum." After several repetitions of this song, he makes up his own song, "This is how you bang your head when you're very mad."

Patty, shaking a maraca in each hand, sings out, "I'm happy, I'm happy as happy as can be."

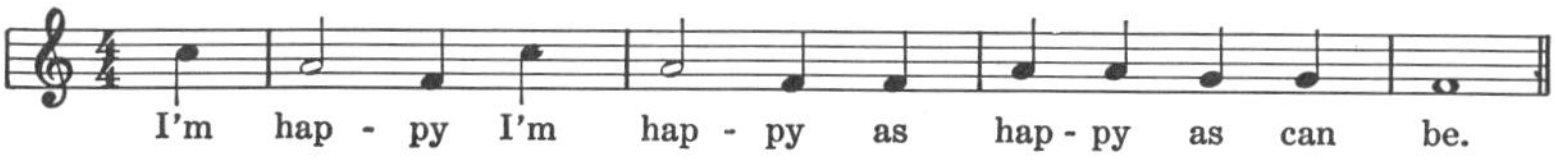


Ellen in the doll corner seems almost to be humming to herself, but there is no vocal sound audible. As she arranges her flowers and puts on the bread, she sings, "Now my dinner's ready."

Jimmy, who is baby-sitting while mother has gone to a party, kneels down by the doll bed, pulls up the covers, and sings, "There, there, don't you cry. Mother's coming by and by."

## Folk Songs

With the revival of interest in folk songs has come an awareness that folk music and children's own musical creative expressions have much in common. This, in turn, has led us to see that folk songs are part of the children's heritage. In an earlier edition of this book, there was a sharp distinction made between folk songs and songs about people, weather, and things which children know about, such as animals, toys, machines, and everyday play experiences. Now we are ready to agree with students of folk music not only that folk songs deal with things children feel and know about but also that their vigorous beauty and fluidity of style make them seem almost like the natural outpouring of children's own music. It is true, too, that the singing of folk songs can span the gap between generations as no other common experience can. In folk songs the kindergarten child has something he and his parents can enjoy together. We must now think of folk songs as a "must" in the kindergarten program. As children learn to enjoy folk music, one of the questions they often ask when a new song is being introduced is, "Is it a folk song?" And sometimes after hearing a song they will say, "It's good. I like it. It *sounds* like a folk tune." In such instances the teacher may reply, "Perhaps one day it will be a folk tune. If you sing it and enjoy it and other people sing and enjoy it, and if you all sing it to your children and your children sing it to their children, perhaps this very song will one day be called a folk song."

Before going on to a consideration of the selection of songs for kindergarten children, let's give a second thought to the idea that there is a fluidity about folk songs that invites improvisations. As we have observed, children just naturally improvise as they go about their play and work, and often a child will burst in the door with a sometimes shockingly modern version of a nursery rhyme or a nursery song. His song or jingle may run something like this (based on "Mary Had a Little Lamb"): "Johnny had an atom bomb, atom bomb, atom bomb, Johnny had an atom bomb, and he blew the works." Some folk tunes fairly challenge singers to go the written or sung text one better. Verse after verse can be made up and added without in most cases detracting from the interest and enjoyment of the verse or the many verses which others have associated with the tune. Sometimes, however, the original verses, or at least the ones we think of as the original verses, can never be enjoyed by a particular group, for every time the tune is heard the modern version sparks a ribald mood.

## Selection of Songs

In choosing songs, the teacher should look first to the range of notes within the song. In general the notes should fall between middle C and E above high C. Some research studies have indicated that the upper part of the vocal range has been stressed too much in songs written for children.[3] If we compare the score of folk songs with the score of songs written especially for young children, we will certainly find this to be true. Middle C to D above high C is more frequently than not the range in folk tunes. In addition to range, the teacher should look for other qualities in songs for young children. The song should have something to do with children's experiences, feelings, or moods; it should be simple, with a single mood or sharply contrasting moods; it should be short or repetitious; it should have a clear-cut melody running throughout; it should be strongly rhythmic and, of course, must be truly artistic.

The list of songs on the following pages merely suggests the types of songs which may be fitted into the kindergarten program. You may have

[3] A. T. Jersild and S. F. Bienstock, "A Study of the Development of Children's Ability to Sing," *Journal of Education Psychology*, October, 1934, 25:481-503.

your own favorites and may feel disappointed because certain songs have been omitted. If so, you may wish to insert an extra page in your copy of this book to be reserved for old favorites not included and new favorites as you come across them.

## Songs to Sing[4]

### ACTION SONGS AND SONGS THAT INVITE ADDITIONAL VERSES

Clapping and Stamping (30)
Dance to Your Daddy (27)
Eency Weency Spider (33) (43)
Follow My Leader (16)
I'm a Little Teapot (18)
John Brown Had a Little Indian (23)
Les Petites Marionettes (23)
Little Red Wagon (20)
London Hill (27)
Mary Wore a Red Dress (20) (33)
Nick Nack Paddy Wack (20)
One Day One Foot Kept Moving (27)
Skip-to-My-Lou (27)
The Spider (18)
This Old Man (29) (33)
Toodala (33)
What Shall We Do When We All Go Out? (33)
Who's That Tapping at the Window? (33)
Who's That Knocking at My Door? (33)

### AIRPLANE, BOAT, TRAIN, AND OTHER SONGS

Aeroplane (4)
Airplane (22)
Auto, The (5)
Canoe, The (10)
Down by the Station (10) (18)
Engine, The (4)
Ferry Boat (10)
Fire Engine (7)
Freight Train (2)
In the Sky (2)
Lovely Little Sail Boat (41)
My Boat Is Rocking (24)
Rocket Ships (43)
Row, Row, Row Your Boat (7) (10) (23) (37)
Sail Boat, The (10)
Train, The (10)
Train Is Coming (33)
Tug Boat, The (24)
Up in a Balloon (21)
Windshield Wiper, The (43)

### ANIMAL, BIRD, FISH, AND OTHER SONGS

All the Birds Are Singing (24)
Baby Birds (7)
Barnyard Songs (24)
Chicadees (18) (30)
Ducks, The (16)
Fly Away Little Birds (24)

[4] Numerals in parentheses refer to music books in which songs appear. See pp. 275–276.

## FOLK AND PATRIOTIC SONGS AND JUST-FOR-FUN SONGS

## HOLIDAYS AND SPECIAL DAYS

### Birthdays

A Birthday Song (5)
A Birthday Song (10)
Happy Birthday (30)

### Easter

Easter (34)
Glad Easter (4)
It's Easter Day (5)

### Christmas

Adeste Fideles (23)
Away in the Manger (42) (23) (30)
Busy Santa Claus (19)
Carol of the Beasts (21)
Christmas Day (15)
Christmas Tree (5)
Christmas Trees (19)
First Noel, The
Here We Come A-Wassailing (21)
Jingle Bells (6) (18) (23) (30)
Mary Had a Baby (23)
O, Little Town of Bethelehem (23) (30)
O Tannenbaum (4) (23)
Oh, Christmas Tree (20)
Santa Claus (15)
Silent Night (4) (15) (23) (24) (27) (30)
We Wish You a Merry Christmas (21)

### Halloween

Brownies and Witches (5)
Halloween (10) (24) (34)
Halloween's Coming (43)
In a Pumpkin Patch (43)
Jack o' Lantern (4)
Jack o' Lantern, Jack o' Lantern (18)
Pumpkin Mellow (24)
Some Funny Little Brownies (34)

### Hanukkah

My Dreydl (21)
Song for Hanukkah (27)

### Thanksgiving

Big Tall Indian (10) (18)
Ducks and Turkeys (27)
Gobble, Gobble (5)
Indians (10) (18)
Thanking God (5)
Thanksgiving (27)
Thanksgiving Is Coming (30)

### St. Valentine's Day

A Valentine (34)
Making Valentines (5)
St. Valentine's Day (19)
Valentine (4)
Valentines (19)

## LULLABIES

All Through the Night (23)
Bye Baby Bunting (23)
Cradle Song (10) (23)
Go to Sleep (10)
Hush, My Babe (23) (24)
Lovely Star, A (7)
Lullaby (5)
Night Song (38)
Rock a Bye Baby (23)
Sleep, Baby Sleep (15) (24) (37)
Stars, The (38)
When We Are Resting (7)

## PLAY, PLAYTHINGS, AND NURSERY RHYMES

Circus Band (34)
Daddy's Fiddle (34)
Dolly, The (4)
Fairies (34)
Gingerbread Boy (10)
Hippity Hop (19) (34)
Jacky Stand Still (16)
Jolly Clown (34)
Just Like a Cowboy (22)
Miss Polly (18)
My Cow Boy Suit (38)
My Drum (34)
My Scooter (35)
Nursery Rhymes (6) (18) (23) (24) (37)
Polly Perkins (16)
See How I'm Jumping (24)
Talking on the Telephone (38)
Teddy Bear (35)
Teeter-Totter (34)

## SEASONS

FALL
Autumn (5)
Autumn Leaves (42)
Brown Leaves (4)
Falling Leaves (5) (10) (24)
Gay Leaves (4)
In the Month of October (24)
In the Woods (11)
My Roadside Stand (22)
Off to School (19)
Red Leaves Falling Down (10) (24)
Shake the Apple Tree (24)

WINTER
Chicadees (18) (30)
Cold Night (4)
How Many Snowflakes (42)
Jack Frost (34)
Jacky Frost (4)
Snow (34)
Snowflakes (4) (38)
Winter (5)
Winter Goodbye (15) (24)

SPRING
In My Garden (19)
Pussy Willow (4) (5) (18)
Seeds (19)
Signs of Spring (38)
Spring (34)
Three Pollywogs (42)
Timothy-Tim-O (19)
Tirra-lirra-lirra (15)
'Tis Raining (24)
Winter's Past (15)
Working (Gardening) (5)

## SONGS ABOUT PEOPLE

Cow Boy Bill (38)
Balloon Man (19)
Carpenter, The (4)
Fireman (4)
Ice Cream Man (42)
Juggler, The (42)
Market Man (10)
Milkman, The (19)
Mister Baker (5)
Postman, The (4) (10) (38)
Traffic Policeman, The (19)

## List of Music Books—Song Books[5]


1. *ABESON, MARION, and CHARITY BAILEY, *Playtime with Music*, New York, Liveright, 1953.
2. Association for Childhood Education and Division of Christian Education, National Council of Churches, *Songs Children Like*, Washington, D.C., Association for Childhood Education International, 1954.
3. *BAILEY, CHARITY, and EUNICE HOLSAERT, *Sing a Song with Charity Bailey*, New York, Plymouth Music Co., 1955.
4. BAKER, CLARA BELLE, and CAROLINE KOHLSAT, *Songs for the Little Child*, New York, Abingdon Press, 1921.
5. *BEATTIE, JOHN W., and OTHERS, *The American Singer*, Book One, New York, American Book, 1944.
6. BERTAIL, INEZ, *Complete Nursery Song Book*, New York, Lothrop, Lee and Shepard, 1947, 1956.
7. BOESEL, ANN STERLING, *Singing with Peter and Patsy*, New York, Oxford, 1944.
8. BONI, MARGARET B., *Fireside Book of Folk Songs*, New York, Simon and Schuster, 1947.
9. BOTWIN, ESTHER, *A Treasury of Songs for Little Children*, New York, Hart Publications, 1954.
10. COLEMAN, SATIS, and ALICE THORN, *Singing Time*, New York, John Day, 1929.
11. COLEMAN, SATIS, and ALICE THORN, *Another Singing Time*, New York, John Day, 1937.
12. COLEMAN, SATIS, and ALICE THORN, *New Singing Time*, New York, John Day, 1956.
13. COMMINS, DOROTHY B., *Lullabies from Many Lands*, New York, Harper, 1941.
14. COMMINS, DOROTHY B., *Favorite Songs for Children*, New York, Grosset & Dunlap, 1951.
15. DAVISON, A. T., and T. W. SURETTE, *One Hundred and Forty Folk Songs*, Concord Series No. 3, Boston, E. C. Schirmer Co., 1921.
16. DUBSKY, DORA, *Sing and Dance*, Toronto, J. M. Dent, 1955.
17. ELKIN, R. H., and H. RÖNTGEN, *Old Dutch Nursery Rhymes*, New York, David McKay, 1917.
18. FLETCHER, MARGARET I., MARGARET DENNISON, and OTHERS, *The High Road of Songs*, Toronto, W. J. Gage, no date given—about 1946.
19. GLENN, H., S. LEAVITT, and V. L. BERMANN, *Sing a Song*, New York, Ginn, 1936.
20. *LANDECK, BEATRICE, *Song to Grow On*, New York, Edward B. Marks Music Corp., and William Sloane Associates, 1950.
21. *LANDECK, BEATRICE, *More Songs to Grow On*, New York, Edward B. Marks Music Corp., and William Sloane Associates, 1954.


[5] Recordings are available for starred books.

22. *LENSKI, LOIS, and CLYDE BULLA, *Songs of Mr. Small*, New York, Henry Z. Walck, 1954.
23. LLOYD, NORMAN, and MARY BLAIR, *The New Golden Song Book* (A Giant Golden Book), New York, Simon and Schuster, 1955.
24. MacCARTNEY, LAURA P., *Songs for the Nursery School*, Cincinnati, Willis Music Co., 1937.
25. MEALY, NORMAN, and MARGARET MEALY, *Sing for Joy*, Greenwich, Conn., Seabury Press, 1961.
26. McCONATHY, O. M., and OTHERS, *Music Hour in the Kindergarten and First Grade*, New York, Silver Burdett, 1938.
27. *McCONATHY, O. M., and OTHERS, *Music for Early Childhood*, New York, Silver Burdett, 1952.
28. MURSELL, J. L., GLADYS TIPTON, and OTHERS, *Music Through the Day*, New York, Silver Burdett, 1956.
29. OHANIAN, PHYLLIS B., and MARJORIE TORREY, *Favorite Nursery Songs*, New York, Random House, 1956.
30. PITTS, LILLA BELLE, MAYBELLE GLENN, LORRAIN E. WATTERS, and LOUIS G. WERSEN, *The Kindergarten Book*, Our Singing World Series, New York, Ginn, 1959.
31. RAY, FLORENCE, *Singing Days of Childhood*, Minneapolis, T. S. Denison, 1958.
32. SALISBURY, HELEN WRIGHT, *Finger Fun Songs and Rhythms for the Very Young*, Los Angeles, Cowman Publications, 1955.
33. *SEEGER, RUTH C., *American Folk Songs for Children*, New York, Doubleday, 1948.
34. SIEBOLD, META, *Happy Songs for Happy Children*, New York, G. Schirmer Co., 1928.
35. SIEBOLD, META, *More Happy Songs for Happy Children*, New York, G. Schirmer Co., 1938.
36. UNGAR, KURTH, and OTHERS, *We Like to Sing*, Toronto, J. M. Dent, 1954.
37. VAN LOON, HENDRICK, *Songs We Sing*, New York, Simon and Schuster, 1936.
38. WEICHARD, ANGELA, *Today's Tunes for Children*, Minneapolis, Paul A. Schmitt Music Co., 1941.
39. WILSON, HARRY, WALTER EHRET, ALICE M. SNYDER, and EDWARD J. HERMANN, *Growing with Music*, Englewood Cliffs, N.J., Prentice-Hall, 1963.
40. *WOLFE, IRVING, and OTHERS, Now Together We Sing Series, *Music Round the Clock*, Chicago, Follett, 1955.
41. *WOLFE, IRVING, and OTHERS, Now Together We Sing Series, *Music Round the Town*, Chicago, Follett, 1955.
42. *WOOD, LUCILLE, and LOUISE BINDER SCOTT, *Singing Fun*, St. Louis, Webster, 1954.
43. *WOOD, LUCILLE, and LOUISE BINDER SCOTT, *More Singing Fun*, St. Louis, Webster, 1961.

## Recordings that Sing and Invite Singing[6]

Autrey, Gene, and Others

*Christmas Fun with Gene Autrey and Others*—Columbia

Rudolph, The Red-Nosed Reindeer; Here Comes Santa Claus; Frosty the Snowman; Up on the Housetop

Bailey, Charity

*Music Time*—Folkways

Brass Wagon (a learning song), Brass Wagon (an activity song), Dormi Mon Enfant (listening to a quiet song), Missie Mouse (a clapping song), Toodela (a wakeup song)

*Play Time Songs*—Young People's Records

Look at Michie Banjo

*Singing in the Kitchen*—Young People's Records

Singing in the Kitchen; Come Dance With Me; Supper Song; We'll Ask Papa, Dear

Bailey, Charity, and Fifteen Children—Decca

Yes Indeed, My Darling; Sambalele; Sleep My Little Bird; Same Train

Chitjian, Howard (26-piece concert band of Los Angeles)

*Patriotic Songs*

Marine Hymn; This Land Is Your Land; Caisson Song; America; Columbia, the Gem of the Ocean; Yankee Doodle; When Johnny Comes Marching Home; Battle Hymn; God Bless America; Star Spangled Banner; Stars and Stripes Forever; You're a Grand Old Flag; This Is My Country; An American; There Are Many Flags in Many Lands

Evans, Dottie, John Anderson, and Others

*All-Time Favorite Disney Songs*—Harmony

Ballad of Davey Crockett, Heigh-Ho!, Hi-Diddle-Dee-Dee, Little Toot, Mickey Mouse's Birthday Party, Dwarf's Yodel Song, When I See An Elephant Fly, When You Wish Upon A Star, Whistle While You Work, Who's Afraid of the Big Bad Wolf?

Ginandes, Shep (with guitar)

*American Folk Songs*—Electra

Billie Boy, Froggie Went a Courting, I Bought Me a Cat, and 6 others

Glazer, Tom

*Collection*—Young People's Records

A Capital Ship, Other Funny Songs, A Hunting We Will Go, The Big Rock Candy Mountain, We Wish You a Merry Christmas, Round and Round the Christmas Tree, Little Bitty Baby, The Twelve Days of Christmas

Glazer, Tom, and Dottie Evans—Science Materials Center

*Space Songs*

Zoom a Little Zoom (Rocket Ship), Constellation Jig, Beep Beep (Here Comes the Satellite), and 11 other astronomical bodies

[6] For additional song recordings, see starred titles in "List of Music Books—Song Books," pp. 275–276.

Guthrie, Woodie (with guitar)
*Songs to Grow On*—Vol. I Nursery Days—Folkways
Put Your Finger in the Air; Come See; Race You Down the Mountain; Car Song; Don't You Push Me Down; My Dolly; How Doo Do; Pick It Up; Merry Go Round; Sleepy Eyes; Wake Up; Clean-O

Hinton, Sam—Folkways
Who Ever Shall Have Some Good Peanuts, The Green Grass Growing All Around, I Had a Little Nut Tree, Crawdad, Michael Finnegan, Jolly Old Roger, Old Dan Tucker, Old Boastun Was Dead, Little Old Woman, All Skin and Bones, Horse Named Billy

Houston, Cisco
*Nursery Rhymes, Games and Folk Songs*—Folkways
London Bridge, My Bonnie Lies Over the Ocean, Pumpkin Eater, Three Blind Mice, Yonder Tree, Cape Cod, and 5 others

Ives, Burl
*Animal Fair*—Columbia
*Mother Goose Songs*—Columbia
*More Songs*—Decca
The Lollipop Tree, The Little Turtle, The Moon Is the North Wind's Cookie, The Little White Duck, Two Little Owls, Fooba Wooba John

Ives, Burl, with Children's Choir
*Blue Tail Fly*—Decca

Jenkins, Ella (School Children in Group Singing — Instruments — Drum Rhythms)
*Call and Response*—Folkways
Zeembah Zeembah, Moon Don't Go, A Chant from American Chain Gang, Arabic Chant

Jenkins, Ella
*Come and See the Peppermint Tree*—Wonderland Records

Kaye, Danny
*Thumbelina*—Decca
*Wonderful Copenhagen*—Decca

Luther, Frank
*Children's Corner Vol. 1*—Decca
a. Betty Blue, The Lock and Key, The Rats and the Mice, I Had a Little Pony, A Little Pink Pig, The Cock and the Hen
b. There Was an Old Owl, Seven Birds Up in a Tree, The Farmer and the Raven, Birds of a Feather, Three Jolly Huntsmen, The Fox Went Out

*Children's Corner Vol. 2*—Decca
a. Burnie Bee, A Hop Skip and a Jump, My Little Tree, Where Did You Come From Baby Dear?
b. Robin Hood; Old Man Persnickety; Sneezing; Obadiah; Hot Codlins; Clap, Clap Handies; Dance to Your Daddy; That's All

*Home on the Range*—Decca
Get Along, Little Dogie

*Mother Goose Circus Time Songs*—Decca
Circus Parade March, Toy Soldier March, Here Come the Clowns, The Elephant Walk, and 12 others
*Thirty-Three Children's Songs*—Decca
A few favorites: There Was a Little Girl; Girls and Boys Come Out to Play; Oh Dear! What Can the Matter Be?; Billy Boy; Bobby Shafto; Old Mother Hubbard; Old King Cole; Little Jack Horner; Winkum, Winkum; Chinese Lullaby; How the Wind Blows
*Winnie the Pooh Songs*—Decca
Buckingham Palace, Hoppity, The King's Breakfast, The Four Friends, At the Zoo, Halfway Down, Vespers

Martin, Mary
*Mary Martin Sings for Children*—Young People's Records
The Sky Is Dark (Train Song); No, I'm Not Sleepy; Sing Soft and Low (A Song of Lullaby); Silly Me, Silly You, Silly We; I Wish We Could Go for a Ride

Miller, Mitch
*Sing Along with Mitch*—Columbia
Aunt Rhody; Billy Boy; Down in the Valley; Goodnight, Irene; Listen to the Mocking Bird; My Darling Clementine; Oh, Suzanna; On Top of Old Smoky; Pop Goes the Weasel; Red River Valley; Skip to My Lou; Bear Went Over the Mountain; The Blue Tail Fly; When Johnny Comes Marching Home

Mills, Alan (with guitar)
*More Songs to Grow On*—Folkways
Ha, Ha, This-a-Way; Up in a Balloon; How Old Are You?; Raisins and Almonds; We Wish You a Merry Christmas; May Day Carol; and 12 others
*French Folk Songs for Children*—Folkways
Sur le Pont d'Avignon, and 19 others (French text—English explanation)

Privette, Jeanne
*Victor Singing Program Vol. I*—Victor
a. The Frog and the Mouse, and 2 others; Mr. and Mrs. Turkey, and 3 others
b. Hey Diddle Diddle, and 5 others; When Little Children Sleep, and 2 others
c. John, John Johnny; and 3 others; Cossack's Lullaby; and 3 others
d. Sing a Song of Six Pence, and 5 others; Diddle Diddle Dumpling, and 5 others

Seeger, Pete (with banjo)
*American Folk Songs for Children*—Folkways
All Around the Kitchen, Jim Crack Corn, This Old Man, Clap Your Hands, Train Is a-Coming, and 6 others

Seeger, Pete
*American Game and Activity Songs for Children*—Folkways
I Know a Little Girl With Red Pajamas, I Want to Be a Farmer, Skip to My Lou, Candy Girl, Shoo Fly, and 7 others

Seeger, Pete
*Song and Play Time*—Folkways
Go In and Out the Window, She'll Be Comin' Round the Mountain, I've Been Working on the Railroad, Mary Wore a Red Dress, Ha, Ha, This-a-Way, and 11 others

Seeger, Pete, Charity Bailey, Adelaide Van Way, and Others
*Songs to Grow On Vol. 2, School Days*—Folkways
By'm By, Mail Boat, Mocking Bird, Skip to My Lou, Fire Down Below, Brass Wagon, Grey Goose, and others

Seeger, Pete, Bess Lomax, Butch Hawes, Cisco Houston, Tom Glazer, Woody Guthrie, Lee Hays (mandolin, banjo, guitars, and fiddle)—Folkways
*Lonesome Valley: A Collection of American Folk Music*
Down in the Valley, Polly Wolly Doodle, On Top of Old Smoky, and 4 others

## SUMMARY

The kindergarten teacher should be alert to the many ways in which children naturally express their thoughts and feelings through song. Although tone and phrase drill have their place in kindergarten, all musical experiences should further the children's enjoyment of music. Children especially enjoy folk music, and many of their chants and story songs have much in common with folk music. Most songs to be learned by kindergarten children should fall between middle C and E above high C. The human voice is the best possible model to use in the teaching of a new song, and repetition of a hearing experience makes the learning of a new song a simple matter. The more informal the singing group can be, the better.

## QUESTIONS AND PROBLEMS

1. Visit a kindergarten during a work or free-time activities period and seek to find the following:
   a. Examples of children singing familiar songs as they work or play.
   b. Examples of children's creative musical expression.
2. Make a list of the song books which you find in any kindergarten and note those which you would especially like to own, explaining why.
3. Observe a group-singing period in a kindergarten.
   a. What was the seating arrangement?
   b. What songs were sung and did the children seem to enjoy any one more than the others? If so, which one?
   c. Was there any effort made by the teacher to raise standards of musical skill?
   d. How long did the period last? Did everyone participate?
4. Find a folk song which is new to you. Try to experience the fun and the

effort, too, which a child might have in first learning the tune. Once having made the tune yours, try to teach it to another person, preferably to a young child.

## SELECTED REFERENCES


Christianson, Helen, and Others, *Music and the Young Child,* Bulletin, Washington, D.C., Association for Childhood Education International, 1936.

Coleman, Satis N., *Creative Music for Children,* New York, G. P. Putnam's Sons, 1922.

Ellison, Alfred, *Music with Children,* New York, McGraw-Hill Book Company, 1959.

Hall, Doreen, *Music for Children,* New York, Associated Music Publishers, Inc., 1960.

Landeck, Beatrice, *Children and Music,* New York, William Sloane Associates, 1952.

Morrison, Ida E., and Ida F. Perry, "Musical Expression Through Singing," *Kindergarten-Primary Teaching Procedures,* New York, The Ronald Press Company, 1961.

Mursell, James L., *Music Education: Principles and Programs,* New York, Silver Burdett Company, 1956.

"Music in the Experience of Young Children," *Teachers Guide to Education in Early Childhod,* Sacramento, California, State Department of Education, 1956.

Pierce, Anne E., *Teaching Music in the Elementary Schools,* New York, Holt, Rinehart and Winston, 1959.

Pitts, Lilla Belle, Mabelle Glenn, Lorrain E. Watters, and Louis G. Wersen, "Teaching Suggestions," *The Kindergarten Book,* New York, Ginn and Company, 1959.

Seashore, Carl E., "Music Before the Age of Six," *Why We Love Music,* Philadelphia, Oliver Ditson Company, 1941.

Seeger, Ruth C., "Introduction," *American Folk Songs for Children,* New York, Doubleday & Company, 1948.

Sheehy, Emma D., *Children Discover Music and Dance,* New York, Henry Holt and Company, 1959.

Sheehy, Emma D., *Music for Young Children,* New York, Henry Holt and Company, 1946, 1952.

Slind, Lloyd H., and D. Evan Davis, *Bringing Music to Children,* New York, Harper and Row, 1964.

Todd, Vivian Edmiston, and Helen Heffernan, "Enjoying Musical Sounds," *The Years Before School: Guiding Preschool Children,* New York, Macmillan, 1964.

# 15

# RHYTHM AND MUSIC APPRECIATION

The rhythm period of the kindergarten program affords opportunities for the child to

- Develop a feeling for and a sense of rhythm.
- Develop motor coordination and grace.
- Cultivate the power of careful attention.
- Express creative ideas and moods through bodily movements.
- Experience the joy of responding in a group to the stimulus of music.
- Develop social habits necessary for group appreciation of music.
- Listen to and enjoy good music.

One has only to watch a group of children to see that their natural response to music lies in bodily activity. Even the baby sitting in his carriage will bounce up and down and wave his hands when the band passes. A rhythmic response serves not only as needed exercise involving bodily coordination but also as evidence of active appreciation of the music.

It is this active appreciation of the music that we are most eager to stimulate through the rhythm and appreciation period. Whether through dancing or through experimenting and playing with simple musical instruments, we want the young child, first, to feel the desire to respond rhythmically, and, second, to be able to translate both his own moods and the moods of the music into rhythmical expression.

If we are to build up musical experiences that will take into account the child's innate feeling for music, we must plan our procedure carefully. It may sound logical to begin by directing the child's motor responses to the music and to advance by building up a series of specific responses to particular bits of music. Such a procedure, however, if given undue stress, would probably crush immediately the child's desire to respond freely and so would defeat the purpose of the rhythm and appreciation period.

The teacher who is fortunate enough to be able to follow the children's own moods and patterns with her music is in a position to foster a true feeling for and honest appreciation of music. But since there are only a few thus favored, this chapter will concern itself with the rhythm and appreciation period as conducted and developed by the teacher of only average musical ability.

## Rhythmic Expression in the Kindergarten

The listening and observant teacher will find rhythmic expression in many of the children's daily activities. She will observe Billy on the rocking horse as he develops an almost breathtaking rhythm; Jean as she transfers beads from the large container into her own basket, dropping her beads in a one-two-three rhythm; Carl chanting, "Now a block and now another" as his block tower grows higher and higher; Barbara as she washes her paint-brushes in a glass jar, accompanying her rhythmic sloshing with a dirge-like chant; Nancy at the finger-painting table moving both hands in a rhythm which is patterned on her paper; Barbara at the workbench repeating this pattern: "Pound, pound, pound-POUND"—"Pound, pound, pound-POUND." And though John, who is leaning against the counter with his chin cupped in his hands, appears to be doing absolutely nothing at all, if the teacher watches carefully she will note that he is raising and lowering his head in a rhythmic pattern. The teacher, by a glance or a word, can indicate her appreciation of these rhythmic activities, or she can save her observations to share with the group at some later time. Frequently it will be possible for her to incorporate some of the observed rhythms into the group rhythm time.

## Rhythms in the Schedule of the Day

Group rhythm time may well follow any one of the more quiet periods of the day—the song or library or story period, or conversation, or rest. The first time rhythms are introduced into the program, it is wise to make the period not more than eight or ten minutes long. Later, as the children become accustomed to some of the social requirements, it may be lengthened to twenty to thirty minutes. Because of the variety of activities engaged in during a rhythm period and because of the diverse moods expressed through the music, the time given to rhythm and music appreciation is frequently greater than that set aside for other organized activities.

Rhythms and music appreciation need not be limited to one period in the day. Music, like poetry, may be introduced anytime it seems to complete a particular group mood or to enrich an experience.

## Arrangement for the Period

The arrangement for the rhythm period is comparatively simple. The first requirement is that there be plenty of floor space in the room, and the second is that there be an instrument to accompany the activities. The instruments used vary from so simple a thing as rhythm sticks or the tambourine to the piano or the phonograph. Rhythm sticks and the tambourine are sometimes used for the appreciation of pure rhythm, quite apart from melodies. The phonograph is used as a supplement to piano music, sometimes as a substitute for it. If the kindergarten teacher is a good pianist, the piano is greatly preferred to the phonograph, for the teacher can then cut the music or regulate the tempo to the activities of the children. If, however, the teacher is a poor pianist or no pianist at all, she will do well to supply herself with a *good* phonograph and build up a library of tested records. Some teachers have worked up amazingly successful rhythm and appreciation periods, through their very careful study and selection of records and their skill in using them.

In most kindergartens one finds some instruments on which the children themselves can experiment. Often the child who is too self-conscious to give free bodily response to music will get great satisfaction and an appreciation and feeling for rhythm if he has an opportunity to experiment and play with drums, rhythm sticks, jingle clogs, tambourines, bells, or cymbals. Such instruments as the piano, xylophone, and tuned bottles will give the child the opportunity to experiment with tune, as well as with rhythm.

At rhythm time the children are usually grouped on the floor near the piano. The piano must be in such a position that the teacher playing can see the children, not only when they are sitting down but also when they are responding to the rhythms.

Since many of the rhythms involve a great deal of bodily activity, there should be an abundance of fresh air in the room during the period.

## A First Rhythm Experience

At some time during the first day or days of kindergarten, the teacher will observe during the free-play period that the children are engaging voluntarily in rhythmic activities. It may be that some children are swinging or teetering, or running, or skipping, or perhaps just walking about. If at the time the activity is observed, the teacher can sit down at the piano and unobtrusively accompany the dominant rhythmic activity with a bit of music, she will give the children their first kindergarten rhythm and appreciation experience. The children will probably leave their activities to listen to the piano, and thus the first rhythm group will be formed.

## A First Rhythm and Appreciation Period

When the children have assembled, the teacher may explain why she happened to play the particular bit of music to which the children have been listening. If some children volunteer to repeat the rhythmic activity, then a repetition may be in order; it is quite probable, however, that no one will volunteer to repeat the activity at this first group meeting. If there are no volunteers, the teacher may turn to the piano and play a lively, strongly accented bit of music in four-four time. Some children may begin to clap in time with the music. If they do, a suggestion may be made that all try clapping to the music. If the children do not respond to the music in any way, then the teacher, on completing the music, may turn to the children and ask them, while the strong rhythm is still in their memory, whether they heard the piano telling the story which her hands are going to tell. Without the music she may clap the rhythm. The children will doubtless feel the rhythm and join in her clapping. As they join in, the teacher may turn to the piano and accompany their clapping with music. After they have acquired the feeling of the rhythm with their hands, the teacher may ask if anyone can make his feet tell the same music story the piano tells. Various demonstrations may be given. The teacher may then ask if anyone has a different way to express the music. Demonstrations such as tapping, swinging the arms, slapping the thighs, and many others may be offered. The teacher must encourage every honest attempt.

Finally the teacher may ask the children whether they can walk about the room and make their feet express the music. It would be wise to suggest the direction in which they should circle the room. If the children become confused, as they often do, and go in both directions, they will immediately see the reason for the suggestion and following it may then become a habit. Once more the children will be asked to walk about the room, this time all in the same general direction.

If the music has been clear-cut and strongly accented, when it stops, the children will stop. The teacher may take this opportunity to compliment the children on the fact that they have really heard exactly what the music has told them to do. They may then walk with the music again, this time giving very particular attention to stopping exactly when the music stops. A signal on the piano will serve to bring the children back together.

A first group experience of this sort will not only give the children the feeling that music has a message and that it is fun to hear the many things it tells, but it will also help them to realize that they have the ability to express themselves in such a way that the music of an instrument can follow and blend with their movements. We do not want children to get the feeling that they must always follow along after the music. Sometimes, indeed, they can "follow along before." All too often the teacher says, "Listen carefully and do what the music tells you to do." The teacher who relies on recordings rather than her own playing is most apt to fall into this habit. The teacher who does not play a musical instrument well enough to accompany the rhythmic activities of children will do well to remember that she can pick up the rhythmic pattern of children's movement by using tone block, rhythmic sticks, or simple hand clapping. It seems a pity to have the teacher sit back and have the recording dictate the children's every movement. The rhythm period then becomes first of kin to the dictated work period.

## General Understandings Regarding Group Rhythms

It is essential for the fullest enjoyment of group rhythms that certain general understandings be developed. Included in these are (a) that individuals should try to find a field of operation large enough so that their activity will not interfere with that of any other individual, (b) that movement about the room should be in one common direction, and (c) that all activity should cease when the music stops. These need not be set up as hard and fast rules, but they can be developed as minor problems or conflicts arise.

## Raising the Standards of the Child's Response

In order to encourage a feeling for and original response to the music, the teacher may observe the whole group in action and then ask a particularly able and responsive child to repeat his performance. The teacher need not suggest that this individual's performance is the best, and certainly she ought not to imply that it is the only desirable response to the music. She can comment, however, on the fact that the child and the music seem to be at one with each other and that the child's way of expressing himself is completely his own. Further, she may suggest that since she enjoyed it so much she feels it only fair to give the rest a chance to enjoy it. When next the group performance is repeated with the same music, the unimaginative child will appreciate having some pattern for his response, and better yet, most of the group will be inspired to create new responses, knowing that a premium is placed on originality.

Sometimes it is well to use simple rhythm without the accompanying melody in order to help the children sense more clearly the effects of changing tempo, intensity, and rhythm. The teacher may tap lightly and quickly with the rhythm sticks, for example, and at the same time ask if any child can run to her tapping. If she makes the tapping clear and distinct, nearly every child can feel the pulse and run in time with the music. The teacher may tap slowly and heavily with the rhythm sticks and at the same time ask if any child can walk to the music. Again the pulse and intensity of music should be so strong that the children can scarcely resist the heavy pounding step of the giant. The tapping may be changed to suggest swinging, skating, or rocking a doll, so that the children can appreciate many differences in tempo and rhythm. This is also a good time for the teacher or a child to see if the various children's rhythms can be repeated in a clapping, drum, or rhythm-stick pattern.

## Rhythm Fun for All

If there are children in the group who are loath to enter into the physical activities of the rhythm period, they may be allowed at first simply to enjoy the emotional satisfaction the music affords them. An effort ought to be made early in the year, however, to get all the children into the activity of the period. The teacher should give particular attention to the child who stays out of the rhythm period and should comment favorably when she observes his slightest rhythmic response, such as nodding his head, tapping his foot, or tapping on the seat of his chair with his fingers. If the child seems pleased with this approbation, the teacher may call the attention of the group to the way the music makes this particular child feel.

Sometimes the extremely self-conscious child will enter more wholeheartedly into the activities of the period if he can have the support of a second child. Often the teacher sets the stage so that a child who responds to the music with abandon will be paired with a less confident child. The teacher must guard against falling into the habit of expecting particular children to be leaders, however. In the first place, the rhythm period may degenerate into one in which the group merely follows the pattern of the leaders, and in the second place, it is not fair for the child who is thrilled by music always to be hampered by being expected to take in tow a less responsive child.

If the music used for particular activities is changed frequently, the children will be led to listen not for certain tunes which may suggest the activity but for the "make-up" of the music. There are certain specific activities, such as running, skipping, galloping, tiptoe dancing, and marching, that will appeal to the kindergarten child throughout the whole year, but in order to assure development and progress, the music used must be varied.

## The Kindergarten Band

Children always enjoy experimenting with beating out rhythm and getting different sound effects on band instruments. The instruments—or at least a sampling of the various kinds of instruments—should be kept where they are easily accessible, and opportunities should be provided during free-time activities period for experimenting with rhythm and sound.

Kindergarten bands differ greatly. Some seem to be little more than an ensemble of pounded-out rhythm. Others seem to be organized chiefly for the gratification of admiring adults. If the band experience is to be musically worthwhile, the teacher must not substitute costuming and program-planning for the musical experience.

As a first step in the organization of the kindergarten band, the children may be asked to demonstrate their ability to respond to the music by clapping. A child who senses not only the rhythm but also some of the feeling of the music may be asked to clap alone to the music. After he has demonstrated his ability to clap, he may be given a set of rhythm sticks and asked if he can make the sticks tell the same story he told with his hands. Other children in turn may demonstrate their ability to clap out the rhythm with their hands and then may be given rhythm sticks. Much can be done through band work in the way of developing a sensitive musical ear.

As other instruments are introduced, the teacher may ask the children to suggest which instrument would best give the feeling of the music being played. For example, light "fairy-like" music will best be accompanied by bells and tambourines, while heavy elephant music will call for such instruments as castanets and Chinese drums.

With practice and emphasis on intelligent listening, the more advanced kindergarten children can learn to choose the instruments which will best give the feeling of the different parts or phrases in the music. Let us consider which instruments might be selected to accompany the old French folk song "Frère Jacques."[1] The first two phrases might well be accompanied by the Chinese drum or castanets, the next two by jingle sticks, the next two by bells, and the last two by the Chinese drum or castanets. While it is sometimes helpful to develop band interpretations around songs, generally it is better for children to learn to be guided by the music rather than by the words of the song, for as Schumann said, "Music must stand on its own."

There is some question as to whether the kindergarten band is or is not complete without a child leader to wield the baton. In many kindergartens the leader with his baton is leader in name only, since the children actually follow the lead given by the piano, and the baton serves only as another device for rhythmic expression. If there is to be a child standing in front of the group beating time, the teacher must make sure that that child is really feeling the music and not just aimlessly waving the stick. Although there is, of course, a definite technique for the use of the baton which may be taught to the children, in many cases it is well to leave it to be learned at a later age.[2]

INSTRUMENTS SUGGESTED FOR A GROUP OF TWENTY CHILDREN

| | | |
|---|---|---|
| 6 pairs of rhythm sticks | 3 jingle sticks | 1 pair of cymbals |
| 2 pairs of maracas | 2 tambourines | 1 triangle |
| 2 bells | 1 castanet | 1 drum and tone block |

SUGGESTED ARRANGEMENT FOR A KINDERGARTEN BAND

| *Left* | *Right* | *Center* |
|---|---|---|
| Cymbals | Jingle sticks | Rhythm sticks |
| Triangle | Tambourine and bells | Tone blocks and drum |
| Castanet | Maracas | Piano |

## Creative Instrumental Music in the Kindergarten

Children of kindergarten age enjoy experimenting and playing with melody. A xylophone, a set of chimes, a row of tuned bottles or bells suspended on a frame, an autoharp, or a piano—each is excellent experi-

[1] See reference, p. 272.

[2] The technique for beating out the time is as follows: Two-four time is directed by holding the baton high, bringing it down on one and raising it on two. Three-four time is directed by bringing the baton down on one, out to the right on two, and up on three. Four-four time is directed by bringing the baton down on one, halfway up and across the body on two, out to the right on three, and up on four.

mental material. Since the child usually accompanies his created melodies with song, the range of the melody is not likely to be great. In order to preserve the melodies, the notes of the scale may be numbered, the number 1 indicating the first note in the scale. An original melody might read thus:

5 1 5 1 5 3 5
Ding dong, ding, dong, Hear my bell.

Though the piano is a very complicated instrument, many kindergarten children get great satisfaction and pleasure in figuring out and inventing simple tunes on it. The children may be expected to use a reasonably light touch and to listen to the sound effect their playing produces. If the teacher will lend an appreciative ear to the interesting tone combinations the child chances to produce, this alone gives the child encouragement to experiment further. Occasionally a child can be helped in his own appreciation if the teacher points out that an agreeable sound may be made by putting down two keys, leaving an intervening key untouched, such as 1–3 or 2–4. It is thrilling to the child to discover that the first two phrases of "Frère Jacques" can be played by putting down in order just three keys and then returning to home base: 1, 2, 3, 1—1, 2, 3, 1. When the children arrive in the morning or afternoon or in other free times during the day, they often avail themselves of the opportunity to experiment on the piano or on other musical instruments. The teacher frequently sees to it that their findings are shared with the group at meeting time.

The experience the children get in this play and experimentation on a variety of instruments develops an appreciative attitude toward music and gives the children a better understanding of the development of music.

## Music Appreciation

Music appreciation for kindergarten children is so closely related to vocal, instrumental, and bodily responses that it can scarcely be considered apart from these activities. Although in all kindergarten music experiences the children are encouraged to listen intelligently, to distinguish between music of different types and moods, and to recognize melodies, the child's immediate response to new music usually is simply "Let's do it" or "Let's sing it."

A story or suggestion, however, of what the child may expect to hear in the music may arouse a keen interest in new music. For example, knowing that at some time while listening to the phonograph record of "In a Clock Store"[3] one may expect to hear tiny clocks, large clocks, and even an alarm clock, is sure to make the child more alert and attentive to the music.

[3] See reference, p. 302.

At times interest in listening may be stimulated by an air of mystery about what the unknown music has to offer. The children may be asked to listen to a single piece of music and then tell rather than show what they saw or what they felt while the music was being played. The "March of the Sleepy-Heads,"[4] by Spaulding, for example, may make the children think of pumpkins rolling along; it may make them think of a giant out for a stroll; or it may even bring to their minds the picture of Old Woman Thaw[5] sweeping and sweeping away the ice and snow. Music such as the "Grand Canyon Suite" by Grofé or "The Waltz of the Flowers" by Tchaikovsky may be effectively introduced in this fashion. What the children see and feel in the music depends largely on what their recent play or story experiences have been.

To be fully appreciated, music, like poetry, must fit a particular mood. A group mood, unless it is developed from a group experience, is very difficult to attain. Pictures are sometimes used in kindergarten as substitutes for actual experiences. To suggest the mood the composer himself may have felt when he wrote the particular bit of music may help establish a fitting group mood. For example, the suggestion that Brahms may have been feeling very comfortable and contented and perhaps a bit dreamy when he wrote his "Cradle Song" may help prepare the children for the lullaby music as it is played.

Most children under six will not profit by attending public musical concerts, or even those called "children's concerts" or "children's symphonies." In the first place, the program is usually too long; in the second place, the seats are uncomfortable for children; and in the third place, since the concert hour offers the children no opportunity for vocal or bodily reaction to the music, they become either bored or overstimulated. A single phonograph record or a few simple numbers played in the kindergarten by skilled people on such instruments as the violin, the cello, the accordion, the flute, or the autoharp will mean more than an hour's concert in a great auditorium. It should also be pointed out that a group of kindergarten children will usually enjoy 78 rpm records more than 33⅓ or 45 rpm records, simply because the listening time is not so prolonged.

The kindergarten children may have some experience as part of a concert audience; they may profitably accept the invitation of another group into their room to listen with them to certain musical numbers offered either by the children themselves or by a visiting artist. The usual auditorium or all-school program is frequently too long for kindergarten children.

Certain children in the group will doubtless enjoy spending more time than others in listening to music. If a phonograph is a part of the room

[4] See reference, p. 295.
[5] Elsa Beskow, *Olle's Ski Trip*, New York, Harper & Brothers, 1928.

equipment, it seems advisable to provide opportunities for the children to use the machine themselves. (We are indeed grateful to the manufacturers for unbreakable records!) During a free-time activities period, it is quite possible that one or two or even a small group of children may profit by playing certain records set aside as playtime records. Incidentally, this gives the teacher an excellent opportunity to help the children establish social courtesies in regard to the phonograph or the radio. In the first place, those children who have chosen to listen to the music must stay close enough to the machine really to enjoy the music. In the second place, they must keep the music tuned down, so that it will not interfere with the pleasure of others. In the third place, the conversation and activities of others in the room must be of such a nature that the music can be enjoyed by the listeners. Blaring, blatting music will make an otherwise peaceful room seem like the midway area of a carnival.

## Measuring the Musical Response

A rating scale set up by Helen Christianson suggests that we may obtain some measure of the child's overt appreciation of music if we observe and score from one to five the following responses:

1. The children's synchronization of bodily movement with the rhythm of the music.
2. The child's social-emotional response as shown in his facial expression, posture, and movement.
3. The dance patterns which the child evolves.
4. The rhythm which the child incorporates in dramatic play patterns.
5. The child's verbal comments indicating his interest in and enjoyment of the musical experience.[6]

## Selecting Material for Musical Experiences

The music to be used in the kindergarten should be of the best quality. The best of the old and the best of the new should be included. The music should be simple, and it should have a strong, well-marked rhythm. The melody should be truly beautiful and with its accompaniment should be full of content, expressing either a single mood or contrasting moods. While it is desirable that the music should arouse emotions, the teacher must

[6] Helen Christianson, *Bodily Rhythmic Movements of Young Children in Relation to Rhythm in Music*, New York, Bureau of Publications, Teachers College, Columbia University, 1938.

guard against overstimulating her group. An exciting, exhilarating bit of music may well be followed by music which will tend to induce a calm and quiet response.

The kindergarten musical experiences should be varied, and the children's musical horizons should be extended as the year progresses. One must remember also, however, that children—and adults as well—enjoy hearing good music over and over again.

In selecting music, one must consider the ability and past experiences of the group, of course. If, for example, children have already had two or three years of group musical experience in the nursery school, probably they will enjoy a wider variety of musical experiences than those who have no such background. All children in our radio and TV age have been exposed to much music—or at least to much sound. But that is quite different from having real listening experiences. It has been said that listening is a skill that must be developed through training. Although music skill and appreciation is an individual asset, it is likely that children who come from music-loving homes will respond with greater verve and freedom to the rhythms and music program than those whose music listening experience has been limited.

## Selected List of Music to Stimulate Rhythmic Activity[7]

### SIMPLE RHYTHMIC PATTERNS

WALKING

"Birthday March" 17
"Chorus" 10
"Christmas Tree March" 17
"Der Kleine Wanderer" 17
"Folk Dance" 10
"Le Pont d'Avignon" 7
'Little Traveler, The" 17
"March" (Hollaender) 17
"Soldiers' March" (Schumann) 3, 17
"Walking Song" 3
"Washington's March" 12

RUNNING

"Airplane, The" 12
"Badinage" 3
"Caterpillar! Caterpillar!" 7
"Gypsy Song" 3
"Pomponette" 10
"Run" 11
"Running" 4
"Will You Come and Play" 17
"Wind, The" 7

GALLOPING

"Allegro" 17
"Au Clair de la Lune" 7
"Gallop" 11
"Galloping" 4
"Horses Galloping" 14
"Hunting Song" 17
"Pony Ride, The" 7
"Presto" 17

[7] Numbers following titles refer to books listed on pp. 296–297.

"Wild Horseman, The" 3, 12

TIPTOEING

"Amaryllis" 17
"Betty Martin" 3
"Tippy-Tip-Toe" 17
"Tip Toe March" 17

SKIPPING

"Ballet Music" 12
"Dance It Merrily" 10
"Pop Goes the Weasel" 3
"Round and Round We're Skipping" 17
"Rustic Dance" 2
"Skip" 11
"Skipping" 4
"Skipping Is Fun" 17
"Spanish Dance" 17
"Thistledown Two Step" 2

JUMPING AND HOPPING

"Bagatelle" 3
"Bunnies Hopping" 4
"Hop Up—Hop Down" 17
"Hopping Harry" 16
"My Pony" 7
"Ramènes tes Moutons" 7
"Salto Mortale" 17
"Secret, The" 12
"Squirrels" 2
"Toad Music" 24

SKATING

"I'll Skate on My Roller Skates" 17
"Reaper's Song, The" 17
"Roller Skating" 3
"Skaters' Waltz" 3
"Skating" 2
"Skating" 4

SWAYING AND SWINGING

"Blue Danube" 3
"Cradle Song" 7, 10, 12, 17
"Papillons No. 8" 17
"Pine Tree Swing, The" 7
"Swaying Tree" 11
"Swing Song" 7
"Swinging" 10
'Tremp'ton Pain, Marie" 7
"Valse Serenade" 17
"Waltz" (Brahms) 3, 17
"Waltz" (Schubert) 10, 17

DANCING

"Air de Ballet" 17
"Chimes of Dunkirk" 17
"Gathering Flowers" 16
"Happy and Light" 17

## RHYTHMIC PATTERNS SUGGESTED BY DRAMATIC INTERPRETATIONS

AIRPLANES

"Aeroplane" 14
"Airplane" 17
"Airplane Song" 14
"Airplanes" 11
'I'd Like to Be" 17
"I'm an Airplane" 17
"My Airplane" 3

BALLS

"Ball Games" 24
"Bounce the Ball" 21
"Bouncing Balls" 10, 11
"My Ball Roll On" 17
"Roll" 16
"Rolling Balls" 2

BELLS

"Bells of Christmas" 18
"Chimes of Christmas" 17
"Jingle Bells" 3, 4
"Jingle Jingle" 3

BICYCLES

"Bicycle Song" 14
"Bicycling" 11
"Cock-a Doodle-doo" 7
"Picnic on the Grass, A" 7

BIRDS

"Fly Away Little Birdie" 14

"Flying Bird" 17
"Sleep My Birdies" 17
"Swallows" 2

Boats

"Gently My Johnny" 17
"My Boat Is Rocking" 14
"Rowing" 4
"Tugboat, The" 14, 17

Brownies

"Brownies" 10
"Dance of the Happy Spirits" 10
"Elfin Dance" (Grieg) 10
"Elves' Dance, The" 7
"Nocturne" 17
"Squirrels, The" 2

Clowns

"Circus Music" 11
"Jolly Clown, The" 19

Ducks

"Alphabet, The" 7
"Ducklings, The" 14

Elephants, Giants, Bears, etc.

"Elephant" 17
"Elephant Music" 24
"Giants" 2
"March of the Sleepy Heads, The" 2

Fairies

"Dancing in the Orchard" 7
"Fairies" 4

Horses

"High Stepping Horses" 14
"High Stepping Ponies" 4
"Horses Galloping" 14
"Little Gray Ponies" 14
"Pony Stepping High" 14
"Wild Horseman" 3, 12

Indians

"Dame Tartine" 7
"Indian Dance" 3, 11
"Indians, The" 18
"Merry-Go-Round" 21

Rabbits

"Bunnies Hopping" 4
"Hop Little Bunny" 14
"Hopping Harry" 16
"Mail Box, The" 7

Squirrels

"Squirrels" 2
"Ramene tes Moutons" 7

Toys

"Dance Dolly Dance" 17
"Dancing Dolls" 11
"Dutch Doll" 24
"I'm a Spinning Top" 17
"Jumping Jack" 15
"Riding a Stick Horse" 17
"Singing Top" 3

Trains, Buses, Steam Shovels, etc.

"Dance of the Moorish Slaves" 17
"Freight Train, The" 3
"In a Bus We Come" 17
"Song of the Train" 13
"Train" 3
"Train Game" 24
"Walking in the Snow" (Wheelbarrow) 17
"Who Will Ride the Bus?" 17

## MUSIC FOR QUIET LISTENING

"All Through the Night" 7
"Golden Boat" 7
"Loch Lomond" 7
"Lullaby" 7
"Moon Song" 7
"Sleep, Baby, Sleep" 7
"Waltz Op. 39, No. 2" (Brahms) 10

## MUSIC FOR THE KINDERGARTEN BAND

WITH STRONG ACCENT

"Bear Went Over the Mountain, The" 14
"Follow the Leader" 16
"My Drum" 3
"Soldiers March" 3, 17

WITH DIFFERENCES IN PITCH

"Happy Little Folks" 16
"March and Skip" 2

WITH DIFFERENCES IN INTENSITY

"Happy Little Folks" 16

WITH DIFFERENCES IN TEMPO

(contrast the two numbers)
"Clouds" 4
"Le Pont d'Avignon" 7

WITH DIFFERENCES IN PHRASING

(showing recurring themes)
"Frère Jacques" (see 6, 23, 37, pp. 275–276.)
"Happy Little Folks" 16

WITH DIFFERENCES IN MOOD

(from major to minor)
"Umbrella Game" 21

## Music for Rhythms and Appreciation


1. ABESON, MARION, and CHARITY BAILEY, *Playtime with Music*, New York, Liveright, 1952.
2. ARNOLD, FRANCIS M., *Rhythms for Home, Kindergarten and Primary*, Cincinnati, Willis Music Co., 1909.
3. BEATTIE, JOHN W., and OTHERS, *The American Singer*, Book One, 2nd Ed., New York, American Book, 1954.
4. BRIGGS, DOROTHY B., *Kindergarten Book*, Philadelphia, Oliver Ditson, 1940.
5. COLEMAN, SATIS, *Another Dancing Time*, New York, John Day, 1954.
6. COLEMAN, SATIS, *Dancing Time, Music for Rhythmic Activities of Children*, New York, John Day, 1952.
7. DAVISON, ARCHIBALD T., and THOMAS W. SURETTE, *One Hundred and Forty Folk Songs*, Boston, E. C. Schirmer Music Co., 1921.
8. DUBSKY, DORA, *Sing and Dance*, Toronto, J. M. Dent, 1955.
9. FLETCHER, MARGARET I., and MARGARET C. DENISON, *The High Road of Song for Nursery and Kindergarten*, Toronto, W. J. Gage, no date—about 1946.
10. GLENN, MABELLE, HELEN LEAVITT, and VICTOR BERMANN, *Play a Tune*, New York, Ginn, 1937.
11. HARVEY, SISTER ANN, *Rhythms and Dances for Pre-School and Kindergarten*, New York, G. Schirmer, 1944.
12. HUGHES, DOROTHY, *Rhythmic Games and Dances*, New York, American Book, 1942.
13. KENAGY, N. M., and FRANCIS, M., *Musical Experiences of Little Children*, Cincinnati, Willis Music, 1932.
14. MACCARTNEY, LAURA P., *Songs for the Nursery School*, Cincinnati, Willis Music Co., 1937.
15. MARTIN, BURNETT, *Rime, Rhythm and Song*, Minneapolis, Schmitt, Hall, McCreary Publishing Co., 1942.

16. NORTON, KATHERINE P., *Rhythm and Action with Music for the Piano*, Philadelphia, Oliver Ditson Co., 1935.
17. PITTS, LILLA BELLE, MABELLE GLENN, LORRAIN E. WATTERS, and LOUIS G. WERSEN, *The Kindergarten Book*. Our Singing World, Boston, Ginn, 1959.
18. RENSTRON, MOISELLE, *Musical Adventures*, Salt Lake City, Deseret Book Co., 1943.
19. SIEBOLD, META, *Happy Songs for Happy Children*, New York, G. Schirmer, 1928.
20. STUART, FRANCIS, R., and KOHN S. LUDLAM, Rhythmic Activity Cards, Series I, Packet for Kindergarten-Third Grade, Minneapolis, Burgess Publishing Co., 1955.
21. WADLEY, FREDERIKA, and MURYL ALLISON, *Discovering Music: Musical Activities for the Pre-School Child*, Boston, Boston Music Co., 1945.
22. WEICHARD, ANGELA, *Today's Tunes for Children*, Minneapolis, Schmitt, Hall, McCreary Publishing Co., 1941.
23. WEILAND, A. N., *Music, Rhythms and Games for Kindergarten and First Grade*, New York, Follett Publishing Co., 1953.
24. WHITLOCK, V. B., *Come and Caper*, New York, G. Schirmer, 1932.
25. WILSON, HARRY, WALTER EHRET, ALICE M. SNYDER, and EDWARD J. HERMANN, *Growing with Music*, Book I, Englewood Cliffs, N.J., Prentice-Hall, 1963.

## List of Recordings

### FUNDAMENTAL ACTIVITY RHYTHMS

*Basic Rhythms Program*—No. 3, Vol. I—Victor

1. March in F Major, Theme for Skipping, Flying Birds, Wheelbarrow Motives, Plain Skip, Tip Toe March, Military March, Galloping Horses, High Stepping Horses, Skipping Theme

*Basic Rhythms Program*—Nos. 1 and 3, Vol. II—Victor

1. Soldiers' March, Schumann; March in D Flat, Hollaender; March, "Nutcracker Suite," Tchaikovsky; March, "Alceste," Gluck
3. Run, Run, Run, Concone; Jumping, Gurlitt; Running Game, Gurlitt; Air de Ballet, Jadassohn; Waltzes Nos. 1, 2, and 9, Brahms

*Basic Rhythm Activities*—Basset, Florence, and Cora Mae Chestnut—Linden Recording Company

Walk, Skip, Slide, Heavy and Light Walk, Small Run, Gallop, Big Run, Swing, Turn-Walk-Hold, Bounce and Swing, Run and Jump, Jump Series, and others

*Childhood Rhythms Records*—Evans, Ruth—Evans Records

Fundamental Rhythms:

Walk, Run, Skip I, March, Jump, Gallop, Skip II

Rhythm Combinations:

Up and Down; Round and Round; Fast and Slow; Walk, Walk, Hop, Hop; Run, Hop, Hop, Stop; Walk and Skip

*Drummer Boy*—Children's Record Guild

March, Gallop

*Free Rhythms*—Phoebe James Rhythms Record Company

Skip, Run, Gallop, Tiptoe, Jump, Hop, Skip and Whirl, Run and Fall Down, Walk and Run, Run and Jump

*Fundamental Rhythms*—Phoebe James Rhythms Record Company

Two Skips, Two Runs, Two Gallops, Three Interpretive Rhythms

*Rhythmic Play*—Dietrich, Sally Tobin—Albums I and II—J. Thomas Egan Sound Recording

Skip, Walk, Glide, Hop, Jump, Gallop, Swing, Run, Bounce, Skip and Turn, Run and Jump, Stretch and Bend, Walk and Bounce, Skip and Jump

*Rhythm Records*—Harvey, Sister Ann—Schmitt Music Company

Skip No. I, Spinning Tops, Skating, Bicycling, Skip No. II

*Rhythm Time*—Wood, Lucille, and Ruth Turner—Bowmar Records

Basic Rhythms:

Walk, Run, Tiptoe, Skip

Combinations:

Skip, Walk, and Whirl; Tiptoe, Run, and Leap

*When the Sun Shines*—Young People's Records

Walking, Running, Swinging, etc.

## DRAMATIC ACTION AND INTERPRETATIVE RHYTHMS

*Activity Songs*, Berman, Marcia—Folkways Records

Birthday Song, Tugboats, Doing Things, Bunny Song, Lullaby, Silly Egg, Ferry Boat, Halloween, Machines, Farm Song

*Animals and Toys*, Evans, Ruth—Evans Record Company

Duck, Camels, Horses, Elephants, Trains, Tops, Soldiers, Airplanes

*Animal Rhythms*, James, Phoebe—Phoebe James Rhythms Record Company

Rabbits, Frogs, Airplanes, Lions, Dogs, Elephants

*Animal Rhythms*, James, Phoebe—Phoebe James Rhythms Record Company

Five Little Ponies, Work Horse, Rabbits, Frogs, Lions, Bears

*Basic Rhythms Program*—No. 2, Vol. II—Victor

2. Boating on the Lake, Kullak; Skating, Kullak; Walzer, Gurlitt; March, Gurlitt; La Bergerenette, Burgmuller; Waltz, Schubert; Scherzo, Gurlitt; L'Arabesque, Burgmuller; Tarantelle, Saint-Saëns

*Basic Rhythms Program*—Nos. 1, 2, 3, and 4, Vol. III—Victor

1. Northern Song, Op. 68, No. 31, Schumann; Song of the Shepherdess, Weber; March, Bach-MacDowell; Papillons, No. 8, Schumann; Dance of the Moorish Slaves—"Aida"—Verdi; Slavonic Dance No. 1, Dvořák; Siciliana—"L'Allegro"—Handel
2. Polly Put the Kettle On, English Folk; Lavender's Blue, English Folk; Waltz, Op. 9a, No. 3, Schubert; Come Lasses and Lads, English Folk;

John Peel, Old Hunting Song; Marche Militaire, Op. 51, No. 1, Schubert

3. Cradle Song, Houser; The Blacksmith, Brahms; Dolly's Funeral, Tchaikovsky; Tarantelle, Op. 46, No. 7, Heller; Berceuse, Ilyinsky; Silhouette, Reinhold; Valse Gracieuse, Dvořák
4. Mirror Dance, Gounod; Elfenspiel, Kjerulf; The Witch, Tchaikovsky; March of the Tin Soldiers, Tchaikovsky; Knight of the Hobby-Horse, Schumann; The Clock, Kullak; The Postillion, Godard; Peasant Dance, Schytte

*Boat Rhythms*, James, Phoebe—Phoebe James Rhythms Record Company
Buoys, Waves, Speed Boat, Row Boat, Sailboat, Tugs and Liners, Deep Sea Fishing Boat

*Building a City*—Young Peoples' Records
Songs for hammering, painting, sawing, etc.

*Christmas Rhythms*, James, Phoebe—Phoebe James Rhythms Record Company
Santa Claus, Toys

*Circus*, Evans, Ruth—Evans Record Company
Grand Entrance into the Circus Ring, Clowns Dancing, Bears Dancing, High Steppin' Ponies, Elephant Walk, Parade and Finale

*Circus Comes to Town*—Young Peoples' Records
Clowns, Tightrope Walkers, etc.

*Circus*, Wood, Lucille, and Ruth Turner—Bowmar
Circus Parade; Merry-Go-Round; Circus Ponies (Gallop and High Step and Trot); Trapeze Performers (Swing, Clown, Shuffle); Walk, Run and Fall; Elephants; Lions; Monkeys

*Circus Fun and Ball Bouncing*, Album IV—Estamae Records
Parade; Band; Clowns; Elephants; Dogs; Jugglers; Ponies; Trapeze Performers; Giraffe; Kangaroo; Lions; Horses; Drum Major; Ringmaster, etc.; Ball Bouncing 2/4 time; Ball Bouncing 3/4 time

*Farm Animals*, James, Phoebe—Phoebe James Rhythms Record Company
Cows, Ducks, Chickens, etc.

*Favorite Action Songs*, James, Phoebe—Phoebe James Rhythms Record Company
Walking, Skipping, Running, Pony Gallop, Merry-Go-Round, etc.

*Fire! Fire! and a March*, James, Phoebe—Phoebe James Rhythms Record Company

*Fun With Music*, Herbert, Donald—Bowmar

Farm:
Riding a Colt, Mother Hen Scolds Her Chicks, Cricket

Seasons:
Autumn, Snowflakes, Sleigh Ride

Birds:
Dove, Woodpecker, Cuckoo, Flying Birds

Playing:
Juggler, Musical Chairs, Yo-Yo

Home:
Suzie Skips to School, Baby Learns to Walk, Ice Cream Man

Toys:
Trains, Top, Rocking Horse
Guess?:
Chattering Monkeys, Dancing, Fireflies, Bouncing Ball, Put a Penny in the Monkey's Cap, Cats

*Garden Varieties*, James, Phoebe—Phoebe James Rhythms Record Company
Bees, Butterflies, Small Birds, Wind, Rain, Sun, Growing Flowers

*Gingerbread Boy and Billy Goats Gruff*, James, Phoebe—Phoebe James Rhythms Record Company
Two Rhythmic Plays

*Grand Canyon Suite*, Grofé—Toscanini, NBC Symphony—Victor
On the Trail, Sunrise, Cloudburst, Painted Desert

*Halloween Rhythms*, James, Phoebe—Phoebe James Rhythms Record Company
Pumpkin, Witches, Black Cats, Dances

*Interpretive Rhythms*, Evans, Ruth—Evans Records
Elevators, Clocks, Jumping Jacks, Step and Point, Heel and Toe, Walk and Bow

*Jump Back Little Toad*—Children's Record Guild

*Let's Be Firemen*—Children's Record Guild

*Let's Play Trains*—Columbia

*Let's Go to the Zoo*—Young People's Records

*Little Gray Ponies*—Young People's Records

*Little Puppet*—Children's Record Guild

*My Playful Scarf*—Children's Record Guild

*Me, Myself and I*—Children's Record Guild
Me, Myself and I; Nothing to Do; The Playful Scarf

*Mechanical Rhythms*, Wood, Lucille, and Ruth Turner—Bowmar
Jet Plane, Mechanical Toys, Clocks

*Play and Character Rhythms*, Evans, Ruth—Evans Record Company
Swing, See-Saw, Bicycles, Rowboats

*Rhythmic Activities for Children*, Basset, Florence, and Cora Mae Chestnut—Linden Recordings
Halloween, Thanksgiving, Christmas, New Year, Valentine's Day, Birthday, Spring, St. Patrick's Day, Easter, Flag Day, Lincoln's and Washington's Birthdays, Fourth of July

*Rhythmic Play Albums III and IV*, Dietrich, Sally Tobin—J. Thomas Egan Sound Recordings
Giants, Ringing Chimes, Elephants, Airplane, Halloween Goblins, Pushing a Swing, Fairies, Grandfather Clock, Swaying Trees, Curling Snake, Mechanical Doll, Lullaby

*Rhythms of Childhood*, Jenkins, Ella (Guitar, Ukulele, Harmonica, and Drum Acc.)—Folkways Records
Rhythms in Nature:
Songs About Trees, Birds, and Water
Rhythms in Dance:
Skip To My Lou, Red River Valley, All Will Be Dancing, and others

Rhythms of Far Away:
African Impression, Kum-Ba-Ya, O-Reign-O, En-Komo-Zee-gah-Ba-Ba

*Songs from the African Veld*, Vol. II sung by Josef Marais—Decca
"Ai, Ai," the Pied Crow Cry; There Comes Alibama; Jan Pieriewiet; Siembamba; There's the Cape Cart; My Heart Is So Sad; Miesiesfontein; Marching to Pretoria; Train to Kimberley; As the Sun Goes Down

*Sunday in the Park*—Children's Record Guild
Playing Tag, Rolling, Stretching, etc.

*This Is Rhythm*, Jenkins, Ella—Folkways Records
Mexican Hand Clapping, Spinning Top, Footsteps, Boat Rowing, Flowers Growing, Wind Blowing, Farmer Hoeing, Woman Sewing, and 4 others

*Toy Shop and other Rhythms for Little Folk*—Album I—Estamae Records
Trombones, Trucks, Balls, Toy Soldiers, Trains, Jumping Jacks, Rocking Horse, Dancing Dolls, Tops, Drums, Wind-up Dogs, Donkeys, Jack-in-the-Box, Cowboy Hat and Lasso, Toy Piano, Roller Skates, Baby Dolls, Tricycles, Airplanes

Rhythms:
Skip, Tip-toe, Walk, Run and Jump, Heel-toe, Gallop

Rhythms:
Tap and Walk, Light Run, Clap, Walk and Run, Slides; Clap Your Hands to the Music So; My Little Broom; My Toes, My Knees; Teddy Bear; One, Two, Buckle My Shoe

*Trains and Planes*, Activity and Dramatic Play—Young People's Records

*Train to the Farm*, Activity and Dramatic Play—Children's Record Guild

*Train to the Zoo*, Activity and Dramatic Play—Children's Record Guild

*Visit to My Little Friend*—Young People's Records
(Orchestra's accented tunes suggest action implied in the story)

*Waltz of the Flowers*, "Nutcracker Suite," Tchaikovsky, Art Gilmore, Narrator —Musical Sound Books

*Who Wants a Ride!*—Young People's Records
(Songs and music suggest different kinds of rides)

"*Whoa! Little Horses, Lie Down!*"—Young People's Records

*Winter Fun*—Young People's Records
(Music suggests different types of winter activities)
Jingle Bells and Skaters' Waltz

## FITNESS EXERCISES

*Fitness for Everyone*, Album 24—Honor Your Partner Records
Bend; Jump; Arm Swinging; Bobbing Head; Rotating Head; Running in Place; Stretching Foot; Flexing Knees; Trunk Bending and Back Stretching; Arm Flinging; Leg Swinging; Jump and Swing; Foot Rocker, Leg Stretch, Body Circle; Run and Hop; Abdominal Contractions; Abdominal Pumping; Sitting-Arm Circling; Double Hand Circling and Hand Grasp

*Rhythmic Activities for the Younger Set*—Kimbo and USA Records
The Elephant, Happy Children, The Rabbit, I'm a Little Book, The Happy Windmill, Jumping Jacks

## MUSIC FOR QUIET LISTENING

*American Bird Songs*—Book Records
*Basic Christmas Album*—Victor
1. Under the Stars, Davis-Brown; I Saw Three Ships, English Traditional Melody; Once in Royal David's City, Alexander-Gauntlett; Jingle Bells, Pierpont; Away in the Manger, Luther; I Heard the Bells on Christmas Day, Gilchrist
2. While Shepherds Watched Their Flocks by Night, Handel; Joy to the World, Handel; It Came Upon the Midnight Clear, Willis; The First Nowell, Old Carol; Deck the Halls with Boughs of Holly, Old Welsh Air
3. O Come, All Ye Faithful, Air from Portugal; O Little Town of Bethlehem, Redner; Silent Night, Grüber; Hark, the Herald Angels Sing, Mendelssohn
4. We Three Kings of Orient Are, Hopkins; Birthday of a King, Neidlinger; O Holy Night, Adam; Nazareth, Gounod

*Basic Listening Program*—Nos. 1, 2, and 3, Vol. I—Victor
1. Lullaby, Brahms; Little Sandman, Brahms; Hush My Babe, Rousseau; Lullaby, Mozart; Cradle Song, Schubert; Sweet and Low, Barnby
2. March of the Little Lead Soldiers, Pierné; Petite Suite, (a) March (Trumpet and Drums), (b) Impromptu (The Top), Bizet
3. Badinage, Herbert; Legend of the Bells, Planquette; Humoresque, Dvořák; Scherzo from 3rd Symphony, Beethoven; Minuet, Paderewski; Gavotte, Popper; Minuet, Beethoven; Rock-a-Bye Baby, Traditional

*Basic Listening Program*—Nos. 1, 2, 3, and 4, Vol. III—Victor
1. Marionettes, "Woodland Sketches," (a) Witch, (b) Clown, (c) Villain, MacDowell; Ol' Br'er Rabbit, MacDowell; To a Water Lily, MacDowell
2. March of the Gnomes, Rebikoff; Allegretto from "Faust Ballet," Gounod; March of the Dwarfs, Grieg
3. Toy Symphony, Haydn
4. The Bee, Schubert; Waltz in D Flat, Chopin; Spring Song, Mendelssohn;

*Cello Solos*, Casals—Victor
Träumerei, The Swan, and others
*Child's Introduction to Folk Music*—Wonderland Records
*"Children's Corner Suite," Debussy*—Musical Sound Books (MSB)
1. Doctor Gradus ad Parnassum, Serenade for the Doll, Jumbo's Lullaby
2. The Snow Is Dancing, The Little Shepherd, Golliwoggs' Cake Walk

*Golden Slumbers, Lullabies from Near and Far*—Sung by Pete Seeger, Jean Ritchie, and others—Folkway Records
*In a Clock Store*—Victor Concert Orchestra—Victor
*Lullabies from Around the World*—Marilyn Horne, soprano—Richard Robinson, tenor—Rhythms Production Company

*Sing We Now of Christmas,* Henry Simeone Chorale—Twentieth Century Fox
*Violin Concert,* Solos by Fritz Kreisler—Victor

## MUSIC FOR STUDIED LISTENING

### MUSIC WITH STRONG ACCENT

(Good Kindergarten Band Music)

*Amaryllis*—Old French Rondo, Ghys; *Minuet in G,* Paderewski—Basic Rhythm Band Album No. 1—Victor

*Knight of the Hobby Horse,* Schumann; *The Clock,* Kullak—Basic Rhythms Program Vol. III, No. 4—Victor

*March in D Flat,* Hollaender—Basic Rhythms Vol. II, No. 1—Victor

*March of the Toys,* Herbert—Decca Album DA 419

*Parade of the Wooden Soldiers*—Decca Album DA 437

*Rataplan,* Donizetti; *Serenata,* Moszkowski; *Waltz No. 5,* Koschat; *With Castanets,* Reinecke; *Shadows,* Schytte—Basic Rhythm Band Album No. 4—Victor

*Rhythm Instruments*—3 albums—Rhythms Production Company, Los Angeles, California (rhythm fun with folk music from many lands)

*Rhythm Orchestra,* James, Phoebe—Phoebe James Rhythms Record Company
Indians (Drums), Clocks (Tone Blocks), Woodpeckers (Rhythm Sticks), Rain (Maracas), In Mexico (Tambourines), Jingle Bells (Bells)

*Stars and Stripes Forever*—Sousa Marches, Vol. I—Decca

### MUSIC DIFFERENTIATING PITCH—HIGH AND LOW

*Csardas* (Xylophone)—Decca

*Drummer Boy*—Young People's Records

*Humoresque,* Dvořák; Minuet, Beethoven—Basic Listening Program Vol. I—Victor

*In the Village from "Caucasian Sketches"*—Decca

*Symphony Orchestra* (woodwind family)—Decca

*Witch, The,* Tchaikovsky—Basic Rhythms Program Vol. III—Victor

### MUSIC DIFFERENTIATING INTENSITY—LOUD AND SOFT

*Hungarian Rhapsody,* Adler—Decca

*Light Cavalry Overture,* von Suppe—Basic Listening Program Vol. II—Victor

*Lullaby,* Brahms—Basic Listening Program Vol. I—Victor

*March of the Little Lead Soldiers,* Pierné—Basic Listening Program Vol. I—Victor

*Turkish March,* Rondo alla Turca—Decca

### MUSIC DIFFERENTIATING TEMPO—FAST AND SLOW

*Amaryllis,* Ghys—Basic Rhythm Band Album—Victor

*Badinage,* Herbert—Basic Listening Program Vol. I—Victor

*Hungarian Dances,* Brahms—Decca Album

### MUSIC DIFFERENTIATING PHRASING AND RECURRING THEME

*Hungarian Folk Song Fantasy*—Decca

*March of the Little Lead Soldiers,* Pierné—Basic Listening Program Vol. I—Victor
*March of the Toys,* Herbert—Decca or Musical Sound Books (MSB)
*Minuet,* Beethoven—Basic Listening Program Vol. I—Victor
*Of a Tailor and a Bear,* MacDowell—Basic Listening Series Vol. II—Victor
*Parade of the Wooden Soldiers*—Decca

Music Analyzing Ensemble Effects and Featuring Individual Instruments

*Big Bass Fiddle, The*—Columbia Records
*Child's Introduction to the Musical Instruments, A*—Golden Records
*Child's Introduction to the Orchestra*—Golden Records
*Fun With Instruments,* Ding Dong School—Victor Records
*Golden Goose, The* (each character a different instrument)—Children's Record Guild
*Happy Instruments*—Columbia Records
*Hot Cross Buns* (Variation on the old Nursery Theme)—Children's Record Guild
*Instrumental Illustrations* (Violin, Cello, and Clarinet, with small orchestra), Bruno, Reibold, conductor—Victor Records
*Little Black Sambo's Jungle Band,* Paul Wing, narrator—Victor Records
*Little Brass Band*—Young People's Records
*Little Fiddle,* with Danny Kaye—Decca
*Little Indian Drum*—Young People's Records
*Little Tune That Ran Away*—Decca
*Meet the Instruments of the Orchestra* (one LP recording and two full color film strips)—Bowmar
  Strings, Woodwinds, Brass, and Percussion
*Music for Young America*—American Book Company
*Pan the Piper*—Columbia Records
*Pee-Wee the Piccolo,* Paul Wing, Narrator—Victor
*Peter and the Wolf* (simplified), Boris Karloff narrator—Mercury Records
*Rusty in Orchestraville,* Henry Blaire and Billy Bletcher—Capitol Records
*Said the Piano to the Harpsichord*—Young People's Records
*Strike Up the Band* (creative use of rhythm instruments)—Children's Record Guild
*Toy Symphony,* Haydn—Victor Records or Musical Sound Books
*Tubby the Tuba,* Victor Jory, narrator—Columbia Records

## SUMMARY

Rhythm is, and music appreciation can be, a part of the everyday living experience of young children. The teacher who is aware of this fact can find and feature rhythm and music appreciation in many phases of the kindergarten program. Group experiences with rhythm and appreciation necessitate the building of social habits which could well be emulated by many adults in our society. Kindergarten children enjoy experimenting with a variety of string and percussion instruments, and their own bodily reactions to music can be both a satisfying experience for them and a pleasurable experience for others. In most instances, kindergarten children get more satisfaction from playing or singing with the music than from simply listening. There is a place in the kindergarten for audience appreciation of music, however, and it is the kindergarten teacher's responsibility to make available to her group the best of the old and the best of the new in the way of music for young children.

## QUESTIONS AND PROBLEMS

1. How can we help children learn to listen carefully in the rhythms and appreciation period?
2. Cite at least ten instances in which you have seen a child give expression to rhythm in activities other than those usually thought of as musical.
3. As you sit in your own room, look about and identify eight objects or articles that could be used to produce rhythm. Bring this list to class and compare it with lists made by others. In the light of your observations, devise a variety of instruments which might be used by young children. What types of instruments do you feel kindergarten children could create for their own use?
4. In some kindergartens the children gather for rhythms in a large open area completely devoid of furniture; in others, the center of the space is occupied by a table. Are there any advantages in the latter arrangement?
5. What did Schumann mean when he said, "Music must stand on its own"?
6. Discuss the relative advantages of using various speeds of records—78, 45, and 33⅓—with kindergarten groups.

## SELECTED REFERENCES

Andrews, Gladys, *Creative Rhythmic Movement for Children,* New York, Prentice-Hall, Inc., 1954.

Association for Childhood Education International, *Music for Children's Living,* Bulletin No. 96, Washington, D.C., Association for Childhood Education International, 1955.

Christianson, Helen, Mary M. Rogers, and Blanche A. Ludlum, *Adventuring in Living and Learning,* Boston, Houghton Mifflin, 1961.

Dale, Ralph A., ed., *Rhythm: Activities and Instruments,* New York, The Arts Co-operative Service, 1955.

Gesell, Arnold, and Others, *The First Five Years of Life*, New York, Harper and Brothers, 1940 (see specifically, "Music Responses of Young Children").

Hood, Marguerite V., and E. J. Schultz, *Learning Music Through Rhythms*, New York, Ginn & Company, 1949.

Jersild, Arthur T., and Sylvia Bienstock, *Development of Rhythm in Young Children*, New York, Bureau of Publications, Teachers College, Columbia University, 1935.

McLaughlin, Roberta, *Music in Everyday Living and Learning*, Bulletin, Washington, D.C., National Education Association, 1960.

McMillan, L. Eileen, *Guiding Children's Growth Through Music*, Boston, Ginn & Company, 1959.

Morrison, Ida, and Ida Perry, *Kindergarten Primary Education: Teaching Procedures*, New York, The Ronald Press, 1961.

Pitts, Lilla Belle, Mabelle Glenn, Lorrain E. Watters, and Louis G. Wersen, *The Kindergarten Book*, Our Singing World, New York, Ginn & Company, 1959 (see specifically Sections II, III, and IV under "Teaching Suggestions").

Sheehy, Emma D., *Children Discover Music and Dance*, New York, Henry Holt & Company, 1959.

Sheehy, Emma D., *There's Music in Children*, New York, Henry Holt & Company, 1954.

Slind, Lloyd H., and D. Evan Davis, *Bringing Music to Children*, New York, Harper and Row, 1964.

Thorn, Alice G., *Music for Young Children*, New York, Charles Scribner's Sons, 1929.

Wills, Clarice D., and William H. Stegeman, *Living in the Kindergarten*, rev., Chicago, Follett Publishing Company, 1956.

# 16

# GAMES IN THE KINDERGARTEN

Through games the kindergarten program attempts to give the child opportunities to

- Experience exhilarating joy.
- Develop habits of fair play and good sportsmanship.
- Develop motor poise, good posture, and good health.
- Quicken sense perceptions.
- Establish both self-confidence and self-control.
- Cooperate as an integral part of a group.

## Games

There are two points of view regarding the place of organized games in the kindergarten. Some authorities think that the five-year-old is not mature enough in his social development to profit by playing group games; they therefore rule out all group games in their kindergartens. Others are so sure that games should be a part of every kindergarten that they would not let a day pass without time for at least two or three games. Since there is no research data strongly in support of either attitude, probably the wisest thing for most kindergarten teachers is to run a middle course. Let's have games in the kindergarten, but not make a fetish of them.

Games best adapted to kindergarten play are those that are loosely organized, frequently of the "ring" or "circle" type. Such games are not dependent on a specific number of players or a permanent casting of parts. There is some evidence that competition begins to be a stimulating factor in the activities of the five-year-old, but that does not mean it should be stressed in group games. At age five there is still little if any team feeling;

competition is pretty much a matter of personal concern. "Our side" and "your side" mean very, very little to the kindergarten child.

All games have rules, and even the simplest require a fairly strict observance of a few definite rules. The essential difference between free play and playing games is that in free play the activity is directed mainly by the materials at hand and the momentary interest of the child, while in playing games the activity is directed by previously established rules, and the interest of the child has to be more than momentary if the game is to be successful.

## The Spirit of Game Time

Apparently the way games are played in the group makes a tremendous difference in both the children's enjoyment and the values that may result from the experience. In some kindergartens, game time is little more than an interminable series of repetitious turns and waits. In others the play is so organized that the children's enjoyment is at high peak and the benefits of the games experience are always apparent. Since the first objective of game time is fun, then surely games ought to be entered into in a gay mood. Nothing is more pathetic than games being played by children who look repressed and glum. Although there are certain rules and regulations which must be observed if the game is to go on, the teacher, in her attempt to organize, must not suppress the fun and thrill of playing. She ought to impress on the children that, while good fun and excitement are a legitimate part of game play, uncontrolled fun and excitement are really a hindrance.

## Time Allotted to Games

In a kindergarten where adequate space, apparatus, and equipment are provided for the number of children enrolled, there will probably be fewer games than in a kindergarten not so ideally set up. If the group is pressed for space and if there is little gymnasium apparatus and other equipment in the room, the teacher will find it necessary to substitute activities involving more organization. Group games generally fill the bill.

## Introducing New Games

In introducing new games, the teacher may adopt either of two policies. She may give a narrative account of the whole game and then give specific

*"The finger play is the thing—and you have to concentrate if you're going to do it right."*

directions for the various parts of the game, or she may simply build up the game step by step, giving directions for each part as it comes. In presenting a new game by verbal direction, the teacher must be sure that each step is clearly set forth before she proceeds with the next step. If a game does not follow set rules it is well to encourage the children to give suggestions as to how they think the game might be played.

It is better for children to follow verbal directions than to imitate the demonstration of the teacher. The practice they get in following verbal directions is excellent training for the many later school experiences that involve understanding and following specific directions. If, however, there is a child in the group who is already familiar with the game, his eagerness to tell *and* show how it is played ought to be taken into account. All too often teachers teach as though they were the only ones who had information to impart. They quite ignore the fact that children too have information and that, in their own way, they too can teach.

## Techniques for Large Groups of Children

Many of the games played in kindergarten have to be adapted to the size of the group. To illustrate with an extreme example, to play "Skipping Tag" in a group of from forty to sixty children, with but one person skipping at a time, would be extremely boring. It would mean also that few children would get a turn during the entire game. One way of adapting the game so that many could have turns in a short time would be to have the first child who skips about the circle tag one child and then have these two children tag two more children, these four remain in the game tagging four more and so on until shortly every child is skipping. A second adaptation might be made by having two individuals, instead of one, start the game. In this case each child returns to his place after having tagged a second child. This, of course, does not speed the turns as much as the other adaptation, but for groups of from thirty to forty children it is probably the better of the two approaches, since it is not quite so confusing as the first. A similar procedure may be followed in adapting "The Farmer in the Dell" for use with a large group. In playing this game, two "farmers" may be chosen to start the game, each farmer choosing for himself a "wife." To avoid confusion, the person may take hold of the hand of the person by whom he was chosen. The last one in the line will always be the one to choose. Other games, such as "Pop Goes the Weasel," "How Do You Do, My Partner?" and "Round and Round the Village," may be adapted to large groups in much the same way.

In large groups it is always difficult to recall which children have had turns and which have not. If those who have had turns sit down as soon as their turn is ended, there will be no misunderstanding, and the game will run more smoothly.

If there are two teachers in the room, it is sometimes well for each teacher to have a game group. If there is not enough space for this in the kindergarten room, perhaps one group can play in the hall or in the gymnasium. The playground affords a great deal of game space in pleasant weather.

There are many games that call for divisions within the group. The divisions are most frequently made on the basis of sex. In fact, it is so often made on this basis that kindergarten children sometimes get the idea that boys and girls must of necessity engage in different activities, an absurd idea, for very little sex difference is found in the game interests of kindergarten children. There are many other ways of dividing the groups which the thoughtful teacher may use. If the children are in a circle, the teacher may ask all those on one side of the circle standing between two named children to be in one group and the rest of the original group to be in the second group. If the children are sitting or standing in a group, the division may be made by grouping all those having one thing in common—red clothes, wearing shoes with laces, having blue eyes, and so on. Sometimes the basis for the division is according to the kind of work the children have done in the work period—all those who worked with crayons, or all those who worked with clay, and so on. Making the division on this somewhat unusual basis not only keeps the children mentally alert but gives them an opportunity to play in different groupings.

Some games call for repeated units of two or three. If the children are standing in a circle, they may be asked to count off by two's or three's. As each group counts off, the pair or group may form its own new unit. In the game of "The Squirrels in the Tree" each unit is made up of three —two children form the tree and the third child is the squirrel. The same device may be used when small groups engage in a game or a turn by themselves. For example, in the game of "The Little White Ponies," the children often count off in groups of five or six. In this case a new group does not count off or leave the circle until the preceding group has had its turn and the individuals have returned to the main group.

## Kinds of Games Played in the Kindergarten

Most games for young children involve a great deal of bodily activity. While the games are not highly organized, this activity usually must be accompanied by mental alertness. Physically the child may throw himself wholeheartedly into the game, but at the same time he realizes that he must be quick of wit if he is to remain in the game or if the game is to proceed. Many, though not all, of the games involving physical activity are accompanied or directed by music.

Games involving considerable bodily activity may be divided into the following classes: imitative games, choosing games, dramatic games, purely social games, games of motor skill, gymnastic or stunt games, and competitive games. Games of a quieter sort, though not nearly so numerous as the more active games, also fill a need in the play program for young children. Most of these quicken sense perceptions and develop mental agility. Games involving little or no bodily activity may be divided into the following classes: games of hearing, games of touch, games of seeing, mental gymnastic games, and guessing games. The rest of the chapter will be devoted to presenting illustrative games of a variety of types.

Many of the games which will be suggested can be played either indoors or outdoors. The teacher ought not overlook the fact that the value of the game is enhanced by being played outside in the air and sunshine. Moreover, the larger area available for games in the playground makes for greater freedom of movement. The fact that on the playground there is usually no objection to loud laughter—or even yells—also contributes to the wholehearted enjoyment of the game period.

## Games Enjoyed by Kindergarten Children

### IMITATIVE GAMES

*Did You Ever See a Lassie?*
Formation: Circle.
Music:

DID YOU EVER SEE A LASSIE?

Did you ever see a lassie (laddie), a lassie, a lassie,
Did you ever see a lassie, do this way and that?
Do this way and that way, and this way and that way,
Did you ever see a lassie do this way and that?

Action: One child in the middle. Other children grasp hands and circle around the child in the center while singing the first two lines. During lines 1 and 4 the children drop hands and imitate the child in the middle, who thinks up some special way to hop, move his head, and so on.

*Looby Loo*
Formation: Circle.
Music:

LOOBY LOO

I put my right hand in.
I put my right hand out.
I give my right hand a shake, shake, shake,

And turn myself about.
Chorus:
Here we dance looby loo,
Here we dance looby light,
Here we dance looby loo,
All on a day so bright.

Verses follow with "I put my left hand (right foot, left foot, round head, whole self) in," and so on.

Action: Children, grasping hands, walk about the circle as they sing the chorus. At the beginning of the verse the children drop hands, put their hands on their own hips, first put right hand into circle, then right hand outside circle, then shake right hand, and with hands on hips turn about in place. Children grasp hands and sing, repeating the action of the chorus.

## OTHER IMITATIVE GAMES

*Toy Man*
*Follow the Leader*
*Polly Perkin*
*Playing farm animals*
*Playing toys*

## CHOOSING GAMES

*Skipping Tag*
Formation: Circle.

Music: Any skipping music.

Action: Children stand with one hand outstretched, palm up. One child skips inside circle to the music, touches second child's hand. Second child starts skipping in opposite direction. Two meet, grasp right hands, and dance about each other. First child goes to his place and second child proceeds as did the first.

*Popcorn Man (The Muffin Man)*
Formation: Circle.

Music:

THE POPCORN MAN (The Muffin Man)

Do you know the popcorn man, the popcorn man, the popcorn man?
Do you know the popcorn man that lives in Drury Lane?
Yes, I know the popcorn man, the popcorn man, the popcorn man.
Yes, I know the popcorn man that lives in Drury Lane.

Action: Child who is to start the game stands in front of child of his own choosing. As lines 1 and 2 are sung, the child dances up and down on his toes, hands on his hips (feet make sound like popping corn). As lines 3 and 4 are sung, the child in front of whom first child was standing dances up and down on his toes, hands on hips. The two children join hands and skip about the circle as they, with the group, sing "Two of us know the popcorn man." Game starts again, this time the two children standing in front of two others. Game continues until eight have had turns. The eight sit down and another person is chosen to start the game.

## OTHER CHOOSING GAMES

*The Farmer in the Dell*
*How Do You Do, My Partner?*
*Walking Tag (like skipping tag)*
*Rig-a-Jig-Jig*

## DRAMATIC ACTION GAMES

*The Little Princess*
Formation: Circle.
Music:

THE LITTLE PRINCESS

1. There was a little princess, princess, princess.
   There was a little princess, long, long ago.
2. She lived in a castle, castle, castle.
   She lived in a castle, long, long ago.
3. The little princess fell asleep, fell asleep, fell asleep.
   The little princess fell asleep, long, long ago.
4. A little prince came galloping, galloping, galloping.
   A little prince came galloping, long, long ago.
5. He woke the little princess, princess, princess.
   He woke the little princess, long, long ago.
6. He took her to his castle, castle, castle.
   He took her to his castle long, long ago.

Action: One child is chosen for the princess and one for the prince.
Verse 1: The little princess walks about inside the circle as the children sing.
Verse 2: The princess continues to walk. Children in the circle form castle by putting hands together high over their heads.
Verse 3: The princess drops down on the floor and pretends to sleep.
Verse 4: The prince gallops about inside the circle. (Music changes tempo to suggest gallop.)
Verse 5: Very gently he stoops down and wakens the princess.
Verse 6: The prince steps in front of the princess and together they gallop about the circle.

## FIVE LITTLE CHICKADEES

Formation: Row of five facing group.

Music:

FIVE LITTLE CHICKADEES

1. Five little chickadees sitting in the door.
   One flew away and then there were four.
2. Four little chickadees sitting in a tree.
   One flew away and then there were three.
3. Three little chickadees looking at you.
   One flew away and then there were two.
4. Two little chickadees sitting in the sun.
   One flew away and then there was one.
5. One little chickadee left all alone.
   He flew away and then there were none.

Action: As each verse is sung the chickadee at the end of the line flies about the room and over to sit with the children who are singing and observing 5, 4, 3, 2, 1.

## OTHER DRAMATIC ACTION GAMES

*Little White Ponies*
*Round and Round the Village*
*Here Comes a Blackbird Through the Window*
*Snail*

*Hickory Dickory Dock*
*Little Miss Muffet*
*Jack Be Nimble*

## PURELY SOCIAL GAMES

*Pop Goes the Weasel*
Formation: Standing in circle.

Music:

POP GOES THE WEASEL

A penny for a spool of thread,
A penny for a needle,
And that's the way the money goes,
Pop goes the weasel.

Action: One child skips around inside the circle. At the word "pop," the group in the circle give a single clap, and the child skipping stops in place. He takes the hand of the child directly in front of him and they skip about in the circle as the music is repeated. On the word "pop," both children stop. They choose the child directly in front of them, form a circle of their own, and skip around in place as the music continues. This time on the word "pop," the first two children to make up the circle of three lift their arms, and the third child skips out under the lifted arms to start the game again.

## BECKONING GAME

Formation: Circle.

Action: One child in the center beckons to child in the circle. The child beckoned to comes into the circle, shakes hands with the first child. The first child goes back into the circle, sits down, and the second child repeats the action of the first child. Game continues until each child has been beckoned to. There seems to be a tremendous fascination about the fact that the whole game proceeds in silence.

## POSTMAN

Formation: Seated in a circle.

Action: A large rubber ball is held by one child. He pretends that the ball is the postman and rolls it across the circle. The child rolling the ball may try to direct it to a certain person but he must accept the fact that the postman "must go where he must" and not just where the child wishes. No child is to pick up the ball (the postman) unless it touches (raps at his door). When a child feels the ball touching him, he picks it up and sends it on its way again.

## OTHER PURELY SOCIAL GAMES

*Here We Go Walking*
*Hey Betty Martin*
*Little Sallie Waters*
*London Bridge*
*Ring Around a Rosie*

## GAMES OF MOTOR SKILL

*Ball*
*Anti-Anti-Over*

Formation: A screen four feet high stands between two players.
Action: As a child throws the ball over a solid screen to his friend, he calls "Anti-Anti-Over." If the friend catches the ball, he tries to run around the screen and touch the first child before the first child can change to the other side of the screen. If a child does not catch the ball, he simply throws it back, each time calling as he throws it "Anti-Anti-Over."

*Bouncing and catching the ball.*
*Bouncing the ball without catching (counting to see how many consecutive times it can be bounced).*
*Standing on a given line and throwing or bouncing the ball into the basket.*
*Throwing the ball into the basket in the middle of the circle.*
*Balloon* (keeping a balloon in the air, using fingertips only).

*Skipping Stooping*
Formation: Informal group.

Music: Any skipping music.

Action: All the children skip with the music. They are to stoop when the music stops. The last one down is out of the game. A player is out also if he (a) stoops too soon, or (b) topples when stooping.

## OTHER GAMES OF MOTOR SKILL

*Crossing the Stream* (Blocks placed at regular intervals, nine inches apart, to form steppingstones.)

*Dodge Ball*
*Hot Potato*
*One, Two, Three, O Larry O*
*Ring Toss*
*Rolling ball through a wicket or arch*
*Rolling ball to knock down block tower*
*Spin the Ring or Platter*
*Tossing the ball into the air* (Teacher calls name of a child. Child dashes to catch ball before it touches the ground.)

## GYMNASTIC OR STUNT GAMES

*Wand Game*
Formation: Informal.

Action: Four or six children are chosen to come to front of group. Each child is given a stick 2½ feet long. He grasps each end of stick in his hands. A variety of true and false statements, such as "chickens bark," "dogs meow," "cats scratch," are made by the teacher. If statement is true, wand is pushed high above head, still grasped in both hands; if false, it is pushed down.

## BICYCLING

*Bicycling*
Formation: Informal.

Action: Children lie on backs, lift feet, and pretend to ride bicycle in the air, using slow, fast, coasting, and stopping motions.

## OTHER GYMNASTIC OR STUNT GAMES

*Getting up from floor without using hands*
*Playing ducks*
*Playing turtle*
*Playing wheelbarrow*
*Playing wooden man*
*Turning cart wheels*
*Turning somersaults*
*Demonstrating on a tumbling mat any "stunt"* (Piano music often accompanies the activity.)

## COMPETITIVE GAMES

*Block Relay* (Bean bags, sponges, or other soft objects may be used.)

Formation: The children not playing sit at the side in a group. Two chairs are placed at one end of the room and two chairs at the opposite end. Three blocks are put on each of the two chairs at one end of the room.

Action: The two players stand by the two chairs with the blocks. On a signal, each child picks up a block and runs with it to the chair at the other end of the room. This is repeated until all three blocks have been transported to the chairs at the opposite end of the room. The players then return and sit on the chairs which first held the blocks. The first one to sit on the empty chair wins the game.

*Duck, Duck, Gray Duck*
Formation: Circle.

Action: The child who is "It" walks around the outside of the circle. As he passes the children he touches certain individuals and says "Duck, Duck, Gray Duck." When he touches the child and says "Gray Duck" he starts to run, and the child tagged follows in pursuit. If the pursued child is caught before he returns to his place in the circle, he must go into the middle of the circle and there, squatting like a duck, must remain until the game is over.

*Robin, Black Bird, BLUE BIRD*
Formation: Circle.

Action: As the person who is "It" walks around the outside of the circle, he touches certain individuals and, as he touches them, gives them the name of a bird. If the child touched is called Blue Bird, he must try to catch the person who touched him before that person returns to his place in the circle. If the pursued child is caught he must go into the cage—the center of the circle. In this game the "It" person tries to use as many different bird names as he can think of.

*Hill Ball*
Formation: Children standing in a line on a hill. (May also be played on level ground.)

Action: Teacher throws the ball down the hill.
Children race down the hill to see who can bring back the ball first.

## OTHER COMPETITIVE GAMES

*Drop the Handkerchief*
*Two Deep*
*Musical Chairs*
*Japanese Tag*
*Surprise Tag*
*Pussy Wants a Corner*
*Cat and Rat*
*Charlie Over the Water*
*Have You Seen My Sheep?*
*Squirrels in the Hollow Trees*
*Fire on the Mountain*
*Touch Ball*
*Color Dodge* (piece of colored paper pinned on back of each two children)
*Wood Tag*

## HEARING GAMES

*Mother Kitty and Baby Kitty*[1]

[1] See p. 148 for tyrannosaurus version of this game.

Formation: Informal grouping or circle.

Story: Mother kitty and baby kitty are fast asleep. Baby kitty wakes up and runs away and hides. Mother kitty wakes up and finds baby kitty gone and calls "Meow." Baby kitty answers "Mew."

Action: Two children, a "mother" and a "baby kitty," lie on the floor. The children in the group repeat the story, and the "baby kitty" and the "mother kitty" dramatize the story as it is told. "Mother kitty" and "baby kitty" supply the "Meow" and the "Mew." Game may be played with 1, 2, 3, and 4 "kittens."

*Ring, Bell, Ring*
Formation: Informal grouping.

Action: One child is chosen to close his eyes. Another is given a bell, which he must hold very carefully, so that no sound will be heard. The child with the bell runs to some distant part of the room. When he is ready, the teacher tells the first child. The first child calls "Ring, bell, ring." The second child rings the bell and the first child points in the direction of the sound. If he points in the right direction, he then becomes the bell ringer. If he does not point in the right direction, the second child remains the bell ringer and a new child takes the first child's place.

*Pattern Clapping Game*
Formation: Circle or informal grouping.

Action: The teacher, using her hands, rhythm sticks, a tom-tom, or drum, taps out a pattern thus:

· · · — · ·
or · — · · ·
or · — · · — · · ·

If the child called on can clap back the same pattern, he may remain standing. If he fails to clap back the same pattern, he must sit down.

## OTHER HEARING GAMES

*Dog and the Bone*
*Who Is Knocking at My Door?*
*Hunting for the Ball* (Music loud and soft directing the hunt.)

## SEEING AND OBSERVING GAMES

*Huckle, Buckle, Bean Stalk*
Formation: Informal grouping.

Action: Five or more children are chosen to leave the room, or all the children may be asked to close their eyes. The teacher or a child puts a ball or some other object, previously selected by the group, in a fairly conspicuous spot.

When all is ready, the teacher gives the signal and the selected children begin the search for the object. When they find it, they walk to their places without touching it, merely calling out "Huckle, buckle, bean stalk." A time limit may be put on the hunt.

*Policeman and Lost Child*
Formation: Circle.

Action: The teacher, playing that she is a mother, calls some child in the group, pretending he is a policeman. The "policeman" answers the call. The mother solicits the aid of the policeman in the search for her lost child. The policeman asks the mother to tell what her lost child is wearing. The mother describes in detail the clothes which her lost child is wearing. The policeman looks about the circle and brings to the mother the child answering the description. Sometimes, in order to make the game more complicated, several lost children (or lost articles) are to be found. With older children the part of the mother may be played by a child.

*Finding a Friend*
Formation: Circle.

Action: One child leaves the room. The others decide which child they will describe as the absent child's new friend. The absent child is called in and, as he walks around the outside of the circle, the children forming the circle sing (to the tune of London Bridge) "Here he comes to find a friend, etc., our own ................ (child's name)." Child seeking a friend steps in the middle and listens further as the group sings the description of the new friend; for example, "Your friend is wearing a bright red dress, bright red dress. . . ."

*"Now try this one."*

Three descriptive verses may be sung in helping the child to identify his new friend. If the new friend is identified correctly, then the child and his new friend skip together in the circle before the new friend leaves the room to play the role of the child who is seeking a friend.

*Color on Color*

Formation: Circle or informal grouping.

Action: Three or five children close their eyes while another child picks a large colored crayon from the box. He shows it to the group (but not to the people whose eyes are supposed to be closed) and then places it somewhere in the room in a fairly conspicuous spot, on a color similar to the crayon. Then he returns to the group, the others open their eyes, and go in search of the crayon. If they see it, they come back to the group and announce "Color on color; blue matches blue," or whatever the original crayon color may have been. The last one to spy the crayon returns the crayon to the box and the game starts again.

## OTHER SEEING AND OBSERVING GAMES

*"I am thinking of something in this room" (description given).*

*"What Is Missing?"*

Formation: Informal grouping.

Action: "Tuck in" and "Take out" pictures may be used in this game or children may hold pictures of birds, flowers, or animals. One child is asked to hold his picture behind him. A child who has had his eyes closed is then asked to look up and name the missing picture.

## GAMES OF TOUCH

*Identifying Objects in a Cloth Bag*

Formation: Informal grouping.

Action: The teacher has a variety of objects, such as a ball, a pencil, a toy automobile, a toy airplane, and various toy animals. She puts from three to six objects in the bag at the same time. Individuals are asked to come up to identify the objects by feeling the bag. After the articles have been placed in the bag —all children watching—one child is invited to close his eyes. One object is removed. The chosen child is expected to identify the missing article by feeling the bag.

*Identifying a Child*

Formation: Informal grouping.

Action: One child is asked to close his eyes (sometimes paper handkerchiefs are used as blindfolds). The teacher beckons to a child in the group. He goes up to and shakes hands with the child. The blindfolded child then tries to identify the child by feeling his head and his clothes.

## OTHER GAMES OF TOUCH (all to be played with eyes closed)

*Counting and placing beads in a bag.* A designated number of balls, squares, and cylinders (from five to ten) are placed in each bag.

*Identifying shapes on form-board puzzles.*
*Matching pieces of cloth.*
*Selecting and placing matching beads into special containers.*

## MENTAL-GYMNASTIC GAMES

*Mrs. Brown's Party*
Formation: Circle.

Story: "Mrs. Brown had a party and at the party she served cake."

Action: One child is chosen to start the story. The child at his right repeats the story as told and adds one more thing which Mrs. Brown served at her party. The game continues around the circle. If a child fails to repeat all the things Mrs. Brown had at her party, or if he fails to repeat them in order, the turn goes to the child on his right. The children may be expected to recall and repeat in order from six to eight articles.

*My Suitcase*
Formation: Informal grouping.

Story: "I went to visit my grandmother and in my suitcase I put my comb."

Action: Each child having a turn repeats the name of the article packed and adds one more article. In this game the teacher designates the turns in relation to the child's apparent mental maturity. A relatively immature child is asked to start the game. As the number of items in the suitcase increases, the teacher selects the more mature children to recall and add items.

*Right and Left Game*
Formation: Children sitting in a group on the floor.

Action: One child is chosen to place two chairs side by side in front of the group. He is asked to place the chairs so that if two children were to sit in the chairs, the children in the group could see only the backs of the two children. Next, a child is given a "steering wheel" and is asked to sit in the left-hand seat —*the seat where the driver* (of an American-made car) *sits.* The driver then beckons to a friend to go for a ride. As they drive along the teacher gives a series of directions to the passenger, "Put your left hand—*your hand which is nearest to the driver*—on your head. . . . Put your right hand—*your hand which is nearest to the door on your side of the car*—on your knee." As the game continues the phrases used to identify the left and right hand are omitted.

If the passenger can carry out the directions correctly, he becomes the driver. After several turns the teacher suggests that the driver turn his car around in order to come back home. When the chairs are placed in a position so that the occupants face the group, the driver is again asked to sit in the left-hand seat, and again he invites a passenger to ride with him. The teacher again gives to the passenger a series of left and right directions. When the trip is ended the teacher asks the driver to take the key out of the ignition and to put it in his left—or perhaps his right—pocket.

*Mr. Bradley's Motor Car*

Formation: Circle or informal grouping.

Action: Each child in the group is assigned to be a part of a car. The teacher "ad libs" a story in the manner of Mr. Bradley's Motor Car, telling about all the parts that fell off as Mr. Bradley drove to town. As each part is mentioined, the child or children representing the part must jump up, turn around and sit down. This must be done quickly, so that the story may continue with as little delay as possible.

This may be the game in its entirety or, as the children come to distinguish left and right and other relationships, it may be played by having the car re-assembled. (Of course, if the car is to be re-assembled, a single child will be assigned to represent a single part.) As the teacher tells about the car pieces being picked up and assembled, each child representing a part must step quickly into his relative position in the car formation. The story might proceed something in this fashion, "Mr. Bradley found the *steering wheel* behind a tree; he found the *front right wheel* over in the cornfield; he found the *left front wheel* in a cabbage patch," and so on.

*Touching Objects About the Room*

Formation: Informal grouping or circle.

Action: This game is played much as "Mrs. Brown's Party," except that the children touch the objects about the room rather than naming articles. The children may volunteer for turns. Usually from eight to ten objects can be touched before the game ends.

*True–False*

Action: The entire group participates. The teacher makes statements such as "Birds fly," "Fish run," "Horses gallop." If the statement is true the children raise their hands; if the statement is false they clap once.

## OTHER MENTAL GYMNASTIC GAMES

*Do As I Say but Not As I Do*
*Simon Says*
*Captain! May I?*

## GAMES THAT INVOLVE A STRETCH OF THE IMAGINATION

*Let's Imagine Sounds*[2]

[2] See Janet Wolff reference, p. 329.

*Let's Imagine Places*[3]
*Let's Imagine Something:*
 Very Soft
 Very Hard
 Very Straight
 Very Crooked
 Very Tall
*Let's Imagine Something:*
 Black
 White
 Red
 Yellow, and so on

## GUESSING GAMES

*Hunt the Slipper*
Formation: Circle.

Music:

HUNT THE SLIPPER

Cobbler, cobbler, mend my shoe;
Have it done by half past two.
Stitch it up and stitch it down:
Now see with whom the shoe is found.

Action: A child stands in the center of the circle, holding an article representing the shoe. He gives the article to a child on the circle saying, "This must be mended quickly." The "cobbler" promises to do just that. The first child sits down to wait for his shoe to be mended. He closes his eyes. The shoe is passed from child to child as the song is chanted. At the last measure of music the child holding the shoe puts it quickly behind himself and resumes a natural position. The "customer" demands his shoe. He must guess who has it. He looks all around the circle and tries to tell by the expression on a child's face whether he is the one who has the shoe. The "customer" can ask three different people but no more. To each he puts the question, "Do you have my shoe?" If the child interrogated has the shoe he must produce it. If he does not have it he must look directly at the "customer" and say, "No, I do not have your shoe."

[3] See Janet Wolff reference, p. 329.

## OTHER GUESSING GAMES

*I Am Very, Very Small—I Am Very, Very Tall*
*Button, Button, Who Has the Button?*
*Twenty Questions*—(reduced to ten)
*Who Is Knocking at My Door?*

## SINGING GAMES AND ACTION FUN[4]

"All Around the Kitchen" (21)
"A-Tisket A-Tasket" (23) (28)
"Cobbler Cobbler" (4) (24)
"Come Let Us Dance" (3)
"Dancing Dollies" (21)
"Did You Ever See a Lassie" (23) (28)
"Farmer in the Dell" (18) (23) (28) (30)
"Frog in the Middle" (30)
"Go In and Out the Windows" (28)
"Here We Go Round the Mulberry Bush" (4) (18) (23) (28)
"Hey, Betty Martin" (20) (33)
"How D'ye Do, My Partner?" (28)
"London Bridge" (23) (28)
"Looby-Loo" (4) (18) (23) (28)
"The Muffin Man" (23) (28)
"My Little Pony" (18)
"My Pigeon House" (18)
"Oats, Peas, Beans and Barley Grow" (23) (28)
"On Our Holiday" (18)
"Open the Gate As High As the Sky" (23)
"Pop Goes the Weasel" (4) (18) (23) (28) (24)
"Princess" (18)
"Punchinello" (21)
"Rig-a-Jig-Jig" (21) (23)
"Ring Around a Rosy" (23) (24) (28) (30)
"Round the Village" (23) (30)
"Sally Go Round the Stars" (24) (30) (33)
"Skip to My Lou" (3) (28) (30)
"Two in the Middle" (21)
"When I Was a Young Maid" (30)
"Where Oh Where Is Pretty Little Susie" (30)

## SINGING GAME RECORDINGS

*American Game and Activity Songs for Children*—Sung by Pete Seeger—Folkways Children's records

I Know a Little Girl with Red Pajamas, I Want to Be a Farmer, Skip to My Lou, Candy Gal, Ring Around the Rosey, Here We Go Round the Mulberry Bush, London Bridge, Shoo Fly, Liza Jane, Pig in the Parlor, New River Train, Yankee Doodle, Jolly Is the Miller

A *Child's First Games*—Sung by Frank Luther—Decca
*Singing Games*—Album 1, Bowmar Records, Los Angeles, California

Cats and Rats; Did You Ever See a Lassie?; The Farmer in the Dell; Charlie Over the Water; Little Polly Flinders; Our Exercise; Go Round

[4] The numbers in parentheses refer to song book listing on pp. 328–329.

and Round the Village; Oats, Peas, and Beans; How D'ye Do, My Partner; When I Was a Shoemaker; Kitty White; Mulberry Bush; Looby Loo; Pussy Cat; The Sleeping Princess

*Singing Games*—Album 2, Bowmar Records, Los Angeles, California
A-Hunting We Will Go; Seven Steps; Dance of Greeting; Come Skip With Me; Lazy Mary; Chimes of Dunkirk; Marusaki; The Snail; Turn Me Round; Nuts in May; Pussy Cat, Pussy Cat; London Bridge; I See You; The Swing

*Singing Games for Primary Grades*—Four Records, Basic Record Library for Elementary Schools, Victor
(1) The Big Grey Cat, Hippity Hop to the Barber Shop, Ten Little Indians, Yankee Doodle, The Snail, Sally Go Round the Moon, A-Hunting We Will Go, The Thread Follows the Needle
(2) Here We Go Round the Mulberry Bush, Soldier Boy, The Muffin Man
(3) The Farmer in the Dell, Did You Ever See a Lassie?, and three others
(4) Looby Loo; Oats, Peas, Beans and Barley Grow; and two others

## SUMMARY

In some kindergartens, organized group games are practically ruled out of the program; in others there is a daily game period. There is no adequate research to support either procedure. Therefore, it is suggested that kindergarten teachers run a middle course by having games but not overemphasizing the game period. Group games best adapted to a five-year-old's play are those which are somewhat loosely organized. The element of competition is still a very personal matter as far as the five-year-old is concerned. It is conceivable that more group games will be played in situations where the physical environment is less ideal than in situations where ample space and equipment are provided for the number of children enrolled in the group.

## QUESTIONS AND PROBLEMS

1. What reasons can you give for having few rather than many games in the kindergarten?
2. The teacher asks Wendy what game she would like to play. Wendy names a game already played by the group earlier in the period. Since the teacher has asked for Wendy's suggestion, should she accept it, even though she feels the group would benefit more from playing another game? How can the teacher avoid a similar situation another time?
3. What specific games can (a) develop motor poise and good posture, (b) quicken sense perceptions, and (c) develop habits of fair play and good sportsmanship?

4. Suppose that a group of twenty-five or thirty five-year-olds is playing "Skipping Tag" (see p. 313). Probably those children who have had turns will become restless before every one has had a turn. How can this situation be prevented?
5. Five-year-olds, at least those approaching six, often talk boastfully in their play of being on "your side" and "my side." Is this an indication that they are ready for group competitive games? From your observations in a kindergarten, cite incidents in support of your answer.

## SELECTED REFERENCES


Andrew, Gladys, Jeanette Sanborn, and Elsa Schneider, *Physical Education for Today's Children*, Boston, Allyn and Bacon, Inc., 1960.

Bley, Edgar S., *The Best Singing Games for Children of All Ages*, New York, Sterling Publishing Company, 1957.

Briggs, Dorothy B., *Kindergarten Book: Games, Rhythms, Songs*, Philadelphia, Oliver Ditson Company, 1940.

Child Craft Vol. 9, *Make and Do*, Chicago, Field Enterprises Educational Corporation, 1964.

Farina, Albert M., Sol H. Furth, and Joseph M. Smith, *Growth Through Play*, Englewood Cliffs, N.J., Prentice-Hall, Inc., 1959.

Forbush, William Byron, and Harry R. Allen, *Book of Games for Home, School and Playground*, rev., Philadelphia, John C. Winston Company, 1954.

Frankel, L. B., and Others, *Giant Book of Games*, New York, Sterling Publishing Company, 1956.

Gordon, Dorothy, *Treasure Bag of Games and Songs*, New York, E. P. Dutton Company, 1939.

Hamlin, Alice, and Margaret Guessford, *Singing Games for Children*, Cincinnati, Willis Music Company, 1951.

Kauffman, Carolyn, and Patricia Farrell, *If You Live With Little Children*, New York, G. P. Putnam's Sons, 1957.

Mulac, Margaret E., *Fun and Games*, New York, Harper & Brothers, 1956.

Sheehy, Emma D., *The Five and Sixes Go to School*, New York, Henry Holt & Company, 1954.

Webb, Marion, *Games for Younger Children*, New York, William Morrow & Company, 1947.

Weiland, Adell M., *Music Rhythms and Games for Kindergartens and First Grade*, Chicago, Follett Publishing Company, 1953.

Wessels, Katherine Tyler, *Songs and Singing Games*, New York, Associated Educational Service Corporation, Golden Branch Division, 1963.

Wolff, Janet, *Let's Imagine Being Places,* New York, E. P. Dutton Company, 1961.

Wolff, Janet, *Let's Imagine Sounds,* New York, E. P. Dutton Company, 1962.

Wolff, Janet, *Let's Imagine Thinking Up Things,* New York, E. P. Dutton Company, 1961.

# 17

# RELAXATION AND REST

The kindergarten program, by providing rest periods as well as a plan for relaxation through change of activity, attempts to

- Establish a balance between activity and quiet.
- Give the child a time of uninterrupted quiet.
- Help the child learn to enjoy quiet.
- Teach the child how to relax.
- Really rest the child.

## Kinds of Relaxation

A distinction may be made between active and passive relaxation. Active relaxation results from a change of activity and is provided for in the kindergarten day by alternating periods of relatively quiet activity with periods in which the output of physical energy is relatively great. For example, a discussion period is followed by a rhythms period, a work period by a library and story period, a free period by a discussion period, and so on.

Periods in which children listen to recordings, listen to the teacher tell or read a story, have books to look at or toys to play with can scarcely be called periods of rest. It is more logical to think of these periods as illustrative of what is meant by providing opportunities for relaxation through alternating periods of relatively quiet activity with periods in which the output of physical energy is relatively great. In this chapter we shall be dealing specifically with that time in the day when children have an opportunity to experience—and, we hope, learn to enjoy—quiet passivity free, for the most part, from external factors which involve activity in the way of looking, listening, or manipulating.

## Types of Rest Periods

There is great difference of opinion concerning the kindergarten rest period. Some feel that it is a waste of the teacher's and the children's time; some feel that it is unwholesome to expect children to be wakefully quiet without occupation or entertainment for as long as ten or fifteen minutes. Others feel that, if properly conducted, it can be one of the most delightful experiences of the day and further, that when twenty-five—and sometimes many more than twenty-five—children live together for daily periods of from two and one-half to four hours they need some few minutes of uninterrupted quiet. The little girl who spoke out in the middle of a rest period and said, "Peath and quiet, ithn't it?" and then added, "I like peath and quiet, don't you?" though she interrupted the peace and quiet herself, spoke for many a kindergarten enrollee.

Certainly if the rest period is approached as time for the teacher's getting things cleaned up and the children are just down—and, hopefully, out—so that they won't bother the teacher, then it *is* a waste of the children's time. Or if the teacher stands by, viewing the group with hawklike eye, trying to spot a possible disturber, it is a waste of the teacher's time. And certainly to ask kindergarten children—or for that matter, anyone—to be rigidly quiet for a period of ten to fifteen minutes would be little short of imposed torture.

The rest period as a time in which everyone in the room, the teacher included, can take time out for relaxing and enjoying uninterrupted moments with his own thoughts is a quite different matter. In setting the stage for this second type of rest period, the teacher needs to make positive suggestions about the satisfaction to be had from having a time when one need not be interrupted or bothered by the sounds and activities of others. In some kindergartens a good feeling for the period has been created by the teacher's sharing with the children Christopher Robin's delight in being alone. In the poem "In the Dark," you will recall, Christopher Robin is thinking to himself, "So here I am in the dark alone. There's nobody here to see. . . . And nobody knows what I say to myself. . . . Nobody here to see. . . . And I can think whatever I like to think. . . . There's nobody here but me."

In the rush and push of today's living, children not only need time to be by themselves but they need to feel that they can enjoy that time. There are too many children—and adults—who have never learned to relax and enjoy their own thoughts. Some, in fact, seem actually afraid to be left alone with their own thoughts! Psychiatrists have been quoted as saying that up to 50 percent of the children referred to neurological clinics have had no traumas, no birth injuries, or other physical problems. Their trouble comes simply from the constant impact of pressures to do this and to do that. We are reminded that children and grown-ups alike need "time to do nothing"; they can really profit by having time to daydream.

An interesting way to encourage "daydreaming" (and an interesting projective technique which reveals much of what is of concern to children) is to ask children to tell what they dreamed or thought about while resting. It is best if this can be done individually, child to teacher, otherwise children may not feel free to tell their thoughts, and chain reporting all too often takes over. One child gets a favorable response from the teacher or a laugh from the group over his remark and then all the reporting which follows follows in a pattern. Too, the teacher has to guard against pushing children into feeling that they *must* give an account of their thoughts. A child ought to be able, in all sincerity, to say that he didn't think of anything. In fact, the child who didn't think of anything may be commended for being able to relax so completely that he could even "let his mind rest."

As implied earlier, reports made in privacy to the teacher may be quite revealing. It would be impossible for a single teacher to experiment with this technique with a group of twenty or more children. But she might each day, very quietly, call one child about a minute or two before calling the others; then as the child gave his report to her, she could jot it down to be reconsidered at a later time. One experiment conducted in this manner resulted in such revealing statements as the following: "I thought about if a satellite crashed into heaven then what would happen?" "I thought about how I could plant some seeds at home and have my own garden." "I thought about how pretty your shoes were." "I thought about my new baby and what if my mother didn't ever come home from the hospital!" "I thought about when are we going to get up." "I thought about how Jimmy could fix his rocket ship." "I didn't fink of nothing." "I thought about if there was nobody in the world but me and then I could do anything I wanted to do." "I thought about when we were at the lake last summer." "I thought about being hungry." "I thought to myself the whole song about 'Old MacDonald Had a Farm' and I made up some new verses too." "I thought about how all the names looked on the lockers." "I thought about me being a doctor like my daddy when I grow up."

Sometimes it is interesting and profitable to throw out suggestions ahead of time relating to some of the many things the children might enjoy thinking about in their resting time. Such suggestions—except on those rare occasions when the children might be asked to think of items of interest to be put in a letter to be dictated immediately following rest, or when they might be asked to review and be ready to report on the things they most enjoyed about an excursion immediately preceding their rest—should not be given as assignments but as leads to help each child enjoy his own thoughts.

## Time

The rest period in the kindergarten is usually scheduled for the middle or the later part of the session. In the morning it usually occurs at about ten-thirty, and in the afternoon between two-thirty and two-forty-five. There are a few kindergartens in which the afternoon children have their rest period immediately on arriving at school. This procedure is followed so that these children may have rest early in the afternoon similar to the nap to which they are accustomed at home.

The rest period observed in schools, though it varies from five to twenty minutes, averages about ten minutes. Research in the kindergarten reveals that the longer the children rest (up to a limit of fifteen minutes), the more quiet they become.[1] Apparently if the children understand that the period is to be one of considerable length, they really settle down to enjoy it. If, on the other hand, they think of it as just a time to lie down and soon bob up, they get little idea of resting and relaxing.[2]

While the rest period is usually scheduled for a definite hour, kindergartens vary greatly in the kind of activity which immediately follows or precedes the period. If there is a mid-morning lunch, milk, or orange juice, then the rest may follow this period. To prevent exhaustion, it may well follow a strenuous game or rhythm period. If it does follow such a period, the teacher must be sure that the children are not overheated when they settle down for their rest. Though more signs of fatigue are shown in those periods in which the group as a unit is being guided by teacher directions than in other periods of the day, it is not wise to have the rest time follow immediately upon such a period: the fatigue which arises is the kind that needs activity, not immobility, as its antidote.

## Physical Preparation for the Period

Before the children settle down to rest, the teacher must make sure that they have had every opportunity to make themselves physically comfort-

[1] H. C. Dawe and J. C. Foster, "The Kindergarten Rest Period," *Childhood Education*, March, 1935, 11:268–270.

[2] Observations from which the above deductions were made were limited to the mid-morning and mid-afternoon relaxation periods. If the observations had been made on rest periods intended to be sleep periods, such as those provided for in an all-day kindergarten, it would have been found that the first children to drop off to sleep usually do so about twenty minutes after they get onto their cots; others may fall asleep at varying times within the hour.

able. If there are toilet and drinking-fountain facilities in the kindergarten unit, it may be assumed that the children have had an opportunity to make use of them. In such a kindergarten, children are usually encouraged to go to the toilet and get their drinks during the unorganized rather than the organized periods of the day. If there are no plumbing facilities in the room, then there should be provision for groups of children to go to the toilet and get their drinks of water before they settle down for rest.

## Room Arrangement

A darkened room is more conducive to rest and relaxation than a light room; yet on occasion it may be well not to darken the room for the rest period, lest the children come to feel that darkness is essential to rest and relaxation. All drafts should be eliminated, and the teacher should, as far as possible, prevent any interruptions of the rest period. The general atmosphere of the room should be conducive to rest. In some schools the children sit on chairs and merely rest their heads on the tables in front of them; in others they stretch out on rugs or rug substitutes, and in still others they lie on cots and cover themselves with blankets.

If the children could lie on cots which appeared and disappeared in some miraculous fashion, that situation would approach the ideal. To date, however, no one has hit on a device which will provide the individual cots without large cost *and* which will dispose of the cots in an economical fashion once they have been supplied. The cost and the difficulty of handling the cots make their use practically out of the question for most kindergartens.

Of course, when the children rest at the tables, they do not get a chance to relax truly, and if they are crowded together there is danger of infection, since their faces are close to each other and they are all breathing on a common surface. All that can be said in favor of resting under such conditions is that the children may have a few minutes of uninterrupted quiet.

Many teachers have made a compromise between a cot and a table by having the children rest on the floor. If the children do rest on the floor —and on the whole this seems the most practical procedure—they should have papers, linoleum strips or, best of all, individual blankets, plastic mats, or rag rugs on which to lie. Blankets, rugs, and mats may be brought from home, but the great variation in size and kind of such equipment poses a real storage problem. If possible kindergartens should provide each child with washable resting equipment which could be used for the duration of the kindergarten year.[3]

[3] See Chapter 7.

*Rugs Are Folded Lengthwise First.*

Each rug or mat should be marked, not only so that the child can identify his own, but so that he can tell on which side to lie and at which end to put his head. For the children themselves, the rug or mat is apparently little more than an indication of space assigned to them. Without suggestion and help from the teacher, they will not see the rug or mat as a means of keeping clean—they may spread it out on the floor and then walk directly across it without giving the matter a thought. For storage, the rugs should be folded first lengthwise, so that the part of the rug on which the head rests does not come in contact with the other part of the rug. It would be more sanitary to roll the plastic mats from top to bottom for storage; but they are easier to store when they are piled or hung on horizontal poles. When horizontal pole units are provided for hanging rugs, taped loops must be fastened at each side of the head portion of the rug.

If the room temperature is below 68 degrees, or if the room is drafty, it is best to omit the floor rest entirely. Parents occasionally object to having their children lie on the floor, but if the windows and door are reasonably tight and if the kindergarten is above a dry, heated basement or other room, there is little cause for their worry. As objective proof of the fact that drafts are not present, one can place a lighted candle on the floor and observe its unwavering flame. Sometimes a folded rug placed in front of a door which leads to the outside will be all that is necessary to alter the situation if the flame does waver. Those school buildings in which radiant heat emanates from the entire floor area provide almost ideal conditions for floor-resting.

## Procedure

When the rest period is first introduced into the program, it is often greeted by one or two with quite earnest objections. For the first day or two, it may be wise to suggest that the objectors sit quietly in chairs and observe the others. The teacher may suggest, in tone at least, that they will soon learn how to relax as well as the others.

For the first few times the teacher may find it less confusing if she calls the children by name to get their rugs or mats. Later they may be expected to remove their rugs from their lockers or obtain them from other storage areas without being called individually. Children need to be encouraged to place their rugs or mats so that each child can have maximum privacy. If heads are too close together communication through words, gestures, or facial expression may be a distracting factor. And, of course, if heads and faces are too close together there is always the possibility of the child who may be coming down with a cold or some other illness breathing directly into the face of another child. From the hygienic point of view, if the children rest with their heads close together, the rest on rugs or mats is no great improvement over having children sit at tables and all put their heads down on the table surface.

If a single light has been left on in the room, or if a single shade has been left up, the teacher may use the light or the shade as a final signal. When everyone is comfortably settled, the light may be turned off or the last shade drawn as an indication that rest time has begun and that there should be no more unnecessary moving about. A few last whispered words will perhaps follow, and then a comfortable silence may be expected.

Usually the teacher remains seated during the period. Occasionally she will move into the vicinity of a restless child. Sometimes it will help the child settle down if the teacher sits near him in a relaxed position. If the teacher walks nervously about or calls out to individual children during rest time, she destroys the atmosphere of the period. She also destroys this atmosphere if she attempts to clean the room or to chat with her assistant. Research findings show that children seem to rest better when there is but one teacher in the room.

Music is sometimes introduced into the period. If so, it is better to limit its use to a certain portion of the period. The music may be played either at the beginning to help the children get into a calm, quiet mood, or after the children have settled down, so that they may have something pleasant and quieting to enjoy while they rest. Music played throughout the period frequently becomes merely a noise to cover commotion.

At the end of the rest period, confusion can be avoided by indicating with a nod or low-spoken name the sequence of risers. If this procedure is used, the teacher tries to make it clear that she is calling first those children who have the appearance of being completely relaxed. She explains that it does not take so long to rest if all parts of the body—head, legs, feet, arms, hands, and even fingers—are resting at the same time. Of course, it is possible to invite all children to rise at the same time, but this procedure is almost bound to result in confusion as the children attempt to put away their resting equipment.

When the children are called individually, the activity following should be one which may be begun before all the group has assembled. For example, the children might look at books, or they might engage in some such game as "Pattern Clapping," "Postman," or "The Beckoning Game."[4] Incidentally, if the rest is followed by such periods as these, the one or two children who have failed to relax will be given incentive to do so in order to join the group fun.

The teacher must guard against building up the idea that rest is a punishment. If it is introduced in the right way and in the right spirit, the child can learn to think of the rest period as a time of undisturbed freedom, a time when he is relieved of all responsibility either to the group or to any individual, a time when he does not have to be disturbed by what anyone else is thinking, and a time when no one has to be disturbed by his thoughts. Rest period may be thought of as a time when one can *enjoy* his own thoughts, when one can review experiences or plan and look forward to future experiences.

## Helping the Child Learn to Relax

Some children find it more difficult to relax than others. A rest period in which the children hold themselves tensely motionless may give the effect of a quiet, calm period, but it does not accomplish for the children what it is supposed to. If the children are really to profit by the rest, they must learn to relax.

Sometimes, in order to help the children, the teacher asks them to stretch their arms and then push up into the air as hard as they can. Then she asks them to let their arms drop to their sides or wherever they chance to fall. This gives the children some notion of how it feels to release control of their muscles.

Occasionally the teacher moves slowly about the group as the children are resting. If she sees a child who looks particularly comfortable, she notes whether his muscles are really relaxed. She explains to the children that

[4] See reference, Chapter 16.

if the parts of the body are completely relaxed, she can do with them exactly what she chooses without feeling any pull or tightening of the muscles. She tries to persuade the children that they don't even need to think about their arms, legs, or feet, for if they are really resting they will stay just where they are until the teacher or someone else moves them. One of the best ways to give children the idea of complete lack of willed control of the muscles is to show how a rag doll just drops its legs and arms when they are lifted. The doll to be used for demonstration purposes must be a very limp creature. It may be placed on a table or a board where the children can observe with ease. After such a demonstration, the teacher may ask all those who think they can relax as the doll does to try resting again. One or two such demonstrations during the semester ought to suffice.

## Positions Most Conducive to Rest

The tendency in kindergarten procedure is to expect the children to rest on their backs. It is probably true that if the individual lies on his back the maximum number of muscles can be relaxed; yet there are figures which show that the children who rest on their stomachs or sides are, throughout the rest period, more quiet and apparently more relaxed.[5] People vary in the position they naturally take for sleeping. For those children who rest naturally on their backs, it is well to encourage that position; but for those children who have formed the habit of resting and sleeping on their sides or stomachs, to change the position and hold the changed position will result in an output of effort that will defeat the purpose of the rest period.

It is easier for the teacher to conduct a quiet rest period if the children are lying on their backs, for when they are in this position they are looking at the ceiling and many distractions are outside the range of vision. Distractions are also shut out if the children close their eyes. However, to ask a child to close his eyes while lying on the floor with some twenty-five or more other children is asking a good deal in the way of self-surrender. Children can rest equally well with their eyes opened or closed. In fact, some children have been known to go to sleep before they closed their eyes.

## Sleep in the Rest Period

In the short kindergarten rest time, it is unusual for a child to go to sleep. If a child does chance to fall asleep while he is resting, it is well to waken

[5] H. C. Dawe and J. C. Foster, "The Kindergarten Rest Period," *Childhood Education*, March, 1935, 11:268–270.

him when the others get up, so that he will not feel embarrassed when he finds that the others are all up and engaged in another activity. If the child does not waken easily, then a group meeting may be called so that the situation may be explained and talked over with the other children. If they realize that the child is tired and probably really in need of rest, they will be more sympathetic and will be willing to engage in quiet activities so that he may rest longer. If the child wakens to find the group sympathetic toward him, he will probably not resent not having been called, nor will he be embarrassed about having fallen asleep.

If a child frequently falls asleep during rest time, the teacher should make it a point to discuss the situation with his mother. It may be that the child needs some medical attention, or simply that he is not getting enough sleep at night.

## Incidental Rest Periods

Resting need not be limited to the one period scheduled in the program. At any time during the day when undue fatigue is shown by loss of emotional control, constant use of high-pitched, tense voices, raucous laughter, or inability to concentrate, a period of rest may profitably be introduced into the program. Perhaps only individual children will need this extra rest, but occasions may arise when the whole group will profit by an unscheduled period of rest and composure.

## The Extended Rest in the All-Day Kindergarten

In those relatively few schools where children spend the entire kindergarten day at school, from eight-thirty in the morning until three-thirty or later in the afternoon, it is customary to include an extended rest period in the afternoon program. In some schools a special rest room is provided, and in others cots are set up and taken down daily in the regular kindergarten room. Each child will have his assigned or chosen resting place in the "rest" room, and the cots should be placed sufficiently far apart so that outstretched arms and legs cannot easily contact other cots. The cots should be so arranged that the head of one cot alternates with the foot of the cot next to it. When cots must be set up and taken down daily, it facilitates matters if the blankets used are fastened to the legs of the bed by means of elastic tape. This keeps the blanket in place, simplifies bed-making, and makes it possible to remove blankets easily for laundering. In the extended rest period, the children should be expected to remove their shoes before getting onto their cots, but the removal of other outer clothing can be a matter of personal choice.

The afternoon rest period follows as soon after luncheon as possible, and is approximately sixty minutes long. If there are some children who seem to need extra rest, they may remain on their cots after the others get up. Occasionally, however, parents request that the child who sleeps longer than the others be called with the others so that nighttime sleep not be delayed.

During the extended rest time, as in the shorter rest time, the children are encouraged to enjoy their own thoughts. There is no particular emphasis placed on sleep, though in some kindergartens a written record is kept of the time the child gets into bed, the time he falls asleep, and the time he wakens or is called. Boys seem to sleep more frequently than girls. It is unusual for the same child to fall asleep on five consecutive days, and it almost never happens that the entire group sleeps on any one day. However, from one-third to two-thirds of a group may be expected to drop off to sleep on any one day.

## SUMMARY

The kindergarten program provides opportunities for both active and passive relaxation. Active relaxation is achieved by alternating relatively quiet and strenuous activities; passive relaxation, through the planned rest period. In any rest period there should be an atmosphere distinctly conducive to rest. The children may rest sitting at tables or lying on mats, rugs, or cots. The rest on mats or rugs seems most practical for the ten- or fifteen-minute period of the morning or the afternoon. The children very seldom sleep at this time. In the extended rest period included in the all-day kindergarten program, cots and blankets are provided for resting, and from a third to two-thirds of the group may be expected to drop off to sleep during any sixty-minute period.

## QUESTIONS AND PROBLEMS

1. What is meant by the statement "Before resting, the teacher must be sure that the children have had an opportunity to make themselves physically comfortable"?
2. Make a diagram of the kindergarten floor area; then, during the rest period record with stick figures the resting position of each child. Indicate each child's posture by code: back—b; left side—ls; right side—rs; stomach—st; sitting—s. Just before the period ends, make a quick check to see how many have changed positions.

3. What factors might enter into the teacher's decision to keep story and rest time as separate experiences?
4. Observe the attitude and activity of the teacher during a rest period. In your estimation, what effect did her demeanor have on the quality of the children's resting?
5. In some kindergartens "the best rester" is designated as the fairy who goes about calling the others by touching them with a wand. What objection would you have to this procedure?
6. Make a list of recordings that might be conducive to rest.

## SELECTED REFERENCES

Gesell, Arnold, and Frances L. Ilg, *The Child From Five to Ten*, New York, Harper and Brothers, 1946.

Hammond, Sarah Lou, Ruth J. Dales, Doris Sikes Skipper, and Ralph L. Witherspoon, *Good Schools for Young Children*, New York, Macmillan Company, 1963.

Lambert, Hazel, *Teaching the Kindergarten Child*, New York, Harcourt, Brace and Company, 1958.

Leonard, Edith, Dorothy Van Deman, and Lillian Miles, *Foundations of Learning in Childhood Education*, Columbus, Ohio, Charles E. Merrill Books, Inc., 1963.

Rand, Winifred, Mary E. Sweeny, and Lee E. Vincent (revised by Breckenridge, Marion, and Margaret Nesbitt Murphy), *Growth and Development of the Young Child*, 7th ed., W. B. Saunders Company, 1963.

Rudolph, Marguerita, and Dorothy H. Cohen, *Kindergarten: A Year of Learning*, New York, Appleton-Century-Crofts, 1964.

Sheehy, Emma D., *The Fives and Sixes Go to School*, New York, Henry Holt and Company, 1954.

"The Kindergarten Rest Period," *Portfolio for Kindergarten Teachers*, Bulletin No. 2, Washington, D.C. Association for Childhood Education International, 1951.

Wills, Clarice D., and William H. Stegeman, *Living in the Kindergarten*, 2nd ed., Chicago, Follett Publishing Company, 1959.

# 18

# LANGUAGE ARTS IN THE KINDERGARTEN

Through many experiences the kindergarten program gives children opportunities to

- Clarify their thoughts through oral expression.
- Acquire an ever larger and more meaningful vocabulary.
- Acquire desirable oral-language habits of correct grammar, clear enunciation, careful pronunciation, pleasing voice.
- Develop the ability to present ideas and to listen to the presentation of ideas.
- Acquire or preserve spontaneity of speech.
- Share the experiences of others in the group.
- Appreciate the significance of both spoken and written words.

## Opportunities for Verbalization

One cannot speak of a language "period" in the kindergarten. Most kindergartens give ample opportunity throughout the daily program for practice in oral expression. The children are encouraged to converse informally, to organize and present their ideas verbally to the group, to listen attentively to the ideas presented by others, to engage in the conversational give-and-take of organized social periods, to make up, tell, and dramatize stories, to interpret pictures, to dictate letters and reports summarizing group experiences, and to make up jingles, rhymes, and riddles.

## Learning Through Talking

When it does not interfere with efficiency or the activities of others, verbalization and conversation are not only permitted in the kindergarten but encouraged. Perhaps it is needless to say that five-year-olds require little encouragement! Of course there may be a silent child in any kindergarten group, but he certainly stands out because of his silence. There is some evidence that the five-year-olds of our radio-television age tend to use more words and longer sentences than the children before this era.[1] Before the advent of radio and television, the children of parents in professional and managerial groupings were exposed to more verbalization than those children whose parents were in other occupations. But now all children are feeling the impact of words. As we listen to five-year-olds today, we are frequently astounded both by the words they use and the extent of their verbalization. Sometimes they seem to be doing all their thinking and learning out loud. And probably there is a great deal of truth in this, for as children talk they really are experimenting with, clarifying, and formulating their ideas.[2] Throughout the year we find, or should find, a steady development in the choice of words, length and complexity of sentences, and adequacy and clarity of expression.

## Conversation with Individuals

During the free-time activities period and work time, there is always much opportunity for conversation. The child converses not only with other children but also "man to man" with the teacher.

In talking with the children, the teacher need not oversimplify her vocabulary. If she is careful to use synonyms or explanatory phrases, she can do much to help the child broaden his own vocabulary. It is amazing to note with what ease some children adopt new words and use them correctly if the meaning is inherent in the context. Two children and a teacher sat quietly observing some Japanese turtles crawling over the sand in a fish bowl. One of the children said, "I would like to pick up those turtles." And the other child added, "Oh, no! They might hurt you!" The teacher entered the conversation at this point, and as an experiment in language she said, "Oh, really, they are perfectly innocuous." She repeated the state-

[1] Mildred C. Templin, *Certain Language Skills in Children: Their Development and Inter-relationships*, Institute of Child Welfare Monograph, No. 26, Minneapolis, University of Minnesota Press, 1957.

[2] Marjorie K. Pyles, "Verbalization as a Factor in Learning," *Child Development*, June, 1932, 3:108–113.

ment and added a synonym for the new word, as she picked a turtle out of the bowl. "See, they really are perfectly innocuous, perfectly harmless. Their claws tickle one's fingers a bit, but that is about all they can possibly do. Really, they're just as innocuous as can be." She replaced the turtle, and all three left the table. A day or two later, one of the two children was heard saying to a third child, "I'm not afraid to pick up that turtle. He's perfectly 'nocuous. He can't hurt you. He only tickles you." The five-year-old has an inordinate interest in new words. He enjoys hearing them, he likes to play with them, and he has little hesitancy about using them in his own conversation.

## Dramatic Play and Word Awareness

The many dramatic and representative-play situations which arise in the free-time activities period offer excellent opportunity for experimenting with unusual words. Sometimes the words used are taken directly from stories, but more often they are simply words the children have heard grown-ups use frequently. Such words as "unconscionable," "exasperating," "splendid," "delicious," "perfectly charming" may enter into a bit of dramatic play when they would never enter easily into the five-year-old's ordinary conversation.

Unfortunately, undesirable as well as desirable words find their way into the conversation of kindergarten children! It is interesting to note, however, how quickly the children learn to use words which meet with approval and to discard, or at least reserve for other occasions, undesirable vocabulary.

## Presenting Ideas Orally to the Group and Listening Attentively to Others

Since reporting an experience in words alone is much more difficult than showing and describing an object, first attempts at speaking before the group are often made in connection with displaying articles brought from home. While in the beginning of the year the children are encouraged to bring and exhibit to the group almost any sort of object, later they are urged to bring chiefly those books, toys, or other items which have a direct bearing on the kindergarten interest of the day or week. Often they show surprising discernment in selecting material to be presented. When gardening is the center of interest for example, the teacher can expect children to bring such things as seeds, fertilizer, gardening tools, plants for transplanting, worms of various kinds, pictures of flowers or vegetables cut from papers and magazines, books about gardening, and picture storybooks which

University of Minnesota

*Listening and Thinking*

have some bearing on the subject. Each of these will call for some sort of verbal statement on the part of the contributor, and it is desirable for the entire group to hear what the contributor has to say about what he has brought. At the group meeting, most of the "reporters," because of the central garden theme, can be expected to speak about gardening. This does not mean that other topics should be completely ruled out, but rather that those children having contributions bearing on the central theme would be invited to make their verbal contribution pretty much in sequence, and that other verbal reports would follow.

## Thought-provoking Verbalization

The alert teacher capitalizes on opportunities to encourage thought-provoking verbalization. The types of questions she asks and the verbal leads she gives do much to make "show and tell" (but let's call it "sharing time" instead of "show and tell" time) a profitable experience. Nothing can be more boring and wasteful of children's time than to have one child after another come before the group "to say his say," call on another child, and then sit down. Nine times out of ten the others are not listening at all but simply waiting and hoping they will, or will not, be chosen next.

As an illustration of the way in which the teacher's participation in the children's sharing time can make the situation thought-provoking, suppose we look at three ways in which teachers might handle a single incident. In each case the situation remains constant, but it is quite apparent that the opportunities for thought-provoking verbalization vary greatly.

THE INCIDENT

On a cold winter day in January, Julie arrives at kindergarten carrying a large brown shopping bag.

THE HANDLING OF THE INCIDENT

*Case I:* After taking off her outside wraps, Julie removes some white sweet peas from her bag and, clutching them in her hands, brings them to the teacher. Miss B. says, "Thank you, Julie. They're beautiful and I'll put them on my desk so everyone can see them." No further comment is made about the flowers.

*Case II:* Miss M. receives the flowers as in Case I, but asks Julie to bring the flowers to the sharing-time meeting. As Julie stands before the group holding the vase of sweet peas, Miss M. says, "Does anyone know the name of Julie's flowers?" In answer the children chorus, "Sweet peas." Miss M. asks, "Julie, do your sweet peas have a nice smell?" Julie smells her flowers, nods her head and says, "Yes." Miss M. says, "Yes, sweet peas are pretty and they have a lovely smell. Now, Julie, will you choose someone else "to show and tell" about his surprise. Put the flowers back on the desk so we can all enjoy them."

*Case III:* Miss G. notes that on her arrival Julie is carrying a large brown shopping bag. She confers with Julie about the contents and then asks her to bring her surprise to the sharing-time meeting. At the meeting Julie removes from the bag a gallon ice-cream container, which she proceeds to show to the children and the teacher:

"It's flowers," says Julie.

"Why did you bring them in an ice cream box?" asks Peter.

"So they wouldn't freeze," says Julie. "If they freezed, they'd die and they wouldn't be pretty."

Jim, "Ice cream is cold. It would freeze them."

Julie, "Silly! Of course there isn't ice cream in the box now. We ate it up." As she removes the cover she says, "See, my mother wrapped them in a wet cloth." Finally Julie produces her flowers and, clutching them in her fist, says, "See, flowers. They're real!"

Miss G., "So they are! They're lovely. I suppose we should put them in water soon. What kind of flowers are they?"

Julie, "White flowers."

Miss G., "But don't they have another name?"

Julie, "I forget the name."

Marsha, "They look like sweet peas."

Julie, "Yes, they are sweet peas."

Miss G., "Beautiful white sweet peas! Where did your mother get them, Julie?"

Julie, "It was my mother's birthday yesterday and my daddy gave them to her."

Miss G., "Flowers make a lovely birthday gift and wasn't it nice of your mother to let you share some of them with us? I for one would like to thank her."

From the group, "Me, too." "I would, too," "Thank her for me, too."

Miss G., "Why do you suppose they call them 'sweet peas'?"

Julie, "Cause they smell sweet."

Miss G., "They do smell sweet. They have a wonderful aroma. I wish we could all have a chance to smell them."

Barbara, "Maybe we could make a circle and Julie could walk around with them."

Miss G., "That's a good idea."

Bob, "Or maybe she could give us each one."

Miss G., "The only trouble there is that if we each had one the pretty bouquet would be gone."

Sally, "And the flowers would die if they didn't have water."

Bob, "I've got it! Why don't we have a few flowers on each of our work tables?"

Miss G., "Good idea. Could we do that, Julie?"

Julie, "O.K."

Miss G., "Probably you had better put the bouquet in a glass of water while we are talking about them, Julie. When it is work time perhaps you could choose someone to help you make little bouquets."

Julie, "How many should we make?"

Rex, "I'll count—1, 2, 3, 4, 5,—. Five. We need five bouquets."

Miss G., "What could we use to put them in?"

Jean, "I've got it! Orange juice cans."

Miss G., "But they are not very pretty."

Julie, "We could put red paper around them."

Miss G., "So we could. Perhaps, Julie, you and your helper could do that for us."

. . . . . . . . . . . . . . . . . .

Miss G., "What other flowers can we think of that are white?"

Class, "Lilies, peonies, roses . . ."

Miss G., "Wait a minute. I'll write them on the easel as you name them." In manuscript she writes the names as dictated. They end with a list of *ten* white flowers, and decide to see if they can think of any more by the next day. They are going to look in flower catalogues and magazines and ask their mothers to write down the names of other white flowers.

. . . . . . . . . . . . . . . . . .

Miss G., "We thought of a reason why we might call them *sweet* peas. Why do you suppose they are called sweet *peas*?"

John, "Because they grow on vines like peas."

Miss G., "You're right about their growing on vines like peas. But I believe there is another reason they might be called peas. Could any one make a guess?"

Miss G., "I'm thinking about the seeds that sweet peas grow from."

Bill, "Oh, maybe the seeds are like peas."

Miss G., "You are so right. They *are* like peas and they grow in pods like peas." As she says this she draws a picture of a pea pod. Then a picture of the inside of the pod showing the peas.

Jim, "We eat the seeds, don't we?"

Miss G., "We eat the seeds of green peas, but I'm not sure whether the seeds of sweet peas would be good to eat or not."

Dorothy, "We have some sweet pea seeds at home. I'll bring some."

Miss G., "But they are all dried up, aren't they? I doubt that they would be good to eat that way. It might be interesting to plant them, though, to see if vines would grow."

. . . . . . . . . . . . . . . . . .

Miss G., "By the way, Julie, where do you suppose these sweet peas came from? They couldn't grow outdoors in your garden now." The children all chuckle. Julie looks puzzled.

Barbara, "Maybe they came from a greenhouse."

Peter, "A greenhouse? My house is painted green."

Miss G., "I think Barbara means they came from the kind of house that has glass walls and a glass roof where green things can grow even in winter."

Billy, "Oh, you mean a hothouse?"

Miss G., "Sometimes a greenhouse is called a hothouse. True, they might have come from a greenhouse or a hothouse. *Or* they might have been flown in to our city from some part of the world that is much warmer than it is in our part of the world. Jim, would you get the globe? Thank you, Jim."

Miss G., "Now let's see. This is north and this is the North Pole. Certainly they couldn't have grown up there where it is all ice and snow."

Jim, "Maybe they grew down at the South Pole."

Miss G., pointing to the South Pole, "It seems as though it might be warm at the South Pole; but it is cold, as cold as it is at the North Pole. It is all ice and snow down there, too. Right here, just halfway between the North Pole and the South Pole, is the hottest place on earth. Right here at the equator."

Peter, "Maybe they came from the equator."

Miss G., "Possibly, or they might even have come from down here in the United States. That's near enough the equator to be quite warm even in winter."

The educational implications seem unending and, counting back, we discover that more than ten children have participated in the few minutes of discussion. The questions asked by both the children and the teacher were thought-provoking, and neither the children's nor the teacher's answers could possibly be classed as echoed responses or idle patter. The experience fostered not only language but honest intellectual development as well.

## Conversational Give-and-Take of the Semi-Organized Social Situation

Probably the best setting for conversational give-and-take is the luncheon or "snack" period. In some kindergartens, milk, or orange juice, or even only water is served. Regardless of the occasion for getting the children together in groups about tables, the period is thoroughly enjoyed if the right spirit of leisurely interchange of ideas is encouraged. A fine opportunity is offered at such a time also for building up social courtesies in speaking and listening.

The subjects which may be introduced are almost innumerable. The following is only a sampling, but it will give some notion of the many subjects which can prove interesting.

Pets
Flowers
Trees
Seeds
Birds
Butterflies
Bees
Cocoons
Polliwogs
Turtles

Moon
Stars
Sun
Ice
Water
Rain
Frost
Snow
Dew
Vacation experiences

Excursions made by groups
Boats
Trains
Steam shovels
Fire engines
Airplanes
Rockets
Astronauts
Homes

Circus
Current events
Movies
TV programs
Milk
Foods
Doctors
Nurses
Birthdays
Holidays

If there is a lull in the conversation or if the conversation seems to be degenerating into idle, foolish talk, the teacher must be ready to save the day by presenting new subject matter. The teacher must always have in mind some worthwhile and interesting topic which she may introduce if necessity arises, but it is well to let the conversation be guided as much as possible by the social situation.

Children, like grown-ups, draw on their past experience and knowledge from books for their social conversation. The sharing of experiences can lead to the dissemination of a tremendous amount of information. One day while a group of children were sitting about drinking their orange juice, a small boy ventured the remark that he was going to Duluth for his vacation. A second child immediately picked up the remark and said, "Oh, Duluth! I've been there. When you go there you will see great big boats. And you will see a bridge that opens right up in the middle." A further discussion of the bridge followed. Then the teacher asked the second child if he had seen the car that takes the people up the steep hill. "Sure," said the little boy, "first my daddy and I went up in a car and then when that car came down we came down and when we were coming down in that car my mother and my sister were going up in the other." A discussion of the pulley system followed. Since the interest was still high in cars which could go up and down steep hills, the teacher told of her experience of riding to the top of a mountain peak in the Italian Alps on a funicular, a cable railway. At the time this incident took place, Virginia Burtons' *Maybelle, The Cable Car* had not been written, but had it been in print this would have been an ideal book to share with the children at story time.

## Reading

When the children are in the library they often comment audibly as they turn the pages of a book. Frequently they pretend to read a story aloud to themselves and on occasion their "reading" is done for the benefit of an audience of three or four children. Sometimes within a kindergarten group there is a child who is able to, and does, read aloud to other children. When the teacher reads the story there is often the "that reminds me" incident which children wish to report, and if a story has been read in part while a child was absent, the need for reviewing the first part of the story calls for verbal expression. These and many other experiences connected with reading offer opportunities for guided oral expression in the kindergarten.[3]

[3] See Chapter 13.

## Dramatizing Stories and Play-Making

In dramatizing stories, children not only repeat portions of the text of the story but also often find it necessary to use words to replace some of the dramatic action. A small girl who was "Goldilocks" once met the situation very well. She sat in the big chair, then the middle-sized chair, and made the fitting remarks. But when she found herself seated in the small chair, she apparently realized that the chair was not going to break as the story suggests. A look of blank despair passed over her face. Finally she smiled, rose from the chair, turned it over and said, "Dear me, this chair is broken all to pieces."

In speaking for plain story figures, stick, shadow, or handpuppets, kindergarten children are often more outspoken and free in their verbalization than they are in playing character parts themselves. This is especially true for the timid child. He seems to find it much easier to speak for the puppet than to speak for himself. The child who seldom ventures to talk before the group or who, when he does do so, speaks in almost a whisper will often come out with a booming voice and a delightfully free and creative flow of words when speaking, behind the screen, for his puppet.

## Original Stories

The original story gives the child unlimited opportunity to play and experiment orally with ideas. The kindergarten child who comes to the front to tell a "make-up" story usually has little or no idea of what he is going to say before he opens his mouth and begins to talk. Just as there is likely to be at least one child with outstanding musical or artistic ability in nearly every large group of kindergarten children, so there is likely to be one who has outstanding storytelling ability. With the artist-storyteller to give the children inspiration, many children will be eager to try to spin tales. Sometimes these tales are really worth preserving. Usually they have in them elements of stories which the children have heard before; but the naïveté and spontaneity of the language and construction used often gives them the charm of folk tales. The following is a tale told by a kindergarten child possessing marked storytelling ability.

John came to the front of the group, smiled at his audience, waited for them to settle themselves comfortably, and then began: "Once upon a time—" A long pause followed. As he gazed about the room, his eyes lighted on a blackboard picture of a huge horse, a small wagon, and a small boy, which had been drawn that morning by a kindergarten child. The story continued ". . . there was a little boy, and he had a big horse and a little wagon. The little boy got in the wagon and said 'Giddy-ap' to the horse. The horse galloped and galloped and galloped, right to a big forest. Then he galloped and galloped and galloped right through the big forest. When he got on the other side of the forest, the little boy said, 'Turn around, horsey, turn around,' but the horse wouldn't turn around. He galloped and galloped and galloped until he came to the ocean. Then the little boy put on his bathing suit and went for a swim. The horse went for a swim, too. Finally the little boy got into his wagon and he said 'Giddy-ap' to the horse. The horse galloped and galloped and galloped right back to the forest. It was getting dark. In the forest they saw a light. It was the robbers' house. The robbers took the little boy's horse and wagon, and the little boy didn't know what to do; but finally he gave the robbers some money and the robbers gave him another horse and wagon. The little boy got into the wagon and he said 'Giddy-ap' to the horse. The horse galloped and galloped and galloped right through the forest and right back to the little boy's house. And then the little boy was back home again and that's all."

## Dream Stories

Telling dream stories offers some children just the opportunity they need for unleashing their imaginations. The really imaginative child will spin his tale almost indefinitely; but the practical, stolid child, even in these stories which suggest no form or bounds, will cling tenaciously to known forms. The following dictated by a five-year-old is an illustration of this last point:

TWO GOATS

Once upon a time two goats went into the woods. They met a rabbit. The rabbit told them to have a race. They all got a line. Then they started. The rabbit thought he would win. (It's something like the story in a book but not just the same—The Hare and the Turtle.) He got tired on the road and fell asleep. The goats went right past him. And when he awoke they were way up nearly to the goal and he ran as fast as he could. He was just as near as they were when they were at the goal.

Sometimes in the dream stories we get an insight into the child's wishes which is most revealing. The story that follows was dictated by a very plain little girl whose mother always dressed her in "just right" but rather severe clothes. See what a lovely, fairylike creature she is in her dreams.

A FAIRY

I dreamed once that I was a fairy. I flew through the sky and no one ever saw me. And the blue sky was so blue that it just matched my dress, when I was a fairy. Then the snow began to fall and my dress turned whiter and whiter as long as the white winter snow did fall. And in the wind the treetops were dancing and dancing. But then the sun began to shine and, do you know, my dress got bluer and bluer again. And the sun got so bright that my dress turned yellow.

Once I had a beautifuler dress than anything. And it was trimmed with lace and it was all full of ruffles and there was a wreath of roses all round the neck. And it had real silvery trimming around the neck, too. And I often put it on when I go to parties and all the people do ask for me. And I had some beautiful shoes on, too; and you never, never saw such pretty ones in your whole life. And that's all.

## Making Up Jingles, Poems, and Riddles

Just the simple fun of playing with words and building up patterns in jingles and rhymes gives the child much practice in oral expression and also affords much satisfaction. Jingles and rhymes are often built on already familiar patterns. One child, for example, played for several days with the pattern found in the song "Who Are You?"[4] Her most satisfying jingle seemed to be:

Oh, Tweedle-dum and Tweedle-dee,
Oh, Tweedle-dum and Tweedle-dee,
Come over to my house today,
Please come and play.

Another child sat at the table mouthing words in a very serious fashion. At last a look of complete radiance came across her face and she said, "I've got it. Listen!" To the tune of "Happy Birthday to You," she laboriously fitted the following words, which were evidently intended to be an expression of her feeling about the cook's food:

Miss-es E-er-ick-son
Miss-es E-er-ick-son
We-e li-ike your foo-ood
Miss-es E-er-ick-son.

Children's poetry—and when we speak of children's poetry in this sense, we usually mean the child's poetical ideas and not his complete verse—is often worth recording, if not for the satisfaction it may bring to other children at least for the newness and freshness it may bring to the adult world.

Making up riddles, having them written down and then read back to the group, is an experience which helps the children both to express themselves

[4] See reference, p. 272.

accurately and to have an appreciation of the written word. Riddles may be made up about any number of things, but in order to help the children express themselves precisely, it is best to limit the subject matter on any given day: one day about animals, another day about toys, another about birds, and so on. Children sometimes make up riddles about pictures they have drawn; then when others fail to guess the riddle, they may look at the picture for the answer. Some examples of kindergarten riddles about birds and animals follow:

BLUEBIRD

I have blue on my back
And my breast is darkish orange;
I build my nest in a hole in the tree.
What am I?

ZEBRA

I am striped, black and white.
I have a black nose.
I live in the jungle.
I can gallop and kick.
I eat grass.
What am I?

## Retelling Stories

Children enjoy telling not only the stories they have heard in kindergarten but those they have heard outside the kindergarten. Excitement can run high when several children try to report or tell the story of a television program each child has seen. It is at times such as this that the kindergarten teacher realizes she will do well to include in her homework the viewing of at least some of the television programs her children watch. Children often get into an argument over the way certain folk tales should be told. When such arguments arise, it is interesting and challenging to have individuals tell the story as it appears in their books or to have them bring in their own books, so that the printed versions can be checked with the oral.

## Interpreting Pictures

Holding a picture before a group of five-year-old children and asking, "What is this picture about?" or "What does the picture tell you?" will usually result in an enumeration of the objects seen in the picture. If, however, the children are presented with a series of pictures for which there is no text, they will be eager to make up a story to go with the pictures.

Picture books with texts in a foreign language, such as *La Plume Mordorée,*[5] *Tant Grön, Tant Brun och Tant Gredelin,*[6] and *Etwas von den Wurzelkindern*[7] and pictures with no text at all such as *What Whiskers Did*[8] are excellent vehicles for original stories based on a series of pictures. The English text of *Peregrin and the Goldfish,* by Dalgliesh, was thus devised by a group of children and their teacher. Still another source of stimulation for original stories is certain ten-cent picture books with illustrations superior to the text. The kindergarten child is not too young to appreciate the fact that not all books are equally good, and while generally the school tries to discourage any mutilation of books, it is quite permissible with these cheap books to write a new story and paste it over the old text.

## Functional Written Language

Letters or reports describing interesting excursions and experiences may be sent to absent teachers or children. Often during the kindergarten year occasions arise for sending dictated invitations, business, and thank-you notes.

When letter-writing is first proposed to the children, the usual response is, "But we can't write." An interesting discussion often follows on the ways in which a person who cannot write might send messages to an individual at some distance. Children in this modern age are likely to propose telephoning, telegraphing, and sending radio or TV messages, or even sending a message by way of Telestar or Early Bird. When the teacher brings the discussion back to the possibility of sending the message on paper, some child will doubtless suggest the possibility of drawing pictures. If composing a letter is decided on, a discussion might then follow of the various things they would want to include. The teacher may volunteer to write down the ideas or to write down what the children would like to say in their pictures. A simple listing of the ideas on the easel or chalkboard will help the children and the teacher know which ideas have been covered and which have been overlooked. Often the children feel that the letter is written when the ideas have been listed. The children could make their pictures immediately after the discussion of ideas, but usually it is wise to let the listing stand for a day before settling down to the actual business of dictating the

[5] Albertine Deletaille, *La Plume Mordorée,* France, Les Album du Pere Castor, Flammarion Editeur, 1960.

[6] Elsa Beskow, *Tant Grön, Tant Brun och Tant Gredelin,* Stockholm, Albert Bonniers Forlag, no date given.

[7] Sibylle v. Olfers, *Etwas von den Wurzelkindern,* Eklingern and Munchen, J. F. Schreiber, no date given.

[8] Ruth Carroll, *What Whiskers Did,* New York, Macmillan Company, 1932.

report or letter. On the following day a review of the ideas and discussion of questions directed by the teacher will help the children decide which ideas seem to belong together. We certainly don't call this outlining and paragraphing at the kindergarten level, but that is exactly what the children are experiencing in this approach to letter-writing. Of course, the teacher will ask leading questions to bring the thinking to a point; but if the letter is to show spontaneity and originality, she must not let herself fall into the habit of questioning and requestioning until she gets from the children the specific response she has in mind. It is well to discuss desirable substitutes for poor English and to encourage the use of a variety of words, but it is not essential that children should express themselves in perfect English, nor is it probable that children of this age will. If the teacher writes down the message in longhand and then has the letter typed, the children can get some appreciation of the two kinds of writing. The first letters to be dictated without the use of pictures are usually very brief; later ones are often quite long and newsy affairs. Here are some examples of these letters and stories:

Dear Mr. B________,

Can we please have the rooster and the chicken back? We might be able to keep them in the squirrel cage or in our barn or we might make a chicken house.

We don't want them forever. We want them for about three days.

When you come with the chickens we will say "thank you" for bringing them. We will help you with them.

Sincerely,
The Kindergarten Children

Dear Dr. H________,

We have been thinking about honeybees all spring. Will they sting us if they get out of their hive and fly in the room instead of outside?

We want honeybees to make honey for us.

Have you any honeybees? Could we have some bees, please, sir?

Would you please teach us how to take care of honeybees?

Please write a letter back to us if you have any honeybees for us or not.

We could come after the bees.

Thank you!

Yours truly,
The University Kindergarten Children

Dear Miss B_________,

We have your card of the soldiers of Buckingham Palace. That was a nice card you sent.

The chickens are getting fatter than they were. The baby chickens can eat big corn. We can put them over the fence now and they are learning to fly.

We made a boat out of blocks. We have a smokestack on the boat.

We gave away our turtles.

We have flowers in our garden. The squash vines are growing big.

We ate lettuce sandwiches down by the river. We ate carrot sandwiches on the knoll on the campus.

Have you forgotten about the book that I gave you? (Bob)

Truly yours,
The Kindergarten Children

## JEAN'S FIRE

Jean had a fire in her roof. Oh! it was terrible. Jean's aunt's housekeeper came in the door hollering, "Fire! Fire! Fire!" Jean's daddy said, "Don't make so much noise, we'll call the fire department."

The neighbors and the students came to the fire. The fire department came. The firemen had to knock a hole in the wall. They put the hose through the hole. The stairway got soaking wet. The firemen went up the ladder and squirted the hose. P—lush, P—lush, Plush. The fire went out. The firemen went away. Now the roof is covered with tarpaper and canvas.

## A TRIP TO THE FIRE STATION[9]

When we had our meeting in the kindergarten, Jean told the children and Miss Smith all about the fire. Miss Smith called the fire station to see if we could come to see the fire barn. The fireman said, "Did you wish to report a fire?" Miss Smith said, "No, we want to come to see the fire barn." The fireman said, "Oh, is that it? All right, come along any time as soon as you want to."

We stood in line and walked to the fire station.

When we went in the fire barn a dog said, "Bow-wow, bow-wow." He was sitting in the seat of the hook-and-ladder truck. Jim put on the fireman's hat. Richard put on the fireman's boots. The boots were too big and too heavy. He almost fell over. John put on the fireman's boots. He walked a little. Some children got on the fire truck. Marnie rang the bell. Some children got on the running board of the truck and some got on the back. John pretended he was driving.

[9] This account was dictated by the children late in the school year. Many of these children were six chronologically and some seven and eight mentally.

The firemen showed us their fire-alarm bell, they showed us their signal board. We saw a fireman slide down the pole.

We went upstairs. We saw the open hole where the firemen slid down the pole. We saw a man dress up fast in his "hitch pants" and boots. Then the fire bell rang. Margaret was scared and covered up her ears. The fireman said, "Fire! Stand back, everybody!" Then he said, "Never mind, there's no fire." We saw the beds with the covers and the mattresses turned over. The firemen sleep upstairs. We saw the big bell that wakes the firemen at night. The bell was about eighteen inches across.

We came downstairs. The firemen lifted the children up a little way into the air and the children slid down the pole.

We saw the kitchen.

We found our partners and walked back to the kindergarten. It was a very windy day.

## Functional Oral Language

If the teacher is careful to use language in such a way that the child needs to listen to the whole statement before he has all his facts, she will be encouraging the child to listen with care to spoken words. All too frequently children know or think they know what we are going to say before we have finished our statements, and so they simply stop listening. The mother or teacher who says the same thing over and over not waiting for a response or who says the same thing in the same words day after day is, in effect, teaching the child to ignore the importance and function of words. The teacher may say, "Betsy, would you walk over to the science table and bring us the magnifying glass with the green frame, the one nearest the salt crystals?" Betsy will have a large order to fill. But if, on Betsy's return, the teacher comments to the group that Betsy did remarkably well to get every single word in the request, and if she then further points out that Betsy *walked* over, brought the magnifying glass with the *green frame* and brought the one *nearest the salt crystals* and not nearest the stones, she will be helping the group appreciate the function of words.

The group's appreciation of the function of words can be further stimulated by such a statement as, "This will be a turn for anyone who is wearing brown oxfords, who lives in The Grove, and who painted a picture this morning." Or, "Let's have all the children who come from across the river and who have brought seeds for the garden sit at the round table." A grandmother observing in a kindergarten once said, "I just don't understand it. Tommy seems to listen and fairly hang on every word the teacher speaks. At home his mother talks and talks and he never pays the slightest attention." We often fall into the habit of forgetting that, in general, words should be functional.

## Colorful Language in Everyday Living

As grown-ups we tend to have stereotyped patterns of speech. We say, for example, "It's as black as pitch," or "It's as cold as ice." The five-year-old whose patterns are not so stereotyped says, "It's as black as the inside of a furnace"; "It's as black as burnt matches"; "It's as black as inside a rhinoceros"; "It's as cold as an attic"; "It's as cold as inside a refrigerator"; "Its as cold as up where Santa Claus comes from." Here are some further illustrations of the refreshing quality of children's speech:

One child, observing the foam on the turbulent, churning waters of a dam said, "Oh look, look. See all the 'soaps' on the water."

Another child, looking meditatively at a crescent-shaped planting in a formal garden, said, "Hm! I guess the *little* moon must be buried there."

And still another child, in discussing rainbows with his teacher, said, "Yes, the rain drops are just like a thousand and thousand prisms in the sky."

## Specific Techniques for Raising the Standards of Oral English in the Kindergarten

The teacher must always remember that her own use of English is one of the greatest factors in improving the language used by the children. Through her example she can do much to help the children appreciate and attempt to use quiet, well-modulated voices, speak clearly, speak to the point, speak with ease and fluency, project their voices, and use well-chosen words and acceptable grammar.

When a child talks before the group, he should learn to make sure that the group is ready to listen before he begins. He should learn, too, that, in order to hold the attention of the group, he needs to present his ideas directly, to look at the group rather than at the teacher, and to speak clearly and distinctly.

In the child's first attempts to express his ideas to the group, the teacher must keep in mind that the idea is much more important than the way it is expressed. Grammar is to language what technique is to art: it is essential for a perfect product, but it should not be stressed too much in the beginning. Whenever corrections of form or pronunciation will not disturb the flow of the child's thought, the teacher can help the child acquire correct grammatical usage, but such instruction should be given, not by citing rules or insisting on the child's repeating the preferred form, but by presenting the correct expression informally. For example, if the child says, "Yesterday I seen a robin," the teacher may come back immediately with,

"Yes, I *saw* a robin, too." If that child or the next child continues to use "I seen," the teacher may well ask if he doesn't mean he "saw" a robin. Or if a child says, "See, it's a pitcher of a flower-rose. I cutted it out of a mazagine," the teacher may say, "It's fun to *cut pic-tures* from *magazines,* isn't it? I suppose you *cut* this from a *magazine* your mother wasn't using, didn't you? Once a little boy came to my house and, without even asking, he *cut a pic-ture* out of a *magazine* I hadn't even read!" Children's coined words and amusing letter substitutions are sometimes so delightful that one is tempted, through imitation, to prolong their use; but as adults it is our responsibilty to set examples of good speech patterns at all times.

## SUMMARY

Throughout the day, with the exception of the rest period, the kindergarten affords opportunities for the child to practice and perfect his language. The child's vocabulary is enlarged and his meanings are clarified through both speaking and listening. He talks with the teachers and his friends, he presents ideas to the group, he listens to the ideas of others. He tells original stories, he makes up rhymes and jingles, he retells stories, he interprets pictures, and he sometimes creates new text material for books already written. He comes to appreciate the function of words both through the letters and reports dictated by the group and through the teacher's own thoughtful use of spoken words. The colorful and refreshing quality of the kindergarten child's vocabulary is something to be cherished. Good grammar is desirable, but it is cramping to both thought and expression to stress it too much. The kindergarten teacher will do well to remember that the most important factor in improving the English of the children is her own use of good English. Through example and substitution, much can be done to help the child use acceptable grammatical forms.

## QUESTIONS AND PROBLEMS

1. Visit a kindergarten and record any words, phrases, or sentences which seem particularly colorful and refreshing.
2. Try to make up a dream story of your own. Are you the practical, stolid type, or the imaginative type?
3. Listen carefully to the vocabulary used by a kindergarten teacher. Does she make any effort to help the children increase their vocabularies? How?
4. Does the teacher ever direct the attention of the group to the function of words? How?
5. Note any instances in which a child (a) attempts to incorporate new

words into his own vocabulary, (b) plays with rhyming words, (c) criticizes others for mispronunciations, (d) inserts or omits sounds in spoken words, (e) inquires about the meaning of words or ideas.

## SELECTED REFERENCES

Applegate, Mauree, *Easy in English*, New York, Harper Brothers, 1960.

Bailey, Matilda, Edna M. Horrocks, and Esther Torreson, *Language Learnings* (Kindergarten, Grade I, Grade II), New York, American Book Company, 1956.

California State Department of Education, Bureau of Elementary Education, *Teachers Guide to Education in Early Childhood*, Sacramento, State Department of Education, 1956 (see particularly Chapter XI).

Commission on English Curriculum of the National Council of Teachers of English, *Language Arts for Today's Children*, New York, Appleton-Century-Crofts, 1954.

Gans, Roma, Celia Stendler, and Millie Almy, *Teaching Young Children in Nursery School, Kindergarten and the Primary Grades*, Yonkers-on-Hudson, World Book Company, 1952.

Herrick, Virgil, and Leland Jacobs (eds.), *Children and the Language Arts*, Englewood Cliffs, N.J., Prentice-Hall, 1959.

Leonard, Edith, Dorothy Van Deman, and Lillian Miles, "Verbal Expression," *Foundations of Learning in Childhood Education*, 1963.

Rudolph, Marguerita, and Dorothy Cohen, "Scope and Variety of Language Expression," *Kindergarten: A Year of Learning*, New York, Appleton-Century-Crofts, 1964.

Shane, Harold, Mary E. Redden, and Margaret Gillespie, *Beginning Language Arts Instruction with Children*, Columbus, Ohio, Charles E. Merrill Books, Inc., 1961.

Strickland, Ruth S., *Language Arts in the Elementary School*, 2nd ed., Boston, D. C. Heath and Company, 1959.

# 19

# SCIENCE AND SOCIAL STUDIES[1]

The title of this chapter may seem amazingly broad. But when we remember that science rightly taught is always enriched with social meanings and when we consider the non-conpartmentalized nature of kindergarten education, it seems next to impossible to consider science and social studies as separate entities. There seems little if any reason to expect children to store up a great body of scientific facts unless those facts have some bearing or application to everyday living. If we think of science as dealing with the biological aspects, forces, and phenomena of the physical universe and social studies as dealing with (a) the impact of climate, geography, and the resources of the universe on man and (b) the interaction of man with man as he attempts to establish workable and satisfying relationships within the physical universe, then we find ample justification for the broad chapter heading.

## Facts Versus Understandings

Children, even young children, can learn an endless number of isolated science and social studies facts but the artist teacher designs and capitalizes on experiences in such a way that learnings evolve from honest and eager questing. Kindergarten children are keenly alert to their environment and are quick to absorb new ideas and new knowledge. It is the kindergarten teacher's responsibility to determine whether the information and understanding they gain under her guidance is worthwhile, inconsequential, incorrect, or actually harmful. Not that we want to suggest that children are like computers, but a popular though inelegant expression, used in connection with computers, makes us stop short to consider the

[1] See pp. 247–258 for books having social studies implications. See pp. 415–420 for children's science books.

kinds of experiences we are "feeding" our children. The expression is "Garbage in—Garbage out," but it can also read, "Gold in—Gold out." Let's make sure that our science and social studies programs can be better characterized by the second than the first expression.

In this chapter and the next we shall be dealing with some of the many worthwhile experiences which kindergartens can provide to encourage children to wonder and speculate. To wonder is to try to relate the known to the unknown and with this in mind we cannot possibly think of the teaching of science and social studies as merely the passing on of a body of facts.

## "Science Is All About Us" and "We Live Social Studies"

In order to alert a group of university students who were preparing to teach in the area of early childhood education to the fact that both science and social studies challenges are all about us, the group was asked to go to the windows. Outside, great white flakes of snow were feathering through the air and adding themselves to the eighteen to twenty-four inch drifts already covering the ground. As the students looked they were asked to think of some of the educational implications which the situation might offer. They immediately began to list poems, songs, stories, rhythms, and "art work" which might be tied in with the experience. Then some of the science implications became apparent. It was not until further questions were suggested, however, that they began to sense any social studies implications in the situation.

Their pattern of attack on the problem was quite typical. They thought immediately of the things they could "teach" the children. They did not think of the situation as one which could be used to foster intellectual questing.

As the students returned to their places they were asked to consider further the leads which a snowstorm might offer for (a) science and (b) social studies questings. The following questings though long are certainly not exhaustive. However, they do serve to alert us to the fact that science and social studies challenges *are all around us.*

## Leads to Science Questions Which Might Evolve from a Snow Experience

What is the difference between rain and snow?
Ice and snow? Frost and snow? Hail and snow?
How cold must it be before we can expect snow?

How do snowflakes form? What shape are they?

Are they identical? Is snow as clean as it looks?

Why do we speak of melted snow as soft water?

Can snow be used to freeze ice cream? How does it freeze the ice cream when it only turns to water itself?

Could one make a snowman and save it for summer? How? Is the snow good for the trees and bushes? When is it not good for them?

Is the snow good for the bulbs planted last fall? Why? Why would the farmer and rancher like snow? Why would he not like snow?

Why is some snow heavy and some snow light?

Why was Mr. Brown shoveling the snow from his porch roof? How many ways can snow be removed from sidewalks and driveways? How is snow going to be removed from the baseball park in time for the opening spring game?

Is there any bodily danger involved in shoveling snow?

How can the knee be used as a fulcrum point to relieve physical strain in shoveling snow?

How can skis and snowshoes keep people from sinking into the snow?

Why can't drivers stop their cars quickly on snow-covered streets?

Why is it difficult to steer a car when going slowly on snow-covered streets?

How can one steer a toboggan on a snow-covered hill?

What are some of the dangers in throwing snowballs? What rules could be established to make snowball fun reasonably safe?

Could the snow ever be used as a shelter from the cold? How?

Why do rivers sometimes overflow in the spring? How can floods be predicted? What provisions can be made to keep the rivers from overflowing? How can the weatherman predict that there will be snow? How can he predict it will stop?

What happens to winter birds when deep snow covers everything? How does the snow help us to know which birds and animals are around us? Which birds come to man-made feeders? What do different birds like to eat? Are squirrels and rabbits usually in evidence in heavy snowstorms? Where are they? How do they get food? What kinds of creatures need no food in winter? Why?

Why did Mr. Brown put burlap and wire around the trunk of his pear tree? Can an airplane fly above a snowstorm? Could you see a snowstorm if you were riding above it? Can an airplane land in a heavy snowstorm? How? What could the pilot do if he couldn't land his plane where he was supposed to land?

Why does the snow on the high south bank of the river stay there long after the snow on the north bank of the river has melted?

## Leads to Social Studies Questions Which Might Evolve from a Snow Experience

Who is responsible for keeping sidewalks cleared?

Who is responsible for keeping streets cleared?

What might happen if doctors, firemen, milkmen, postmen, and repairmen couldn't get about on the city streets?

Where does the money come from to pay the men who clear the streets? Where does the money come from to buy big snowplows? Why is sand put on the streets during or after a snowstorm? Does the city provide places for sand storages? Why couldn't anyone who needed sand on his own driveway help himself to the sand stored at intersections?

Why are automatic traffic signals sometimes operated by police officers during or after heavy snowfalls?

How do snow tires help in driving in snow? Where do we get snow tires? Why is our state legislature currently concerned with whether snow tires should have spikes or cleats like football shoes? Who should decide this?

What are the hazards involved in snow covering holes in streets left by frost bubbles? Who is responsible for marking and filling the holes?

If the snow were so deep that cattle couldn't be cared for, and food and medical supplies couldn't be brought into an area, on whom could the people call for help?

Does the United States government ever help in snow emergencies? How? Where does the money come from to pay for help supplied by the federal government?

Does the Red Cross ever help in snow and flood emergencies? Where does the Red Cross get its funds? Who contributes to the Red Cross?

How do helicopters serve in snowbound areas? How do radio and television stations help when storms are approaching or when ice and snow make travel hazardous?

Who decides when school will be closed because of a storm? How do they get word to the teachers and the children?

Does the mailman have a vacation when snow makes traveling difficult?

What might happen if the fire hydrants in the cities got snowed under? Who keeps them uncovered? Do the Boy Scouts in our community ever help? Why do city workmen have to keep the drains along the curbs open in winter? Where does all the melted snow go when it disappears down the drains? Why do city trucks carry great loads of snow to be dumped in open fields, rivers, or lakes?

How do snow fences help to keep the highway safe? Who puts up the snow fences? Why do highway snowplows always have a special colored flashing light?

Why do men working in the streets wear bright orange-red jackets or hats?

Since drivers cannot stop their cars quickly on the snow and ice what precautions must pedestrians—both children and adults—take?

In addition to the people who earn money removing the snow what other people would have opportunities to make money because of the presence of snow?

What kinds of clothes are designed, manufactured, and sold for snowy weather? What kinds of machinery are designed, manufactured, and sold for snow removal?

Could the people who operate ski resorts make money if they had to rely on artificial snow? Where, how, and by whom is the artificial snow made?

Would it be possible to find real snow near a community where the thermometer seldom if ever goes below thirty-two degrees above zero?

How can we have snow on mountaintops when we know that warm air rises and when we know that the mountaintops are nearer the sun than the lowlands?

Why would the people living in the arctic zone have little time for snow sports such as skiing and tobogganing?

In which countries might we expect to find many snow sports?

At the time of the Olympics in Japan many countries competed for skiing and tobogganing honors. Try to find these countries on a map or globe.

## Varied Opportunities for Science and Social Studies Challenges

Certainly the snowstorm experience would not be one common to children the world around; but as an experience it serves as an illustration of the fact that opportunities for science and social studies learnings can be found in the immediate environment. Science and social studies learnings can be based on a wide variety of experiences. The specific experiences and the kinds of observations children will be able to make will depend to a large extent upon the part of the world in which they live. Lines, real or imaginary, drawn between the geographic locales listed below and the words denoting experiences and concerns which might be thought of as common to the locales will indicate but a few of the vast variety of experiences which might be expected to afford science and social studies leads.

| | |
|---|---|
| Alaska | Fjords |
| Arizona | Islands |
| British Columbia | Monorail |

| | |
|---|---|
| California | Geysers |
| China | Cowboys |
| Georgia | Oil wells |
| Hawaii | Rice fields |
| Japan | Maple syrup |
| London | Salmon fishing |
| Montana | Subways |
| New York | Forests and Lumber |
| Norway | Cotton fields |
| Oklahoma | Fog |
| Oregon | Long nights |
| Pennsylvania | Desert |
| Texas | Mountains |
| Vermont | Orange groves |
| Wyoming | Coal Mines |

## How Much Science and Social Studies in the Kindergarten?

There can be no hard-and-fast rules as to how much should be offered in the way of science and social studies in the kindergarten. The amount and the kind of science and social studies experience and information must be adapted to the needs of the children. Recently rather extensive "units" on science and on social studies have been developed by specialists in the subject matter areas. In most instances they have been designed to convey information in a very logical fashion; but all too often their design is such that the timing factor, that factor so important to learning, is completely ignored. A contrived experience, for example, might give kindergarten children a great deal of information about fulcrums and levers but—so what? To know or discover that a nail which has been inadvertently pounded part way into the workbench can be removed by using a block of wood as the fulcrum and the hammer handle as a lever will make the principle much more meaningful. To make an extensive study of the effect of temperature changes on liquids would certainly be untimely. Yet if the kindergarten is near a waterfront where the water freezes in the late fall, it will be both appropriate and desirable to set up an experiment to show that at thirty degrees, and slightly lower, water will freeze over but will not support anything comparable to the weight of a child. And to point out because of this, "No Skating" signs are posted by the park board for the safety of individuals rather than to deprive individuals of pleasure will help children appreciate that rules and laws are designed for the good of individuals.

From the point of timely learning the teacher who helps thirty-pound

Alice and forty-five pound Bill figure out a way they can teeter-totter; the teacher who helps Jeff see that he can sit or lie on a cot, but that the same cot may not support his standing weight; the teacher who helps Susan and others to see that climatic conditions and not the demands of the teacher call for snow boots; and the teacher who initiates map reading by designing with the children or posting a floor plan of the kindergarten room—this teacher is providing opportunities for children to build science and social studies understandings.

## Where Does the Young Child Get Science and Social Studies Information?

There are four main sources of science and social studies information: (1) the spoken words of others, (2) the written words of others (interpreted, of course, through the reading done by adults), (3) pictures—posted pictures, periodical and book illustrations, filmstrips, films, and television, and (4) actual experience and observation. The adult is frequently amazed to find some of the things that children have learned through listening to radio and television and just overhearing the conversations of grown-ups. Sometimes the information is somewhat distorted, but frequently it is approximately correct even down to the interpretation of adult attitudes. Unfortunately, in talking with children and answering their quesions, we often overlook the opportunities to foster science and social studies learnings.

We now have many science pictures and picture storybooks directed to the interest of young children.[2] There was a time when it was almost impossible to find such books and most of the science information had to be digested by adults and then passed on. We are now living in a day when young children are often getting information from their books which they are actually passing on to adults. In the past fifteen years we have had a deluge of picture books designed specifically to convey science ideas. Probably the best social studies books for young children are to be found in the picture storybooks classified under the heading of children's literature. Virginia Burton's, *The Little House* and *Katy and the Big Snow;* Ezra Keats' *The Snowy Day;* Elsa Beskow's *Pelle's New Suit;* Golden MacDonald's (Margaret Wise Brown), *Little Island;* and Norman Bate's *Who Built the Bridge* are examples of such books.[3]

[2] See pp. 415–420, "Science Books for Children (and Teachers!)."
[3] See "Story and Picture Story Books" pp. 247–258. Titles having social studies significance are specially marked.

*"When I Grow up . . ."*

St. Paul Public Schools, St. Paul, Minnesota

Filmstrip and films,[4] including television presentations, are another source of science and social studies information available to today's children. Here especially it is important that the kindergarten teacher be selective and educationally alert. It is all too easy for her to feel that having provided science and social studies films she has fulfilled her science and social studies responsibilities. To be educationally significant, such visual experiences must be integrated with other phases of the learning program.

The most effective way for children to gain information relating to science and social studies is, of course, through firsthand experimentation accompanied by problem-solving challenges. Spoken words, written words, pictorial presentations, no matter how well presented, cannot possibly stand as satisfactory substitutes for firsthand learning experience. Words and pictures can direct interest to or summarize and supplement firsthand science and social studies experiences, but they ought never to be thought of as sufficient in themselves.

## Know Your Community

No kindergarten teacher can make a wise plan for profitable learning experiences for her group without knowing the resources of the neighbor-

[4] See "Filmstrips and Films" pp. 432–443.

hood or the community. It is time well spent for any teacher new to a community to spend a day or more making some sort of survey of its available science and social studies resources.

Almost every kindergarten is within reach of some or many of the following resources for science and social studies:

Airport
Aviary
Bakery
Bank
Barber Shop
Barges
Birdhouses
Bird Nests
Boats
Book Store
Bookbinding Shop
Bottling Company
Bridges
Churches
City Dump
Clay Pit
Community Center
Construction Work
- Bridges
- Buildings
- Heating Tunnels
- Highways
- Parking Areas
- Power Lines
- Sewers
- Shelters
- Streets

Creamery
Dam
Docks
Drug Store
Elevators
Escalators
Factories
Farms
Filling Station
Fire Alarm Box
Fire Station
Florist Shop
Flour Mill
Fountain
Fruit Depot
Garage (public with ramps)
Garden Store
Grain Elevator
Greenhouse
Grocery
Hardware Store
Hatchery
High Buildings (view)
Hills
Homes of Children
Hospital
Hydrant (street)
Island
Lake
Laundry
Library
Locks
Lumber Yard
Machines in Operation
- Cement Mixer
- Crane
- Dredge
- Electric Repair Truck
- Hoist
- Pile Driver
- Road Grader
- Snowplow
- Steam Shovel
- Street Sweeper
- Street Sprinkler
- Telephone Repair Truck
- Tractor
  - Combine
  - Corn Picker
  - Cultivator
  - Harrow
  - Plow
  - Seeder
- Tree Trimming Equipment

Mailbox

Market
Milk and other delivery trucks
Mountains
Museum (art, science, history)
Oil Storage Tanks
Orchard
Park
Pet Shop
Playgrounds
Private Gardens
Police (Security and Traffic)
Ponds
Postal Station
Power Station
Print Shop
Public Gardens
Public Library
Public Waterworks
Quarry
Radio and TV Station
Railroad Station and Yards
Ranch
Restaurant
River
Roadside Market
Sandpit
Sawmill
School
Shoe Repair Shop
Snack Vendor
Steamship Line
Stream
Supermarket
Swimming Pool
Taxi Garage and Stands
Telephone Booths
Telephone Exchange
Tile Factory
Toy Shop
Tree Nursery
Trees
Truck Farm
Trucks
Tunnel
Vacant Lot
Vegetable and Fruit Shop
Waterfalls
Weather Indicators
  Instruments for measuring rainfall
  Large Thermometers
  Weather Balls
  Weather Vanes
Wildflower Gardens
Woods
Yards
Zoological Gardens

## Excursions and Excursion Technicalities

The teacher who knows her community will be aware of some of the many opportunities for learning outside the classroom and beyond the school premises, and she will want to make some of these opportunities available to her group of children. It is to be hoped that parents will have already made or can be encouraged to make some of the many opportunities available to children. Because the teacher will want to make some of the opportunities available to her entire group she will plan group excursions. If wisely planned and conducted an excursion can greatly enrich kindergarten living. If not wisely planned and conducted, it can be just another "get up and go" experience—and of these, many of today's children already seem to have far too many! It is to be hoped that kindergarten teachers will choose wisely and plan well the excursions to be made during any one year.

Before considering excursion procedures, it might be wise to examine some of the technicalities involved. First of all the teacher should acquaint herself with school policies concerning excursions and with the state law regarding personal liability in case of accident.[5] In some states the teacher herself is liable in case of an accident which might befall a child if the child has been taken by the teacher from the school premises. In certain instances there is an insurance arrangement whereby the school, not the teacher, will be responsible in case of accidents. When the transportation is provided by the school, school vehicular insurance provides coverage for accidents. These are facts of which the teacher should be aware.

Whenever the excursion is to be made beyond walking distance, the teacher should have for her own security the parent's signed permission to take each child. In many school systems, a blanket yearly coverage is made on excursions by securing a parent's signature permitting the child to participate in any and all excursions to be made by the group during the school year. Even though the signature for blanket yearly coverage is on file it is well for the teacher to advise the parents of particular excursions. The children can cooperate in this by dictating to the teacher a statement of the plans. The letter, when duplicated, can then be taken home by the children to their parents. One such letter follows below:[6]

> Dear Mother:
> We are planning to go to see the animals at Como Park. We expect to be going on Monday, May 6, at two o'clock. Miss ____________________, Mr. ____________________ and Mrs. ____________________ are planning to take us in their cars. If you want me to go, will you please put your name on this paper under my name? I will take the paper back to school. I hope I may go.*
>
> ____________________
>
> ____________________
>
> *Teacher's P.S.
> If you do not want your child to go on this particular trip please indicate what provision you are making for his care during the time we are on the trip.
>
> Parent's Signature ____________________

## Planning the Excursion

Before any excursion is undertaken, both the teacher and the children

[5] Gauerke, Warren E., *Legal and Ethical Responsibilities of School Personnel*, Englewood Cliffs, New Jersey, Prentice-Hall, 1959.

[6] See also p. 177.

must be prepared. The teacher must have the goals of the excursion clearly in mind, and she must be familiar with the place where the group plans to go. The children, through previous experience, conversation, discussion, and information supplied by the teacher and facts gleaned from stories, science and picture storybooks and films, must have an attitude that will make them both eager to verify their present information and alert to make new observations and findings.

If the group is to visit either a private or publicly operated establishment, such as a fire station, a chicken hatchery, a bakery, or a farm, permission must be obtained from the proper authorities and arrangements made in advance. Trips to the woods, to a sandpit, to a construction site and business trips to the florist, grocery, hardware store, and the like can usually be made without special appointments. However, in making any group excursions to such places as stores and markets, the teacher should plan the trip so that the group will not be underfoot during rush hours.

## Some Excursion Techniques

Most excursions within the neighborhood can be made on foot. Taking large groups of kindergarten children out into the traffic and confusion of the city places a tremendous responsibility on the teacher. There are, therefore, certain rules which must be outlined before the excursion is undertaken. First of all, it must be understood that the group will always stay together. This does not mean that the children have to walk hand in hand in military rows, but it does mean there will be no dashing ahead and no straggling behind. It is well, before starting out on an excursion, to choose one or two leaders and back captains. No one is to go ahead of the leaders or drop behind the back captains. Wisely chosen leaders and captains will share the teacher's responsibility. It is understood that groups going on an excursion will always stop at the street corners so that the group can cross the street together. This is, of course, a safety measure, but when put to the children not only as a safety measure but also as a matter of helping car and bus drivers, greater respect is shown the rule. If the group has both leaders and back captains, the teacher can move up and down in the group, discussing matters of interest with various small groups.

Sometimes the group may be kept as a unit by dramatizing the experience, pretending, for example, they are all riding on a large bus. In this case, no child gets off the bus before the destination is reached—that is, no one gets separated from the group; no child changes seats while the bus is in transit—that is, the children remain in their same positions in the line; and, since the space between the bus seats is always the same, the spaces between the children must be kept reasonably constant.

If a guide or conductor for the party is furnished by the establishment visited, the children must understand his function. They must feel free to ask questions, but they must also be ready to listen to his directions and to the information he may have for them. It is to be hoped that out of real appreciation, the children will feel moved to thank the individual who has extended the hospitality of the establishment to the group. Often the teacher's own sincere words of thanks will inspire the children to express their gratitude. For example, if the teacher says, "Mr. Jones, I—for one—certainly want to thank you," then it is quite probable that others will add, "And I want to thank you, too.". . ."And me, too.". . ."Thank you, Mr. Jones.". . ."Thank you ever so much.". . ."Thanks for showing us everything." Notes of thanks will be appreciated as well.

## Excursions to Points Too Distant for Walking

Probably not more than one or two excursions during the kindergarten year will necessitate the use of cars or buses. If the school has a bus, it is a reasonably simple matter to load a whole kindergarten group into the one vehicle and set forth.

Public buses are a possible, but not very practical, means of transportation for kindergarten excursions. In the first place, there is the matter of transportation fare, though it is sometimes possible to obtain passes; in the second place, there is the concern for safety; and in the third, there is the problem of interfering with and being interfered with by other passengers. If public conveyances are to be used, trips should certainly be planned in relation to the heavy flow of traffic.

One of the most satisfactory ways of making trips to points at any distance, though still a questionable one from the point of view of liability, is to solicit the aid and cooperation of parents who are known to be expert and cautious drivers. It is well to have two adults in each car, in case of a flat tire or engine trouble. Car trouble and a half a dozen five-year-olds do not make a good combination!

Sometimes, if the distance is not great and a sufficient number of cars are not available, the excursion can be made by having one or two cars make the trip twice. A group of fifteen children once made a very satisfactory excursion to a point some two miles away by using only one car for transportation. The driver, with a second adult and a group of eight children, started out, leaving a third adult and the remaining seven children to start walking in the direction of the destination. The driver unloaded her group three blocks from the destination and returned to pick up the other group, which had progressed about two blocks on its way. They all arrived at their destination at the same time, and no group had to walk more than five blocks on the whole trip. This particular excursion gave the children the opportunity to see and ride on an old-fashioned paddle wheel riverboat.

### The Kindergarten Science and Social Studies Program Is a Challenge to the Teacher.

Most teachers, somewhere along the way, have had courses in biology, botany, astronomy, meteorology, chemistry, and physics, and most teachers have had courses in physical and human geography and courses in the humanities, psychology and sociology—or at least they have had some general science and general social studies courses. From their courses they have gleaned a tremendous number of facts; but all too often these facts have seemed unrelated to either the business of everyday living or teaching young children. The test of good science and good social studies teaching lies, not in the learner's ability to recite principles glibly but in his being able to use his acquired information and knowledge in related situations.

The kindergarten science and social studies program challenges the teacher to use already acquired knowledge in situations which may seem to bear little similarity to orthodox classroom procedures. The kindergarten teacher never knows from hour to hour or, for that matter, from minute to minute, when some bit of information or understanding that she has picked up along the way may be the exact clue to aid in the solution of the problem at hand. Many times the teacher finds it profitable to break down the problem so that the child can use his already acquired information to arrive at new understandings. So far as we know, no one person has ever had on hand enough information to meet the challenge of kindergarten children's questings satisfactorily. The teacher should always feel free to acknowledge frankly her ignorance or uncertainty about facts but, if the information is of such a nature that it will be useful to the child, she should be willing and eager to seek it either in books or from other sources. Those teachers who simply "feed" science and social studies facts to kindergarten children will probably feel that a handbook of facts or a detailed outline of a "unit" is all that they need for teaching science and social studies. But those who accept the responsibility of helping kindergarten children develop science and social studies understandings will find the science and social studies program a *most* stimulating challenge.

## SUMMARY

There are many elements in every environment which afford rich opportunities for science and social studies learnings. It is the teacher's responsibility to direct children's attention to those that will be rewarding learning experiences. The number and kind of science and social studies experiences that will be offered will be determined by the general geographic locale, the offerings of the immediate neighborhood, the maturity of the children and the educational background and alertness of the teacher. It is most important for the teacher to know the resources within the community, to have accurate science information, and to perceive that there are science and social studies implications in a wide variety of experiences. The ill-prepared teacher is inclined to pass on science and social studies facts and then post signs which say "science is all around us" and "we live social studies." The alert and adequately prepared teacher does not need to post such signs because in her teaching she demonstrates the truth of such statements.

## QUESTIONS AND PROBLEMS

1. In the seventeenth century, Comenius presented the following beliefs.

   > A boy, during the first six years, can be brought to know what are water, earth, air, fire, rain . . . iron, trees, birds, fish . . . and pave the way for natural science. A boy learns the elements of optics when he distinguishes and calls by their names, light, darkness . . . white, black, red, etc. The rudiments of astronomy consist in knowing what is meant by . . . the sun, the moon and the stars . . . the elements of geography when he learns the nature of mountains, valleys, rivers, villages, citadels or states. The basis of chronology . . . what is meant by an hour, a day, a week . . . etc. The seeds of arithmetic will be planted if the child understands what is meant by "much" and "little," can count to ten, can see that three are more than two, and that one added to three makes four. The elements of static will have been learned if they see objects weighed in scales . . . The elements of the process of reasoning . . . are learned when the child observes that conversations are carried on by means of questions and answers and he himself acquires the habit of asking and answering questions . . . A handbook should contain a brief description of the various subjects in which children should be educated, and should state the occasions that are most suitable for each . . . Some children of two years old can speak with ease and display great intelligence while others are scarcely equal to them when five years old.[7]

   Find in a modern kindergarten or in the experiences and experiments cited in this and other chapters in this book illustrations of the learnings and principles referred to in the above beliefs of Comenius.

[7] M. W. Keatinge, *The Great Didatic of Comenius*, London, Adam and Charles Black, 1896, pp. 410–417.

2. For each of the following experiences which might be had or reported by kindergarten children, list possible science and/or social studies implications:
   a. As Susan struggles to pull on her snow boots she says, "I wish I lived where my mother lived when she was a little girl. She didn't even have to wear snow boots."
   b. George has spilled a whole box of metal paper clips down a register. They can be seen but they are too far down to be reached. How can they be retrieved?
   c. The teacher, without comment, has posted a detailed floor plan of the kindergarten room on the easel. Jim and Jean study the "picture." Jim says, "What is it?" Jean studies it more carefully; then placing her finger on the figure that represents the easel she calls out excitedly, "Hey, look! We're standing right here!"
   d. The electric company is taking down a light pole in the street in front of the school building.
   e. Alice is up in the air on the teeter-totter. Bill on the other end sits quietly gloating over the fact that she can't get down. Alice is leaning forward and clinging to the handle in front of her. The teacher, noting the situation, says, "Alice, try sitting up straight and sliding way back to the end of your board."
   f. A guest from India dressed in a beautiful sari appears to have the undivided attention of the kindergarten group as she tells about a monkey that came down from a tree and stole a pie which she had placed in the window to cool. As she finishes, Ann says, "What is that red spot on your forehead?"
   g. A sunflower plant appears in the children's garden but they had not planted any sunflower seeds.
   h. Judd is showing the children a coconut which his grandfather has sent him from Florida.
   i. Douglas and Jim are struggling to get the heavy wagon up the steps. The teacher suggests they use a couple of planks.
   j. Jeff reports that he is going to spend his vacation on Star Island.
   k. Todd is showing the group a picture of a man placing a flag on the summit of a snowclad mountain in Alaska.
   l. James reports that his big brother didn't go to school and Lisa adds, "I know, neither did my brother go to school. All the big boys are helping to put sandbags by the river so we won't have a flood."
   m. Teresa observes a policeman putting a tag on a car parked by the play yard fence. She races over, kicks at the fence and says, "You shouldn't do that! That's not nice! You're mean!"
   n. Chris is trying to remove a nail from the workbench. The head of

the nail is about an inch above the bench and he is pulling at it with the pliers. The teacher places a small block of wood near the nail and hands him a claw hammer.

## SELECTED REFERENCES

Association for Childhood Education International, Washington, D.C.:
*Science for Teachers and Children,* Bulletin No. 91, 1953.
*Social Studies for Children,* Bulletin No. 97, 1956.
*Young Children and Science,* Bulletin No. 12-A, 1964

Blough, Glenn O., *You and Your Child and Science,* Bulletin, Washington, D.C., National Education Association, Department of Elementary School Principals and National Science Teachers Association, 1963.

Greenlee, Julius, *Teaching Science to Children,* Dubuque, Iowa, William G. Brown Company, 1958.

Hochman, Vivienne, and Mildred Greenwald, *Science Experience in Early Childhood Education,* Bulletin No. 54, New York, Bank Street Bureau of Publications, no date given.

Hubler, Clark, *Working with Children in Science,* Boston, Houghton Mifflin Company, 1956.

Merritt, Edith, *Working with Children in Social Studies,* San Francisco, Wadsworth Publishing Company, 1961.

Navarra, J. C., *Development of Scientific Concepts in Young Children,* New York, Bureau of Publications, Teachers College, Columbia University, 1955.

Rudolph, Marguerita, and Dorothy H. Cohen, "Science Experiences for Children and Teachers," *Kindergarten: A Year of Learning,* New York, Appleton-Century-Crofts, 1964.

Wann, Kenneth D., Miriam S. Dorn, and Elizabeth Ann Liddle, "Children Want to Understand the World Beyond the Here and Now," and "Children Want to Know about the Phenomena that Surround Them," *Fostering Intellectual Development in Young Children,* New York, Bureau of Publications, Teachers College, Columbia University, 1962.

# 20

# THE HERE AND NOW OF THE KINDERGARTEN SCIENCE PROGRAM

This chapter is devoted to the presentation of a wide variety of here-and-now experiences from which children can gain science information and understanding. The letter "A" in each case stands for the activity or experience and the letter "O" stands for some of the observations which might be made by the children and the teacher. Obviously there should be no attempt to offer in the kindergarten such courses as astronomy, biology, entomology, meteorology, physiology, or ornithology; yet all these and other areas of science as well will be featured in one way or another in the good kindergarten science program.

The suggested activities are not to be thought of as experiments and demonstrations to be made by the teacher *to teach* science. Instead they are to be thought of as some of the many experiences which the teacher can capitalize on in extending children's understanding in the field of science. In some instances the experiences are followed by possible discussion paragraphs. This has been done to remind the reader that both the science and social studies implications of an experience, like eddies produced by an oar dipping in otherwise unperturbed waters, can extend far beyond the immediate experience. Do not neglect to give thought to some of the many leads for discussion which may not have been suggested.

It is assumed, of course, that no kindergarten teacher will have occasion to deal with all or even half of the listed experiences in any one school year. It is also obvious that many experiences not mentioned in this chapter will arise and can be used to extend children's science understanding. If the list does no more than alert the reader to the fact that opportunities for extending children science understanding are all about us it will have served a purpose.

## Elements and Forces of Nature

### AIR

**A.** Take a deep breath of air into your lungs.

**O.** You can feel the air pushing out and expanding your lungs. Air can fill space. Air can push.

**A.** Blow up a balloon.

**O.** Air fills the balloon just the way it fills your lungs.

**A.** Watch the man at the filling station putting air into tires.

**O.** Air fills the tires. It makes them stretch. Air can hold up great loads. It can even lift the car up from the ground.

**A.** Weigh an inner tube before it has been inflated; then weigh it after the air has been put into it.

**O.** Air seems light, but quantities of air have weight.

**A.** Breathe on the bulb of a thermometer that has recently been removed from a refrigerator.

**O.** As the mercury in the thermometer becomes warmer, it expands and rises, thus indicating a warmer temperature.

**A.** Put a cork stopper in an empty bottle. Try to float the bottle in a pan of water. Put a cork stopper in a bottle filled with water. Try to float this bottle.

**O.** The bottle filled with air will float. The one filled with water will not. Why?

**A.** Blow into a small bottle.

**O.** A whistling sound comes from the bottle. People make music by blowing through such instruments as the tuba, piccolo, flute, saxophone, and oboe.

**A.** Watch or help the teacher siphon the water from the fishbowl. Submerge a piece of rubber hose in water. Pinch the hose while both ends are under water. Observe the air bubbles in the water. When there are no more air bubbles, that means that all of the air is out of the hose. Only water remains in the hose. The teacher places her two thumbs over the ends of the hose so that no water can get out and no air can get in. Now she puts one end into the water in the fishbowl and the other into a container which is on a lower level than the fishbowl.

**O.** As she removes her thumbs from the ends of the hose,.the water rushes through the hose. Since no air can get in, the water from the fishbowl continues to run out into the container. It keeps rushing until all the water is out. Now the hose fills with air. Put it back into the water and pinch it again. What happens?

**A.** Make your own siphon. Bend a straw so that it looks like a "U."

Put one end into a glass. Put the other into your mouth and draw all the air out of the straw.

**O.** The water will rush into the straw, and it will continue to rush out until the glass is empty or until the straw is removed.

**A.** At a time when it seems rather cold in your kindergarten room, climb up to the top of the jungle gym or, if you have a balcony in the room, go up into it.

**O.** It will feel much warmer up there because the warm air rises.

*Possible discussion:* Air is all about us. All space not filled with something else is filled with air. An exception to this is a vacuum, a space from which all air has been exhausted. Could you live in a vacuum? Do plants need air? Do animals? Do fish? What is the difference between dead air and fresh air?

## WIND

**A.** Fan yourself with a piece of paper.

**O.** The air moves back and forth before your face. It makes a breeze, a small wind. Wind is simply air in motion.

**A.** Watch the wind blowing leaves, bits of paper, or snowflakes.

**O.** It lifts them up, whirls them about, carries them a little way, and then drops them. Often it blows them in circles. Air often moves in upward currents.

**A.** Open a milkweed case and toss it into the wind.

**O.** The seeds open like little parachutes, and the wind carries them up and off. Some drop near and some are carried great distances.

**A.** Toss soap bubbles into the air.

**O.** If the wind is gentle it will lift them and carry them high into the air. If the wind is too strong it may break the bubble.

**A.** Watch to see what the wind does with the smoke as it comes from the chimney.

**O.** Sometimes the smoke will be lifted up and up. Sometimes it is blown far away, and sometimes there is so little motion in the air that the heavy smoke just settles all around.

**A.** Make a paper windmill and hold it in the wind. Blow on it.

**O.** The speed of the windmill will change as the force of the wind changes.

**A.** Run with a paper windmill.

**O.** When you run, you push the air aside, and the motion of the moving air turns the windmill very fast.

**A.** Make a small sailboat of wood, paper, cork, or a walnut shell. Put it outside in a pan of water.

**O.** If there is a wind, it will push the boat. If the wind is not moving, you can make a breeze either by fanning or by blowing the air.

**A.** Make a kite, or perhaps watch some older child with his kite.

**O.** As the child runs into the wind with the kite, the wind carries the kite high into the air. Pulling on the string makes the kite stay up because then the wind has something to push against. If you did not have the string attached, the wind might blow the kite for a bit; but then in some spot where the air was still, the kite would simply drop to the ground.

**A.** Recall your experience in an airplane.

**O.** Occasionally the airplane made a sudden dip or drop. This was when the plane went through a bit of air that was not very active.

**A.** Wet two sponges. Hang one in the wind and the other in a sheltered corner.

**O.** The sponge in the wind will dry more quickly than the other. The bits of water vapor are carried away more quickly by the wind than by the comparatively still air.

### CLOUDS

**A.** Watch the clouds, either from your window or by lying on resting rugs on the grass.

**O.** Some clouds are dark and heavy looking. Some are light and fluffy. When the dark clouds pass over the sun, they make shadows on the earth and hide the sun. The clouds move sometimes fast and sometimes slowly, depending on air currents. Clouds are made up of tiny drops of moisture.

**A.** Imagine various forms in the clouds—ships, trees, or animals, for example.

**O.** Clouds are ever-changing in shape, because of the movement of air.

### FOG

**A.** On a foggy day, try to see the shape of certain familiar buildings or nearby trees.

**O.** It is difficult to see through the fog. A cloud near the earth is called fog.

**A.** With the teacher's help, make some fog. Fill a milk bottle with hot, but not boiling, water. Over this hold a pan filled with ice or ice water.

**O.** The warm air rises from the bottle; as it strikes the bottom of the cold pan, the tiny drops of water in the air suddenly cool, and you are looking at fog.

### DEW

**A.** Feel the grass very early on a still, warm summer morning. Feel it again after the sun has been shining for some time.

**O.** At first the grass is wet, as if it had been rained on. The cooler air, touching the warm earth, has caused dew to form. Later the sun causes the dew to evaporate.

## EVAPORATION

**A.** Set a saucer of water in the sun, or note the puddles of water left on the sidewalk after a rain.

**O.** The sun and the wind will help take the water away. The air, warmed by the sun, will change the water into tiny vapor drops. The warm vapor will rise, and the wind will blow it away.

## RAIN

**A.** Watch the rain from the window.

**O.** Sometimes it rains hard, sometimes gently. The rain may sink into the ground, it may evaporate, or it may run off into the gutters. Rain is moisture falling from the clouds. When the clouds can hold the moisture no longer, it falls to earth.

**A.** Wash a fishbowl inside and out and polish it until it is absolutely free from moisture. Place a shallow dish of water in the bowl, and then put a piece of glass over the top of the bowl. Let it stand overnight.

**O.** As the water evaporates, the drops of vapor will condense on the inside of the glass which covers the bowl. Tap the glass gently and you will find you are making it "rain" in the bowl. The moisture collected on the glass is like the moisture in the clouds. When the clouds are disturbed, when they move through cold air, and when they can hold the moisture no longer, then we have rain.

**A.** On a rainy day, put a broad, shallow pan outside, away from the trees and buildings.

**O.** Note or actually measure the amount of water that falls into the pan in an hour or during the school session.

**A.** Try to hold an umbrella on a rainy, windy day.

**O.** The umbrella must be moved from side to side because sometimes the wind blows the rain this way and sometimes that.

**A.** Watch the storm clouds that are heavy with moisture.

**O.** Sometimes they drop their moisture over us, and sometimes the wind blows them to another part of the town or city. Have you ever observed that it has rained in your block and not in the block where your friend lives?

**A.** After a rain, watch for a rainbow.

**O.** The rainbow appears only when the sun shines while there is much moisture in the air. The rainbow is made by the light shining on millions and millions of separate drops of moisture. Watch for a rainbow when the sun is shining on a spray, watering your lawn.

**A.** Hang a prism in the window on a sunny day.

**O.** As the sun shines on the many surfaces of the glass, rainbow colors appear.

*Possible discussion:* Why do we need rain, or what does the rain do for us? It waters the earth's vegetation, washes plants, pavings, and buildings free of dust, makes puddles in which to sail boats, provides water for drinking, washing, and bathing. We can be thankful for rain because it returns to the earth the moisture which has been taken away by evaporation. What happens in countries where there is very little rain? where there is a great deal?

## THUNDER AND LIGHTNING

**A.** Watch the patterns made in the sky by the lightning.

**O.** Sometimes there is just a glow in the sky. Sometimes lightning makes clear-cut veins of light, and sometimes zigzag patterns. The lightning is really great electric sparks in the air. Thunder is the noise that goes with the giant electric spark of lightning.

**A.** Listen to the thunder in a rainstorm.

**O.** Sometimes it sounds like rolling and rumbling, and sometimes like crackling and banging. Thunder is the noise caused by the expansion of air when it is disturbed by lightning.

**A.** Try to decide which you notice first, thunder or lightning. Actually, they occur at almost the same moment.

**O.** Sometimes the thunder seems to follow many seconds after the lightning. That is because light travels much faster than sound. When the storm is very near, the sound of the thunder comes to us very shortly after the lightning. When the storm is very far away, it takes the sound longer to come to us. We can tell roughly by measuring the time between the lightning flash and the thunder how far the storm is from us.

**A.** Blow into a paper bag. Twist the top so that the air is held in the bag. Hold the bag in one hand and strike it with the palm of the other hand.

**O.** A loud crash results. Thunder is something like this; it, too, results from the sudden pushings of air.

## HAIL

**A.** During a summer rain when the air seems suddenly to turn cool, look for hail.

**O.** The hail "stones" will vary from the size of tiny peas to those as large as great cherries. A hailstone *can* weigh more than a half pound, but most of those we see are no larger than cherries or marbles. Hail is formed as the raindrops pass through cold air. These frozen drops get tossed again and again into the air, and get coating after coating of ice and snow. A hailstone may have as many as twenty-five coatings of ice and snow before it drops to the earth.

*Possible discussion:* What is the difference between hail and rain? Can hail do any damage to gardens? to windows? Could you use hail to freeze ice cream? Does hail stay on the ground for a long time? Why or why not?

## FROST

**A.** Note the sparkling white crystals on the grass on the first fall morning when the thermometer registers about thirty-two degrees above zero.

**O.** The frost melts very quickly in the sun. Frost forms on the grass and other surfaces when the temperature is low enough to change the vapor of the fog into tiny ice particles.

**A.** Breathe on the windowpane on a very, very cold day.

**O.** If the day is not cold enough, steam will form on the pane. If the day is one on which the temperature is around zero, the droplets of moisture from your breath will freeze, and the frost will be left on the window.

**A.** Watch the steam from the teakettle rise and settle on a very cold windowpane. Do not have the teakettle too near the glass.

**O.** Heavy frost may form on the window. Frost patterns can be very beautiful. Sometimes when the frost forms a thick, white coating on the window, you can etch designs with your fingernail.

## ICE

**A.** On a day in late fall or early winter when the temperature is somewhat below thirty-two degrees, observe a small pond, a lake, and a river.

**O.** Ice forms in quiet water more quickly than where there is current. Ice forms on shallow water more quickly than on deep water.

**A.** On a spring day when the temperature is somewhat above thirty-two degrees, observe a pond, a lake, and a river.

**O.** The ice melts first where the water is shallow. The ice breaks up more quickly where there is a current.

**A.** On a day when the temperature is around zero, put out a pan of water and watch the water turn to ice. Or watch the water as it turns to ice in a refrigerator.

**O.** At first, needle-like crystals of ice will appear. Later the water will freeze into a solid block of ice.

**A.** On a very cold day (preferably a sub-zero day), place outdoors two bottles filled with water. Seal one tightly and leave the other unsealed. After the water has had time to freeze, look at the bottles. The same experience may be had by placing the bottles in the freezing compartment of the refrigerator.

**O.** The bottle that was sealed, if it was *completely filled* with water, has broken. The bottle which was not sealed is whole, but it has a cap of ice which has been pushed up from the bottle. Water expands when it freezes into ice.

**A.** Bring the unsealed bottle into the room and let the ice melt.

**O.** When it melts, there is only enough water to fill the bottle again.

**A.** Melt in separate glasses a piece of ice which you may find somewhere outside and melt a piece of ice which has been frozen in the refrigerator.

**O.** The water from the artificially made ice is clean and clear. In all probability the piece of ice which you picked up outside has left a residue of dirt.

**A.** Observe icicles hanging from the roof or bushes. Bring one inside. Watch it drip.

**O.** The icicle drips from the point. Icicles are formed by one drop running down over the other drops and freezing there.

**A.** Bring in a clod of frozen earth and let it thaw in a pan.

**O.** The frozen earth is very hard. When it melts it becomes soft and can easily be broken apart. Sometimes there are tiny seeds and roots in the clod. These will grow again if given a chance.

*Possible discussion:* What are some of the values of ice? Ice keeps food cold and fresh, can be used to freeze ice cream, is good for skating, and is beautiful to look at. What are some of the dangers? Ice makes the streets slippery, makes both walking and driving difficult. Ice which is not frozen hard enough does not support much weight and is therefore a safety risk. Heavy ice on wires and branches sometimes breaks them. Water freezing in car radiators and other nonexpandable containers may cause great damage.

## SNOW

**A.** Watch a snowstorm.

**O.** The snow seems to be pure white. The little flakes pile up and cover the ground with whiteness. When the wind blows the snow on the ground, the snow forms drifts. The snow is moisture dropping from the clouds. The flakes are formed high in the cold air.

**A.** Catch snowflakes on a dark surface, on your snowsuit, or on a dark sheet of paper.

**O.** Each snowflake is beautifully patterned; each has three or six points.

Snowflakes formed at different distances above the earth are of varying shapes.

**A.** Fill a glass bowl with fresh white snow. Bring it indoors.

**O.** The snow turns to water. The snow filled the bowl, but the water does not. Probably you will find particles of soot and dirt in the water. Let the water evaporate and you will be almost sure to find a residue of soot and dirt in the bowl. The snow which has come through the air over a city will be dirtier than the snow which has come through the country air.

**A.** Play in the snow.

**O.** Sleds and skis slide over the snow. Snowshoes hold weights on top of the snow. When the snow is moist—that is, when the temperature is slightly above or around the melting point—the snow can be made into balls, snowmen, and snowhouses. Artists can model in snow.

*Possible discussion:* What does the snow do for us? It gives us a chance to have lots of fun. It covers the ground, protecting the roots and seeds from hard freezes. It provides moisture for the land in the spring. Why do some parts of the world have snow and others not? How can there be snow on mountaintops in the summer? How does life in those parts of the world with a great deal of snow differ from life in those parts of the world with no snow?

## SLEET

**A.** Notice how the sleet beats on the windows and how it stings your face or freezes on the windshield.

**O.** Sleet sometimes gives trees and bushes sparkling coverings. It melts into water or freezes into sheets of ice. It is made up of droplets of ice that have been formed from partially melted snowflakes.

## FIRE

**A.** Rub your hands together very fast.

**O.** They get very warm. They feel almost burning hot. Rubbing two sticks together will make them so hot they will catch fire, but it takes much rubbing time to produce fire in this manner.

**A.** Watch someone striking a match.

**O.** The flame bursts forth immediately. Certain chemicals combined with friction (rubbing things together) will produce fire instantly.

**A.** Watch some adult as he lets the sun shine through a magnifying glass onto small bits of paper.

**O.** The paper will begin to smoke, and then it will burst into flames. Fire can be made in this way by concentrating heat rays.

**A.** Watch an adult place a glass over a lighted candle which he has set on a saucer.

**O.** The flame will burn for a few seconds and then go out. Fire must have oxygen to burn. Oxygen is in the air. When the oxygen under the glass has been used up, the candle goes out.

**A.** Watch an adult place a lighted stubby candle on a saucer. Observe how he scatters baking powder on the lighted candle.

**O.** The flames goes out immediately. Fire needs air, and the baking powder crowds the air away from the fire. It smothers the fire.

**A.** With the teacher, examine the fire extinguisher in your room. Observe how it works.

**O.** Note how the force stored up in the extinguisher sends the spray many feet. The spray may be the kind that smothers the fire, or it may be the kind that sets up a chemical interaction to put out the fire.

*Possible discussion:* Fire is NOT a plaything! Extreme caution must be used in any situation where fire is concerned. What else can you use to smother fire besides baking powder? Sand, wet towels, or woolen blankets. In case of fire, how can you get the fire department quickly? How do the firemen work to put out a fire? Who pays the firemen? How do people who live outside cities get help in fighting fire? Fire is not always something to be extinguished—name as many situations as you can where fire can be used constructively.

## Electricity

**A.** On a day when the air is cold and dry, walk across the rug, dragging your feet as you go. Then touch something made of metal, or touch another person.

**O.** An electric shock results. Sometimes a spark may even be seen. Electricity is all about us. Electricity which is moving can be made to light bulbs, ring bells, and do many other things.

**A.** Hold a piece of paper in your hand as you drag your feet across the rug.

**O.** Put the paper against the wall. The electricity will make the paper stick to the wall.

**A.** With the help of an adult, connect a three-volt bulb to the two binding posts of a dry cell.

**O.** The bulb will give light because the electricity from the battery is moving through the bulb and back through the battery. Electricity must always go in a complete circle in order to give light or furnish power. If you remove one of the wires, the light goes out.

**A.** Turn on the light switch in the room.

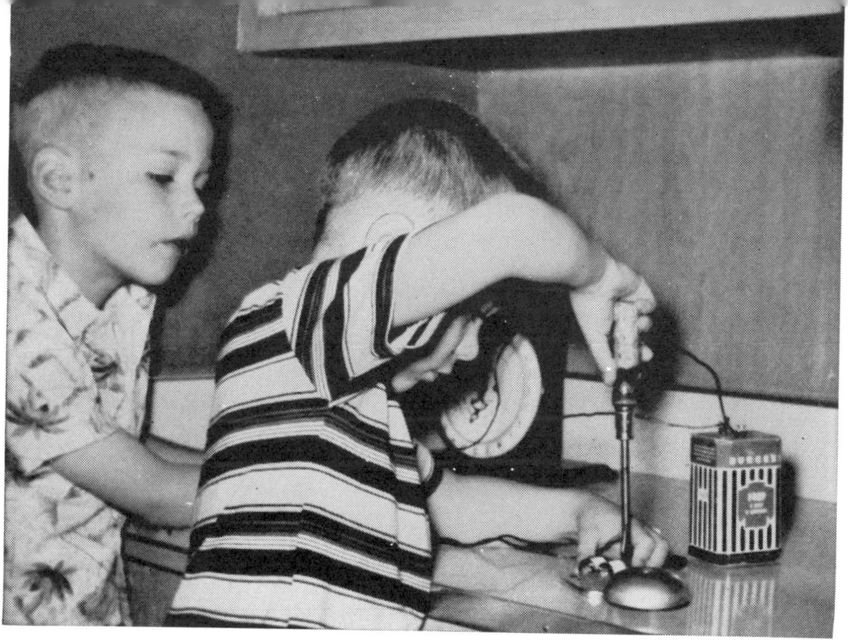

University of Minnesota

*"Just tighten it here and I think she'll ring."*

**O.** The light goes on because the electricity is coming in through one wire, passing through the light, and going out through another wire. As the electricity goes through the tiny wire filament in the bulb, the electricity rubs so fast that it makes a great deal of heat. The wire becomes not red hot but "white hot," and thus it gives light.

*Possible discussion:* When you comb your hair, do you ever hear or see the electric sparks jump from your hair to the comb? Did you ever see the electric sparks which sometimes are produced when the plug is being put into the iron? Think of all the things you have in your house which are operated by electricity: lights, toaster, razor, vacuum cleaner, radio, TV, and so on. What would happen if we had no electricity over a period of several days?

## MAGNETIC ATTRACTION

**A.** Hold a magnet (horseshoe or bar) over some nails.

**O.** The nails will cling to the magnet. The magnet has within it the power to attract certain metals. Iron and steel are most easily attracted.

**A.** Rub a screwdriver with a magnet. Now try to pick up nails with the screwdriver.

**O.** The newly magnetized screwdriver will now pick up nails. Magnetism can be transferred from one magnetic substance to another, or it can be induced electrically.

**A.** Place a needle, nail, or paper clip in a tiny boat made of paper or cork. Move a magnet through the air immediately above the boat.

**O.** The boat will move across the water because of the magnetic force. Magnetism is a force which we cannot see, but it can be made to work for us.

**A.** Place a nail between two equally strong magnets.

**O.** The nail will not move because the two magnets are pulling with equal strength. It is as though two children were pulling equally hard on two ends of a rope.

## Gravity

**A.** Throw a ball high into the air.

**O.** The ball, as you know, will come back to the ground. This is the force of gravity at work.

**A.** Suspend a magnet from a string. Toss some paper clips up toward the magnet.

**O.** If the magnet is strong enough (and if you get any one of the paper clips close enough to the magnet) the clips will cling to it. The magnetic attraction in this case is stronger than the force of gravity.

## Sound

**A.** Close your eyes and try to enumerate all the sounds you hear.

**O.** *Sounds of nature:* Bird calls, animal sounds, gurgling water, acorns dropping, wind sighing.

*Human sounds:* Talking, singing, laughing, crying, walking, running.

*Mechanical sounds:* Hammering, sawing, put-put of motors, car brakes.

**A.** Make a funnel out of a piece of paper. Talk through the funnel.

**O.** Your voice sounds much louder. It is amplified. It goes, not in many directions, but all in one direction.

**A.** Hold a watch as far away from your ear as you can reach. Listen to the watch. Now put the watch on the wooden table. Put your ear close to the table.

**O.** You can hear the watch more readily when it is on the table and your ear is close to the table. Sound can travel through certain materials better than it can travel through air.

**A.** Put a nail hole in the bottom of two small cans. Run a long string from the bottom of one can to the bottom of the other. Tie large knots on the inside of each can. Stretch the string tight, so that one child has a can to speak into and the other has a can to put to his ear.

O. The child at the far end of the string will hear very well, even though the words are spoken very softly. Not the sound but the vibrations set up in the bottom of the can are carried along the string. The vibrations are set up then in the other can, and the child hears the words made by the vibration pattern. Over the telephone the vibrations are carried by electricity along the wire.
*Possible discussion:* Some sounds are pleasant, others unpleasant. Why? Noise is produced by irregular vibrations, music by patterned vibrations. Why do some rooms have echoes? Some surfaces reflect sounds; some ceilings are made to absorb sound and do not let it come back.

## Stones

A. Gather stones and pebbles, preferably from the shore of an ocean, a lake, or a stream.

O. Some have sharp edges, some smooth. They have different colors and shapes.

A. Break a piece of chalk and note its sharp edges. Put many small pieces of chalk into a bottle and shake them.

O. Sharp edges get worn down. The sharp edges of stones get worn down by much bumping against other stones.

A. Look at the side of a cliff.

O. Stones seem to run in stripes, or strata.

A. Rub two pieces of soft chalk or lime together for some time.

O. A pile of sand remains.

A. Observe stones which appear to be made of many parts, many crystals. Experiment with making crystal formations by putting together a few drops of water and a tablespoon or more of any one of the following: salt, sugar, or alum. Boil the mixture and let it stand in the air.

O. The moisture will evaporate, leaving crystals in the pan. A piece of thread placed in the pan while the moisture is evaporating will cause the crystals to form round the string. The string may then be lifted and the crystals readily observed through a magnifying glass.

A. Bring in a piece of polished granite.

O. Granite is a very hard stone that will take a high polish.

A. Inspect a statue or monument in the neighborhood.

O. It is made of hard stone.

A. Visit a stone quarry.

O. Stone comes in such great pieces that it has to be cut up before it is used. It is so heavy that big derricks are used to lift it.
*Possible discussion:* Stones have many uses. Strong stone can be used for

building. Why wouldn't chalk be a good kind of stone for making a house? How did we use stones in planting flowers in flower pots? How, then, are stones valuable in a garden? Why do some cities use stone for paving?

## Soil

**A.** Compare a lump of school clay with a handful of mud and a handful of sand.

**O.** Clay holds together better than mud does. Mud cracks apart when it is dry. Sand just drops apart when it is dry. They are all different kinds of earth.

**A.** Visit a clay pit and a tile factory.

**O.** Clay is used to make bricks. It must be heated.

**A.** Visit a sand pit and a glass factory.

**O.** Sand is used to make glass. It must be heated.

**A.** Notice piles of dust along the roadside.

**O.** Dust is very fine earth which is blown about from one place to another.

**A.** Notice tiny dust particles in the air.

**O.** Sometimes there is only a little and it sparkles in the sun. Sometimes there is so much dust in the air that it hides the sun.

**A.** Hang a wet towel in the window on a day when dust is blowing.

**O.** If the towel fits closely, it will catch the dust and not let it come through, and the air in the room will not be dusty.

*Possible discussion:* Dust storms. What will prevent much dust? Effect of grass on the yard. Bringing mud into the schoolroom makes the room dirty and gives extra work to the janitor.

## The Sun

**A.** Watch a sunrise or a sunset.

**O.** The sun rises in the east, sets in the west. There are beautiful colors in the sky at these times.

**A.** Follow the course of the sun through the day.

**O.** In the morning, the sun shines in the east windows; at noon it is high in the sky and shines in through the southern windows if through any; in the afternoon, it shines in the west windows.

**A.** Try to see the sun on a cloudy day.

**O.** If the clouds are not too thick, the sun can be seen as a round, bright spot behind the clouds.

**A.** Try to get away from your shadow.

**O.** The shadow moves when the object making the shadow moves.

**A.** Standing in a given spot on the sidewalk, have someone draw an outline of your shadow in the morning, at noon, and in the late afternoon.

**O.** The shadow changes in size and position as the sun changes its position.

**A.** Place a thermometer in the sun; then move it to the shade.

**O.** It is much cooler in the shade.

**A.** In the spring, note the ice on the south and north sides of the building.

**O.** The ice and snow melt more quickly where it is sunny.

**A.** Place one plant in sunlight, another in the dark. Inspect them after a few weeks.

**O.** The plant in the sunlight is bright green and healthy; that in the dark is yellow and weak.

**A.** Place a plant in the window and after a few days turn it around.

**O.** The plant leans toward the sun. The plant turns itself toward the sun.

**A.** Shine a flashlight on a large beach ball on which you have placed a mark representing your part of the world. Keep the flashlight still but turn the ball on a north-south axis.

**O.** As the ball, representing the earth, turns, we find that the flashlight (the sun) shines on different parts of it. This is like night and day.

**A.** Wet two sponges. Hang one in the sun, the other in the shade. Inspect them after an hour or so.

**O.** A sponge dries more quickly in the sun than in the shade.

## The Moon[1]

(*Note:* If the teacher wishes to call the attention of the children to the changing shapes of the moon, she must be sure that she selects a season when the moon will rise before their bedtime.)

**A.** Look at the moon every night for five or six nights. Draw or get one of your parents to draw a picture of the way the moon looks each night. Bring these pictures to the kindergarten.

**O.** The moon changes its position and appears to change its shape every night.

(If it is possible to carry on the observation long enough, the childlren will see that the horns of the new moon point to the left, of the old to the

[1] See Franklyn Branley references at the end of this chapter.

right. If the child sees the moon sometimes near the horizon and sometimes near the zenith, he may notice that it seems larger and more reddish or golden when near the horizon.)

**A.** Look at the moon, or at pictures or models of the moon. Share information about the moon's surface, which may have been picked up from Ranger moon shots.

**O.** The moon has hills and valleys and great craters. The sun shining on these makes shadows. These shadows are the dark places on the moon. They form the face of the "man in the moon." The United States has thousands of pictures of the moon. Wo do not know much about the moon's "soil," but we hope to be able to send a man to the moon within five years and when he comes back he will tell us all about the atmospheric conditions and the surface of the soil.

**A.** Look at the moon on four consecutive Mondays.

**O.** If it is a waning moon, it seems to get smaller and smaller. If it is a new moon, it seems to get larger and larger. Really it does not change in shape. The moon has no light of its own, and when the sun is on the side of the moon away from the earth, the side facing the earth has no light and therefore we cannot see it.

## The Stars[2]

**A.** Look into the sky on any clear night.

**O.** There are millions of stars. Some are brighter than others. They change position during the night and from night to night.

**A.** Notice the lights on a car. They look very small when the car is far away.

**O.** When the car comes nearer, the light looks larger. Stars that we can see are really larger than our earth; but they look small because they are so very far away. Many stars, though huge, are so far away that they cannot be seen from the earth.

**A.** Look for the stars in the sky in the daytime. Now look at a lighted streetlight in the daytime.

**O.** The streetlight is scarcely noticeable in the brightness of the daylight. The stars are not visible at all in the daylight, but they are there all the time.

*Possible discussion:* The relationship of the earth, sun, moon, and stars. Too-detailed discussion is inadvisable, but kindergarten children can understand that the stars are suns like our sun, only many, many millions of miles away. They will probably be interested in other planets and the

[2] See Franklyn Branley references at the end of this chapter.

possibility of animal life on them. Space travel and the adventures of earth satellites will no doubt come into the children's discussion.

## Vegetable Kingdom

### SEEDS

**A.** Collect seeds of all kinds.

**O.** Seeds may be gathered from flowers, vines, trees, grain, and weeds.

**A.** Make small paper boxes, cellophane or plastic envelopes, or obtain transparent plastic boxes, and sort the seeds so that each kind is in a separate container.

**O.** Seeds are different in size, shape, and color. The size of a seed does not indicate the size of the fruit, flower, plant, or tree it may grow into.

**A.** Put bean seeds on moist blotting paper or a moist sponge; watch them day after day.

**O.** The seed softens and breaks open; then sprouts appear.

**A.** In the spring, plant some seeds in pots inside the building, and plant others out-of-doors.

**O.** Seeds grow faster in the warm air of the room than in the cooler air outside.

**A** Scatter wheat for the birds in winter. Feed the canary his grain. Bring corn for the school's chickens. Bring sunflower seeds for the school's white rats.

**O.** Some kinds of seeds are eaten by birds and animals.

**A.** Bring to school a variety of nuts. Open them and look inside.

**O.** Some kinds of seeds are eaten by people.

**A.** Bring to school fruit and berries, such as apples, peaches, grapes, strawberries.

**O.** Some seeds have coverings which we eat, while we throw away the seed itself.

**A.** Observe different ways in which seeds are scattered and sown.

**O.** Some (like maple, box elder, and ash) have winglike parts and sail through the air. Some (like dandelions, poplar, and thistles) have fluffy, feathery parts which help them sail through the air. Some (like burdocks and stickseeds) stick to the clothes of people and the fur of animals and are thus carried about. Still others (like bean, pea, catalpa, and locust seeds) grow in pods which burst open and in that way become scattered.

### FRUITS

**A.** Make a collection of different kinds of fruits.

**O.** Fruits vary in size, color, and shape. Each fruit has a special name.

Some common fruits (such as apples) have names for the different varieties.

**A.** Visit a grocery store and list the kinds of fruit found there. Note which are grown locally.

**O.** Some fruits can be grown in this vicinity; others are shipped from far away.

**A.** Visit an orchard in the spring.

**O.** Fruit trees have blossoms in the spring. Each kind of fruit has its own kind of blossom.

**A.** Cut several kinds of fruit open.

**O.** Every fruit has its own special kind of seed arrangement.

## VEGETABLES

**A.** Bring to school samples of many vegetables.

**O.** Vegetables differ in size, shape, and color.

**A.** Visit a grocery store and list the kinds of fresh vegetables there. Note which are grown locally.

**O.** Some vegetables can be grown in your vicinity. Others are shipped from far away.

**A.** Visit the same grocery store a month or two later in the year. Note that some vegetables which were grown locally a month ago are now being shipped in.

**O.** Even if a vegetable will grow in your climate, it will not grow there at all seasons of the year.

**A.** Visit a grocery store and list the kinds of canned or frozen fruits and vegetables on sale.

**O.** Some foods can be kept fresh easily; others keep best when canned, dried, or frozen.

**A.** Visit a vegetable garden if the school has no vegetable garden of its own.

**O.** Some vegetables (like peas and beans) grow on vines. Some (like potatoes and carrots) grow beneath the ground. Some (like lettuce and cabbage) grow on the ground.

**A.** Have a picnic on which you use the vegetables from the school garden.

**O.** Vegetables are good to eat. Many vegetables are good to eat raw. (Carrot sandwiches are particularly enjoyable, especially when the carrots have been raised by the kindergarten group.)

**A.** Wash and scrub vegetables such as carrots, potatoes; shuck peas; snap beans. Add salt. Boil in a pyrex kettle so that all can see the activity. Let cool to comfortable temperature. Serve in cups at snack time.

**O.** Even the most prosaic food when cleaned and prepared by the children themselves tastes better than the chef's specialty.

**A.** Make a basket or bowl arrangement of vegetables, using eggplant, summer and acorn squash, cauliflower, cabbage (green and purple) carrots, corn, or other vegetables.

**O.** Vegetables have artistic as well as nutritional qualities.

*Possible discussion:* The value of seeds, fruits, and vegetables to mankind. The necessity in certain climates for preserving such food. Changes in attitudes toward food (tomatoes, once thought to be poison, now recognized as excellent food). The value of fruits and vegetables in the diet. Industries of various sections are greatly affected by what is raised there (flour in the Upper-Midwest, apples in the state of Washington, potatoes in Maine and Idaho, oranges in California and Florida). Transportation is affected by new demand for certain foods—refrigerated cars, faster freight trains, air express, and new kinds of trucks.

## TREES

**A.** Collect from the neighborhood samples of leaves from different trees. Mount one of each kind on the bulletin board.

**O.** There are many kinds of trees in the neighborhood. Each one has a name and a special kind of leaf and bark.

**A.** In the fall, bring in beautifully colored leaves.

**O.** Many trees lose their green coloring in the fall. Some turn brown, others red and yellow. Later the leaves drop to the ground.

**A.** Play in the fallen leaves.

**O.** The leaves which fall to the ground are dry. They rustle when you walk through them. They crumple and break when handled.

**A.** Dip bright-colored leaves in warm melted wax or press them between sheets of heavy waxed paper.

**O.** Shapes and colors may be preserved for weeks if the air is kept from drying the leaves.

**A.** Bring in a few twigs from which the leaves have fallen.

**O.** A scar left where the leaf dropped may be seen. Just where the leaf dropped off is a tiny winter bud.

**A.** In the late winter or early spring, bring in twigs and place them in water which is changed frequently.

**O.** The leaf bud begins to swell, and then the leaf unfolds.

**A.** Put pussywillow branches in water.

**O.** The fuzzy gray pussywillow changes to a great catkin, and later a leaf forms.

**A.** Notice twigs of different kinds.

**O.** On some, the leaf buds are opposite each other; on others they alternate, like steps.

**A.** Bring in twigs from apple and plum trees.

**O.** On the apple tree, the leaves come out first; on the plum tree, the blossoms come first.

**A.** Note the change in the coloring of the elm trees as spring advances.

**O.** The buds are red, then yellow. Finally the leaves become green.

**A.** Watch men cutting or chopping down a tree, or look at wood that has been sawed.

**O.** Different woods have different barks and different grains. Every tree shows rings of growth. From these we can count the years that a tree has been growing.

*Possible dicussion:* Trees give us shade. They are used by squirrels as homes and by birds as foundations for their nests. Trees keep the wind off. Some trees give us fruits. Other trees give us wood. Wood is important as a source of warmth in stoves. Wood is used for making such things as houses, furniture, boats, bridges, carts, pencils, toys, and paper. Some men who work with trees and wood are called lumbermen, carpenters, and cabinetmakers. Some men, called forest rangers, fly over the forest or watch from high towers to guard the forest so that fires will not get underway or out of control.

## GRASS

**A.** Pull up a blade of grass and examine the roots.

**O.** The roots are very tender and will not grow if stepped on.

**A.** Feed grass to the rabbits. Watch cows, sheep, or horses grazing.

**O.** They are using grass for food.

**A.** Slip a blade of grass from its rootcase and eat it.

**O.** It has a pleasing taste. It might be good in a sandwich or salad.

**A.** Scatter some grass seed on black earth, and keep the earth well watered.

**O.** Grass grows quickly under moist conditions.

**A.** Drop grass seeds into a moist sponge. Keep the sponge moist by spraying every day.

**O.** In a day or two, the sponge will be covered with new grass.

*Possible discussion:* Value of grass as fodder. Value of grass in holding down the dirt and keeping the lawn clean. Signs such as "Keep off the Grass" are put there to remind us that grass will not grow if the roots are destroyed. Bare spots in yards and parks detract from their beauty.

## FLOWERS AND GARDENS

**A.** Walk in the woods and bring back a sample of each kind of wild flower seen (except for those which it is unlawful to pick).

**O.** Wild flowers differ in shape, color, and size. Every flower has a name of its own.

**A.** If it is permissible in your state, bring in a few wild-flower plants, roots and all; transplant these into your school garden.

**O.** If the garden, soil, shade, sunlight, and other conditions are at all like the area from which the flower came and if the plant is transplanted carefully, it will continue its growth.

**A.** Notice particularly wild crocus and anemone.

**O.** They are protected from the early spring cold by a soft fuzz.

**A.** Plan a school garden of either flowers or vegetables or both. Consider the things to be planted, how and in what order they should be planted.

**O.** Some things grow more quickly and easily than others. Radishes grow quickly, tomatoes slowly.

**A.** Draw a plan of the garden plot on a large piece of paper. Plan a space for planting each kind of seed, and follow the chart.

**O.** Some things take more room than others. Summer squash and pumpkin vines will run over much space.

**A.** Prepare the ground by spading it up, breaking up lumps, perhaps adding fertilizer. Rake it smooth.

**O.** Ground must be prepared before a garden is planted if the plants are to grow well.

**A.** Use a long board or a string to guide the planting or, better yet, place a sheet of heavy corrugated paper on the soil. Planting may be done on either edge of the corrugated strip, and the children may walk on the strip. The paper, of course, is removed after each two rows have been planted. Even when corrugated paper is used, it is well to mark the planted rows by stretching a string from stick to stick over the planted row.

**O.** Rows must be straight, so that one can walk in the garden without stepping on the plants.

**A.** Scatter some seeds in rows, plant others in holes at distances suggested on the package of seeds.

**O.** Some seeds, such as radish and carrot seeds, grow best when planted thickly and later thinned. Others, such as pumpkin and tomato seeds, need much space from the beginning.

**A.** Water the garden frequently but gently.

**O.** Plants need moisture. Water from a hose held too near the ground will dig up the seeds and young plants.

**A.** Hoe the garden.

**O.** The ground must be kept loose, so that the roots can get moisture and air.

**A.** Pull out the weeds.

**O.** Weeds choke other plant life. They are very sturdy and have tough roots.

**A.** Bring into the kindergarten some of the pretty weeds (thistle, smart weed, dandelions, devil's paintbrush).

O. Many weeds are pretty, but they should be destroyed in places where we want more useful plants to grow.

A. Find the seeds in the weeds.

O. Some weeds have many seeds and so can spread rapidly.

A. If an outdoor school garden is impossible, plant seeds inside in an old sandbox or in flowerpots or cans. Keep in the sun or under fluorescent light and water well.

O. Seeds germinate and plants grow if they are warm and have light and water.

A. Make a rock garden in an old sandbox by using a pan of water for fish or turtles, arranging a few small potted plants, and filling in the space with stones and sand.

O. Compare miniature Japanese gardens with outdoor rock gardens. Why should anyone have a rock garden?

A. Visit a greenhouse.

O. Different temperatures are kept for different plants. The air in most of the rooms is warm and moist. No weeds are allowed to grow. The stage of development of the different plants depends on the date they were planted.

A. Make a simple terrarium by stretching Saran Wrap over and around four-corner boards which have been fastened securely to a heavy wooden base. Cover the base with heavy aluminum foil. Plant grass and grain seeds in your terrarium.

O. In many ways, your terrarium is like the large greenhouse you visited. Since the moisture cannot evaporate, the plants are kept constantly moist.

A. Cut the bottom from a carrot. Scoop out some of the remaining part of the carrot. Turn it upside down, fill with water, and hang it in a window.

O. The foliage will start to grow from what is now the bottom.

*Possible discussion:* If we want to keep on having wild flowers in our woods, we must take care of them and not pull up the roots. Flowers are beautiful. Many flowers have pleasant odors. To be successful, a garden must be carefully tended. What are the advantages of greenhouses? What things have people made that are copies or imitations of flowers? (Wallpaper, dress goods, perfumes, artificial flowers for hat or dress trimming, or table decoration.)

## PLANTS

A. Start pansy, aster, and tomato plants from seeds. Start geranium plants by leaving slips of the plant in water. Start a sweet-potato vine by placing a sprouted sweet potato in a jar partly filled with water, setting it for several days in a dark place, and then bringing it out to the light.

**O.** Each plant can be rooted easily with some special kind of treatment.

**A.** Make some paper boxes. Dip them in wax to make them waterproof —cut-down milk cartons will serve the same purpose. Transplant into these cartons any plants which cannot be used in the school garden, so that they may be taken home.

**O.** With care, plants can be moved (transplanted) from one place to another without injury.

### BULBS

**A.** In the fall, bring to school a variety of bulbs.

**O.** All the bulbs are hard and dry. The different kinds vary in size and shape. Some bulbs are planted in the fall. Others will be killed if the winter weather is too severe.

**A.** Plant bulbs (tulip, crocus, and the like) outdoors in the fall. Watch them early in the spring.

**O.** The green shoots appear almost before the snow is gone.

**A.** During the winter, plant bulbs (narcissus and hyacinth) in flower-pots, using pebbles to support them and giving them plenty of water. Keep in a dark place.

**O.** The root side of the bulb must be down. The roots will start in the dark.

**A.** Move the rooted bulbs from the dark to a place in the sunshine.

**O.** The yellowish color of the plant soon turns to green.

**A.** Continue to observe the growing plant.

**O.** Soon flower buds appear. After a time, the flower disappears. With some plants, seed pods will form. The narcissus will form seed pods if pollen from one flower is introduced into another. Most bulbs multiply by growing a second bulb beside the original one.

**A.** Put the bulb of a paper narcissus on a plate.

**O.** This bulb will grow without water or dirt. It takes nourishment from air.

*Possible discussion:* The bulb is the form in which the plant rests through the winter. The bulb contains food for the plant, which will start to grow when the rest period is finished. What kinds of bulbs can you think of which are really plants at rest? (Tulips, hyacinths, crocus, narcissus, tuberous begonias, onions.)

## Animal Kingdom

### BIRDS

**A.** Watch for birds in the late fall.

**O.** Some are flying south. Some stay in the North all winter.

**A.** Plan some way to feed the birds in the winter. Put melted suet and

*"She likes me — she doesn't even want to fly away."*

St. Paul Public Schools

seeds in half an orange skin, then hang it on a bush. Tie pieces of suet to the branches of trees. Put a sheaf of wheat on a high post in the schoolyard. Scatter crumbs. Build a feeding station for birds. Trim a birds' Christmas tree with strings of popcorn and dried fruit.

**O.** When the earth is frozen and covered with snow, the birds have difficulty finding food. Birds will keep coming to a place where they are fed. Birds eat suet, crumbs, dry berries, and seeds.

**A.** In the spring, watch for the robins, and observe them.

**O.** Robins have reddish-orange breasts. They look unusually plump in the spring. Robins sing little during the day, but much in the early morning and at sunset. They have various calls. When the robin flies, he steers and balances himself with his tail. He cocks his head, looking and listening for worms. When he finds a worm, he braces himself and tugs and pulls at it. The robin hops and runs.

**A.** Observe the robins building their nest.

**O.** Mother and father work together. They put dry grass, twigs, and string in the crotch of a tree or on a post or window sill, and then bring mud to cement it. The robin sits in the nest and turns round and round, smoothing it with her breast. Nests are seldom used twice.

**A.** Watch the birds sitting on the nest.

**O.** Underneath the bird are usually four blue-green eggs. Mother and father take turns sitting on the eggs. It takes from eleven to fourteen days for the eggs to hatch.

**A.** Watch the baby robins.

**O.** The tiny babies have no feathers and cannot see. Their mouths are open all the time, chirruping and crying for food. Later the feathers appear. The breast of the young robin is speckled. His tail is not yet long enough to let him balance well. He is awkward when he first tries to fly, but learns quickly.

**A.** Watch other birds common to the locality.

**O.** Each kind of bird has its own coloring and its own habits in nest-making.

*Possible discussion:* What do the birds do for us? Why does the government sometimes make laws prohibiting the killing of some kinds of birds?

## SQUIRRELS

**A.** When squirrels are near, put out peanuts and nuts with very hard shells. Observe the squirrels.

**O.** The squirrel picks up the peanut with his front paws. He turns it round and round, cracks the nut, drops the shell, and eats the nut. When he is satisfied, he tucks another nut into his mouth and scuttles off in a hurry.

**A.** Follow the squirrel and watch him bury the nut.

**O.** Usually he buries the nuts with hard shells and the peanuts he has not eaten.

**A.** Sit very quietly on the ground, holding a peanut in your outstretched hand.

**O.** If you are very, very still, a squirrel may come and take the nut.

**A.** Invite squirrels into the kindergarten by first placing a basket of peanuts by the door and later moving them just inside.

**O.** If you do not frighten them and if you feed them, squirrels will become friendly.

**A.** Trim a Christmas tree for squirrels by tying peanuts on the tree. Place it outside the window.

**O.** Several squirrels may come to it.

*Possible discussion:* Squirrels like to eat nuts. If there are no nut trees in the vicinity, what do squirrels eat when we do not feed them? The ground will soften the hard shell of a nut. How do they store food for winter? How do we store our food for winter?

## FARM ANIMALS

**A.** Visit a farm in the spring after the baby animals have been born (cow, sheep, pig, horse, duck, chicken, turkey). Listen to the mothers and the babies.

Lilly from F. P. G.

*"Which comes first . . . ?"*

**O.** Each animal is different from the others. Each mother uses different sounds when she wants the babies to come to her.

**A.** Compare the babies with their mothers.

**O.** The babies are smaller. They are sometimes a different color. They are clumsy.

**A.** Note the homes prepared for each kind of animal.

**O.** Each animal thrives best in some special kind of home.

**A.** See what kind of food each animal eats.

**O.** Different animals eat different things.

**A.** Hunt for eggs if the farm is one where the hens roam over the barnyard.

**O.** Hens lay eggs in strange places, though usually they lay in the nests the farmer provides.

**A.** See the eggs (chicken, turkey, duck) in the incubator.

**O.** The air in the incubator is kept at an even temperature. Every day the farmer turns the eggs. Eggs of different fowl are different. You can tell what will hatch from an egg by its size, color, and shape.

**A.** Watch a cow being milked.

**O.** The cow must be milked twice every day. If she does not have good grass and other good food, she will not give much or rich milk.

**A.** Watch the milk being separated.

**O.** This is a quicker way to get the cream than by waiting for it to rise to the top of the milk. The stable, pails, and everything that touches the milk are kept very clean.

**A.** Inspect the barns and silos.

**O.** Food is stored for the animals to eat in winter.

**A.** Bring a setting hen and eggs to the kindergarten. Build a nest for her in a large cage, using hay, excelsior, or the grass from Easter baskets. Place the cage in a quiet place and visit the cage once a day.

**O.** The mother hen gets off her nest only to eat and drink. She turns the eggs with her feet and wings. The eggs hatch in three weeks.

**A.** Keep the mother hen supplied with food and water.

**O.** The mother hen likes corn, lettuce, and fresh grass.

**A.** Build a chicken house and yard outdoors for the mother hen and her chickens. Watch them there and feed them.

**O.** The baby chicks like well-chopped hard-boiled eggs, milk, lettuce, and a mash prepared from cracked wheat and corn. The mother hen teaches the chickens to scratch for worms and bugs.

**A.** If you cannot get a setting hen, or if you do not wish to wait the three long weeks for the eggs to hatch, get from a hatchery either (a) eggs which are about ready to hatch and keep them in an incubator in the room, or (b) some baby chicks that have just hatched. The baby chicks can be kept in a box or, better yet, a dry aquarium with an electric gooseneck lamp to keep them warm.

**O.** Even without a mother they know how to feed themselves and get about.

**A.** Watch the chickens as they develop.

**O.** When they are first hatched, they are all wet and thin. Soon their down dries and they look fluffy. As soon as the chickens are dry, they can run about. When they are three or four weeks old, their feathers begin to grow. Then they try to fly.

**A.** Put up some poles for roosts.

**O.** When they are big enough, the chickens like to go to roost. When they are little, they sleep under the mothers' wings.

**A.** Watch the chickens drink.

**O.** They have no muscles in their throats, and so they hold up their heads and let the water run down.

**A.** After the chickens have been taken back to the farm, bring some turkeys, ducks, geese, or guinea hens to take their place in the yard.

**O.** Different fowl have different appearances and different habits and calls.

*Possible discussion:* What does each of the animals do for people? Why do many farmers use machinery instead of horses? Why are most farms out in the country instead of in the city? Does a city need to have farmers near it? Why? How does the city get its milk?

## DOGS

**A.** Go to see a mother dog and her new puppies.

**O.** The puppies are very wobbly on their legs when they are young. The mother dog has milk for them. She needs to have good food while she is nursing the puppies. She teaches her puppies. She calls to them, noses them around to put them where she wants them, and picks them up in her mouth. The puppies do not all look alike.

**A.** Bring a dog to kindergarten for a day's visit.[3] Build a play yard for him with blocks. Have milk, dog biscuits, and a bone ready for him.

**O.** The puppy likes to be petted for a while, but grows tired of being handled too much. He needs a time for quiet and rest. Care must be taken in picking up the puppy. Support him by putting your arm under his legs as you pick him up.

**A.** Let the dog exercise at rhythm time.

**O.** He will walk and run with children. He cannot skip or dance.

## WHITE RATS[4]

**A.** Bring a pair of white rats or mice to kindergarten. Keep them in an empty sandbox and provide a cage in which there is a wheel.

**O.** The rats will run about the sandbox but will not jump out unless it is on the floor or very near a chair or other piece of furniture. They need exercise and get it by running in the wheel.

**A.** Keep a supply of food for them.

**O.** Rats like milk, bread, something green like lettuce, apples, sunflower seeds. A mash may be purchased for them. In winter it is well to give them cod-liver oil.

**A.** Notice their long sharp teeth. Put a bone in their cage.

**O.** They like to have something to gnaw on. If they do not wear down their teeth by gnawing, the teeth will grow too long.

**A.** Watch them clean themselves.

**O.** They lick and wash with their paws. They are very neat.

[3] Pet rabbits, kittens, lambs, and goats also may be visited or brought to kindergarten for short visits.

[4] White mice, guinea pigs, hamsters, and chipmunks may be used in place of white rats. Chipmunks are interesting to watch and study, but they cannot be handled, and they are not so likely to reproduce in the kindergarten, as are the mice, rats, guinea pigs and hamsters. The hamster is the most prolific of the animals mentioned; the gestation period is but eighteen days.

**A.** Keep paper in the cage. Just before nesting time, put in an empty chalk box.

**O.** The rats like to tear up papers. Just before the mother is to have her babies, the rats will busy themselves by making a nest of torn paper. The mother rat likes to hide her babies in the torn paper. She will fill the chalk box with the torn paper and keep the babies snug and warm and hidden there.

**A.** When the babies are born, remove the father rat from the cage.

**O.** The father rat is no help to the mother at this time. Sometimes he even does harm to the babies.

**A.** Watch the baby rats.

**O.** The mother has from eight to fourteen babies. The babies are tiny pink things without fur. They have long tails. They cannot see or run. They squeak for food.

**A.** Watch the mother feed her babies.

**O.** The mother rat has milk for the babies.

## UNUSUAL ANIMALS

**A.** Visit a zoo. Observe the different animals.

**O.** There are many kinds of animals which do not naturally live in this vicinity but which can live here if special arrangements for homes and food are made. The raccoons need trees to climb. The monkeys must be kept warm in winter. The bears need a pool to splash in so that they may keep cool during the warm days. Each animal makes a different noise.

**A.** Report on animals seen at a circus. Make models of them from plasticine.

**O.** Elephants, ponies, monkeys, bears, zebras, tigers, lions, and giraffes all have distinguishing characteristics. Where do the animals come from? How do they get to the United States?

## GOLDFISH[5]

**A.** Select an aquarium, rectangular in shape if possible, and with a wide top open to the air. Prepare it for goldfish. Have an inch of coarse sand in the bottom. Plant green waterweeds in this sand. Put a small amount of water in it until the weeds become rooted. Then add more water, very gently, so as not to disturb the weeds.

**O.** The fish need air. The weeds help aerate the water and serve as a food. The gravel or sand holds the roots of the weeds in place and makes the aquarium look neat and clean.

[5] Source for plants, fish, and other items—General Biological Supply House, 761–63 East 69th Place, Chicago, Illinois.

**A.** Put some snails into the aquarium.

**O.** The snails eat the green scum which forms on the sides of the aquarium and so help keep it clean. The snails are interesting to watch.

**A.** Feed the fish a few grains of prepared fish food once a day or every other day.

**O.** Fish will overeat and die if too much food is given them.

**A.** Watch the fish to see if any of them get spotted or if any begin to tip over on their sides. If this happens, take out the sick fish and put it in a bath of salt water for a day.

**O.** Water with considerable salt in it will often cure a sick goldfish.

## GUPPY FISH

**A.** Set up an aquarium in a warm place or insert a heating unit. Place the guppies inside.

**O.** Guppies are tropical fish and need warm water if they are to grow. Keep the water temperature 70° or above.

**A.** Try to count the guppy fish.

**O.** They are so tiny that it is hard to count them. Sometimes they are as long as half an inch, but usually they are smaller.

**A.** Watch the babies growing inside the mother.

**O.** You can see right through the mother. The babies are no bigger than a pinhead.

**A.** Keep many weeds in the aquarium.

**O.** The babies hide in the weeds so that the big fish cannot catch and eat them.

*Possible discussion:* Different fish grow best in different surroundings. Some like warm water, and some cold. Most fish lay eggs, but guppies are born directly from the mother's body. What do we use fish for?

## TURTLES

**A.** Bring a variety of turtles into the kindergarten.

**O.** There are snapping turtles, mud turtles, Japanese turtles, and other less common varieties. The Japanese turtles are small, with green backs and an under shell of yellow design. The snapping turtle has a sharp, saw-like ridge on its back. The painted terrapin or pond turtle has a mottled red border on its upper shell and beautiful markings on the under shell.

**A.** Build a pen for turtles out of blocks. Put a large pan of water into the pen.

**O.** Some of the turtles like to be in the water practically all the time, others only part of the time.

**A.** Feed the turtles.

**O.** Turtles have no teeth. They like to eat earthworms and green water plants. Japanese turtles like ant eggs. Some turtles feed only under water.

**A.** Bring in and examine a turtle egg.

**O.** The egg is soft, white, and leathery. The mother buries the eggs in the sand.

**A.** In the fall, put turtles in a box of dirt in a cool place.

**O.** The turtles will burrow down into the earth and remain there for the winter.

## FROGS AND TOADS

**A.** From a slough or pond bring in toad or frog eggs.[6] Place them in an aquarium filled with water from a pond. The water should contain mud, stones, and sticks.

**O.** There are hundreds of little white eggs in a jelly-like string. They will not develop in ordinary city water.

**A.** Watch the tadpoles as they hatch and develop.

**O.** At first the tadpoles are tiny, wriggling, jelly-like things. Then they take the form of a body and a long tail. The back legs develop first, then the front ones. The tail grows shorter as the legs and a distinct head develop. It takes from twenty-five to sixty days for a tadpole to develop the features of the grown toad or frog. In July or thereabouts the toad or frog will be ready to leave the water.

*Possible discussion:* There are some animals which live partly in the water and partly on dry land. How long can a frog or a turtle keep its head under water? How do frog and turtle eggs differ from hens' eggs? How do toads help the farmer? Of what use are turtles and frogs? Where do frogs and turtles go in winter?

## COCOONS AND MOTHS[7]

**A.** In the fall, collect caterpillars of various kinds.

**O.** The woolly caterpillar does not normally spin his cocoon until spring, but sometimes, if he is brought into a warm room, he will spin it in the fall. If the Promethea caterpillar (large and green) is supplied with ash, wild cherry, or lilac leaves, he will make his cocoon by folding the leaf around him. The Cecropia caterpillar is a fat, warty creature most often found in orchards. If he is brought in on a branch of his chosen tree, he may spin a cocoon inside.

[6] Frogs' eggs may often be purchased from fish stores. The frog is a little slower than the toad in attaining maturity.

[7] The development of butterflies, bagworms, and praying mantises may be followed in similar fashion. See footnote, p. 407.

**A.** Watch the caterpillar spinning its cocoon.

**O.** The sticky thread is spun from the region of the head.

**A.** Gather cocoons in the late fall or early spring. Look for special kinds on special bushes or trees. Keep cocoons cool and moist through the winter by sprinkling them occasionally.

**O.** Different kinds of caterpillars spin different kinds of cocoons in different kinds of places. If left in the woods, the cocoons would be dampened by winter snows and rains. We must make their surroundings indoors as much as possible like their natural home if they are to develop normally.

**A.** In April or May, bring in twigs of the bushes which serve as food for the kind of moth you are trying to raise. Put them in water to force the development of the leaves. Bring the cocoons into the warm room. Inspect the cocoons every day. Hold a cocoon for a few minutes in a gently closed hand.

**O.** Someday you will feel something move inside the cocoon. This is the pupa wriggling. After days of wriggling, he will break a little hole in the end of the cocoon.

**A.** Watch the moth work its way out of the cocoon.

**O.** The moth comes out of the end of the cocoon. At first the wings seem small and wet, and folded close to its caterpillar shape. After an hour or so, they will be stretched out. The male and female have different wing markings.

**A.** Cut open a pupa case which shows no sign of life.

**O.** Each kind of moth, each cocoon, and each pupa case is different from that of other kinds.

**A.** Watch the mother laying her eggs. If a piece of soft silk is provided, she will probably lay them on that.

**O.** The eggs are fastened onto the surface with a sticky substance. The eggs are brownish white. The moth lives only a few days.

**A.** Watch the eggs hatch. Put them near the young leaves.

**O.** The tiny grubs must have food if they are to develop. If you do not have the right kind of leaves for them, they will die.

*Possible discussion:* In how many forms do we find most living creatures? What advantage is there to different forms? Compare different creatures which have wings. What advantage have winged creatures over those which have no wings? Is there any advantage for the creature which makes a cocoon that is hard to find?

### BEES[8]

**A.** In May, get a glass exhibit case containing a section of hive and a swarm of bees. This case may be placed in the room or just outside a

[8] Ants and grasshoppers may also be observed in glass cases in the schoolroom.

closed window. If it is placed in the room, the bees' exit and entrance may be provided for by inserting a clear plastic hose into the hive and running the hose through a hole in a board which fills an aperture made by the slightly open window.

**O.** The bees go in and out through the tube, bringing back pollen (or bee bread) and nectar from nearby flowers. They carry the pollen in leg pockets and nectar in honey stomachs. They store these foods in the cells.

**A.** Watch the queen bee.

**O.** The queen is longer and thinner than the other bees. Her markings are different. She puts eggs into each of the cells which have been made ready by the worker bees.

**A.** Watch the other bees at work.

**O.** The workers bring pollen and nectar. The drones are idlers.

**A.** Observe the cells of the queen bee.

**O.** They are larger than the ordinary cells. The bees which are to be queens are fed different food by the workers.

**A.** Watch the bees "dance."

**O.** The dances seem to mean different things, such as "Come, there is much nectar or much pollen" or "Dust off my wings and clean me."

**A.** Watch the new bees emerge from the cells.

**O.** They are practically as large as the grown bees. They begin to work almost immediately.

*Possible discussion:* What advantages are there in working together? Why should there be so many worker bees when there is only one queen? Why do we call some people "drones"? What other creatures live in groups or colonies? In what ways is life made easier by group living? What happens to the bees if their honey is taken away from them? How does the farmer prepare the honey for sale? What happens to the bees in the winter time?

## PEOPLE

**A.** Look at your skin.

**O.** Your skin is lighter or darker than the skin of some of the other children in the group. Some people have very much darker or very much lighter skin than yours. Different families have different skin coloring. Different groups of people, different races, have different skin coloring. Their blood is like yours but the color of their skin happens to be different.

**A.** Are your eyes blue, brown, gray, or green? Are they large or small? Do you have light or dark hair? Is your hair straight or curly? Are you tall or short compared with the other children in the group?

**O.** Every person, except in the case of identical twins, has a different appearance from every other person. Wouldn't it be uninteresting if we all looked alike? How could we tell one person from the other?

**A.** Feel the bones in your legs. In your arms. In your back. In your head.

**O.** Your bones are like the frame of a house. They hold you up. If you did not have bones—that is, a skeleton—you could not stand up.

**A.** Look at a model of a human skeleton. Find matching bones.

**O.** For every bone in one arm there is a matching bone in the other arm and the same is true of the leg bones.

**A.** Try to move the bones in the skeleton model. Try to move your own bones. Some bones move and some do not move.

**O.** One bone fits into another or onto another so that all parts of the skeleton are connected. The sockets make it possible for us to move some bones. The parts of a broken bone must be kept absolutely in their proper place while the "knitting" takes place.

**A.** Look at your teeth in the mirror.

**O.** You have matching teeth on either side of your mouth just as you have matching bones in your arms and legs. Different teeth are used for different purposes. Teeth are harder than bones but even so they can break. Teeth will not "knit" as bones do.

**A.** Look at a model of a set of teeth.

**O.** Note the matching teeth. If this is a model of a five-year-old's teeth then there will be fewer teeth than would be found in the model of an adult's teeth. Also these teeth will be "baby" teeth, the ones that will be pushed out when the permanent teeth are ready to appear. Permanent teeth usually begin to appear sometime around a child's sixth birthday. Both baby teeth and permanent teeth need to be brushed daily. Good food helps teeth and bones to develop properly.

**A.** Put your hand on your heart.

**O.** If you have your hand in the right place you can feel your heart pumping. It is pumping in order to circulate the blood to all parts of your body. If you cannot feel it pumping then jump up and down or run a bit. Your heart has to pump faster and work harder when you exercise.

**A.** Hold a bell in your hand and ring it.

**O.** You can enjoy the bell by feeling it, by looking at it, and by hearing it. You use three of your five senses to enjoy the bell. You *touch* the bell. You *see* the bell and *hear* the bell.

**A.** Close your eyes and listen to a musical recording.

**O.** This time you are using only one sense. You *hear* the music; you are using your sense of hearing.

**A.** Try to think of all the senses you might use if you were to eat a stick of peppermint candy.

**O.** You would probably enjoy the shape and color of the candy with your *eyes;* you would enjoy its pungent aroma with your *nose;* you would feel its shape with your hands; you would enjoy its taste with the *taste buds* in your mouth, and with your *ears* it is probable that you would hear the crunching as you ate the stick. In this one simple experience you would have used all of your five senses.

## A Few Simple Mechanical Forces and Devices

**A.** Try to move a very heavy box of blocks. Now put the same load on a truck.

**O.** The load can be carried much more easily on wheels.

**A.** Suspend a pulley from the top of the jungle gym or some other high place. Put a rope around the pulley and fasten to it a weight which is almost too heavy for you to lift. Now pull on the other end of the rope.

**O.** You can lift fairly easily with the pulley and rope the same weight which you could scarcely lift by hand.

**A.** Try to pry up a piece of wood which has been firmly nailed to a plank.

**O.** The longer the prying tool, the less force you will have to use to separate the two pieces.

**A.** Tie a basket onto one end of the teeter-totter and put some heavy blocks in the basket. Now go to the end of the teeter-totter and try to make the basket go up in the air.

**O.** At first the basket may be very hard to raise, but if you will pull the board toward you so that you have more and more board on your side of the balancing frame, you will find that the load becomes increasingly easy to lift.

**A.** Try to get a wagon up the steps without lifting both ends at the same time.

**O.** The task is difficult. Now place two boards on the steps to form a ramp. The inclined plane makes it easy to bring the wagon to the top of the steps.

**A.** Ride a tricycle very slowly up to a line. Try to stop exactly on the line. Now ride it very fast and try to stop on the line.

**O.** It is much easier to stop when going slowly than when going fast.

**A.** Ride a tricycle up to a line on a dry sidewalk and try to stop exactly on the line. Now pour some water on the sidewalk and try to stop just on the line.

**O.** It takes longer to stop on the wet than on the dry pavement. The wheels slip and slide on the wet pavement and do not hold the tricycle back.

**A.** Using the same kind of blocks, build two towers of equal height. Make the first tower with a small base and the second with a broad base.

**O.** The tower with the broad base is much more steady than the tower with the small base.

**A.** On a set of table scales, place one at a time a cup of steel ball bearings, a cup of sand, and a cup of sunflower seeds.

**O.** No two of the filled cups will weigh the same.

**A.** Make a weighing device by fastening the exact center of a long block to a half cylinder. Place objects on the opposite ends of the long block of wood.

**O.** The end of the block on which the heavier weight rests will go down first. Check the accuracy of your scales with real scales.

**A.** Make a parachute. Tie strings to the four corners of a handkerchief, or any square of cloth. Tie the ends of the pieces of string to a single weight, such as a metal washer. Hold the string, the cloth, and the weight in your hand, and throw the parachute into the air.

**O.** As the force of gravity starts to bring the parachute down, the air will push against the cloth and the parachute will sail rather than fall to the ground.

**A.** Make a pointed boat from a flat piece of wood. Work with or watch the teacher as she helps you make it into a paddle-wheel boat. Insert the paddle wheel between the two arms, which are formed by sawing out the back middle section of the boat. Before inserting the paddle wheel, put two slightly twisted rubber binders around the axle of the paddle wheel. When the axle is in place, fasten the other ends of the binders to the back of the boat. Turn the paddle wheel round and round so that the binders have to stretch to their limit. Put the boat in a tub of water.

**O.** The boat will rush forward as the paddle wheel unwinds. The paddle wheel makes the boat move as the paddles push against the water.

**A.** Enumerate as many devices as you can think of which help people move.

**O.** Scooter, roller skates, tricycles, cars, boats, escalators, airplanes, for example.

**A.** Try to push a nail into a piece of wood.

**O.** Even if the wood is soft pushing will do little more than make a slight indentation on the wood. When you hold a hammer near the head the effect is like pushing the nail in. But if you grasp the hammer near the end of the handle the force of the blow will send the nail into the wood.

**A.** Enumerate as many devices or machines as you can think of which help people do their work.

**O.** Steam shovels, derricks, cement mixers, pile drivers, vacuum cleaners, sewing machines, telephones, lawn mowers, and the like.

*Possible discussion:* All these devices have been developed because people have experimented and kept studying and learning more and more about how to control and utilize the elements and forces of nature. Scientists are constantly learning to utilize new elements and to produce new forces.

## Science Books for Children (and Teachers!)


| | |
|---|---|
| Ballard, Lois | 1. *True Book of Reptiles*, Chicago, Children's Press, 1957. |
| Bancroft, Henrietta, and Richard G. Van Gelder | 2. *Animals in Winter*, New York, Thomas Y. Crowell, 1963. |
| Bartlett, Margaret Farrington | 3. *Where the Brook Begins*, New York, Thomas Y. Crowell, 1961. |
| Beauchamp, Wilbur and Others | 4. *Look and Learn: All Around Us: How Do We Know*; New York, Scott, Foresman, 1952. |
| Bendick, Jeanne | 5. *All Around You*, New York, Whittlesey House, 1951. |
| Blough, Glenn | 6. *Christmas Trees and How They Grow*, New York, Whittlesey House, 1961. |
| | 7. *Not only for Ducks*, New York, McGraw-Hill, 1954. |
| | 8. *Who Lives at the Seashore?* New York, Whittlesey House, 1962. |
| Blough, Glenn | 9. *Wait for the Sunshine*, New York, McGraw-Hill, 1954. |
| Borten, Helen | 10. *Do You Hear What I Hear?* New York, Abelard-Schuman, 1960. |
| Branley, Franklyn | 11. *A Book of Planets for You*, New York, Thomas Y. Crowell, 1961. |
| | 12. *The Big Dipper*, New York, Thomas Y. Crowell, 1962. |
| | 13. *Mickey's Magnet*, New York, Thomas Y. Crowell, 1956. |
| | 14. *Rain and Hail*, New York, Thomas Y. Crowell, 1963. |
| | 15. *Rockets and Satellites*, New York, Thomas Y. Crowell, 1961. |
| | 16. *Snow Is Falling*, New York, Thomas Y. Crowell, 1963. |
| | 17. *What the Moon Is Like*, New York, Thomas Y. Crowell, 1963. |
| | 18. *What Makes Day and Night*, New York, Thomas Y. Crowell, 1961. |
| Broekel, Ray | 19. *True Book of Tropical Fish*, Chicago, Children's Press, 1957. |

| | | |
|---|---|---|
| Bulla, Clyde R. | 20. | *What Makes a Shadow?* New York, Thomas Y. Crowell, 1962. |
| Carter, Katherine | 21. | *True Book of Houses,* Chicago, Children's Press, 1954. |
| Collier, Ethel | 22. | *Who Goes There In My Garden?* New York, William R. Scott, 1963. |
| Craig, Gerald | 23. | *Science Near You*—A Book of Science for Today and Tomorrow Series, New York, Ginn, 1954. |
| de Regniers, Beatrice | 24. | *The Shadow Book* (photographs), New York, Harcourt, Brace, 1960. |
| Fisher, Aileen | 25. | *I Like Weather,* New York, Thomas Y. Crowell, 1963. |
| Foster, Doris | 26. | *A Pocketful of Seasons,* New York, Lothrop, Lee and Shepard, 1961. |
| Fox, Charles Philip | 27. | *When Winter Comes* (photographs), Chicago, Reilly and Lee, 1962. |
| Friskey, Margaret | 28. | *True Book of Birds We Know,* Chicago, Children's Press, 1954. |
| Fuller, Elizabeth, and Mary Ellis | 29. | *Springboards to Science,* Minneapolis, T. S. Denison, 1959. |
| | 30. | *Wading Into Science,* Minneapolis, T. S. Denison, 1961. |
| Gans, Roma | 31. | *Birds Eat and Eat and Eat,* New York, Thomas Y. Crowell, 1963. |
| | 32. | *It's Nesting Time,* New York, Thomas Y. Crowell, 1964. |
| | 33. | *The Wonder of Stones,* New York, Thomas Y. Crowell, 1963. |
| Goudey, Alice | 34. | *The Day We Saw the Sun Come Up,* New York, Scribner's, 1961. |
| Hutchinson, William M. | 35. | *A Child's Book of Sea Shells,* New York, Maxton Publishers, 1954. |
| Huntington, Harriet | 36. | *Let's Go Outdoors,* New York, Doubleday, 1939. |
| | 37. | *Let's Go to the Brook,* New York, Doubleday, 1952. |
| Jordan, Jelene J. | 38. | *Let's Go to the Desert,* New York, Doubleday, 1949. |
| | 39. | *Let's Go to the Seashore,* New York, Doubleday, 1941. |
| | 40. | *Seeds by Wind and Water,* New York, Thomas Y. Crowell, 1962. |
| Larrick, Nancy | 41. | *Rain, Hail, Sleet and Snow,* New York, Grosset & Dunlap, 1961. |
| Lewellen, John | 42. | *Tommy Learns to Fly,* New York, Thomas Y. Crowell, 1956. |

Marchen, Marion
43. *Monarch Butterfly*, New York, Holiday House, 1954.

Miller, Patricia, and Iran L. Seligman
44. *Baby Elephant*, New York, Holt, Rinehart and Winston, 1963.
45. *Big Frogs and Little Frogs*, New York, Holt, Rinehart and Winston, 1963.
46. *You Can Find Out*, New York, Holt, Rinehart and Winston, 1963.

Miner, Irene
47. *The True Book of Plants We Know*, Chicago, Children's Press, 1953.
48. *The True Book of Policeman and Fireman*, Chicago, Children's Press, 1954.

Ozone, Lucy
49. *Winter Birds*, Chicago, Albert Whitman, 1956.

Peterson, John (ill.)
50. *Tulips* (Science Story Without Words), New York, Holt, Rinehart and Winston, 1963.

Pistorius, Anna
51. *What Butterfly Is It?* Chicago, Wilcox and Follett, 1949.
52. *What Tree Is It?* Chicago, Wilcox and Follett, 1955.
53. *What Wildflower Is It?* Chicago, Wilcox and Follett, 1950.

Podendorf, Illa
54. *True Book of Electricity*, Chicago, Children's Press, 1961.
55. *True Book of Pebbles and Shells*, Chicago, Children's Press, 1954.

Russell, Solveig
56. *About Nuts*, New York, Melmont, 1963.

Schlein, Miriam
57. *Go With the Sun*, New York, William R. Scott, 1952.
58. *How Do You Travel?* New York, Abingdon Press, 1954.

Schneider, Herman, and Nina Schneider
59. *How Big Is Big?* New York, William R. Scott, 1950.
60. *Let's Find Out*, New York, William R. Scott, 1948.
61. *Let's Look Inside Your House*, New York, William R. Scott, 1948.
62. *Let's Look Under the City*, New York, William R. Scott, 1951.
63. *Science for Work and Play*, New York, John Day, 1955.

Selsam, Millicent
64. *All About Eggs*, New York, William R. Scott, 1952.
65. *All Kinds of Babies and How They Grow*, New York, William R. Scott, 1953.

66. *The Doubleday First Guide to Wildflowers,* New York, Doubleday, 1964.

67. *Greg's Microscope,* New York, Harper and Row, 1963.

68. *You and the World Around You,* New York, Doubleday, 1963.

Shapp, Martha, and Charles Shapp — 69. *Let's Find Out About Air,* New York, Franklin Watts, 1963.

Showers, Paul — 70. *The Listening Walk,* New York, Thomas Y. Crowell, 1961.

Shuttlesworth, Dorothy — 71. *Doubleday First Guide to Rocks,* New York, Doubleday, 1963.

Swain, Su Zan Noguchi — 72. *The Doubleday First Guide to Insects,* New York, Doubleday, 1964.

Webber, Irma — 73. *Bits That Grow Big,* New York, William R. Scott, 1949.

74. *Thanks to Trees,* New York, William R. Scott, 1942.

75. *Travelers All,* New York, William R. Scott, 1944.

76. *Up Above and Down Below,* New York, William R. Scott, 1943.

Williamson, Margaret — 77. *The First Book of Birds,* New York, Franklin Watts, 1957.

Wing, Henry R. — 78. *What Is Big?* New York, Holt, Rinehart and Winston, 1963.

Zaffo, George — 79. *The Big Book of Real Wrecking Machines,* New York, Grosset & Dunlap, 1951.

80. *Giant Nursery Book of Things That Go,* New York, Doubleday, 1959.

Zim, Herbert — 81. *Lightning and Thunder,* New York, William Morrow, 1952.

82. *What's Inside Plants?* New York, William Morrow, 1952.

Zolotow, Charlotte — 83. *In My Garden,* New York, Lothrop, Lee and Shepard, 1961.

84. *The Storm Book,* New York, Harper & Brothers, 1952.


## SERIES


Gans, Roma, and Franklyn M. Branley (editors) Let's-Read-And-Find-Out. Science Book. New York, Thomas Y. Crowell Company, 1960 and on.

Astronomy — *The Big Dipper; The Moon Seems to Change; Rockets and Satellites; The Sun; Our Nearest Star; What Makes Day and Night; What the Moon is Like.*

| | |
|---|---|
| Botany | *Down Come the Leaves; How a Seed Grows; Seeds by Wind and Water; A Tree is a Plant.* |
| Earth Science | *The Clean Brook; Icebergs; The Wonder Stones; Where the Brook Begins.* |
| Entomology | *Bees and Beelines; Fireflies in the Night; Spider Talk; Watch Honeybees with Me.* |
| Meteorology | *Air is All Around Us; Flash, Crash, Rumble, and Roll; Rain and Hail; Snow is Falling.* |
| Ornithology | *Birds Eat and Eat and Eat; It's Nesting Time; Sandpipers.* |
| Physiology | *Find Out by Touching; Follow Your Nose; How Many Teeth? In the Night; Look at Your Eyes; My Five Senses; My Hands.* |
| Physics | *The Listening Walk; Upstairs and Downstairs; What Makes a Shadow?* |
| Zoology | *Animals in Winter; Big Tracks, Little Tracks; Starfish.* |

Parker, Bertha, Glenn O. Blough, and Mabel O'Donnell. Today's Basic Science Education Series, Evanston, Illinois, Harper and Row, 1941 and on. (Although the following listing includes books recommended for primary *and* intermediate groups, many of these are of interest to kindergarten children as pictures or "reference books")

| | |
|---|---|
| Primary | *Animals and Their Young; Animals Round the Year; Animals That Live Together; Aquarium; Birds in the Big Woods; Birds in Your Back Yard; Doing Work; How the Sun Helps Us; Insect Parade; Leaves; Pet Show; Plants Round the Year;* Seasons: *Fall is Here; Winter is Here; Spring is Here; Summer is Here; Six Legged Neighbors; Toys; Useful Plants and Animals; Water Appears and Disappears.* |
| Intermediate | *Air About Us; Animals of the Seashore; Animals of Yesterday; Animals We Know; Animal Travels; Birds; Clouds, Rain and Snow; Dependent Plants; Earth a Great Storehouse; Electricity; Fire; Fishes; Flowers, Fruits, Seeds; Garden and Its Friends; Garden Indoors; Gravity; Insects and Their Ways; Living Things; Machines; Magnets; Plant and Animal Partnerships; Plant Factories; Reptiles; Saving Our Wild Life; Scientist and His Tools; Seeds and Seed Travels; Sky Above Us; Sound; Spiders; Stories Read from the Rocks; Thermometers; Heat and Cold; Toads and Frogs; Trees; Water; What Things Are Made Of; You as a Machine.* |

Basic Science Program, Curriculum Foundation Series, New York, Scott, Foresman and Co.

"Doubleday First Guide to—" Series, New York, Doubleday & Co., Inc.

"The First Book" Series, New York, Franklin Watts, Inc.

Golden Nature Guides, New York, Harper and Row.

"The Little Owl" Series, Holt, Rinehart and Winston, Inc.

Science and Conservation Series, Chicago, Benefic Press.
"The True Book" Series, Chicago, Children's Press.
"What Is It?" Series, Chicago, Benefic Press.

## SUMMARY

Common everyday experiences, which for today's children may range from digging in the soil and finding an earthworm to sitting in front of a television set and seeing an astronaut emerging from his capsule, afford many opportunities for building science understandings. The artist teacher capitalizes on these experiences. She helps bring simple problems into focus and then challenges children to use their present knowledge and understanding to build new concepts. The richness of the kindergarten science program will depend to a great extent on two factors: (a) the teacher's awareness of the science implication in an experience and (b) the teacher's own science background.

## SELECTED REFERENCES

Atkin, J. Myron, and R. Will Burnett, *Working with Animals*, Elementary School Science Activity Series, New York, Rinehart and Company, 1959.

Blough, Glenn, Julius Schwartz, and Albert Huggett, *Elementary School Science*, 3rd ed., New York, Holt, Rinehart and Winston, 1964.

Comstock, Anna B., *Handbook of Nature Study*, 24th ed., Ithaca, New York, Cornell University Press, 1939.

Craig, Gerald, *Science for the Elementary School Teacher*, rev., New York, Blaisdell Publishing Co., 1962.

Ellis, Mary Jackson, Elizabeth M. Fuller, and Robert L. Shrigley, *Wading into Science*, Minneapolis, Denison Company, 1961.

Fuller, Elizabeth M., and Mary Jackson Ellis, *Springboards to Science*, Minneapolis, Denison Company, 1959.

Hudspeth, Jack C., and Frances Hudspeth, *Handbook for Teachers of Elementary Science*, Austin, Texas, Steck Company, 1949.

Tannenbaum, Harold E., and Nathan Stillman, *Science Education for Elementary School Teachers*, Boston, Allyn and Bacon, 1960.

# 21

# AUDIO-VISUAL EXPERIENCES IN THE KINDERGARTEN

The kindergarten has used audio-visual methods in education at least as extensively as any other unit in the school system. The term *audio-visual* has not always been employed to describe these uses, but when one analyzes the kindergarten program, it becomes obvious that most of the activities engaged in by the five-year-olds afford opportunities for learning through a variety of sensory experiences. If, for example, the kindergarten group is discussing squirrels and the way they prepare for winter, the information is not limited to that supplied by spoken and written words. Rather, the children go outside to observe and to listen to the squirrels as they scurry about the yard gathering acorns or coming to take the peanuts which the children offer. The children observe as the squirrels eat their fill and then tuck the extras into their cheek pouches and scuttle off to bury them in the ground or store them in their holes in the trees. These firsthand experiences and observations are supplemented by posted pictures, book illustrations, dramatizations, art materials, story and song experiences and, whenever possible, projected still or motion pictures.

## Learning Through a Variety of Experiences

The whole history of early childhood education is filled with the efforts of educators to provide opportunities for learning through a variety of experiences rather than through verbal and visual symbols alone. As far back as the fourteen hundreds and early fifteen hundreds, Desiderius

Erasmus tried to combat verbalism in education by advocating that children become acquainted with familiar objects and animals. Erasmus not only discouraged mere word and memory learning, but suggested that such things as stories, pictures, games, and other informal materials of teaching be used in the education of young children. In the sixteen hundreds, John Comenius produced the first picture book for children. Called *Orbis Pictus*, this book compares in some respects quite favorably with some of our newer pictorial educational materials.[1] Each item in the pictures is numbered, and below each picture can be found both the English and the Latin names of the items depicted. Many of the statements Comenius made about education are as modern as their counterparts in our own education and child-development books. Comenius suggested, for instance, that children should have pictures before they go to school, for both their pleasure and their enlightenment; that they should have pictures in order that they might associate the name with the picture and the picture with the name. He suggested that models or actual samples of the things studied be in the school, and he made a plea for the children to have opportunities to express what they know through pictorial delineation.

Jean Jacques Rousseau, in the seventeen hundreds, criticized the sheer verbalism in the education of his day. He suggested that the child's most profitable learning came through firsthand experience, and he deplored the fact that so much emphasis was put on memorizing. Late in the seventeen and early in the eighteen hundreds, Johann Pestalozzi became interested in the "object method," the method of sense perception in teaching. He found untold opportunities for children to learn through actual experiences rather than simply through verbal symbols. He and others of his time made great fun of some of the parrot-like repetition of facts often called learning.

Friedrich Froebel in the eighteen hundreds stressed the importance of sensory experience in learning, and Madame Maria Montessori in the early nineteen hundreds went so far as to contend that a great part of early childhood education might well be a matter of training through sense perceptions. John Dewey and many of our own time have stressed the importance of building up learnings, and corroborating facts through a variety of media and experiences. Through the centuries, those who have best understood young children have pointed out the futility of trying to teach solely through the use of abstract symbols; they have stoutly contended that the most profitable learning comes through a variety of experiences.

[1] John Amos Comenius, *Orbis Pictus*, Nuremberg, 1657, English edition; C. W. Bardeen, ed., Syracuse, New York, C. W. Bardeen Publisher, 1887.

## Audio-Visual Education in Its Broadest Sense

We must guard against the error of thinking of audio-visual education as restricted to the materials and tools of the field. So much emphasis has been put on the modern tools and so many of the tools are so startlingly new to education that the error is understandable. Our scientific age has provided us with radios, recorders, slides, motion pictures, stereoscopes, and television. As educators we must familiarize ourselves with all these, but we must not overlook the many other experiences in our daily living which also provide opportunities for audio-visual education.

In its broader sense, audio-visual education includes many types of experience. Edgar Dale, in his *Audio-Visual Methods in Teaching,*[2] has set up what he calls the "cone of experience." Each of the divisions in his cone represents a stage between direct experience and pure abstraction. The cone, he suggests, "is merely a visual aid to explain the interrelationships of the various types of audio-visual materials . . . and shows that the sensory materials can be readily classified as they move from the most direct to the most abstract kind of learning." At the broad base of the cone we find that learning involves *doing,* and that direct experience, contrived experience, and dramatic participation form ascending levels of the base of the cone. In the middle section of the cone we find that the experiences are less direct, and that learning results from *observing* rather than doing. In rising levels, those experiences which provide opportunities for new learning include demonstrations, field trips, exhibits, motion pictures, radio programs, recordings, and still pictures. At the tip of the cone we find that the experiences are increasingly abstract in their nature and that new learning results from the *interpretation of visual and verbal symbols.* Many of the experiences may overlap and blend into each other, but roughly the "cone of experience" can be conveniently subdivided into experiences involving (a) doing, (b) observing, and (c) symbolizing.

## Kindergarten Experiences Which Provide Opportunities for Audio-Visual Education

There are, of course, hundreds of kindergarten experiences which provide opportunities for audio-visual education. But for the purpose of clarifying our own thinking, let's consider just a few of those experiences which might fit into the categories mentioned above. Because the concrete and

[2] See selected references at end of chapter.

direct experiences are at the broad base of the cone, it may have been assumed that these experiences are first and always the most desirable. At the outset, suppose we look into this assumption.

Concrete and direct experiences are valuable. We do need many firsthand experiences, and yet it is conceivable that in some instances the firsthand experience would be relatively meaningless if it were not broken down or supplemented by other experiences. Suppose the question arose as to how a locomotive can make a "whistle sound." It is probable that, even if the children were taken to a locomotive and permitted to operate or observe the operation of the whistle control, they would learn very little about how the "whistle" sound is produced. They could probably learn much more about how a whistle sound is produced if an adult were to help them see and hear what happens (a) when air is forced through a small opening, as through a small bottle or the lips; or (b) when steam forces its way through a small opening, as in the whistling teakettle. In this instance, is it not quite obvious that the observation of the demonstration would offer a better learning opportunity than the direct experience?

Again, it is quite possible that a firsthand experience might be relatively meaningless if it were not supplemented by a variety of other experiences. For example, a group of children might have the opportunity to go to a fire station to see exactly how every piece of equipment worked, and yet if the group did not have their firsthand experiences supplemented, organized, and summarized through other experiences, such as discussions, dramatizations, picture-story materials, and still and moving pictures, their learning might be incomplete. As we note the following sampling of experiences, we must remember not only that in specific instances one kind of experience may provide a better learning situation than another, but also that in general those experiences which supplement each other tend to strengthen the learning.

## SPECIFIC KINDERGARTEN EXPERIENCES INVOLVING DOING

### Direct Experiences

Planting a garden
Making a collection of seeds
Making place mats for a party
Setting tables for luncheon
Caring for pets or sharing housekeeping responsibilities
Making furniture for the play corner
Making Christmas gifts

### Contrived Experiences

Setting up a store in the kindergarten
Experimenting with models of trains, derricks, elevators, and the like

Making a fire engine, train, bus, or launching pad
Making models of harbor or street traffic
Building with blocks a city, farm, county fair, station, or airport

### Dramatic Participation

Playing house in the doll corner
Playing traffic officer, pilot, fireman, deliveryman, storekeeper
Staging a play radio performance
Dramatizing stories from books, or making up and dramatizing a story
Playing teacher, doctor, nurse, and so on

## SPECIFIC KINDERGARTEN EXPERIENCES INVOLVING OBSERVING

### Demonstrations

Observing a demonstration of how the fire extinguisher works
Watching and listening as a guest musician plays his instrument
Watching a guest artist as he models in clay, sketches, or paints
Observing as the teacher cuts open a cocoon from which the moth has already emerged
Observing how a certain child has made a particular article
Watching the rhythmic demonstrations or gymnastic stunts of others

### Field Trips

Going out into the neighborhood to see how a steam shovel works
Going outside to observe the signs of seasonal change
Making a trip to the greenhouse to get rainwater for the fish
Going to a museum
Going to an aviary or a zoo
Exploring the building, health unit, principal's office, custodian's quarters

### Exhibits

Having in the room a special museum case and changing exhibit materials, such as birds, animals, insects
Having a place for collections of such things as birds' nests, cocoons, seeds, leaves, and stones
Going to other rooms to see special exhibits—Easter eggs, dolls and toys of different lands, and so on
Having models of different modes of transportation on display
Having samples of processes on display, such as cotton in the boll, ginned cotton, baled cotton, cotton twisted into thread and woven into cloth

### Motion Pictures

Watching movies of the children's own school experiences
Watching movies of the school experiences of other children
Watching movies which portray action in stories or songs
Watching pictures showing the wonders of nature, of bird and animal life in particular

*"The bat is stretching his wings—look, he's too big for this jar!"*

Following, through a movie, an extensive process, such as making a house, running a farm, taking a train, boat, or plane journey

Radio and Television

Tuning in on educational and other programs presenting stories, dramatization, travelogues, science reports and demonstrations, music and art experiences

Recordings

Listening to both old and new stories
Listening to the recordings which sometimes accompany slides or filmstrips
Listening to dramatizations
Listening to music
Listening to recordings which may have come over the radio when the children were not in school

Still Pictures

Looking at illustrated text or story books
Looking at posted pictures, photographs, paintings, or drawings
Looking at pictures through the stereoscope
Looking at projected opaque pictures
Looking at film slides or filmstrips

## SPECIFIC KINDERGARTEN EXPERIENCES INVOLVING SYMBOLIZING

Visual Symbols

Making and following with the teacher a large chart of the garden planting
Referring to room charts which give the location of individual lockers, beds, table arrangements, and so on

Picking out specific buildings or streets on pictorial maps
Following on the map or globe a journey being made by one of the group
Outlining on paper or the blackboard the imaginary boundaries of the play yard
"Reading" (enumerating, describing, and interpreting) pictures, cartoons, and comic strips
Identifying locker tags, page numbers, familiar words or phrases in a picture storybook

Verbal Symbols

Reporting an experience to the group—a great step beyond showing and telling
Grasping meanings of new words through context or supplementary material
Grasping meanings of new words through the teacher's seemingly casual use of synonyms
Playing games in which words must bear meanings before right action can be produced—for example, "True-False": "Clap once if the statement you hear is false. Raise your hand if it is true."
Playing games such as "Do as I say but not as I do," in which words and not actions must be followed
Following directions in which of all the words spoken a single word or phrase is the key—for example, "This is to be a turn for anyone who belongs to this kindergarten, who is sitting on the floor, who worked with clay today, who lives at 3416 Smith Avenue."

As we follow the kindergarten experiences all the way from the base of the cone up to the tip, it is obvious that words are constantly acquiring content and, in so doing, crystallizing experiences. As words become meaningful, we are relieved of dependence on objects and things. When we can manipulate ideas with words, we have achieved a certain degree of freedom. The broader and more universal our experiences, the more readily we will be able to use words as a medium for conveying ideas accurately.

One of the greatest difficulties with words, however, is that they sometimes come to symbolize or stand for different experiences for different people. Once while driving in London, I was doing what seemed to me very well considering the "keep-to-the-left traffic" and all the "circuses" I had to contend with. But as I prepared to make a particular turn, a man stepped up, tipped his hat, and said, "That's a dumb turn you're making, madam." It made me furious to have him comment so scathingly on my driving. It wasn't until I had proceeded halfway up the block and found a sign saying "Dumb Turn" that I appreciated his courtesy, for "Dumb Turn" in England is synonymous with "Dead End Street" in America.

It should be a purpose of the teacher to help children add not only new words but also new meanings to their words. One of our chief responsibilities is providing a variety of experiences for all children so that words can truly communicate. Audio-visual education provides this resource. In the days and years to come, if the new tools and materials are used widely, audio-visual education will do much to bring to many people common understandings.

## Some of the Newer Tools of Audio-Visual Education

### THE STEREOSCOPE

The stereoscope, though it was sometimes found in our grandmothers' or great-grandmothers' parlors, is today an instrument which can be classed among the newer visual education tools. The modern stereoscope is made in several sizes; the one best adapted to the use of kindergarten children is a plastic instrument only slightly larger than a pair of binoculars. It can be purchased at either department stores or camera shops, and it costs only $1.50 to $2.50. A disc or reel containing seven pairs of stereoptic Kodachrome pictures may be slipped easily into the instrument and then, when the viewer simply clicks a tiny lever and holds the instruments up to his eyes, the pictures appear in full color and in three dimensions. There are over 150 film discs available, with subject matter ranging from the "Story of the Three Bears" to Colonial Williamsburg and the Marine Studios. The reels themselves are not expensive. They can be purchased for as little as 3 for $1.25. The instrument is light in weight and can be easily handled by kindergarten children. There is also available a projector —The Junior Projector—for these stereoptic Kodachrome pictures. This, of course, means that children can now enjoy viewing the pictures together. Some phonograph records have accompanying stereoptic reels with which the projector can be used effectively.

### THE OPAQUE PROJECTOR

The opaque projector is a machine which permits a picture from a book, a postcard, or any flat picture not larger than 6 in. x 6 in. to be flashed on the screen in its original color. It is sometimes also called a Delineascope, a Baloptican, or a Reflectoscope. The opaque projector is excellent for use in connection with either science or storytelling experiences. Sometimes illustrations from old books can be salvaged for use. The machine is bulky, however, and not easily transported; in most cases the children would go to the room where the machine is set up to view the pictures.

### FILMSTRIP PROJECTOR[3]

The filmstrip projector is used for projecting 35 mm. films. The pictures shown on the screen are still. In many ways this is an advantage, for it facilitates detailed observation and discussion. The film rolls cost from $2.00 to $6.00

[3] See reference, p. 119.

apiece, and each roll contains from fifteen to fifty pictures. The films come in black and white and in color. Sometimes the filmstrip machine can be adapted for showing the small 2 in. x 2 in. slides which are available also in black and white and in color. It is becoming more and more common for children to have at home photographic slides which they like to share with the school if a machine is available for their projection. The machine itself is light in weight and is easily transported and operated. The range of subject matter depicted in still films and small film slides is already great, and many new strips and slides are being placed on the market.

## THE SLIDE PROJECTOR[4]

The slide projector, a modern form of the old magic lantern, is frequently found in classrooms. Both photographic and handmade slides can be used with the machine. The slides are transparent and are usually 3½ in. x 4 in. in size, though the 2 in. x 2 in. slides mentioned above are becoming very popular. Handmade slides can be made by placing glass or cellophane over the picture to be copied, tracing the outline, and coloring the picture with transparent colors. For materials to be used in making slides, see the Keystone catalogue listed under sources of audio-visual materials at the end of this chapter. Professionally made slides may be purchased for from \$.55 to \$1.35 per slide.

## MOTION-PICTURE PROJECTORS

The motion-picture projector is seldom the property of a kindergarten. The machine is usually owned either by the school or by the school system. Motion pictures provide wonderful educational opportunities for older children, but so far as kindergarten children are concerned, they are often confusing. The action, in most cases, moves so quickly before the eyes and so much takes place in a short period of time that the five-year-old often gets a very distorted idea of what is really happening in the film. If the five-year-olds as a group are to see moving pictures, it is well to limit the experience to very brief showings which can be run through more than a single time. It is not a really valuable experience for five-year-olds to go to a general school assembly for the viewing of a forty-five to ninety-minute film. There are, of course, some movie films which supply in a simple and direct way desirable information and interesting entertainment for five-year-olds; but most of the materials could better be presented to the kindergarten children through still films. Movie films cost from \$50 to \$60 or can be rented for approximately \$3.50 per day.

## STILL FILMS WITH RECORDINGS

There are some still films, slide films, and filmstrips which are accompanied by their own recordings. The recordings can be played on the phonograph while the pictures are flashed on the screen. The combined experience seems very

[4] See reference, p. 119.

satisfying to five-year-olds. The recordings, however, are expensive (approximately $6.00 per volume), and in many cases a story read or told by the teacher can be quite as satisfying an experience, though sometimes the musical accompaniment on the record adds much which cannot be supplied by spoken words.

## RECORDINGS

Almost daily, new material is coming to us on records. Many of the newer records for young children are being made of an unbreakable substance. There are some excellent recordings of songs, stories, and dramatizations, as well as some fine new orchestral performances for young children. For specific references, see the listing of records at the end of Chapters 14, 15, and 16.

## RADIO PROGRAMS

There is still not a great deal on the radio that is adapted to the group listening of five-year-olds. Some of the "school-of-the-air" stories and dramatizations and some of the newer musical recordings and the art and science presentations are excellent, but even many of these are better reserved for older children.

## TELEVISION PROGRAMS

Television, which has been generally thought of as a news and entertainment medium, is fast developing educational value. All over the country, television not only is finding its way into homes as an educational medium but is being used by universities, colleges, and schools as a teaching aid. So far, most of the educational experiments involving the use of television as a mass teaching medium have been directed to children older than those in nursery school, kindergarten, and primary groups. Yet television experiences can be profitable for young children. In fact, some commercial stations in the United States and Canada have proved that television experiences can be directed effectively to preschool children. This does not imply that television can ever take the place of group living or firsthand experiences, but it does suggest that it can do some things as well as or even better than firsthand experiences. Perhaps this means that we need expert teachers who will be willing to turn their thoughts and attention to the new field.

Let's briefly consider one or two situations in which the viewing of an experience on television may be more meaningful to a young child than actually being at the scene of the action. Suppose, for example, that a group of young children were to have the opportunity of seeing the shearing of a sheep. It is probable that the position of the children would be such that some would have little chance to see well or, if turns were to be taken in having a good viewing position, each child could see only portions of the process. Now if this same process were to be televised and projected onto a large screen, each child could not only see the whole process equally well but could hear equally well what the television teacher was saying.

Suppose a group of kindergarten children were to take a walk through the woods. The mere presence of the children would detract from the peace and quiet, and further, only children nearest an adult could have their attention directed to those things the teacher would hope to have the group observe. Of course, no television experience can give the feel of the earth under foot, the smell of the air, or the joy of finding, firsthand, the many surprises the woodlands offer. But, sitting quietly before a television screen, the children can view what has taken the cameraman hours, days, and perhaps even months to catch and record. Through both words and pictures, the attention of the children can be directed to high points in the experience.

Perhaps educational television will do for young children what it seems to be doing for adults in the way of making them seek further information or firsthand experiences related to their television viewing. As an outgrowth of interests fostered by television, family groups may make more excursions and thus provide many of those direct experiences for their young children which the school has tried, rather ineffectively, to offer.

There is still another factor in considering the possible values of educational television for young children. Many of the interests of young children are seasonal, and few school systems could hope to provide enough in the way of visual-aid materials to meet the needs of each group at the time such interests as Halloween, Christmas, seeds, birds, or spring gardening are at their peak. Educational television could bring to every group a viewing and listening experience that would be timely.

Tuning in a television set is a simple enough operation; however, as with radio programs, there is the problem of timing activities to meet the broadcasting schedule. We will always have the problem of the "repeat performance," however. Young children do enjoy hearing and seeing again what they have once enjoyed.

## The Mechanics of Handling Audio-Visual Materials

In our American schools we look to our public libraries as distributors of much supplementary educational material. From some of the libraries in our larger cities, we can obtain not only books but also exhibit materials, films, and records. As the field of audio-visual education has broadened, the schools themselves have come to recognize the need of having within their own organizations a system for handling the many new materials now considered essential to modern education. Every school and every schoolroom should have some equipment and material of its own, but to have on hand all the materials that might conceivably be used in any one year would be a waste of both money and space. Many school systems now have a teacher or committee that functions as the coordinator of audio-visual materials. Through this teacher or committee, materials are distributed and kept in repair. The individual teacher can make her request for loan materials directly to them. Functioning much as our public libraries now function, they will be able either to provide the materials or to tell her when the materials will be available. Sometimes the teacher can make a tentative list of materials she feels she may need during the semester or year; this list, however, ought not to be final. In many instances, experiences will arise throughout the year which will make certain materials more profitable to use than others. The teacher should have the privilege of canceling her orders or requesting additional materials as the year progresses.

## Story Filmstrips for Children[5]

Andy and the Lion,* 42 fr-si-color, Weston Woods, 1959
Angus and the Ducks, 35 fr-si-color, Weston Woods, 1962
The Big Snow,* 50 fr-si-color, Weston Woods, 1961
The Biggest Bear,* 47 fr-si-color, Weston Woods, 1959
Biggest Frog in the World, 27 fr-si-color, Curriculum Films, 1951
Blueberries for Sal, 47 fr-si-color, Weston Woods, 1963
Bob's Goldfish, 27 fr-si-color, Curriculum Films, 1951
Bobby the Squirrel, 42 fr-sd-color-disc 33⅓ rpm-7′, Dukane Corporation, 1955
Boy and His Goat, 35 fr-si-color, Young America Films, 1947
The Camel Who Took a Walk,* 42 fr-si-color, Weston Woods, 1959
Caps for Sale,* 34 fr-si-color, Weston Woods, 1960
Chanticler and the Fox*, 44 fr-si-color, Weston Woods, 1961
Christmas in Piney Woods, 34 fr-si-color, Church Screen Productions, 1953
Christmas—Little Shepherd's Gift, 28 fr-si-color, Society for Visual Education, 1951
Christmas—When the Littlest Camel Knelt, 45 fr-sd-color, disc 78 rpm-20′ Society for Visual Education, 1947
The Circus Baby,* 36 fr-si-color, Weston Woods, 1959
Crow Boy, 53 fr-si-color, Weston Woods, 1963
Curious George Rides a Bike,* 58 fr-si-color, Weston Woods, 1960
Don't Count Your Chicks, 38 fr-si-color, Weston Woods, 1963
Finders Keepers,* 37 fr-si-color, Weston Woods, 1961
Five Chinese Brothers,* 56 fr-si-color, Weston Woods, 1960
Flicka, Ricka, Dicka, and Their New Friend, 26 fr-si-color, Popular Science, 1949
Four Musicians, 51 fr-si-color, Young America Films, 1947
Frog Went A-Courtin,* 31 fr-si-color, Weston Woods, 1961
Fun on a Picnic, 26 fr-si-color, photograph, Curriculum Films, 1951
Georgie,* 40 fr-si-color, Weston Woods, 1957
Harold and the Purple Crayon, 64 fr-si-color, Weston Woods, 1963
Hercules,* 52 fr-si-color, Weston Woods, 1957
In the Forest,* 39 fr-si-color, Weston Woods, 1960
Jenny's Birthday Book, 33 fr-si-color, Weston Woods, 1960

[5] Recordings are available for starred filmstrips. Abbreviations: fr = frames; si = silent; sd = sound; b-w = black and white; ′ = minutes.

Kathy's Cat Has Kittens, 40 fr-si-color, photographs, McGraw-Hill Text Film Dept., 1956
Kitten, The, 38 fr-si-color, Young America Films, 1956
Kittens, 38 fr-si-color, Young America Films, 1956
Lentil,* 41 fr-si-color, Weston Woods, 1959
Little Black Sambo, 30 fr-si-color, Stillfilm, 1948
Little Island,* 36 fr-si-color, Weston Woods, 1961
Little Red Lighthouse, The,* 41 fr-si-color, Weston Woods, 1959
Little Lost Angel, 53 fr-si-color, Society for Visual Education, 1954
Little Pine Tree, 35 fr-si-color, Society for Visual Education, 1955
Little Toot,* 52 fr-si-color, Weston Woods, 1959
Madeline's Rescue,* 50 fr-si-color, Weston Woods, 1961
Magic Michael,* 40 fr-si-color, Weston Woods, 1960
Make Way for Ducklings,* 47 fr-si-color, Weston Woods, 1957
Mike Mulligan and His Steam Shovel,* 59 fr-si-color, Weston Woods, 1957
Millions of Cats,* 44 fr-si-color, Weston Woods, 1957
Old Woman and Her Pig, 51 fr-si-color, Weston Woods, 1962
Pancho,* 48 fr-si-color, Weston Woods, 1960
Petunia, 50 fr-si-color, Weston Woods, 1963
Play With Me, 50 fr-si-color-35′, Weston Woods, 1963
Rabbit Who Wanted Red Wings, 28 fr-si-color, Curriculum Films, 1947
Red Carpet, The,* 56 fr-si-color, Weston Woods, 1957
Seven Sneezes, 28 fr-si-color, Young America Films, 1951
Shoemaker and the Elves, 26 fr-si-color, Jam Handy Organization, 1954
Snipp, Snapp, Snurr, and the Big Farm, 21 fr-si-color, Popular Science, 1949
Snipp, Snapp, Snurr, and the Red Shoes, 21 fr-si-color, Popular Science, 1949.
Stone Soup,* 46 fr-si-color, Weston Woods, 1957
The Story About Ping,* 45 fr-si-color, Weston Woods, 1957
Tale of Peter Rabbit, The, 33 fr-si-color, Weston Woods, 1962
Thanksgiving—The Story of Thanksgiving, 33 fr-si-color, Society for Visual Education, 1948
Three Bears, 45 fr-si-color, Young America Films, 1947
Three Billy Goats Gruff, 32 fr-si-color, Jam Handy Organization, 1955
Three Billy Goats Gruff, The, 28 fr-si-color, Weston Woods, 1963
Three Little Pigs, 51 fr-si-color, Young America Films, 1947
Time of Wonder,* 55 fr-si-color, Weston Woods, 1961
A Tree Is Nice,* 27 fr-si-color, Weston Woods, 1961
White Snow Bright Snow,* 35 fr-si-color, Weston Woods, 1960.

## Story Films[6]

Adventures of Two Little Goats, sd-b-w-11′, Coronet, 1956
Adventures of Willie Skunk, sd-b-w-11′, McGraw-Hill, 1951

[6] The Weston Woods films are all iconographic motion pictures—that is, they are produced by filming the original book illustrations.

Andy and the Lion, sd-color-10′, Weston Woods, 1955
Apryl and Her Lamb, sd-color-7′, Atlantis Productions, 1955
Big Snow, The, sd, Weston Woods, 1961
Camel That Took a Walk, The, sd-color-10′ Weston Woods, 1957
Caps for Sale, sd-color-5′, Weston Woods, 1960
Circus Baby, The, sd-color-5′, Weston Woods, 1959
Curious George Rides a Bike, sd-color-10′, Weston Woods, 1958
Easter Surprise, sd-color-6′, Encyclopædia Britannica, 1953
Five Chinese Brothers, sd-color-10′, Weston Woods, 1958
Georgie, sd-b-w-6′, Weston Woods, 1956
Hercules, sd-color-11′, Weston Woods, 1955
I Wanted Red Wings (Puppet Story), sd-b-w-11′, Gateway, 1940
In the Forest, sd-b-w-6′, Weston Woods, 1960
Jenny's Birthday, sd-color-6′, Weston Woods, 1956
Lentil, sd-color-10′, Weston Woods, 1957
Little Red Lighthouse, sd-color-9′, Weston Woods, 1956
Magic Michael, sd-color-11′, Weston Woods, 1960
Make Way for Ducklings, sd-color-11′, Weston Woods, 1955
Mike Mulligan and His Steam Shovel, sd-color-11′, Weston Woods, 1956
Millions of Cats, sd-b-w-10′, Weston Woods, 1955
Mr. Hare and Mr. Hedgehog, sd-color-11′, Portefilms, 1959
Pancho, si-color-10′, Weston Woods, 1960
Raindrop Splash, sd-b-w-15′, Weston Woods, 1955
Red Carpet, sd-color-9′, Weston Woods, 1955
Rumpelstiltskins (Marionettes), sd-b-w-15′, Sterling, 1951
Spirit of Christmas, The (Marionettes), sd-color-20′, Association Films, 1953
The Snowy Day, sd-color-6′, Weston Woods, 1965
Stone Soup, sd-color-11′, Weston Woods, 1957
Story About Ping, The, sd-color-10′, Weston Woods, 1955
Talking Valentine, A, sd-color-5′, Weston Woods, 1953
This Is New York, sd-color-12′, Weston Woods, 1962
Time of Wonder, sd-color-13′, Weston Woods, 1961
Whistle for Willie, sd-color-6′, Weston Woods, 1965

## Science and Social Studies Filmstrips for Young Children

Airplane Trip, 17 fr-si-color, Jam Handy Organization, 1956
Airplanes at Work, 27 fr-si-color, photographs, Curriculum Films, 1951
All Kinds of Houses, 32 fr-color, Encyclopædia Britannica Films, 1960
All Kinds of Weather, 48 fr-color, Eye Gate House, 1951
Animal Babies, 30 fr-si-color, Children's Press Films, 1959
Animals in Four Seasons, 25 fr-si-color, Eye Gate House, 1951
Animals of the Forest, 37 fr-si-color captions, Encyclopædia Britannica Films, 1961
Animals of the Pond, 24 fr-si-color, Curriculum Films, 1949
Animals of the Shore, 30 fr-si-color, Children's Press Films, 1959

Animals of the Zoo, 31 fr-si-color, Society for Visual Education, 1951
Ann Visits the Zoo, 26 fr-si-color, Curriculum Films, 1949
Backward Insects, 31 fr-si-color, photographs, Society for Visual Education, 1951
Baker, The, 34 fr-si-color, photographs, Long Filmslide Service, 1956
Beach Birds, 30 fr-si-color, Stillfilm, 1948
Bird and Animal Babies, 32 fr-si-color, Society for Visual Education, 1951
Birds at Their Nests, 26 fr-si-b-w, Society for Visual Education, 1947
Birds Grow, 26 fr-si-color, Jam Handy Organization, 1953
Birds of Our Community, 29 fr-si-color, photographs, Society for Visual Education, 1951
Birds of the City, 42 fr-si-color, National Film Board of Canada, 1960
Birds We Know, 30 fr-si-color, Children's Press Films, 1959
Building a House, 30 fr-si-color, Curriculum Films, 1951
Busdriver, The, 41 fr-si-color, Young America Films, 1954
Buses at Work, 27 fr-si-color, photographs, Curriculum Films, 1951
Butterflies and Moths, 42 fr-si-b-w, Society for Visual Education, 1947
Butterflies Grow, 24 fr-si-color, Jam Handy Organization, 1953
Buying a Pet, 11 fr-si-color, Jam Handy Organization, 1954
Carol's Apartment House, 25 fr-si-color, Curriculum Films, 1951
Children's Zoo, The, 27 fr-si-color, Curriculum Materials, 1958
Common Animals of the Woods, 52 fr-si-color, Encyclopædia Britannica Films, 1947
Day at the Light House, A, 26 fr-si-color, Curriculum Films, 1949
Doctor, The, 34 fr-si-color, photographs, Long Filmslide Service, 1956
Doctor, The, 39 fr-si-color, Young America Films, 1954
Elephants, 52 fr-si-color, Encyclopædia Britannica Films, 1947
Family Fun, 45 fr-si-color, photographs, Encyclopædia Britannica Films, 1953
Family Shopping Trip, 52 fr-si-color, Society for Visual Education, 1956
Farm Animals and Pets, 30 fr-si-color, photographs, Society for Visual Education, 1951
Feeding of the Animals, 45 fr-si-color, Encyclopædia Britannica Films, 1953
Fire House, 26 fr-si-b-w, Curriculum Films, 1951
Fireman, The, 41 fr-si-color, Young America Films, 1954
Freight Trains at Work, 27 fr-si-color, photographs, Curriculum Films, 1951
Gathering Eggs, 45 fr-si-color, Encyclopædia Britannica Films, 1953
Goat Farm, 30 fr-si-color, Curriculum Films, 1951
Going Down Town, 29 fr-si-color captions, Encyclopædia Britannica Films, 1960
Going Shopping, 29 fr-si-color captions, Encyclopædia Britannica Films, 1960
Going to the Country, 29 fr-si-color captions, Encyclopædia Britannica Films, 1960
Going to the Zoo, 29 fr-si-color captions, Encyclopædia Britannica Films, 1960
Gray Squirrel, 52 fr-si-color, Encyclopædia Britannica Films, 1947
Grocer, The, 34 fr-si-color, Long Filmslide Service, 1956
Grocer, The, 41 fr-si-color, Young America Films, 1954
Growing Up, 45 fr-si-color, photographs, Encyclopædia Britannica Films, 1953

Harbor Boats at Work, 27 fr-si-color, photographs, Curriculum Films, 1951
Haying, 45 fr-si-color, Encyclopædia Britannica Films, 1953
Helping Mother, 45 fr-si-color, photographs, Encyclopædia Britannica Films, 1953
Homes of Birds, 37 fr-si-color, Society for Visual Education, 1951
Honey Bees, 30 fr-si-b-w, Stillfilm, 1948
Horse, The, 52 fr-si-color, Encyclopædia Britannica Films, 1947
In Autumn, 30 fr-si-color, Young America Films, 1953
In Spring, 30 fr-si-color, Young America Films, 1953
In Summer, 30 fr-si-color, Young America Films, 1953
In Winter, 30 fr-si-color, Young America Films, 1953
Janet's Ducks and Geese, 26 fr-si-color, photographs, Curriculum Films, 1951
Janet Helps Mother, 25 fr-si-color, photographs, Curriculum Films, 1951
Janet Visits a Dairy Farm, 28 fr-si-color, photographs, Curriculum Films, 1951
Keeping Busy, 45 fr-si-color, photographs, Encyclopædia Britannica Films, 1953
Large Animals of the Zoo, 39 fr-si-color, Encyclopædia Britannica Films, 1962
Learning About Kinds of Workers, 35 fr-color, Audio Education.
Let's Go to the Zoo, 12 fr-si-color, Jam Handy Organization, 1954
Let's Visit an Ocean Liner, 37 fr-si-b-w, Popular Science, 1948
Let's Visit Some Animals of the Woods (2 parts)
    Story of the Golden Fawn, 34 fr-si-color, Creative Arts Studio, 1955
    Golden Fawn and New Acquaintances, 35 fr-si-color, Creative Arts Studio, 1955
Librarian, The, 31 fr-si-color, Long Filmslide Service, 1956
Loose Tooth, 9 fr-si-color, Jam Handy Organization, 1954
Low Tide at the Beach, 27 fr-si-color, Curriculum Films, 1951
Magnets, 46 fr-si-b-w, Young America Films, 1947
Mailman, The, 41 fr-si-color, Young America Films, 1954
Making Gingerbread Boys with Janet and Peggy, 25 fr-si-color, Curriculum Films, 1955
Making Maple Syrup, 27 fr-si-color, Curriculum Films, 1951
Making Maple Syrup, 68 fr-si-color, Photo Lab, 1955
Mother Duck and Her Family, 14 fr-color, Encyclopædia Britannica Films, 1961
Mother Grey Squirrel, 14 fr-color, Encyclopædia Britannica Films, 1961
Mother Rabbit and Her Family, 14 fr-color, Encyclopædia Britannica Films, 1961
Mr. and Mrs. Robin's Springtime Family, 31 fr-color, Society for Visual Education, 1960
Nature in Four Seasons, 25 fr-si-color, Eye Gate House, 1951
Our Family, 45 fr-si-color, photographs, Encyclopædia Britannica Films, 1953
Our Neighborhood Store, 25-30 fr-si-color, photographs, Eye Gate House, 1954
Parakeet, 38 fr-si-color, photographs, Young America Films, 1956
Passenger Trains at Work, 27 fr-si-color, photographs, Curriculum Films, 1951
Picking Fruit, 45 fr-si-color, Encyclopædia Brittanica Films, 1953

Picking Vegetables, 45 fr-si-color, Encyclopædia Films, 1953
Plants and Animals in Spring, 35 fr-si-color, photographs, Society for Visual Education, 1951
Plants Grow, 25 fr-si-color, Jam Handy Organization, 1953
Plants We Know, 30 fr-si-color, Children's Press Films, 1959
Policeman, The, 39 fr-si-color, Young America Films, 1954
Policeman at Work, 28 fr-si-b-w, Curriculum Films, 1948
Postman, The, 30 fr-color, Long Filmslide Service, 1956
Postman, The, 32 fr-si-color, Society for Visual Education, 1948
Puppy Plays a Trick, 9 fr-si-color, Jam Handy Organization, 1954
Rabbits, 36 fr-si-color, photographs, Young America Films, 1956
Rabbits Grow, 24 fr-si-color, Jam Handy Organization, 1953
Reptiles, 27 fr-si-color, Curriculum Films, 1950
Rocks We Know, 30 fr-si-color, Children's Press Films, 1959
Share the Ball, 21 fr-si-b-w, Society for Visual Education, 1934
Share the Sand, 24 fr-si-b-w, Society for Visual Education, 1954
Shep, the Farm Dog, 52 fr-si-color, Encyclopædia Britannica Films, 1947
Spiders and Their Work, 29 fr-si-b-w, Society for Visual Education, 1947
Spring Is Here, 27 fr-si-color, photographs, Society for Visual Education, 1954
Squirrel's Picnic, 10 fr-si-color, Jam Handy Organization, 1954
Summer on the Farm, 35 fr-si-color, photographs, Society for Visual Education, 1951
Surprise for Daddy, 12 fr-si-color, Jam Handy Organization, 1954
Susan and Peter Go to Market, 34 fr-si-color, Society for Visual Education, 1948
Toads Grow, 25 fr-si-color, Jam Handy Organization, 1953
Trailers at Work, 27 fr-si-color, photographs, Curriculum Films, 1951
Trees Grow, 24 fr-si-color, Jam Handy Organization, 1953
Trees in Four Seasons, 25 fr-si-color, Eye Gate House, 1951
Trip to the Autumn Woods, 35 fr-si-color, Society for Visual Education, 1951
Trip to the Beach, 36 fr-si-color, photographs, Young America Films, 1956
Trip to the Fair, 42 fr-si-color, photographs, Young America Films, 1956
Trip to the Museum, 41 fr-si-color, photographs, Young America Films, 1956
Trip to the Zoo, 43 fr-si-color, photographs, Young America Films, 1956
Trucks at Work, 27 fr-si-color, photographs, Curriculum Films, 1951
Turtle, The, 37 fr-si-color, photographs, Young America Films, 1956
Turtles, The, 29 fr-si-color, Curriculum Films 1951
Vegetables, 25 fr-si-color, Curriculum Films, 1951
Vegetables for the City, 24 fr-si-color, Curriculum Films, 1951
Visiting Grandma, 24 fr-si-color, Curriculum Films, 1951
Walk in the Woods, 24 fr-si-color, Curriculum Films, 1952
We Grow, 25 fr-si-color, Jam Handy Organization, 1953
We Make Stick Puppets, 49 fr-si-color, Encyclopædia Britannica Films, 1954
We Work with Clay, 49 fr-si-color, Encyclopædia Britannica Films, 1954
We Work with Designs and Pictures, 49 fr-si-color, Encyclopædia Britannica Films, 1954

We Work with Paper and Scissors, 49 fr-si-color, Encyclopædia Britannica Films, 1954
What Are Satellites? 28 fr-si-captions and text in color, Jam Handy Organization, 1961
What Are Space Stations For? 28 fr-si-captions and text in color, Jam Handy Organization, 1961
What Is in Space? 31 fr-si-captions and text in color, Jam Handy Organization, 1961
Why Do We Have Day and Night? 30 fr-si-color, drawings, Filmstrip House, 1956
Why Do We Have Rain? 30 fr-si-color, drawings, Filmstrip House, 1956
Why Do We Have Warm and Cold Days? 30 fr-si-color, drawings, Filmstrip House, 1956
Why Do We Have Wind? 30 fr-si-color, drawings, Filmstrip House, 1956
Wild Flowers Everyone Should Know, 39 fr-si-color, photographs, Society for Visual Education, 1951
Winter in the Country, 32 fr-si-color, photographs, Society for Visual Education, 1951
Woodland Friends, 27 fr-si-color captions, Encyclopædia Britannica Films, 1960
Woods in Autumn, 25 fr-si-color, Eye Gate House, 1951
Woods in Spring, 26 fr-si-color, Eye Gate House, 1951
Woods in Summer, 26 fr-si-color, Eye Gate House, 1951
Workers in Four Seasons, 25 fr-si-color, Eye Gate House, 1951

## Science and Social Studies Films for Young Children

Air Around Us, sd-color-35′, Children's Press, 1959
Airplane Trip, sd-color-11′, United Airlines, 1954 (free loan)
Airplane Trip by Jet, sd-color-11′, Encyclopædia Britannica, 1961
Airport in the Jet Age, sd-color-11′, Encyclopædia Britannica, 1962
Animal Friends, sd-color-11′, Coronet, 1956
Animal Homes, sd-color-11′, Churchill and Wexler, 1954
Animal Tracks and Signs, sd-color-11′, Encyclopædia Britannica, 1962
Animals and Their Food, sd-color-11′, Coronet, 1955
Animals and Their Homes, sd-color-10′, Coronet, 1955
Animals and Their Homes, sd-b-w-11′, McGraw-Hill, 1958
Animals in Winter, sd-b-w-11′, Encyclopædia Britannica, 1950
Assembling a Freight Train, sd-color-10′, Santa Fe Railroad, 1955 (free loan)
Big Wide Highway, The, sd-color-10′, Coronet, 1955
Billy's Helicopter Ride, sd-color-11′, Coronet, 1962
Birds in Winter, sd-color-11′, Encyclopædia Britannica, 1958
Birds of Our Story Books, sd-color-12½′, Coronet, 1952
Birds of the Dooryard, sd-color-12½′, Coronet, 1954
Boy of the Circus, sd-color-14′, Coronet, 1956

Boy of the Navajos, A (present day), sd-color-11′, Coronet, 1956
Building a House, sd-b-w-10′, Encyclopædia Britannica, 1947
Busy Airport, The, sd-color-11′, Coronet, 1963
Busy Day at the County Fair, A, sd-color-11′, Coronet, 1963
Busy Harbor, The, sd-color-11′, Coronet, 1960
Christmas for the Birds, sd-color-16′, Wilmar Films, 1955
Christmas Gift, sd-color-6′, Wilmar Films, 1953
Circus Animals, sd-color-10′ Academy Films, 1947
Circus Baby, The, sd-color-5′, Weston Woods, 1956
Circus Day in Our Town, sd-color-15′, Encyclopædia Britannica Films, 1949
Circus People, sd-color-10′, Academy Films, 1947
Circus Wakes Up, sd-color-10′, Sterling Films, 1949
City Bus Driver, sd-color-11′, Encyclopædia Britannica, 1962
City Fire Fighters, sd-color-11′, Coronet, 1947
Clown, The, sd-color-30′, released by National Education Television Film Service, 1956
Electricity for Beginners, sd-color-11′, Coronet, 1963
Farm Babies and Their Mothers, sd-b-w-10′, Film Associates, 1954
Farmyard Babies, sd-color-11′, Coronet, 1952
Fathers Go Away to Work, sd-color-11′, Pat Dowling Pictures, 1959
Firehouse, sd-color-11′, Coronet, 1956
Foodstore, sd-b-w-11′, Encyclopædia Britannica, 1945
Frank and His Dog, sd-color-5′, Encyclopædia Britannica, 1952
Freight Yard, sd-b-w-20′, New York Central Line, 1947 (free loan)
Frisky the Calf, sd-color-10′, Coronet, 1950
Fun at the Zoo, sd-b-w-12′, United World Education, 1954
George's New Suit, sd-color-11′, Coronet, 1955
Gravity and How It Affects Us, sd-color-14′ Encyclopædia Britannica, 1960
Grey Squirrel, sd-b-w-11′, Encyclopædia Britannica, 1938
Helpers Who Come to Our House, sd-color-11′, Coronet, 1955
How Air Helps Us, sd-color-11′, Coronet, 1963
How Animals Live in Winter, sd-color-11′, Coronet, 1955
How Birds Help Us, sd-color-11′, Coronet, 1957
How Insects Help Us, sd-color-11′, Coronet, 1957
How Machines Help Us, sd-color-11′, Coronet, 1957
How Simple Machines Make Work Easier, sd-color-11′, Coronet, 1964
Judy Learns About Milk, sd-b-w-10′, Young America Films, 1948
Ice Cream, sd-b-w-11′, Encyclopædia Britannica, 1948
Jimmy Visits the City, sd-color-11′, Coronet, 1954
Let's Look at Levers, sd-color-10′, Journal Films, 1961
Light for Beginners, sd-b-w-11′, Coronet, 1960
Little Garden, sd-b-w-11′, Instructional Films, 1952
Mother Hen's Family, sd-color-11′, Coronet, 1953
Mr. and Mrs. Robin's Family, sd-color-11′, Coronet, 1957
On the Way to School, sd-color-11′, Coronet, 1952
One Rainy Day, sd-color-10′, Coronet, 1953

Peppy the Puppy, sd-color-11′, Coronet, 1952
Prehistoric Animals of the Tar Pits, sd-color-11′, Film Associates, 1957
Prove It With the Magnifying Glass, sd-color-11′, Film Associates
Rocks: Where They Come From, sd-color-11′, Coronet, 1963
Seasons of the Year, sd-color-11′, Coronet, 1952
Seeds Grow Into Plants, sd-color-10′, Coronet, 1956
Snappy Turtle, The, sd-b-w-11′, Encyclopædia Britannica, 1940
Snow Flakes, sd-b-w-7′, Moody Institute of Science, 1956
Sound for Beginners, sd-color-11′, Coronet, 1960
Sparky the Colt, sd-b-w-11′, Coronet
Spotty: the Fawn in Winter, sd-color-11′, Coronet, 1958
Spotty: the Story of a Fawn, sd-color-11′, Coronet
Spring Is an Adventure, sd-color-11′, Coronet, 1955
Stores in Our Community, sd-b-w-10′, Coronet, 1954
Summer Is an Adventure, sd-color-11′, Coronet, 1957
Train Trip with Dick and Sandra, sd-color-16½′, Academy Films, 1955
Trip to the Zoo, sd-color-10′, Educational Films, 1955
Truck Driver, The, sd-b-w-16′, Encyclopædia Britannica, 1958
Truck Farm, The, sd-color-11′, Coronet, 1957
Trucks and Trains, sd-color-11′, Churchill Film Productions, 1961
Tugboats and Harbors, sd-color-11′, Churchill Film Productions, 1961
Visit With Cowboys, A, sd-b-w-10′, Encyclopædia Britannica, 1949
We Explore the Beach, sd-color-11′, Coronet, 1955
We Explore the Field and Meadow, sd-color-11′, Coronet, 1961
We Explore the Stream, sd-color-11′, Coronet, 1960
We Explore the Woodlands, sd-color-11′, Coronet, 1957
What Do We See in the Sky? sd-color-11′, Coronet, 1957
What the Frost Does, sd-color-10′, Coronet, 1953
Where Do Our Letters Go? sd-color-11′, Coronet, 1956
Where Does Our Food Come From? sd-color-11′, Coronet, 1956
Where Does Our Meat Come From? sd-color-11′, Coronet, 1960
Winter Comes to the Forest, sd-color-11′, Coronet, 1964
Wonders in a Country Stream, sd-color-10′, Churchill and Wexler, 1949
World Is Born, A, sd-color-20′, Disney Production, 1955
Zoo Babies, sd-color-11′, Coronet, 1955
Zoo Families, sd-color-11′, Film Associates of California, 1956

## Filmstrips Relating to Teaching and Child Development

### ADULT FILMSTRIPS

Art and the Growing Child, 68 fr-sd-color-disc 33⅓ rpm-13′, Films for Education, 1956
Busy Morning in School, A, 27 fr-si-color, Society for Visual Education, 1954

Fear, 28 fr-si-captions-color, Bowman, 1955
Growing Through Art, 50-fr-sd-color-disc 33⅓ rpm-15′, Jewish Education Committee of New York, 1954
Keeping an Aquarium, 70 fr-si-color, Jam Handy Organization, 1948
Kindergarten and Your Child, 40 fr-si-b-w, Wayne University, 1951
Kindergarten Way Is to Learn Each Day, 65 fr-color-photographs, sd-disc 33⅓ rpm, Books That Talk Program, 1956
Primary Grade Art Series:
 Clay Modeling, 32 fr-si-color, Young America Films, 1952
 Cutting and Pasting, 34 fr-si-color, Young America Films, 1952
 Drawing, 35 fr-si-color, Young America Films, 1952
 Finger Painting, 35 fr-si-color, Young America Films, 1952
 Painting, 30 fr-si-color, Young America Films, 1952
 Water Color Painting, 31 fr-si-color, Young America Films, 1952
Tommy Goes to Kindergarten, 35 fr-si-captions-color, photographs, Eye Gate House, 1954
We Plan Together, 27 fr-si-b-w, Young America Films, 1952
We Work Together, 32 fr-si-b-w, Young America Films, 1952
Why and How of Guidance (2 strips), 49 fr-si-color, Popular Science, 1949

## Films Relating to Teaching and Child Development

### ADULT FILMS

All About Fives, sd-b-w-20′, Released by Michigan Education Association, Association for Childhood Education, 1959
Answering the Child's Why, sd-b-w-13′, Encyclopædia Britannica Films, 1951
Balloon Aggression and Destruction Games, sd-b-w-20′, Educational Film Library Association, New York University, 1941
Beginning of Picture Making, sd-color-6′, International Film Bureau, 1951
Building Children's Personalities with Creative Dancing, sd-color-30′, California University Films Sales Dept., 1954
Child at Play, The, sd-b-w-18′, Bureau of Publications, Teachers College, Columbia University, 1952
Child Grows Up, The, sd-b-w-10′, Knowledge Builders, 1938
Children's Fantasies, sd-b-w-21′, McGraw-Hill, 1956
Children's Play, sd-b-w-27′, McGraw-Hill Text Film Dept., 1956
Child's World, A, sd-b-w-19′, Educator Films, 1952
Christmas Through the Ages, sd-color-14′, Encyclopædia Britannica Films, 1954
Curriculum Based on Child Development, sd-b-w-12′, McGraw-Hill Text Film Dept., 1954
Day in the Life of a Five-Year-Old, A, sd-b-w-20′, Bureau of Publications, Teachers College, Columbia University, 1949

Don't Be Afraid, sd-color-12′, Encyclopædia Britannica Films, 1953
Don't Get Angry, sd-color-12′, Encyclopædia Britannica Films, 1953
Fears of Children, sd-b-w-30′, International Film Bureau, 1951
Felt Board in Teaching, sd-color,-9′, Wayne University, 1951
Finger Painting, sd-color-10′, Association Film, 1950 (free loan)
Finger Painting, sd-b-w-5½′, International Film Bureau, 1949
Flannelgraph, sd-color-27′, University of Minnesota, 1956
From Sociable Six to Noisy Nine, sd-color-22′, McGraw-Hill Text Film Dept., 1954
Frustrating Fours and the Fascinating Fives, The, sd-b-w-22′, McGraw-Hill Text Films Dept., 1952
Good Day in Kindergarten, A, Released by California Association for Childhood Education, 1955
He Acts His Age, sd-b-w-35′, McGraw-Hill Text Film Dept., 1951
Helping the Child to Accept the Do's, sd-b-w-11′, Encyclopædia Britannica Films, 1948
Helping the Child to Accept the Don'ts, sd-b-w-11′, Encyclopædia Britannica Films, 1946
Helping Our First Grade Children to Learn, sd-color-32′, New York City Board of Education, 1950
House of the Child, sd-b-w-25′, Contemporary Films, 1953
Individual Differences, sd-b-w-23′, McGraw-Hill Text Films Dept., 1951
It's a Small World, sd-b-w-38′, Columbia University Press, 1951
Let Us Grow In Human Understanding, si-b-w-30′, Harmon Foundation, Inc., 1946
Life with Baby, sd-b-w-18′, McGraw-Hill Text Film Dept., 1946
Long Time to Grow, Part II—Four and Five-Year-Olds, sd-b-w-35′, Child Study Dept. of Vassar, New York University Film Library, 1954
Making a Balanced Aquarium, sd-b-w-8′, Coronet, 1955
Meaning in Child Art, sd-color-10′, Penn State Audio Visual Aids, 1955
Our Teacher, sd-color-10′, Coronet, 1951
Play Is Our Business, sd-b-w-20′, Sun Dial Films, 1946
Pre-school Incidents, No. 1—When Should Grownups Stop Fights, sd-b-w-15′, Child Study Dept. of Vassar, New York University Film Library, 1952
Purple Turtle, The, sd-color-14′, ACI Production and Association Films, 1962
Roots of Happiness, sd-b-w-25′, Mental Health Film Board, 1953
Schools for Tomorrow, sd-color-16′, Wayne University, 1956
Search, The, sd-b-w-25′, Yale University (Child Development), Young America Films, 1955
Sibling Relations and Personality (based on Hurlock), sd-b-w-22′, McGraw-Hill Text Film Dept., 1956
Sibling Rivalries and Parents (based on Hurlock), sd-b-w-11′, McGraw-Hill Text Film Dept., 1956
Skippy and the Three R's, sd-color-29′, National Education Association and Affiliated State Associations, 1953
Story Telling—Can You Tell It in Order, sd-b-w-11′, Coronet, 1953

Terrible Twos and Trusting Threes, The, sd-color-22′, McGraw-Hill Text Film Dept., 1950
Time of Their Lives, The, sd-b-w-30′, Released by National Education Association, 1962
Understanding Children's Drawings, sd-b-w-10′, A. F. Films, 1949
Understanding Children's Play, sd-b-w-10′, Educational Film Library Association and New York University Film Library, 1948
We Go to School, sd-color-10′, Coronet, 1948
Your Children's Play, sd-b-w-21′, McGraw-Hill Text Film Dept., 1952

## SUMMARY

Audio-visual materials are not new to early childhood education. Those who have best understood children through the centuries have contended that the most profitable learning comes through a variety of experiences. In its broadest sense, audio-visual education is concerned with many experiences, the main categories of which may be listed under three headings: (1) doing, (2) observing, (3) symbolizing. Audio-visual experience should not be confined to a single category. Since experiences sooner or later tend to be crystallized in words, educators should make an effort to see that words come to be symbols for a variety of experiences. As words become meaningful, they make it possible to communicate without the presence of objects and things. Every teacher should acquaint herself with the new tools of audio-visual education. Since it would be a waste of both space and funds to attempt to have each building supplied with all audio-visual equipment, schools and school systems need some sort of organization whereby audio-visual materials can be most profitably used by the greatest number of teachers and children.

## QUESTIONS AND PROBLEMS

1. Design for yourself a "cone of experience" based on the categories set up by Edgar Dale. From your observation, or from your teaching experience, select those experiences in any twelve-week period that might be classified in the ascending levels of the cone.
2. Why are many motion-picture experiences not adapted to a group of five-year-olds? What are the advantages of still films over motion pictures? Of some motion pictures over still films?
3. Cite a firsthand experience which you feel would not be a good learning experience for kindergarten children. Why would it not be a good learning experience?
4. Recall from your own childhood an instance in which a particular word or group of words became crystallized into a narrow and perhaps erroneous understanding.

5. Why might it be better for a group of five-year-olds to listen to a recording on a phonograph rather than to listen to the same recording on the radio?

## SELECTED REFERENCES


Association for Childhood Education International, Washington, D.C.:
*Children and TV—Making the Most of It,* Bulletin No. 93, 1954.
*Portfolio in Audio-Visual Materials,* Bulletin No. 7, 1951.

Brown, James W., and Others, A.V. *Instructional Materials and Methods,* New York, McGraw-Hill Book Company, 1959.

Dale, Edgar, *Audio-Visual Methods in Teaching,* rev., New York, Holt, Rinehart and Winston, 1954.

*Education Guide to:*
*Films*
*Filmstrips*
*Tape Scripts and Transcriptions*
Educator Progress Service, Randolph, Wisconsin, 1964 and earlier.

*Educational Film Guide,* New York, H. W. Wilson Company, 1953–1962.

*Educational Film Strips,* New York, H. W. Wilson Company, 1954–1962.

*Educational Media Index,* Pre-School and Primary, K-3, New York, McGraw-Hill, 1964.

*Free and Inexpensive Learning Materials,* 12th ed., Nashville, Tennessee, George Peabody College for Teachers, 1964–1965.

Kinder, James S., *Audio-Visual Materials and Techniques,* 2nd ed., New York, American Book Company, 1959.
*Using Audio-Visual Materials in Education,* New York, American Book Company, 1965.

Library of Congress Catalog, *Music and Phonorecords,* Washington, D.C. (semi-yearly supplements).
*Where to Buy 2" x 2" Slides, Baltimore,* Enoch Pratt Library, 1953.

Williams, Catherine, *Learning From Pictures,* Washington, D.C., Department of Audio-Visual Instruction, National Education Association, 1963.

Review columns in the following periodicals:
*Childhood Education,* "Films Seen and Liked."
*Elementary English,* "Look and Listen."
*Parents' Magazine,* "Family Movie Guide," "Records for Your Children and You."
*Saturday Review,* "TV and Radio," "SR Goes to the Movies."
*School Executive,* "Audio-Visual Aids."
*School Life,* "Aids to Education by Sight and Sound."

# 22

# THE CHILD WHO NEEDS SPECIAL ATTENTION

We noted in an earlier chapter that at no point in their school progress are children in any one class so dissimilar as during their year in kindergarten. That this is so is due in part to the fact that the children have no common school experience, also to the fact that, in most school systems, all five-year-olds are expected to attend the regular kindergarten while in later years some children will be enrolled in special classes of one kind or another. The result is that almost any kindergarten group will include one or more children who may need a great deal of individual attention.

Sometimes the difficulty is purely physical; sometimes it is sheer immaturity—intellectual, social, or emotional—and sometimes it is purely a problem of mental attitude. Usually, however, many factors contribute to making a child a deviate. While some are easily recognized others will be noted only by the alert, understanding teacher. If a child has a leg in a metal brace, obviously every teacher will be aware of the problem; but if the deviate in the group is a bully or perhaps a very timid child, many teachers overlook the fact that they have an obligation to help the child cope with his problem. The present chapter deals with some of the challenges presented by children who need special attention.

## The Crippled Child

The child who is crippled but able to walk is usually enrolled in classes with normal children. Often such children are somewhat delayed in entering school, but many start at the usual entrance age. If the parents are intelligent and supplied with sufficient means, they have probably done all that can be done for the unfortunate child. But if the parents are uninformed or financially handicapped it is quite possible that the kindergarten teacher and the school nurse can be of assistance to the parents by referring them to clinics or welfare agencies where the child's handicap can be studied and perhaps lessened.

Whether or not there is medical aid for the disabled child, the kindergarten teacher can make special provision for him in the school. If the child has difficulty climbing steps, it may be possible to arrange a few wide planks as a ramp or to arrange for him to enter and leave the school building by the entrance with fewest steps. In some schools the kindergarten children use a basement gymnasium for their games. If there is a child in the group who has difficulty with stairs, it may be possible to have the games in the kindergarten room instead of going downstairs, or else to plan activities for the crippled child upstairs while the others go down to the basement.

The teacher may be able to plan games into which the disabled child can enter without disturbing the play of the other children. Perhaps he can play with balls and marbles and quoits. He may be able to march but not skip. He may be able to play with a wagon though not with a velocipede. Such children usually need more rest than normal children. If the child walks a long way from home to school, he may need a rest period when he reaches school.

The attitudes of many crippled children need special attention. These children suffer from defects which will always make them objects of curious interest to the thoughtless. Other children are particularly prone to open-mouthed interest in abnormal bodies, and such scrutiny is naturally highly unpleasant for the unfortunate victims. At the kindergarten level, there is little we can do to persuade the other children to ignore defects, but if we feature the crippled child's outstandingly good qualities and appreciate and admire the ways in which he compensates for his handicaps, the children will tend to do the same. If some child asks, "What makes John's leg like that?" John can either give the answer himself or the teacher, including John in the conversation, can give the facts as she knows them and then can ask John to verify or correct her statements. Fortunately this curiosity passes quickly for children. After the first few days they accept John for his real worth and ignore his disability except, perhaps, to be very proud of him when he learns to do something the rest have been able to do for a long time.

Often such children are sheltered at home to an extent which actually interferes with their normal development. The mother often is so distressed over the child's difficulties that she endeavors to do more for him than for a normal child. The result is that he becomes more and more dependent instead of assuming his own share of work. The disabled child craves an equal share in the work and responsibility of the world. There are many things he can do happily for himself if he is given opportunity and time. In the kindergarten room the teacher can observe the child in order to find just what limitations he has, and can then encourage him to engage in every activity within his ability. Since we want to make this child just as close to normal as he can be, we make special provisions and exceptions for him only when it is absolutely necessary to do so. The child should have a reasonably accurate understanding of his own abilities, and he needs a mental outlook that will insure as happy a life as possible.

## The Child Who Looks Unusual

There are certain children whose personal appearance is so odd as to attract attention. If there is nothing actually wrong physically or mentally, the special task of the teacher is to help the child ignore his handicap or see it as something not very important. The cross-eyed child fascinates other children. If the condition can be remedied by glasses or medical care, then, of course, it should receive attention from specialists. If it cannot, the teacher can keep the interest of other children occupied until they take the crossed eyes for granted. In one kindergarten Tommy had a most peculiar and most ugly shaped head. The teacher tried to see the child and not his head; she tried to look deep into his eyes as she spoke to him. Children seemed to sense what she was doing and they tended to adopt the same manner when talking with him. In time they came to completely disregard the irregularities of Tommy's skull and Tommy came to be appreciated for what he could do—he could, as one child put it, "draw better 'an anybody," and before the end of the term he became quite a leader in the group. It was only the occasional visitor who had to be told of the automobile accident that had left him disfigured. Flaming red hair, enormous and numerous freckles, very thick glasses, and even something unusual in the way of clothing, such as mother's old hat forced on a little girl, may cause considerable agony to a child unless the teacher is quick to help the children accept such things as of little importance.

## The Child Who Is of an Uncommon Race

In various sections of the country children of certain ethnic groups tend, to a greater or lesser degree, to be confronted with social ostracism. But the average five-year-old who has not been a part of or witness to racial antagonism tends to accept the child with different skin pigment or different racial features without questioning. Usually, in a short time the child comes to be accepted for his worth and not his appearance. The more the teacher can do to feature the outstanding contributions or the outstandingly desirable characteristics of the child whose ethnic background is different from that of the majority of the group the more she will be doing to help children appreciate that racial differences mean little so far as the contributions which individuals can make to society are concerned. Good foreign picture storybooks as well as periodicals such as the Japanese *Kinderbook*[1] can be of real significance in developing an awareness that people the world around have and enjoy many things in common. The teacher in the kindergarten in which the following incident occurred is to be congratulated on what she must have done in the way of building an appreciation for human beings as contributing social entities. A child trying to recall the name of a Japanese boy who had recently joined the group said, "Oh, you know! The one with the black hair. He smiles a lot and he makes good boats."

The teacher has an opportunity to enrich the experience of her group through their personal contact with people of other races. If a new child and his parents are willing to tell something about the language, the customs, and perhaps the games of their native land, the experience can be most broadening. A picture storybook from the library written in the language of the newcomer can be a key to mutual understanding. Mother or father will probably be more than glad to translate the text or get friends to make a translation for the kindergarten. The kindergarten teacher can do much to acquaint the newcomer with the most common English words and with only a little extra care and thought on her part the foreign-speaking child will, in a surprisingly short time, build up a working vocabulary. Then, too, there are many kindergarten activities which the child can engage in without having a knowledge of English. He can watch other children and follow their actions and he can understand the simple gestures which the teacher and the children use. He can play with puzzles, look at picture books, listen to music, engage in rhythmic activities, use materials such as crayons, paint, clay and wood, and he can cooperate with others in feeding the goldfish or other room pets, watering the plants, putting the room in order and being responsible for his own personal needs. A good kindergarten will be set up so that the challenge of the environment and the routine of the day will carry him comfortably along. He will, of course, understand spoken words long before he is able to speak with any fluency.

[1] See periodicals for children listed in Appendix.

## The Culturally Disadvantaged Child

We are hearing a great deal these days about those children whose cultural background is such that they are deprived of many of the experiences which seem but natural forerunners to learning to read and cope with other school challenges. In the United States, currently, vast sums of federal money are being allocated to provide nursery and other group experiences designed to compensate for the cultural disadvantages so evident in some areas.

The cultural advantages or disadvantages reflected in any kindergarten group offer leads for curriculum development and program planning. A diversity of cultural backgrounds represented in a kindergarten can be an enrichment factor, but sometimes the diversity leads the teacher to feel that although the children speak the same language, that is English, yet they cannot communicate because their experience has been so vastly different. When, in addition, the language is a barrier between children or between teacher and children it is most difficult to arrive at common understandings.

The kindergarten teacher who is working with children whose language and experience is different from her own needs to make every effort to learn as much as possible about both the language and the culture of her group. Even when she has a single or but a few children whose language or culture differs from that of the majority of the group, she needs to acquaint herself with the language and the culture of the few. A word or a smile indicating common understanding often does much to dispel apprehension.

## The Child Who Has Defective Vision

The blind child—that is the totally blind child—does not usually enter the regular public-school kindergarten. There have been experiments, however, that indicate that an able child even without vision can greatly profit by being a member of a nursery school or kindergarten group made up of sighted children. Some school systems are making provision for preschool blind children to have group experience under the guidance of specially trained teachers. In some cases the blind child spends all his time with the special teacher but in other cases he spends part of his time with other blind children and part of his time in a group of sighted children.

Many children have seriously defective vision unknown to their parents. If the child's vision has always been poor and if he has nothing better to compare it with, he simply assumes that he is seeing what everyone else is seeing and he does not complain. We find some young children who think that "bird" means a noise which a tree makes, because they fail to see the actual bird which an adult points out as the source of the song. Small children uncertain of their own judgment, accept the adult's remarks without criticism or question. When, for example, the adult points to the sky and says, "See the airplane," if the child fails to see the small figure moving across the blue sky, he feels quite justified in assuming that the blue sky is all the adult sees too. Sometimes it is difficult to recognize poor eyesight in a small child. Those who have worked with blind and partially sighted children remind us that the following kinds of behavior may indicate poor vision:

1. The child rubs his eyes frequently or attempts to brush something away from them.
2. When inspecting nearby objects, he blinks continuously or screws up his face, shuts or covers one eye, or tips his head to one side.
3. When trying to see distant objects, he holds his body tense, thrusts his body forward, screws up his face, or shows no interest, whereas the other children are very much interested.
4. He fails to catch and tends to fend off a ball thrown to him.
5. He cries frequently, has frequent fits of temper, fatigues unduly, and is irritable.

The teacher must bear in mind that any child who is alert in some ways but seems stupid when confronted with any situation involving vision may not be stupid or contrary, but merely partly blind. It is possible to ascertain acuity of vision in kindergarten by use of the "E" chart.[2] If there is time, this test should be given to all kindergarten children as soon as possible after they have become accustomed to school ways.

When the teacher suspects a child's inability to see as others see, she should report her suspicions to the school nurse or directly to the parents so that they may take the child for an examination. In the schoolroom itself, the teacher can make sure that the child with poor vision sits in the most favorable place, has proper lighting and working surfaces free from glare, and seldom engages in work involving detail. Besides this, she can talk to him somewhat more than to the other children. The child with poor vision should learn much through hearing.

Often the recognition and treatment of a visual defect will make an enormous difference in the behavior of the child. In a public-school kindergarten, Charles, a rather undersized boy in the group, seemed friendly and talked intelligently for his age. As the days passed, however, he showed little interest in most of the kindergarten activities, was unwilling to undertake anything new, offered no comments on the work of other children and, unless forced into some other activity, spent his days playing at the sand

[2] See bibliography of tests in Appendix.

table. After some weeks had passed, the children were all given a routine vision test by the school nurse. On this test, Charles was discovered to have exceedingly defective vision. The parents were informed, and they took Charles to the oculist at once. Beginning with the first day of wearing his new glasses in school, Charles' whole attitude changed. He left the sand table and approached blocks, paper, scissors, and crayons with great interest and joy. It was quite evident that Charles had previously been unable to see what the teacher had shown the group and, not realizing what his difficulty was, had felt hopelessly at sea.

## The Deaf Child

Technically the child who has never heard is the only one who should be called deaf. The child who has lost his hearing after speech has been acquired is called "deafened," and the child whose acuity of hearing has been impaired in any way is called "hard-of-hearing." The deaf and the deafened children are not often found in regular public-school groups, though recent studies have pointed out that the deaf and deafened child can greatly profit by group experience with children whose hearing is normal. There is a growing trend, as in the case of the blind child, for large public-school systems to make provisions for the deaf and deafened child to have "preschool" group experience.

All too frequently, a child's hearing defects are not recognized even in the kindergarten; in fact, he may have suffered from his handicap since infancy without its being recognized. He may never have heard well and so, like the blind child, may have had no basis for comparison. Even if his hearing difficulty is of recent origin, perhaps due to a cold or some more severe illness, its approach may have been so gradual that the child has been unaware of his increasing disability.

The hard-of-hearing child is inclined to be inconsistent in his behavior. He may be the child who seems to be rather stupid, but when given mental tests, rates fairly high. The teacher may be inclined to be provoked at his inattention, his irrelevant interruptions, his seeming denseness, when the truth of the matter is that the child simply does not hear what is being said. In the games in the kindergarten, it should be possible for the alert teacher to recognize those children who have difficulty in hearing. A simple test with a watch or with whispered words may give the teacher a clue to those children with poor hearing. If a defect is even suspected, the child should be referred to the nurse for examination, and recommendations should be made to the parents.

When the teacher finds a hard-of-hearing child in her group, she can help matters considerably by encouraging the child to sit near the front of the group during discussions. It is quite possible that such a shift in position will make the difference between hearing and not hearing.

In addition to being placed in a favorable position in the group, the hard-of-hearing child needs other special attention. He needs to learn to "read lips." The teacher can tell the child to watch the face of the person who is speaking to him. Many young children pick up considerable lip-reading ability simply from this procedure. They may not realize that the movements of the speaker's lips are helping them, but they find that they "hear" better when they watch the speaker's face.

The child who is hard of hearing is likely to become solitary in his play because he is cut off from much conversation. To prevent such an unfortunate eventuality, he should be helped early in life to improve his capacity to understand others and to interest himself in things that do not require hearing. The kindergarten can assist greatly not only in helping the child understand others but also in acquainting him with types of handicraft and physical play which involve group participation.

## The Child in Poor Physical Condition

In any kindergarten group there will be some children who are less robust than the others. If a child is listless and tires easily, the teacher should refer him to the nurse or school doctor or should ask the parents to have their family physician examine him. If such examinations are not available, there will be little difficulty in at least obtaining measures of the child's height and weight and consulting the height-weight-age charts (see p. 4) to discover whether or not he is greatly underweight. Whether or not a definite physical difficulty can be found, the child who tires easily needs special rest periods, either in school or at home. He needs also the right kind and amount of food (perhaps an extra lunch in the middle of the morning, if this is possible); he needs fresh air, warm but light clothing, suitable room temperature, and above all, ample rest. The fatigued child often feels cold in a room which is warm enough for his more robust classmates. An extra sweater then will help.

Sometimes children with lowered vitality have trouble keeping up with their group and so feign or exaggerate their physical shortcomings for the sake of being allowed to remain at home. Such a procedure constitutes a vicious circle, of course, for the more frequent the child's absences, the farther behind his group he will fall and the greater will be his difficulties when he does return. The kindergarten program should be flexible enough and individual enough, however, to preclude such a response on the part of the child. Obviously, such frail children should not be expected to go through school at a normal rate.

## The Child with a Speech Defect

It has been estimated that some 5 percent of school children have defective speech. Such a figure would doubtless be much too small for the kindergarten group, since in that group we have not only the stuttering, the letter substitutions, huskiness, shrillness, lisping, oral inactivity, and imperfect breathing of the older children but also the last remnants of baby talk in children who may eventually speak correctly.

Speech defects may be "functional" or "organic." Functional disorders are caused by such conditions as poor coordination, late maturation, poor speech standards at home, and the influence of foreign speech. Organic disorders are those which have a physical basis. Children with functional disorders may be expected to respond to remedial instruction, while those with disorders of an organic nature will need the help of medical specialists.

Speech difficulties in kindergarten children usually fall into three classes: stuttering, inaccuracies in sound production, and improper voice placement. Stuttering often persists only a few weeks or months but, whether it is temporary or lasting, the teacher can help the child in his endeavor to overcome the difficulty by her own unemotional attitude. He needs practice in talking to people who are sympathetic but who treat the stuttering as if it were of practically no importance and certainly not a matter for either ridicule or pity. Above all, the stutterer needs confidence in his own ability to overcome his difficulty. If the stuttering persists and the blockings become accompanied by secondary manifestations such as shaking the head, clenching the fists, or using other mannerisms, medical advice should be sought. The child who stutters is often reported to be a "nervous" child. Sometimes "nervousness" is the result of inadequate nutrition and sleep; therefore, special care should be taken to see that the "nervous" child gets proper food and rest.

Many kindergarten children mispronounce words—that is, they omit, interchange, or substitute letters or syllables for others, saying, for example, "muvver" for "mother" and "ith" for "with." The letters and combinations most commonly mispronounced by young children are ch, d, f, g, k (or c), l, n, r, s, sh, sz, t, v, and zh. If the teacher is unable to recognize exactly which sounds cause the child trouble, she can check his speech with an articulation test.[3] Often the child is not aware of his own mispronunciation.

[3] See Templin reference in bibliography of tests in Appendix.

He may be speaking as well as his family speaks, or he may be persisting in some baby-talk sounds which his family has never helped him overcome. It is important that, so far as possible, the family help the child develop acceptable forms of speech before he becomes socially sensitive.

Once the child's difficulties have been discovered, either through observation or the use of diagnostic articulation tests, the kindergarten teacher can help him in many informal situations. In her own conversation with the child she can see that she pronounces slowly, carefully, and distinctly the sounds with which he has particular difficulty. She can initiate games or introduce rhymes in which these sounds are emphasized, and she can stress them through exaggerated tongue and lip movements. Speech improvement records may be used to help the child hear in a somewhat exaggerated fashion such sounds as "SSS," "RRR," "TH TH," "L," "G," "K," and "SH."[4] If the faulty speech seems to be causing personality problems, the teacher might want to recommend that the child do special work with the speech teacher. Frequent short practice on some words, rhymes, and jingles containing the difficult sound can result in definite improvement. Many speech specialists think it better to postpone formal speech work, however, until the child is in the first grade or even the second grade. The child with improper voice placement—for example, the child who speaks in too-loud or too-soft tones, in a too-high or too-low register, or with a whine—is not always thought of as having speech difficulties. Yet he is establishing faulty patterns of vocalization, and he should be encouraged and helped to appreciate pleasing, clear, resonant tones. The causes underlying the childs persistent use of husky, whining, harsh, strained, or very nasal tones should be looked into.

## The Child Who Is Somewhat Immature

Most public schools admit children to kindergarten on the basis of chronological age, without reference to mental maturity. This means that a certain number of somewhat immature children may be expected in any kindergarten group. Such children tend to be playful and inattentive, to wander away from group discussions or stories. They often fail to follow directions or they give up after a slight attempt and can be held, only with difficulty, to finishing a task. Often the immature children seem dependent on the teacher or more advanced children; they follow them around the room and are happy only when they feel the support of a more mature person. Sometimes the immature child lacks muscular strength or coordina-

[4] *Speech Improvement Records*, by Elaine Mikelson, "Listen and Learn," Vols. 1 and 2. See also other speech records listed in record catalogs. Records may be purchased at or through local music shops.

tion and is unable to use the tools or to perform on gymnastic apparatus as well as the other children of the group. Frequently an immature child is a hindrance to the group because of his inability and unwillingness to cooperate and persevere. The teacher's task is to adapt the program so that the immature child will have something he can do with satisfaction and without disturbing the rest of the group. The other children will quickly come to recognize his lack of ability and will not lower their standards just because one child in the group is not able to meet them.

Another problem which arises is the contact with the parents of immature children. Usually parents are surprised to find that their child is less mature than other children of the same chronological age. But most parents can be helped to understand that some children develop more rapidly than others, and they can be shown that pushing the slower children through school at the rate expected of more mature children will result in nothing but failure and unhappiness for the slow child. Sometimes the child who seems immature in the kindergarten in later years catches up to or even surpasses not only the average but even some of the seemingly precocious children.[5] But often, of course, the child who appears immature is really the retarded child who never will be able to reach the stage of development achieved by the average child of his own age.

## The Child Who Is Mentally Retarded

Statistics show that somewhat over two children in every hundred are sufficiently retarded mentally to require special methods of education. The school systems of larger cities provide special schools or classes for these handicapped children. Since children of kindergarten age are not ordinarily placed in a special class, it is not unusual for a public-school kindergarten group to include at least one child with an IQ in the 70's or even 60's. Such children should probably be kept at home or in a nursery school for another year. In systems which admit children solely on the basis of chronological age, such a postponement of kindergarten entrance is almost impossible. It is interesting to note that there is a trend toward providing public-school experience for those children whose mental retardation is quite apparent at three or four years of age, the thinking being that teachers who are trained to work with these handicapped children can help them reach their potential. All too often these children's potentials are not realized and they are allowed, as it were, to vegetate in an environment which offers them no challenge.

What can be done for the retarded child in the kindergarten group?

[5] Nancy Bayley, "Individual Patterns of Development," *Child Development*, March, 1956, 27: 45–74.

First, if possible, we must secure some measure of his retardation and make sure that there is no remediable physical cause which is giving a false impression of his intellectual attainment. A deaf child or a child from a foreign-speaking home or an emotionally disturbed child may easily give the impression of backwardness. If, however, the child gives every evidence of being retarded, then the teacher can modify her program to allow for his incapacity. Perhaps he can be given a special type of work. Surely he can be treated with extreme patience and held to standards considerably lower than those set for the rest of the group.

Personal and social traits vary among the mentally retarded just as among normal children, and it is exceedingly important to help the less bright child develop a pleasing personality. Obviously he can never compare favorably with others mentally and for that reason he needs more than others to have pleasing manners, an attractive appearance, and desirable habits. Retarded children acquire good habits with less ease than do normal children; but once the habits have been acquired they have little difficulty in retaining them. Because retarded children cannot always understand the reasons for certain types of behavior we appeal to their reason somewhat less than we would to normal five-year-olds.

We must find out what the retarded child can do, where his abilities and interests lie, and try to give him things to do that will offer him an honest challenge. The retarded child has often been confronted with nagging and criticism; this is especially likely if he has normal or particularly able brothers and sisters. He should feel that kindergarten is a friendly place where people like him and appreciate his efforts. He needs to be encouraged and praised for his accomplishments rather than being compared unfavorably with more able children. The retarded child needs to see things concretely. He needs opportunities to handle, manipulate, and arrange play materials and other objects in order to gain understanding. Theory and abstract generalization will mean little to him. In some physical activities he may be as skilled as the other children, though usually he will need special training in good posture and physical coordination. Most book work will never be a happy occupation for him, but there will be many things he can enjoy doing with his hands. In music, art, natural science in its simple forms, and even in dramatics, he may show special ability which does not correlate with his ability to solve difficult intellectual problems. Some of the worthiest citizens are less capable than the average man and even in kindergarten we can help the retarded child gain an understanding of the responsibility which he has for being a good citizen. He may not aspire to be President but he may hope to and be proud of assuming many another responsibility.

Parents often fail or refuse to recognize that a child is retarded mentally. It is a difficult task for even the most tactful teacher or principal to tell parents that their child is less capable than the average child of his age; yet, if the information is not given the child runs a chance of suffering acutely from being held by his parents to standards far beyond his ability. Since we know relatively little about the course of the mental development of even typical children, we cannot say flatly to the family that their child will never be able, for instance, to finish high school or go into training for a certain occupation. We would be very unwise to disclose to parents their child's exact IQ rating. We know that IQ ratings may vary slightly from one week to another and that they occasionally change astoundingly from one year to another. We certainly do not want to brand a child as deficient when there is any possibility that he is merely slow in developing. We can tell the parents that a child seems somewhat less mature than most of the other children in his group. We can perhaps suggest another year of growing up in the kindergarten situation, and in some cases, if the test scores have not been too low, we can point out that in another year he may find it as easy to learn to read as most of the others in his first-grade group. We can definitely stress the fact that if he enters the first grade this next school year he will almost certainly become one of the slowest in the group. We can point out how discouraging it is for any individual, no matter how much effort he puts forth, always to find himself at the bottom.

If the child is at the lower level of the group chronologically, this is a point which should make his classmates, parents, and the child himself appreciate the wisdom of providing another year for growing up before he tries to do those things which children who are many months older are expected to do. In some instances, however, the child is socially so much a part of his group that he will gain more from staying with the group than from another year in kindergarten. If, however, a slow-developing child moves to a new community at the end of his kindergarten year, there is little question about the wisdom of giving him another year in which to grow before transferring him to a first-grade group.

If the parents are seriously concerned, we can point out the many differences between persons and suggest that there are many different kinds of ability. We can let the parents know that, in cooperation with them, we are interested in making a study of the child's particular abilities and disabilities and that we are eager to help the child. If the parents are concerned with doing the best thing for their child, they will think of him as an individual who is in no way responsible for his retardation and who deserves all the help he can get in his endeavor to become a worthy citizen and a happy person. If the child appears definitely not to belong in the regular school classes, the school psychologist or principal can recommend that the parents get advice on placement from a child-guidance clinic or, in many states, from the state testing department.

## The Superior Child

The kindergarten teacher meets the definitely superior child less often and for shorter lengths of time than the retarded child. In some cities, for example, a child who has already learned to read enters first grade without attending kindergarten at all; and in some places a child who is outstanding in the kindergarten is promoted to first grade after only half a year of kindergarten. To the person who lays great stress on completing school at as early an age as possible, such rapid advancement seems highly advantageous. Others feel that there are distinct disadvantages in allowing a child to progress too rapidly through school. The child who passes all tests brilliantly at an early age may be precocious rather than permanently superior. Even if his superiority is lasting, he may be immature socially and so fail to benefit greatly from the more advanced schoolwork.

Particularly in kindergarten we may find a child who is keen and alert mentally but who is lacking in poise, in motor coordination, or in ability to get along happily with his fellows. If such a child is pushed ahead, he may become a prodigy who is almost completely out of touch with his own generation. In later years his fellows may catch up with him mentally, and the prodigy may always lack the joy of true companionship. For such a child the kindergarten may be very beneficial. While recognizing the child's unusual ability, the teacher will encourage him in those areas in which his development is less mature. The fact that he has learned to read is no reason why he cannot still be happy and challenged in the kindergarten. He may have little time for reading in kindergarten; but he will be busily engaged in all sorts of other activities and, if he is in the right kind of kindergarten, he will be challenged with problems that will require him to exert his every effort in their solution. He will be planning and testing his theories. He will be acquiring skill in handling tools, crayons, and scissors. He will be learning the fun of expressing his ideas and clarifying his understanding through words, music, clay, crayons, paints, paper, and other media. He will be discovering how best to get along with other children. In the kindergarten *laboratory* he will be constantly experimenting with his environment, both persons and things.

## The Child Who Is Left-Handed

Most things in this world are planned for right-handed people. The person who cannot cut without special left-handed scissors, who cannot play golf without special left-handed clubs, and who cannot eat comfortably at a dinner table unless he is seated at the corner is under a handicap.

Left-handedness appears in all degrees. By the time the child is five years old, hand dominance is usually well established. Studies have shown that approximately 6 percent of all school children show a definite preference for the left hand and that between 4 and 5 percent show no strong hand preference. There are some activities which may be done as well with the left hand as with the right. It makes no difference, for example, whether a hammer is held with one hand or the other. But it is a nuisance to have to secure a special pair of scissors before cutting, or to ask for a particular seat in order to avoid bumping elbows with the next person.

If the kindergarten teacher has some children in her group who are vacillating in hand preference, she will want to try to determine which, if either, seems to be the dominant hand. It is helpful to observe and record the child's apparent hand preference in such activities as pulling down a shade, winding a mechanical toy, pounding a nail, throwing a ball, screwing a jar lid, carrying a bottle of paint, and using a paintbrush. For more accurate determination of hand preference, see the Iowa Scale for Measuring Hand Preference or other scientifically developed scales.[6] If the child appears to use either hand equally well, the teacher probably will not be at fault if she points out that it will be easier for him if he would use his right hand for such things as eating, cutting, or drawing. If he exhibits a distinct preference for his left hand, this usage should be accepted, and the teacher should be ready with suggestions that will help him adapt himself most efficiently and effectively to our strongly right-handed civilization. If the left- or right-handed preference is marked and if annoying attempts are made to shift hand usage, or if, because of accident, it is necessary to shift hand usage, certain nervous symptoms, such as tics, nail-biting, and stuttering, may appear. Interfering with hand dominance is likely to make a child confused and upset.

## The Child Who Misbehaves

Behavior difficulties usually cannot be traced to one underlying physical cause—they are often symptoms of a deep-seated difficulty. If the teacher will remember that there is always a cause behind troublesome behavior and if she will seek out and treat that cause, she will achieve much more improvement in behavior than if she confines her attention to the overt behavior itself.

[6] Florence L. Goodenough, *Developmental Psychology*, 3rd ed., New York, D. Appleton-Century Company, 1959.

## The Child Who Cannot Sit Still

The child who squirms continually is a nuisance in the room, a constant irritant to teacher and to other children. The most natural response on the part of the teacher is to keep reminding the child that he must sit still. But perhaps he can't sit still! The child suffering from chorea is often an offender. He may tell the teacher that he can't help wriggling; but if she doesn't understand these matters, she will probably reply in caustic tones that anyone can sit still. The unfortunate child, however, cannot keep still despite all his efforts, and he has to conclude, if he thinks about it, that he is inferior to the other children. Or the squirming child may have some itching skin trouble. Even the calmest of adults cannot sit still when suffering from eczema, and yet we boldly assure children of five that "anybody can sit still." If we are sure there is no physical or emotional cause behind the restlessness, then we have the task of gradually teaching the child to relax and control his muscles for short periods of time. Any group will become restless after prolonged quiet. Suggesting a run on the playground or a skip about the room will be more effective than nagging.

## The Child Who Is Highly Distractible

The child who is too easily distracted may upset a group. The pictures on page 461 illustrate this point. Illustration "A" is a drawing which Byron made when he was sitting at the table with Manly. Manly is an erratic boy, who, although average in mental ability, has little interest in completing anything he begins, and who apparently gets most pleasure out of acting silly on all occasions. The boys sat together, and the pictures, which had been planned as decorations for the walls of the new playhouse, turned into mere scribbles. The kindergarten teacher looked at Byron's work, told him that she was sorry he had forgotten what he was planning to make, and thought he might be able to do better work if he were to have a table by himself, where he could keep his attention on what he was trying to do. Byron moved his paper and crayons to a secluded corner of the room, and ten minutes later returned with the drawing in Illustration "B."

We need to help the distractible child not only for the sake of other members of the group but for his own sake as well. The "scatterbrain" individual is no asset to society and no great satisfaction to himself. Kindergarten is probably the first situation in which this child is expected to control himself. Up to this time, he has been allowed to flit from one occupation to another as fancy suggested. From now on, he will be expected to stick to one task for longer and longer periods as necessity demands. The kindergarten, therefore, is an enormously important stepping-stone for such a child.

(A) *Byron's Picture When He Was Distracted by a Child Who Was Acting Silly*

(B) *Byron's Second Picture, Made Five Minutes After the Distraction Was Lured Away*

The kindergarten teacher helps the child by seeing that he does not undertake tasks that are too difficult for him, and by seeing that the simple undertakings, once begun, are carried through. If the child becomes highly excited and cannot stay at his task, she offers him the opportunity to stretch out and rest quietly on his rug until he can "get hold of himself." If the teacher will frequently point out that the child's present work is an improvement over his earlier efforts, she will do much to help him feel that he can and does make progress.

## The Child Who Is Irresponsible

Many children coming into kindergarten have never learned to take any responsibility. Frequently this is the direct fault of the family rather than any inclination of the child. In one kindergarten a new child was overheard to say, "Gee! I like to put on my own coat. You know, I can't do it at home because my mother likes to put it on for me." Such a child delights in responsibility when he is offered an opportunity to assume it. Other children have become so overdependent on the mother that they cry when separated from her or cling to the skirts of the teacher, expecting baby talk and much attention. They feel deserted and helpless in a group of strange children, and they attach themselves first to one person and then to another, hoping to locate someone under whose wing they may be sheltered. Sometimes these children hesitate to express or even to formulate an opinion of their own until they ascertain just what certain respected adults think. Such children need constantly to be encouraged to become more self-reliant. Step by step these children need to be confronted with situations which will necessitate decision and constructive action on their part. They need praise for every new step they take, and they need to learn the respect the group feels for individuals able to look out for themselves.

## The Child Who Makes Excuses

Many children of kindergarten age have learned through experience certain methods for meeting correction and criticism. Some children stall when confronted with an embarrassing question. They say, "What did you say?" or "Who? Me?" or pretend not to hear in an effort to gain time to invent a satisfactory answer. By the age of five, excuses are all too common. The more clever children sometimes attempt to change the subject and so direct the teacher's attention from themselves. Jimmy, when reminded that he should not have interrupted Catherine's work, looked up brightly and said, "My, that was an interesting story you read us this morning, Miss Smith!" Some children habitually attempt to shift the blame to some companion. Others say penitently (or at least with apparent remorse), "I forgot." Still others have learned to escape criticism by displays of temper, in the hope that the experience will be so unpleasant for the adults that they will avoid the risk of repeating it.

Usually children experiment with methods of avoiding the unpleasant results of their own behavior. The method which, from the child's point of view, is most effective is the one upon which he patterns his later behavior.

It is important that children be helped to learn to face a situation, to acknowledge their shortcomings, and to attempt to improve their behavior. If the child is naturally shy, a kindly word from the teacher will do more at this time than scolding or finding fault. If the difficulty persists, then at each appearance it must be met firmly and justly. Every time the child "gets by" with evading the responsibility for his acts, his character becomes so much less desirable. Sometimes it may be necessary for the teacher to check the veracity of the child's remarks before she passes judgment. Always, of course, she must be sure of what happened and must make the child see the relative importance of the incident.

## The Bully

The kindergarten group may and often does contain a bully, or a child who is domineering. There is almost always an unfortunate home situation behind this type of behavior. The teacher needs to know the habits and ideals of the family of the bully. Sometimes she will find older brothers and sisters who have tormented the five-year-old for months without end. The smaller child is wholly unable to compete with them on the physical level and is as yet so unlearned in the ways of the world that he does not know any other method of combat. His one aim may be to treat a smaller child as he himself has been treated. Sometimes we find that the family members preach to the children that only through the exertion of physical strength can one hope to "get anywhere in the world." These children are unsuccessful in their fights with larger and older children, and so they naturally select smaller and weaker foes. Sometimes the bully is a direct copy of an admired bad boy of the neighborhood.

In attempting to help such children become acceptable members of a group, the teacher needs first of all to discover, if she can, the real reason for the undesirable behavior, and then to treat the cause. If she can note one or two outstandingly good qualities of the child's behavior—for example, his generosity, his awareness of details, or perhaps even his physical strength—she should feature these with the group. So doing often helps the bully see himself in a *new* role.

## The Timid Child

Contrasting with the domineering child is the timid, fearful child, usually small in stature but not necessarily lacking in mental ability. This child may fear everything, may be the shrinking sort of individual whose one ambition is to escape notice. Again, the history of the child in the home is most important. Is the child the victim of severe punishment, perhaps at the hands of a strict father? Is the child a wide-eyed auditor at family tales of horror or of crime? Is he taken to see terrifying movies? Is he constantly warned with vague though frightful threats, or has he had some unhappy experience which has left him timid and fearful? One kindergarten child showed so much anxiety during the first week of school that the teacher made a special visit to the mother. Apparently the reason for the behavior was the fact that a few months before the child had been taken, without warning, to the hospital for an operation which kept him there in considerable discomfort for several weeks, and he was in constant fear of the reoccurrence of such an experience. With this knowledge, the teacher took particular care to reassure the child and alleviate his worries.

The timid child needs to be assured not only by words but by experience. His time needs to be filled with activities and getting satisfaction from them. He needs to know what he can count on and that others have confidence in and can count on him.

## The Child Who Is Overemotional

Occasionally a kindergarten child exhibits a specialized fear, as of dogs or of fire. Such a fear can sometimes be alleviated by encouraging the child to form pleasant associations with a mild form of the feared objects, perhaps with pictures of dogs or toy dogs or puppies or, for fire, with a single tiny candle on a birthday cake.

Displays of anger, even temper tantrums, do appear, but they are uncommon at the kindergarten age. The kindergarten setup is not one which encourages such displays, but the teacher need not be surprised if they appear. A group offers the teacher an excellent opportunity to show the child that such behavior as an extreme display of temper is not acceptable in a social situation and that an individual acting in this manner is not

*Clay Lends Itself to Emotional Release.*

Jump from F. P. G.

a desirable member of the group. Temporary isolation will ordinarily quiet outbursts of temper, but occasionally it is better to let the child take out his feelings on inanimate objects. There is the possibility that isolation will only result in pent-up feelings. If unreasonable outbursts of anger persist, a play therapy session with a good psychologist may result in the release of tensions and may also uncover the hidden source of tension. If the services of a school psychologist are not available, the teacher can perhaps get some clue to the child's pent-up feelings by observing the kinds of things he does with dolls, puppets, crayons, and paints. Frequently the child will tell much about his own feelings in his dramatic play or in chatting about his pictures.

## The Child Who Uses Undesirable Language

A child who causes consternation among some of the mothers is the one who uses bad language, whether vulgar or profane. Such language will vary greatly from one school to another. In some districts it is merely the type of language occasionally used by many adults of the community. In this case, it is perhaps hopeless to try to do much to change the child's expressions. Certain words and phrases may be understood as "not allowed" in the schoolroom, but the teacher must realize that she is probably giving the child, not a change in his language habits, but a second language, which is to be used on special occasions.

Often there is a child who stands out as being particularly vulgar in his language. Such a child is a menace to the group and needs more attention than if he were merely one of a group all using the same kind of undesirable speech. A small boy who was known the neighborhood over for his unrepeatable street vocabulary was once enrolled as a member of a somewhat select kindergarten group. Mothers shook their heads and threatened to withdraw their children if the child continued to attend. The teacher, being forewarned, was forearmed! On the second or third day of kindergarten she heard the small boy say in a loud voice to his table companion, "That's a damn dumb thing you're making." With another child the teacher would probably either have completely overlooked his speech or would have brought favorable attention to the good qualities of the work being done by the child whose work was being criticized. In this case, however, she quietly and calmly, but with no uncertainty, picked up the work of the loud speaker and, asking him to bring his chair, ushered the boy, work, chair, and all to a table in a remote section of the room. As she helped him settle in his new working quarters, she explained to him that they did not enjoy having him with the group when he talked like that. There was apparently no ill feeling on the part of the child, and from that day until the kindergarten year was ended, the only other time this child's language slipped from grace was once under great duress.

## SUMMARY

In any kindergarten group, there are likely to be a number of children who need special attention from the teacher. For each of these cases, the teacher will need to discover the underlying cause. If the cause is physical, she may need to urge the parents to take steps toward remedial work. If the cause is mental, she will need to change the attitude of the child and, perhaps, the attitude of other children toward him. Whether or not the condition is remediable, the teacher should strive to give the child a mental outlook and forms of response that will further his own happiness and his social adjustments in the group.

## QUESTIONS AND PROBLEMS

1. What are the arguments for and against having handicapped children taught in separate schools?
2. Parents of handicapped children may (a) fail to realize that there is any difficulty; (2) expect special attention for the child; (c) become upset at any discussion of the child's difficulties; (d) try to smooth out all difficulties which the child encounters. What attitude should the teacher take in response to each of these?
3. If the kindergarten teacher is called on to furnish part of a "program"

for the school, should she favor the children who are most attractive, should she try to include all the unattractive and handicapped children, or should she adopt some other procedure? Discuss.

## SELECTED REFERENCES


Baker, Harry J., *Introduction to Exceptional Children,* New York, Macmillan Company, 1953.

Baynham, Dorsey, "The Great Cities Projects," *NEA Journal,* April, 1963, 52:17–20.

Capa, Cornell, and Maya Pines, *Retarded Children Can Be Helped,* New York, Channel Press, 1957.

Cruichshank, William M., and G. Orville Johnson, eds., *Education of Exceptional Children and Youth,* Englewood Cliffs, New Jersey, Prentice-Hall, 1958.

Cutts, Warren G., "Reading Unreadiness in the Underprivileged," *NEA Journal,* April, 1963, 52:23–24.

D'Evelyn, Katherine E., *Meeting Children's Emotional Needs,* Englewood Cliffs, New Jersey, Prentice-Hall, 1957.

Friedler, Miriam F., *Deaf Children in a Hearing World,* New York, The Ronald Press, 1952.

High, Jane, *Children Who Should Not Be In School,* New York, Exposition Press, 1957.

Jenkins, Gladys G., *Helping Children Reach Their Potential,* Chicago, Scott, Foresman and Company, 1961.

Krimsky, Emanuel, *Children's Eye Problems,* New York, Grune and Stratton, 1956.

Larson, Richard, and James L. Olson, "A Method of Identifying Culturally Deprived Children in Kindergarten," *Exceptional Children,* November, 1963, 30:130–134.

Magary, James F., and John B. Eichorn, *The Exceptional Child: A Book of Readings,* New York, Holt, Rinehart and Winston, Inc., 1960.

Mayer, Greta, *When Children Need Help With Emotional Problems* (pamphlet), New York, Child Study Association of America, 1961.

National Society for the Study of Education, *Education for the Gifted,* 57th Yearbook, Part II, Chicago, University of Chicago Press, 1958.

Olson, Willard C., *Child Development,* 2nd ed., Boston, D. C. Heath and Co., 1959.

Riessman, Frank, *The Culturally Deprived Child,* New York, Harper and Row, 1962.

Screiber, F. R., *Your Child's Speech,* New York, G. P. Putnam's Sons, 1956.

Slaughter, Stella, *The Educable Mentally Retarded Child and His Teacher*, Philadelphia, F. A. Davis Co., 1964.

Stern, Catherine, and Elsa Castendyck, *The Handicapped Child: Educating by Insight*, New York, A. A. Wyn, 1952.

Strang, Ruth, "The Gifted Child," *Nursery-Kindergarten Education*, Jerome E. Leavitt, ed., New York, McGraw-Hill, 1958.

Wallin, J. E., *Children with Mental and Physical Handicaps*, Englewood Cliffs, New Jersey, Prentice-Hall, 1949.

Wright, Beatrice A., *Physical Disabilities: A Psychological Approach* (pamphlet), New York, Child Study Association of America, n.d.

# 23

# KINDERGARTEN RECORDS AND REPORTS

Within any group of experienced teachers the topic of record-keeping is bound to provoke lively discussion. Some teachers can see nothing of value in keeping records, and accept them as necessary red tape. Others are enthusiastic about the value of many kinds of records. The first type of teacher probably thinks of records as an end in themselves. She derives no benefit either from the records she has made or those made by others. She fails to understand that records are kept for a variety of purposes. We will grant that record-keeping can be a time-consuming business and that in many cases the teacher has the right to feel that she is being asked to keep too many records. But a few reasonably simple ones, intelligently kept and intelligently used, can be one of the teacher's most valuable assets.

## Why Keep Records?

Those who question the usefulness of records would do well to read Chapter X in the *Forty-sixth Yearbook of the National Society for the Study of Education.*[1] In that chapter, Ethel Kawin sets forth eleven uses to which records may be put: (1) to help teachers understand the child; (2) to help parents understand the child; (3) to secure evidence of growth and development; (4) to discover and meet special needs; (5) to discover personality and behavior difficulties; (6) to determine school placement; (7) to provide a basis for confidential reports to outside specialists and clinics; (8) to provide data for reports to other schools; (9) to serve as guides in cur-

[1] See selected references, p. 521.

riculum planning; (10) to provide in-service education for teachers; and (11) to provide data for research. In this chapter we shall discuss the kinds of records the kindergarten teacher should find helpful.

## Cumulative Records

It is desirable to have a cumulative record folder for each child enrolled in the school. One of the best ways to bridge the gap between kindergarten and first grade is to have adequate materials in each child's cumulative record folder. The kindergarten stands in a strategic position in regard to cumulative records. To the kindergarten teacher falls the lot of (1) summarizing the significant events in the child's preschool life; (2) assembling scientific data in regard to the child's development; (3) contributing observations of the child as a developing personality; and (4) making probably the first recorded estimate of the child's behavior in a society of his peers.

## Contents of the Cumulative Record Folders

The first material to go into the folder is the initial enrollment card, on which will be recorded such information as the child's name, birth date, address, father's and mother's occupations, and date on which the child was enrolled in the school. On this card there will be space in which a record of any later school transfer can be made. In the folder will also be further information about the child's preschool life, the record of his routine physical and dental examinations, records of any mental tests given, the teacher's scoring of the child on available standardized rating items, anecdotal records, brief accounts of parent contacts with the school, the teacher's record of the child's progress, and an account of the teacher's report to the parent. In some cases there may also be records of readiness-for-learning tests.

## Records from the Home for Use in the School

The kindergarten child spends some two-and-a-half to three hours a day at school (seven hours in an all-day kindergarten). He is in kindergarten on about half of all the days of the year. The rest, the great majority of his time, is spent in an environment about which the kindergarten teacher knows all too little. If the child is to be given help in developing his potentialities to the utmost, the school and the home must work together. Such cooperation can result only when each comes to know more about the environment of the other and how the child reacts in it. A child with generations of cultured, well-educated ancestors, a child from a family of unlettered but simple, worthy, self-respecting citizens, and a child only a few weeks out of an orphan's home, adopted by a childless and wealthy couple, may appear much the same outwardly. Yet their background of experience and their present environments may be so different from one another that the new kindergarten experiences will have quite different significance for each of them.

## Procuring the Information

In many communities, the school conducts a spring or summer roundup for those children who will be entering kindergarten in the fall. At that time the teacher has a chance to see the child with at least one of his parents. Frequently a conference with the parent can be held then or scheduled for a later date. In at least one city school system, the first two or three days of the semester are devoted to conferences. The group of children does not come together as a unit until the teacher has met each child and talked with at least one person who has intimate knowledge of the child and his home environment.[2] If the interviews are scheduled at fifteen-minute intervals it is possible for the teacher to talk with from eighteen to twenty parents a day between the hours of nine and three-thirty. A strenuous schedule? Yes! But one which seems to pay good dividends as the year progresses. In some instances, after an opening conversation, the parents can continue on their own jotting down the bits of information sought by the school.

## Members of the Family

The school needs to know something of each child's parents. Were they born in this country? If they were born in a non-English-speaking land, we need to know how long they have lived in the United States, whether they speak English or the native tongue at home, and how closely they cling to the customs of their former country.

We need to know also whether both parents are living and whether or

[2] The child, of course, does not sit in on the interview. He is encouraged to explore the room and generally familiarize himself with his new environment.

not they are living together. Many children who come from broken homes suffer a social or emotional handicap. If we can know just how much happiness there is in the home, how much discord and sorrow, it will help us understand the child. Obviously we cannot ask for such information directly from the parent, but obviously, also, if the information is volunteered we should not neglect to record that the father is a problem, for instance, or that the mother hates housework and doesn't cook when she can avoid it, that the grandmother sides with the child in all arguments, and so on. Such remarks may be given outright by the parent in conferences with the teacher, but they appear more often in the casual remarks of the kindergarten child. Many a kindergarten teacher, despite great efforts to keep personal affairs out of the kindergarten discussion, cannot help overhearing such statements as "Gee, but my Daddy was so drunk last night! And we had company, too. Mother was so mad at him," and "You ought to have seen the fight my mother and Mrs. Smith had. They looked just like chickens with their heads stuck way out."

It is important to know whether a kindergarten child has older or younger brothers and sisters or whether he is an only child. If older children attend the same school, the teacher may know more of the family situation through her acquaintance with them. She may have to remind herself that simply being members of the same family will not necessarily mean similarity in disposition or in mental ability, though it will probably mean the appearance of certain family traits. She will recognize, too, occasional bits of seeming erudition as mere parrot-like repetition of the words of the older sibling. One kindergarten child startled adults by her completely unusual art work. She made picture after picture of characters whose nationalities could be identified by their costumes and general racial characteristics. The productions were to be wondered at under any condition, but when one learned that this child had a high-school brother who was absorbedly interested in designing posters for his international-relations club, the marvel of the productions did not seem quite so great. An only child may have some difficulty adjusting to the group. The youngest member of a big family may try to treat other children as he has been treated at home. We cannot predict from mere knowledge of home situation what the child's behavior at school will be like; but knowledge of the home may help us understand underlying causes and help us guide the child's behavior into acceptable forms.

The presence of persons other than the immediate family in the home frequently presents problems. The child who has two grandparents with opposing views living in the home may suffer. Janice's maternal grandmother and paternal grandfather were both members of her home. Grandmother was very religious and, whenever she could catch Janice, insisted on her learning long hymns and psalms. Grandfather was openly derisive of such doctrines and lay in wait for an opportunity to demand that Janice recite the last thing Grandma had taught her so that he could roar with laughter at the performance. No wonder Janice learned to avoid all elderly people!

Gwendolyn was naturally a rather clever child, quick to pick up new slang and pert phrases that provoked laughter. Her mother was the housekeeper for a fraternity house, and the college boys who lived there soon found they could have great fun quizzing Gwendolyn and teaching her all sorts of "slick" words and expressions. For some weeks the kindergarten teacher despaired of ever helping the child learn not to show off and not to use many of the expressions which came so easily to her. An understanding of the home situation and a talk with Gwendolyn's mother resulted in her keeping the child in their own apartment while she was at home and preventing further exposure to the thoughtless teaching of the college students.

## The Status of the Family

The teacher can help the child more effectively if she knows also the social, cultural, and economic conditions in the home. If the family is living in a neighborhood of similar families, the child is probably an acceptable member of a neighborhood group of children. But if the neighbors consider the family "different," the child may suffer the humilities of ostracism. If the family is a superior one settled for some reason in an inferior community, the parents may try to prevent intimacy between the child and other children to a point which makes for serious emotional upset in the child.

What is the education of the parents, and what are their leisure-time interests? Is the home one where the child is exposed to cultural conversation on matters of interest politically, historically, and socially? Or is the only talk he hears concerned with the freshest crime, the juiciest scandal, the petty squabbles of the neighborhood, or senseless backbiting among the older members of the family? Does he hear clever, stimulating wit, or are the conversations limited to gross ridicule of the misfortunes of others or the repetition of smutty jokes? Whether or not the child enters into the conversations of the home, he will absorb much of their vocabulary and, more important still, their attitude. Perhaps in no way is the cultural status of the family so fully revealed as in their leisure-time occupations. The parents who are limited in their amusements to the movies and television programs, card-playing, and newspaper-reading are not likely to inspire worthier recreations in their children. The child who sees his parents read, and who hears good books read aloud, who hears fine music and the discussion of music, who joins in family trips to museums, to zoos, to the woods and country, who learns which television programs and which movies the parents enjoy, who watches in rapt admiration while his father or mother carves a bit of wood or soap, or models clay, draws a design, fashions a dress, or hunts up information in the dictionary or encyclopedia, is ready for a far different type of schoolwork than the child who has learned to accept the cheapest types of ready-made entertainment.

The atmosphere of the home may be altered by the financial status of the family. While the school is not concerned, of course, with the actual income of the family nor with their budget and spending, still it is of great importance to know whether the family is on the relief rolls of the city, whether it is barely managing on meager and uncertain funds, or whether it is comfortably secure or very wealthy. The children from the poorest groups may come to school ill-nourished and thinly clad; they may need help from the school in learning how to secure necessary medical care, glasses, or dental work; they may need help in obtaining sufficient warm clothing. Apart from actual help, the teacher will modify her attitude toward individual children if she knows they are probably breakfastless and hungry. If the family owns its own home, it is probably at least not in dire need, and the child may be expected to be a fairly permanent member of the school.

## The Past History of the Child

If admission to school is based on chronological age, the most important piece of information is the child's date of birth. If the school rules require that dates of birth be checked, the place of birth should also be noted, so that the records can be consulted. Sometimes parents, in the belief that early school entrance is an advantage to the child, deliberately misstate the date of birth. In one kindergarten, no checking of birth dates was required, and the school accepted Ruth's age as stated by the mother. Ruth was well above average for her age in physical development and for that reason gave no indication of misplacement. As the year progressed, however, it became more and more evident that she seemed less mature than the rest of the group in many ways. A mental test, administered at the teacher's request, gave her an IQ of 89. When the time came for the group to be transferred to the morning session, the teacher suggested to the mother that, because Ruth seemed less mature than the other five-and-a-half-year-olds in the group, it would be better for her to remain in the afternoon group. She hastened to point out that Ruth might well have opportunities to be an occasional leader in that group, whereas with the older group she seemed inevitably to be a follower. The mother exhibited considerable embarrassment when she heard this and at last falteringly admitted that she had given Ruth's age as six months older than she actually was because "Ruth was so large for her age and she seemed just as smart as other children who were entering kindergarten," and it had seemed that the school entrance rule was foolish anyway. The mother had not realized that her falsification of the birth date would result in an injustice to her child. When she understood the situation, she was perfectly happy to have Ruth remain in the group of younger children. Ruth made an excellent adjustment to her new group and, with her corrected IQ of 99, seemed not a slow but a very normal child.

When asking a parent about the date and place of birth, it is a simple matter to ask also whether or not there was anything unusual about the child's birth or infancy. A history of extreme delicacy in babyhood may explain later physical or emotional difficulties. Surely the school needs to have a record of immunizations or the contagious diseases the child has had. In a time of epidemic it is extremely important to know just which children in a certain room are immune and which are susceptible to the disease. Sometimes it is possible to record the age at which the child first walked and first talked. The occurrence of very precocious or much delayed development may presage advanced or retarded development in other areas.

## Present Condition of the Child

If the child is given a routine physical examination at the school, his weight and height will be recorded, but if he has no such examination, the parents can be asked to supply the information. The teacher needs to know something of the child's home routine. What is his usual bedtime? His usual rising time? How good is his appetite? What does he usually have to eat during the day? If he is sleepy and tired in the kindergarten, if he is listless and inactive, it may be the direct result of insufficient rest or inadequate food at home.

The teacher needs to know something of the child's speech. Perhaps she can make records of stuttering and letter-substitutions in the schoolroom, but she needs to know also whether or not the parents recognize any inadequacies in the child's speech.

Sometimes a knowledge of the child's emotional responses at home will help the teacher cope with school situations. Particularly she needs to know whether or not he has any intense fears. A child, for example, who has for months shown terror at the approach of a dog would not be happy about meeting a dog in the schoolyard. Temper tantrums may be frequent at home and perhaps never appear at school. It will give the teacher a clearer understanding of the child if she knows the differences between his behavior at home and at school.

An awareness of the child's particular interests will give the teacher a key for interesting him in new occupations. A girl who scorns dolls and adores steam engines must be reached by an approach quite different from the one used with the dainty, domestic type of young lady. Favorite toys, stories, radio, TV programs, and the like all give the teacher insight into a child's character.

Sometimes it is possible to obtain, even at an early date, an account of the child's attitude toward school. David gave the impression during the early weeks at kindergarten that he simply "couldn't be bothered" doing any of the things the other children were doing. When the teacher interviewed the mother, she learned that David's attendance at the school was only temporary, that the family was to move out of the state in a month or two. The mother had deliberately warned David not to get too much interested in school in the belief that she was thus protecting him from too great disappointment at leaving school later on.

In the original interview with parents, the teacher must be sure to convey the idea that the information is being assembled in order that the home and the school can work together for the good of the child. One somewhat inexperienced teacher who failed in doing this gave the father the impression that she was simply prying into the private affairs of the family. At the conclusion of the interview, she was faced with a barrage of facetious questions from him.

Most schools find it advisable to set up their own home-interview blank. One which can meet the needs of many schools in its major design is the following, which has been adapted from the Initial Information Blank used in the Preschool Laboratories of the State University of Iowa.

HOME INFORMATION INTERVIEW

Child ______ ______ ______ ______
Last Name First Name Middle Name Name Used

Sex ______ Date of Birth ______ Place of Birth ______ Nationality ______

Address ______ Phone number ______

Previous school experience ______

Father ______ Place of Birth ______ Date ______

Place of birth of paternal grandparents (if outside U.S.) ______

Education: Grammar School ______ High School ______

College ______ Advanced Degree ______

Occupation ______ Address ______ Business Phone ______

Mother ______ Place of Birth ______ Date ______

Place of birth of maternal grandparents (if outside U.S.) ______
Mother's maiden name ______
Education: Grammar School ______ High School ______
College ______ Advanced Degree ______
Occupation before marriage ______
Present occupation outside home (if any) ______
Hours employed outside home ______
Business address ______ Business Phone ______

Are the father and mother living together? ______

Siblings—list below:

| Name | Sex | Date of Birth | If deceased, date, cause |
|---|---|---|---|
| | | | |
| | | | |
| | | | |

Members of household other than parents and own children:

| Name | Sex | Approximate age | Position in household |
|---|---|---|---|
| | | | |
| | | | |
| | | | |

Dwelling: House ______ Duplex ______ Apartment ______ Rooms ______
Does the child have a room of his own? If not, shared with whom? ______

Special interests
Favorite play activities ______
Favorite radio, TV programs ______
Favorite books and stories ______

Social activities
Is child's play limited to the yard? ______ to the block? ______
Into how many homes does the child go frequently? ______
How many playmates come to the child's home frequently? ______
Does the child attend movies? ______ Number of times a month ______
Does the child attend Sunday School? ______ Number of times a month ______
Is he enrolled in any special groups? (rhythms, play, art) ______
What travel experiences has the child had? ______
How does the child get along with other children? ______ with adults? ______

Health
Name of family doctor or child's doctor ______ Address ______
Estimate of present general physical condition ______
Anything unusual about birth? ______
Serious illnesses or accidents to date? ______
Contagious diseases: Measles ______ chickenpox ______ mumps ______
scarlet fever ______ whooping cough ______ others ______
Immunizations to date ______
Usual routine for sleep and rest
Night: In bed ______ Asleep ______ Up ______
*Rest: In bed ______ Asleep ______ Up ______
Foods
Appetite: Poor ______ Fair ______ Good ______ Very good ______ Excellent ______
Strong likes ______
Strong dislikes ______

What (if any) points are most often issues between parents and child?
What types of control are most frequently used?
What is the child's attitude toward his new school experience?

Information given by ______
Information recorded by ______
Date ______

* If child does not take a rest, how long has it been since daytime rest was discontinued?

## Records of Physical Condition

Early in the year, the school needs to know about the child's physical condition. All examinations by the school doctor should be reported, of course, to the home, though it may be advisable to make the report general and, in case of special difficulty, to refer the parents to the family physician. The report might read: "The school physician reports that Henry is in good physical condition" or, "The school physician recommends that Henry be taken to your family physician for treatment of eczema," or "to investigate his persistent cough," or, "Vision tests show that Henry should be taken to an oculist for examination."

Records of the child's height and weight made two or three times during the year will tell the school and the home much about the child's physical condition. A failure to gain during one period may mean nothing, but persistent failure to gain or actual loss in weight is sufficient reason for recommending a complete physical examination.

Periodic examinations of teeth can sometimes prevent serious dental problems later on, and checks on vision and hearing are essential if the handicapped child is to be understood and helped. It is exceedingly difficult for the untrained parent to recognize weakness in vision and hearing, and the young child, of course, does not realize that he sees or hears less well than any other person.

A record of absences from school, with the reasons for the absences, will give a good picture of the child's health and will often explain why, at the end of the year, a child does not seem to have gained as much as others from his year's experience.

## Records of Intelligence Tests[3]

While there is a tendency for some teachers to take individual test scores too seriously, the fact remains that tests given over a series of years are a reasonably good measure of an individual's mental stature at various stages in his development. If we can have a battery of reliable tests administered by trained examiners, and if we can know the tests given, the dates on which the tests were given, the scores or mental ages attained, and the trustworthiness of the test experience, we can better adapt our teaching to the mental development of individual children.

Some tests give us not only a measure of the child's mental stature but

[3] See bibliography of tests in Appendix. For a comprehensive list of tests and ratings for young children, see Hildreth, G. H., compiler. A *Bibliography of Mental Tests and Rating Scales*, New York, Psychological Corporation, 1933, 1939, 1945, 1949, and supplements.

also an indication of the areas in which the child shows special abilities and shortcomings. In the SRA Primary Mental Abilities test, for example, the child is given a score on comprehension of verbal meanings, speed of perception, quantitative awareness, motor skill, and space awareness. In the Minnesota Pre-School Test the child is given one score on the verbal and another on the nonverbal part of his test. These scores indicate the abilities of the child who is unusually capable in his use of language and the child who is more clever with his hands than with his tongue.

The policy of most testing centers is that parents should not be told the child's actual IQ. It is only with considerable experience and understanding of the difficulties in obtaining a reliable test score that we now know that, though a child's IQ usually stays in the same range, it may vary a number of points from one examination to another. The parent who hears in September that his child has an IQ of 105 and in May that it is 102 may feel that his child is regressing. The untrained person does not understand such variations and should be told that the child on both tests "tested normal for his age" or something to that effect. If the IQ rating is above 110, the parent can be told that the child is "above average," and perhaps we can say that the child who tests above 120 or 125 is "distinctly above average." Such reports will prevent many unhappy comparisons with children in the neighborhood when one child is known as the brightest simply because his IQ is a point or two above some other child's.

A simple technique for obtaining a reasonably objective measure of individual intelligence lies in the analysis of children's drawings. Each child, supplied with a single dark crayon and a piece of 9 in. x 12 in. Manila paper, may be asked to draw the best picture of a man he can. When these pictures are scored on the basis of the Goodenough Drawing Test,[4] it is found that the scores have a very high correlation with scores obtained on other intelligence tests. Even if the teacher is not prepared to do the scientific scoring, she will find that she can obtain a fairly accurate range of the mental ability in her group by merely arranging the drawings in piles in relation to the number of details included in each child's portrayal of the human figure.

## Rating Scales

If such rating scales as those dealing with introversion-extroversion (Marston) or with problem tendencies (Haggerty-Olson-Wickman) are available, it proves both interesting and valuable to check the individuals

[4] See bibliography of tests in Appendix.

of the group on these standardized scales. The ratings thus obtained give the teacher a picture of the behavior tendencies of her group in relation to those of other groups.

In addition any records which the teacher might have on the child's readiness for future learning should also be included, of course, in the cumulative record folder. Different types of readiness may be indicated objectively by the child's performance on a modification of the Probst Information Test, the Brueckner Readiness Test in Arithmetic, and the Metropolitan Reading Readiness Test. This is, of course, not a complete list of tests; there are many others, particularly in the area of reading readiness.

## Anecdotal Material and Behavioral Jottings

The kindergarten teacher will find it very helpful to keep a record of behavior which reflects desirable and undesirable attitudes on the part of the child. A single event will have little if any significance. But if, through a year, we get such a record as the following from a child's folder, we can feel that it tells us much about the child, her personality, and her problems.

10/ 4 Lois brought an army whistle to school. Gene claimed it as his. There seemed no available solution to the problem. Lois took the whistle home.

10/25 Lois went out the door doubled up in a jackknife fashion. Casual observation revealed that she was concealing a rubber boat which belonged in the locker next to hers. Upon request she cheerfully returned the boat to the locker.

11/24 Lois was the last child to leave the kindergarten. She talked enthusiastically about the watch she had in her hand. "My Daddy gave it to me last Christmas. He gave my sister one, too. I just *love* my watch."

11/25 Arnold reported the loss of a watch from his locker. Lois hastened to say, "I didn't take it." The others chimed in, "She did, too," "I saw her with it in her pocket at rest time," "She always takes everything."

3/ 4 Lois brought a very attractive puppet doll to the group meeting. She explained she had found it on the floor by her locker and wondered whose it was. Betty: "It's mine, but you can play with it if you want to." Lois: "Oh, thank you, Betty. I think I'll sit by you. We're friends, aren't we?"

It might be a good plan to single out each week two or perhaps three children for special observation. To clarify the problem and to simplify the recording, it is convenient to have on hand mimeographed sheets, perhaps set up in the following fashion:

BEHAVORIAL JOTTINGS

Child's name ______________________ Age: Years ____ Mo. ____ Days ____

Enrolled in ______________________ Observed by ______________________

Record below observed and dated instances of behavior which would seem to indicate that this child has characteristics which would make his presence a distinct asset to the group:

______________________________________________

______________________________________________

Suggestions for further developing and utilizing these good qualities:

______________________________________________

______________________________________________

Record below observed and dated instances of behavior which would seem to indicate that this child has characteristics which might profitably be modified by his kindergarten experience:

______________________________________________

______________________________________________

Suggestions for modifying these qualities:

______________________________________________

______________________________________________

## Records of Achievement in School

One of the things we want to know about every kindergarten child is whether or not he is showing growth and progress. It is desirable to keep samples of various sorts of achievement at different periods in the year, so that we can demonstrate the change in ability. Drawings are, of course, the easiest to store. We need only note the child's name and the date in the corner of the sheet and then drop it into a file for comparison with later drawings. Sometimes it is possible to keep samples of work done in wood and clay, but the wood constructions frequently soon fall apart, and the clay crumbles away. If the school has a photographer (or if the teacher is sufficiently interested to use her own camera), pictures of these constructions are more satisfactory than attempts to store the actual articles.

The child is improving not only in his use of materials but also in the use of language. If the teacher or an assistant can write down the first three or four remarks a child makes on a day in the fall, in the winter, and in the spring, she should be able to see a distinct advance in pronunciation, length of sentence, and use of words. It is also possible to record the child's use of language by taking down at intervals through the year his own dictation of the "story" that goes with his picture. The dictation may be recorded directly on the back of the drawing.

*Levels of Maturity Clearly Indicated in Picture-Making*

*(Top) Drawings—Pictures Made by a Two-Year-Old, a Three-Year-Old, a Four-Year-Old, and a Five-Year-Old*

*(Bottom) Paintings—Pictures Made by a Two-Year-Old, a Three-Year-Old, a Four-Year-Old, and a Five-Year-Old*

## Records of Behavior in School

Although accurate tests are a great help to the teacher, a lack of them need not handicap her seriously in following the development of a child. There are many evidences of development which she may record during the year and then later compare to discover whether or not a child seems to be gaining.

One form on which the kindergarten teacher can record the child's school behavior is on pp. 484–485, adapted from the blank used in the kindergarten of the Elementary School at the University of Minnesota. The record is merely a guide to aid the teacher in setting down her impressions of the child's behavior as she sees the child in a group of his peers. It includes a number of items and would probably be too cumbersome to be used in a public-school system, where the enrollment totals are sometimes staggering. Each school system can develop its own blank for recording school behavior. The blanks will of necessity be much more brief than this, but each in essence will probably include the major items indicated.

## A Record Showing the Total Picture of the Human Resources of the Group

As the teacher comes to know her group, she will do well to make an inventory of the human resources which it represents. Perhaps by the end of the first semester she will have made enough observations and assembled enough data so that she can plot her chart of human resources. This chart is not only valuable to the teacher herself but also has predictive value. It gives the school principal and those who will be working with the group later an estimate of the kind of performance to be expected from the group as it progresses through the grades. The chart may also serve as evidence in later years of why the group is able to perform above or below grade norms established on certain achievement tests. Items included on the chart are the name of the child, chronological age, scores on mental tests, physical and behavioral characteristics, earlier school experience, siblings, occupations of father and mother, standards which the family sets for the child and, most important of all, what the child can do for the kindergarten—special interests and abilities—and what the kindergarten can do for the child—special needs or shortcomings.

## Records for the Use of the Child

It is sometimes desirable, though not always, to have records of accomplishment which the child himself can follow. All of us occasionally enjoy surpassing our own previous record. The child referred to in the anecdotal

KINDERGARTEN RECORD BLANK

Report on ______________________

Enrolled in ______________________ Group. Date ______________

Days absent first semester ______________ Second semester ______________

Enrollment transferred to ______________________ Group. Date ______________

Teacher ______________ Date ________ Teacher ______________ Date ________

| | Date | Date |
|---|---|---|
| *I. *Intellectual Behavior* | | |
| Initiates own activities: (1) wholly; (4) at times; (7) seldom | | |
| Contributes ideas which are: (1) very useful; (4) useful; (7) useless | | |
| Carries out plans: (1) almost exactly; (4) approximately; (7) with many changes | | |
| Judges worth of own work: (1) accurately; (4) approximately; (7) inaccurately | | |
| Expresses own thoughts: (1) very clearly; (4) clearly; (7) vaguely | | |
| Uses correct English: (1) consistently; (4) usually; (7) seldom | | |
| Shows originality in stories: (1) great; (4) average; (7) little | | |
| Retells stories, rhymes, etc.: (1) very well; (4) moderately well; (7) poorly | | |
| Shows appreciation of the value of numbers: (1) keen; (4) average; (7) vague | | |
| Shows interest in printed words: (1) keen; (4) average; (7) little | | |
| Alert to his environment: (1) markedly; (4) moderately; (7) little | | |
| II. *Social Behavior* | | |
| Displays leadership: (1) marked; (4) average; (7) slight | | |
| Appreciates rights of others: (1) clearly; (4) fairly clearly; (7) vaguely | | |
| Respects rights of others: (1) uniformly; (4) when politic; (7) when necessary | | |
| Shows a give-and-take spirit: (1) consistently; (4) within limits; (7) seldom | | |
| Offers negative criticism: (1) seldom; (4) occasionally; (7) frequently | | |
| Offers positive criticism: (1) frequently; (4) occasionally; (7) seldom | | |
| Profits by the criticism of others: (1) markedly; (4) somewhat; (7) little | | |
| Exhibits courteous habits (please, thank you, etc.): (1) consistently; (4) to some degree; (7) seldom | | |
| Responds to signals and directions: (1) alertly; (4) adequately; (7) sluggishly | | |
| Takes responsibility for carrying on own routine activities: (1) completely; (4) at times; (7) seldom | | |
| Enters into the joys and sorrows of others: (1) markedly; (4) somewhat; (7) little | | |
| Enters into play with others: (1) wholeheartedly; (4) adequately (7) little | | |
| Is accepted by the other children: (1) enthusiastically; (4) as a matter of course; (7) with reservations | | |
| III. *Emotional Behavior* | | |
| Displays anger: (1) justifiably; (4a) somewhat excessively; (7a) excessively; (4b) somewhat insufficiently; (7b) insufficiently | | |
| Displays self-assertion: (1) justifiably; (4a) somewhat excessively; (7a) excessively; (4b) somewhat insufficiently; (7b) insufficiently | | |

* The numbers indicate directional tendencies only. They are not indications of specific gradations.

| | Date | Date |
|---|---|---|
| Displays fear or timidity: (1) justifiably; (4a) somewhat excessively; (4b) somewhat insufficiently; (7a) excessively (7b) insufficiently | | |
| Displays affection: (1) justifiably; (4a) somewhat excessively; (4b) somewhat insufficiently; (7a) excessively (7b) insufficiently | | |
| Displays joy or happiness: (1) justifiably; (4a) somewhat excessively; (4b) somewhat insufficiently; (7a) excessively (7b) insufficiently | | |
| Displays discouragement: (1) justifiably; (4a) somewhat excessively; (4b) somewhat insufficiently; (7a) excessively (7b) insufficiently | | |
| Displays excitability: (1) justifiably; (4a) somewhat excessively; (4b) somewhat insufficiently; (7a) excessively (7b) insufficiently | | |
| Shifts moods: (1) justifiably; (4a) somewhat excessively; (4b) somewhat insufficiently; (7a) excessively (7b) insufficiently | | |
| IV. *Skills* | | |
| Adjusts own outside wraps: (1) easily; (4) fairly easily; (7) awkwardly | | |
| Moves about the room: (1) gracefully; (4) with average ease; (7) awkwardly | | |
| Responds to rhythms: (1) feelingly; (4) adequately; (7) uncertainly | | |
| Relaxes at rest time: (1) completely; (4) partially; (7) but little | | |
| Matches musical tones: (1) skillfully; (4) fairly well; (7) poorly | | |
| Carries a tune alone: (1) skillfully; (4) fairly well; (7) poorly | | |
| Handles hammer and saw: (1) skillfully; (4) fairly well; (7) poorly | | |
| Handles scissors: (1) skillfully; (4) fairly well; (7) poorly | | |
| Handles crayons: (1) skillfully; (4) fairly well; (7) poorly | | |
| Handles paints: (1) skillfully; (4) fairly well; (7) poorly | | |
| Handles modeling materials: (1) skillfully; (4) fairly well; (7) poorly | | |

V. *Interests*

Physical activities: (1) marked; (4) average; (7) slight ______

Manual arts: (1) marked; (4) average; (7) slight ______

Imaginative play: (1) marked; (4) average; (7) slight ______

Music: (1) marked; (4) average; (7) slight ______

Books and stories: (1) marked; (4) average; (7) slight ______

VI. *Special Abilities or Assets*

Date ______

VII. *Features of Conditions Which Might Warrant Special Consideration*

Date ______

VIII. *Physical Growth Record*

| Height in Inches | Date | Weight in Pounds | Date |
|---|---|---|---|
| | | | |
| | | | |

IX. *General Physical Condition at Time of Last Physical Examination*

Date ______ ______

Date ______ ______

records on p. 480 was delighted when the teacher volunteered to help her win back her reputation by keeping a record of both the disagreeable and agreeable incidents in her daily behavior. The agreeable column soon outgrew the other, and Lois seemed to take great pride in studying the two columns.

It is often difficult to know when to terminate such a record; if it is continued too long, it loses its significance. In this particular case, however, the problem was not a difficult one. The record-keeping terminated promptly when the mother reported that in a bedtime conversation Lois had said, "Mother, I do have fun being agreeable!" and then added somewhat meditatively, "But I *don't* want to get like Evelyn. You know she's too agreeable. Why, she's just *too darned* agreeable."

## Special Records for Research

Although most teachers find their time fully taken up with the immediate demands of the kindergarten day, a few manage and are sufficiently well trained to carry out their own bits of scientific research. Others who have not the training themselves can cooperate with the research workers by keeping records and collecting data. In some school systems, usually those located near a university or teachers college, the teachers are called on to make provision in their program for research workers to come in to collect data. If such research studies do not greatly interrupt the program of the day, the teacher should be ready and eager to assist.

## Reports from the School to the Home

If parents are to help their child achieve a development commensurate with his potentialities, the more they know about the child, the better. The first aim, then, in making reports to the home should be to give the parents a better understanding of their child. Ideally, a report shared with the parents should help them appreciate (1) where their child stands in relation to his previous growth and progress; (2) where he stands in relation to the development and growth of his present class; (3) where he stands in relation to the development of all other children of his own age; (4) where he stands in relation to his own capacity for growth; and (5) where he may be expected to stand if he performs up to his capacity in the years to come. To attempt to make a report of this nature seems at first like undertaking the impossible; yet if the teacher will go back over her cumulative record material and if she will keep in mind the outline which guided her in rating the child's school behavior, she will find that it is really not difficult to make a worthwhile report.

## Written Reports

It has already been suggested that the report to the home should be a simplification of the report on school behavior kept in the cumulative record folder. How far one goes in simplifying the report will depend in part on the type of parent to whom the report is being sent and in part on the purpose of the report. Sometimes the linear rating on qualities is retained in the report sent to the parents, and sometimes the substance of the long report is simply condensed into the pattern of an informal letter. In addition to the routine record of attendance, the report will include some summary of the physical and dental examinations. Some reference will be made to any outstandingly desirable qualities the child may possess and to the child's intellectual, social, emotional, and motor behavior. Special interests will be pointed out, and if there are indications of present or impending difficulties, these also will be noted. In every respect it will be evident that the school is interested in cooperating with the parent in helping the child make the most of his native endowment. Some schools encourage the parents to come in for conferences following receipt of the school report. In fact, the written report often makes a very good opening for the conference. If the parents are asked to share with the school their observations of the child's out-of-school behavior, they have the assurance that they are helping round out the child's total developmental picture.

## Oral Reports

Even the best written reports cannot take the place of the personal conference. Sympathetic listening on the part of the teacher will give her insight and understanding which she could not possibly gain otherwise. The points touched on in the conference will be the same as those considered in the written report. If the parents have already had a written report, questions raised in reading it may well be discussed. The written report often raises questions in the minds of the parents which, if it were not for the conference, would have to go unanswered. Schools have changed greatly since the parents of present-day children were young, and these changes need to be pointed out and interpreted to the parents. Factors which loomed as great problems often seem to vanish if the situation can be talked over. It has been said that the teacher's estimate of the degree to which a child is a problem tends to vary in direct proportion to the degree to which she knows the family—that is, the better the teacher knows the family, the less Johnny seems to be a problem.

## Time for Oral Reports

If kindergarten reports are to be made orally, the teacher must be allowed time for the conferences. One group of kindergarten teachers, together with their supervisor and their principals, have been experimenting with a plan whereby the teacher is entirely free from teaching responsibilities on Fridays until the conferences have been completed. It is understood by the parents that the kindergarten will not be in session for the first three or four successive Fridays.

## Other Opportunities for Parent-Teacher Contacts

The least time-consuming and probably the least effective form of parent-teacher conference is found in the meetings of the Parent-Teacher Association. Such meetings are excellent places for the presentation of the aims of the school in general, and for the discussion of plans wherein parents and teachers can cooperate in improving the work of the school. They are poor places, however, for discussing the problems of any individual child.

In serious cases of "discipline" it is often the custom to ask the parents to come to the school for a conference with the principal or the teacher. There is no reason to have such discussions only for grave difficulties. It may be quite as important to ask parents to come to the school to hear how well their child has done as to call them in when the performance of the child has been very poor. If the schedule of the teacher is not exhausting, she may be able to set aside certain late afternoons for fifteen- or twenty-minute conferences.

Perhaps most important of all are the casual contacts between mother and teacher. If a parent brings the child to school, the minute or two of greeting and the occasional query and answer will build up an understanding and frequently a real friendship which will help both teacher and parent in their guidance of the child. If the parents can come to spend an hour or so in the kindergarten, they will see their child in comparison with others of his age and in a situation quite different from the one at home.

Not to be forgotten are the chance meetings of parents and teachers at the grocery store, on the bus, or at church, which help to make each feel a little more friendly toward the other. If the child happens to be with the parent at the time, the meeting is even more fortunate.

Many parents plan to invite the teachers to their homes for a meal sometime during the year. Some mothers are shy about giving such invitations, for they fear the teachers will interpret them as a request for special treatment of their child. Other mothers are quick to make the teachers realize that the purpose of the invitation is to allow parents and teachers to become better acquainted or to give the children the pleasure of entertaining the teacher in their own home. Although the conversation is likely to refer occasionally to the child, it is important to keep the conversation general, to exchange points of view on major interests, and to make teacher, parents, and children all members of an informal social group.

In some schools, teachers are asked to make at least one visit to the home during the school year. Teachers who go to the home must remember that it is courteous to make an appointment with the mother before the call. The child is usually delighted to have the teacher visit. When they next meet at the school, there is a new kind of kinship, and for both child and teacher there is a new and closer bond between the home and the school.

## SUMMARY

Records are kept for a variety of purposes. For each child there should be a cumulative record folder, with contributions from both school and home. Records are for use, not for storage. The report to the parents, whether written or oral, should convey information which will help them better understand and provide for their child's development. The conference has an advantage over the written report, for it results in the mutual benefit of parents and teachers. It is to the advantage of teachers, children, and parents that a wholesome school-home bond be established.

## QUESTIONS AND PROBLEMS

1. What can a kindergarten teacher learn from watching the records of her children as they progress through the grades?
2. If a child transfers from one kindergarten to another in the middle of the year and fails to make a good adjustment in the second school, what information does the second teacher need from the first?
3. Secure copies of the kindergarten report used in several schools. What improvements can you suggest?
4. Devise a brief report to be sent in confidence to the first-grade teacher, and one to be sent to the parents.

## SELECTED REFERENCES

Association for Childhood Education International, Washington, D.C.:
"Recording and Reporting Children's Growth," Primary School Portfolio No. 3, 1956.
"Records Aid Good Teaching," Nursery School Portfolio No. 1, 1953.
"The Why and How of Kindergarten Records," Kindergarten Teacher's Portfolio No. 2, 1951.

Berson, Minnie Perrin, *Kindergarten—Your Child's Big Step,* New York, E. P. Dutton Company, 1959.

Davis, David C., *Patterns of Primary Education,* New York, Harper and Row, 1963.

Hammond, Sara Lou, Ruth J. Dales, Dora Sikes Skipper, and Ralph L. Witherspoon, *Good Schools for Young Children,* New York, Macmillan Company, 1963.

Imhoff, Myrtle M., "Report Forms," *Early Elementary Education,* New York, Appleton-Century-Crofts, 1959.

Kawin, Ethel, *A Guide for Child Study Groups,* Chicago, Science Research Associates, 1959.

Kopp, O. W., "Building Good Home-School Relationships," *Those First School Years,* Washington, D.C., National Education Association, 1960.

Langdon, Grace, and Irving W. Stout, *Helping Parents Understand Their Child's School: A Handbook for Teachers,* New York, Prentice-Hall, 1957.

Langdon, Grace, and Irving W. Stout, *Teacher-Parent Interviews,* New York, Prentice-Hall, 1954.

Leonard, Edith M., Dorothy VanDeman, and Lillian Miles, *Counseling with Parents,* New York, Macmillan Company, 1954.

Moore, Sallie Beth, and Phyllis Richards, *Teaching in the Nursery School,* New York, Harper and Brothers, 1959.

Osborne, Ernest, *The Parent-Teacher Partnership,* New York, Bureau of Publications, Teachers College, Columbia University, 1959

Rudolph, Marguerite, and Dorothy H. Cohen, *Kindergarten: A Year of Learning,* New York, Appleton-Century-Crofts, 1964.

Strang, Ruth, *Reporting to Parents,* New York, Bureau of Publications, Teachers College, Columbia University, 1947.

# 24

# FOUNDATION LEARNING AND READINESS FOR FIRST-GRADE LIVING

In the early part of this century, our schools began to evince great interest in and concern for the physical development and welfare of the child. In the nineteen twenties and thirties great stress was placed on social development. In the forties and fifties, the emotional side of the child's development attracted the educational spotlight. In the early nineteen sixties, following the launching of Sputnik I, pressures from all sides came to bear on the schools demanding that they do more about stepping up the intellectual challenge of their program. Much was published, and is still being published, in both popular and professional periodicals about what could and should be done in the way of speeding up learning. Studies have been made and evidence has been presented proving that children can acquire certain academic skills at a very early age. To date, however, no one has evidence to support the contention that "can" means "should." Great strides have been taken in providing intellectual challenges for gifted children and much is being said and written about the need for providing an honest intellectual challenge for all children. Now at the midpoint of the nineteen sixties there is national concern for enriching the backgrounds of those children who for one reason or another appear to be culturally disadvantaged. Fortunately, along with this concern has come a growing awareness of the fact that creativity plays an important part in achievement.

Interestingly enough the kindergarten has always shown great concern for background enrichment *and* creativity. It is hoped that in meeting society's demands for academic achievement it will not lose sight of its honest concern for both background enrichment and creativity. The kindergarten has always been concerned with offering children an intellectual challenge; but it has somewhat shied away from speaking about the intellectual or academic side of its program. Probably this has been the case for two reasons: (1) the non-compartmentalized nature of its academic program makes it difficult to explain, and (2) if the academic side of its program were featured, the lay public and many educators as well might tend to think of it as a "sit down, be quiet, and I'll teach you" program. Today the kindergarten stands ready to proclaim and defend its academic program. Some have felt that having an academic program means bringing the recognition of the printed page and the use of pencils and other formal reading-readiness procedures and materials down into the kindergarten. Others have felt that we meet the challenge of providing intellectual stimulation for kindergarten children by simply being aware of the educational implications of many experiences that are naturally a part of kindergarten living.

This chapter presents a thesis which contends that (a) the kindergarten should and does have an academic program, and (b) the academic program of the kindergarten is developed through everyday experience living rather than through isolated rote learning or artificially contrived problems designed to provoke thought and develop paper and pencil techniques.

Although the kindergarten program is not subject-matter oriented and the subject matter dealt with is not compartmentalized, yet through planned experiences and the teacher's awareness of the educational implications of casual experiences, foundations for further learning are constantly being built. One of the delights of teaching in the kindergarten is that the curriculum is not rigidly circumscribed. In the experience program the teacher and the children can touch on great bodies of subject matter. Let's take phonics as an example. The teacher calls the names of Marcia and Martha, and Marcia says, "Say, we better be careful, 'cause Marcia and Martha start just alike. If we don't be listening we might get mixed up." The teacher does not overlook the educational implication of the situation. She knows that the place of phonics is a moot question in the teaching of beginning reading, but she recognizes that experience with phonics may begin at any time. And so she says, "That's good listening, Marcia," and then, printing the names of Marcia and Martha on a large piece of paper on a nearby easel, she says, "They *sound* very much alike and look, MAR-cia and MAR-tha, they *look* a good bit alike too, don't they? And I can think of two other names in our group that start the same way that MAR-cia and MAR-tha start." Meeting the challenge, the children discover that MAR-k and MAR-vel also start the same way. John, after some scrutinizing and mouthing of syllables says, "Say, and also Mary, that's my sister's name, starts the same way, MAR-y, but it doesn't sound the same."

Louise M. Gross

*Picture Writing Develops Eye-Hand Coordination.*

In the course of any one day in the kindergarten, there may arise experiences bearing on reading, arithmetic, writing, biology, geology, geography, physics, chemistry, history, or any other knowledge to be found in the arts or the natural, physical, or social sciences. If the teacher is aware of the opportunities which the kindergarten year provides for each child's development, then most of the children in her group will enter first grade ready for that phase of reading which focuses special interest on printed symbols as conveyors of thought and ideas.

The kindergarten teacher is mindful, of course, of the fact that most five-year-olds, as they approach six or six and one-half years, are just coming into that stage of their development in which they exhibit a great eagerness to read and write. She has a great academic responsibility in seeing that five-year-olds have experiences which will pave the way for a logical and comfortable next step toward the acquisition of new tools of learning.

On the following pages you will find examples of foundation experiences in various areas of interest. Notc that in providing such experiences, the teacher must exercise considerable skill and judgment in knowing when, where, and how to emphasize their academic aspects. Nothing could be more deadly than having a teacher break the continuity of an experience to say, "And now, children, from this experience you can learn . . ." The teacher must also be selective in the kind and amount of information she chooses to share. Too many experiences and too much information are probably more harmful to children than too few experiences and too little information.

## Foundation Experiences in Reading[1]

1. Tr. "S., will you please bring the mail box over to the piano?"
   S. returns carrying a box of nails.
   S. (looking doubtful) "Is this what you wanted?"
   Tr. (holding a sealed letter in a conspicuous position) "Why did you think we wanted nails?"
   S. "Oh, oh—I thought you said nail box. Nail. Mail? It was the mail box you needed for the letters."
   Tr. "Nail and mail? They do sound a great deal alike, don't they? Nail and mail rhyme exactly, don't they? I can easily see how you would confuse the two."

2. As the teacher shows the pictures and reads *The Little Gardeners*, the fence in the story appears first as blue and then as green.
   C. "But look, they changed the color of the fence."
   Tr. "Maybe the blue color was just the first coat of paint."
   C. "And look, the little girl doesn't have the same dress on she had in the other picture. They made a mistake."
   Tr. "That's a careful observation, C. But you know it takes a long time, many days to make a garden. Maybe this is many days later and she is wearing another dress."

3. B. "In what row shall I plant the carrot seeds?"
   Tr. "Frankly, I don't know—I think it is either row two or three. You had better look on our garden plan to make sure."
   B. looks but says, "I can't tell."
   J. "I'll go help you."
   Both children return carrying a 2 x 3 foot bulletin board on which the plan is posted.
   J. "Here it is, but this word has an 'S' on it and B.'s (referring to his seed package) doesn't."

[1] Following each section is a list of references related to the type of experience described.

Tr. "J., you certainly do observe details! B.'s package says 'carrot,' but when I wrote the word I was thinking not of *a* carrot but of many carrots so I wrote carrots instead of carrot."

B. "Now I see! Then carrots go in row three. And do we put them in holes or shake them in?"

Tr. (reading the directions aloud) " 'Make a line ¼ inch deep (measuring with her finger and thumb) and scatter.' We can shake them in."

4. C. has a sealed envelope on which she has printed her name. This she opens at the group meeting, saying, "When I was looking in a mazagine I saw these pictures and 'cause we're interested in flowers I cut them out and brought them." She has a small rose, violets, and a large rose.

Tr. "That was thoughtful of you. There are often interesting pictures of flowers in magazines, aren't there? Let's all of us keep looking in magazines and if nobody needs the magazine any more maybe we could cut out enough flowers to make an attractive bulletin board."

5. M. has brought a bouquet of bleeding hearts to kindergarten.

J. "When I was helping Miss T. fix the library books, I saw a Snipp, Snapp, and Snurr book and in that book the princess was under a tree that had flowers on it that looked like this."

Tr. "I believe you are right, J. Not now, but later, could you get the book and put it in our library? I think the children would enjoy seeing that picture."

J. "I'll do that."

6. Teacher rereading typed letter which had been dictated by the children. She runs her finger under the lines as she reads.

Tr. "And here, I see, is the beginning of a new idea; it's a new paragraph." She reads further. "And here I see we have another idea and another paragraph. There are many different ideas and many different paragraphs in our letter, but they are all telling about the rabbit. Let's count the paragraphs." As she points to the indentations, the children count.

7. E., eating a morning snack of milk and crackers, "Look, the cookie has my initial on it!" And sure enough, he has eaten all except the part on which the "E" was raised.

8. As the teacher starts to read at the top of the page about Pet, L. turns to a friend and says in a clear voice, "Pet, let, bet, set."

Tr. "Those words do rhyme, don't they? But since the first sentence on the page was interrupted, suppose I begin again, so that you can enjoy every bit of the story."

9. M. has brought the *Golden Encyclopedia* to show the picture of the moth or butterfly which seemed to be like the one J. caught and put in a jar on the science table. She has her page marked and, sure enough, the picture looks like J.'s.

Tr. "Have you checked on the markings or the spots on the wings?"
M. checked and reported that J.'s had six spots, three on each side.

Tr. "Your picture is surprisingly like J.'s."
Together M. and the teacher look but cannot find a picture of one exactly like J.'s.

10. Tr. "I'm thinking of something in your kitchen that you let the water go down."
Ch. "Sink."
Tr. "Now I'm thinking of something that sounds like sink. It is something you write with."
Ch. "Ink."
Tr. "And now I am thinking of something that sounds like ink and it's something you do with your eyes."
Ch. "Blink."

11. Each child has a 3 x 5 card on which are written his name and plans for his Christmas gifts in this fashion: Carol: spindle—clay.
When the gift was started this sign was put on the card: —.
When it was finished this sign was made: +.
When the article was wrapped, this sign followed: ⊕.
The cards are placed on the piano but there is not enough room for all to be spread out.

S. "Why don't we put all the name cards that start with the same letter together?"

12. M. "I'm thinking of a word that rhymes with green."
R. "Bean?"
M. "No."
G. "Queen?"
M. "No."
Tr. "Tangerine?"
M. "No, it is dream."
Tr. "But does it rhyme? Look, when I say *green*, my lips are like this for 'n,' and when I say *dream*, my lips are like this for 'm.'

They do sound something alike, but if they are going to rhyme they have to come out of your mouth the same way."

13. M. is trying to tell her mother where Miss Z., a Spanish-speaking guest, is from. She cannot remember but goes to the family dictionary to find the light blue and white flag which the guest had pointed out as being her flag.
M. said, "She comes from here. This is her flag; what is the name of her country?"
"San Salvador," reads her mother.

14. Plans are being made for making applesauce. As the group lists articles needed, the teacher writes them on a large sheet of paper on the easel.
Apples Pan Spoon
M. says, "Why don't you draw the pictures too?" and the teacher attempts to do so.
Sugar Cinnamon Knife Stove
Tr. "As I put the number in front of the article, will you say the name of the article—just read it." The teacher numbers and the group "reads" words and pictures without difficulty.

15. M. and G. are asked by the teacher to bring from the library the book called *Runaway Rabbit*. They bring three rabbit books before coming to the right one.
M. "Maybe we had better look at the picture to see if the rabbit is running away," said M.
They return with the right book. The teacher runs her finger under the title and points out her own error saying the title reads *Runaway Bunny*, not *Runaway Rabbit*. They compare the title of the *Velveteen Rabbit* with the title of *Runaway Bunny*.

16. The teacher is holding up a Japanese picture storybook before the group. As she opens it, D. says, "But you're looking at it backwards."
M. "Not for a Japanese book. They do it that way. When you use their things you do it the way they do."
The teacher runs her finger along the words and then runs her finger across the page as one would follow the words in English.
S. "*Two* things are different about Japanese books. They begin at the back and they read up and down."
D. "Read it."
Tr. "I'm sorry; I can't read this."
B. "But we can read the pictures anyway, huh?"

17. Ann W. has picked up a green paper chain which she thinks is hers.
Ann M. looks at the name on the chain and says, "That's mine."
Both girls carry the chain and carefully examine another green chain. Finally they take the two chains over to their lockers and look at their name tags.
"Here, this one is yours," said Ann M.
They check with the teacher; Ann M. has identified her initial correctly.

## SELECTED REFERENCES


Association for Childhood Education International, Washington, D.C.:
*Basic Human Values,* Bulletin 8-A, 1962.
*Implications of Basic Human Values,* Bulletin 10-A, 1964.
*Reading in the Kindergarten??* 6-A, 1962.

Blakely, Paul W., and Emma Shadle, "A Study of Two-Readiness for Reading Programs in the Kindergarten," *Elementary English,* November, 1961, 37:502–509.

Cowin, Shirley H., "Reading Readiness Through Kindergarten Experiences," *Elementary School Journal,* October, 1951, 52:96–99.

Downing, John, *ITA Reading Experiment,* Toronto, Canada, British Book Service, Ltd., 1964.

Ploghoft, Milton H., "Do Reading Readiness Workbooks Promote Readiness?" *Elementary English,* October, 1959, 36:424–426.

Smith, Nila B., *Reading Instruction for Today's Children,* Englewood Cliffs, New Jersey, Prentice-Hall, 1963 (see particularly chapters 3, 4, and 15).

Smith, Nila B., *Shall We Teach Reading in the Kindergarten?,* Bulletin H, Washington, D.C., Association for Childhood Education, 1964.

Vernon, P. E., M. B. O'Gorman, and T. McClellan, "Comparative Story of Educational Attainments in England and Scotland," *British Journal of Educational Psychology,* 1955, 25:195–203.


## Foundation Experiences in Arithmetic

1. Since the clock indicates that there is no more time for story reading, the teacher presents this problem.

Tr. "Let's see, on which page are we having to stop?" She runs her finger under "25" and some join her in saying, "Twenty-five."
"Now, how are we going to remember that?"

J. "It comes right before 26."
D. "It comes right after 24."
Tr. "You're both right. But suppose we forget the numeral?"
K. "We could remember that we stopped where the picture of the rabbit is."
F. "Wait a minute." F. leaves the group and returns carrying a piece of Kleenex. "Here, put this right where it says '25' and then if we forget the numerals we can just look for the marker."

2. The children are standing in a circle; each child has two place mats in his hands, one that he has made for a guest and one that he has made for himself. The teacher, as she moves around the circle, starts counting: "Two, four, six, eight," and so on. Some of the children look mystified, others mouth the words, and about four of the group of thirty count along easily with the teacher.
Tr. "I was just counting by twos because I knew each of you had two place mats in his hands. Let's check our count to see if we get the same number when we count by ones."

3. The group is ready to go over to get fruit juice.
B. "Let's go the hard way."
The teacher designates a space for line "A" and line "B" and then she says, "C., will you be number 1 in line 'B'?". . . , "J., will you be number 5 in line 'A'?". . . , "D., . . . number 3 in line 'B'?". . . , "G., . . . number 1 in line 'A'?". . . , and so on until line "A" and line "B" each is complete with five children. These two lines go over to get their fruit juice as two other lines are formed.

4. The group is gathering by the piano. Those already assembled with the teacher, do rote counting. They accent the number on which individuals arrive to sit with the group. *1*, 2, *3*, 4, 5, 6, *7*, 8, 9, *10* . . . *15*, *16* . . . 22 . . . 29 . . . *50*, and so on until J. joins the group at 99.

5. Tr. "K., if I fold this paper, will you cut it so we will have two pieces the same size—will you cut it in half?"
K. "There, now they're just the same size, and we have two pieces instead of one."
Tr. "Thank you! Just right—two halves. That is just what we need."

6. E. has been explaining at some length the picture he has painted, telling about a cowboy, a hideout, a sunset, and so on. In one

corner he has a vertical and horizontal line crossing each other. "And that," said E., "is a 'venus' or, I mean a 'plus.' "

Tr. "It does look like a plus sign, E."

"What does plus mean?" ask several children.

Tr. "Perhaps I can show you," and picking up two books she continues, "This book and this one added to it—or this one book *plus* this book would give us—would make us have two books." Then on the back of E.'s picture, with his permission, she writes:

| | | |
|---|---|---|
| 1 book | then 2 books | 4 |
| + 1 book | + 2 books | + 4 |
| 2 books | "4 books" call the children | "8" call some of the children. |

Tr. "Now I'm going to make it hard and I'm going to put four here and I'm going to write *minus* or take away two here." "Two," call about six of the twenty-seven children. Then, for the benefit of those who seem mystified by this higher mathematics, she picks up four books and then takes away two. Problems continue for as much as five minutes, and even then some of the group are loath to have them discontinued.

S. "Let's do it again tomorrow."

7. After a group meeting, the teacher suggests that the group go back to work for just ten minutes—or until the big hand of the clock would be on numeral twelve.

J. "Until twelve o'clock?"

Tr. "No, until two o'clock. The little hand, you see, is almost on numeral two. When it is really on two and the big hand is on numeral twelve, then it will be just exactly two o'clock. The little hand always tells us the hour and the big hand always tells us how many minutes it is before or after the hour. Now it is ten minutes—or nearly nine minutes—before the hour of two."

8. M. "C., I can count 100 faster than you can. One—one hundred!"

Tr. "And then if you wanted to go on counting by one hundreds you would have 200 next, then . . . ?"

C. and M. continued, "300, 400, 500, . . . 900," and the teacher supplied "1000."

M. "Let's go on by thousands, '2000, 3000, 4000, . . .' " Counting continues into the millions and billions. Finally J., who has been standing nearby, says, "And then if you kept on going, it would be 'finity."

9. R. comes up from the garden saying that a stick, a row marker, is missing.

Tr. "Which one, R.?"
R. "I don't know; I'll go down and see."
R. returns saying, "There wasn't any marker on the row. But I looked on the next row to it and that was '11,' so now I know that it's '10' that is missing."
Tr. "R., I'm glad you noticed that the marker was missing. Would you put a '10' on this stick, and here is some string to mark the line of the row."

10. J. "I'll be six in a few weeks."
P. "I'm six already."
J. "We aren't babies any more."
Tr. "That's so true; you have long since left your baby days behind. C. has a brother who hasn't even had his first birthday. He isn't even a year old, is he, C.? Is he months old?"
C. "No, only weeks old and before that he was only days old."
Tr. "And before that he was only hours old."
A. "And before that he was only minutes old. And before that only only seconds old."
Tr. "Right!—First he was ____, then ____, then ____." (The children supply the missing words up to years.)

11. Tr. "I don't believe that the soil in our garden is very rich."
Ch. "We could put some fertilizer in it the way they did in the story."
Tr. "If I'm not mistaken there is a bag of fertilizer in the cupboard. Sure enough, a full bag. But I am sure we wouldn't need as many pounds as this for our little garden."
"I wonder how many pounds are in this bag?"
E. "We could find out on those things we weighed our pumpkins on."
Tr. "Why don't you get the scales, E.—I think they are in the science cupboard."
E. returns with the scales and the teacher sets the bag on the scales. "Five, five," call the children.
Tr. "You are right—five pounds. I'm almost sure that one pound of fertilizer would be enough for our small garden. How could we measure so we would have just one pound?"
After much discussion they decide to "take away" some so that there will be only four pounds left in the bag.

12. J. and G. are trying to divide the blocks so that each will have an equal number of the various shapes. They run into mathematical difficulties and tempers flare.

*"Eight pounds!"*

Tr. "Perhaps these would help to settle your problem.". . . And she offers them two sets of sturdy 8″ braces.

J. "Where is the equal sign?"

G. "Here! We can use these pieces from the felt board."

Tr. "You could use those pieces but they might get dirty on the floor. How about using these pegs?"

The boys like the idea and immediately begin constructing equal sets of blocks.

{□ △ ▭} = {□ △ ▭}

13. As the teacher watches J. and G. constructing equal sets of blocks and putting them in two separate piles, she draws a picture of the set on the chalkboard.

Tr. "It would be interesting to see how many sets you can make. Suppose I put John's name here on the chalkboard and Gregg's name here. Then every time you put a set in your own pile you can just make a mark under your name like this '/'."

J. "OK. But I can write my own name."

G. "And so can I."

John erases the name the teacher made for him and prints his own name in capitals. Gregg studies each letter in his name and laboriously prints his name using both upper and lower case forms. Then he erases the name made by the teacher.

Tr. "When you have finished making your sets we can count the lines that represent the sets you have made. I think you may have as many as six sets . . . maybe more . . . maybe less. We'll just have to wait to get our answer. I wonder what numeral we'll have to write?"

14. J. and G. have arranged the blocks so that each has 8 sets and now they find they have many cubes and a few oblong bricks left.

Tr. "Could you make sets out of these?"

G. "I've got it! We could make sets like this:

The teacher draws a picture of this set on the chalkboard and the boys continue as in example 13 above making and recording the number of sets each has.

When they finish, J. counts the lines.

J. "I have six sets and G. has six sets."

Tr. "How many sets do you suppose you have altogether?" The boys count all the lines under the two pictures made by the teacher.

J. "We made 8 sets like this and we made 6 sets like this."

Tr. "Eight sets and six sets? That means you made *14* sets altogether!" The boys look at their two big piles of blocks.

G. "How many blocks do you suppose we have altogether?"

Tr. "Let's count G.'s blocks."

J. "Count mine too."

Tr. "We could. But we really don't have to because we know that your set is equal to G.'s set."

J. is still doubtful so when they have finished counting G.'s 48 blocks the teacher helps J. count his blocks.

J. "Wow! We each have 48 blocks. How many altogether?"

Tr. "Almost 50 blocks in each pile." She waits to see if this offers a challenge to either child.

Tr. "Fifty and fifty more blocks would be . . . *100* blocks."

J. "But we don't have fifty blocks. We just have 48 blocks."

Tr. "If you each had two more blocks in your pile then you would each have 50 blocks."

G. "Let's add 2 of these—referring to some arc-shaped blocks—and then we'll have 100 blocks altogether."

Tr. "There! You each have 50 blocks and together you have 100 blocks. . . . Someday we must count all the blocks—all the shapes we have in this set of blocks. If we counted all the shapes and sizes there might be as many as three hundred or even more!"

## SELECTED REFERENCES

Deans, Edwina, *Arithmetic—Children Use It*, Bulletin No. 94, Washington, D.C., Association for Childhood Education International, 1954.

"Development of Arithmetical Ideas in Young Children, The," *Teacher's Guide to Education in Early Childhood*, Sacramento, California, State Department of Education, 1956.

Suppes, Patrick, *K I Sets and Numbers*, Syracuse, New York, L. W. Singer and Company (Division of Random House), 1962.

Swenson, Esther, *Making Primary Arithmetic Meaningful*, Bulletin, Washington, D.C., National Education Association, 1961.

Swenson, Esther, *Teaching Arithmetic to Children*, New York, Macmillan Company, 1964.

Wann, Kenneth D., Miriam S. Dorn, and Elizabeth Ann Liddle, *Fostering Intellectual Development in Young Children*, New York, Bureau of Publications, Teachers College, Columbia University, 1962.

## Foundation Experiences in Science

1. Tr. "Q. and J., when you were watering the transplanted morning glories this morning, how did they look?"
   J. "Some were growing fine; but some were just on the ground."
   Tr. "Perhaps they had been broken, either in transplanting or by the wind. In that case the roots couldn't send food up to make them grow. They were very delicate."
   Q. "Or maybe a cutworm cut off the top and the root couldn't send up food."
   Tr. "Possibly, but I think it is more likely that, even though we tried very hard to be careful, we might have injured the delicate plants."

2. E. "Say, if an egg or if the life in an egg doesn't develop, the egg can't go back inside a duck can it?"
   Tr. "No, it can't; you are right about that."
   D. "Just like a baby. When a baby is born, it can't go back inside its mother."
   Tr. "That's true too. But sometimes if a baby is born and it isn't quite strong enough to live in the big world it can go on developing in an incubator—a warm, snug, soft, quiet enclosure somewhat like a box or a basket with a cover on it. Then when the baby has developed enough to live outside the incubator, it can be moved into a bassinet or crib."

3. A., watching J. put a moth in a glass jar, says, "I suppose it was in a cocoon before it was a moth. We had a moth at home that came out of a cocoon."

Tr. (listening in) "Did you know that N. had a moth come out of its cocoon right in her kitchen?"

A. "Yes, but they *killed* it!"

Tr. "Perhaps they did that so that they could study its wings and color. If it had stayed alive in the jar it probably would have battered its wings to pieces. Or perhaps it just died naturally. You know some moths only live a few days—just long enough to lay their eggs so that little grubs, and then more moths, can develop."

4. J. comes into the kindergarten saying, "Look, I don't know whether it is a stone or a seed."

Tr. (after feeling it) "It might be a dried pea seed."

J. "We could plant it to find out." Whereupon he goes over to the window and pokes the seed into dirt in a flower pot.

5. L. "Let's study about the temperature." He presents a wooden thermometer with a red adjustable tape on it. The teacher sets the thermometer at 33°, which was the reported temperature for the morning. They discuss the possibility of leaf buds and flowers freezing if the temperature goes below 32°. The teacher reports having seen some plants protected with sheets and papers.
S. suggests putting the wooden thermometer outdoors to see if it is freezing outside.

Tr. "This thermometer couldn't tell us that because there is no mercury in it. Mercury is something like the gas-filled balloon we had last winter. It shrinks—gets smaller—when it gets cold, and it expands—gets larger—when it gets warm. Mercury, that red liquid down here on our real thermometer, expands when it gets warm and, because it doesn't have any other place to go, it goes higher up in the glass. The warmer it gets, the higher it goes. And the colder it gets, the _____ it goes." (The children supply the missing word.)

6. The teacher and the children are working together trying to get shadow pictures of children's heads. The shadow on the paper is very light and really difficult to see.

M. "I know. I'll pull the curtain over there." Still the shadow seems faint.

R. "You need a brighter light. I'll get the bright light from your office." As R. returns from the office, he says, "I turned it off in case you would get a shock when you plugged it in." The shadow was now very clear but much too big for the 12 x 18 paper.

Tr. "Let's see what the shadow does when I move the light farther away."

Ch. "It's getting smaller. It's getting smaller. Stop! It's just right."

7. J. has brought to kindergarten a bag of buffalo bones. As he picks up the bones, he names each one and the children with the teacher locate corresponding bones in their own bodies—that is, leg, rib, vertebrae, jawbone, and so on.

8. The children are about to throw away their old potato puppets when K. says, "Wait a minute; what's this funny thing?" The potato is sprouting. So, instead of throwing them all away, they cut off the sections where they find sprouts and a few other sections where they find "eyes" and plant these sections in their garden. By the time school closes the potato plants will be almost a foot high. In connection with this same experiment they have also planted pumpkin seeds saved from October jack-o'-lanterns. As future first-graders, they will look forward to their harvest.

9. D. "Want to see something?" And D. proceeds to suck in on the paper cup which he was about to throw in the wastebasket. The paper cup, as if by magic, clings to his face, even though he isn't touching it with his hands.

W. "It's 'cause he blows on it—it's the pressure you know."

Tr. "You're right about the pressure; but the pressure change makes it stay there because he has sucked the air out of the cup. I suppose if he whistles—if he blows into the cup—the pressure change will make it go away." D. blows and, of course, the cup gets pushed away.

10. The group has been discussing the fact that many trees like apple trees, peach trees, and plum trees have flowers before they have fruit.

S. "Do banana trees have flowers?"

Tr. "I suppose so, but I don't really know. I have seen banana plants —I believe they call them banana plants and not banana trees— growing down in Guatemala, but when I saw them they already had bananas on them. We'll have to find out about that."

A. "We've got some books at home and they tell lots of things. They have pictures too. Maybe I can see a picture in there." The next day A. says, "I brought one of our 'cyclopedias. This one tells all about things that start with 'B.' And it has a little picture, but not a very good one."

Several days later the group takes a walk to a greenhouse to look at a banana plant. Upon arrival at the greenhouse, S. is commissioned to go in to inquire about the banana plant. The greenhouse attendant replies, "Yes, we do have a banana plant, but I am sorry to say it hasn't any bananas on it. It just has a blossom now." The group, including the teacher, is ecstatic over the news and, on the attendant's invitation, go in to see the long head of clustered and rather tightly wrapped pink flowers.

## SELECTED REFERENCES

Association for Childhood Education International, Washington, D.C.: *Science for Teachers and Children*, Bulletin No. 91, 1953.
*This Is Science*, Bulletin (No no.), 1945.

Blough, Glenn, Julius Schwartz, and Albert Huggett, *Elementary School Science and How to Teach It*, rev., New York, Holt, Rinehart and Winston, Inc., 1964 (See particularly Chapter I).

Greenlee, Julius, *Teaching Science to Children*, Dubuque, Iowa, William C. Brown Company, 1958.

Tannenbaum, Harold E., and Nathan Stillman, *Science Education for Elementary School Teachers*, Boston, Allyn and Bacon, 1960.

Wann, Kenneth D., Miriam S. Dorn, and Elizabeth Ann Liddle, "Children Want to Know About the Phenomena That Surround Them," *Fostering Intellectual Development in Young Children*, New York, Bureau of Publications, Teachers College, Columbia University, 1962.

After reading this sampling of experiences and knowing that thousands of other such experiences might be cited, could anyone question the presence of opportunities for academic learning or a readiness program in the kindergarten? Let us never confuse this kind of readiness with that which concerns itself solely with the recognition and interpretation of little black symbols and making crosses in a workbook.

## Readiness for First-Grade Living

If a child has had the opportunity to build, and if he has been capable of building for himself a broad base of understanding in the kindergarten, his first-grade experiences will seem natural and satisfying extensions of earlier experiences. His new learnings will extend and deepen his present base of understanding. Most children who have had the opportunity to experience nine or ten months of kindergarten living at its best will find the transition from kindergarten to first grade a comfortable though most thrilling experience. There may be individuals, however, who, for one or more reasons, are just not ready to meet the challenges of first-grade living.

## Promotion Policies

Promotion from kindergarten to the first grade was and still is, to a great extent, based almost entirely on the child's chronological age. In many schools, if the child has attained or is within a few weeks or months of six years at the time of his entrance into first grade, it is assumed that he is ready to learn to read. Little thought is given to the fact that, regardless of chronological age, each child has his own pattern and rate of development.[2] The child's mental age, his physical development, his health record, his degree of emotional stability, and his social adaptability ought all to be considered in relation to his readiness to undertake a reading program. Readiness to walk, readiness to talk, and many other factors are commonly accepted by parents as patterns of development which show great variation among individual children. In filling out a medical history, parents may calmly report a difference of from three to twelve or more months in the ages at which their children learned to walk or talk. Yet, often these same parents seem greatly distressed to find that not all children have developed a readiness to read by their sixth birthday.

The solution to the problem seems fairly obvious—simply permit the child to have another year or part of a year in which to mature before expecting him to be ready to read. This may be done in either of two ways: (a) by providing an opportunity for another year of kindergarten living in an environment which will be challenging to the child, preferably in a setting outside his present school environment, or (b) by enrolling him in a first-grade group in which the enrollment is sufficiently small and the teacher is sufficiently aware of individual patterns of development for the child to be challenged at his own level.

Since kindergarten attendance is not compulsory, it will probably be some time before any kindergarten report on a child's development and behavior can definitely defer his entrance into a regular first grade. To defer his entrance on the basis of observed development and behavior while permitting other children of the same chronological age but with no kindergarten experience to enter the first grade is, from the lay point of view, to penalize the child for attending kindergarten. However, to enroll children in the first grade on the basis of chronological age and then to fail from

[2] See Bayley reference in Appendix.

15 to 25 percent solely because of their difficulties in identifying black symbols on a white page is, from the point of view of those concerned with the psychology of education, a sad waste of both teacher's and child's time. In addition, it is a procedure which may well result in grave personality difficulties for the child.

Parents and the public in general need to broaden their understanding of the readiness factor in learning. In recommending any special school placement for an individual child—that is, any placement which implies that the child could profit by further maturity before undertaking the challenge of a particular educational venture—one must be sure that the parents' attitude toward the child's placement will be a wholesome one.[3] If, for example, the parents will be greatly disturbed by the proposal to pace the child's learning to his maurity level, or if they are going to make life miserable for him because he "failed to pass," such factors must be considered in relation to the child's wholesome adjustment to school. It is unfortunate that having one's child learn to read at an early age has become almost a status symbol for parents!

## Learning to Read

We have always known that some children, even without formal instruction, learn to read at an early age. Recently it has been brought to our attention that under certain conditions and usually with a great deal of individual guidance—machine or human—many normal and less than normal children can be taught to read at a very early age. New systems of teaching reading have been developed.[4] Some, such as the ITA system, greatly simplify the problem of learning to read but, by and large, success in learning to read in a group situation is still based largely on general maturity and the absence of a complexity of visual problems.

## Prediction of First-Grade Success

Many efforts have been made to find scientific measures for predicting the child's ability to cope with the challenges of the first grade and, as a result, a variety of standardized intelligence, ability, and readiness tests have been developed and used.[5] In addition the question which always

[3] Willard C. Olson, "Parents Request an Extra Promotion," *Childhood Education*, September, 1941, 18:24–29.

[4] See section on research studies and articles in Appendix.

[5] See bibliography of tests in Appendix.

used to be, "Is the child ready for first grade?" is frequently changed to, "Is the first grade ready for the child?" Even so, records from many schools indicate that success in first grade depends on a variety of factors. Of these, chronological age, mental maturity, the child's social and emotional adjustment, the child's physical maturity, fitness and stamina, and the child's home environment and cultural background seem most important. Table 7,[6] although based on data gathered some years ago still proves helpful to both teachers and parents as they try to solve the problem of pacing learning to the maturity level of the individual child.

**Table 7** Prediction of Degree of Success in First Grade

| CHRONOLOGICAL AGE | IQ | MENTAL AGE | PROBABILITY OF SUCCESS IN FIRST GRADE |
|---|---|---|---|
| Below 6 yr. | Below 110 | Below 6 yr. | Small chance of success. Better postpone entrance. |
| Below 6 yr. | 110–119 | 6 yr. 0 mo. to 6 yr. 7 mo. | Fair chance of success. Postpone entrance if any question of social, emotional, or physical immaturity, or if home conditions are unfavorable. |
| Below 6 yr. | | 6 yr. 8 mo. or 6 yr. 9 mo. | A good chance. |
| Below 6 yr. | 120 or over | 6 yr. 10 mo. or over | High probability of success, but personality factors must be taken into consideration. |
| 6 yr. 0 mo. to 6 yr. 4 mo. | Below 100 | Below 6 yr. | Practically no chance. Better postpone entrance. |
| 6 yr. 0 mo. to 6 yr. 4 mo. | 100–109 | 6 yr. to 6 yr. 3 mo. | Fair chance of success. Postpone entrance if any question of social, emotional, or physical immaturity, or if home conditions are unfavorable. |
| 6 yr. 0 mo. to 6 yr. 4 mo. | 110 or over | | Almost certain to succeed. |

It will be noted that frequent reference has been made to the fact that personality factors, such as social and emotional maturity, should be considered along with mental and chronological age. There are at present no reliable measures of personality traits, but the extreme cases, where social and emotional factors are likely to interfere greatly with the child's progress, are not difficult to recognize. If the child is given to severe and

[6] Elizabeth B. Bigelow, "School Progress of Under-Age Children," *Elementary School Journal*, November, 1934, 35:192.

uncontrolled bursts of temper, if he is easily overcome with embarrassment, if he cannot work and play without constant friction with other children, if he is too dependent on other children or adults, if normal effort produces undue fatigue, or if he is excitable and tense under the slightest strain, it can be assumed that first-grade success will be most unlikely.

### Further Guides to Promotion

It would probably be helpful to all of us in planning for the child's good if we could have before us a picture of his total development as plotted on an organismic[7] or some other growth chart. Practically, it is not now possible for most of us to have such data available, but if we did, it is conceivable that we could more clearly appreciate the diversity displayed in the development of individual children. Placement and expectancy would then be on the basis of many clear-cut factors, rather than on chronological age and seeming or tested intelligence. If such material were available, it is quite possible that schools would be happier places for all. May the research people continue to provide teachers with data from which more and more working generalizations can be derived, and may kindergarten teachers in the light of these guides, continue to strive to pace kindergarten education to the maturity levels of the children to be found in their groups.

## SUMMARY

The good kindergarten is designed to meet the physical, social, emotional, *and* intellectual needs of its children. Because the curriculum of the kindergarten is not circumscribed, the teacher feels free—insofar as she is intellectually able herself—to cut across any and all bodies of subject matter. This she does, not by way of "lessons" and paper-and-pencil techniques, but by drawing knowledge of all kinds from the ordinary experiences of the kindergarten. The good kindergarten teacher is alert to educational implications in all experiences, and through these she helps children build for themselves a broad base of understanding. Most children who have attended a good kindergarten will find the transition from kindergarten to first grade a natural and comfortable extension of their earlier experiences. Because of the varying rates of maturing among individuals, however, some children will not be as ready as others to meet the challenges of first-grade living. Lack of readiness at this age should not be considered a failure. Parents and teachers should work together to provide that program which will best pace the educational challenge to the maturity level of the child.

[7] See Olson reference, p. 513.

## QUESTIONS AND PROBLEMS

1. How might each of the following experiences be made educationally significant?
   a. The teacher observes that Billy has a dollar bill. She assumes that it is play money. Later she notes that it is real money, and that he has shared it with his friends by tearing it into four approximately equal parts.
   b. Three children have discovered a milkweed seed floating in the room and they are frantically trying to catch it. There are other seeds in pods in a fall bouquet which the teacher has brought into the room earlier the same day.
   c. Two children have brought books from home. The books bear the same title, but each book is illustrated by a different person.
   d. Mike and Jean are on the teeter-totter. Mike jumps off without warning Jean.
   e. Jim observes that the fish in the aquarium are all swimming near the top and seem to be trying to jump out of the water.
   f. Barbara and Judy are wearing dresses made from the same material but fashioned differently.
   g. The children are going to make applesauce in kindergarten. It is hoped that each child will bring one large or two small apples.
   h. Rebecca Jones and Rebecca Christiansen are in the same kindergarten group. Each is used to being called "Becca."
2. What does the following tell you?
   Each child in the group is supplied with a workbook and a marking pencil. (a) Three children in the group progress happily and successfully through the book as the days go by; (b) ten children look forward to the part of the day when they use their workbooks, but they need a great deal of individual help in carrying out the directions; (c) eight children need almost constant individual attention, and day after day they become more and more restless; (d) two children try hard but invariably meet with failure—one cries frequently, the other seemingly ignores his failures; and (e) one child makes only random scribble marks in his book.
3. Jean's parents are disturbed because she is not bringing home from kindergarten the "cute" cutouts and other items which are being brought home by her cousin, who is attending another kindergarten. Is this an indication that Jean's teacher is doing a poor teaching job? What would you need to know about the kindergarten before passing judgment on the quality of her teaching.
4. Barbara, who is enrolled in a kindergarten of twenty-four children, is

a quiet but seemingly well-adjusted child. She was five years old on October 6. On a November day, quite by chance, the teacher discovers that Barbara is reading fluently. Does this mean that she should be transferred at this time from the kindergarten to the first grade? On what grounds do you base your answer?

5. James is chronologically the youngest child in the group; he will be five early in January. Tests indicate that he has an IQ of about 120. James cries easily, and frequently through the first semester he has said, "But you shouldn't expect a little four-year-old to do this." What are the probabilities of his adjustment and success in the first grade next September? Explain your answer.

## SELECTED REFERENCES

Almy, Millie, *Children's Experiences Prior to First Grade and Success in Beginning Reading,* New York, Bureau of Publications, Teachers College, Columbia University, 1949.

Hildreth, Gertrude H., *Readiness for School Beginners,* Yonkers-on-Hudson, World Book Cmpany, 1950.

Lambert, Hazel, *Early Childhood Education,* Boston, Allyn and Bacon, 1960.

Langdon, Grace, and Irving W. Stout, *Teaching in the Primary Grades,* New York, Macmillan, 1964.

Lee, J. Murray, and Dorris Lee, *The Child and His Curriculum,* 3rd ed., New York, Appleton-Century-Crofts, 1960.

Monroe, Marion, *Growing into Reading,* New York, Scott, Foresman and Company, 1954.

Morrison, Ida E., and Ida Perry, *Kindergarten Primary Procedures,* New York, The Ronald Press, 1961.

National Education Association, *Foundation Learnings in the Kindergarten* (bulletin), 1958.

*Your Child and Reading* (pamphlet) incorporated in the *NEA Journal,* January, 1963.

National Education Association, Department of Elementary School Principals, *Those First School Years,* Washington, D.C., National Education Association, 1960.

Olson, Willard C., *Child Development,* 2nd ed., New York, D. C. Heath and Company, 1959.

Rudolph, Marguerite, and Dorothy H. Cohen, "Kindergarten Is School," *Kindergarten: A Year of Learning,* New York, Appleton-Century-Crofts, 1964.

Smith, Nila B., *Reading Instruction for Today's Children,* Englewood Cliffs, New Jersey, Prentice-Hall, 1963.

# APPENDIX

## General Bibliography[1]


ALMY, MILLIE C., *Child Development,* New York, Henry Holt and Company, 1955.

————, *Children's Experiences Prior to First Grade and Success in Beginning Reading,* New York, Bureau of Publications, Teachers College, Columbia University, 1949.

ALMY, MILLIE C., AND AGNES SNYDER, "The Staff and Its Preparation," Chapter VIII, *Forty-sixth Yearbook, Part II: Early Childhood Education,* Chicago, National Society for the Study of Education, University of Chicago Press, 1947.

ALSCHULER, ROSE H., AND LA BERTA W. HATTWICK, *Painting and Personality: A Study of Young Children,* Chicago, University of Chicago Press, 1947.

ANDERSON, JOHN E., "Child Development: An Historical Perspective," *Child Development,* June, 1956, 27:181–196.

————, "The Limitations of Infant and Pre-School Tests in the Measurement of Intelligence," *Readings in Child Development,* Martin and Stendler, eds., New York, Harcourt, Brace and Company, 1954.

————, "The Theory of Early Childhood Education," Chapter V, *Forty-sixth Yearbook, Part II: Early Childhood Education,* Chicago, National Society for the Study of Education, University of Chicago Press, 1947.

————, *The Psychology of Development and Personality Adjustment,* New York, Henry Holt and Company, 1949.

APPLEGATE, MAUREE, *Everybody's Business—Our Children,* Evanston, Illinois, Row Peterson and Company, 1952.

ARBUTHNOT, MAY HILL, *Anthology of Children's Literature,* Chicago, Scott, Foresman and Company, rev. ed., 1961.


[1] In addition to and inclusive of some of the selected references found at the end of each chapter.

———, *Children and Books*, Chicago, Scott, Foresman and Company, 3rd ed., 1964.

ARNOLD, ARNOLD, *How to Play with Your Child*, New York, Ballantine Books, 1955.

ASHTON-WARNER, SYLVIA, *Teacher*, New York, Simon and Schuster, 1963.

ASSOCIATION FOR CHILDHOOD EDUCATION INTERNATIONAL—Bulletins, 3615 Wisconsin Avenue, N.W., Washington, D.C., 20016:

*Basic Human Values*, 8-A, 1962.

*Bibliography of Books for Children*, 37, rev. ed., 1962.

*Don't Push Me*, 1-A, 1960.

*Equipment and Supplies*, 39, rev. ed., 1964.

*How Good Is Our Kindergarten?* 65, 1959.

*Implications of Basic Human Values for Education*, 10-A, 1964.

*Kindergarten Graduation? No and Why Not* (flyer), –C, n.d. (about 1962).

*The Color Book Craze* (leaflet), –F, 1964.

*Kindergarten Portfolio*, –2, 1951.

*More About Reading*, –29, 1959.

*Reading in the Kindergarten??* 6-A, 1962.

*Space, Arrangement, Beauty in School*, 102, 1961.

*What Are Kindergartens For?* (leaflet), –A, 1961.

*Young Children and Science*, –12 –A, 1964.

AXLINE, VIRGINIA MAE, *Play Therapy: Inner Dynamics of Childhood*, Boston, Houghton Mifflin Company, 1947.

BACMEISTER, RHODA W., *Your Child and Other People: At Home, At School, At Play*, Boston, Little, Brown and Company, 1950.

BARNOUW, ELSA, AND ARTHUR SWAN, *Adventuring with Children in Nursery School and Kindergarten*, New York, Thomas Y. Crowell and Company, 1959.

BAXTER, BERNICE, GERTRUDE M. LEWIS, AND ANN CROSBY, *The Role of Elementary Education*, Boston, D. C. Heath and Company, 1952.

BECK, ROBERT, AND OTHERS, *Three R's Plus: What Today's Schools Are Trying to Do and Why*, 2nd ed., Minneapolis, University of Minnesota Press, 1960.

BERSON, MINNIE PERRIN, *Kindergarten, Your Child's Big Step*, New York, E. P. Dutton and Company, 1959.

BOND, GUY L., AND EVA BOND, *Teaching the Child to Read*, New York, Macmillan Company, 3rd ed., 1960.

BROGAN, PEGGY, AND LORENE K. FOX, *Helping Children Learn*, Yonkers-on-Hudson, World Book Company, 1955.

BROWN, JAMES W., RICHARD LEWIS, AND FRED HARCLEROAD, *A–V Instruction: Materials and Methods*, New York, McGraw-Hill Book Company, 1959.

BRUNER, JEROME, *The Process of Education*, Cambridge, Massachusetts, Harvard University Press, 1960.

BUROS, OSCAR K., *Mental Measurements Yearbook*, Highland Park, N.J., The Gryphon Press, 6th ed., 1965.

BURR, JAMES B., AND OTHERS, *Student Teaching in the Elementary Schools*, New York, Appleton-Century-Crofts, 2nd ed., 1958.

BUSH, ROBERT N., *The Teacher-Pupil Relationship*, Englewood Cliffs, N.J., Prentice-Hall, 1954.

CALIFORNIA STATE DEPARTMENT OF EDUCATION, BUREAU OF ELEMENTARY EDUCATION, STATE CURRICULUM COMMISSION, *Teachers Guide to Education in Early Childhood*, Sacramento, California, 1956.

CARDOZO, PETER, *A Wonderful World for Children*, New York, Bantam Books, 1956 (paper).

CARMICHAEL, LEONARD (ed.), *Manual of Child Psychology*, New York, John Wiley and Sons, 2nd ed., 1954.

CASSEL, RUSSELL, W., *The Psychology of Child Discipline*, Cincinnati, C. A. Gregory Company, 1956.

CAUDILL, WILLIAM W., *Toward Better School Design*, New York, F. W. Dodge Company, 1954.

CHILD STUDY ASSOCIATION—Pamphlets, 9 E. 89th Street, New York, 10028:

*The Children's Bookshelf: A Parents Guide to Good Books for Boys and Girls, K-10.*

*Behavior—The Unspoken Language*, CSAA Staff.

*How to Give Your Child A Good Start*, Aline B. Auerbach.

*How to Protect Your Child Against Prejudice*, Kenneth B. Clark.

*When Children Need Help with Emotional Problems*, Greta Mayer and Mary Hoover.

*The Why and How of Discipline*, Aline B. Auerbach.

CHITTENDEN, GERTRUDE E., *Living with Children*, New York, Macmillan Company, 1944.

CHRISTIANSON, HELEN M., MARY M. ROGERS, AND BLANCHE A. LUDLUM, *Nursery School: Adventures in Living and Learning*, New York, Houghton Mifflin, 1961.

CHUKUVSKY, KORNEI, *From Two to Five*, Berkeley and Los Angeles, University of California Press, 1963.

COHEN, DOROTHY H., AND VIRGINIA STERN, *Observing and Recording the Behavior of Young Children*, New York, Bureau of Publications, Teachers College, Columbia University, 1958.

COLE, NATALIE R., *Arts in the Classroom*, New York, John Day Company, 1940.

COMSTOCK, ANNA B., *Handbook of Nature Study*, Ithaca, New York, Cornell University Press, 24th ed., 1939.

CONRAD, GEORGE, *The Process of Art Education in the Elementary School*, Englewood Cliffs, N.J., Prentice-Hall, 1964.

COREY, STEPHEN, *Action Research to Improve School Practices*, New York, Bureau of Publications, Teachers College, Columbia University, 1953.

COX, DORIS, AND BARBARA WEISMAN, *Creative Hands*, New York, John Wiley and Sons, 2nd ed., 1951.

CRAIG, GERALD S., *Science for the Elementary Teacher*, Boston, Ginn and Company, rev. ed., 1962.

CROW, LESTER D., AND ALICE CROW, *Human Development and Learning*, New York, American Book Company, rev. ed., 1965.

CROXTON, W. C., *Science in the Elementary School,* New York, McGraw-Hill Book Company, 1939.
CULKIN, MABEL L., *Teaching the Youngest,* New York, Macmillan Company, 1949.
DALE, EDGAR, *Audio-Visual Methods in Teaching,* New York, Holt, Rinehart & Winston, 3rd ed., 1965.
DALGLIESH, ALICE, *First Experiences with Literature,* New York, Charles Scribner's Sons, 1932.
D'AMICO, VICTOR, *Creative Teaching in Art,* Scranton, Pennsylvania, International Text Book Company, rev. ed., 1953.
————, *Experiments in Creative Art Teaching,* New York, Doubleday, 1960.
D'AMICO, VICTOR, AND OTHERS, *Art for the Family,* New York, Doubleday, 1958.
DAVIS, DAVID, *Patterns of Primary Education,* New York, Harper and Row, 1963.
D'EVELYN, KATHERINE E., *Individual Parent-Teacher Conferences,* New York, Bureau of Publications, Teachers College, Columbia University, rev. ed., 1963.
————, *Meeting Children's Emotional Needs,* Englewood Cliffs, N.J., Prentice-Hall, 1957.
DEWEY, JOHN, *Art as Experience,* New York, G. P. Putnam's Sons, 1959.
————, *Experience and Education,* New York, Macmillan Company, 1938, Collier (paper).
DIXON, MADELINE C., *The Power of the Dance: Dance and Related Arts for Children,* New York, John Day Company, 1939.
DUFF, ANNIS, *Bequest of Wings,* New York, Viking Press, 1944.
*Early Childhood Education, Forty-sixth Yearbook of the National Society for the Study of Education,* Part II, Chicago, University of Chicago Press, 1947.
EATON, ANNE T., *Treasure for the Taking,* New York, Viking Press, rev., ed., 1957.
ELKINS, FREDERICK, *The Child and Society: The Process of Socialization,* New York, Random House, 1960.
ELLIS, MARY JACKSON, *The Kindergarten Log,* Minneapolis, T. S. Denison and Company, Vol. I, 1955; Vol. II, 1960.
ENGELHARDT, N. L., N. L. ENGELHARDT, JR., AND STANTON LEGGETT, *Planning Elementary School Buildings: An Architectural Record Book,* New York, F. W. Dodge Company, 1953.
FACULTY OF THE UNIVERSITY SCHOOL, *How Children Develop,* University School Series, No. 3, Columbus, Ohio, College of Education, Ohio State University, 1946.
FAEGRE, MARION L., AND JOHN E. ANDERSON, *Child Care and Training,* Minneapolis, University of Minnesota Press, 8th ed., 1958.
FARINA, ALBERT M., SOL H. FURTH, JOSEPH M. SMITH, *Growing Through Play,* Englewood Cliffs, N.J., Prentice-Hall, 1959.
FLEMING, ROBERT S., *Curriculum for Today's Boys and Girls,* Columbus, Ohio, Charles E. Merrill Books, Inc., 1963.

FOREST, ILSE, *Child Development*, New York, McGraw-Hill Book Company, 1954.

————, *Early Years at School, New York*, McGraw-Hill Book Company, 1949.

————, *The School and the Child From Two to Eight*, Boston, Ginn and Company, 1935.

FRAIBERG, SELMA H., *The Magic Years*, New York, Charles Scribner's Sons, 1959.

FOWLKES, JOHN G., AND D. A. MORGAD (editors), *Elementary Teachers Guide to Free Curriculum Materials*, Randolph, Wisconsin, Educators Progressive Service, 1948, 1951, and later.

FRANK, JOSETTE, *Your Child's Reading Today*, New York, Doubleday and Company, rev. ed., 1960.

FRANK, LAWRENCE, "Mental Health in the Classroom," Chapter I, *Thirteenth Yearbook of the Department of Supervisors and Directors of Instruction*, Washington, D.C., National Education Association, 1940.

FRANK, MARY, AND LAWRENCE FRANK, *How to Help Your Child in School*, New York, Viking Press, 1950 (Signet, paper, 1954).

*Free and Inexpensive Learning Materials*, Nashville, Tennessee, Division of Surveys and Field Services, George Peabody College for Teachers, 7th ed., 1957.

FROEBEL, FRIEDRICH, *Pedagogies of the Kindergarten*, New York, D. Appleton and Company, 1895.

FULLER, ELIZABETH M., AND OTHERS, "Practices and Resources," *Chapter 6, Forty-sixth Yearbook, Part II; Early Childhood Education*, Chicago, National Society for the Study of Education, University of Chicago Press, 1947.

FULLER, ELIZABETH M., *Values in Early Childhood Education*, Washington, D.C., National Education Association, 1960. Second edition revised by Evangeline Burgess, 1965.

GABBARD, HAZEL, "Status and Trend in Early Childhood Education," *Those First School Years*, Washington, D.C., National Education Association, 1960.

GANS, ROMA, *Common Sense in Teaching Reading*, New York, Bobbs-Merrill Company, 1963.

————, *Reading Is Fun*, New York, Bureau of Publications, Teachers College, Columbia University, 1949.

GANS, ROMA, CELIA STENDLER, MILLIE ALMY, *Teaching Young Children—Nursery School, Kindergarten and the Primary Grades*, Yonkers-on-Hudson, World Book Company, 1952.

GARRISON, CHARLOTTE G., AND OTHERS, *Horace Mann Kindergarten for Five-Year-Old Children*, New York, Bureau of Publications, Teachers College, Columbia University, 1937.

GESELL, ARNOLD, AND FRANCES L. ILG, *The Child from Five to Ten*, New York, Harper and Brothers, 1946.

GESELL, ARNOLD, AND OTHERS, *The First Five Years of Life*, New York, Harper and Brothers, 1940.

*Good Education for Young Children,* Albany, New York, New York State Association for Childhood Education and the New York State Association for Nursery School Education, 1946.

GOODENOUGH, FLORENCE L., AND LEONA E. TYLER, *Developmental Psychology,* New York, D. Appleton-Century Company, 3rd ed., 1959.

GRIM, PAUL R., AND JOHN U. MICHAELIS, *The Student Teacher in the Elementary School,* Englewood Cliffs, N.J., Prentice-Hall, 1953.

GROUT, RUTH E., *Health Teaching in Schools,* Philadelphia, W. B. Saunders Company, 4th ed., 1963.

GRUENBERG, SIDONIE (ed.), *Encyclopedia of Child Care and Guidance,* New York, Doubleday and Company, 1954.

GRUENBERG, SIDONIE, *Our Children Today,* Child Association of America, New York, Viking Press, 1952.

————, *Parents' Guide to Everyday Problems of Boys and Girls,* New York, Random House, 1958.

HAMMOND, SARAH LOU, RUTH J. DALES, DORA SIKES SKIPPER, AND RALPH L. WITHERSPOON, *Good Schools for Young Children,* New York, Macmillan Company, 1963.

HARRIS, DALE, *Children's Drawings as Measures of Intellectual Maturity,* New York, Harcourt, Brace and World, Inc., 1963.

HARTLEY, RUTH E., AND ROBERT M. GOLDENSON, *A Complete Book of Children's Play,* New York, Thomas Y. Crowell Company, 1957.

HARTLEY, RUTH E., LAWRENCE K. FRANK, AND ROBERT GOLDENSON, *Understanding Children's Play,* New York, Bureau of Publications, Teachers College, Columbia University, rev. ed., 1963.

HARTMAN, GERTRUDE, AND ANN SHUMAKER, *Creative Expression,* Milwaukee, E. M. Hale and Company, 1930.

HAVIGHURST, ROBERT J., *Developmental Tasks in Education,* Chicago, University of Chicago Press, 2nd ed., 1959 (paper).

HAWKES, GLENN R., AND DAMARIS PEASE, *Behavior and Development from 5–12,* New York, Harper and Brothers, 1962.

HAZARD, PAUL, *Books, Children and Men, Boston,* Horn Book Publishers, 1948.

HEADLEY, NEITH, *The Kindergarten: Its Place in the Program of Education,* Englewood Cliffs, N.J., Prentice-Hall, 1965.

HEFFERNAN, HELEN (ed.), *Guiding the Young Child,* Boston, D. C. Heath and Company, 2nd ed., 1959.

HEFFERNAN, HELEN, AND VIVIAN TODD, *The Kindergarten Teacher,* Boston, D. C. Heath and Company, 1960.

HEINZ, MAMIE W., *Growing and Learning in the Kindergarten,* Richmond, Virginia, John Knox Press, 1959.

HILDRETH, GERTRUDE H., *A Bibliography of Mental Tests and Rating Scales,* New York, Psychological Corporation, 1949 and supplements.

————, *Child Growth Through Education,* New York, The Ronald Press, 1948.

————, "Readiness for Learning," *Forty-eighth Yearbook,* Part II, Chicago, National Society for the Study of Education, University of Chicago Press, 1949.

———, *Readiness for School Beginners,* Yonkers-on-Hudson, World Book Company, 1950.

HILLIARD, PAULINE, *Improving Social Learnings in the Elementary School,* New York, Bureau of Publications, Teachers College, Columbia University, 1954.

HOCHMAN, VIVIENNE, *Trips in Early Childhood Education,* New York, Bank Street Publications, 1957.

HUBLER, CLARK, *Working with Children in Science,* Boston, Houghton Mifflin, 1956.

HURD, HELEN D., *Teaching in the Kindergarten,* Minneapolis, Burgess Publishing Company, rev. ed., 1959.

HURLEY, BEATRICE D., *Curriculum for Elementary School Children,* New York, The Ronald Press, 1957.

HURLOCK, ELIZABETH B., *Child Development,* New York, McGraw-Hill Book Company, 3rd ed., 1956.

HYMES, JAMES L., JR., *Behavior and Misbehavior,* Englewood Cliffs, N.J., Prentice-Hall, 1955.

———, *Effective Home-School Relations,* Englewood Cliffs, N.J., Prentice-Hall, 1953.

———, *Three to Six: Your Child Starts School* (pamphlet), New York, Public Affairs Committee, Doubleday and Company, 1950.

———, *Understanding Your Child,* Englewood Cliffs, N.J., Prentice-Hall, 1952.

ILG., FRANCES L., AND LOUISE BATES AMES, *Child Behavior,* New York, Harper and Brothers, 1955.

———, *The Gesell Institute's Child Behavior,* New York, Dell Publishing Company, 1960 (paper).

IMHOFF, MYRTLE, *Early Elementary Education,* New York, Appleton-Century-Crofts, 1959.

JENKINS, GLADYS G., *Helping Children Reach Their Potential,* Chicago, Scott, Foresman and Company, 1961.

JENKINS, GLADYS G., AND OTHERS, *These Are Your Children,* Chicago, Scott, Foresman and Company, rev. ed., 1953.

JERSILD, ARTHUR T., *Child Psychology,* Englewood Cliffs, N.J., Prentice-Hall, 3rd ed., 1960.

———, *When Teachers Face Themselves,* New York, Bureau of Publications, Teachers College, Columbia University, 1955.

JERSILD, ARTHUR T., AND ASSOCIATES, *Child Development and the Curriculum,* New York, Bureau of Publications, Teachers College, Columbia University, 1946.

JOHNSON, EDNA, EVELYN R. SICKLES, AND FRANCES CLARKE SAYERS, *Anthology of Children's Literature,* Boston, Houghton Mifflin Company, 3rd ed., 1960.

JOHNSON, JUNE S., *Home Play for the Pre-School Child,* New York, Harper and Brothers, 1957.

KANNER, LEO, *Child Psychiatry,* Springfield, Illinois, Charles C. Thomas Company, 3rd ed., 1960.

KAUFFMAN, CAROLYN, AND PATRICIA FARREL, *If You Live with Little Children*, New York, G. P. Putnam's Sons, 1957.

KAWIN, ETHEL, "Records and Reports: Observations, Tests and Measurements" Chapter X, *Forty-sixth Yearbook, Part II; Early Childhood Education*, Chicago, National Society for the Study of Education, University of Chicago Press, 1947.

———, *The Wise Choice of Toys*, Chicago, University of Chicago Press, 1938.

KEPLER, HAZEL, *The Child and His Play: A Planning Guide for Parents and Teachers*, New York, Funk and Wagnalls, 1952.

KINDER, JAMES, *Audio-Visual Materials and Techniques*, New York, American Book Company, 2nd ed., 1959.

———, *Using Audio-Visual Materials in Education*, New York, American Book Company, 1965 (paper).

KINDERGARTEN HANDBOOKS:

*Children in the Elementary Schools*, Lansing, Michigan, Lansing Public Schools.

*A Good Start for the School Year*, River Forest, Illinois, River Forest Public School.

*A Good Start in the Pittsburgh Schools*, Pittsburgh, Pennsylvania, Pittsburgh Public Schools.

*Come With Us*, Concord, Massachusetts, Concord Public Schools.

*Getting Ready for School*, Kalamazoo, Michigan, Kalamazoo Public Schools.

*Getting Ready for School in Great Neck*, Great Neck, New York, Great Neck Public Schools.

*Going to Kindergarten and Going to First Grade*, Cincinnati, Ohio, Cincinnati Public Schools.

*Handbook and Curriculum Guide for Kindergarten*, Richmond, Indiana, Department of Elementary Education.

*Handbook*, Emporia, Kansas, Elementary Laboratory School, Kansas State Teachers College.

*Happy Days in Kindergarten*, Bakersfield, California, Bakersfield City School District.

*In Our Kindergarten*, San Diego, California, San Diego County Schools.

*In the Kindergarten*, Baltimore, Maryland, Baltimore Public Schools.

*Kindergarten for Your Child*, Minneapolis, Minnesota, Minneapolis Public Schools.

*Kindergarten Handbook*, Madison, Wisconsin, Madison Public Schools.

*Kindergarten Handbook*, Wilmington, Delaware, Wilmington Public Schools.

*Kindergarten Registration and Entrance Procedures*, Canton, Ohio, Canton Public Schools.

*Kindergarten—What We Do*, Youngstown, Ohio, Youngstown Public Schools.

*Let's Go To Kindergarten*, Atlanta, Georgia, Atlanta Public Schools.

*Looking Forward to Kindergarten*, Peoria, Illinois, Peoria Public Schools.

*Meeting the Kindergarten*, St. Louis, Missouri, Normandy School District.
*Off To School*, Des Moines, Iowa, Des Moines Public Schools.
*Parent's Handbook*, A, Duluth, Minnesota, Duluth Public Schools.
*Preparing Your Child for School*, Washington, D.C., U.S. Office of Education.
*School Begins with Kindergarten*, The Subject Field Series, Bulletin C-1, Springfield, Illinois, Illinois Curriculum Program, Superintendent of Public Instruction.
*School Days Are Happy Days*, Chicago, Illinois, Chicago Public Schools.
*So You're Going to School*, Tyler, Texas, Tyler Public Schools.
*Starting to School*, Richmond, Indiana, City of Richmond.
*Through the Doorway of Kindergarten to School*, Niagara Falls, New York, Division of Elementary Education, Board of Education.
*Understanding Your Kindergarten*, Hammond, Indiana, Kindergarten Committee.
*Welcome to Kindergarten at the Glencoe Schools*, Glencoe, Illinois, Glencoe Public Schools.
*Welcome to Kindergarten*, Cedar Falls, Iowa, Campus Laboratory School, Iowa State Teachers College.
*We Start to School*, Lansing, Michigan, Lansing Public Schools.
*When Children Go to Kindergarten*, Santa Cruz, California, California Committee of Early Childhood Education, Central Coast Section.
*Will Your Child Be Ready for School?* Panama City, Florida, Bay County Public Schools.
*Your Child and His Kindergarten: A Handbook of Information for Parents of School and Kindergarten Children*, Manitowac, Wisconsin, Board of Education of Manitowac Public Schools.
*Your Child Goes to Kindergarten*, Honolulu, Hawaii, Hawaii Department of Public Instruction.
*Your Child, Your School and You*, Grand Rapids, Michigan, Grand Rapids Board of Education.
*Your Child in Kindergarten*, Pasadena, California, Pasadena City Schools.

KOEHRING, DOROTHY, *Getting Ready to Read*, Cedar Falls, Iowa, The Extension Service, State College of Iowa, rev. ed., 1964.

LAMBERT, CLARA, AND STAFF MEMBERS OF THE PLAY SCHOOL ASSOCIATION, *School's Out*, New York, Harper and Brothers, 1944.

LAMBERT, HAZEL, *Early Childhood Education*, Boston, Allyn and Bacon, Inc., 1960.

————, *Teaching the Kindergarten Child*, New York, Harcourt, Brace, and Company, 1958.

LANDECK, BEATRICE, *Children and Music*, New York, William Sloane Associates, 1952.

LANDRETH, CATHERINE, *Education of the Young Child*, New York, John Wiley and Sons, rev. ed., 1952.

————, *The Psychology of Early Childhood*, New York, Alfred Knopf, 1958.

LANE, HOWARD, *Understanding Human Development*, Englewood Cliffs, N.J., Prentice-Hall, 1959.

LANE, HOWARD, AND MARY BEAUCHAMP, *Human Relations in Teaching: The Dynamics of Helping Children Grow,* Englewood Cliffs, N.J., Prentice-Hall, 1955.

LANGDON, GRACE, AND IRVING W. STOUT, *Teacher-Parent Interviews,* Englewood Cliffs, N.J., Prentice-Hall, 1957.

———, *Teaching in the Primary Grades,* New York, Macmillan, 1964.

LANGFORD, LOUISE, *Guidance of the Young Child,* New York, John Wiley and Sons, 1960.

LEASE, RUTH, AND GERALDINE SIKS, *Creative Dramatics in Home, School and Community,* New York, Harper and Brothers, 1952.

LEAVITT, JEROME E. (ed.), *Nursery-Kindergarten Education,* New York, McGraw-Hill Book Company, 1958.

LEE, J. MURRAY, AND DORRIS LEE, *The Child and His Curriculum,* New York, Appleton-Century-Crofts, 3rd ed., 1960.

———, *The Child and His Development,* New York, Appleton-Century-Crofts, 1958.

LEONARD, EDITH M., DOROTHY VANDEMAN, AND LILLIAN MILES, *Counseling with Parents,* New York, Macmillan, 1954.

———, *Foundations of Learning in Childhood Education,* Columbus, Ohio, Charles E. Merrill Books, Inc., 1963.

LINDBERG, LUCILE, *A Democratic Classroom: A Guide for Teachers,* New York, Bureau of Publications, Teachers College, Columbia University, 1954.

LOGAN, LILLIAN M., *Teaching the Young Child: Methods of Preschool and Primary Education,* Boston, Houghton Mifflin, 1960.

LOWENFELD, VIKTOR, *Creative and Mental Growth,* New York, Macmillan, 4th ed., 1964. (Revised by W. L. Brittain.)

———, *The Nature of Creative Activity,* New York, Humanities Press, 1954.

———, *Your Child and His Art: A Guide for Parents,* New York, Macmillan, 1954.

MARTIGNONI, MARGARET, *Illustrated Treasury of Children's Literature,* New York, Grosset and Dunlap, 1955.

MARTIN, W. EDGAR, *Children's Body Measurements for Planning and Equipping Schools,* Washington, D.C., U.S. Department of Health, Education, and Welfare, Office of Education, 1955.

———, *The Functional Body Measurement of School Age Children,* Chicago, National Service Institute, 1954.

MARTIN, WILLIAM E., AND CELIA B. STENDLER, *Child Behavior and Development,* New York, Harcourt, Brace and Company, rev. ed., 1959.

MATHIAS, MARGARET E., *The Beginnings of Art in the Public Schools,* New York, Charles Scribner's Sons, 1924.

MEAD, MARGARET, AND MARTHA WOLFENSTEIN (eds.), *Childhood in Contemporary Cultures,* Chicago, University of Chicago Press, 1955. (1963 paper.)

MEARNS, HUGHES, *The Creative Adult,* New York, Doubleday, 1940.

———, *Creative Power,* New York, Dover Publications, 2nd ed., 1959 (paper).

MEIGS, CORNELIA, ELIZABETH NESBITT, ANN EATON, AND RUTH HILL VIGUERS, *A Critical History of Children's Literature,* New York, Macmillan, 1953.

MERRITT, EDITH, *Working with Children in Social Studies,* San Francisco, Wadsworth Publishing Company, 1961.

MERRY, FRIEDA KIEFER, AND R. V. MERRY, *First Two Decades of Life,* New York, Harper and Brothers, 2nd ed., 1958.

MITCHELL, LUCY SPRAGUE, *Know Your Children in School,* New York, Macmillan, 1954.

————, *Our Children and Our Schools,* New York, Simon and Schuster, 1950.

MONROE, MARION, *Foundations for Reading,* Chicago, Scott, Foresman, 1964.

————, *Growing into Reading,* Chicago, Scott, Foresman, 1954.

MOORE, ELEANORA HAEGELE, *Fives at School,* New York, G. P. Putnam's Sons, 1959.

MOORE, SALLIE BETH, AND PHYLLIS RICHARDS, *Teaching in the Nursery School,* New York, Harper and Brothers, 1959.

MORRISON, IDA E., AND IDA F. PERRY, *Kindergarten-Primary Education,* New York, The Ronald Press, 1961.

MOUSTAKAS, CLARK E., *Children in Play Therapy,* New York, McGraw-Hill, 1953.

————, *Teacher and the Child: Personal Interaction in the Classroom,* New York, McGraw-Hill, 1956.

MOUSTAKAS, CLARK E., AND MINNIE P. BERSON, *The Young Child in School,* New York, Whiteside and William Morrow, 1956.

MURPHY, GARDENER, *Freeing Intelligence Through Teaching,* New York, Harper and Brothers, 1961.

MURPHY, LOIS BARKLEY, AND OTHERS, *Personality in Young Children,* Vol. I, Toronto, Irwin Clarke and Company, 1956.

————, *The Widening World of Childhood: Paths Toward Mastery,* New York, Child Study Association, Inc., 1962.

MURSELL, JAMES L., *Education for Musical Growth,* New York, Ginn and Company, 1948.

MUSSEN, PAUL HENRY, JOHN JANEWAY CONGER, JEROME KAGAN, *Readings in Child Development and Personality,* New York, Harper and Row, 2nd ed., 1965.

NATIONAL CONFERENCE ON RESEARCH IN ENGLISH, *Readiness for Reading and Related Language Arts,* Chicago, National Council of Teachers of English, 1950.

NATIONAL EDUCATION ASSOCIATION, Department of Elementary-Kindergarten-Nursery Education, Bulletins, 1201 Sixteenth Street, N.W., Washington, D.C., 20036:

*Block Building in the Kindergarten,* 1960.

*Creativity: The Step Beyond,* 1964.

*Current Approaches to Teaching Reading,* Elementary Instructional Service Leaflet, 1965.

*Foundation Learning in the Kindergarten,* 1958.

*Freedom to Move,* 1962.

*Let's Look at Kindergartens,* 1959.

*Kindergarten Today,* 1963.

*Teaching Resources for the Kindergarten-Primary Teacher,* 1960.
*Thinking, Feeling, Experiencing: Towards Realization of Full Potential,* 1962.
*Values in Early Childhood Education,* 2nd ed., 1965.
*Why Kindergarten?* 1959.
*Your Child and Reading,* pamphlet incorporated in *NEA Journal,* January, 1960.

NATIONAL EDUCATION ASSOCIATION, Department of Elementary School Principals, *Those First School Years,* Washington, D.C., National Education Association, 1960.

NESBITT, MARION, *A Public School for Tomorrow,* New York, Harper and Brothers, 1953.

NICHOLS, JOHN E., AND OTHERS, "Sites, Buildings and Equipment," Chapter IX, *Forty-sixth Yearbook, Part II; Early Childhood Education,* Chicago, National Society for the Study of Education, 1947.

OLSON, WILLARD C., *Child Development,* New York, D. C. Heath and Co., 2nd ed., 1959.

————, "Parents Request an Extra Promotion," *Childhood Education,* September, 1941, 18:24–28.

OTTO, HENRY, *Curriculum Enrichment for Gifted Elementary School Children in Regular Classes,* Austin, Texas, University of Texas Press, 1955.

PERRINE, VAN DEARING, *Let the Child Draw,* New York, Frederick A. Stokes, 1936.

POURVEUR, L., *A l'Ecole Maternelle: Essai de Methodologie,* Paris, H. Dessain, 1964 (paper).

PETERSON, HELEN T., *Kindergarten: The Key to Child Growth,* New York, Exposition Press, 1958.

PFEIFFER, ROBERT, *Working with Student Teachers,* Bulletin No. 9, East Lansing, Michigan, Department of Teacher Education, Bureau of Research and Service, School of Education, Michigan State University, 1955.

PLANT, JAMES S., *The Envelope: A Study of the Impact of the World upon the Child,* New York, Commonwealth Fund, 1950.

PRATT, CAROLINE, *I Learn from Children,* New York, Simon and Schuster, 1948. 1956 (paper).

RAMBUSH, NANCY, *Learning How to Learn,* Baltimore, Helicon Press, 1962.

RAND, WINIFRED, MARY SWEENEY, AND E. LEE VINCENT (Revised by BRECKINRIDGE, MARION, AND MARGARET NESBITT MURPHY), *Growth and Development of the Young Child,* Philadelphia, W. B. Saunders Company, 7th ed., 1963.

RASEY, MARIE I., AND J. W. MENGE, *What We Learn from Children,* New York, Harper and Brothers, 1956.

READ, KATHERINE, *The Nursery School: A Human Relations Laboratory,* Philadelphia, W. B. Saunders, 3rd ed., 1960.

REDL, FRITZ, AND WILLIAM WATTENBERG, *Mental Hygiene in Teaching,* New York, Harcourt, Brace and Company, 2nd ed., 1959.

REDL, FRITZ, AND DAVID WINEMAN, *Controls from Within,* New York, The Free Press, 1952.

REYNOLDS, MARTHA M., *Children from Seed to Saplings,* New York, McGraw-Hill, 1951.

RIBBLE, MARGARET, *The Personality of the Young Child,* New York, Bureau of Publications, Teachers College, Columbia University, 1955.

ROGERS, DOROTHY, *Mental Hygiene in Elementary Education,* Boston, Houghton Mifflin Company, 1957.

RUDOLPH, MARGUERITA, AND DOROTHY H. COHEN, *Kindergarten: A Year of Learning,* New York, Appleton-Century-Crofts, 1964.

RUDOLPH, MARGUERITA, *Living and Learning in Nursery School,* New York, Harper & Brothers, 1954.

RUGG, HAROLD, *Foundations for American Education,* Yonkers-on-Hudson, World Book Company, 1947.

RUGG, HAROLD, AND ANN SHUMAKER, "The Copy Book Regime" and "The Creative Artist Enters," *The Child Centered School,* Yonkers-on-Hudson, World Book Company, 1928.

RUSSELL, DAVID, *Children's Thinking,* New York, Ginn & Company, 1956.

RUSSELL, WILLIAM F., *How to Judge a School: A Handbook for Puzzled Parents and Taxpayers,* New York, Harper & Brothers, 1954.

SAWYER, RUTH, *The Way of the Story Teller,* New York, The Viking Press, rev., 1962. 1964 (paper.)

SCIENCE RESEARCH ASSOCIATES, *Better Living Booklets,* Chicago, Science Research Associates, Inc.

*Building Self-Confidence in Children,* 1959.
*Developing Responsibility in Children,* 1953.
*Guide for Child Study Groups, A,* 1952.
*Guilding Children's Social Growth,* 1951.
*Helping Children Develop Moral Values,* 1953.
*Helping Children Get Along in School,* 1955.
*Helping Children Solve Problems,* 1953.
*How Children Grow and Develop,* 1953.
*Self-Understanding—A First Step to Understanding Children,* 1951.
*Understanding Hostility in Children,* 1954.
*Your Child and the People Around Him,* 1953.

SCOTT, LOUISE B., AND J. J. THOMPSON, *Speechways,* St. Louis, Missouri, Webster Publishing Company, 1955.

SEASHORE, CARL E., "Music Before the Age of Six," *Why We Love Music,* Philadelphia, Oliver Ditson Company, 1941.

SHACTER, HELEN, *Understanding Ourselves,* Bloomington, Illinois, McKnight and McKnight, 1959 (paper).

SHANE, HAROLD, MARY F. REDDIN, AND MARGARET GILLESPIE, *Beginning Language Arts Instruction with Children,* Columbus, Ohio, Charles Merrill Books, Inc., 1961.

SHAW, RUTH F., *Finger Painting,* Boston, Little, Brown and Company, 1939.

SHEDLOCK, MARIE, *The Art of the Story Teller,* New York, Dover Publications, 1951 (paper).

SHEEHY, EMMA D., *Children Discover Music and Dance,* New York, Henry Holt and Company, 1959.

————, *The Fives and Sixes Go to School,* New York, Henry Holt and Company, 1954.

————, *There's Music in Children,* New York, Henry Holt and Company, 1946.

SHERER, LORRAINE, *Their First Years in School,* Los Angeles, Los Angeles Board of Education, 1939.

SHOEMAKER, ROWENA, AND CLARA LAMBERT, *Let Them Play,* New York, Play School Association, 1943.

SHUTTLESWORTH, DOROTHY EDWARDS, *Exploring Nature with Your Child,* New York, Greystone Press, 1952.

SIKS, GERALDINE B., *Creative Dramatics: An Art for Children,* New York, Harper and Brothers, 1958.

SMITH, MARION, AND ARTHUR J. BURKS, *Teaching the Slow Learning Child,* New York, Harper and Brothers, 1954.

SMITH, NILA B., *Reading Instruction for Today's Children,* Englewood Cliffs, N.J., Prentice-Hall, 1963.

SPOCK, BENJAMIN, *The Common Sense Book of Baby and Child Care,* New York, Duell, Sloan and Pearce, 1957 (paper).

————, *Talking with Mothers,* Boston, Houghton Mifflin, 1961.

STENDLER, CELIA B., AND WILLIAM E. MARTIN, *Intergroup Education in Kindergarten and Primary Grades,* New York, Macmillan, 1953.

STEPHENS, ADA D., *Providing Developmental Experience for Young Children,* New York, Bureau of Publications, Teachers College, Columbia University, 1952.

STERN, EDITH M., AND TONI S. GOULD, *The Early Years of Childhood,* New York, Harper and Brothers, 1955.

STEWART, M. S. (ed.), *Growing Family,* New York, Harper and Brothers, 1955.

STONE, L. JOSEPH, AND JOSEPH CHURCH, *Childhood and Adolescence: A Psychology of the Growing Person,* New York, Random House, 1959.

STRANG, RUTH M., *An Introduction to Child Study,* New York, Macmillan, 4th ed., 1959.

————, *Reporting to Parents,* New York, Bureau of Publications, Teachers College, Columbia University, 1948.

STRATEMEYER, FLORENCE B., H. L. FORKNER, M. G. McKIM AND ASSOCIATES, *Developing a Curriculum for Modern Living,* Bureau of Publications, Teachers College, Columbia University, 2nd ed., 1957.

STRICKLAND, RUTH S., *The Language Arts in the Elementary School,* Boston, D. C. Heath and Company, 2nd ed., 1959.

TEICHER, JOSEPH D., *Your Child and His Problems: A Basic Guide for Parents,* Boston, Little, Brown and Company, 1953.

THEMAN, VIOLA, *A Good School Day,* New York, Bureau of Publications, Teachers College, Columbia University, 1950.

TODD, VIVIAN EDMISTON, AND HELEN HEFFERNAN, *The Years Before School: Guiding Pre-School Children,* New York, Macmillan, 1964.

TOOZE, RUTH, *Story Telling,* Englewood Cliffs, N.J., Prentice-Hall, 1959.

TORRANCE, E. PAUL, *Education and the Creative Potential,* Minneapolis, University of Minnesota Press, 1963.

TRAGER, HELEN G., AND MARION H. YARROW, *They Learn What They Live: Prejudice in Young Children,* New York, Harper and Brothers, 1952.

TRAXLER, ARTHUR E., *How to Use Cumulative Records,* Chicago, Science Research Associates, 1947.

———, *Techniques of Guidance,* New York, Harper and Brothers, rev. ed., 1957.

UNITED STATES DEPARTMENT OF HEALTH, EDUCATION, AND WELFARE, Washington, D.C., Office of Education, School Designing:

*Designing Elementary Classrooms,* Special Publication No. 1, 1953.

*Good and Bad School Plans in the U.S. As Revealed by School Facilities Survey,* Special Publication No. 2, 1954.

UPDEGRAFF, RUTH, AND OTHERS, *Practice in Preschool Education,* New York, McGraw-Hill Book Company, 1938.

WAECHTER, H. H., AND ELIZABETH WAECHTER, *Schools for the Very Young,* New York, F. W. Dodge Company, 1951.

WANN KENNETH, MIRIAM S. DORN, AND ELIZABETH ANN LIDDLE, *Fostering Intellectual Development in Young Children,* New York, Bureau of Publications, Teachers College, Columbia University, 1962.

WARD, WINIFRED, *Playmaking with Children from Kindergarten to High School,* New York, Appleton-Century-Crofts, 2nd ed., 1957.

———, *Stories to Dramatize,* Anchorage, Kentucky, Children's Theatre Press, 1952.

WASHBURNE, CARLETON, *What Is Progressive Education?* New York, John Day Company, 1952.

WASHBURNE, RUTH W., *Children Have Their Reasons,* New York, D. Appleton-Century Company, 1942.

———, *Children Know Their Friends,* New York, William Morrow and Company, 1949.

WHITE HOUSE CONFERENCE ON CHILDREN AND YOUTH, *Children in a Changing World,* Washington, D.C., White House Conference on Children and Youth, Inc., 1960.

WILLS, CLARICE D., AND WILLIAM STEGEMAN, *Living in the Kindergarten,* Chicago, Follett Publishing Company, 2nd ed., 1956.

WINGO, GLENN M., AND RALEIGH SCHORLING, *Elementary School Student Teaching,* New York, McGraw-Hill Book Company, 3rd ed., 1960.

WITMER, HELEN LELAND, AND RUTH KOTINSKY, *Personality in the Making,* New York, Harper and Brothers, 1952.

WITTY, PAUL, *Reading in Modern Education,* Boston, D. C. Heath and Company, 1949.

WOLFF, WERNER, *Personality of the Preschool Child,* New York, Grune and Stratton, 1946.

WOOD, ALICE L., *Sound Games: Speech Correction for Very Young Children,* New York, E. P. Dutton and Company, 1948.

*Working with the Child from Two to Six,* Ohio Curriculum Bulletin No. 5, Columbus, Ohio, State Department of Education, 1944.

ZEDLER, EMPRESS YOUNG, *Listening for Speech Sounds,* New York, Doubleday and Company, 1955.

## A Bibliography of Standardized Tests, Rating Scales and Checklists for Kindergarten Children and Teachers[1]

### *General Intelligence Tests*

I* ARTHUR, GRACE, *Arthur Point Scale of Performance*, C. H. Stoelting Company, 1925–1947.

ARTHUR, GRACE, *Leiter International Performance Scale: Arthur Adaptation*, C. H. Stoelting Company, 1952–1956.

BAKER, H. J., AND H. KAUFMAN, *Detroit Kindergarten Test*, World Book Company, 1922–1925.

GOODENOUGH, FLORENCE L., "Drawing a Man," *The Measurement of Intelligence by Drawing*, World Book Company, 1926.

I* GOODENOUGH, FLORENCE L., JOSEPHINE C. FOSTER, KATHERINE MAURER, AND M. J. VAN WAGENEN, *Minnesota Pre-School Scale*, Educational Test Bureau, 1932–1946.

I* KUHLMAN, F., AND ROSE C. ANDERSON, *Kuhlman Anderson Test*, Personnel Press, 1927–1952.

LANTS, BEATRICE, *Easel Age*, California Test Bureau, 1955.

I PORTEUS, STANLEY, *Porteus Maze Test*, C. H. Stoelting Company, 1914–1959.

I* STUTSMAN, RACHEL, *Merrill-Palmer Scale of Mental Tests*, C. H. Stoelting Company, 1926–1931.

PINTNER, RUDOLPH, AND BESS CUNNINGHAM, *Pintner Cunningham Primary Mental Test*, World Book Company, 1923, 1946.

I RAVEN, J. C., *Raven's Progressive Matrices*, H. K. Lewis & Company, 1938–1956.

SULLIVAN, ELIZABETH T., WILLIS W. CLARK, AND ERNEST TIEG, *California Test of Mental Maturity and Adaptations*, California Test Bureau, 1936–1957.

I* TERMAN, L. M., AND MAUD A. MERRILL, *Stanford Revision of the Binet Scale*, Forms L and M, Houghton Mifflin Company, 1916–1960.

THURSTONE, L. L., AND THELMA G. THURSTONE, *Test of Primary Mental Abilities for Ages Five and Six*, Science Research Associates, 1947.

VALENTINE, C. W., *Intelligence Tests for Children*, 4th ed., Methuen & Company, 1945–1958.

I* WECHSLER, DAVID, *Wechsler Intelligence Scale for Children* (WISC), Psychological Corporation, 1949.

### *Personality and Adjustment*

BELLAK, LEOPOLD, AND SONYA SOREL BELLAK, *Children's Appreciation Test*, C. P. S. Company, 1949–1961.

[1] This symbol, "I," indicates that the test is designed to be given to individual children. The asterisk indicates that the test so marked is to be administered only by certified testers, psychometricians, or psychologists.

Addresses of publishers cited are listed on pp. 533–534.

BENE, EVA, AND JAMES ANTHONY, *Family Relations Test: An Objective Technique for Exploring Emotional Attitudes in Children,* National Foundation for Educational Research in England and Wales, 1957.

DOLL, E. A., *Vineland Social Maturity Scale,* Educational Test Bureau, 1935–1953.

FLANAGAN, JOHN C., *The Personal and Social Development Program: with Performance Record,* Science Research Associates, 1947–1956.

HAGGERTY, M. E., W. C. OLSON, AND E. K. WICKMAN, *Haggerty-Olson-Wickman Behavior Rating Schedules,* World Book Company, 1930.

HOLTZMAN, WAYNE H., *Holtzman Inkblot Technique,* Psychological Corporation, 1958–1961.

LYNN, DAVID B., *Structured Doll Play,* Test Developments, 1959–1960.

MARSTON, L. R., *Marston Introversion-Extroversion Tests,* University of Iowa Studies in Child Welfare, C. H. Stoelting Company, 1932.

MECHAM, MERLIN J., *Verbal Language Development Scale* (extension of the communications section of the Vineland maturity scale), Educational Test Bureau, 1958–1959.

REYMERT, MARTIN L., *The Wishes and Fears Inventory,* Mooseheart Laboratory for Child Research, 1949.

THORPE, L. P., W. W. CLARK, AND E. W. TIEGS, *California Test of Personality—Primary, Form* A, California Test Bureau, 1939–1953.

TWITCHELL-ALLEN, DORIS, *Twitchell-Allen Three Dimensional Personality Test* (formerly *Three Dimensional Appreciation Test*), C. H. Stoelting Company, 1948–1958.

### General Information

PROBST, CATHRYN, A., "A General Information Test for Kindergarten Children," *Child Development,* June, 1931, 2:81–85.

SANGREN, P. V., *Information Test for Young Children,* World Book Company, 1930.

SMITH, JANET, "Test of General Information for Children of Pre-School Age," *Journal of Experimental Education,* December, 1943, 12:92–105.

TEMPLIN, MILDRED, "General Information of Kindergarten Children; A Comparison With Probst Study after Twenty-six Years," *Child Development,* March, 1958, 29:87–96.

### Vision and Hearing

*A-B-C Test for Oscular Dominance,* Psychological Corporation, 1927–1946.

EAMES, THOMAS, *Eames Eye Test,* Harcourt, Brace and World, 1938–1960.

FREEMAN, ELLIS, *Freeman Acuity Tests,* Freeman Technical Association, 1954.

*Keystone Visual Service for Schools and Colleges* (originally *Betts Ready to Read Tests*), Keystone View Company, 1933–1938.

*Maico Audiometer,* Maico Audiometer, Inc., 1949–1959.

*Massachusetts Vision Test,* Massachusetts Department of Public Health, Welck Allyn, Inc., 1943–1954.

MEYERSON, LEE, *Hearing for Speech: A Verbal Audiometric Test,* Copenhagen, 1956.

*Michigan Pre-School T/O Vision Tester* (Ages 3-5 years), Titmus Optical Co., 1958–1960.

MOORE, JOSEPH E., *Moore Eye Hand Coordination and Color Matching (Pre-School form 2-6 years)*, Joseph E. Moore and Associates, 1949–1955.

*New York Vision Tester*, Bausch and Lomb, Inc., 1957.

ROBBINS, SAMUEL, AND ROSA SEYMOUR ROBBINS, *Robbins Speech Sound Discrimination and Verbal Imagery Type Tests*, Expression Company, 1948–1958.

SHERIDAN, MARY D., *Stycar Hearing Tests*, National Foundation for Educational Research in England and Wales, 1958–1959.

*Snellen "E" Chart Test*, Buffalo, New York, American Optical Company.

SULLIVAN, ELIZABETH, WILLIS W. CLARK, AND ERNEST TIEGS, *Pretest of Vision, Hearing and Motor Coordination* (formerly part of the California Test of Motor Maturity) California Test Bureau, 1936–1951.

WEPMAN, JOSEPH M., *Auditory Discrimination Test*, Language and Research Association, 1958.

### Speech and Language

AMBCO, *Speech Tests Records*, Ambco, Inc., 1958.

BRYNGELSON, BRYNG, AND GLASPEY, ESTHER, *Speech in the Classroom and Speech Improvement Cards*, Scott, Foresman & Company, 1941–1951.

MEACHAM, MERLIN J., *Speech Articulation Test for Young Children*, University Press, Brigham Young University, 1955–1959.

TEMPLIN, MILDRED, AND FREDERIC L. DARLEY, *Templin-Darley Screening and Diagnostic Tests of Articulation* (Ages 3-8), Bureau of Educational Research Service, 1960.

### General School Readiness, Reading, and Arithmetic Readiness

BANHAM, KATHERINE M., *Maturity Level for School Entrance and Reading Readiness*, Educational Test Bureau, 1950–1959.

BRENNER, ANTON, *Brenner-Gestalt Developmental Test of School Readiness*, Western Psychological Services, 1964.

BRUECKNER, LEO J., *Co-ordinated Scale of Attainment—Battery I, Primary Arithmetic* (ages 5½ to 6½), Educational Test Bureau, 1947.

Dominion Tests, *Group Test of Reading Readiness*, Vocational Guidance Center, 1945–1954.

COLE, L. W., AND LEONA VINCENT, *Cole-Vincent Test for School Entrants*, Bureau of Educational Measurements and Standards, Kansas State Teachers College, 1924–1928.

GATES, ARTHUR, *Gates Reading Readiness Tests*, Teachers College, Columbia University, 1939–1949.

*Group Test of Reading Readiness: Dominion Tests*, Department of Research, Ontario College of Education, University of Toronto, 1949–1959.

HARRISON, M. LUCILE, AND JAMES B. STROUD, *Harrison-Stroud, Reading Readiness Test*, Houghton Mifflin Company, 1949–1956.

HILDRETH, GERTRUDE H., AND N. I. GRIFFITHS, *Metropolitan Readiness Tests*, World Book Company, 1932–1950.

ILG, FRANCES L., AND LOUISE BATES AMES, *School Readiness Tests Used at the Gesell Institute*, Harper and Row, 1964.

LEE, J. M., AND W. M. CLARK, *Lee-Clark Reading Readiness Tests*, California Test Bureau, 1931–1951.

MONROE, MARION, *Reading Aptitude Tests, Primary Form*, Houghton Mifflin Company, 1935.

PRATT, WILLIS, AND OTHERS, *American School Reading Readiness Test*, Public School Publishing Company, 1941–1955.

THURSTONE, L. L., AND THELMA G. THURSTONE, *Tests of Primary Mental Abilities for Ages Five and Six* (see especially, Verbal Meaning, Perception, Quantitative, and Number Portions of the Test), Science Research Associates, 1947.

TIEGS, ERNEST, AND WILLIS W. CLARK, *California Arithmetic Test*, California Test Bureau, 1933–1950.

VAN WAGENEN, M. J., *Van Wagenen Reading Readiness Tests*, Educational Test Bureau, 1932.

VOTAW, DAVID V., AND PEGGY LOU MOSES, *Reading Readiness Test*, Steck Company, 1957.

WATSON, G. MILTON, *Watson Reading Readiness Tests*, Book Society of Canada, Ltd., U.S.-C.S. Hammond Co., 1960.

WECHSLER, DAVID, *Wechsler Intelligence Scale for Children* (WISC), (see particularly sections concerned with comprehension, arithmetic, similarities, and vocabulary), Psychological Corporation, 1947.

WITTICH, W. A., "A Number Readiness Test," *School Executive*, March, 1942, 61:11–13.

YOUNG, ROBERT V., AND OTHERS, *American School Achievement Test: Arithmetic Readiness*, Public School Publications Company, 1941–1955.

### *Teacher Rating Scales and Checklists*

ANDERSON, H. H., "Mental Hygiene Scale for Teachers," *American Journal of Orthopsychiatry*, 1940, 10:253–264.

ANDERSON, T. H., "Techniques for Recording Dominative and Integrative Contacts Which Teachers Have with Kindergarten Children," *Child Development*, 1939, 10:73–89.

BAXTER, B., "Teacher Rating Scale," *National Educational Association Journal*, 1938, 27:81.

COOK, WALTER, AND OTHERS, *Minnesota Teacher Attitude Inventory*, Psychological Corporation, 1951.

FLORY, C. D., "Self Rating Scale for Prospective Teachers," *Educational Administration and Supervision*, 1930, 16:135–143.

HEADLEY, NEITH, "Qualities and Abilities of a Good Kindergarten Teacher," *The Kindergarten: Its Place in the Program of Education*, Prentice-Hall, 1965.

National Teacher Examination, *Early Childhood Education*, Educational Testing Service, 1940–1961.

SANDERSON, M., "A Personal Check List for the Teacher," *National Education Association Journal*, 1939, 28:183.

UPDEGRAFF, R., "Rating Scale for Nursery School Teachers," *Practice in Preschool Education*, McGraw-Hill Book Company, 1938.

VOTAW, DAVID F., *Test of Adult Attitudes Toward Children*, Steck Company, 1957.

WILSON, HOWARD EUGENE, *Self Appraisal Scale for Teachers*, Administrative Research Associates, 1957.

## NAMES AND ADDRESSES OF CITED TEST PUBLISHERS[1]

Administrative Research Associates, PO Box 1160, Chicago, Illinois 60690.

Ambco, Inc., West Washington Boulevard, Los Angeles, California 90007.

American Optical Company, Buffalo, New York 14215.

Bausch and Lomb Optical Company, Rochester, New York 14002.

Book Society of Canada, Ltd., 4386 Shepard Avenue, Agincourt, Ontario, Canada.

Brigham Young University Press, Brigham Young University, Provo, Utah 84601.

Bureau of Educational Measurements, Kansas State Teachers College, Emporia, Kansas 66801.

Bureau of Educational Research and Service, State University of Iowa, Iowa City, Iowa 52240.

Bureau of Publications, Teachers College, Columbia University, New York, New York 10027.

California Test Bureau, Del Monte Research Park, Monterey Park, Monterey, California 93940.

C. P. S. Company, PO Box 83, Larchmont, New York 10538.

Educational Test Bureau, 720 Washington Avenue S.E., Minneapolis, Minnesota 55414.

Educational Testing Service, Princeton, New Jersey 08540.

Expression Company, Magnolia, Massachusetts 01348.

Freeman Technical Associates, 1206 Benjamin Franklin Drive, Sarasota, Florida 33577.

Guidance Centre, College of Education, University of Toronto, 371 Bloor Street West, Toronto 5, Ontario, Canada.

Harper & Row, Publishers, 49 E. 33 Street, New York, New York 10016.

Hammond, C. S., and Company, Maplewood, New Jersey 07040.

Houghton Mifflin Company, 2 Park Street, Boston, Mass. 02107.

Keystone View Company, Meadville, Pennsylvania 16335.

Language Research Associates, 950 E. 59th Street, Chicago, Illinois 60637.

Lewis, H. K., and Company, Ltd., 136 Gower Street, London W.C.1., England.

Maico Electronics, Inc., 21 North Third Street, Minneapolis 55401.

McGraw-Hill Book Company, 330 W. 42 Street, New York, New York 10036.

Methuen and Company, Ltd., 36 Essex Street, Strand, London W.C.2, England.

[1] See *Tests in Print*, Oscar K. Buros (ed.), Highland Park, New Jersey, The Gryphon Press, 1966, for additional tests.

Mooseheart Laboratory for Child Research, Mooseheart, Illinois 60539.

Moore, Joseph F., and Associates, 4406 Jett Road, N.W., Atlanta, Georgia 30305.

National Foundation for Educational Research in England and Wales, 79 Wimpole Street, London W.1, England.

Personnel Press, Inc., 188 Nassau Street, Princeton, New Jersey 08540.

Prentice-Hall, Inc., Englewood Cliffs, New Jersey 07632.

Psychological Corporation, 304 East 45th Street, New York, New York 10017.

Public School Publishing Company, Test Division of Bobbs-Merrill Company, Inc., 1720 East 38th Street, Indianapolis, Indiana 46206.

Science Research Associates, Inc., 259 East Erie Street, Chicago, Illinois 60611.

Scott, Foresman & Company, 433 Erie Street, Chicago, Illinois 60611.

Steck Company, Austin, Texas 78901.

Stoelting, C. H., Company, 424 North Homan Avenue, Chicago, Illinois 60624.

Test Developments, Box 8306, Denver, Colorado 80200.

Titmus Optical Company, Inc., Petersburg, Virginia 26747.

Western Psychological Services, 10655 Santa Monica Blvd., Los Angeles, California 90025.

World Publishing Company, 2231 W. 110 Street, Cleveland, Ohio 44102.

## Research Reports and Articles Helpful to Kindergarten Teachers

ADLERBLUM, EVELYN D., "Mental Hygiene in the Kindergarten," *NEA Journal*, February, 1955, 44:80–82.

ALBERA, R. G., "Validity of Early School Entrance into Kindergarten," *Journal of Educational Research*, September, 1962, 56:53–54.

AMES, LOUISE B., AND FRANCES L. ILG, "Developmental Trends in Writing Behavior," *Journal of Genetic Psychology*, September, 1951, 79:29–46.

AMMONS, MARGARET P., AND J. I. GOODLAD, "When to Begin," *Childhood Education*, May, 1955, 32:21–26.

AMMONS, R. B., "Reaction in a Projective Doll Interview of White Males Two to Six Years of Age to Differences in Skin Color and Facial Features," *Journal of Genetic Psychology*, 1950, 76:232–241.

BACCI, W., "Children Can Read in Kindergarten," *School Management*, May, 1961, 5:120.

BAIN, WINIFRED E., "With Life So Long Why Shorten Childhood?" *Childhood Education*, September, 1961, 38:15–18.

BARNES, FRED P., editor, *School Begins with Kindergarten*, Bulletin No. C-1, Springfield, Illinois: Superintendent of Public Instruction, 1957. (Kindergarten Handbook, Illinois Curriculum Program.)

BAYLEY, NANCY, "Individual Patterns of Development," *Child Development*, March, 1956, 27:45–74.

BERGAMINI, YOLANDA, AND WALTER SWANSON, "Does Kindergarten Make a Difference?" *School Executive*, December, 1954, 74:54–55.

BETTELHEIM, BRUNO, "What Children Learn from Play," *Parents' Magazine*, July, 1964, 49:101–102.

BIBER, BARBARA, AND CLAUDIA LEWIS, "What Young Children Expect From Their Teachers," *Genetic Psychology Monographs*, 1948, 40:228.

BIRCH, JACK W., "Early School Admission for Mentally Advanced Children," *Exceptional Children*, December, 1954, 21:84–87.

BLAIR, ABBE, "Kindergarten: Trouble Shooters," *Parents' Magazine*, May, 1962, 37:58–59.

BLAKELY, W. PAUL, AND ERMA SHADLE, "A Study of Two Readiness for Reading Programs in Kindergarten," *Elementary English*, November, 1961, 38:502–505.

BLOCK, JEANNE, AND BARCLAY MARTIN, "Predicting the Behavior of Children Under Frustration," *Journal of Abnormal and Social Psychology*, September, 1955, 51:281–285.

BLUM, L., AND J. RATHS, "Can Kindergarten Teachers Be Trained to Identify Emotionally Handicapped Children?" *Elementary School Journal*, February, 1964, 64:242–245.

BRADLEY, BEATRICE E., "An Experimental Study of the Readiness Approach to Reading," *Elementary School Journal*, February, 1956, 56:262–267.

BEVERLY, M. L., "Role of the Kindergarten in the Space Age," *Ohio Schools*, December, 1961, 39:10–11.

BROOM, LEONARD, "Need for 'Preschool Schools,'" *U. S. News and World Report*, June, 1964, LVI:60–61.

BROWN, DANIEL G., "Sex-Role Preference in Young Children," *Psychological Monographs*, 1956, Vol. 70, 14:1–19.

BUTLER, ANNIE L., "Hurry! Hurry! Hurry! Why?" *Childhood Education*, September, 1962, 39:10–13.

CANTOR, GORDON N., et al., "Observing Behavior in Preschool Children as a Function of Stimulus Complexity," *Child Development*, September, 1963, 34:683–689.

"Characteristics of Kindergarten Children," *California Journal of Elementary Education*, May, 1963, 31:197–207.

COLEMAN, M. E., "Phonics Learning as a Concomitant Learning," *Education*, May, 1962, 82:521–524.

COUNCIL OF CHIEF STATE SCHOOL OFFICERS, *Responsibilities of State Departments of Education for Nursery School and Kindergarten*, Washington, D.C.: The Council (1202 Sixteenth St., N.W.), 1961. (21 p.)

COUSINS, NORMAN, "Not So Fast," *Saturday Review*, July 6, 1963, XLVI:14.

CUTTS, WARREN G., "Reading Unreadiness in the Underprivileged," *NEA Journal*, April, 1963, 52:23–24.

DALE, D. G., "Love of Literature Begins in Kindergarten," *Elementary English Journal*, January, 1958, 35:28–29.

DAVIS, H. M., "Don't Push Your School Beginners," *Parents' Magazine*, October, 1956, 27:140–141.

DELOURDES, SISTER MARY, "Importance of Readiness at the Kindergarten Level," *National Catholic Education Association Bulletin*, August, 1963, 60:537–543.

DINKMEYER, DON, "Understanding Childrens' Behavior," *Elementary School Journal*, March, 1961, 61:314–316.

DOLLINS, JOSEPH G., HENRY ANDELINE, AND EDMUND MECH, "With Words of Praise," *The Elementary School Journal*, May, 1960, 60:446–450.

DOMAN, GLENN, GEORGE L. STEVENS, AND REGINALD C. OREM, "You Can Teach Your Baby to Read," *Ladies Home Journal*, May, 1963, 62:124–126.

DOWNING, JOHN A., "A New Phonetic Alphabet Is Put To Test," *Parents' Magazine*, January, 1963, 38:48–49, 93–95.

DOWNING, JOHN A., "The Augmented Roman Alphabet for Learning to Read," *The Reading Teacher*, March, 1963, 16:325–36.

DURKIN, DOLORES, "Children Who Read Before Grade One: A Second Study," *Elementary School Journal*, December, 1963, 64:143–148.

————, "Kindergarten and Reading," *Elementary English*, March, 1962, 39:274–276.

————, "Reading Instruction and the Five-Year-Old," *Scholastic Teacher*, April 24, 1963, 7–8.

DURKIN, DOLORES, AND WILLIAM D. SHELDON, "Should the Very Young Be Taught to Read?" *NEA Journal*, November, 1963, 52:20–24.

DURRELL, DONALD, AND HELEN A. MURPHY, "Reading Readiness," *Journal of Education*, December, 1963, 46:3–10.

DUTTON, WILBUR H., "Growth of Number Readiness in Kindergarten Children," *Arithmetic Teacher*, May, 1963, 10:251–255.

EAST, J. K., "Kindergarten Is a Good Investment," *School Executive*, May, 1953, 72:52–53.

ENGELHARDT, N. L., JR., "The Working Heights of Elementary School Children," *American School and University*, 1950–1951, 344–350.

"The Educational Program," *Early and Middle Childhood Review of Educational Research*, Vol. 23, No. 2, Washington, D.C., American Educational Research Association, 1953.

ESTES, BETSY WORTH, "Some Mathematical and Logical Concepts in Children," *Journal of Genetic Psychology*, June, 1956, 88:219–222.

FANCHER, BETSY, "Speaking Out: Let's Stop Cheating Our Children Out of Their Childhood," *Saturday Evening Post*, September 29, 1962, 235:10.

FAST, I., "Kindergarten Training and Grade 1 Reading," *Journal of Educational Psychology*, January, 1957, 48:52–57 (with bibliography).

FERGUSON, E. D., "Evaluation of Two Types of Kindergarten Attendance Programs," *Journal of Educational Psychology*, May, 1957, 48:287–301.

FORESTER, JOHN, "At What Age Should a Child Start School?" *School Executive*, March, 1953, 72:80–81.

FOX, R. B., AND M. POWELL, "Evaluating Kindergarten Experiences," *The Reading Teacher*, November, 1964, 18:118–120.

FULLER, ELIZABETH M., *About the Kindergarten: What Research Says to the Teacher*, Bulletin No. 22, Washington, D.C., National Education Association, Department of Classroom Teachers, 1961.

GABBARD, HAZEL, "Nation's Concern for Kindergartens," *School Life*, May, 1959, 41:10–12.

GUNTHER, MAX, "Cracking the Grown Ups Code," (ITA Initial Teaching Alphabet), *Saturday Evening Post*, June, 1964, 24:34–35.

HAMALAINEN, ARTHUR E., "Kindergarten-Primary Entrance Age in Relation to Later School Adjustment," *Elementary School Journal*, March, 1952, 52:406–411.

HAMMOND, SARAH L., "What Happens to the Five-Year-Olds?" *Educational Leadership*, October, 1954, 12:9–14.

HANSON, EARL H., "Let's Use Common Sense to End the Reading War," *NEA Journal*, February, 1962, 51:41–44.

———, "There's No Magic Formula for Learning to R-r-r-r-read," *Parents' Magazine*, February, 1963, 38:56–57.

HEADLEY, NEITH E., "Good Education for Five-Year-Olds," *Childhood Education*, March, 1954, 30:314–316.

———, "Kindergarten Comes of Age," *NEA Journal*, March, 1954, 43:153–154. Condensed: *Education Digest*, May, 1954, 19:49–51.

———, "The Content of the Kindergarten," *NEA Journal*, October, 1959, 48:47–49.

———, "To Write or Not to Write," *Childhood Education*, February, 1961, 37:260–263.

HEFFERNAN, HELEN, "Fullness of Living Here and Now," *Reading in the Kindergarten?* Bulletin 6-A, Association for Childhood Education, 1962, 6–12.

———, "Keeping the Curriculum Up to Date," *Arizona Teacher*, March, 1960, 48:14–16.

———, "Kindergarten; A Growing-Up Year," *Grade Teacher*, June, 1958, 75:14.

———, "Pressures on Children and Youth," *California Schools*, August, 1962, 289–306.

———, "Pressures to Start Formal Instruction Early," *Childhood Education*, October, 1960, 37:57–60.

———, "Significance of Kindergarten Education," *Childhood Education*, March, 1960, 36:313–319.

HELTIBRIDLE, MARY E., "What, No Kindergartens?" *NEA Journal*, January, 1957, 46:12–14.

HILLMAN, ROSEMARY, "In Defense of Five-Year-Olds," *Saturday Review*, November ,1963, XLVI: 76, 89.

HOPPOCK, ANNE, "What Are Kindergartens For?" *The Compass*, January, 1959, publication of State Department of Education, New Jersey. Reprinted by the Association for Childhood Education as an 8-page pamphlet.

HYMES, JAMES L., JR., "How Are the Fives Faring in Your Town?" *Childhood Education*, September, 1958, 35:25–26.

———, "How Can You Tell About Readiness?" *Grade Teacher*, March, 1963, 80:17.

———, "The Importance of Pre-Primary Education," *Childhood Education*, September, 1962, 39:5–9.

———, "Most Solid Learnings," *Grade Teacher*, September, 1961, 79:17.

———, "One Good Way to Teach Fives to Read," *Grade Teacher*, December, 1961, 79:15, 88, 90.

———, "Phonics in the Kindergarten," *Grade Teacher*, November, 1962, 80:22, 131.

———, *Public Kindergartens*, Elementary Instructional Service Leaflet, Washington, D.C.: National Education Association, Summer, 1960.

———, "Wide World of Fives," *Grade Teacher*, January, 1962, 79:15.

"I am Tired of—: A Private Explosion," *Childhood Education*, November, 1963, 40:147–148.

"Intellectual Leap," *Newsweek*, June 24, 1963, 61:106.

KEISTER, MARY ELIZABETH, "Relation of Mid-morning Feeding to the Behavior of Nursery School Children," *Journal of American Dietetic Association*, 1950, 26:25–29.

KELIHER, ALICE, "Alice Keliher Says" [re pressures], *Grade Teacher*, December, 1963, 81:102.

KELLEY, MARJORIE L., "When Are Children Ready to Read?" *Saturday Review*, July 20, 1963, 46:58.

KIESSEL, WILLIAM C., JR., "Kindergarten in America," *Education*, April, 1955, 75:540–544.

KOHN, MARTIN, "Importance of the Beginning: Kindergarten," *National Elementary Principal*, April, 1962, 41:18–22.

KOLSON, C. J., "Oral Arithmetic Vocabulary of Kindergarten Children," *Arithmetic Teacher*, February, 1962, 10:81–82.

KUNKLE, E. W., "What Are Sound Learning Experiences For the Young Child?" *Teachers College Journal*, May, 1961, 32:139–141.

LAGEMANN, JOHN KORD, "How We Discourage Creative Children," *Redbook Magazine*, March, 1963, 120:44–45.

———, "A New Way for Children to Learn," *Redbook Magazine*, February, 1964, 122:42–43.

LANGERAK, ROBERT W., "Don't Let the Tax Swing the Axe on Our Kindergarten Program," *Midland Schools*, May, 1960, 14:29–30.

LARSON, A., "Early Admission Experiment of the Fund for the Advancement of Education," *Education Forum*, November, 1958, 2:101–108.

LARSON, R., AND J. OLSON, "A Method of Identifying the Culturally Deprived Children in Kindergarten," *Exceptional Children*, November, 1963, 30:130–134.

LOBSENZ, NORMAN M., "The Plot to Abolish Childhood," *Redbook*, June, 1962, 119:31.

MAAS, JEANNETTE, AND WILLIAM B. MICHAEL, "The Relationship of Interest Choices of Kindergarten Children to Social Group Membership and to Sex Differences," *California Journal of Educational Research*, January, 1964, 15:24–33.

MARGOLIN, E. B., AND D. A. LETON, "Interest of Kindergarten Children in Block Play," *Journal of Educational Research*, September, 1961, 55:13–18.

MARTIN, W. EDGAR, *Children's Bodily Measurements for Planning and Equipping Schools: A Handbook for School Officials and Architects*, Special Publication No. 4, Washington, D.C., United States Department of Health, Welfare, and Education, Office of Education, 1955.

———, *Functional Body Measurements of School Age Children*, Chicago, National School Service Institute, 1954.

MARTIN, WILLIAM E., "Quantitative Expressions in Young Children," *Genetic Psychology Monographs*, 1951, 44:147–219.

MATTHEW, EUNICE S., "What Is Expected of the Soviet Kindergarten?" *Harvard Educational Review*, Winter, 1959, 29:43–53.

McCONKIE, GWEN W., AND MARIE M. HUGHES, "Quality of Classroom Living Related to Size of Kindergarten Group," *Childhood Education*, May, 1956, 32:428–432.

McGINLEY, PHYLLIS, "In One Era—Out the Other," *Ladies Home Journal*, April, 1964, 81:42–44.

MICUCCI, PAT, "Let's Not Teach Reading in the Kindergarten," *Elementary English*, March, 1964, 41:246–250.

MONTAGUE, DAVID O., "Arithmetic Concepts of Kindergarten Children in Contrasting Socio-Economic Areas," *Elementary School Journal*, April, 1954, 64:393–397.

MONTAGUE, PATSY, "Kindergarten and First Grade Programs for Today," *Educational Leadership*, 1959, 16:292–295.

MOORE, SALLIE BETH, "The Use of Commands, Suggestions and Requests by Nursery School and Kindergarten Teachers," *Child Development*, March, 1938, 9:185–201.

MURPHY, L. B., AND B. M. CALDWELL, "World Stands Out" (Review of *Widening World of Childhood*), *Children*, July, 1963, 10:153–155.

NATIONAL EDUCATION ASSOCIATION, *Admission Policies for Kindergarten and First Grade*, Circular No. 3, Washington, D.C.: The Association, 1958.

NATIONAL EDUCATION ASSOCIATION, RESEARCH DIVISION, *Kindergarten Practices, 1961*, Research Monograph 1962-M2, Washington, D.C.: The Association, April, 1962, 36 p.

NEISSER, EDITH G., "Preschools Are Not Just For Play," *Parents' Magazine*, February, 1964, 39:72, 120, 128.

NUMNICHT, G., J. SPARKS, AND J. MORTENSEN, "Is There a Right Admission Age?" *The Education Digest*, May, 1963, 28:34–36.

NUNNALLY, NANCY, "Are the First Grades Ready for Our Kindergarteners?" *Childhood Education*, September, 1962, 39:14–18.

OJEMANN, RALPH H., "Personality Adjustment of Individual Children"—*What Research Says to the Teacher*, Bulletin No. 5, Washington, D.C., National Education Association, 1954.

PAULEY, FRANK R., "Sex Differences and Legal School Entrance Age," *Journal of Educational Research*, September, 1951, 45:1–9.

PINES, MAYA, "How Three-Year-Olds Teach Themselves to Read—and Love It," *Harper's Magazine*, May, 1963, 226:58–64.

PITCHER, EVELYN GOODENOUGH, "Male and Female," *Atlantic*, March, 1963, 211:87–91.

————, "Learning Academic Subjects in the Kindergarten," *Journal of Nursery Education*, September, 1963, 18:250–252.

PLOGHOFT, MILTON H., "Do Reading Readiness Workbooks Promote Readiness?" *Elementary English*, October, 1959, 36:424–426.

PRATT, WILLIS E., "A Study of the Difference in the Prediction of Reading Success of Kindergarten and Non-Kindergarten Children," *Journal of Educational Research*, March, 1949, 42:525–535.

PRESCOTT, GEORGE A., "Sex Differences in Metropolitan Readiness Test Results," *Journal of Educational Research*, April, 1955, 48:605–610.

RABBAN, MEYER, "Sex Role Identification in Young Children in Two Diverse Social Groups," *Genetic Psychology Monographs*, 1950, 42:81–158.

———, "Reading All of a Sudden. I.T.A.," *Life*, November, 1963, 55:45–46.

*Research Relating to Children: An Inventory of Studies in Progress*, Washington, D.C., The Clearing House for Research in Child Life, Children's Bureau, United States Department of Health, Education, and Welfare, 1949–1960.

ROBBINS, JOHN, AND JUNE ROBBINS, "Do Our Schools Demand Enough of Our Children?" *Redbook*, October, 1961, 117:50–51.

ROBINOWITZ, RALPH, "Learning Relation of Opposites as Related to Scores on the Wechsler Intelligence Scale for Children," *Journal of Genetic Psychology*, March, 1956, 88:26–30.

ROBINSON HELEN F., "Clarifying Ideas in the Kindergarten," *Instructor*, May, 1964, LXXIII: 32, 95.

ROTH, B. A., AND G. W. WAGNER, "Promising Practices in Kindergarten Education," *Midland Schools*, March, 1960, 74:18–19.

SASSMAN, E. G., "Kindergarten and the Forward Look," *Education Digest*, March, 1963, 28:32–33.

SCARFE, N. V., "Play Is Education," *Childhood Education*, November, 1962, 39:117–121.

SCHINDLER, A., "School Admission and Promotion," Washington, D.C., *National Education Association Research Bulletin*, 37, 1959, pp. 13–15.

SEGAL, JULIUS, "Children Are People Too," *Family Circle*, May, 1963, 27:99–100.

SHELDON, WILLIAM D., "Reading . . . Where Do We Stand? Where Are We Going?" *Grade Teacher*, April, 1961, 78:40–41.

———, "Reading for the Very Young; Is It Worth It?" *Times (London), Edition Supplement*, October 19, 1962, 2474:486.

———, "Teaching the Very Young to Read," *The Reading Teacher*, December, 1962, 16:163–169.

SIEGEL, ALBERTA E., "Film-mediated Fantasy Aggression and Strength of Aggression Drive," *Child Development*, September, 1956, 27:365–378.

SMITH, NILA BANTON, *Shall We Teach Reading in the Kindergarten?* Leaflet-H, Washington, D.C., Association for Childhood Education, 1964.

SPAYDE, P. E., "Kindergarten Children's Familiarity with Measurement," *Education Research Bulletin*, December, 1954, 32:234–238.

SPODECK, B., "Developing Social Science Concepts in the Kindergarten," *Social Education*, May, 1963, 27:353–356.

SPRINGER, DORIS V., "Awareness of Racial Differences by Preschool Children in Hawaii," *Genetic Psychology Monographs*, 1950, 51, 215–270.

———, "Development in Young Children of an Understanding of Time and the Clock," *Journal of Genetic Psychology*, March, 1952, 80:83–96.

STERN, D. A., AND R. MUKERJI, "Creating with Words," *Educational Leadership*, January, 1956, 15:221–227.

STEWART, EVELYN, "The Big Question of Creativity," *Parents' Magazine*, June, 1963, 38:62–65.

SUTTON, MARJORIE HUNT, "Readiness for Reading at the Kindergarten Level," *The Reading Teacher*, January, 1964, 17:234–240.

————, "Listen to the Little Ones," *The Education Digest*, May, 1964, 29:36–38.

SWENSON, ESTHER J., "Making Primary Arithmetic Meaningful to Children," *NEA Journal*, April, 1961, 50:43–44.

TEMPLIN, MILDRED C. *Certain Language Skills in Children*, Institute of Child Development, Monograph Series XXVI, Minneapolis, University of Minnesota Press, 1957.

TEMPLIN, MILDRED C., et al., "Selected References on Kindergarten-Primary Education," *Elementary School Journal*, January, 1964, 64:231–233.

THOMPSON, ETHEL, "Effective Practices in the Kindergartens," *Education: Intellectual, Moral, Physical—48th Annual School Newsweek Proceedings*, Philadelphia, University of Pennsylvania Press, 1961, 175–182.

THOMPSON, GEORGE C., "The Social and Emotional Development of Preschool Children Under Two Types of Educational Programs," *Psychological Monographs*, Iowa City, University of Iowa, 1944, 56:5.

THOMPSON, J. M., AND C. J. FINLEY, "Relationship Between the Goodenough *Draw a Man Test* and the *Stanford-Binet-Forms L and M*," *California Journal of Educational Research*, January, 1963, 14:19–22.

TILLMAN, RODNEY, "What Is Good About Public School Programs for Children," *Teachers College Journal*, October, 1964, 36:19–20.

TORRANCE, E. PAUL, "Priming Creative Thinking in the Primary Grades," *Elementary School Journal*, October, 1961, 62:34–41.

TOWNSEND, AGATHA, "What Research Says to the Reading Teacher," *The Reading Teacher*, January, 1962, 15:267–270.

TRILLINGHAM, C. C., "An Administrator Views the Kindergarten," *NEA Journal*, April, 1961, 50:37–39.

TROW, WILLIAM CLARK, "The Learning Process," *What Research Says to The Teacher*, Bulletin No. 66, Washington, D.C., National Education Association, 1954.

TRUSAL, MAURICE E., "The Effect of Kindergarten Experience Upon Social Readiness and Total Readiness for the First Grade; and the Effect of Kindergarten Experience Upon First Grade Achievement in Reading and Numbers in the Williamsport, Pennsylvania, Public Schools" (Doctoral Dissertation), Pennsylvania State University, *Review of Education Research*, November, 1955.

VANWIE, E. K., AND D. M. LAMMERS, "Are We Being Fair to Our Kindergarteners?" *Elementary School Journal*, April, 1962, 62:348–351.

WASNER, G., "What Schools Are Doing: Kindergarten," *Education*, December, 1963, 84:253–254.

WEISMAN, DOROTHY, "Is Play Obsolete?" *Saturday Review*, November 16, 1963, XLVI: 77-78.

WEISS, ROSALEE G., "The Validity of Early Entrance into Kindergarten," *Journal of Educational Research*, September, 1962, 56:53–54.

WILLIAMS, GERTHA, "The Kindergarten and Reading," *Childhood Education*, October, 1963, 40:77–78.

WILSON, J. A. R., AND M. C. ROBECK, "Comparison of the Kindergarten Evaluation of Learning Potential (KELP)—Readiness, Mental Maturity, Achievement and Ratings by First Grade Teachers," *Educational Psychological Measurement*," Summer, 1964, 24:409–414.

WINEBRENNER, D. KENNETH, "Let Them Be Children," *School Arts*, September, 1962, 62:1 (editorial page).

WITTROCK, M. C., AND OTHERS, "Verbal Cues in Concept Identification," *Journal of Educational Psychology*, August, 1964, 55:195–200.

ZAPOROZHETS, A., "New Educational Curriculum in the Kindergarten," *Soviet Education*, December, 1962, 5:3–6.

ZIMMERMAN, V. V., "Five Year Olds Need Kindergarten," *International Journal of Religious Education*, March, 1962, 38:16–17.

## Periodicals for Children

*Child Life*, Child Life, Inc., 817 W. Market St., Louisville, Kentucky 40202, 10 issues, $5.00 (5–10 years).

*Children's Digest*, Parents' Magazine Enterprises, Inc., Bergenfield, New Jersey 07621, 12 issues, $5.00 (6–12 years).

*Children's Playmate*, Children's Playmate Magazine, Inc., 629 Union Avenue, Cleveland, Ohio 44105, 10 issues, $5.00 (6–12 years).

*Highlights for Children*, Highlights for Children, 2300 W. 5th Avenue, Columbus, Ohio 43200, 10 issues, $5.00 (3–12 years).

*Humpty Dumpty's Magazine for Little Children*, Parents' Magazine Enterprises, Inc., Bergenfield, New Jersey 07621, 10 issues, $5.00 (3–7 years).

*Jack and Jill*, Curtis Publishing Company, Independence Square, Philadelphia, Pennsylvania 19100, 12 issues, $3.95 (4–10 years).

*Kinderbook*, Froebel-Kan Company, Ltd., No. 1, 3-chome, Kanda, Ogowa-machi, Tokyo, Japan, 12 issues, approximately $2.00 (3–7 years).

*Wee Wisdom* Unity School of Christianity, Lee's Summit, Missouri 64063, 12 issues, $2.00 (6–11 years).

## A Guide to Current Thinking in the Area of Early Childhood Education

### *Abstracts, Bulletins, Educational Indexes, Pamphlets, Periodicals, Reviews*

*American School Board Journal*, Bruce Publishing Company, 44 Broadway, Milwaukee, Wisconsin 53201, 12 issues, $4.00.

Association for Childhood Education International (bulletins, pamphlets, and journals), 3615 Wisconsin Ave., N.W., Washington, D.C. 20016.

*Audio-Visual Communications Review*, Department of Audio Visual Instruction, National Education Association, 1201 16th St., N.W., Washington, D.C. 20006, 4 issues, $6.00.

Bank Street Bureau of Publications (bulletins and pamphlets), 69 Bank St., New York, New York 10014.

Bureau of Publications, Teachers College, Columbia University (monographs, bulletins, and pamphlets), 501 W. 120 St., New York, New York 10027.

*Bulletin of the Center for Children's Books*, University of Chicago Press, 5835 Kimbark Ave., Chicago, Illinois 60637, 11 issues, $4.50.

*California Journal of Educational Research*, California Teachers Association, 693 Sutter St., San Francisco, California 94100, 5 issues, $6.00.

*Child Development* (Society for Research in Child Development), Child Development Publications, 1341 Euclid, University of Illinois, Champaign, Illinois, 4 issues, $12.00.

Child Development Abstracts and Bibliography (Society for Research in Child Development), Child Development Publications, 1341 Euclid, University of Illinois, Champaign, Illinois, 6 issues, $6.00.

*Childhood Education*, Association for Childhood Education International, 3615 Wisconsin Ave., N.W., Washington, D.C. 20016, 9 issues, $5.50.

Children's Bureau (bulletins and pamphlets), United States Department of Health, Education, and Welfare, Washington, D.C. 20202.

Children's Book Council, Inc., Book Notices, Book Week and other display materials, 175 Fifth Ave., New York, New York 10003.

Child Study Association (bulletins and pamphlets), 9 East 89th St., New York, New York 10028.

*Child Study*, Child Study Association, 9 East 89th St., New York, New York 10028.

*Children—An Inter-Disciplinary Journal for Professions Serving Children*, United States Children's Bureau, Superintendent of Documents, Washington, D.C. 20202, 6 issues, $1.25.

Cornell University Extension Department (bulletins and pamphlets), Ithaca, New York 14850.

*Education Abstracts* (English, French, and Spanish editions), UNESCO Publications Center, 801 Third Ave., New York, New York 10022, 4 issues, $2.00.

*Education Digest*, 330 Thompson St., Ann Arbor, Michigan, 48103, 9 issues, $5.00.

*Education Film Guide, Annual Cumulative*, H. W. Wilson and Company, 450 University Ave., New York, New York 10052.

*Elementary English Journal*, Naional Council of Teachers of English, 509 S. Sixth St., Champaign, Illinois 61822, 8 issues, $5.00.

Elementary Instructional Service, National Education Association, 1201 16th St., N.W., Washington, D.C. 20016.

*Elementary School Journal*, University of Chicago Press, 5835 Kimbark Ave., Chicago, Illinois 60637, 8 issues, $4.50.

*Encyclopedia of Child Guidance*, Philosophical Library, 15 E. 40th St., New York, New York 10016.

*Encyclopedia of Modern Educational Research*, 60 Fifth Ave., Macmillan Company, New York, New York 10111.

*Film World and Audio Visual World*, 672 S. Lafayette Park, Los Angeles, California 90057, 12 issues, $4.00.

*Grade Teacher,* Educational Publishing Corporation, Darien, Connecticut 06820, 10 issues, $5.50.

*The Horn Book Magazine,* The Horn Book, Inc., 585 Boylston St., Boston, Massachusetts 02116, 6 issues, $5.00.

Institute of Child Development, University of Minnesota (pamphlets), University of Minnesota, Minneapolis, Minnesota 55455.

*International Child Welfare Review* (English and French editions), Internanational Union for Child Welfare, 1 rue Varamble, Geneva, Switzerland, 4 issues, 10 fr, $2.50.

*Instructor,* F. A. Owen Publishing Company, Instructor Park, Dansville, New York 14437, 10 issues, $6.00.

*Journal of Educational Research,* Dembar Publications, Box 737, Madison, Wisconsin 53703, 9 issues, $7.50.

*Journal of Experimental Education,* University of Wisconsin, Madison, Wisconsin 53706, 4 issues, $5.00.

*Keeping Up with Early Education,* Newsletter published by the Department of Elementary-Kindergarten-Nursery Education, National Education Association, 1201 16th St., N.W., Washington, D.C. 20036, 4 issues, $2.00.

Merrill-Palmer (bulletins and pamphlets), 71 E. Ferry Ave., Detroit, Michigan 48200.

*National Association for the Education of Young Children* (formerly National Association for Nursery Education), (bulletins, pamphlets, and journal), 104 East 25th St., New York, New York, 10010.

National Committee for Mental Hygiene (bulletins and pamphlets), 1790 Broadway, New York, New York 10019.

*National Education Association Research Bulletin,* NEA Research Division, National Education Association, 1201 16th Street, N.W., Washington, D.C. 20036, 4 issues, $2.00.

*National Education Journal,* National Education Association, 1201 16th St., N.W., Washington, D.C. 20036, 10 issues (with membership).

*NEA News,* National Education Association, 1201 16th St., N.W., Washington, D.C. 20036, irregular issues, no price given.

*National Parent-Teacher,* The PTA Magazine, National Congress of Parents and Teachers, 700 Rush St., Chicago, Illinois 60611, 10 issues, $1.25.

*News Letter* (radio, TV, press, and motion pictures), Bureau of Educational Research, Ohio State University, Columbus, Ohio 43200, 8 issues, no price given.

New York Committee on Mental Health (bulletins and pamphlets), 105 E. 22nd St., New York, New York 10010.

Office of Education, United States Department of Health, Education, and Welfare (bulletins and pamphlets), Washington, D.C. 20202.

*Parents' Magazine,* Parents' Magazine Enterprises, Inc., 52 Vanderbilt Ave., New York, New York 10017, 12 issues, $4.00.

Play School Association (bulletins and pamphlets), 119 W. 57th St., New York, New York 10019.

Public Affairs Committee (pamphlets), 22 E. 38th St., New York, New York 10010.

*Review of Educational Research*, American Educational Research Association, National Education Association, 1201 16th St., N.W., Washington, D.C. 20036, 5 issues, nonmembers $7.00.

*Saturday Review*, Saturday Review, Inc., 380 Madison Ave., New York, New York 10017, 52 issues, $8.00 (monthly educational column).

*School and Society*, Society for the Advancement of Education, 1834 Broadway, New York, New York 10023, 24 issues, $7.50.

*School Arts: The Art Education Magazine*, 44 Portland St., Worcester, Massachusetts 01600, 10 issues, $5.00.

*School Equipment News*, American School Publishing Corporation, 470 Fourth Ave., New York, New York 10016, 12 issues, no price given.

*School Executive*, American Publishing Corporation, 470 Fourth Ave., New York, New York 10016, 12 issues, $4.00.

*School Life*, United States Office of Education, Superintendent of Documents, Washington, D.C. 20202, 9 issues, $1.75.

*Science and Children*, National Science Teachers Association, 1201 16th St., N.W., Washington, D.C. 20036, 8 issues, $4.00.

*Science News Letter*, 1719 N St., N.W., Washington, D.C. 20036, 52 issues, $5.50.

Science Research Associates (tests, bulletins, and pamphlets), 228 Wabash Ave., Chicago, Illinois 60604.

*Story Art: A Magazine for Story Tellers*, National Story League, 5835 Marttel Ave., Dallas, Texas 75200, 6 issues, $2.00.

*Teachers College Record*, Teachers College, Columbia University, New York, New York 10027, 8 issues, $3.00.

*Today's Child*, 1225 Broadway, New York, New York 10001, 12 issues, $3.00.

*Two to Five World Newsletter*, 127 E. 56th St., New York, New York 10020, 6 issues, $0.50.

*Understanding the Child*, National Association for Mental Health, 1790 Broadway, New York, New York 10001, 4 issues, $1.50.

*Young Children* (formerly *Journal of Nursery Education*), National Association for the Education of Young Children (formerly National Association for Nursery Education), 104 E. 25th St., New York, New York 10010, 6 issues, $3.50.

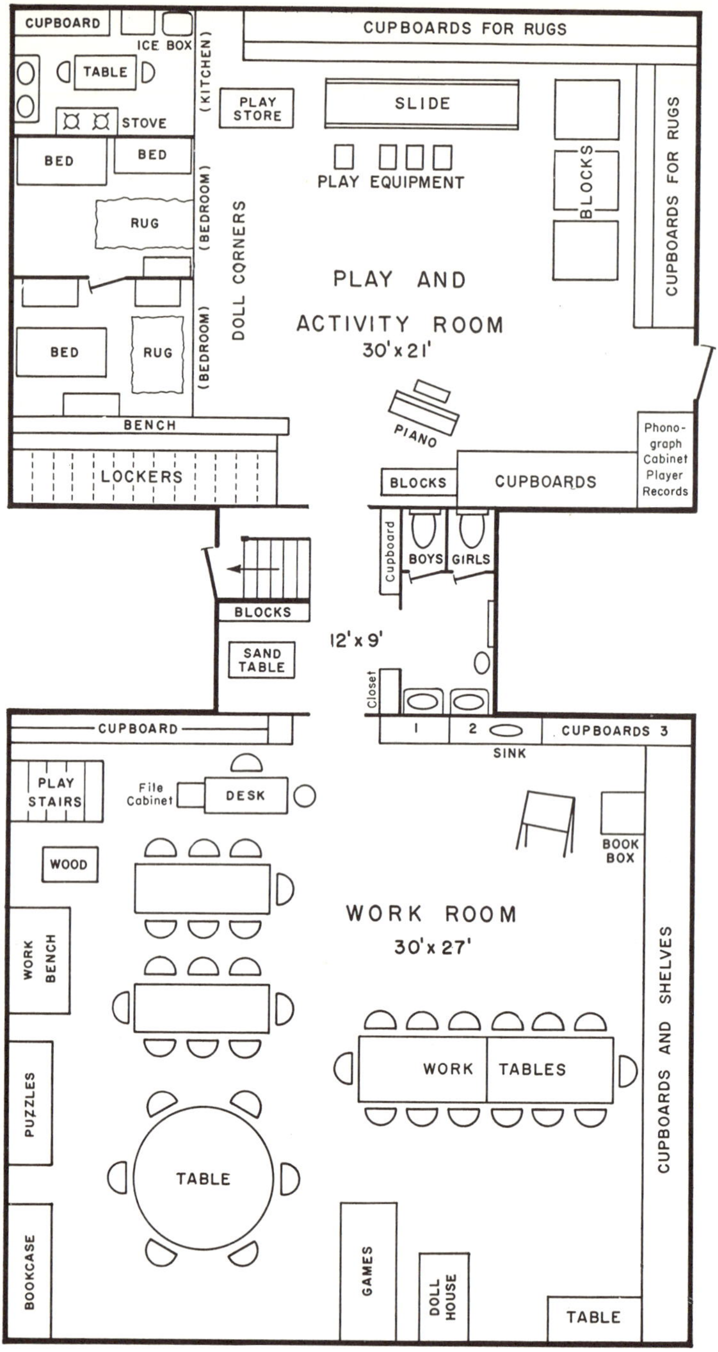


*Kindergarten Floor Plan*

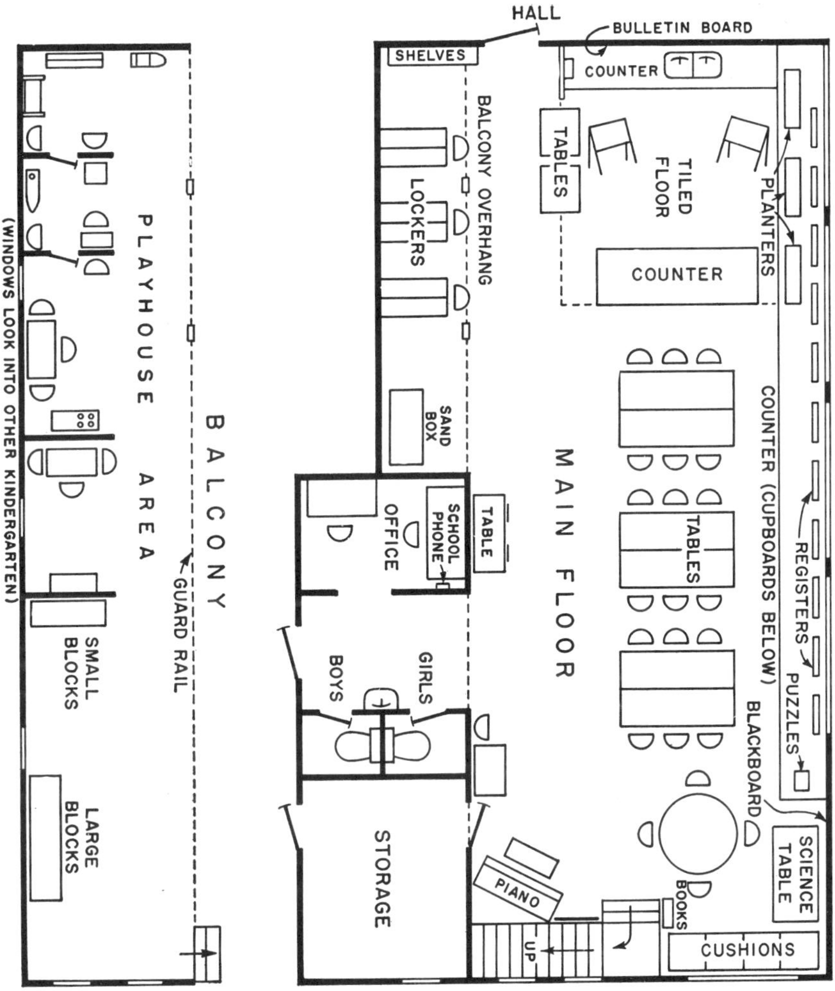


*Kindergarten Floor Plan*

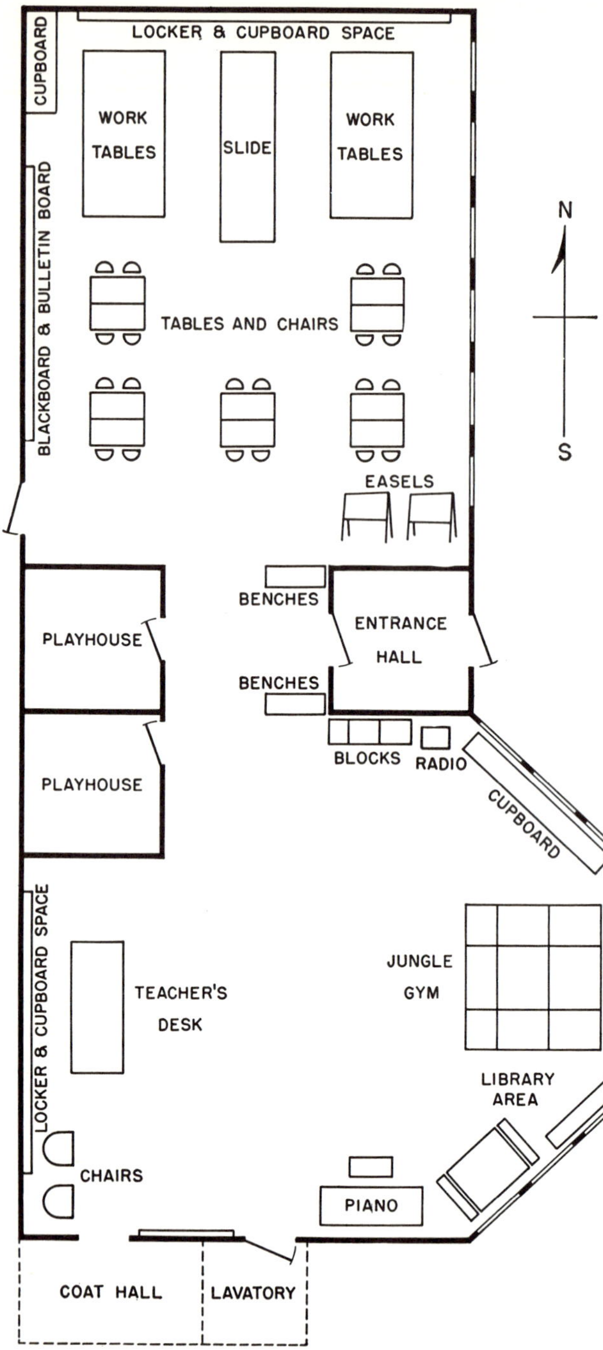


*Kindergarten Floor Plan*

# INDEX

Faithway Baptist College
Library
Memphis, Mich. 48041

This book may be kept